MIDWAY INQUEST

Richard K.L. Mok

Twentieth-Century Battles
Spencer C. Tucker, editor

MIDWAY INQUEST

Why the Japanese Lost the Battle of Midway

Dallas Woodbury Isom

INDIANA UNIVERSITY PRESS

BLOOMINGTON AND INDIANAPOLIS

This book is a publication of

Indiana University Press
601 North Morton Street
Bloomington, IN 47404-3797 USA

Manufactured in the United States of America

ISBN 978-0-253-34904-0

CONTENTS

PREFACE

THIS BOOK ON THE pivotal naval battle of the Pacific War—and perhaps the most famous naval battle in American history—is the product of over ten years of research, much of it in Japan. I embarked on this project after concluding that none of the existing accounts on the Battle of Midway satisfactorily explained why the Japanese lost that battle; indeed, some presented scenarios that made sense only if it was assumed that the Japanese were grossly incompetent, or just plain stupid. Although it may seem odd to some that a law professor would be writing a book about a naval battle, I concluded that *that* was precisely what was needed. The subject has entered the realm of legend— even epic saga—and much of what has been written on the battle in America is jingoistic and condescending toward the Japanese. (Some accounts read more like hagiography than mere history.) What was now needed—over sixty years after the battle—I believed, was the kind of objective, detached analysis of the Japanese side of the battle that a crusty old law professor was peculiarly equipped to provide.

When I say that the existing accounts of the battle do not satisfactorily explain why the Japanese lost, what I mean more specifically is that there has been no satisfactory explanation for what I believe is the central mystery of the battle: why the Japanese could not get a carrier plane strike force launched against the American carriers before their own carriers were attacked and destroyed by American dive-bombers from *Enterprise* and *Yorktown*. Although that American dive-bomber attack had the appearance of an ambush, in fact the American carrier force had been discovered by a Japanese search plane nearly three hours before the fatal bombing.

While it is well known that the Japanese were unable to launch an immediate attack because they were in the process of changing the armament on their torpedo planes from torpedoes to "land" bombs for a second strike on Midway, none of the published accounts of the battle give any good reason why the re-arming operation could not have been reversed in time for an attack to be launched before the American dive-bombers arrived. (One recent book takes the position that the rearming operation had actually been reversed in time for such an attack to be launched, but that the Japanese carrier force com-mander—Vice Admiral Chuichi Nagumo—declined to spot the strike force on the flight decks of his carriers because he wanted to keep those flight decks clear for anticipated combat air patrol operations.)*

In point of fact, the torpedoes did not get restored to the Japanese torpedo planes in time for a strike to be launched against the American carriers before the fatal bombing. I believe that I have solved the mystery of why they were not. My reconstruction of what actually happened on the Japanese carriers during those critical hours on the morning of the battle before the American dive-bombers arrived is based on my analysis of Japanese records (chiefly, Na-gumo's official report), on Japanese literature on the battle (much of which has not been translated into English), and on interviews with almost two dozen Japanese veterans from the carrier air groups at Midway.

I freely admit, however, that I do not know exactly what really went on in Na-gumo's headquarters: why—and even when—some of the decisions crucial to the outcome of the battle were made. Nor do I think anyone else alive knows. The record is inconsistent and in some cases vague. Deductions occasionally have to be made from fairly slender evidence; ambiguities have to be resolved by analysis of the record as a whole. It is very much lawyer's work. In a few cases it even comes down to a matter of whether one chooses to give the Japanese commanders the benefit of the doubt that they acted intelligently under the circumstances.

I think it is fairly easy to construct a scenario for why the Japanese lost the battle if one assumes that they were incompetent; it is more of a challenge when one assumes that they were generally competent and intelligent. I might be out on a limb, but I have made the assumption that the principal Japanese officers in the flagship headquarters—Ryunosuke Kusaka, chief of staff, Minoru Genda, air officer, and even the much criticized Chuichi Nagumo, were intelligent pro-fessionals and generally acted reasonably under the circumstances. I reject sce-narios premised on their being stupid. Not that they did not commit blunders; they did. But under my scenario, those blunders were at a higher level than are the ones commonly ascribed. Thus, what I have endeavored to do is reconstruct a scenario for why Nagumo could not get his strike force launched in time that is plausible *if* it is assumed that he and his staff were reasonably responsive to the various exigencies that popped up on the morning of the battle.

---

*Japanese names are given in Western order, family name last.

Many of my findings will be surprising to devotees of the battle, and some are bound to be controversial in the military history community. Many cherished myths surrounding that legendary battle will be debunked. My approach to this contentious subject has been that of a detached jurist attempting to objectively assess the evidence to determine whether anyone was to blame for the disaster that befell the Japanese at Midway (which is why I call it an "inquest.")

The scope of this book, however, is broader than just the Battle of Midway. To give historical context to that battle, key events leading to the war between Japan and America are summarized (such as the Japanese aggressions in China and southeast Asia, and the American oil embargo.) So is the attack on Pearl Harbor (where the failure to catch the Pacific Fleet carriers in port and destroy them is what made the later Midway operation necessary in the first place.) And so is the aftermath of the battle—to show just why Midway was the pivotal battle of the Pacific War.

After concluding that had the Japanese got their strike force off their carriers in time they probably would have won the battle, I then end the book with a chapter of "what ifs" where I speculate on how a Japanese victory at Midway might have altered the course of the war. (Not to fear: America still would have won the war in the Pacific, but it probably would have taken at least a year longer. I come to the ironical conclusion that Japan was lucky to lose that battle; had she won, her inevitable defeat would have been even more devastating than it actually was.)

A personal note: I got interested in the Battle of Midway after my father—Orville Isom—died in 1990. A few years before that he had written his memoirs—with one of the chapters devoted to his experiences as a Marine in the South Pacific during World War Two. (He was a country lawyer in Cedar City, Utah, with four kids when he was drafted in 1943.) Before his death, what interest I had in military history had been mostly limited to the European theater of the war. After then, spurred on by my father's account of his sojourns on those storied but bloody islands from the Solomons to the Marianas, I decided to learn more about the Pacific theater. (It turns out that he landed on the island of Saipan just days after Nagumo had committed suicide there.)

After he returned home from the war, it was apparent that he bore the Japanese people no particular animosity even though our two countries had been bitter enemies. He had even somehow managed to gain a certain respect for them (which I found curious given the intensity of anti-Japanese feeling at the time.) Perhaps this was from insights gained through his work in military intelligence in the South Pacific. I seem to have acquired my own attitude toward the Japanese—which I believe readers will find less chauvinistic and somewhat more respectful than is typical among American commentators on Midway—from him. Although my father joined the war over a year after the Battle of Midway, I believe he would have enjoyed my account of it. In any case, I dedicate this book to him.

ACKNOWLEDGMENTS

WHEN I GOT THE IDEA for this project to discover what really happened on the Japanese aircraft carriers during the crucial hours of the Battle of Midway, I realized I would not get very far unless I could link up with someone in Japan who could track down Japanese veterans of the battle and arrange interviews with them. Fortunately, there was an American branch of a Japanese University (Tokyo International University) right next to Willamette University in Salem, Oregon, where I was teaching law. It was Dean Kawashima, of Tokyo International University America, who provided the vital connection to Japan.

Through him, I was put in contact with Professor Sinichirou Hagimoto at Tokyo International University's main campus in Kawagoe, Japan, who sponsored my proposal to that university for research in Japan. He linked me up with the one truly indispensable person in this entire project: Munehiro Miwa. Miwa was a Japanese military historian on the faculty of Nihon University who was familiar with the various Japanese veterans organizations. He located a considerable number of veterans of the Battle of Midway and arranged for interviews. As he was bilingual, he was able to translate my written questions into Japanese and serve as interpreter during the interviews. Together, we traversed the length and breadth of the Japanese islands in 1992 and 1993 to meet with about two dozen veterans. (While several were in the Tokyo metro area, most were scattered around the country—some in remote mountain villages in the southern island of Kyushu.)

Miwa not only assisted me with the interviews, but provided me with essential Japanese language material on the battle—and even translated some of it. Moreover, as he was well versed in the literature on the battle—American as well as Japanese—he was able to give me insights that proved invaluable. (He was also the first person to read and critique my early draft of the book, and steered me away from some potentially embarrassing missteps.)

Regarding the Japanese veterans, though all provided me with useful information (and are listed in the book), there were two who went out of their way to give me extra-special assistance and, thus, deserve special mention: Tatsuya Ohtawa (torpedo plane pilot, *Soryu*) and Hiseo Mandai (engineer, *Hiryu*). Ohtawa met with me on several occasions during which he provided me with printed material on the Japanese carriers and carrier aircraft—most notably, material portraying aerial torpedo-launch technique; he even drew sketches of the equipment used in the operation to arm torpedo planes with torpedoes. Mandai also met with me several times and put me in touch with other veterans. He located every surviving member of *Hiryu*'s air group and sent a set of my questions to all those who were unavailable for interviews. Their responses supplemented the fruits of the in-person interviews and made a substantial contribution to my understanding of Japanese carrier operations.

Apart from the veterans of the battle, there were others in Japan I want to thank: Koichi Mera, Dean, International Center, Tokyo International University, who provided me with a research grant and generally looked after my needs while I was in Kawagoe, Japan; Noritaka Kitazawa, Librarian, Military History Department, National Institute for Defense Studies in Tokyo, who helped me understand some of the finer points of the original Japanese version of Admiral Nagumo's official report on the Battle of Midway; and Hitoshi Tsunoda, who served as a staff officer at the Imperial Japanese Navy headquarters in Tokyo during the war, and who was the principal author of the Senshi Sosho (official war history) volume on the Battle of Midway. Tsunoda—though almost ninety years old and in declining health—most kindly met with me on several occasions and proved to be a treasure trove of information on the battle.

My first interview of Midway veterans in Japan—that with Tatsuya Ohtawa—took place following a reunion of Japanese carrier air group veterans at Kasumi-gaura, the site of the Imperial Japanese Navy's basic pilot training facility (which is located about 50 miles northeast of Tokyo outside the town of Tsuchi-ura). The interview was held at the home—near Tsuchiura—of a young Japanese family, who treated Miwa, Ohtawa, and myself to a most delicious traditional Japanese meal. I want to thank them for their hospitality, though I cannot do so by name because the note paper containing that information has, embarrassingly, been lost. I hope this book somehow comes to their attention.

Now, turning to my compatriots in the United States who made special contributions to this book: Robert Misner was my law school dean at Willamette University back in 1992 when I conceived of this project. I had been granted a sabbatical leave for autumn of that year to do research on a legal subject quite unrelated to the Battle of Midway. After Dean Kawashima of TIUA had opened the door for me to travel to Japan that fall to interview Midway veterans, Bob Misner interceded with the university administration to allow me to amend my sabbatical project. (Fortunately, the presidents of the two universities had just reached an agreement to foster joint research projects between members of their respective faculties.) But for that fortuitous alteration in my sabbatical plans, this project probably would not have gotten off the ground, and for that I owe a debt of gratitude to Bob Misner and also to Jerry Hudson, the then president of Willamette University.

A book like this one cannot be written without access to the primary sources—most importantly, translations of the original Japanese action reports and other documents. For those, I thank the staff of the Naval Historical Center, Operational Archives Branch, at the Washington Navy Yard in Washington, D.C., and specifically Bernard F. Cavalcante and Mike Walker.

From John B. Lundstrom I also acquired primary source material, mostly action reports and other documents from the American side of the battle. John is generally regarded as the doyen of the Pacific War historians—not just because he has written extensively in the field, but rather because of his generosity in sharing documents from his vast collection with other authors, and his willingness to engage in extensive e-mail dialogues with them. Though we have disagreed on some things, John has sharpened my thinking on a number of points.

Finally, a word of thanks to my publishers and editors: To Thomas B. Grassey and Pelham G. Boyer of the Naval War College Review, who published my article "The Battle of Midway: Why the Japanese Lost" in their Summer 2000 issue. This was a precursor to this book, which has benefited greatly from Pelham Boyer's rigorous editing of my article. And lastly, and most importantly, to Robert J. Sloan and his fine editorial staff at Indiana University Press: the eagle-eyed Dawn Ollila, Senior Project Editor, who saved me from a number of potentially embarrassing mistakes, Brian Herrmann, who was my final editor, Miki Bird, and the always helpful Beth Marsh. Special thanks to Bob Sloan for having the courage to take a chance on what may well be a controversial book.

MIDWAY INQUEST

Pacific Theater of Operations

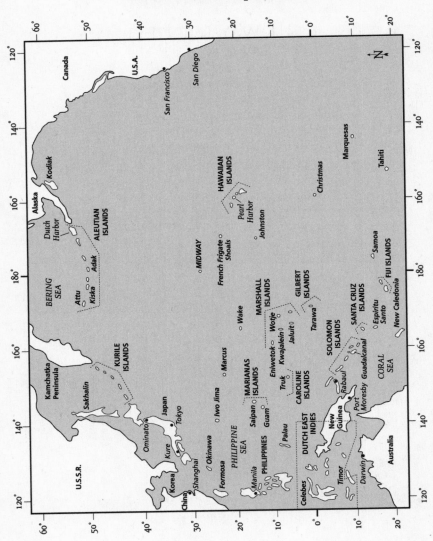

Battle of Midway Search & Course Chart
0430-1030 June 4

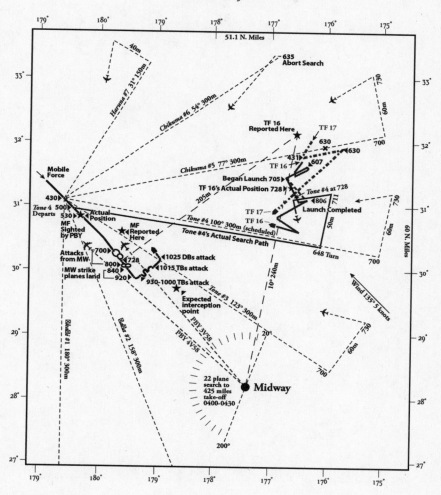

CHAPTER ONE

WHY THIS INQUEST

A GREAT MANY BOOKS HAVE already been written about the Battle of Midway. It continues to grip the imaginations of those interested in World War II because it had all the ingredients of an epic saga: it was the pivotal battle of the Pacific, and the underdog won. Not only did the Americans win this legendary battle of June 4, 1942, but they won by one of the most lopsided margins in naval history. Even Nelson's victory at Trafalgar and Togo's at Tsushima Strait—where outnumbered naval forces also won spectacular victories—pale in comparison with the most striking aspect of the Battle of Midway: the lethal damage that determined the outcome was done during a two-minute period when three of the four Japanese aircraft carriers were set ablaze by American dive-bombers.

When the battle was finally over, all four of the Japanese carriers were at the bottom of the ocean. With four of the six fleet carriers in her navy now gone, along with about 250 carrier planes and more than 100 irreplaceable pilots, Japan's naval air power was decimated. What little chance Japan had of winning the war in the Pacific went up in the smoke of her burning carriers. The titles of the three most widely read books on the subject sum it up: "Miracle at Midway," "Incredible Victory," and "Midway—The Battle That Doomed Japan."

Then why another book about the battle? Has not the subject been exhausted, the sources mined out? Although the story of the American side of the battle has been told and retold in great detail, and with stirring drama, there is no satisfactory account of what happened on the Japanese side—and, in the final analysis, no satisfactory explanation of why they lost the battle. The commander of the Japanese carrier force, Vice Admiral Chuichi Nagumo, has been roundly criticized and belittled for making a series of decisions that resulted in catastrophe in a battle that he was supposed to have won. But the books available, on both sides of the Pacific, give inconsistent—and in some cases implausible—accounts of those decisions. It became clear that much more needed to be known about the nature of those crucial decisions and the circumstances surrounding them. What really happened on the Japanese carriers of Nagumo's Mobile Force during the hours just before they were destroyed?

It is generally agreed that had Nagumo been able to launch a strike against the American carrier force before his own carriers were destroyed by American dive-bombers, he probably would have won the battle. However, as will shortly be seen, existing accounts fail to provide a plausible explanation for why that could not be done. In order to better explain why the existing accounts of what happened on the Japanese carriers before they were destroyed do not make sense—and why a fresh look is needed at why the Japanese lost the battle—let us first set the scene.

PREVIEW OF THE BATTLE

The Midway operation was masterminded by Admiral Isoroku Yamamoto, commander in chief of the Japanese Combined Fleet. It sprung from the failure of the attack on Pearl Harbor to catch and destroy the American carriers that Yamamoto had expected to be there with the rest of the Pacific Fleet. The Doolittle raid on Tokyo and other Japanese cities in April 1942, in which sixteen B-25 bombers were launched from the carrier *Hornet*, had crystalized support in the Japanese high command for an operation to eliminate the American carrier force in the Pacific. Yamamoto's objective was to entice—by attacking and occupying Midway atoll with its vital naval base—the American carriers into a decisive battle in which they could be destroyed. Midway, about 1,100 miles northwest of Pearl Harbor, was regarded by the Japanese as the "sentry for Hawaii," too valuable an asset for the Americans to lose without a fight.

Yamamoto's plan—which included an attack in the Aleutians—was unprecedented in its complexity and scale, involving almost every combatant ship in the Japanese navy, almost 140 in all, along with dozens of support ships. The "Teeth," however, were the four fleet carriers in Nagumo's Mobile Force: *Akagi*, *Kaga*, *Hiryu*, and *Soryu*.[1] Between them, these ships embarked around 250 carrier planes, of which 230 were operational (and another 21 land-based Zero fighters that were being ferried for use on Midway after its capture.) It was these four carriers, with their supporting ships, of the Mobile Force that were involved in what is popularly called the Battle of Midway.

On the American side, code breakers at Pacific Fleet headquarters in Hawaii had deduced the general outline and approximate date of Yamamoto's Midway operation. Admiral Chester W. Nimitz, commander in chief of the U.S. Pacific Fleet, planned to ambush Nagumo's carrier force. For this he had three carriers available: *Enterprise* and *Hornet* in Task Force 16, under the command of Rear Admiral Raymond Spruance, and *Yorktown* in Task Force 17, under Rear Admiral Frank Fletcher. (*Yorktown*, damaged three weeks earlier in the battle of the Coral Sea, and assumed to be out of action by Yamamoto, had been miraculously repaired in less than three days.) The three carriers collectively carried 234 planes, of which 221 were operational.[2] In addition, there were about eighty land-based combat planes and thirty-two PBY Catalina flying boats for reconnaissance on Midway itself.

Thus Nimitz actually had more planes at his disposal in the immediate arena of the battle than Yamamoto, but Nagumo's planes—especially his torpedo planes—could potentially deliver far more ship-sinking firepower, and his pilots were generally much more experienced. If the Americans were to have a reasonable chance of winning, their planes had to strike Nagumo's carriers before they could launch their own attack against the American carriers. That, of course, is exactly what happened—but just barely. Why could the Japanese not get an attack launched in time?

THE CRUCIAL PERIOD

The period that determined the outcome of the battle was the little over three hours between 0715 and 1025 on the morning of June 4, 1942.[*] Prior to that, at 0430, a "first wave" of thirty-six torpedo planes armed with land bombs, thirty-six dive-bombers, and thirty-six Zero fighters had been launched from the four carriers to attack Midway. Also, between 0430 and 0500, seven search planes had been launched to canvas the area for American ships. At 0715, Nagumo had on his carriers a "second wave" of at least thirty-six torpedo planes armed with torpedoes and thirty-six dive-bombers armed with antiship bombs standing ready to attack any American ships that might show up. He also had a sufficient number of Zero fighters on hand at that time, in addition to those needed for air defense, to provide an effective escort for those torpedo planes and bombers.

Had the American carriers been discovered by that time, Nagumo could have launched a full-scale strike, which most likely would have knocked them

---

[*]All dates and times used in this book will be those for Midway. Japanese sources use Tokyo time, which is one day later and three hours earlier. These will be converted to Midway time. (0430, June 4 at Midway is 0130, June 5 in Tokyo.)

out of the battle. This is because the Japanese Navy possessed a deadly ship-sinking weapon—an aerial torpedo that was very accurate and reliable, and so fast that it was difficult to evade. (The American aerial torpedo at that time in the war was extremely unreliable and slow—it essentially did not work.) More-over, had such a strike been launched, then even if Nagumo's four carriers were later attacked by American carrier planes exactly as happened, those car-riers probably would have sustained only a fraction of the damage actually inflicted because their flight decks and hangars would have been clear of planes and the hazardous gasoline and ordnance they carried.

But, as it turned out, at around 1025 his carriers were caught by American dive-bombers in the most vulnerable condition a carrier can be in: crammed with armed and fueled bombers—the hangar decks littered with bombs. In two minutes, three carriers were hit by nine high-explosive bombs, most of them 1,000-pounders. Those bombs by themselves would not necessarily have been fatal. Unlike the Japanese, the Americans lacked armor-piercing, delayed-fuse bombs that could penetrate into the bowels of a ship before exploding.[3] It was the burning gasoline from ruptured fuel tanks and the secondary explosions of their own ordnance that turned those carriers into funeral pyres. (It is possible that a well-placed hand grenade could have destroyed a 36,000-ton carrier in that condition.) By 1030 in the morning—the time his own strike force had originally been scheduled for launch—Nagumo had lost the battle.

The disaster that befell the Japanese at 1025 on June 4 is exactly what would be expected from an ambush. That clearly was what Admiral Nimitz had planned. But there was no ambush. The American naval presence had been discovered by a Japanese search plane—the infamous *Tone* 4—three hours ear-lier at 0728, and Nagumo was aware of at least one American carrier in the area two hours before the fatal attack. Had Nagumo gotten his strike off before 1025 he most probably would have won the battle. Nimitz's ambush plan depended on his carriers not being discovered until he had hit Nagumo's carriers. It was a gamble that Nimitz lost—but he still won the battle because Nagumo could not take advantage of the unexpected discovery. Again, why was Nagumo un-able to get his attack launched before 1025?

The problem, as is well known, is that at the time the American fleet was first discovered—at 0728—Nagumo's carrier torpedo planes were in the process of being rearmed with land bombs for a second strike on Midway, and thus were temporarily out of action.[4] But, still, it does seem incredible that with such lead time Nagumo could not have reversed the armament back to torpedoes and launched his planes before the American strike. What went wrong in Na-gumo's headquarters; why were the torpedoes not restored in time for an attack to have been launched before 1025? That is a mystery that has not been satisfac-torily explained to this day, and is the central focus of this book.

The widely accepted chronology of key events during this crucial period—

given by the leading American and Japanese authorities—is as follows: At 0715 Nagumo issued the order to rearm his standby torpedo planes and dive-bombers with land bombs for a second strike on Midway. The planes on the flight decks were stricken below to the hangars, and work began to remove the torpedoes on the torpedo planes and antiship bombs on the dive-bombers. Then, at 0728, the *Tone* 4 search plane discovered elements of the American fleet, and sent back a vague sighting report merely stating that "ten ships" were seen. That report was supposedly received by Nagumo at around 0740. At 0745, Nagumo issued an order to suspend the rearming operation, and at 0747 he radioed a request to *Tone* 4 to specify the ship types and maintain contact. A second request to specify ship types was made at 0800. At 0809, *Tone* 4 reported back that the ships consisted of five cruisers and five destroyers. Then, at 0820, it sent another report identifying an aircraft carrier. Nagumo received that report at about 0830.

Instead of launching an immediate attack at that time against the American carrier with what was readily available—dive-bombers without a fighter escort—Nagumo chose to postpone his attack until after the Midway strike force, which had just returned, had been recovered. The launch of a coordinated strike force, with rearmed torpedo planes along with the dive-bombers and a Zero escort, was then scheduled for 1030. At around 1025, American dive-bombers from *Enterprise* and *Yorktown* attacked and destroyed *Akagi*, *Kaga*, and *Soryu*. Most readers of this book will be familiar with this chronology of events. For that reason this chronology, and the decisions supposedly made by Nagumo during that period, will be referred to as the "standard scenario." But, as will be seen, much of that scenario is myth.

THE CRUCIAL DECISIONS

In order to show why existing accounts, Japanese as well as American, fail to explain the central mystery of why Nagumo could not get his attack launched before the fatal American bombing, it might be helpful to review the decisions made by Nagumo during the crucial period prior to 1025. The following is a summary of the various, and often contradictory, versions given of those decisions, and the facts upon which they were based, by the leading American and Japanese commentators on the battle. Many readers will be familiar with the principal American sources.[5] However, the principal Japanese reference on the battle has received little mention in America. It is *The Midway Sea Battle*, published by the Japanese government in 1971 as part of a one-hundred-volume war history series popularly known as Senshi Sosho.[6] The scenario it gives differs from the American standard scenario on a number of points, as will be noted, but it also contains some irrationalities of its own.

Three decisions made by the admiral determined the course of the battle.

THE FIRST DECISION—TO REARM THE TORPEDO PLANES

It is generally agreed by the commentators—all American, and most Japanese (including Senshi Sosho)—that the decision by Nagumo to rearm his "second-wave" torpedo planes with land bombs was made at 0715. It was made pursuant to a report sent at 0700 by the commander of the Midway strike force, Joichi Tomonaga, that a second strike on Midway was needed. Such a strike was needed primarily because the American planes based on Midway had not been caught on the ground and destroyed, as had been hoped.

This decision contravened a "standing order" by Yamamoto that half the torpedo planes in the Mobile Force remain armed with torpedoes at all times—and be on standby in a state of readiness to attack any American carriers that might turn up.[7] Tomonaga's request coincided with the first attack by Midway-based torpedo bombers on Nagumo's carriers, which, no doubt, made Tomonaga's recommendation more persuasive. The admiral hoped that these bombers—and others expected to follow—could then be caught on the ground and destroyed after their return to Midway from the attack on his carriers.

Although this is generally regarded as the fatal decision, it has also been judged by most commentators to have been reasonable under the circumstances—this, despite the fact that it contravened Yamamoto's standing order, and was made before the search operation to look for American carriers was completed. Nagumo opted to forgo readiness against a possible American carrier threat that he deemed unlikely in favor of dealing immediately with a threat from Midway that had already materialized.

There is, however, a dissenting view in Japan that has a considerable following among younger Japanese historians—though it is vehemently challenged by most veterans of the war. Hisae Sawachi, in her *Record of the Midway Sea Battle*,[8] contends that Nagumo made his decision to rearm the torpedo planes with land bombs for a second strike on Midway not at 0715, but almost two hours earlier at 0520.[9] The main basis for this surprising conclusion is a somewhat cryptic order from Nagumo, recorded in Nagumo's battle report as having been issued at 0520, stating that "unless unforeseen changes in the situation occur, the second attack wave . . . will be carried out today." This had been interpreted by Senshi Sosho as being merely a "precautionary order," informing the carrier air group commanders that a second strike on Midway might be necessary.[10] While Senshi Sosho accepts that certain preliminary steps were taken pursuant to this order, such as hauling 800-kilogram land bombs from the magazines up to the hangar decks of *Akagi* and *Kaga*, it insists that the actual rearming of the torpedo planes did not begin until 0715. Sawachi rejects the "precautionary order" theory, and contends that it was interpreted as an order to begin rearming the second-wave torpedo planes.

Her interpretation of the 0520 order is astonishing because, if true, it means that Nagumo had decided that a second strike would be necessary even before the first strike had reached Midway, and even before his carrier force had been discovered by American search planes. It also means that Nagumo was so convinced that no American carriers could be in the area that he had totally discounted such a possibility even though his search effort had barely begun.

Thus, Sawachi has Nagumo flagrantly disobeying Admiral Yamamoto's standing order to keep half the torpedo planes armed with torpedoes in case American carriers showed up. She contends that the "official version" of the rearming order in Nagumo's battle report, which has the decision made at 0715, was fabricated to cover up this rank insubordination.[11] (She also contends that the message from the Midway strike force leader recommending a second strike on Midway—recorded in Nagumo's report at 0700—was likewise a fabrication, and notes that it cannot be found in the original message logs.)

For reasons that I will explain later, I reject Sawachi's theory. I mention it because it is taken seriously in Japan, and does—better than any other scenario advanced so far—explain why the torpedoes on Nagumo's torpedo planes never got restored in time for a strike to be launched against the American carriers before 1025.

Getting back to the more generally accepted scenario that the rearming operation was not ordered until 0715, there have been differing views of the scope of the rearming operation (whether dive-bombers were included along with the torpedo planes), and the length of time it would take. Some of the early American commentators believed that only the torpedo planes were ordered to be rearmed with land bombs, that the dive-bombers remained armed with antiship bombs.[12] This interpretation probably resulted from the fact that the rearming order recorded in Nagumo's battle report makes no mention of dive-bombers; it merely says that "Orders were issued for the ship-based attack planes to remove their torpedoes and replace them with [800-kilogram] land bombs."[13]

Senshi Sosho and later American commentators take the position that the dive-bombers were rearmed along with the torpedo planes—that the antiship bombs (armor-piercing, delayed-fuse) were replaced by land bombs (instant detonation, fragmentation). Indeed, it would have been irrational not to include dive-bombers equipped with land bombs in a second attack on Midway as they were better suited for destroying most of the intended targets than were torpedo planes. The reason the rearming of the dive-bombers is not explicitly mentioned in Nagumo's battle report is probably because it—as will be described in detail later—was a relatively simple and quick procedure.

As for how long it would take to rearm the torpedo planes, most American commentators have stated one hour or less.[14] Senshi Sosho, however, provides convincing evidence—based on an experiment conducted in the Indian Ocean campaign in April—that it took considerably longer: one and a half hours to change from torpedoes to 800-kilogram land bombs, and two hours to change back to torpedoes.[15] (And these times assume that the land bombs—as well as the planes—were already in the hangar.) Moreover, while most American accounts have the torpedo planes stricken below from the flight deck at 0715 to be rearmed in the hangars, Senshi Sosho makes no mention of any such striking below and appears to assume that the planes were already in the hangars at 0715.

As mentioned, most commentators (including Senshi Sosho) have judged Nagumo's decision at 0715 to rearm his "second wave" planes to have been a reasonable one, given the circumstances at that time. Clearly, Midway had not been sufficiently neutralized by the first strike, and the aircraft based there and the gun emplacements still standing had to be dealt with. But one might ask whether there was a less risky alternative available for doing this that would also have preserved Nagumo's ability to respond to a sudden American carrier threat. Was it necessary to rearm the torpedo planes—or could dive-bombers and Zeros alone have done the job?

THE SECOND DECISION—TO COUNTERMAND THE REARMING ORDER

At 0728, a formation of ten American warships was sighted by a search plane from the cruiser *Tone* (referred to as *Tone* 4.) There are two keys points on which the commentators disagree. First, and most crucial, is the matter of when Nagumo received this report. Nagumo claimed in his battle report that he did not receive it until "about 0800," and went on to say that the delay in getting it to him "greatly affected our subsequent attack preparations."[16] However, this claim has been almost universally rejected by historians—all American ones and Senshi Sosho as well—largely because it is inconsistent with two entries in the message log of that same report.

The first entry is Nagumo's order, logged at 0745, countermanding the 0715 rearming order. The second is an order, logged at 0747, by Nagumo to *Tone* 4 to "ascertain ship types." These orders, of course, make no sense unless Nagumo had already received the sighting report. It was the doyen of American naval history, Samuel Eliot Morison, who commented back in 1949 that Nagumo's claim of an 0800 receipt was "belied" by his countermand order logged at 0745.[17]

The earliest American commentators assumed that the radio room on Nagumo's flagship *Akagi* received *Tone* 4's sighting report directly, and thus Nagumo received it around 0730. Senshi Sosho, however, offers convincing evidence that *Tone* 4's report was first received by its mother ship—the cruiser *Tone*—and was then deciphered and relayed to *Akagi*.[18] Accordingly, most modern commentators, unwilling to accept that this procedure could take much longer than ten minutes, assume that Nagumo received it around 0740.[19]

The second controversy is over what Nagumo did in response to this report. All American commentators, and Senshi Sosho, say he issued an order at 0745 countermanding the 0715 rearming order. But did this order reverse the rearming procedure (back to torpedoes and antiship bombs) or merely suspend the procedure—freezing, for the time being, the armament status of the bombers? (The order logged in Nagumo's battle report is ambiguous: "Prepare to carry out attacks on enemy fleet units. Leave torpedoes on those attack planes which have not as yet been changed to bombs.")[20]

Most American authorities say that the rearming operation was merely "halted"—either because Nagumo was not convinced that the unidentified ships presented a threat and was waiting for further information from the search plane or because he was frozen into indecision by the shock of the bad news.[21] The failure to reverse the rearming operation—for whatever reason— is considered by some a prime example of Nagumo's indecisiveness and "dithering." Senshi Sosho, on the other hand, takes the position that the order was interpreted as ordering the rearming operation to immediately be reversed, that torpedoes were to be restored to any planes from which they had been removed.[22] The decision to reverse the rearming procedure was made by Nagumo just minutes after receiving the sighting report; there was no "dithering" according to Senshi Sosho, and mere suspension was not considered.

However, Sawachi takes a dismissive approach to the whole rearmament controversy: she says that no countermand order of any kind was issued at 0745 (just as no rearming order had been issued at 0715). No reversal of the rearming operation—which, according to her, had commenced at 0520—was ordered until after 0830, when Nagumo learned for certain that at least one American carrier was in the area. She accepts Nagumo's claim that he did not receive the initial *Tone* 4 sighting report until about 0800—by which time the torpedo planes would have all been rearmed with 800-kilogram land bombs. She contends that the entire scenario of the "change, change back again" of the armament between 0715 and 0745 depicted in Nagumo's battle report and Senshi Sosho is myth—fabricated to make Nagumo appear less insubordinate to Yamamoto's "standing order" regarding the torpedo planes, and more responsive to the American carrier threat, than he actually was.[23]

Even if one rejects the Sawachi thesis, it is still clear that something is very wrong with the chronology of the "standard scenario." If the rearming operation began at 0715 and was suspended at 0745, as portrayed in that scenario, only thirty minutes of work would have been done on the torpedo planes. Even if the work to restore the torpedoes did not begin until a little after 0830, surely the torpedo squadrons on *Akagi* and *Kaga* could have been made ready for launch well before 1025. (At 1000, as we will see, there was a fifteen-minute "window" between the American torpedo bomber attacks during which a strike force could have been launched.)

This, then, is the nub of the problem: why could not what had been done in thirty minutes be undone in less than one and a half hours? A timely reloading of the torpedoes should have been possible, even though for much of the hour and a half after 0830 the Mobile Force was recovering the Midway strike force and fending off attacks by American carrier-based torpedo bombers; under the standard scenario's chronology, there simply would not have been that much to do.

If the rearming operation was actually reversed at 0745, as Senshi Sosho has it, this inability to get the torpedoes back on in time is even more incredible. Even though attacks by American dive-bombers began at 0805—which, because of evasive maneuvering by the carriers to avoid the bombs, would have disrupted efforts to restore the torpedoes—there still would have been fifteen to twenty minutes of clear time after 0745 in which to begin reversing the rearming operation. (Senshi Sosho fudges this by implying that the American attacks began almost immediately after 0745,[24] but American accounts—which are more credible on this issue—have the dive-bombers not making their first dives until about 0805.) Thus, under Senshi Sosho's scenario, when the attacks by American dive-bombers (and then B-17s, and then more dive-bombers) were over at around 0835, there would only would have been about fifteen minutes worth of work left to restore the torpedoes. If the rearming procedure was in fact reversed at 0745, operations to raise the torpedo plane squadrons to the flight decks of *Akagi* and *Kaga* should have been possible as soon as the Midway strike force had been landed shortly after 0900.

But the torpedo squadrons were not ready to be deployed to the flight decks soon after 0900. In fact, according to Senshi Sosho, most of the torpedo planes were still in the hangars of *Akagi* and *Kaga* at 1025 when those carriers were bombed.[25] (Though early American and Japanese commentators have the Japanese strike force on the flight decks about to be launched at 1025, this turns out to be myth.) The fact that the torpedo planes were still in the hangars at 1025 is what appears to have led Sawachi to hypothesize that the rearming operation began long before 0715, and conclude that the entries in Nagumo's battle report showing that the rearming operation was ordered at 0715 and countermanded at 0745 were fabrications to put Nagumo in a better light.

Sawachi's thesis is beguiling, but there are two things wrong with it. First, for it to be true, a lot of people—including the staff officers who compiled Nagumo's battle report—had to be lying. Her theory is based, in part at least, on a conspiracy among Nagumo and his staff to cover up the true chronology of the rearming operation. Such a conspiracy would had to have been kept secret by Nagumo's staff officers for many decades after the war. This seems highly implausible; surely somebody would eventually have spilled the beans. (Ryunosuke Kusaka, Nagumo's chief of staff, and Minoru Genda, his air officer, both wrote books and gave many interviews after the war. Even had they been intent on keeping the secret, it would seem that Mitsuo Fuchida—who had been designated to lead the attack on Midway until he was laid up on *Akagi* with appendicitis—would have ferreted out such a cover-up. He later wrote the book *Mid-*

way, the Battle That Doomed Japan, which was highly critical of Nagumo, and then moved to America.)

Second, her thesis proves too much. If the operation to rearm the torpedo planes with land bombs began shortly after 0520, as she contends, the rearming would almost certainly have been completed before 0800. It would then have taken about two hours to change the torpedo planes from 800-kilogram land bombs back to torpedoes, assuming no disruptions from air attacks. As Sawachi also contends that operations to change back to torpedoes were not ordered by Nagumo until 0840, it therefore would take until 1040 to complete if there were no disruptions.

But there were disruptions, the most serious of which were the two American torpedo bomber attacks between 0930 and 1000. These again required Nagumo's carriers to maneuver radically at battle speed to avoid the torpedoes; the sharp turns and heeling decks made it almost impossible to move the 1,872-pound torpedoes, let alone jack them up and attach them to the planes. At 1015, such operations would again terminate—this time for good—when the third wave of American torpedo bombers attacked. There would still have been almost an hour's work left to be done to completely restore the torpedoes. Yet there is substantial evidence that at the time of the fatal American bombing, the torpedoes had been fully restored to the torpedo planes (though most of the planes still remained in the hangars).

Thus, while under the American standard scenario (and especially Senshi Sosho's) there would not have been enough left to do after 0830 to explain why the torpedo planes were not ready for launch before 1000, under Sawachi's scenario there would have been too much to do to account for the armament status that appears to have existed at 1025. Is there another scenario for the rearming operation that would be consistent with that armament status? What if the rearming operation on the torpedo planes, ordered by Nagumo at 0715, actually continued until a little after 0800 before it was countermanded? That would have left forty-five minutes worth of work to be undone, commencing at a little after 0830 when the attacks from Midway were over. We will see that even with the disruptions caused by the American torpedo bomber attacks there still would have been time to get the torpedoes back on by soon after 1000 (though not enough time to get the torpedo squadrons up to the flight decks before 1025).

Is there any evidence that the rearming operation continued until at least 0800? We have seen that Nagumo's claim that he did not receive the *Tone* 4 sighting report until "about 0800" (and therefore would not have countermanded the rearming operation before then) has been discounted by the American commentators, as well as Senshi Sosho. Even though the claim of an 0800 receipt time was later supported by Kusaka and Genda,[26] it has been rejected because it is said to be "belied" by entries in the "composite log" of

Nagumo's own battle report indicating that the countermand order was issued at 0745, and a request for details as to ship types was sent to *Tone* 4 at 0747.

But what if Nagumo actually did not receive the *Tone* 4 sighting report until 0800, as he claimed? Is it possible that there is something wrong with the times recorded in the "composite log" of Nagumo's battle report for those two conflicting entries? I am not suggesting deliberate fabrication, as does Sawachi, but simply the kind of honest logging mistakes commonly made in the chaos and fog of battle.

In any case, to continue with the accepted chronology, after Nagumo had received the initial vague sighting report he sought clarification from the search plane crew as to the types of American ships spotted. At 0809, the search plane reported back that the formation consisted only of five cruisers and five destroyers—no carriers. Most commentators have Nagumo's staff expressing great relief at this,[27] but some have noted that at least one key staff officer held reservations as to whether carriers could be ruled out by this report. (After all, what would these ships be doing in the area if not to escort carriers, Kusaka is reported to had said.)[28] At the time Nagumo received this more specific report, the Mobile Force was under attack by sixteen dive-bombers from Midway. As soon as it ended, fourteen B-17s from Midway began—at about 0814—their bombing runs. Most authorities agree that at this time the last Zeros remaining in the "second wave" were deployed for air defense.

THE THIRD DECISION—TO POSTPONE ATTACK

At 0820 the *Tone* search plane reported a shocking addition to its 0809 report: there "appeared" to be an aircraft carrier in the American task force! Nagumo received this report ten minutes later at 0830, at the time the Midway strike force had just returned and was requesting an immediate landing (some of the planes were shot up, and many were low on fuel.) A quick decision had to be made whether to launch an immediate attack or postpone until the planes back from Midway were recovered. At about this time, Rear Admiral Tamon Yamaguchi, commander of the Second Carrier Division (containing *Hiryu* and *Soryu*) stepped in to urge that a strike be launched immediately against the American carrier, regardless of the armament condition of the torpedo planes and regardless of the lack of a fighter escort.[29] His dive-bombers were properly armed to attack ships and could be launched in very short order. But Nagumo's air officer, Genda, counseled in favor of an immediate landing of the Midway strike force as he feared that a delay would result in many of its planes running out of fuel and having to ditch in the ocean.

At around 0835 Nagumo decided against launching an immediate attack. Instead, he chose to land the Midway strike force, restore the torpedoes to his second-wave torpedo planes, and then launch a "grand-scale" coordinated attack with an adequate Zero escort. This decision not to launch an immediate strike against the American carrier force is the one most harshly criticized by most American commentators. If an effective strike could have been launched, the failure to do it would certainly stand as Nagumo's signal blunder of the battle. He had known since before 0600 that his carriers had been discovered by American reconnaissance planes.[30] Thus, it would seem that he had to assume that an American carrier-based attack was imminent. A launch, even if substantially less than full strength, would have done some damage to the American carrier force. But, perhaps more important, it would have gotten the planes off his own carriers and prevented most of the damage that resulted from the American dive-bomber attack a little under two hours later.

Why, then, did he not launch at 0835? The reasons given by the American standard scenario are the following: lack of Zeros to provide an adequate escort for the bombers—because combat air patrols had used them all up to fend off the attacks from Midway; pressure from his air officer to land the recently returned Midway strike force to avoid ditching; and Nagumo's disdain for launching a "half-cocked" strike when "with a little more time" a much deadlier grand-scale attack could be made.[31] One might wonder what made Nagumo think that he had the time to organize such an attack force before he himself was attacked, but this is not addressed in any of the American accounts except for the suggestion that he was arrogantly confident that his combat air patrol could fend off any American attack.

Given the seriousness of the American carrier threat facing Nagumo, it would seem that the key issue in assessing the reasonableness of this third decision is whether he had the resources available at 0830—or soon afterward—to launch an effective strike. What then was available? There is near unanimity by commentators from both sides of the Pacific that the thirty-six dive-bombers on *Hiryu* and *Soryu* were properly armed and could have been launched fairly soon after 0830 (at least some may have already been on the flight decks). However, most American authorities say that there were no Zeros remaining on board to escort them. This was difficult to understand from the earlier accounts, which had as many as ninety operational Zeros on the four carriers going into the battle.[32] As only thirty-six were in the Midway strike force, one was given to wonder why some of the remaining fifty-four could not have been spared from the combat air patrol to provide at least a minimal escort for the dive-bombers.

Senshi Sosho provides a credible answer. There were only seventy-two operational Zeros in the carrier air groups—eighteen on each carrier—plus a few "spares" without pilots.[33] In addition, there were twenty-one Zeros of the land-based Sixth Air Group being ferried for use on Midway after its capture.[34] But it appears that very few of their pilots were carrier-qualified; Senshi Sosho mentions only two being used to reinforce the combat air patrol. Thus, according to Senshi Sosho, Nagumo had only seventy-four Zeros available for the battle.

(This low number has been accepted by the later American commentators.) After the Midway strike force departed, only thirty-eight remained on board, and, according to Senshi Sosho, all of these had been committed to the combat air patrol by 0830.[35] (As there is continuing controversy over whether there actually were some Zeros available for escort—despite Senshi Sosho's contention to the contrary—in chapter 6 I will reconstruct the CAP activity from Japanese primary records in an attempt to resolve this issue.)

According to Senshi Sosho, Nagumo was loath to send the dive-bombers to attack unescorted. It was feared that without escorts most of the dive-bombers would be shot down by American combat air patrol before dropping their bombs—a sacrifice of irreplaceable pilots that Japan could not afford. The just witnessed sacrifice of the unescorted Midway-based American dive-bombers is said to have made an impression. Nagumo was also reluctant to send the dive-bombers without torpedo planes. The two bomber-types attacking together would split the defenses between high and low level, making both less vulnerable to American combat air patrol and antiaircraft gunfire. Thus, not only would an attack by just dive-bombers be ineffective and wasteful of dive-bombers, but a later attack by torpedo planes without dive-bombers would be less effective and more wasteful of torpedo planes.

Therefore, in assessing whether an effective strike was available to Nagumo at 0830, or soon after, we must determine not only the state of readiness of the dive-bombers on *Hiryu* and *Soryu*, but the armament status of the torpedo planes on *Akagi* and *Kaga*. Torpedo planes, when equipped with torpedoes, were the most important component of Nagumo's strike force (in contrast to the American carrier air groups, in which dive-bombers were paramount). Aerial torpedoes were Japan's secret weapon for sinking American carriers. Not only were they very accurate, reliable and deadly, but if the torpedo planes were equipped only with 800-kilogram land bombs it was almost impossible for those bombs to be delivered to a rapidly maneuvering ship by level bombing—the Kate torpedo plane could not dive-bomb. However, despite the critical role torpedo planes played in an attack, the armament status of the torpedo planes on *Akagi* and *Kaga* as described in the existing literature is very murky. Did any still have torpedoes on them?

We have seen that most American commentators state that the rearming operation was suspended at 0745, by which time the rearming of the torpedo planes was "about half" completed. Many assume this means that about half the planes still had torpedoes attached (but that they were in the hangars), and about half had been rearmed with 800-kilogram land bombs. Some say that those torpedo planes equipped with land bombs had been brought up to the flight decks before 0830.[36] Thus, under the American standard scenario, it would appear that some bomb-laden torpedo planes could have been launched almost immediately and that many others with torpedoes attached—perhaps half the squadrons—could have been brought up from the hangars and launched fairly soon after 0830. If that were indeed the case, Nagumo's decision to postpone his strike would seem highly questionable—even foolhardy.

Senshi Sosho's version of the armament status of the torpedo planes at 0830 is even more difficult to fathom. We have seen that under its scenario the rearming operation was reversed—not just suspended—at 0745. Moreover, as the operation would have taken one and one-half hours—not just one—there would not have been any torpedo planes rearmed with land bombs and returned to the flight decks by 0830; all the planes would have been in the hangars. It does not comment on the actual armament status of the torpedo planes at 0830, other than to say that they "were not rearmed for ships." (It does note, though, that even had they all had been equipped with torpedoes it would have taken forty minutes to get them up to the flight decks and made ready for launch.)[37]

Senshi Sosho's dismissal of the torpedo planes is curious. We have seen that if the rearming operation was, in fact, reversed at 0745—and work to restore the torpedoes continued until the dive-bomber attacks from Midway made further progress impossible at a little after 0800—then it would seem that quite a few of the planes, perhaps two-thirds, could have had torpedoes attached at 0830. (Indeed, under Senshi Sosho's chronology, there should have been only about an additional fifteen minutes worth of work required to completely restore the torpedoes.)

Moreover, although it took forty minutes to raise a squadron of torpedo planes to the flight decks of *Akagi* and *Kaga* and prepare them for launch, we will see that this was the case only when one elevator (the aft) was used, the normal situation when the hangar also contained a squadron of dive-bombers. However, when the dive-bombers were out of the hangars of those carriers—as they were at 0830—then it would seem that the midship elevator could also be used to raise the torpedo planes. In that case, two-thirds of a squadron (twelve planes) could be raised and spotted on the flight deck in about fifteen minutes. All this simply does not jibe with Senshi Sosho's vague statement that the torpedo planes "were not rearmed for ships."

But, as we will see, it is now clear that the torpedoes were nowhere near being restored to the planes at 0830. There was so much work left to do that they were not ready even at 1000 (and, in fact, their launch had been scheduled for 1030 even before the American torpedo bomber attacks disrupted that timetable). This armament status is far more consistent with a scenario in which the rearming operation began at 0715, and continued, unabated, until shortly after 0800— which would have been the case had Nagumo not received the initial *Tone* 4 sighting report until 0800. In that event, it will be seen that had the rearming operation continued until 0800, it is almost certain that all the torpedoes would have been removed from the torpedo plane squadrons on *Akagi* and *Kaga*. Neither the American accounts nor Senshi Sosho provide a plausible scenario for their armament status at 0830. Is it possible that at 0830 none of the torpedo planes had any torpedoes on them?

Though Senshi Sosho is very vague about the armament status of the torpedo planes, according to it, the unavailability of the torpedo planes was a key factor (along with the unavailability of Zeros for escort) in the decision by Nagumo and his staff to forgo launching an attack at 0830. In view of the unavailability of an effective attack at that time, the superior option, it was agreed by all in the headquarters staff, was to wait. First land the Midway strike force, properly arm the second-wave torpedo planes, and then organize an adequate Zero escort. This would provide for a coordinated grand-scale attack that could inflict far more damage, with much smaller losses, than an immediate attack by dive-bombers alone. All that was needed was a little time.

But the bedeviling question—unanswered by the American literature—is what made Nagumo think he had the time to do all this before American carrier planes attacked? (As already mentioned, it would seem that at 0830 an attack was imminent, as Nagumo knew that his Mobile Force had been discovered almost three hours earlier.) Senshi Sosho is the only authority to give an explanation for this conundrum: the Mobile Force was believed to be beyond the range of the American Wildcat fighter plane.[38] Based on *Tone* 4's sighting report, Nagumo's staff estimated that—at 0728—the American carrier force was over 200 miles away. While it was assumed that the American dive-bombers had the range to attack from this distance and return to their carrier, it was believed that the Wildcat fighter did not. (In fact, the Wildcat's combat radius was only about 175 miles.) This, it was hoped, meant that the Wildcats probably would not be sent from that distance to escort the dive-bombers.

Therefore, it was reasoned that if the American dive-bombers attacked without escorts, it would be easy to shoot most of them down before they could release their bombs; the carriers of the Mobile Force would most likely survive such an attack. (There is, of course, an irony here: the American dive-bombers did attack without escorts, but the Mobile Force did not survive the attack. However, as will be explained in chapter 7, the circumstances that led to this were so bizarre as to have been unimaginable to Nagumo and his staff at 0830.) If, on the other hand, the American commander opted to attack with escorts, it was reckoned that he would have to steam closer to the Mobile Force, delaying a launch until much later than 0730. This, it was reckoned, would give "plenty of time" to rearm the torpedo planes and get them launched before the American attack arrived.[39] Such a delayed attack was deemed the more likely option. Senshi Sosho does not say when the American attack was expected, but it appears that it was not expected to arrive until at least 1000. (We will see that when

Nagumo made his decision to postpone, he contemplated a launch by then; the 1030 launch time was scheduled later.)

Thus, according to Senshi Sosho, at 0830 Nagumo and his staff actually had reason to believe that they had the time to organize a grand-scale attack. Though this might seem unconvincing to many, Yoshioka, the staff officer who compiled the composite log of Nagumo's battle report, is quoted as saying "this decision was easily made according to my recollection."[40]

But we will see in chapter 6 that the problem with Nagumo's calculation was that *Tone* 4's navigator had mislocated the position of the American task force. It actually was 30 miles closer to the Mobile Force—only about 175 miles away at 0728. Senshi Sosho acknowledges that the flaw in Nagumo's supposition that he had time to organize a grand-scale attack was the unquestioned assumption that *Tone* 4's report of the location of the American force was accurate. It states that nobody in the headquarters of either *Akagi* or cruiser *Tone* noticed that if the *Tone* 4 search plane was on course it could not possibly have seen the American fleet at the location reported.

Senshi Sosho's explanation of why Nagumo thought he had time to land the Midway strike force and organize a grand-scale attack may still seem unconvincing if it is assumed—as some commentators have—that at 0830 Nagumo thought he had at least two hours, and scheduled the launch for 1030 at *that* time. However, Senshi Sosho suggests that the decision at 0830 was merely to wait until the Midway strike force was landed, along with those Zeros on combat air patrol that were low on fuel and ammunition. This could be done before 0920. It appears that Nagumo assumed that by that time the torpedo planes would have their torpedoes restored and that the deployment of the strike force to the flight decks would be under way. Thus, at 0830, Nagumo may have contemplated a postponement of his launch for only a little over an hour.

But the torpedo planes were not ready at 0920. Indeed, it was at about that time, according to Senshi Sosho, that he was told by his air group commanders that the torpedo planes on *Akagi* and *Kaga* would not be ready for launch until 1030. (It would appear that at 0830 Nagumo's staff had no idea what the armament status of the torpedo planes actually was.) As it turned out, they would not be ready for launch even at 1030. Thus, in retrospect, the decision to postpone the attack was a disaster—which makes it easy to say, as most American commentators have, that the decision was the cardinal blunder by Nagumo. However, Senshi Sosho maintains that it was still the best option available under the circumstances existing at 0830, when the decision was made.

Was it reasonable for Nagumo to postpone? In chapter 6 I will compare the two options: an immediate attack with dive-bombers alone or a later coordinated attack, in terms of the likely damage that would have been inflicted on the American carrier force and the likely costs to the Japanese in aircraft and pilots.

THE SEARCH EFFORT

Along with scorn for Nagumo's decisions—especially the postponement of his attack—the Japanese search effort on the morning of the battle has also taken a lambasting by many proponents of the American standard scenario. It is said that Nagumo's search plan for the morning of June 4 was grossly inadequate and sloppily executed and that the performance of the *Tone* 4 crew was woefully inept. It is assumed that with a more adequate search effort the American fleet would probably have been discovered before 0728, thus preventing the fatal rearming order; and with a more observant search plane crew in *Tone* 4, one or more carriers would have been seen in the initial sighting—sharpening Nagumo's response. As will be seen, both of these assumptions are dubious.

THE SEARCH PLAN

It consisted of seven lines, covering an arc from 20 degrees north to 180 degrees south at a distance of 300 nautical miles. At the end of their lines, the search planes were to make a 60-mile dogleg to the left before returning to their mother ships. Criticisms of the adequacy of Nagumo's search plan focus on two points: density of the search lines and timeliness of the departure of the search planes.

It is true that Nagumo's search plan on the morning of June 4 was skimpy compared with the Americans'—which employed twenty-two search planes. However, this comparison might not be entirely fair. The Americans were expecting to find Japanese carriers in the Midway area, and thus the purpose of their search was to find them as early as possible. Nagumo, on the other hand, was not expecting American carriers to be in the area. His search effort was merely precautionary, and it can be argued that compared with similar routine searches by both sides during the war, it was reasonably adequate. In any event, is the assumption that a more extensive search effort would probably have resulted in an earlier discovery of the American fleet a sound one?

Second, many American commentators make much of the fact that *Tone* 4 was launched thirty minutes late. (The reason, whether engine trouble or a catapult malfunction, is in dispute.) An assumption of the standard scenario is that had it been launched on time—at 0430 instead of 0500—the American fleet would have been discovered thirty minutes earlier, which would have avoided the whole rearming problem. Is this assumption sound?

Senshi Sosho sheds some fascinating new light on this matter: it concludes that *Tone* 4's search path had been substantially shortened en route from the scheduled course. Senshi Sosho's reconstruction of the actual course flown shows that *Tone* 4 turned north after flying only about 240 miles of its scheduled 300-mile outbound path.[41] Senshi Sosho could not determine the reason for this. *Tone* 4's crew did not survive the war, and the surviving officers from cruiser *Tone*'s headquarters could not explain it. *Tone* 4's crew had not been instructed to shorten their course. Senshi Sosho suggests that it may have been done by the pilot to make up for the time lost by the late launch.

Whatever the reason, the shortened course proved most fortuitous. After making a dogleg to the north, *Tone* 4 turned west; it had proceeded several miles on its return path when it spotted the American fleet. Its shortened course enabled *Tone* 4 to find the American fleet over an hour earlier than it otherwise would have, had it flown the scheduled course. This highly ironical conclusion refutes the criticism leveled in most American commentaries that had *Tone* 4 been launched on time—at 0430 instead of 0500—the American fleet would have been discovered thirty minutes earlier—at 0700 instead of 0728—thus preventing the fatal rearming order at 0715.

However fortuitous the sighting was, the fact remains that *Tone* 4 reported the American task force's position as being about 55 miles north of its actual position. Senshi Sosho has no good explanation for this navigation error. However, it should be noted that their navigational error was not particularly unusual when compared with other sighting reports early in the war. (We will see that the American PBY search plane that discovered Nagumo's carrier force earlier that morning mislocated it by 40 miles, and reconnaissance by both sides in the Battle of the Coral Sea a month earlier was equally inaccurate.) Because navigational instruments were primitive at that time, reconnaissance at sea was notoriously unreliable. Indeed, it is difficult to find a sighting report from the first year of the war that places ships within 30 miles of their actual location. *Tone* 4's faulty navigation, however, had serious consequences: it resulted in *Tone* 4 placing the American ships 30 miles further away from the Mobile Force than they actually were. This misled Nagumo into thinking he had more time before being attacked than he actually had, which, according to Senshi Sosho, was a major reason for his decision to postpone.

THE PERFORMANCE OF THE *TONE* 4 CREW

They have been made the principal scapegoats for the Japanese disaster at Midway. No one, including Nagumo, has been subjected to more ridicule. And like Nagumo, they did not survive the war to tell their side of the story. The main criticism of them arises from the fact that it took fifty-two minutes—until 0820—after the first sighting of American ships at 0728 to identify an aircraft carrier, and then, only one of the three actually present. The standard scenario condemns the crew as obviously incompetent. Even those commentators more charitable toward the Japanese than the earliest critics have difficulty understanding why it took fifty-two minutes—"nobody could miss anything that big for long," it is said.[42]

However, Senshi Sosho gives a finding not noted by any other account of the battle, which, if true, requires a completely new assessment of the reason why no carriers were spotted on the initial contact at 0728. It has been generally assumed by American commentators that the first sighting by *Tone* 4 was made from a considerable distance—at least 30 miles. At that distance aircraft carriers would be difficult to distinguish from cruisers, especially if the search plane was at fairly low altitude (such as five thousand feet or lower), and visibility was somewhat hazy. However, Senshi Sosho concludes that *Tone* 4 was quite close to the American fleet when it first spotted it, perhaps less than 10 miles.[43]

The basis of this startling conclusion is that, in addition to cloudiness in the area that would have prevented a long-distance sighting, *Tone* 4's sighting report gave the course of the American ships in precise degrees rather than general direction (150 degrees rather than merely "southeasterly"). This is something the crew could not have done had they been at a distance approaching the limit of visibility. If this was indeed the case, then the exact composition of the "ten ships" spotted should have been easily discernable.

Thus, why it took so long to identify a carrier is still a mystery; Senshi Sosho attributes it to inexperience and carelessness on the part of the crew, but concedes that limited visibility caused by cloudiness in the vicinity of the American fleet may have also been a factor. But is it just possible that the *Tone* 4 crew reported exactly what they saw and that there were no carriers with the "ten ships" they saw before 0820? There has been a tendency to assume that the entire panorama of the American fleet was visible to a competent observer, but there was much more cloudiness in the area before 0800 than is generally recognized. As will be seen, many of the American ships could have been hidden by clouds, especially if fleet elements became separated during launch operations between 0705 and 0806.

TOWARD A MORE PLAUSIBLE SCENARIO

As can be seen, there are too many things that do not make sense in the existing literature on the Battle of Midway. Even Senshi Sosho, though it fills in many of the gaps in the American standard scenario, fails to provide a satisfactory explanation for the most perplexing mystery of Midway: why Nagumo could not get an attack force launched before he was bombed at 1025.

But before addressing that question, mention must be made of a recent book that purports to render such an inquiry moot: *Shattered Sword: The Untold Story of the Battle of Midway*, by Jonathan Parshall and Anthony Tully.[44] This book advances the thesis that the torpedoes had, in fact, been fully restored to the torpedo planes on *Akagi* and *Kaga* by around 0917,[45] which means that the entire strike force could have been deployed to the flight decks of the Mobile Force beginning at that time. Had that been the case, it would have been possible to commence the launch of a strike against the American carrier force a little after 1000, with the planes off the flight decks by 1010–1015—at least ten minutes before the fatal bombing at 1025. (We have seen that when Nagumo made his decision, at a little after 0830, to postpone his attack until after the Midway strike force had been recovered, he did so with the hope that a grand-scale strike force could then be deployed to the flight decks at that time. The Midway strike force, along with a number of Zeros on combat air patrol (CAP) needing reservicing, had been landed by 0918.)

Thus, if Parshall and Tully's conclusion that the torpedo planes had been re-armed with torpedoes by 0917 is true, this should have been very good news for Nagumo. But, according to those authors, Nagumo declined to deploy his strike force at that opportunity. Why? Because at 0918 a squadron of American tor-pedo bombers had been spotted coming in about 20 miles out, and this suppos-edly precluded spotting the strike force; Japanese "carrier doctrine" required that the flight decks be kept clear for CAP operations until the threat from enemy planes was over.

As a general principle this, at first blush, does not seem too unreasonable — until we look at precisely what CAP operations would be necessary between 0918 and 1010. The most obvious one would be the launch of Zeros to reinforce the CAP. Indeed, the Japanese records show that over thirty Zeros were launched from the four carriers between 0920 and 1000. Parshall and Tully seem to imply that this would preclude deployment of attack planes to the flight decks. But Zeros required only the forward third or so of the flight deck to take off (and were deployed from the front hangar via the forward elevator). Thus, such CAP operations would in no way be impeded by the spotting of at-tack aircraft on the rear of the flight deck (via the aft and midship elevators). Even Parshall and Tully concede that fighters could take off from the bow dur-ing spotting operations at the rear, but they go on to say "in practice we know of no instances where this was done."[46] As there is no other instance during the war where the Japanese were attempting to spot a strike force while under at-tack, this is not surprising. But it has no bearing on what Nagumo might do when presented with such an emergency.

Landings of Zeros on CAP would, however, be another matter. Clearly, if it was expected that a substantial number of Zeros would have to be landed be-tween 0918 and 1010, it would not be advisable to have bombers spotted at the rear of the flight decks. But as those Zeros on CAP in need of reservicing had already been landed by 0918, along with the Midway strike force, it would seem that those still aloft can be assumed to have had sufficient fuel to last until after 1010. (Typically, when Zeros were refueled for CAP duty they were given enough fuel to last for at least three hours.) The only servicing they would be expected to need during the period it would take to spot and launch the strike force would be for rearming their guns should ammunition be exhausted dur-ing air combat.

Japanese records show that only *four* Zeros were actually landed during that period. Two of these came down, apparently for refueling, at 0930. As they had been launched 0710, it is most likely that they could have stayed aloft until after 1010. But as the flight deck of their carrier was clear at 0930, there was no reason to wait. (Just because Zeros were landed for refueling when their flight deck was clear does not mean that it would have been necessary to land them to avoid ditching had their flight deck been occupied by attack aircraft.) The other two came down at 0951. As they had been in the air less than one hour and twenty minutes, it is likely that they landed to have their guns rearmed after having exhausted their ammunition (at least their 20-mm cannon shells) in attacks on American torpedo bombers.

Are we to believe that the deployment of a strike force on the flight decks would have been scuttled because two Zeros ran out of ammunition? Or, more to the point, are we to believe that at 0918 Nagumo would have postponed the deployment of a grand-scale strike force ready to go because two or more Zeros might run out of ammunition during the next fifty minutes? There are, no doubt, some readers who will accept Parshall and Tully's thesis that the Japanese were so hidebound by "doctrine," or so stupid, that Nagumo would have postponed deployment of a fully ready strike force at 0918. I prefer to credit the Japanese with enough moxie to have found a way to get such a strike force spotted and launched before 1025 — even at the risk of a few Zeros running out of ammunition — had they, in fact, had one ready to go at 0918.

In any case, this is a completely academic issue: absolutely no evidence is presented in *Shattered Sword* to show that the torpedo planes on *Akagi* and *Kaga* were rearmed with torpedoes by around 0917. The evidence, primarily from Nagumo's official report (but also from many other Japanese sources), is that they were not ready. In fact, it was at about this time that Nagumo was explicitly informed by his air group commanders that the torpedo planes on *Akagi* and *Kaga* would not be "ready for take-off" until 1030. Parshall and Tully dismiss this, and strongly imply that Nagumo simply lied in his official report. (As discussed earlier, Sawachi also made that allegation concerning a different issue.)

With regard to both of these charges it should be noted that the Office of Naval Intelligence, which published the translation of Nagumo's official report, states in a preface: "There is nothing to indicate that the Japanese were not perfectly frank in this report. It was intended only for the highest echelons in the Japanese Navy and Government, and was guarded very closely throughout the war." I might be accused of naivety, but I accept this and generally reject all scenarios — Sawachi's as well as Parshall and Tully's — premised on flagrant fabrications in Nagumo's official report. Therefore, we must return to the question of why the torpedo planes were not ready in time to be launched before *Akagi* and *Kaga* were destroyed at around 1025.

I believe I can reconstruct a more plausible scenario of what happened on the Japanese side of the battle — especially during the period between 0700 and

1030 when the outcome of the battle was determined. It will be based on material either unavailable to previous American commentators or underutilized by them: untranslated Japanese literature, the Japanese primary records, and new testimony from Japanese veterans of the battle.

JAPANESE LITERATURE

As this book primarily deals with the Japanese side of the battle, not surprisingly it relies heavily on Japanese sources. Two of the most productive such sources have already been mentioned: Senshi Sosho's *The Midway Sea Battle*, and Sawachi's *Record of the Midway Sea Battle*. The Senshi Sosho volume is the most detailed Japanese account of the battle ever produced. It has been cited to by several more recent American commentators, but there is no reference to many of its more illuminating findings. Although Senshi Sosho has its defects (and I have taken issue with its timing of the reversal of the rearming operation), a plausible scenario of what happened on the Japanese side of the battle cannot, nevertheless, be reconstructed without taking it into account.

Sawachi's book is a more revisionist, and certainly a more provocative, account of the decisions made by Nagumo, and appears to be largely a critique of Senshi Sosho. Her contribution is useful as it exposes what are some of the irrationalities of the accepted view of events in Nagumo's headquarters, and why they utterly fail to explain why the Japanese carriers were caught so unprepared to meet the American carrier threat. While I reject much of her scenario as too extreme, I was spurred on by it to come up with a new alternative scenario—one not predicated on deliberate falsification of the record or conspiracy theories—to explain why Nagumo could not get an attack launched in time.

Resort has also been made to other Japanese language books, most notably those by Kusaka and Genda. There was one Japanese source—Fuchida and Okumiya's original *Midway*—that produced a surprise.[47] It had been translated into English and published in America in 1955, and became one of the cornerstones of the American standard scenario. However, some of the chronology had been changed by the editors to conform to the early American scenario propounded by Morison. In particular, the time of Nagumo's receipt of the *Tone* 4 sighting report was changed by the editors from around 0800 to around 0740, and although the original text makes no mention of an order by Nagumo countermanding the rearming order at 0745, this time was inserted into the American version.[48] (The editors were frank in admitting that the original text had been extensively revised and that details concerning chronology that "have long been known" in the United States were inserted to flesh out the otherwise skimpy account.)[49]

PRIMARY RECORDS

There are two Japanese primary records of the battle that have been translated into English. The most important is Nagumo's official battle report, entitled

"Mobile Force's Detailed Battle Report #6," dated 15 June 1942, translated and published by the Office of Naval Intelligence in 1947 under the title "The Japanese Story of the Battle of Midway."[50] (This is referred to as Nagumo's battle report or simply "Official Report.") Also useful are the Action Reports of the air groups of the four carriers, but they are fragmentary and were never published.[51]

All serious inquiries into what happened on the Japanese side of the battle — especially during the three and a half hour period before the fatal bombing at 1025 — must begin with an analysis of the Official Report. However, the portion relied upon most heavily by American commentators — the composite message log — is ambiguous and full of inconsistencies. The staff officer, Chuichi Yoshioka, who compiled the message log portion of the report later explained why: the headquarters log of the flagship *Akagi* had been lost in the battle; he had to reconstruct the record of communications to and from headquarters from the message logs of the surviving support ships. This resulted in many inconsistencies in the "composite log," and Yoshioka cautioned against placing undue reliance on its accuracy.[52] Early American commentators lacked the benefit of this caveat and assumed that the times given for certain key events — such as the order countermanding the rearming operation — were accurate.

It should be noted that the narrative portion of the Official Report, unlike the "composite log," is tightly written and internally consistent. It is there that Nagumo states that he did not receive the *Tone* 4 sighting report until about 0800 and goes on to complain that the delay in its delivery "greatly affected our subsequent attack preparations." Is it possible that the times indicated in the composite log for the two orders that appear to impeach Nagumo's claim of an 0800 receipt time — the countermand order recorded at 0745, and the first request to *Tone* 4 to identify ship types recorded at 0747 — were mislogged? Is it possible that the countermand order was actually issued after 0800? As will be seen in chapter 5, this is indeed likely.

There is a third document that is tantamount to a primary record: Japanese Monograph No. 93, "Midway Operations May–June 1942."[53] It was produced in 1947 by the Demobilization Bureau, to which records from the War Ministry and Naval General Staff had been transferred. It is very detailed and was prepared by some of Nagumo's staff officers, but has rarely been cited by American commentators. Although it largely parallels Nagumo's official report, it omits the "composite log" and instead incorporates key events from it into the narrative. Notably, however, it gives a different chronology for some of the key events concerning Nagumo's decisions.

For example, as for the contentious issue of the time when Nagumo received the 0728 sighting report, the monograph says it was at "about 0800," and Nagumo's request to *Tone* 4 for details of "ship types" was sent at 0800. There is no mention of any prior order or communication by Nagumo that would be inconsistent with this time. According to it, the countermand order was issued after 0830.[54] Although this chronology would help provide a more convincing explanation for why no attack was launched by Nagumo before most of his carriers were destroyed (and is consistent with the narrative in his official report) this scenario was apparently deemed not credible by American scholars who read it; there is scarcely any reference to it in the English-language accounts of the battle. However, in Japan it appears that this record is treated almost as a primary source along with Nagumo's Official Report.[55]

A fresh reanalysis of the Official Report and other Japanese primary records is needed. It can now be made in light of new information garnered from the Japanese literature not available to earlier American commentators, such as Senshi Sosho, Sawachi, Kusaka, and Genda. Also, new evidence from the Japanese veterans of the battle—pilots and mechanics—clarifies many of the ambiguities in the report.

TESTIMONY FROM JAPANESE VETERANS

The third pillar for my new scenario for Japanese carrier operations on the morning of the battle is testimony from the veterans of the carrier air groups of the Mobile Force. As has been seen, very little is known of the armament status of the torpedo planes on *Akagi* and *Kaga* at key times when crucial decisions had to be made by Nagumo, such as whether to launch a strike at 0830. But a fair assessment of Nagumo's decision to postpone at 0835 cannot be made without knowing the armament status of those torpedo planes at that time—how many, if any, had torpedoes attached. Nor is it possible to understand why the torpedo planes were not ready for launch before the fatal bombing at 1025 without knowing the procedures for rearming the torpedo planes.

As no direct evidence of the armament status of the torpedo planes at the relevant times is available from the Japanese record, it can only be deduced from knowledge of the various procedures required to change those planes from torpedoes to 800-kilogram land bombs and the time it usually took for each procedure. Although the torpedo plane pilots were somewhat familiar with the procedures, the principal witnesses were the weapons mechanics—they were the ones down in the hangar decks literally doing the "heavy lifting."

In the course of three trips to Japan, I conducted oral interviews with almost two dozen veterans of the battle.[56] Another dozen responded by letter to written questions. Most were mechanics who served in the "ground crews" of the torpedo and dive-bomber squadrons of the four carriers sunk at Midway. (Only five torpedo plane pilots could be found—grim testament to the mortality rate of Japanese carrier pilots in the war.)

When one attempts to interview someone about events that occurred fifty years earlier, memory is an obvious problem. To help penetrate the murkiness of this large span of time, I attempted to make use of two types of long-term memory: "flash-bulb" memory, a term descriptive of the phenomenon that people tend to forever remember where they were and what they were doing at the time of a shocking event (such as the Kennedy assassination or the terrorist attack on the World Trade Center), and memory for a procedure that one had once performed regularly.

The shocking event I was relying on for "flash-bulb" memory was the fatal bombing of the carriers just before 1030. Among the questions I thought might be answered were how many torpedo planes were on the flight decks of *Akagi* and *Kaga* at that time and whether any were still in the hangar decks being re-armed. It seemed to me that the pilots would remember whether they were in their planes on the flight deck or not when "all hell broke loose," and the torpedo mechanics would remember whether they were in the hangar deck install-ing torpedoes.

Significantly, most of the pilots remembered being in the hangar with their planes, or being on the flight deck waiting for their planes to be brought up, when the bombs hit. This indicated that the torpedo plane squadrons—for the most part anyway—were not on the flight decks ready for launch at the time their carriers were bombed at around 1025. The weapons mechanics, on the other hand, mostly remembered doing quite mundane things like eating, rest-ing, or standing on the flight deck getting fresh air. None remembered arming planes with torpedoes or bombs at the time of the bombing. This strongly indi-cated that the rearming operation had already been completed by that time, though the planes were mostly still in the hangars.

The memory for procedures regularly done was even more fruitful. I had hoped that by learning about the various operations involved in arming planes with bombs and torpedoes, and approximately how long each operation took (and on how many planes it was performed simultaneously) I could deduce the probable armament status of a squadron of dive-bombers or torpedo planes at each of the times when crucial decisions were made. For example, if it could be learned what could be done to a squadron of torpedo planes thirty minutes into a rearming procedure, it would be possible to determine the likely arma-ment status of those planes at 0745; forty-five minutes into the procedure, the status at 0800; and so on. This would provide a better picture of what Nagumo's options were at those times, especially at 0830 when the decision to launch or postpone had to be made. Recollections of procedures regularly done, though not performed for fifty years, were surprisingly detailed.

However, it must be noted that the various recollections of the veterans con-cerning the arming procedure—especially the times certain procedures took—were not entirely consistent, as one might expect, but general patterns did emerge. New facts were discovered that not only filled in many of the gaps in the records and literature of the battle, but provided a plausible resolution of most of the unresolved questions. The following is a summary of the key findings.

SUMMARY OF KEY FINDINGS FROM THE VETERANS

The rearming operation for torpedo planes was more complicated and took longer than is commonly assumed by American commentators on the battle. The planes were neither rearmed one at a time nor simultaneously for the entire squadron, as has been variously stated, but rather were rearmed one *chutai* (division) at a time—six planes simultaneously on *Akagi* and perhaps nine on *Kaga*. (While *Akagi*'s torpedo squadron had eighteen planes, *Kaga*'s had twenty-seven—though it appears from the testimony that it is possible that only eighteen may have been equipped with torpedoes earlier in the morning, with the remainder standing by unarmed as a reserve.) The reason why an entire squadron of torpedo planes could not be rearmed simultaneously was because of the limited number of heavy weapons "carrier cars" (as the mechanics called them). The carrier cars were large nonmotorized carts that had double jacks for raising the 800-kilogram ordnance—torpedoes or bombs—to the belly of the plane, or lowering them after they had been detached from the release mechanism.

After the carrier car was positioned under the torpedo, the torpedo was disarmed (by removing its detonator) and disengaged from the release mechanism. It was then lowered to the bed of the carrier car by manually cranking the double jacks. These operations took at least five minutes, though less than ten. The loaded carrier car was then rolled to the heavy weapons rack near the elevator to the magazine where the torpedo was deposited. As the torpedo weighed 1,872 pounds, five to six men were required to manhandle it off the carrier car. This operation took about five minutes. Thus, the total time to remove a torpedo from the plane and deposit it on the rack was close to fifteen minutes.

Before a bomb could be installed on the torpedo plane, the "launcher" (as the mechanics called it) had to be changed. This was the ribbed rack on the belly of the plane to which ordnance was attached. There were different launchers for torpedoes and bombs; Japanese aerial torpedoes were long and slender, but 800-kilogram land bombs were short and stubby. It required a surprisingly long time to change the launcher—at least twenty minutes, and perhaps as many as thirty. While the launchers were being changed on the first division of torpedo planes, the carrier cars were used to remove the torpedoes from the next division. The launcher change was, by far, the most time-consuming procedure in the rearming operation for the torpedo planes—taking a large part of the total one and one-half hours required to change a squadron of torpedo planes from torpedoes to land bombs. It is a key factor in deducing the armament status of the torpedo planes at various times after the rearming operation began (yet the necessity of changing launchers had not been mentioned in American literature on the battle until very recently).

I will give a detailed description of the rearming procedures in chapter 4. But at this point it should be apparent that thirty minutes into the rearming operation on the torpedo planes—at 0745, when the standard scenario and Senshi Sosho say that the operation was countermanded—torpedoes could have been removed from as many as two-thirds (two six-plane divisions) of *Akagi*'s planes. However, it is also apparent that no 800-kilogram land bombs could have been put on any of those planes by then because there would not have been time to change the launchers. Had the rearming operation been suspended at 0745—as claimed by the American standard scenario—this would have been the status of the torpedo planes at 0830, when Nagumo had to decide whether to launch an immediate attack or postpone. Had the rearming operation actually been reversed at 0745, as contended by Senshi Sosho, it is apparent that there would not have been very much left to do at 0830 to completely restore the torpedoes (though it would have taken additional time to get the torpedo planes up to the flight deck).

On the other hand, had the rearming operation continued, without interruption, for forty-five minutes (until 0800), it is apparent from the testimony of the veterans that the torpedoes could have been removed from *all* the planes, and the launchers changed on one-third to two-thirds of them. It is unlikely that any land bombs would have been installed on *Akagi*'s planes (but a few could possibly have been attached to *Kaga*'s if only two nine-plane divisions had originally been equipped with torpedoes). Moreover, had the rearming operation been countermanded at 0800, it would have required at least one hour, free of disruptions, to change the launchers back and restore the torpedoes to the planes on *Akagi* and *Kaga* (it took longer to install torpedoes than to remove them).

However, after 0800 there were disruptions caused by American attacks, first from Midway for most of the period between 0800 and 0840, and then from the American carriers between 0930 and 1000. During attacks on the carriers, evasive maneuvers to avoid being hit by bombs or torpedoes disrupted rearming operations—especially on the torpedo planes—much more than has been realized by American commentators on the battle. According to the veterans, it was impossible to attach a torpedo to the torpedo plane, and hazardous even to jack them up on the heavy-weapons carrier cars, while the aircraft carrier was swerving sharply. (Rearming operations on the dive-bombers were slowed down, but did not have to be suspended, because of the much smaller size of those bombs—250 kilograms rather than 800.)

Therefore, it is unlikely that operations to restore the torpedoes would have commenced until all the attacks from Midway were over—at around 0840. They would again have been suspended between 0930 and 1000 when two waves of American carrier-launched torpedo bombers attacked. This means that if the rearming continued until 0800, and operations to reverse it did not begin until around 0840, it would have been very difficult to complete the job of restoring all the torpedoes by 1000.

As for operations with dive-bombers to change from armor-piercing to high-explosive bombs, they were quickly done—taking only about thirty minutes, a third the time required for torpedo planes. There were several reasons, according to the veterans, for this: the 250-kilogram bombs, being less than a third the weight of torpedoes or 800-kilogram bombs, were easily manipulated; there were more of the smaller "dollies" to transport the bombs; it was not necessary to change the launcher; they could be rearmed on the flight deck as well as in the hangar; and only two-thirds of the dive-bombers had to be rearmed with land bombs. (When dive-bombers were armed for attacks on ships, a third of them were equipped with high-explosive bombs for the purpose of knocking out antiaircraft gun batteries and holing flight decks.)

Because of the relative ease with which dive-bombers were rearmed, not only would the change to land bombs have been completed at around 0745, but the dive-bombers could have been switched back for attacks on ships by soon after 0830—even if the countermand order was not issued until around 0800. This is consistent with the generally held view that the dive-bombers were properly armed for ships at the time Nagumo made his decision to postpone his attack.

* * *

In this chapter I have attempted to explain why the existing accounts of what happened on the Japanese carriers on the morning of the battle do not make sense. The most serious problem with them has been highlighted: if the rearming operation began at 0715 and was countermanded at 0745, as claimed by most commentators except Sawachi, no good reason has been given for why the torpedoes could not have been restored to the torpedo squadrons of *Akagi* and *Kaga* in time for a launch to have been made before the fatal bombing at 1025. (We have seen that Parshall and Tully finesse this problem by assuming that the torpedoes had, in fact, been restored by around 917, but have Nagumo declining to deploy the strike force to the flight decks in order to keep them clear for CAP operations.)

I have suggested, through a series of rhetorical questions, that a new and more plausible scenario for what happened on the Japanese side of the battle can be constructed, based on a reanalysis of the primary record and new evidence from the veterans. A better understanding of the mechanics of the rearming operation for torpedo planes will enable us to reconstruct a scenario that better explains Nagumo's decisions after he learned of the American carrier threat and, most important, provides a better answer to the perplexing question of why he never got his grand-scale attack launched. What is now needed is evidence for that new scenario.

My findings relating to Nagumo's three crucial decisions, and the circumstances surrounding them, will be set out in detail in three chapters. Chapter 4,

"The Fatal Decision," will deal with his decision to rearm his torpedo planes for a second strike on Midway, and discuss whether a less risky option was available. The adequacy of the search operation on the morning of the battle will also be analyzed. The details of the rearming operation will be set out so it can be seen how Nagumo got himself in such a bind when the American carrier fleet was unexpectedly discovered. Chapter 5, "Gamble Lost," will deal with the order countermanding the rearming operation. It will also address the vital issue of when Nagumo received the *Tone* 4 sighting report, and present the evidence—pro and con—for the 0800 receipt time he claimed. The performance of the *Tone* 4 crew will be evaluated. Chapter 6, "To Launch or Not to Launch," will deal with the decision to postpone the attack on the American carrier force. The resources available to Nagumo at 0830 will be discussed in detail, especially the armament status of his torpedo planes. We will also see why his strike force never got ready for launch.

Then chapter 7, "Ironies," will deal with the ironies in the assumptions underpinning Nagumo's decision to postpone. The interplay between that decision and those of his main tactical counterpart, Spruance, will be detailed—with ironies revealed in Spruance's decisions as well. We will see why American dive-bombers had such a difficult time finding Nagumo's carriers and why there was no combat air patrol protecting the Mobile Force—as Nagumo had assumed there would be—when the American dive-bombers finally arrived.

But before we get to the chapters on Nagumo's crucial decisions, some context is in order. Chapter 2, "Prelude," will deal with the seeds of the conflict between the two nations and give a brief summary of Japanese-American relations that led to Pearl Harbor. The Pearl Harbor operation will be reviewed, and we will see how the failure to catch and destroy the American carriers Yamamoto had hoped would be there was the main impetus for the Midway operation. We will also see that lessons learned from lack of adequate intelligence and from underestimating Japanese naval capabilities at the beginning of the war helped Nimitz ensure that America would not be caught by surprise again. Chapter 3, "The Run-up to Midway," will deal with the battles that followed Pearl Harbor —including the Doolittle raid on Tokyo and the Battle of the Coral Sea— which convinced the Japanese high naval command to accede to Yamamoto's Midway operation plan. It will then deal with the sortie of Yamamoto's fleets from Japan, and discuss the communications failures en route—and other defects in the Midway operation plan—that proved to be the seeds of disaster.

The chapters after those addressing Nagumo's crucial decisions will deal with the carrier battle itself, and the aftermath. Chapter 8, "Denouement," will describe the climactic battle that resulted in the sinking of all four of Nagumo's carriers, as well as the *Yorktown*. New details of Japanese and American aircraft and pilot losses in the battle will be given. The Aleutian phase of the overall operation will also be dealt with briefly to assess the impact that the diversion of resources to that phase may have had on the outcome of the Battle of Midway. Chapter 9, "Aftermath," will deal with the consequences of the battle—the change from an offensive to a defensive posture forced on the Japanese—and the impact their losses at Midway had on the subsequent carrier battles in the Solomon Islands. Chapter 10, "Postmortem," deals with the blunders that cost the Japanese the battle, and poses some "what ifs"—the most important being whether Nagumo could have won the battle had he got his grand-scale attack against the American carriers launched. (After concluding that he would have won in such an event, I refer to a war-gaming exercise presented in an appendix to illustrate a likely scenario for a Japanese victory.) This final chapter will then end with a comparison of the subsequent course of the war with that which might have occurred had Japan won the battle—and ponder the likely consequences for history.

Finally, a word about my approach in writing this book. It has been that of an investigator attempting to solve a mystery: why Nagumo's strike force could not be launched in time. As Admiral Nagumo and the crew of *Tone* 4 have been charged with serious malfeasance, or at least with gross negligence, I have also taken on the role of a lawyer conducting an inquest into a "crime," hence the title *Midway Inquest*. But, also as a lawyer, I have applied a more rigorous standard to evidence than have other commentators: some evidence from documents and other sources that has been accepted as establishing a particular point by other authors has been rejected by me where its reliability is highly dubious. I have endeavored to be as objective and evenhanded as possible in this account.

CHAPTER TWO

PRELUDE

THE DECISION TO GO TO WAR

On September 6, 1941, the Japanese government decided to go to war with America. (Japan had been preparing for the possibility of war for several years, but at this time the Japanese Cabinet resolved to complete preparations.) Though the final decision to actually go to war was deferred, pending a possible but unlikely diplomatic breakthrough, the machinery for war, especially in the Imperial Japanese Navy, was put in motion; what had previously been contingency plans now took on the urgency of operation plans. The decision—and "fateful" is an apt description here—was made by the Imperial Council in the presence of the emperor. The leading personalities present were Prince Fumimaro Konoye, the prime minister; General Hideki Tojo, war minister; and Admiral Osami Nagano, chief of the naval general staff.

The event that occasioned (most Japanese would say provoked) this decision to prepare for war was the executive order by President Roosevelt, six weeks earlier on July 26, freezing Japanese assets in the United States. This was quickly followed by similar freezes by Great Britain and the Netherlands. Within days this resulted in an almost total trade embargo on Japan, with oil being the most vital commodity cut off. Not only could Japan no longer buy oil and aviation fuel from what had been its largest supplier, the United States, but it now lacked the foreign exchange reserves to buy oil from anyone else—including the Dutch East Indies, which had been Japan's second largest supplier. (A follow-up executive order from the President on August 1 completely banned the exportation of all petroleum products from the United States to Japan.)

These executive orders effectively imposing a total oil embargo on Japan were, in turn, in response to the Japanese move into southern French Indochina. The French Vichy government had acceded to a Japanese ultimatum to be granted bases in the south and be given a joint protectorate of all of Indochina. (Japan had been given access to the north of the colony the previous year.) This move was seen as especially threatening to American and British interests—as bases in the south of the peninsula would put Japan in a position to launch attacks on Malaya, the Dutch East Indies, and the Philippines.

However, the move into southern Indochina, by itself, probably would not have provoked such a draconian response by Roosevelt. It was just the last in a series of recent aggressions by Japan, which began in China in 1937, and which had led to a series of economic sanctions by the United States, beginning with the "moral embargo" of aircraft and aircraft parts to Japan in July of 1938. (That action by the American government had been taken largely in response to American public outrage over the Japanese bombing of Chinese cities and, especially, the "Rape of Nanking" in December 1937.) This had been followed in 1940 by outright embargos of iron and steel scrap, and aviation fuel and lubricants.

Although since 1938 American shipowners had been "morally" dissuaded from shipping fuel oil to Japan, there had been no real embargo of crude oil; large quantities of American—along with Dutch East Indies and Latin American—oil was reaching Japan in Japanese and neutral tankers. (However, the proportion of petroleum products imported from the United States had declined from 80 percent in 1937 to less than 60 percent by summer of 1941.)[1] The Japanese move into southern Indochina was simply the last straw. And as the previous embargos had proved ineffectual to deter Japanese expansion, the American administration decided it was time to do something that would really hurt, even at the risk of provoking a war in the Pacific.

And hurt it did. Japan was almost totally dependent on imported oil—about 90 percent of her needs had been imported, most of it still from the United States. (In those days America was the "OPEC" of the oil world, accounting for over 60 percent of global crude oil production.) As of September 1941, Japan's annual consumption of petroleum products was around 30 million barrels. (Though it was technically still "peacetime," Japan was on a war-preparation footing, with extensive naval training exercises underway and severe rationing of civilian gasoline in place.) Estimated wartime consumption was 33–35 million barrels per year (an estimate that turned to be woefully short: in the first

year of war around 52 million barrels were actually consumed—over 30 million
by the navy alone). In 1941 Japan produced only about 3 million barrels of oil,
including synthetic production. However, the embargo of 90 percent of Japan's
petroleum product needs did not cause an immediate shortage; in recent years
much more oil had been imported than was required for current use, with the
excess put into reserve. By September 1941, the reserve stock was around 50 million barrels; but this was enough to last only about one and a half years of current consumption.[2]

If Japan went to war with America and Great Britain, the lion's share of this
stockpile would be eaten up by the navy (it held three-quarters of the petroleum
reserves). Consequently, the share of oil and gasoline reserves allocated to the
general economy, including the industrial sector—and even to the army—
could be expected to run out in less than a year. After those reserves were exhausted the economy would grind to a halt—and even the navy would become
immobilized in the following year. This all was a most grim prospect. Thus, it
was widely accepted in Japan that if the embargo could not be lifted soon it
would be necessary for Japan to invade the East Indies and take by force the oil
she needed to remain a world naval and industrial power. Crude oil production
in the Dutch East Indies was more than enough to make Japan self-sufficient in
oil—even during wartime.[3] The South Seas region also contained other strategic materials such as rubber, iron, tin, and bauxite (for aluminum).

At the time of the Imperial Council's decision to prepare for war, it was becoming increasingly evident that the American government had no intention of
lifting the embargo unless Japan was willing to withdraw its armed forces from
not only Indochina, but China as well. But even if the Japanese government was
willing to do that (and Prime Minister Konoye was open to negotiations, as the
war in China had become bogged down and was losing popular support), it was
also clear that the Japanese army would countenance no such concession. In
the eyes of the Army high command—especially General Tojo—the humilia-
tion would be too unbearable. Any Japanese prime minister who agreed to for-
sake Japan's imperial ambitions would surely be assassinated, and the civilian
government would be ousted and replaced by the military.

There was thus deadlock between the two governments over a matter that
threatened Japan's survival—access to oil. In the Imperial Conference, Admiral Nagano—arguing in favor of immediate preparations for war—had likened
Japan "to a patient who was certain to die if you did nothing, but might be saved
by a dangerous operation."[4]

That dangerous operation, of course, would be war with the United States
and Great Britain. The tactical details had yet to be worked out, but the broad
outline of the strategic plan was straightforward: Malaya and the Philippines
would be invaded, followed by conquest of the oil-rich East Indies. This could
be fairly easily done, but to protect the operation from interference, and later

safeguard the sea lanes between the newly acquired South Seas colonies and Japan, and the American navy would have to be knocked out of the Pacific Ocean, and the British navy would have to be knocked out of the Southeast Asian seas. The most dangerous part of the operation would be an attack on Pearl Harbor to destroy the American Pacific Fleet, and for this the surgeon would be Isoroku Yamamoto.

At the Imperial Conference in early September, the military leadership, now dominated by Tojo, gave the prime minister until mid-October to work out an acceptable arrangement with the United States that would restore oil imports. On October 14, Prime Minister Konoye asked Tojo for his consent to withdraw troops from China. Tojo flatly refused. He had made up his mind to invade the South Seas and told Konoye that he was not worried about war with America because he believed Japan would win. Konoye resigned, and two days later Tojo became prime minister (as well as retaining his post as war minister). Japan had crossed the Rubicon.

Although negotiations in Washington between the Japanese ambassador and the American secretary of state continued for another six weeks, neither side had any realistic hope of resolving the impasse. The American government had no intention of lifting the embargo unless Japan withdrew from China. The Japanese government had no intention of withdrawing from China. Japan had already resolved to take, by force, the oil fields of the East Indies—and, to preclude American interference with this endeavor, to attack Pearl Harbor and the Philippines. However, the Japanese navy was not yet ready to attack Pearl Harbor. Thus, both sides used the negotiations to play for time.

The Japanese needed more time to work out the details of the multipronged attack on Pearl Harbor, Malaya, and the Philippines. As for the most complex and risky of these attacks—Pearl Harbor—several problems remained to be solved: Not all of the six carriers in the Pearl Harbor Striking Force were ready. The newly completed attack carriers—the *Shokaku* and *Zuikaku*—would not have aircrews on board until November. Also, an attack on Pearl Harbor would require aerial torpedoes specially modified to run in the shallow waters of the harbor. The first batch of these torpedoes would not be delivered to the Striking Force until the end of October,[5] and several weeks of practice with them would be necessary before the torpedo plane crews would be ready to attack Pearl Harbor.

Finally, in order to provide air support for the attacks on Malaya and the Philippines without using some of the carriers needed for Pearl Harbor, the range of the Zero fighter had to be extended so Zeros could escort bombers from land bases in Indochina and Formosa. This would be done by adding new drop tanks to increase the range of the Zero (to an incredible 1,930 miles). But the new drop tanks would not be fitted until early November.[6] (As will later be seen, the American navy was totally unaware of any of these new "secret weapons.")

All this meant that an attack on Pearl Harbor could not be made until early December. Thus, Japan had nothing to lose and everything to gain by stalling negotiations until then—but, as will be seen, an attack on Pearl Harbor could not be delayed beyond December.

As of the fall of 1941, the Americans needed even more time than the Japanese to prepare for war. The Philippines needed to be reinforced with troops and aircraft. The newly commissioned fleet carrier *Hornet* needed even more time than the *Shokaku* and *Zuikaku* to be equipped with an aircrew and made operational. Likewise, the newly commissioned fast battleships—the *North Carolina* and the *Washington*—needed several months to be made operational. In an effort to delay the onset of war, the American government attempted to reach at least a temporary modus vivendi by holding out the possibility of a partial lifting of the embargo in return for a partial disengagement in China by Japan.

Thus, both sides used the negotiations to buy time—but unbeknownst to Washington, the Japanese needed much less time and were facing an end-of-the-year deadline. On November 26 the negotiations, for all practical purposes, ended. Roosevelt had just received clear evidence of a major move south by the Japanese army and navy and abruptly called off efforts to reach a modus vivendi. The Japanese ambassador was brusquely told that a complete withdrawal from China—along with Japanese acceptance of Chiang Kai-shek's government—was now required for America to lift the oil embargo. That day, the Pearl Harbor Striking Force set sail, and on December 1, the American "ultimatum" having been rejected out of hand by Tojo, the final decision to attack the United States was ratified by the Imperial Conference.

THE SEEDS OF CONFLICT

What brought these two nations to such a state of affairs? Until less than twenty years earlier relations between Japan and America had been generally amicable. After the Meiji Restoration in 1868, Japan had industrialized rapidly—largely with the aid of technology gained from extensive trade with Europe and America. (Also imported, along with the technology, was a great deal of Western culture and liberal attitudes in philosophy and politics.) But along with this modernization, Japan had begun—immediately after the Restoration—building a navy to protect its new maritime interests.

Several key events that began in the 1890s—most involving China—would later be seen as the seeds of the war between Japan and the United States. In that decade both countries began using their navies to project military power in East Asia and the Pacific—and began to acquire colonies there. The first of these colonial acquisitions by Japan came from a war with China over Korea in 1894. Korea had long been a "tributary" state of China, but was in rebellion for independence. Japan intervened, resulting in war with China. The next year, China sued for peace and yielded Korea to Japan's sphere of influence, and as a war indemnity also gave Japan Formosa (Taiwan).

In 1898 the United States also used her navy for the first time to acquire overseas possessions. It went to war with Spain, not for the purpose of acquiring colonies, but to intervene in a rebellion for independence by Cuba. But by time it was over, the American navy had sunk the Spanish navy—attacking it first in Manila Bay and then off the coast of Cuba—and had gone on to acquire not only Spanish possessions in the Caribbean, including Puerto Rico, but the Spanish colonies of the Philippines and Guam in the western Pacific. Thus, in what many regarded as pursuit of its "manifest destiny," the United States had suddenly become a Pacific Ocean imperial power along with Japan.

Although there was potential for conflict, with America having acquired territory on Japan's side of the Pacific, relations between the two countries nevertheless remained generally friendly. Japan's relations with Britain were even more cordial. In 1902 the two countries entered into a treaty whereby Britain pledged to come to the aid of Japan against any third powers that allied themselves to Russia in event of a war between Japan and Russia. Not only had that made Japan's upcoming attack on Russia in 1904 feasible, but the new relationship had resulted in substantial British assistance in modernizing the Japanese navy.

The second territorial expansion for Japan on the Asian mainland began in 1904. Russia had earlier taken control of Manchuria and was now seeking influence in Korea. The Japanese government had resolved to eject Russia from those provinces, but it had first been necessary to strengthen the navy. (Unlike China, Russia was a world-class naval power—ranking third after Britain and the United States.) Since 1898, Japan had deployed six battleships with 12-inch guns and nine armored cruisers (all built in Western shipyards). However, Russia's navy possessed about three times as many capital ships as Japan's—though most were in the Baltic Sea. After attempts at mediation—urged by Britain—had failed, and after then receiving assurances from Great Britain and the United States that no other powers would be permitted to intervene, Japan decided to go to war against Russia.

The Russo-Japanese War began on February 8, 1904. The Japanese navy cleared the way for invasion of Korea by a surprise night attack on the Russian Pacific Squadron (an attack later seen as a harbinger of Pearl Harbor). The next day the Japanese landed troops near Seoul, Korea. It drove the Russians out of Korea and then advanced into Manchuria, and by July was laying siege to Port Arthur. A savage trench-warfare battle for Port Arthur lasted nearly six months (presaging the kind of machine-gun carnage that ten years later would characterize the Western Front of World War I). By the time the fortress surrendered to the Japanese in January 1905, the Japanese had suffered sixty thousand casualties.

In the meantime, the Russian Baltic Fleet had been dispatched in October of the previous year to come to the rescue of the beleaguered Port Arthur and what was left of the Pacific Squadron holed up in its harbor. The voyage of the Baltic Fleet had been long and tortuous because the British, in the spirit of the treaty of 1902, had denied the Russian fleet use of British coaling stations along the way. After the surrender of Port Arthur, and with the Asiatic Fleet mostly destroyed, the rescue mission of the Baltic Fleet was no longer needed, so when it reached Pacific waters in May 1905 it was ordered to break through to Vladivostok. The shortest route would take it through the Tsushima Strait, between the southern Japanese island of Kyushu and Korea. The Japanese battle fleet was lying in wait.

TSUSHIMA

The Battle of Tsushima Strait was the most legendary sea battle in Japanese naval history. It is for the Japanese what Trafalgar is for the British and what the Battle of Midway is for the Americans. A large part of the mystique of the battle is the fact that the Japanese fleet, led by Admiral Togo, was greatly outnumbered and outgunned but still won a crushing victory by sheer guile and superior discipline. The battle is relevant to the Pacific War thirty-six years later because it instilled in the minds of the Japanese navy leadership the conviction that their navy was invincible—even against a numerically superior foe.

Togo entered the battle on May 27, 1905, with four battleships and eight armored cruisers. He was opposed by a Baltic Fleet consisting of eight battleships, eight armored cruisers, and four "coastal defense ironclads" (actually smaller battleships). Before the battle, Togo signaled to his fleet an admonition that echoed Nelson's: "The fate of the Empire depends on this battle. Let every man do his utmost." Togo then executed a classic "crossing of the T" maneuver so as to better concentrate his gunfire on the Russian ships, hoping that the superior gunnery skills of his men would overcome his numerical disadvantage.

He was not disappointed. Togo lost *none* of his capital ships (only three torpedo boats went down), but sank six of the eight Russian battleships, four of their eight cruisers, and two of their four ironclads—twelve capital ships in all. The two remaining battleships and the two remaining ironclads were captured, and three of the surviving cruisers fled to neutral ports, where they were interned. Only one capital ship—a cruiser—escaped to a Russian port. Thus, nineteen of the twenty capital ships in the Baltic Fleet were lost to the Russians, against none for the Japanese—making the Battle of Tsushima Strait an even more lopsided victory than its storied counterparts. It was for the Japanese, indeed, the stuff of legends.

After "Tsushima," Russia had had enough of the war with Japan, but would not formally sue for peace. The American president, Theodore Roosevelt, stepped in and arranged a negotiated peace to end the Russo-Japanese War (for which he later won the Nobel Peace Prize). Under the terms of the treaty signed on September 6, 1905, Russia vacated Manchuria, ceded to Japan the Liaotung Peninsula of Manchuria—including Port Arthur—and the southern half of Sakhalin Island, and explicitly recognized Korea as being in Japan's sphere of influence. (Korea was formally annexed by Japan in 1910 and renamed Chosen.)

Thus, in less than forty years since the Restoration, Japan went from being a quaint island backwater to having acquired an empire and having become a world military power. Its territory had roughly doubled in size and ranged from Sakhalin in the north to Taiwan in the south, and from the Japanese islands to the Asian mainland. Japan's population had increased from 30 million to over 70 million in "Greater" Japan as of 1905 (by comparison, the United States then had about 100 million). Japan's early imperial expansion had been substantially aided and abetted by Great Britain and the United States, for which Japan was grateful.

WORLD WAR I

When World War I broke out in August 1914, Japan joined the Allies. Although it sent no troops to the Western Front, it attacked German possessions in China and the southwest Pacific. However, Japan's role in the war must be described as opportunistic. It had no grievance against Germany and was not a party to any agreement involving the balance of power in Europe. Even though Tokyo had close diplomatic relations with Britain, ideologically the emperor and most of his advisers sympathized with the Germans and their kaiser.[7] They had similar forms of government and shared many cultural values. On the other hand, Japan had designs on China and Manchuria and coveted the German-held islands in the west and southwest Pacific. It was hoped that if Japan allied itself with Britain against Germany, Britain would not object too strenuously to Japanese moves into China and Manchuria. And Japan was certain to acquire most of the German possessions in the Far East and Pacific—most importantly the German leasehold on the Shantung Peninsula on the north China coast, with its thriving port of Tsingtao.

This is exactly what transpired. However, attempts to wrest all of Manchuria away from China failed, as did a later attempt to grab a piece of mineral-rich Siberia from Russia during the Russian civil war. But, all in all, Japan made out very well from World War I—and at a minimal cost in blood and treasure. At the Peace Conference of 1919, Japan was awarded Shantung and a mandate over all German possessions in the Pacific north of the equator. The most important of these—on which naval bases would later be constructed—were the Marshall, Mariana, and Caroline island groups.

During the war, Japan had also substantially strengthened her navy. To the ten old-fashion battleships—with 12-inch guns—built before World War I, were added eight much larger and faster battleships and battle cruisers mounting 14-inch guns. These were the four battleships of the *Fuso* and *Ise* classes—the first capital ships built entirely in Japan—and the four battle cruisers of the *Kongo* class. (All would see service in World War II.) During the war, Japan had also begun construction of the world's first battleships with 16-inch guns: the *Nagato* and *Mutsu*.

Thus, after World War I, Japan was the leading imperial power in East Asia and the western Pacific Ocean and possessed the world's third largest navy. (The large German navy had ceased to exist, and the Russian navy had been destroyed in 1905—not to be rebuilt until after the Second World War.) In its rise to this lofty status it had received considerable assistance from Britain and the United States. Up to this point, Japan was a leading member of the community of democratic industrial nations and had enjoyed friendly relations with the United States, notwithstanding competing interests in East Asia. Soon after the war—during the 1920s—this all changed.

THE FALLING OUT

The new decade began auspiciously for Japan and its relations with the West. The country had avoided the crushing war debts the other major powers had incurred, and its economy was buoyant. The government, led by a liberal, pro-Western prime minister—Takashi Hara (known as the "Great Commoner")—not only cooperated with arms reduction but even renounced Japan's longstanding ambition for hegemony over China. Hara's government began the process of democratization of Japanese politics. It also promised to evacuate Shantung and agree to a new "open doors" status for China.

However, even at the beginning of the decade, there were ominous signs under the surface that not all was rosy in Japan. In 1920 a book, *Reconstruction Program for Japan* by Ikki Kita, had been published. In it, Kita proposed abolition of the Diet, nationalization of important industries, the institution of military government, and Japanese hegemony of the Far East. (This, collectively, was known as *Kodo*—the Imperial Way.) The liberal government of the day tried to suppress the book, but now it was gaining considerable influence in the army and among many young intellectuals. It has been called the Japanese *Mein Kampf*.[8] In November 1921 Hara was assassinated by a disgruntled railroad employee who believed that he was too pro-Western and was selling out Japan's imperial interests, especially in China. The assassin would later be glorified by right-wing militarists.

Two events in the early years of the decade soured the Japanese populace's attitudes toward the United States and were exploited by the militarists: the Washington Naval Limitation Treaty in 1922 and the American Immigration Act of 1924. As the Naval Limitation Treaty not only had a major effect on

Japanese-American relations, but shaped the warship-building programs of the two countries in the run-up to World War II, some details here are in order.

NAVAL LIMITATION TREATY

The Washington Conference of 1921–22 was convened to arrive at an agreement among the major powers for a limitation on warship building that would avoid the kind of naval arms race that had gone on between Britain and Germany before the war. Britain was especially interested in naval limitations as it had been almost bankrupted by the war and could not afford to match the warship-building programs already underway in Japan and America. The Japanese government did not object to a general naval limitation. However, the proposal before the conference to limit the Japanese navy to just three-fifths of the capital ships the American and British navies could possess (known as the 5-5-3 formula) came as a shock.

In 1921, Japan had ten battleships and battle cruisers with 14-inch or larger guns. The United States had fourteen battleships with 14-inch or larger guns (including two battleships with 16-inch guns, which had been launched but not yet completed). Britain had fifteen battleships and battle cruisers with 14-inch guns or larger (all with 15-inch guns). The Japanese Diet had approved in 1918 a plan to build the Imperial Japanese Navy up to parity in capital ships with the navies of the United States and Britain. Two battleships (the *Kaga* class) displacing almost 40,000 tons and carrying ten 16-inch guns, and four large battle cruisers (the *Akagi* class) displacing over 40,000 tons, also with ten 16-inch guns, had already been laid down. In 1921 the Diet had approved a budget for four more *Kaga*-class battleships and, more ominously for the West, four superbattleships with 18-inch guns were being planned.[9] Thus, when completed, these programs would add fourteen new capital ships—with 16- to 18-inch guns—to the ten capital ships Japan already had.

America had already laid down six battleships (the *South Dakota* I class) displacing over 40,000 tons and carrying twelve 16-inch guns, and six large battle cruisers (the *Lexington* class), also displacing over 40,000 tons and carrying eight 16-inch guns.[10] This would give the United States a total of twenty-seven capital ships—three more than Japan would have—but as none would mount 18-inch guns the two sides would be roughly equal in firepower. The British parliament did not want to finance a ship-building program to match these numbers; it wanted to retain its naval superiority without having to build any more capital ships.

Under the 5-5-3 plan, the United States and Britain could have fifteen capital ships each, and Japan nine. This meant that each country would break up or decommission a large number of older battleships with guns less than 14 inches. The United States was initially permitted to complete a 16-inch battleship nearing completion, but as a compromise to assuage the Japanese it agreed to substitute the old 12-inch-gunned *Arkansas*.[11] It was also proposed at the conference that a ten-year "holiday" be adopted during which no more capital ships would be built. This meant that none of the older (14-inch-gunned) capital ships in each country's allotment could be replaced by more powerful types.

Thus, the United States and Japan would be required to destroy most of the new ship hulls recently laid down under their postwar building programs—though two for each country could be converted to aircraft carriers. As Britain had no new hulls laid, she was delighted with these terms. (Moreover, because she had no ships with 16-inch guns, she was given an exemption from the "holiday" provisions to later replace two small battle cruisers with 16-inch-gunned battleships—which emerged in 1927 as the *Nelson* class.) The treaty also placed limitations on building aircraft carriers, and, again, the limitations were discriminatory against Japan: 135,000 tons for the United States, and 60 percent of that—81,000 tons—for Japan.[12] But, as Japan only had one small carrier under construction at the time, the limitation left plenty of carriers that could be built, so this limitation did not, at first, pinch as much.

While the refusal by the United States and Britain to accord Japan equal naval status offended many Japanese, there were some in the Japanese navy—such as the young Isoroku Yamamoto—who realized that the lower capital ship quota for Japan was actually a blessing in disguise. Forward-looking naval strategists realized that with the advent of aircraft the days of the battleship as *the* capital ship were numbered. They saw that the future capital ship would be in the form (not yet fully configured) of an aircraft carrier. They realized that Japan simply would not have the resources to build a fleet of aircraft carriers on top of the enormously expensive battleship-building program that had been planned before the Naval Limitation Treaty.

At the time the treaty was signed in February 1922, Japan was already building its first aircraft carrier, the *Hosho*. (Britain had already built two, and the United States was converting a collier—renamed *Langley*—into its first aircraft carrier.) Now with the limitation on traditional capital ships, resources would be freed up for Japan to stay abreast of the Anglo-Americans in this new type of warship—at least until the 81,000-ton limit had been reached.

In 1923, pursuant to the Treaty, Japan began converting the hulls of the large battle cruisers *Akagi* and *Amagi* into carriers. The United States also began converting the hulls of the battle cruisers *Lexington* and *Saratoga* into carriers. On September 1, 1923, a devastating earthquake struck the Tokyo Bay area, setting off fires that burned most of Tokyo and Yokohama to the ground. At the nearby Yokosuka shipyard, *Amagi* was badly damaged by the quake and had to be abandoned; the hull of a battleship scheduled to be destroyed under the treaty, *Kaga*, being substituted. (This is why *Kaga* was slower than *Akagi*, but had greater fuel capacity—asymmetries that would later cause problems in the deployment of the carrier force for the Battle of Midway.)

IMMIGRATION LAW

The 1923 earthquake brought an outpouring of sympathy and financial assistance from the United States, which softened the resentment still felt in Japan over the snub dealt in Washington a year earlier, but a second insult came the next year. In 1924, the United States Congress passed a new immigration law that totally excluded Japanese from entering the United States. The mood of renewed good feeling in Japan toward America resulting from the earthquake relief quickly dissipated. The Japanese would have been satisfied with a low quota like the "white" nations of Europe were given—not that many Japanese wished to emigrate—but to be completely excluded along with the Chinese and people from other economically less developed Asian countries deeply offended their pride. Because Japan had achieved the highest literacy rate in the world, and a Western level of economic and military power, the Japanese considered themselves the equal of Europeans and had deluded themselves into believing they would be treated as such by America.

These two events—the discriminatory Naval Limitation Treaty and the even more discriminatory immigration law—caused an emergence, for the first time, of widespread anti-American sentiment in Japan. The resentment played right into the hands of right-wing demagogues. Those arguing for a return to the Samurai Code of Bushido and other creeds of self-sufficiency and militarism found receptive ears—especially among young army and navy officers and cadets and university students, who began to believe that the Americans intended to keep Japan forever inferior.

However, it is an exaggeration to suggest—as many, especially in Japan, have—that without these two events in the early 1920s Japan would not have embraced ultranationalism and embarked on its expansionist program. One must look at the total context of those times. World War I had destroyed not only the old world order, but also the trend toward greater liberalism and democracy in the industrialized countries. In the years following the war, Germany descended into chaos; so did Italy and, worst of all, Russia. Moreover, the revolution in Russia had raised the specter of communist ideology spreading around the world—including Japan. Countervailing right-wing ideology was ascendant, not only in Germany and Italy, but in Japan as well. World trade had become more restrictive, and America had retreated into isolationism—content to just look after its own economic interests. In this climate, it would be surprising indeed had Japan not moved toward nationalism and began seeking economic self-sufficiency. However, not even this made the rupture of Japanese-American relations inevitable. That would occur in the following decade, over China.

THE MOVE INTO CHINA

If the decade of the twenties began hopefully for Japanese-American relations and then soured, the decade of the thirties began bleakly and got worse. By 1930 the world was in a depression (which hurt Japan's economy more than most because of its dependence on manufactured exports), Germany was moving toward Nazism, and militarism was on the rise in Japan. The Japanese army would soon begin a colonial expansion in China that a decade later would lead to the Pacific war with the United States.

In September 1931 a bomb exploded on the tracks of the Japanese South Manchuria Railway. Though blamed on Manchurian terrorists by the army, it was actually the work of junior army officers. Nevertheless, the army used this "incident" to move into Manchuria. Though the Japanese government did not authorize this, it decided to accept it as a fait accompli. However, in doing this, it also had to accept that effective control of the government was being yielded to the Japanese army.

The Japanese army quickly defeated the Chinese forces in Manchuria and annexed the area, renaming it "Manchukuo." The United States strenuously protested this aggression as a violation of the Kellogg-Briand Pact (the treaty to outlaw war signed by Japan in 1928), and the League of Nations appointed a commission of inquiry to investigate it. Japan replied by formally recognizing the independence of Manchukuo in February 1932, but set up a puppet government under a nominal Manchu emperor, Pu-Yi (the former boy emperor of China).

Japanese government officials and business leaders who showed less than total enthusiasm for the Manchurian venture were simply eliminated by secret-society cabals of junior military officers mentored by the militarists—referred to as the *Kodo* men. Several high-ranking politicians—including the prime minister—were assassinated (the period became known as "government by assassination"). Although this rash of killings shocked most of the Japanese public, it consolidated the power of the militarists. At the end of September 1932 the League of Nations condemned the Japanese aggression in Manchuria. Japan responded the following February by withdrawing from the League. Japan was quickly becoming an outcast nation.

On February 26, 1936, the military extremists struck again with a new wave of assassinations that turned into a mutiny. The army *Kodo* men were intent on destroying the entire group of elder statesmen advising the emperor who were deemed constitutionalists, and instituting a military dictatorship that would implement the domestic reforms and foreign policies advocated by Kita. They were rabidly anticommunist and favored war with the Soviet Union rather than with China. This was known as the "Strike North" faction, as opposed to the "Strike South" faction, which favored an immediate move into China. (The

Strike South faction also favored conquest of the Dutch East Indies and other South Seas colonies of the Western powers to gain for Japan self-sufficiency in natural resources, most importantly oil.) Most in the navy leaned toward the Strike South policy, as the navy was by far the largest consumer of oil.

A new war with China started on July 7, 1937, with a firefight at the Marco Polo bridge near Peking (it is not clear who fired the first shot, but it does not really matter). Peking was quickly taken, and the focus shifted south to Shanghai. The assault on the city by the army was preceded by an aerial bombardment by the navy, which shocked the world with its ferocity and obvious targeting of civilian population—including the foreign communities. Chiang Kai-shek's army fought tenaciously, and the city was not taken until November. Most of Chiang's army escaped, but the Japanese army then pushed them up the Yangtze valley toward Nanking—the Chinese capital—180 miles west of Shanghai. The retreat of Chiang's army turned into a rout. By December 7 the Japanese army was at the gates of the capital. That day, Chiang, with three-quarters of his army, abandoned Nanking and retreated west further up the Yangtze. But 75,000 of his troops were trapped in the city.

THE RAPE OF NANKING

On December 12, Nanking capitulated. That same day, an American river gunship—the *Panay*—was bombed and strafed by two dozen Japanese navy planes. It and two of the three American oil barges it was escorting were sunk. It was obvious at the time that the American vessels had been deliberately attacked. (It later turned out that the Japanese army officer who had ordered the attack had intended to provoke the United States into declaring war.)[13]

President Roosevelt communicated his outrage directly to the emperor. The Japanese government, though claiming mistake, immediately offered profuse apologies and indemnity for the families of the victims. Vice Admiral Isoroku Yamamoto—who would later mastermind the attack on Pearl Harbor—was privately outraged that an army officer had ordered his naval airmen to carry out the attack, but publicly accepted full responsibility for the embarrassing incident. It could have been another *Maine* or *Lusitania*, but so eager was the United States to avoid war at that time that the incident was allowed to pass.

The Rape of Nanking began two days after it fell. When the first Japanese troops entered the city on the day of its capture they were fairly restrained, but on the 14th of December the Sixteenth Division, notorious for its brutality, rolled in.[14] Over the next six weeks, the inhabitants of Nanking were subjected to a reign of terror without precedent in the modern history of war. When it was over virtually all of the 75,000 Chinese soldiers who had been trapped in the city had been killed—along with at least that number of civilians, who were massacred with barely believable savagery. (No one knows the exact body count— credible estimates range between 40,000 [Japanese estimate] and 300,000 [Chinese estimate]—but a good guess for the combined military and civilian tally was around 150,000.)[15] At least 5,000 (some say 20,000) women were raped and most of them thereafter killed.

Word of the atrocity—with photographs—began to leak out of the city by the end of December through the foreign contingent trapped in the city. What horrified the American public was not so much that a massacre had taken place—soldiers run amok in every war—but the scale of this massacre and the fact that the atrocities were systematic and prolonged; it seemed obvious that this one had been carefully planned at a high level.[16]

The Rape of Nanking had a profound affect on popular opinion in the United States. More than anything else up to that time—Manchuria or even the *Panay*—it served to sway American sentiment in a decidedly anti-Japanese direction. This produced public support for the American government's later policy of aiding China and ratcheting up economic sanctions against Japan. Roosevelt had commented that "the Japanese hate us—sooner or later they will come after us." After Nanking, it began to dawn on the Japanese that the Americans were beginning to hate them and sooner or later might come after *them*.

THE BUILD-UP OF THE NAVIES

During the period of rising tensions between the two countries caused by Japanese expansion into China and political upheaval in Japan, a naval arms race got underway. When Franklin D. Roosevelt took office in 1933 he announced that he would build up the navy—especially aircraft carriers—to treaty strength. The Japanese Diet had already authorized, in 1932, a naval "supplementary" program to enlarge the carrier fleet. As most of the carriers involved in this build-up would see action in the Battle of Midway, a certain amount of detail on the building of the carrier fleets—and the capabilities of the individual carriers—may be useful.

In 1934, before the hulls of the new carriers on both sides were laid down, Japan and the United States each possessed four aircraft carriers. None of Japan's carriers was "modern" by World War II standards in that none could carry more than sixty aircraft. Their largest, *Kaga* and *Akagi*—built on battleship and battle cruiser hulls, respectively—displaced just under 27,000 tons, but were configured with an antiquated flight deck design of three short, stepped (terrace-like) decks. The *Ryujo*, the first purpose-built carrier, had a single flight deck, but it was short (513 feet compared with 730 on its American counterpart *Ranger*). It was an experimental design that turned out to be impractical—its two hangar decks, which gave the small carrier a capacity of forty-eight planes, made it top-heavy and dangerously unstable because of its light displacement of only 8,000 tons.

The carriers of the United States navy, in comparison, were considerably more "modern." The *Lexington* and *Saratoga*, which had also been converted from battle cruisers, displaced 33,000 tons and had a single full-length flight deck 875 feet long; each could carry over one hundred planes. However, *Ranger*, America's first purpose-built carrier, though more modern than the Japanese carriers, was also an experimental design that would prove inadequate to perform as a full-fledged attack carrier when war came. Although it could carry eighty planes, it later turned out to be too light—at 14,500 tons—to be a stable platform for landing the heavier carrier bombers that would be deployed during the war. Even worse, it had arresting gear too weak to safely land those heavier planes.[17] It would not be operationally deployed in the Pacific.

In comparative total carrier tonnage, in 1934 the United States had 91,500 and Japan had 68,400. Both countries were still below their Washington Treaty limits of 135,000 tons and 81,000 tons respectively. In May and July 1934, *Yorktown* and *Enterprise* were laid down, followed in 1936 by *Wasp*. With the first two displacing 19,900 tons each and *Wasp* displacing 14,700—and with *Langley* being retired as an aircraft carrier—the United States' carrier tonnage reached 135,000 in 1939.

In 1934 Japan also began to build up her navy (and at the end of that year gave notice that the naval limitation treaty would be allowed to lapse at the end of 1936). *Kaga* and *Akagi* were to be radically reconstructed: the flight decks of both carriers were converted to single long decks of over 800 feet, with the two lower flight decks on each converted into large double-decked hangars capable of holding ninety aircraft. Displacement was increased to 38,200 tons for *Kaga* and 36,500 for *Akagi*. (*Ryujo* was also rebuilt to make it more stable—its displacement was increased to 10,600 tons.) Most significantly, Japan's first truly modern purpose-built carrier—*Soryu*—was laid down in November 1934. It displaced 15,900 tons and carried seventy-one planes (though only fifty-seven operationally). It was followed in 1936 by *Hiryu*, displacing 17,300 tons, and carrying seventy-three planes (but also only fifty-seven operationally). The outstanding feature of these two relatively small fleet carriers was the power of their engines: 152,000 horsepower, giving them a speed of over 34 knots. (By comparison, the larger *Yorktown* class had engines of 120,000 horsepower.) The high speed gave these carriers the capability of launching far more planes in a single deckload than would be expected from carriers with flight decks only 711 feet long. Thus, despite their relatively light displacement they were full-fledged fleet attack carriers.[18]

The total tonnage of Japan's carrier fleet, on completion in 1939 of this building program, was 126,000—almost that of the American carrier fleet. After the naval limitation treaty expired, the size and aircraft-carrying capacity of their carriers were kept secret. They continued to claim 26,000 and 26,900 tons, respectively, for *Kaga* and *Akagi*—with just sixty aircraft each—and 7,100 tons for *Ryujo*. But most deceptively, they announced that *Soryu* and

Hiryu were merely light carriers displacing 10,500 tons each—with aircraft capacities of forty planes each. (For this reason they were designated as light fleet carriers [CVLs] in books and official documents produced during the war rather than the full fleet carriers [CVs] they actually were.)

At the completion of the building program begun in 1934, Japan was still behind the United States. By 1939—when *Hiryu* was completed and *Wasp* launched—the United States had five modern attack carriers (excluding *Ranger*) with a total displacement of 120,500 tons and an operational plane-carrying capacity of almost 360 aircraft. Japan now had four modern attack carriers (excluding *Hosho* and *Ryujo*) with a total displacement of 107,900 tons and an operational plane capacity of about 260 aircraft. This disparity, however, would soon be reversed.

In 1937, with a new era of hostility beginning between Japan and the United States over China, both countries began to prepare for a Pacific war. But Japan's commitment to that prospect was much stronger. The more progressive leaders of Japan's navy—most notably Yamamoto—realized earlier and more clearly than their American counterparts that the era of the battleship as the principal capital ship had passed, and that the next war—in the Pacific at least—would be decided by carrier-based naval air power. In 1937 Japan began the second phase of its naval build-up in a quest to overtake America in this new capital ship arena.

At that time Japan's carrier force not only was still quantitatively inferior to that of the American navy, but—in a class-by-class comparison—was qualitatively inferior as well. *Kaga* and *Akagi*, even after reconstruction, were not as fast as *Saratoga* and *Lexington* and had shorter flight decks; they could not launch as many planes in a single deckload. *Soryu* and *Hiryu*, though faster than *Yorktown* and *Enterprise*, were lighter and carried substantially fewer planes. (The *Yorktown*-class carriers carried seventy-two operational planes—increased to over eighty when the folding-wing model of the Wildcat fighter was introduced.) Japan's qualitative deficit was to be cured with the laying down of the *Shokaku* in December 1937 and her sister ship *Zuikaku* a few months later. Thus, in 1937 a building program designed to overtake the United States in carrier strength was begun.

The *Shokaku* class carriers were heavier, faster, and better armed and armored, and had the same plane-carrying capacity as the American *Yorktown*-class carriers. They were regarded as "super-carriers" by the Japanese navy, and though that might be a slight exaggeration, they were clearly the best carriers afloat when the war broke out. Each displaced 25,675 tons (standard) and was 844 feet long; their engines produced 160,000 horsepower, giving them a speed of over 34 knots (the lighter *Yorktown* class could do thirty-three); and each could carry eighty-four planes—seventy-two operational. And, unlike the other Japanese carriers, they would be able to take a lot of punishment in battle. Even though the limitation treaties had expired, Japan still decided to keep the actual specifications secret. After they were launched it was announced that the carriers displaced 20,000 tons and carried sixty planes each.[19]

The only American carrier laid down after the Washington Treaty expired—and before war broke out in Europe—was *Hornet*. It was essentially a *Yorktown*-class carrier, but with a larger flight deck and displacing 20,000 tons. It was commissioned in October 1941—a month after *Zuikaku*—but did not get an air group and become operational until spring of 1942. Thus, on the eve of the attack on Pearl Harbor, Japan had six operational attack carriers, totaling 139,250 tons in displacement and embarking 423 planes (around 400 operational); the United States had five, totaling 120,500 tons and embarking around 390 planes (354 operational). (In addition to attack carriers, Japan had also built several light carriers for use in supporting amphibious landing operations.)[20] Japan had finally achieved its goal set in 1937 of overtaking the United States in carriers.

The warship building programs between 1934 and 1941 extended, of course, to other types of ships as well. Japan, hoping to make up the deficit in numbers of battleships with quality, laid down in 1937 the mammoth *Yamato*—followed a few months later by her sister ship, *Musashi*. These ships were by far the largest and most heavily gunned battleships ever built. *Yamato* displaced 64,000 tons (71,659 full load—roughly double that of the largest American battleship afloat) and carried nine 18.1-inch guns in three triple turrets. (The size of the guns was kept secret—they were reported as being 16-inch.)[21] It was expected that these two behemoths could sink most of the American battleships in a single gun battle if given the chance. (But one of the mysteries and ironies of World War II is that neither of these ships ever fired a shot in anger against another warship, and they were ignominiously sunk by aircraft.)

More relevant to the carrier fleet was the reconstruction of the four *Kongo*-class battle cruisers. They were increased in size and engine power to become fast battleships, with a speed of 30 knots. This would enable them to serve as escorts to the carrier striking force—carrying an antiaircraft armament double that of a heavy cruiser, and much more difficult to sink. (None of the American battleships could do more than 21 knots, and thus they were useless for escorting attack carriers.) As for heavy cruisers, Japan was able to match the United States in numbers (eighteen each) by converting six large "treaty light cruisers" carrying 6-inch guns to heavy cruisers with 8-inch guns.[22] Two of these—*Tone* and *Chikuma*—had been specially designed to escort carriers, by increasing to five the number of catapult-launched seaplanes that could be accommodated for search operations.

During this time, the United States also laid down its first modern fast battleships capable of escorting carriers. They were the *North Carolina* and *Washington*, with a speed of 28 knots, displacing 37,500 tons and carrying nine 16-inch guns in three triple turrets. These were followed by four more battleships of the

South Dakota class, which were similar in size, speed, and armament to the *North Carolina* class (except that they were shorter). However, none of these six ships was completed in time to serve as carrier escorts until after the Battle of Midway.

THE EMERGENCE OF NAVAL AIR POWER

In 1937, when *Shokaku* was laid down, the naval aircraft carried by aircraft carriers were still mostly slow, cloth-covered biplanes not much different in appearance from the airplanes of World War I. Although all-metal monoplanes had made their debut in the early 1930s as land-based and sea-based planes, the aircraft engines of the day were not powerful enough to propel an all-metal monoplane bomber into the air from a carrier deck (and the catapults were too inefficient to launch an entire squadron of carrier bombers in a reasonable time). But by the mid-1930s, quantum advances in aircraft engine and propeller technology (supercharging and variable-pitch propellers) had made an all-metal monoplane for carriers feasible.[23]

The first of two remarkable carrier aircraft to be produced by Japan was the Nakajima B5N2 torpedo plane (actually an "attack" plane as it also served as a level bomber) known to the American navy as the "Kate." It went into production November 1937—five months after the American navy's first all-metal torpedo bomber, the Douglas "Devastator." But while the Devastator was clunky and slow, and very short-ranged, the Kate was sleek and fast, and very long-ranged. It had fully retractable landing gear (the Devastator's only partially retracted), folding wings (as did the Devastator), and a top speed of 235 mph (compared to 207). Morever, it had a maximum range of over 1,200 miles (compared with around 700 for the Devastator). It was by far the best torpedo bomber in the world when the war broke out. With its 1,000-horsepower engine for a 9,000-pound machine, and long wings, it could lift off from a fairly short carrier deck with an almost 2,000-pound torpedo or bomb load. (The Devastator was underpowered; with only 900 h.p. for a plane over 1,000 pounds heavier, it required a long flight deck to lift off with a similar load.)

Even more remarkable than the plane was the aerial torpedo that had been developed for the Kate—the Type 91. It could be dropped from over 250 feet above the water at an air speed of over 250 knots. In the water, it had a speed of 42 knots and was extremely accurate and reliable.[24] By contrast, the American navy's aerial torpedo—the Mark 13—had to be dropped from 50 feet at an air speed of no more than 100 knots. With a speed of only 33 knots, it could be outrun by the fastest Japanese carriers. But worse than all that, it had a defective firing pin, which meant that even if it hit a ship (it often went underneath them) as often as not it would not explode. It was so hard to deliver and so unreliable that it is not unfair to say that, essentially, it did not work. Incredibly, these deficiencies were not discovered until after the war began.[25] The United States Congress had been so parsimonious with the navy's budget that the navy could not afford to purchase enough of the torpedoes to adequately test them in practice runs.

By contrast, the Japanese navy was able to drop hundreds of their Type 91s in practice runs. This not only ensured that they worked, and could be constantly improved, but honed the skills of the torpedo plane aircrews. The performance of the Type 91 was kept secret from the American navy. It would turn out to be a secret weapon that, when delivered by the Kate, gave the Japanese navy the capability to knock the American navy out of the Pacific.

The other remarkable Japanese carrier plane was, of course, the Mitsubishi "Zero" fighter. It can be said to be Japan's other secret weapon in its war with the United States. It went into production in July 1940. The Zero's performance outclassed that of any other fighter in the world that could be launched from a carrier. It was faster (332 mph) and had a higher rate of climb and a much sharper turning radius than its American counterpart—the Grumman Wildcat F4F. It gave the Japanese navy air superiority for most of the first year of the war. Perhaps most remarkable, however, was its range; that high performance was coupled with the capability of staying in the air for almost 2,000 miles. It was the world's first strategic fighter plane. Even under fuel-guzzling combat conditions (and without its drop tanks), its combat radius was over 300 miles. (The Wildcat, in comparison, was severely hampered by its short range—giving it a combat radius of only about 175 miles.)[26] Prior to the production of the Zero and Kate, the Japanese had largely copied Western aircraft designs. But not only were these two planes revolutionary, they were of uniquely original designs.

However, with the third class of carrier planes, dive-bombers, the balance of superiority was reversed. Here, it was the Japanese Aichi D3A1—"Val"—that was clunky, with its fixed landing gear, and it normally carried only a 550-pound bomb (though it proved to be a surprisingly effective dive-bomber). By contrast, its counterpart, the Douglas SBD dive-bomber—the "Dauntless"—had fully retractable wheels and a top speed of 250 mph (compared with 240 for the Val), and could carry a 1,000-pound bomb. It was easy to fly and very forgiving; its pilots loved it. Its only serious deficiency for carrier service was lack of folding wings. It probably is not an exaggeration to say that without the Dauntless, the American navy would have lost the Battle of Midway and been knocked out of the Pacific, at least for the first year of the war.

Of the three things needed for naval air power—carriers, carrier planes, and carrier pilots—the last may be the most crucial. In 1937, the year Japan began its quest to overtake the United States in naval air power, the Japanese navy also doubled the number of pilot trainees admitted to its pilot training programs.[27] These programs had 177 graduates in 1937. The following year, when the classes admitted after July 1937 graduated, there were 362, and this number increased steadily in subsequent years.[28]

Most of the graduates (at least most of those who survived the attrition of the advanced training programs) went on to become land-based or seaplane pilots. But those who survived the rigors of the more intense and hazardous advanced carrier training to become carrier pilots numbered just under 500 by December 1941.[29] Of these, about 400 would be considered first-line pilots, most with over seven hundred hours of flight time, who would serve on the six attack carriers. (The elite of this group were the 250 pilots in the First and Second Carrier Divisions—*Akagi*, *Kaga*, *Hiryu*, and *Soryu*; the pilots of the new Fifth Carrier Division—*Shokaku* and *Zuikaku*—were less experienced.) This was a more highly trained cadre of carrier pilots than the American navy would have on hand at the outbreak of the war. (Again, as with the aerial torpedoes, the United States Congress's penny-pinching with the navy curtailed the number of hours American carrier pilots could spend training with the fleet—they averaged only about three hundred hours.)[30] Thus, with the build-up begun in 1937, it would turn out that by December 7, 1941, the Japanese navy had overtaken the American navy, at least qualitatively, in ships, planes, ordnance, and pilots. But, unfortunately, this was not realized in Washington when negotiations to forestall war were taking place.

As impressive as these new aircraft carriers, carrier planes, and pilots were, by themselves they did not automatically form into a formidable naval war machine. To combine them into a decisive striking force required a reorganization of a battleship-oriented navy into one centered around aircraft carriers. That is what Isoroku Yamamoto did when he took over as commander in chief of the Combined Fleet on August 30, 1939. This was revolutionary, and Yamamoto had to overcome fierce resistance from the naval traditionalists. But with the assistance of a brilliant young naval air officer—Minoru Genda—he created a new carrier-oriented navy with a "first strike" capability. The critical innovation was to assemble all the fleet attack carriers into a single striking force—the First Air Fleet (also later called the "Mobile Force" or "Striking Force"—*Kido Butai* in Japanese). The role of fast battleships and cruisers was to support the carriers, rather than the other way around as had been traditional. (By contrast, the American navy, at that time, deployed its carriers into a number of small task forces.)[31]

This new reorganization of the Japanese navy—completed April 1941 with the deployment of the First Air Fleet—provided it with a perhaps even more deadly offensive capability than did its "secret weapons." It was analogous in many respects to the German army's innovation of massing its tanks into special Panzer divisions and supporting them with tactical aircraft to achieve the blitzkrieg capability that astounded the world at the beginning of the war in Europe. The *Kido Butai* would likewise astound the world at the beginning of the Pacific War.

TABLE 1

Comparative aircraft complements of carriers—December 1941
(Normal operational planes, excluding spares)[32]

US		JAPAN	
Lexington: 18 F, 36 DB, 18 TB	= 72	Kaga:18 F, 27 DB, 27 TB	= 72
Saratoga: 18 F, 36 DB, 18 TB	= 72	Akagi: 18 F, 18 DB, 27 TB	= 63
Ranger: 36 F, 30 DB	= 66	Ryujo: 18 F, 18 TB	= 36
Yorktown: 18 F, 36 DB, 18 TB	= 72	Soryu: 18 F, 18 DB, 18 TB	= 54
Enterprise: 18 F, 36 DB, 18 TB	= 72	Hiryu: 18 F, 18 DB, 18 TB	= 54
Wasp: 27 F, 30 DB, 9 TB	= 66	Zuiho: 12 F, 12 DB	= 24
		Shokaku: 18 F, 27 DB, 27 TB	= 72
		Zuikaku: 18 F, 27 DB, 27 TB	= 72
	420		**447**

(Excluded from this tally are escort carriers—one for each side; the obsolete
Hosho; and the new *Hornet,* which though commissioned lacked an air
group.)

THE OUTBREAK OF WORLD WAR II

In 1939, while the final stages of a naval build-up that would propel the Japanese navy past that of the United States by the end of 1941 were proceeding
apace, war broke out in Europe. Until this time, although Japan was preparing
for war it was not clear with whom it would go to war—America and the other
Western powers, or its old foe Russia. (Moreover, the Japanese government
had entered into an alliance with Nazi Germany against the Soviet Union under the so-called anti-Comintern pact signed in November 1936. Although the
"treaty" was without real teeth, it at least obligated Japan to pose a semblance of
a threat against the Soviets.) As we have seen, the military leadership—especially
in the army—had been divided between the Strike North (against Russia) and
Strike South factions. Although the former had incurred a serious setback
with the abortive coup in 1936, and with the move into China the following
year, they were not yet out of the picture.

Two events immediately preceding the German invasion of Poland on September 1, 1939, further isolated the "strike northers." A month before, while the
world's attention was focused on Germany, a little-noticed battle was being
fought between Japan and Soviet Russia on the Manchurian border. On August 20, the Russian army, under the later to become legendary Marshal Georgi
Zhukov, decisively defeated the Japanese army in a battle on the Khalka River.
Four days later, Germany and the Soviet Union signed their infamous nonaggression pact, which left Hitler free to invade Poland. The Japanese govern-

ment was shocked. It had not been consulted by its supposed anti-Comintern pact ally, and the nonaggression treaty meant that the Soviet Union was free to devote even more military resources to the Far East against Japan.

The significance of these two events for the prospects of war between Japan and the United States was that they provided a humiliating and final setback for the Strike North faction in the Japanese army. This left, as the only feasible course for expansion, a move south into the resource-rich peninsulas and islands of the British, French, and Dutch colonies—even though that would most likely lead to war with the United States. When Germany invaded Poland, and Britain and France declared war on Germany two days later, the prospects for a strike south became even more inviting, as two of the colonial powers in southeast Asia—Britain and France—would have their hands full fighting Germany.

In the spring of 1940, all-out war finally came to western Europe. Hitler had shelved the anti-Comintern pact with Japan, not only to clear the way for the attack on Poland, but to take care of business with France and Britain before turning against the Soviet Union. In April, Germany occupied Denmark and invaded Norway, and on May 10 it invaded the Low Countries and France. After France was defeated—after just six weeks—the new puppet Vichy government consented to a Japanese army occupation of northern French Indochina on August 30, which Japan then used to construct airfields for attacks on southern China. As previously mentioned, the United States extended the limited embargo begun two years before to include aviation gasoline, lubricating oil, scrap iron, and various strategic minerals and chemicals (but not crude oil).

Meanwhile, domestic measures were taken in Japan to put the population on a war footing. In July, a relatively moderate government had been replaced by one headed by the more military-friendly Prince Konoye. General Hideki Tojo became minister of war. The new administration began immediately to impose a near-totalitarian "New Structure" in Japan.[33] All political parties and labor unions were suppressed, censorship was tightened, workers were required to work longer hours in the war industries, and many luxuries were forbidden.

On September 27, 1940, Japan signed the Tripartite Pact, nominally allying itself to Germany and Italy. The pact pledged each signatory to declare war on any third country that joined the war against any of the "axis" countries. It was intended primarily to deter the United States from entering the war against Germany or Japan. (It was the reason Hitler later declared war on the United States after the attack on Pearl Harbor; this seemingly foolish act was in reality one of the few times Hitler honored a treaty commitment.) Notably, the pact did not apply to either country's involvement in a war with Soviet Russia.

Because of this, the Tripartite Pact must rank among the most feeble military alliances in history. It would not deter the United States from making war against Germany or Japan when the time for that came, and it did not apply to the most obvious common enemy of the two countries—Soviet Russia—where military cooperation could have made a possibly decisive difference in the outcome of the war. Japan once would have welcomed a meaningful military alliance against Russia, but the double-cross of the Hitler-Stalin pact slammed the door on that. Japan was left free to follow her own interests quite independently of Germany's, a consequence Hitler would soon rue. In April 1941, Japan signed her own nonaggression treaty with Russia (the Neutrality Agreement)—just two months before Germany invaded Russia. The purpose was to free up pressure on the Manchurian border so Japanese troops could be redeployed south. But it also freed Soviet troops in the Far East to be transferred to western Russia should the need arise.

On June 22, 1941, Hitler repudiated his nonaggression pact with Stalin and launched Operation Barbarossa against Russia. Within weeks the German blitzkrieg had moved so fast and so far into the Soviet Union—destroying entire army groups of dozens of divisions along the way—that most foreign observers believed that it would be a short war and that Germany would soon be master of all of Europe. The affect in Japan of the German success was to intensify eagerness to get on the bandwagon of impending Axis triumph by grabbing the resource-rich South Seas lands and become master of all of East Asia.

However, in late August, the German offensive stalled on the southern front around Kiev. Hitler—through his foreign minister and ambassador in Tokyo—pleaded with the Japanese government to attack Russia in the east. Tokyo declined, having shifted its interest to the South Seas area (and, in any case, was confident that Germany would defeat Russia without Japanese assistance). The German army, after shifting Panzer units south from the center front, was finally able to envelop and destroy the Soviet armies defending Kiev, and in early October resumed its drive on Moscow.

But as December approached, the German army got bogged down in front of Moscow by stiffened Red Army resistance, aided by the fierce Russian winter. Soviet troops that had been on the Manchurian border had been transferred west—thanks to the neutrality pact with Japan—and arrived in time to save Moscow from capture. Two days before the Pearl Harbor attack, Zhukov launched a counteroffensive that pushed the Germans on the Moscow front back almost 200 miles. Though it was not fully realized at the time, this effectively doomed Germany to eventual defeat. (While the German defeat at Stalingrad a year later is generally regarded as the turning point on the Eastern Front, it is unlikely that the Soviets would have been able to rebuild their armies to sufficient strength at prevail at Stalingrad had they lost Moscow—their railroad hub and central marshalling yard—in December 1941.)

One cannot help but note that had Japan repudiated its neutrality pact with the Soviet government and joined in Germany's attack on Russia—the dream of the Strike North faction in the army—not only would the German army most likely have taken Moscow in the winter of 1941, but Germany probably would have gone on to win its war against the Soviet Union. In such a case Japan might not have felt compelled to go to war with the United States—at least not in 1941. Apart from lacking the manpower and resources to fight in Russia, China, and South Asia at the same time, Japan's likely share of Russian spoils—including oil—might have at least temporarily satisfied her imperial ambitions and quest for self-sufficiency in natural resources. But fortunately for Russia (and perhaps Britain as well) Germany and Japan were poor allies.

"OPERATION HAWAII"

Formal planning for an attack on Pearl Harbor had been under way by Yamamoto since January 1941. He had been intrigued by the British navy's torpedo plane attack against Italian battleships in the harbor of Taranto the previous November, and had begun to toy with the idea that perhaps something even more dramatic could be carried out against the American Pacific Fleet. This idea took on added impetus in February when the United States permanently moved the Pacific Fleet from San Diego to Pearl Harbor. While Yamamoto had been pessimistic about his capability to wipe out most of the American fleet by a surprise attack all the way to the American west coast, Pearl Harbor was a much more inviting target.[34]

The Pearl Harbor plan had been merely a contingency plan until the decision by the Imperial Council on September 6 to prepare for war, in response to the American oil embargo in July. After then it became a deadly serious operational plan for Yamamoto. But more time was needed to perfect it and, especially, to sell it to a skeptical Naval General Staff.

As mentioned earlier, there were still a number of technical problems to be worked out. The trickiest was how to make aerial torpedoes work in the shallow waters of Pearl Harbor. The harbor was estimated by the Japanese to be only forty feet deep, and aerial torpedoes normally plunged much deeper than that when they first hit the water—at least seventy-five feet—even when launched at low altitude and low speed.[35] (The harbor at Taranto, Italy, where the British had successfully used aerial torpedoes in November of 1940 was much deeper than that.) By September, some torpedoes had been specially modified—by attaching supplementary fins—to keep them from plunging more than thirty-five feet, but they had to be dropped in a special, very precise manner.

The first batch of these special torpedoes would not be delivered to the First Air Fleet until the end of October and would require weeks of practice by the torpedo plane aircrews before they became an effective weapon for Pearl Harbor.[36] Another problem involving ordnance was that Japan lacked a bomb capable of piercing the deck of an American battleship. It was believed that an armor-piercing bomb of 800 kilograms would be required. Experiments had been underway to test a special armor-piercing 800-kilogram bomb converted from 16-inch battleship gun shells used by the *Nagato*-class battleships. However, these bombs would not be delivered to the fleet until the end of September,[37] and much practice would be required by the Kate level-bomber aircrews before these, too, would become an effective weapon.

While the Japanese envoys were in Washington unwittingly buying time to complete these preparations, Japan could not afford to delay her attack beyond the end of 1941. American lack of preparedness had given the Japanese navy the opportunity to gain superiority over the American navy by the end of the year. By then it would have developed the capability to knock the American navy out of the Pacific — a task that might take a year — but the Japanese navy's advantage over the American navy would quickly erode after the beginning of 1943. The Japanese were aware that the United States had begun — in the summer of 1941 — to lay down a new and formidable class of aircraft carriers, the *Essex* class. They also knew that a new generation of carrier aircraft were under development and that the American naval pilot training program had been enormously enlarged. (Unlike Japan's, American naval procurement programs and specifications of ships, aircraft, and weaponry were not closely held secrets.)

Moreover, the clock was ticking against Japan on oil: stockpiles had been declining since September; without a new source of oil Japan's economy, and even its navy, could be facing crippling shortages by the end of 1942.[38] It was therefore considered imperative to seize the oil fields of the East Indies in early 1942 so that production from the oil fields — which were expected to be badly damaged by the retreating Dutch and British — could be restored before the end of the year. Then, of course, it had to be possible to safely transport that oil back to Japan. This could be achieved only by eliminating American naval power in the western Pacific by the end of 1942. Thus, all these factors made it apparent that there was only about a twelve-month window of opportunity — beginning December 1941 — to accomplish all this.

In addition to these strategic considerations, there was a more immediate problem on the tactical level that imposed a December deadline for the opening attack — weather. The monsoon season in the South Seas, especially in the Malaya and Philippines areas, would begin before the end of December. It was reckoned that large-scale amphibious landings on Malaya and the Philippines would be next to impossible in January and February.[39] A delay of those invasions until spring of 1942 would throw the whole timetable for the twelve-month window off track. And, as the invasions and occupations of the targeted South Seas areas had to be protected from interference by the American and British navies, all these considerations dictated an attack on Pearl Harbor before the end of the year. Thus, come December it would be now or never.

Yamamoto, however, had a hard sell for his Pearl Harbor scheme. The Naval General Staff — and even his carrier striking force commander, Chuichi Nagumo, and Nagumo's chief of staff, Ryunosuke Kusaka—opposed it as not being feasible and, even if the means could be developed to make it technically possible, as being too risky. When war came, they favored using the carrier force to support the paramount southern operation. Everyone agreed that the American Pacific Fleet had to be destroyed to prevent flank attacks on the Japanese convoys from the South Seas. But the Naval General Staff wanted that to be done in waters closer to home, where the Japanese navy would enjoy the advantages of shorter supply lines and air supremacy. Moreover, it was assumed that after the Philippines was taken, America would send its fleet across the Pacific in an attempt to recapture those islands, where the fleet could be engaged in a "great decisive battle."

Yamamoto, on the other hand, did not believe that the Americans would accommodate Japan by engaging in a single "great decisive battle" at a place advantageous to Japan. He feared that his Combined Fleet would find itself involved in a more drawn-out series of battles of attrition that would result in the Pacific Fleet surviving long enough for America to deploy the new generation of ships and naval air power it was developing. In such a case, he feared Japan would surely lose the war. He believed that Japan's only hope for success was in destroying the Pacific Fleet quickly—and that only his Pearl Harbor scheme offered that prospect, however risky.

As the new techniques required for attacking a fleet in a shallow harbor began to take shape by the fall of 1941 (under the tutelage of Minoru Genda), Yamamoto became convinced that he had a good chance of knocking out most of the American Pacific Fleet in a single strike. It would take luck—such as the three American carriers in the Pacific being at Pearl Harbor when he attacked— but it appeared to Yamamoto to be worth the risk. If it was successful, American naval power could be eliminated from the Pacific Ocean in the first year of the war. This would then buy time to take the oil fields of the East Indies, repair them, and get the oil back to Japan before stockpiles ran out.

Although by the end of September Yamamoto had garnered the cooperation of Kusaka (and more reluctantly Nagumo) for his Pearl Harbor plan, the Naval General Staff still opposed it and, in any event, insisted that half the carriers of the carrier striking force be committed to the Southern Operation.[40] The Second Carrier Division (*Hiryu* and *Soryu*) commanded by Rear Admiral Tamon Yamaguchi was then scheduled to participate in the Southern Operation. (This not only infuriated the aggressive and volatile Yamaguchi, but was bitterly ironical as he had been the most ardent supporter of Yamamoto's plan.)

On October 13, at a conference that included key members of the Naval General Staff, the Pearl Harbor operation was war-gamed using just three carriers— *Kaga*, *Shokaku*, and *Zuikaku*. The results produced by the exercise were adjudged to have inflicted only "moderate damage" on the American fleet, results that pleased no one. It was clear to Yamamoto and Genda that the operation was not worth carrying out unless it could be done with all six carriers of the First Air Fleet. A crisis point had been reached: either the Naval General Staff gave its support for a full-scale attack on Pearl Harbor or the operation would be aborted and Yamamoto would resign.

On October 18, Yamamoto sent his senior staff officer, Captain Kameto Kuroshima, to Tokyo to make a final plea to the Naval General Staff for its support of an operation that would have the participation of all six carriers. Kuroshima was armed with a secret weapon: if he could not obtain support by ordinary means of persuasion he was to inform the Naval General Staff that Yamamoto and the entire staff of the Combined Fleet would resign.[41] When he was met with continued stiff resistance by the key members of the general staff Kuroshima dropped his bomb shell. They were shocked, but such was Yamamoto's prestige that by the end of the day they gave in. Formal approval of the Naval General Staff came in early November, when it incorporated the Pearl Harbor operation into its Combined Fleet Operation Order No. 1— barely a month before the date scheduled for the attack.

A development, almost at the last moment, had made it possible to provide air support for the Southern Operation without using carriers: the range of the Zero fighter had been vastly increased by the addition of drop tanks. It could now escort bombers to Malaya from land bases in Indochina, and to the Philippines from Formosa. The stage was finally set for the attack on Pearl Harbor.

WHAT MADE THE JAPANESE THINK THEY COULD WIN

Did the Japanese leadership and naval high command actually believe they could defeat the United States in a Pacific war? From the American perspective —especially after the fact—it seems obvious that Japan had no chance, that waging war on America was suicidal. Yamamoto's statement to Prince Konoye in August of 1940 has been often—and variously—quoted as evidence that he did not think Japan could win such a war: "If I am told to fight regardless of consequence, I shall run wild for the first six months or a year and win victory upon victory. But I have utterly no confidence for the second or third years. I hope you will endeavor to avoid a war with America."[42]

Yamamoto had traveled widely in the United States in the early 1920s and was awed by its immense size and industrial might. At the times he expressed his "run wild" opinion in 1940 he saw no practical way to eliminate American naval power from the Pacific in the first few months of the war—which he believed essential for Japan to have a chance. However, by the fall of 1941 things had changed that shifted Yamamoto's thinking: the Pacific Fleet had been moved to Pearl Harbor, and special new weapons—torpedoes and bombs—were being devised that would make it possible to sink any battleships and aircraft carriers anchored there. While a series of ordinary naval victories probably would not achieve victory in the long run, the destruction of the bulk of the Pacific Fleet in a stunning single blow might just do the trick.[43]

But while this augured well if the war was a short one, what if the United States did not throw in the towel even if its Pacific Fleet was destroyed, but kept fighting until its new generation of carriers, battleships, and aircraft came on line? Did anybody in Japan seriously think that Japan could win a long war with America? There were in fact many (and not just Tojo) who believed she could. That may seem foolhardy—even irrational—from today's perspective, but if one looks at the world situation in the fall of 1941, the prospects for Japan actually did not appear that hopeless. At that time, the German army was rolling across the Russian steppes like a juggernaut, Rommel was threatening to run the British army out of North Africa, and German U-boats were threatening to cut off Britain's supply lines from America.

From that perspective, it looked like Germany would quickly defeat the Soviet Union, and then go on to knock Britain out of the war. This would leave America without any allies, and with a powerful Germany across the Atlantic. These alarming prospects were visible to the American government as well, but what was not visible from Washington was a Japan that posed a serious threat to American naval power in the Pacific. As the screws were being tightened on Japan by the latest series of embargoes, what was not known in Washington was the Japanese navy had overtaken the American navy—especially in naval air power—and had aerial torpedoes capable of sinking the United States Pacific Fleet.

It was reckoned in Tokyo that if the American Pacific Fleet—especially its carrier force—could be knocked out of the Pacific Ocean in the first few months of the war, and if ample stockpiles of strategic materials from the South Seas—especially oil—could then be built up, Japan had a good chance to hold out against America for the long haul. In such a case, even after America rebuilt its battleship and carrier forces, it was assumed that much of the American navy would be tied up in the Atlantic against Germany. This raised the hope, even for Yamamoto, that the United States might then be persuaded to come to terms that would yield the western Pacific and east Asia to Japan.[44] But this promising scenario was largely predicated on something beyond Japan's control: Germany winning its war in Europe.

While Japan's prospects from its vantage point in the autumn of 1941 were not as hopeless as it has become fashionable to assume, there were, nevertheless, some obvious and terrifying risks in going to war with the United States. One of them is known to have caused Yamamoto many sleepless nights: the Japanese attack on Pearl Harbor might not catch the American carriers. In such a case, even if Germany eventually won the war in Europe, in the meantime the American navy could still disrupt Japanese plans in the South Seas. An even more serious risk was that Germany might not defeat the Soviets. In that event, even if Yamamoto succeeded in destroying the American carrier force, the United States could still stay in the war until its navy was rebuilt. The new carrier force could then be deployed exclusively in the Pacific, where it would eventually overwhelm the Japanese fleet. Thus, Japan's only hope of winning the war in the Pacific rested on two precarious premises: quick destruction of the American carrier force and quick victory by Germany over the Soviet Union.

However, in late November 1941, when the Pearl Harbor striking force set sail, neither of these assumptions seemed farfetched—though it would take some luck for *both* to come off in the crucial next few months. (No one contemplated that *neither* would occur.) In any event, the Japanese leadership believed it had no choice but to risk it. The clock was ticking on oil. While nothing could be done immediately to affect the situation in Russia—that opportunity was now lost—the Japanese navy had the means to destroy the American Pacific Fleet. Immense treasure had been invested to create that capability, and now this was the time to put it to the test.

THE ATTACK ON PEARL HARBOR

THE SORTIE OF THE STRIKING FORCE

On November 26, 1941, the Pearl Harbor Striking Force sortied from Hitokappu Wan (Tankan Bay) in the northern Japanese Kurile Islands. Its carriers and supporting ships had rendezvoused there on the 22nd after having departed from Kure on the inland sea near Hiroshima. There had been strict radio silence, and American and British radio intelligence personnel who had been monitoring the Combined Fleet had lost track of the carrier divisions.[45] The Kuriles had been chosen for the departure point of the sortie because a northern route to Hawaii had been decided on. Although this route would be much more difficult this time of year than a southern one because of rough seas and fog—making navigation and especially refueling hazardous—it was chosen in the interests of stealth.

The stealth paid off. Although the American government received intelligence that a major move south by the Japanese navy was afoot—and that Malaya and the Philippines would probably be invaded—there is no credible evidence that a carrier force was suspected to be heading for Hawaii.[46] The next day, November 27, Admiral Stark, chief of naval operations, sent his famous "war warning" to Admiral Thomas C. Hart in the Philippines and Admiral Husband E. Kimmel at Pearl Harbor. It said:

> This dispatch is to be considered a war warning. Negotiations with Japan looking toward stabilization of conditions in the Pacific have ceased. An aggressive move by Japan is expected within the next few days. The number

and equipment of Japanese troops and the organization of naval task forces indicates an amphibious expedition against either the Philippines, Thai or Kra Peninsula or possibly Borneo. Execute appropriate defensive deployment preparatory to carrying out the tasks assigned in WPL 46.[47]

(It might seem curious that there was no mention of Pearl Harbor; but, as will be seen later, the American naval high command did not believe the Japanese navy had the capability to carry out a serious strike on that base.)

On December 1, the Imperial Council ratified Tojo's decision to attack Pearl Harbor, Malaya, and the Philippines. The Japanese envoys in Washington—Ambassador Nomura and special envoy Kurusu—were to be notified that a declaration of war was to be given to the American government a half an hour before the attack on Pearl Harbor began.[48] The next day, Yamamoto from his flagship *Nagato* back in the inland sea broadcast to his Striking Force the prearranged code for proceeding with the attack on Pearl Harbor: "Climb Mount Niitaka 1208" (the numbers announcing the date as December 8 in Japan).

The Striking Force was commanded by Vice Admiral Chuichi Nagumo. He would seem an odd choice to lead this force; he was not a carrier commander or naval airman by profession and was leery about the Pearl Harbor operation. He had been given the appointment because of seniority—which was the general Japanese practice—though he was regarded as an able commander and was a torpedo expert. Yamamoto, who had originally sought the job but was refused, had considered replacing him with someone more carrier-oriented and more enthusiastic about the operation, but had decided against it because he did not want to upset morale at the last moment—Nagumo was a popular commander. Another asset Nagumo had was Minoru Genda as his air officer; Genda had been the real brains behind the Pearl Harbor operation. (But how differently things might have turned out had someone like the aggressive Yamaguchi been in command.)

The nucleus of the Striking Force consisted of all six of Japan's attack carriers: *Akagi* ("Red Castle") and *Kaga* ("Increased Joy"), *Hiryu* ("Flying Dragon") and *Soryu* ("Green Dragon"), and the new super-carriers *Shokaku* ("Soaring Crane") and *Zuikaku* ("Happy Crane"). They embarked 423 aircraft—405 "operational" (that is, with pilots). Three hundred sixty planes were scheduled for the attack on Pearl Harbor[49]—though only 355 would eventually be assigned for the strike due to pilot disabilities—plus 45 operational planes for combat air patrol, and the remaining 18 planes as "spares." (The "operational" aircraft complements appear to have been: 67 for *Akagi*,[50] 76 for *Kaga*, 57 for *Hiryu*, 56 for *Soryu*, 72 for *Shokaku*, and 72 for *Zuikaku*.) Supporting the carriers were the two fast battleships *Hiei* and *Kirishima*, the heavy cruisers *Tone* and *Chikuma* (which had been specially designed to carry five float planes each for reconnaissance), and a screen of nine destroyers led by a light cruiser.

The Pearl Harbor Striking Force was essentially the First Air Fleet but had been modified in two ways: First, the number of supporting ships assigned to the First Air Fleet had been reduced; the other two *Kongo*-class fast battleships, some heavy cruisers, and a squadron of destroyers that normally would be with the Mobile Force had been detached to support the Southern Operation. (This also had the virtue of minimizing the risk of detection en route to Hawaii and conserving fuel.) The second modification was the augmentation of the First Air Fleet's normal complement of about 385 operational aircraft with about 20 planes and pilots taken from the light carriers *Ryujo* and *Zuiho*.[51] The slightly more than 400 pilots in the Striking Force were pretty much the entire contingent of "first-line" carrier pilots the Imperial Japanese Navy possessed.

THE ATTACK

In the early hours of December 7, Genda, on the flagship *Akagi*, pored over the latest radio intelligence on the conditions at Pearl Harbor received from the Naval General Staff in Tokyo. (This intelligence had come from the Japanese consulate in Honolulu—which had been sending reports regularly for weeks— and from scout submarines that had recently been stationed near the mouth of the harbor.) This last-minute intelligence reported that, as of December 6, while there were nine battleships (and a number of light cruisers and destroyers) in the harbor, there were no carriers. This was disturbing news indeed. The number-one priority target of the operation had been the three carriers of the Pacific Fleet (*Lexington*, *Saratoga*, and *Enterprise*); the destruction of the battleships, while important, probably would not have justified the operation.

However, it had been decided that if the Striking Force was not discovered before the day set for the attack, the strike would still be carried out on whatever targets were available. In addition to the American capital ships, air power in Hawaii was to be destroyed. To obtain literally last-minute intelligence Genda had scheduled the launch of two float-plane scouts—one each from the cruisers *Tone* and *Chikuma*—a half hour before the launch of the strike force to reconnoiter Pearl Harbor. When they were launched at 0530, it was no doubt hoped that they would spot some carriers in or near the harbor— but it was not to be. The *Lexington* had departed two days earlier to ferry planes to Guam; the *Enterprise* had left on November 28 to ferry planes to Wake Island—and though returning was still over 200 miles west of Oahu; the *Saratoga* was at San Diego, having undergone some minor repairs.[52]*

---

*Although details of the Pearl Harbor attack might seem out of place in a book on the Battle of Midway, I believe they provide useful context for some of the decisions later made by Nagumo at Midway. Details such as the allocation of tasks among the carriers and the carrier aircraft and Nagumo's refusal to send a third strike against shore-based installations—mainly the oil tank farms—have a bearing on what would happen at Midway.

At 0550, the carriers of the Striking Force reached their launch point—about 220 miles north of Oahu—and turned into the wind. The first plane took off just minutes after 0600. The first to be launched were forty-five Zeros from all six carriers. (Only forty-three made it into the air—one crashed on takeoff and another aborted with engine failure.) Following them were eighty-nine Kate attack planes from *Akagi*, *Kaga*, *Hiryu*, and *Soryu*—forty-nine loaded with 800-kilogram armor-piercing bombs and forty loaded with torpedoes. The Zeros from *Shokaku* and *Zuikaku* were followed by fifty-one Val dive-bombers armed with 250-kilogram land bombs. These first-wave planes—183 in all—were launched in fifteen minutes, formed up and at 0620—led by Commander Mitsuo Fuchida—set course for Oahu. The first combat air patrol of fifteen Zeros was then launched—most from *Shokaku* and *Zuikaku*.

The second-wave strike force—numbering 170 planes—was then raised to the flight decks. Launch began about 0715—thirty-six Zeros, nine each from *Akagi*, *Kaga*, *Hiryu*, and *Soryu*, followed by eighty dive-bombers from those same carriers (two of which aborted) carrying 242-kilogram armor-piercing bombs. Fifty-four Kate attack planes, most carrying two 250-kilogram land bombs each, were launched. The planes—now numbering 168—formed up and headed for Oahu around 0730.

Two waves, totaling 351 planes, were now winging their way toward their targets: the forty Kates carrying torpedoes, along with the forty-nine other Kates in the first wave carrying 800-kilogram bombs, would attack the battleships; the dive-bombers and Zeros of the first wave would attack the airfields of Hickam, Wheeler, Ford Island, Barber's Point, and Kaneohe. The dive-bombers of the second wave would hit cruisers and destroyers, and any battleships that needed finishing off. The Kates and Zeros of the second wave would hit the airfields to mop up any planes still left. (It will be noted that none of the planes from the green Fifth Carrier Division—*Shokaku* and *Zuikaku*—were targeted for ships, though they must be given credit for destroying most of the aircraft on the ground.)

As Pearl Harbor came into view of the first wave at 0753, Fuchida jubilantly radioed the code for announcing to Nagumo that the Americans had been taken by surprise: "Tora! Tora! Tora!" The first bomb exploded at 0755, and the first torpedo hit the water a minute later. There were, indeed, nine battleships moored in the harbor as confirmed by the *Chikuma* scout plane at 0735. One of the battleships was the decommissioned *Utah*—used as a target ship—but the other eight constituted the Battle Force of the Pacific Fleet. Lined up, some in double rows, along "Battleship Row" on the southeastern side of Ford Island were *Nevada*, *Arizona*, *Tennessee*, *West Virginia*, *Maryland*, *Oklahoma*, and *California*. The *Pennsylvania* was in dry dock across the channel. (The ninth battleship of the Pacific Fleet—*Colorado*—was safely at the Bremerton shipyard in Washington State undergoing overhaul.)

Forty torpedo planes and forty-nine more Kates as high-level bombers attacked these battleships and other ships around the periphery of Ford Island. Thirty-six torpedoes were launched, and eighteen struck the battleships, with two more hitting light cruisers. (The four torpedo planes that did not launch were probably hit by antiaircraft gunfire and were shot down.) Of the forty-nine high-level Kates armed with 800-kilogram armor-piercing bombs, only thirteen managed to drop their bombs on or near a ship (though none of these planes were shot down). Four battleships eventually were sunk—*Arizona*, *Oklahoma*, *West Virginia*, and *California*—and the *Nevada* ran aground while attempting to escape after taking a torpedo hit. (The decommissioned *Utah* was also sunk.) *Maryland* and *Tennessee* sustained moderate damage, while *Pennsylvania*—in dry dock—avoided being hit by the first wave.[53]

The fifty-one Val dive-bombers from *Shokaku* and *Zuikaku*, along with the forty-five Zeros in the first wave, attacked the airfields—both army and navy. About sixty-five army and ninety-three navy planes were destroyed on the ground, with dozens more damaged.[54] The first wave attack was over at 0825, and, except for a few stragglers, the planes returned to their carriers. Only nine Japanese planes had been lost—five Kates, three, Zeros and one Val dive-bomber. This would stand as the most deadly-efficient air raid in naval history and the high point of the Imperial Japanese Navy; it would be downhill thereafter.

At 0840, the second wave arrived. Seventy-eight dive-bombers from *Akagi*, *Kaga*, *Hiryu*, and *Soryu* armed with 242-kilogram armor-piercing bombs attacked ships in the harbor, and fifty-four Kates from *Shokaku* and *Zuikaku* armed, primarily, with 250-kilogram land bombs—along with thirty-six Zeros from the First and Second Carrier Divisions—bombed and strafed the airfields again. The Vals went after the crippled *Nevada* attempting to flee the harbor and hit her with five bombs—causing her to beach, ripping open her hull. *Pennsylvania*, in dry dock, was hit with one bomb, causing only minor damage. Even *Arizona*, already irreparably damaged and sinking with most of her crew already dead, was apparently pummeled with several more bombs. Three light cruisers and several destroyers were also hit and severely damaged.

As for the airfields, with most of the planes already destroyed, the Kates concentrated on hangars and other buildings (they would have been better employed hitting the oil tank farms). The attack was over at 0945, and it was the last attack that would be made on Pearl Harbor. The second wave attack added very little to the carnage, and turned out to be mostly redundant. However, as the antiaircraft gun crews were able to get organized during the fifteen-minute lull between the two attacks, the second attack was much more costly to the Japanese: twenty planes were shot down—fourteen Vals and six Zeros. This was almost as many as the number of additional American planes destroyed on the ground; the total number of American aircraft destroyed at the end of the day was around 188.

THE RETIREMENT

After the two waves of the strike force returned to their carriers—the last plane landed about noon—work immediately began to rearm the torpedo planes and bombers with torpedoes and antiship bombs to attack any American carriers that might be found.[55] In Nagumo's command center on *Akagi*, debate immediately began on whether a third attack wave should be sent to attack the oil tank farms and dockyards around the harbor. Fuchida later claimed that he argued in favor of such an attack to maximize the damage to the base; Nagumo's chief of staff, Ryunosuke Kusaka, was opposed. After listening to the pros and cons, Nagumo decided against another attack. He was satisfied with the results of the first two attacks—which had greatly exceeded his expectations—and did not want to put his carriers at risk from an American counterattack. He also did not want to lose any more planes and aircrews to American antiaircraft gunfire (the sharp increase in casualties between the first and second waves indicated that another attack could be very costly). Nagumo preferred to retire north to get out of range of any American bombers that might have survived his attack and postpone until the next day any decision on what to do about the missing American carriers.

This decision not to send another attack to destroy the oil tank farms and dockyard facilities has been justly criticized as one of the most fateful made by the Japanese in the war. (It ranks with Nagumo's decision six months later at Midway to rearm his torpedo planes with land bombs for a second strike on Midway—ironically, the opposite of his decision at Hawaii.) The oil tanks around Pearl Harbor were extremely vulnerable to an air attack as all of them were above ground. Had they been destroyed it would have taken months to rebuild and replenish them as everything would had to have been shipped from the mainland. The submarine pens and repair facilities were almost as vulnerable and difficult to rebuild. Pearl Harbor would have been rendered useless as a forward naval base. Until it was rebuilt and replenished with oil (and Japanese submarines could have made that difficult) the Pacific Fleet would have had to operate from San Diego and other west coast ports—adding over 2,000 miles to the deployment of submarines and carrier task forces to the western Pacific to harry the Japanese navy in the area of the Southern Operation. This would probably have delayed Nimitz's later counteroffensive across the Pacific by as much as a year.[56]

Yamamoto's operation order for the attack on Pearl Harbor did not call for an additional attack to destroy the fuel and repair facilities. The reason is simple: he had no idea what would be encountered in the first attack and what its results might be. He thought it quite possible that the Americans might be prepared for it and that his planes would have to fight their way to the target, incurring heavy losses (he had contemplated losing as much as a third of his strike force). He had also expected that American carriers would be in the area, requiring additional attacks against them if they were not all caught by surprise and destroyed in the harbor in the first attack.

Therefore, he had to leave further operations after the scheduled two attack waves to Nagumo's discretion. There can be no doubt, however, that had he foreseen the loss of only twenty-nine planes in those attacks he would have insisted on a further attack to finish the job of destroying Pearl Harbor as a functioning base. He later blamed Nagumo for failing to make that additional attack, even though he had not been ordered to do so.[57] Nevertheless, Yamamoto must be accorded a large share of the blame, for not including the oil tank farms as a priority target. (The green Fifth Carrier Division could have covered itself with unexpected glory had its second-wave bombers been assigned to that task—rather than a virtually redundant second attack on the airfields.) Yamamoto's focus had been exclusively on the carriers and battleships in the harbor, not the harbor facilities themselves—which turned out to be much more valuable to the Pacific Fleet than the battleships lost.

Although Nagumo wanted to find and destroy any American carriers in the area, his reconnaissance effort was not very aggressive. *Enterprise* had been only 200 miles west of Oahu on the morning of the attack on Pearl Harbor, and the commander of its task force, the pugnacious William F. Halsey, was trying to find the Japanese carrier force and take it on even though he was heavily outnumbered.[58] An extensive armed search effort using torpedo-bearing Kates might well have found the *Enterprise*—and Halsey was doing his best to accommodate this possibility. But when Nagumo decided to retire to the north the afternoon of the 7th, he had, by the next day, put his strike force 600 miles north of Oahu—leaving *Enterprise* out of range of reconnaissance planes. As his ships were running low on fuel, he was eager to get his Strike Force back to Japan unscathed.

VERDICT

Because of the failure to destroy any American carriers and to put Pearl Harbor out of commission, the Hawaii operation must be judged a failure. The battleships sunk were obsolete because of their sluggish speed and would have been of little use in attacking the more mobile Japanese battle fleet. (Six months later Nimitz would, for this reason, eschew sending the three battleships that survived and had been repaired[59]—along with other equally obsolete battleships then available—to Midway and the Aleutians to take on the Japanese battle fleet that was known to be bearing down on those two outposts.)

Although there was great jubilation in Japan over the sinking of at least four battleships at Pearl Harbor, Yamamoto, Genda, and Fuchida knew that the attack actually had been a failure—though they kept this knowledge to themselves. Yamamoto was bitterly disappointed that the American carriers had not been destroyed—not even one. He knew that the attack had stirred up a hornet's nest in America without achieving the only goal that justified it. ("We have awakened a sleeping giant and filled him with a terrible resolve" was the metaphor he supposedly used.) Had even one American carrier been sunk, or had the oil tanks been destroyed, the operation could have been judged at least a qualified success. Actually, Yamamoto was quite unlucky: the *Lexington* had left the harbor only two days before his attack, and *Enterprise* was scheduled to return the day after. An attack forty-eight hours on either side of December 7 would almost certainly have netted a carrier. (One can only speculate on how the loss of *Enterprise*—which was actually within Nagumo's grasp the afternoon of his attack—would have affected American carrier operations the following spring.)

The Pearl Harbor operation, though brilliantly conceived, thus failed to achieve its goal of eliminating American naval power from the Pacific because of mediocre execution. An admittedly risky operation had come up a loser. And when this is combined with the Red Army's counteroffensive on the Moscow front two days earlier, which pushed the German army back and blunted the hope of a quick German victory over the Soviets, it must be said that Japan's Pacific War certainly got off to a bad start.

WHY "AT DAWN WE SLEPT"

On the American side, there was shock, grief, and rage over the loss of the battleships and especially the deaths of 2,403 sailors, soldiers, and civilians (1,103 on *Arizona* alone). In addition to hatred against the perfidious Japanese, there was also outrage against the American commanders at Pearl Harbor—Admiral Kimmel and General Short—for being caught so woefully unprepared. Why, indeed, was Kimmel caught—almost literally—with his pants down on the morning of December 7? While it is beyond the scope of this work to reiterate in detail the case for or against those commanders, or speculate on the various conspiracy theories relating to President Roosevelt, there is one point that has not been adequately dealt with, and that is why the attack on Pearl Harbor *was* such a surprise. Japanese attack was not expected by the Americans simply because Kimmel, Short, Admiral Stark (the chief of naval operations), and President Roosevelt did not believe that the Japanese navy had the *capability* to deliver a devastating strike against the Pacific Fleet at Pearl Harbor.

Numerous war games and "fleet problems" had shown to the navy that while a carrier plane attack could be made on Pearl Harbor, very few capital ships were likely to be sunk or even seriously damaged. Therefore, it was thought, a Japanese attack without the prospect of wiping out the Pacific Fleet would be irrational—and speculation over it should not be taken seriously. Let us briefly review why a devastating attack was considered a virtual impossibility. First, it was believed that aerial torpedoes would not work in the shallow harbor. (Even the Japanese believed this until just weeks before the attack.) American aerial torpedoes certainly would not work in the harbor, so it was assumed that Japanese ones would not work either.[60] Second, America did not have a bomb that could pierce the heavily armored decks of American battleships, so it was assumed that the Japanese did not have one either.[61] It simply did not occur to the American naval commanders of the time that those "slant-eyed, buck-toothed little Japs" could possess weapons with capabilities far beyond those produced by the American naval ordnance industry.[62]

Lack of knowledge about the Japanese navy's special weapons capabilities was not the only reason the Americans believed that an attack by the Japanese on Pearl Harbor was not feasible. It was also believed that the Japanese did not have enough carriers and carrier aircraft crews to mount an attack on Pearl Harbor while at the same time supporting the Southern Operation. A move south by the Japanese in early December *was* expected by the American high command—as clearly shown by Admiral Stark's "war warning" of November 27—and for it the Japanese would need air superiority over the area. This would, it was believed, require a substantial carrier force to be attached to the Southern Operation.

The assumption that Japan lacked the capacity to deploy carriers in two separate theaters at the same time was based on a gross misapprehension of Japanese carrier strength. As already explained, the Americans believed that the Japanese had fewer carriers than they actually had and, moreover, that their carriers embarked far fewer planes than they actually did. This, as we have seen, had been due to a long course of misrepresentations by the Japanese about the size of their ships (and inadequate naval intelligence by the Americans to discover the truth). Because of this, the American navy counted on the Japanese carrier force embarking around 280 operational aircraft—only about 60 percent of the approximately 450 they actually had.[63] The assumption was that most of this limited carrier air power would have to be used to support the Southern Operation, especially if the Philippines were to be attacked.

But what was not realized was that carriers were no longer needed to provide air support for the Southern Operation—even for attacking American airfields in the Philippines. This is because the range of the Zero fighter had been extended—almost at the last minute—so that it could escort land-based bombers all the way from Formosa to the Philippines (and from Indochina to Malaya). The American naval high command was completely unaware of this. The new long-range Zero, then, was the third secret weapon that—along with the specially modified aerial torpedo and the heavy-armor-piercing bomb—made the Pearl Harbor operation feasible. This meant that Nagumo's entire carrier force (which was already over half again larger than estimated) was freed up to be deployed at Hawaii.

It is really no wonder that the American naval high command was caught by surprise. But this ignorance of the various Japanese capabilities that made the

Pearl Harbor operation a serious possibility also has not been given sufficient weight in the popular postmortems about Pearl Harbor written long after the war.

This is why all the supposedly telltale signs of an impending attack, recounted with hindsight after the war, were ignored in 1941: Ambassador Grew in Tokyo cabled Washington in January 1941 about rumors of a plan to attack Pearl Harbor. It was ignored; the very idea of such an attack was derided as "ridiculous."[64] In September, a coded message was sent from Tokyo to the Japanese consul in Honolulu, who had been monitoring the ships in Pearl Harbor, instructing him that in future reports he was to identify their location according to a coded plot that divided the harbor into sectors. This message was intercepted and decoded by the Army Signal Intelligence Service in Washington. Although later dubbed the "Bomb Plot" and, with hindsight, seen as an obvious preparation for aerial bombing of Pearl Harbor, no significance was attached to it at the time; it was not even sent back to the commanders in Hawaii.[65]

Even in late November, when radio traffic from Yamamoto to his Combined Fleet indicated that the Japanese fleets were on the move to somewhere, and the American and British naval intelligence agencies had lost track of Nagumo's carrier fleet, there still was no alarm at Pearl Harbor. (The most telling message from Yamamoto—in retrospect—was to an unidentified task force departing November 26 from an anchorage in the northern Kurile Islands to a destination far enough away to require refueling after eight days. Whether or not the American government received this message is in dispute, but even if it had there would have been no reason at the time to believe that a carrier force was heading for Hawaii—Malaya would have been a more likely possibility.)[66] This conviction that no serious attack on Pearl Harbor was possible is why Admiral Stark's "war warning" sent to Kimmel on November 27 mentioned about every possible target for a Japanese attack except Pearl Harbor.

In 1941 the Japanese had been grossly underestimated by the Americans. This was the product of attitudes that today would be considered blatantly and scandalously racist, but in 1941 were pretty much the norm—even among "liberal" elements in America. These attitudes, going back to the early 1920s, had long chafed the pride of the Japanese people. If what the Japanese wanted out of the stunning feat at Pearl Harbor was respect—and of course that is not all they wanted, but if they did—they certainly got it (along with a good measure of hatred). They were never underestimated again.

Thus, while the Hawaii operation was a strategic failure, its mere accomplishment justified the jubilation in Japan. The Japanese would, however, end up paying an awful price for never being underestimated again: they were no longer able to mount further surprise attacks against the United States navy and, because of that, Yamamoto's dream of knocking the American navy out of the Pacific would be rudely shattered six months later at Midway.

CHAPTER THREE

THE RUN-UP TO MIDWAY

As we have seen, the impetus for the Midway operation was the failure of the Pearl Harbor operation to catch and destroy the American carriers of the Pacific Fleet. But this failure lost its sting in the immediate post–Pearl Harbor euphoria in Japan over the stunning achievements by its navy at Hawaii and the army in the Southern Operation. Things were proceeding so well in the South Seas and western Pacific that the Japanese naval high command hoped that the American Pacific Fleet would soon be reduced to insignificance by attrition.

THE SOUTHERN OPERATION

Almost simultaneously with the attack on Pearl Harbor, attacks were unleashed on Hong Kong, Malaya, Singapore, Guam, and the Philippines. They had been expected by the British, Dutch, and Americans, and, indeed, the attack on Malaya began with a seaborne landing on the Kra Isthmus of Thailand—just as predicted by British intelligence on November 25. In the Philippines, although General Douglas MacArthur had been specifically warned about a possible attack on his bases—unlike the commanders at Pearl Harbor—and he had even heard about the Pearl Harbor attack, his air force was caught on the ground and almost half of it destroyed in the first attack against his air bases.

This might seem curious—and even more curious is the fact that MacArthur escaped the kind of criticism endured by Kimmel and Short. However, there is a reason for it: after MacArthur got word of the Pearl Harbor Attack at 0400 on December 8—one hour after the attack—he sent his planes aloft soon after dawn broke. But the anticipated air attack did not come; a heavy fog over the air bases in Formosa prevented the Japanese from launching an air strike until later in the morning. When no attack arrived by 1000, he landed his aircraft. At 1245, 192 planes from the Eleventh Air Fleet (108 bombers and 84 Zeros) finally arrived and attacked Clark Field and other army air fields in the Manila area while the planes were still on the ground. Communications with the radar stations had managed to fail at this critical moment. Seventeen B-17s and more than thirty P-40 fighters were destroyed at a cost of only seven planes for the Japanese.

One might ask why a combat air patrol was not maintained throughout the morning. It appears that MacArthur was lulled into thinking that because almost all the Japanese carrier strength was apparently in Hawaiian waters the Japanese lacked the means to mount a significant air attack on his bases around Manila. As has been mentioned, the Americans were unaware of the newly increased range of the Zero fighter and thus did not believe that bombers from as far away as Formosa could be escorted by Zeros for attacks on the Manila area. (Already that morning an air strike from the light carrier *Ryujo* by dive-bombers escorted by Zeros had been launched against Davao far to the south on the island of Mindanao.)[1]

Two days later, on the 10th, Japanese troops landed on Luzon, commanded by General Homma and supported by the Second Fleet. Little armed resistance was met, and by the 27th troops approached Manila from two directions. MacArthur decided to spare the city from bombardment, so he declared Manila an open city and evacuated his army to the Bataan Peninsula. By then his air power had been wiped out, and the small Asiatic Fleet was in shambles. At Bataan, his army soon became trapped—with no prospect of relief. About 30,000 American and 110,000 Philippine troops held out in the fortress of Corregidor, an island off the peninsula, until May 6, when exhausted supplies and disease compelled them to surrender to General Homma's army.

On the same day Luzon was invaded, December 10, the Japanese entered Hong Kong and landed on Guam in the Marianas—America's main outpost for protecting the Philippines. Guam, virtually undefended, fell within hours. The small British contingent in Hong Kong held out for two weeks before surrendering on Christmas Day. But the most shocking loss to the British on December 10 was off the coast of Malaya.

A task force consisting of the new battleship *Prince of Wales* and the battle cruiser *Repulse* (accompanied by four destroyers) had been sent from Singapore to interdict Japanese troop transports destined for Malaya. After it became clear that they had been discovered by Japanese reconnaissance planes and were being shadowed by submarines, and after the task force commander had been told by headquarters in Singapore that the promised fighter cover could no longer be sent, the task force turned back. While on the way to Singapore, *Prince of Wales* and *Repulse* were attacked by eighty-five Japanese twin-engine naval bombers ("Nells" and "Bettys.") These were from the elite Kanoye Air Group based on airfields near Saigon. Fifty-one of the bombers were equipped with torpedoes, and thirty-four carried bombs.

In the level bombing attack from high altitude, none of the bombs hit, but the torpedoes proved more deadly. Of the forty-eight torpedoes launched, nine struck home—five on the thinly armored *Repulse*, which sank almost immediately, and four on *Prince of Wales*. The *Prince of Wales* had been designed to be invulnerable to an air attack. Yet it and *Repulse* had been sunk while maneuvering at battle speed in open ocean (not merely sitting moored in an anchorage as were the American battleships at Pearl Harbor), a feat thought impossible. In fact, *Prince of Wales* was the first battleship to be sunk at sea by aircraft—an achievement that stands as one of the most impressive of the war for Japanese naval air power. After the debacle survivors of the *Prince of Wales* were asked why the ship was sent into hostile waters without air support. The replies were to the effect "we did not think those funny little yellow men could sink a battleship at sea with aircraft."[2] This racist mentality was, of course, precisely what had led to the American disaster at Pearl Harbor three days earlier.

After the sinking of *Prince of Wales* and *Repulse*, there were no allied capital ships left in the western Pacific to bother the Japanese in their Southern Operation. They were able to continue their landings unchecked and begin pushing down the five-hundred-mile length of the Malaya Peninsula. A month later— on January 11—the American carrier *Saratoga* (the Japanese thought it was *Lexington*) was torpedoed by a Japanese submarine near Hawaii. It was believed by the Japanese to have been sunk—giving hope that the American carrier force could be eliminated by attrition.

The Japanese army reached the southern tip of Malaya by the end of January, and a week later crossed the narrow channel to Singapore Island. On February 15, Singapore fell. (Its heavy guns had been pointed seaward, the British having not expected the Japanese army to hack its way through the Malayan jungle to attack the city by the back door.) For over two months jubilant cries of *"Banzai"* reverberated throughout southeast Asia from Hong Kong to Burma.

Meanwhile, Nagumo's First Air Fleet had returned to Japan from Pearl Harbor to an ecstatic welcome as it steamed into Hashirajima anchorage in the Inland Sea off Hiroshima on Christmas Day. The *Hiryu* and *Soryu* had been detached on the way back to support landings on Wake Island in mid-December, and returned several days later. On January 5, the Mobile Force—less the *Hiryu* and *Soryu*—departed for Truk in the Caroline Islands to support future operations in the South Seas. On January 20, ninety carrier airplanes attacked

Australian-held Rabaul in New Britain, and the next day they attacked Australian airstrips on the northern New Guinea coast. As they were only lightly defended, within days both targets fell to the Japanese, who then proceeded to build a major naval base at Rabaul. However, Fuchida was furious that the Mobile Force was used on such minor targets. (He likened it to using a sledgehammer to crack an egg.)[3] He had advocated using it for another attack on Pearl Harbor, but was turned down because without the element of surprise it would be too risky—and surprise was by then highly unlikely.

While the conquest of the Philippines and the march down Malaya had been proceeding apace, another Japanese army, supported by the Third Fleet, began the invasion of the principal objective of the Southern Operation: the oil-rich Dutch East Indies and Borneo. Landings on British Borneo (Brunei today) had begun on December 17; invasion of Celebes in the Dutch East Indies followed on January 11. And on February 18 operations against the main island of Java began. A little over a week later the first large-scale naval battle of the Pacific war took place—the Battle of the Java Sea.

The Allies attempted to block the final Japanese landings on Java with a force that included two heavy and three light cruisers and a squadron of destroyers. The Japanese countered with a somewhat smaller force—two heavy and two light cruisers (Japanese light cruisers had much less fire power than the allied ones, though their heavy cruisers were more powerful than the allied ones) and a similar number of destroyers. They had, however, the considerable advantage of air superiority over the area. On the 27th, the battle raged for a good part of the day, and at the end the Allies, after losing two light cruisers (the Dutch *De Ruyter* and *Java*) and several destroyers—against no losses for the Japanese— disengaged and attempted to escape. (On the same day, in a separate battle, the *Langley*—America's first carrier but now an aircraft ferry ship—was also sunk.)

On the night of the 28th, in the Sunda Strait, the surviving cruisers (heavy cruisers *Houston* and H.M.S. *Exeter* and light cruiser H.M.A.S. *Perth*) ran into four more Japanese heavy cruisers, accompanied by destroyers, and were sunk. No Japanese warships were sunk (though some were damaged), but the *Houston* managed to sink four transports before going down. These two battles were disastrous for the Allies. Allied naval power in the southwestern Pacific was destroyed, leaving the door wide open for the Japanese to complete their conquest of the Dutch East Indies, British Borneo, New Guinea, the Solomons, and other islands in the South Seas.

On March 11, Dutch resistance on Java collapsed. Although the oil fields in the Indies had been set ablaze by the Dutch and British, and most of the oil refineries and storage facilities had been destroyed, the Japanese expected oil production to begin resuming before the end of the year.[4] With American naval and air power in the Philippines destroyed, and British and Dutch naval and air power in the southeastern Pacific now gone, the Japanese hoped that the treasure trove of resources from the region—especially oil—could soon be safely transported back to Japan. This, after all, had been the purpose for going to war against the United States.

At this point in the Pacific War the main naval threat to the Japanese flanks in the South Seas region was the British navy in the Indian Ocean. The Japanese high command believed that there were at least three battleships, two carriers, over a dozen cruisers, and several airfields—principally based on the island of Ceylon (Sri Lanka today). The destruction of this naval and air power would secure the Japanese conquests from attack from the west and also pave the way for an invasion of India—to rid all of Asia of Western presence. On March 26, the Mobile Force—now including the *Hiryu* and *Soryu, but* less the *Kaga,* which had been taken in for repairs—departed from Celebes and headed for the Indian Ocean. The five carriers were protected by all four of the *Kongo*-class fast battleships, along with the heavy cruisers *Tone* and *Chikuma* and eight destroyers led by a light cruiser.

On April 5, Nagumo launched an air strike against the British naval base at Colombo on Ceylon. He was sorely disappointed, however, by the fact that the Indian Ocean Fleet was not in the harbor (unlike the Americans at Pearl Harbor, the British had advance warning and were well prepared for the attack). But the Japanese were favored by a nice piece of luck: while the strike force was returning, a float search plane spotted the heavy cruisers *Cornwall* and *Dorsetshire,* which were steaming to get out of the area. After landing and refueling, Commander Egusa—of *Soryu*—led fifty-three dive-bombers to attack these ships. In the most accurate dive-bombing display of the entire Pacific war, both cruisers—maneuvering evasively at battle speed—were sunk. Forty-six hits (out of fifty-three drops) were claimed by the pilots, an incredible 87 percent. Though the number of actual direct hits was probably only about half that, it was still a remarkable performance.[5] (One hit in four would be closer to the average for Japanese dive-bombers against American carriers in subsequent battles the first year of the war.) Egusa's dive-bomber squadron was the most skilled in the Japanese navy. It was most fortunate for America in the upcoming battle of Midway that *Soryu* was bombed before Egusa's squadron could be launched.

Although the bagging of two cruisers was satisfying, Nagumo's mission was to destroy the battleships and carriers in the area. The next day he headed for Trincomalee, the other British naval base on the Island, in hopes of finding the bulk of the British fleet. That fleet was even larger than Japanese intelligence had estimated; it contained five battleships, instead of three, and three carriers (including two of the new armored-deck *Illustrious* class) instead of two. At dawn on April 9, Fuchida led a strike force of ninety Kate attack planes escorted by thirty-eight Zeros to Trincomalee (the dive-bombers were held in reserve). Port facilities and merchant shipping in the harbor were heavily bombed, but the fleet was not there. However, a float search plane from the battleship *Haruna* found the light carrier *Hermes*—steaming without her air group—65 miles south of Trincomalee. Eighty-five Val dive-bombers were dispatched, and in another remarkable performance delivered at least forty bombs (by British count) on the carrier and a destroyer escort, sinking them in minutes.

Hermes was the first carrier sunk by the Japanese. At this point in the Pacific War the British had, arguably, suffered more grievous losses at the hands of the Japanese than had the Americans. Counting just large warships, the Americans had lost five battleships (including the gutted and beached *Nevada*) and the heavy cruiser *Houston* at Java. But the American battleships lost were so slow as to be obsolete—and, in any case, three of them were later salvaged. The British, on the other hand, had lost one modern battleship, one fast battle cruiser (both to land-based naval aircraft), a light aircraft carrier, and three heavy cruisers; an Australian light cruiser under British command had also been lost.

After sinking *Hermes*, the Mobile Force was ordered back to Japan. In a little over three months since Pearl Harbor its record had been spectacular—even if it had underachieved at Hawaii. It had sunk four American battleships, two British heavy cruisers, a light carrier, and nine destroyers—without any of its ships taking so much as even a single hit. In addition, it had shot down or destroyed on the ground more than three hundred aircraft while losing less than sixty of its own planes (twenty-nine at Pearl Harbor, seventeen in the Indian Ocean, and about a dozen at Rabaul, Darwin, and other places in the South Pacific). It had all seemed so easy; but things were about to get a little tougher.

AMERICA STRIKES BACK

While the Japanese navy had been rampaging throughout the South Seas and Indian Ocean regions, the American navy had been recovering from the shock of Pearl Harbor; the British navy had provided most of the Allies' resistance to Yamamoto's naval juggernaut. But a new man had arrived on the scene: on the last day of December 1941, Admiral Chester W. Nimitz had replaced the disgraced Kimmel as commander in chief of the Pacific Fleet. The calm, decisive, but gentle man was just what America needed to rebuild the strength and, especially, the morale of a shattered fleet. But within days—as we have seen—Nimitz's fleet suffered another blow when *Saratoga* was torpedoed. Although (contrary to Japanese hopes that it had been sunk) it was able to limp back to Pearl Harbor, it was severely damaged and would be out of commission for almost five months. This temporarily reduced Nimitz's carrier strength to two carriers—*Enterprise* and *Lexington*—but reinforcements soon arrived in the form of a new carrier task force assembled around *Yorktown*, which had been transferred from the Atlantic Fleet.

This still gave Nimitz only three fleet attack carriers to Yamamoto's six (and the recently completed *Shoho* also increased the number of light carriers at Yamamoto's disposal to three, not counting the obsolete *Hosho*). The newly commissioned *Hornet* was still in the Atlantic undergoing a shakedown cruise and assembling its air group; it would not be operational for another couple of months. *Wasp*, in the Atlantic, was operational but did not have a full offensive air group; it would not be transferred to the Pacific until early June. Along with the *Yorktown*, Nimitz also got three battleships (of the *New Mexico* class) from the Atlantic Fleet, but as these were as slow and obsolete as those lost at Pearl Harbor, they were not of much use for offensive operations against the Japanese navy. (The two new *Washington*-class battleships would not be operational until the summer.) What Nimitz did have, however, to provide shellfire in support of his carrier force was a full complement of heavy cruisers. They, like the carriers, had been at sea on December 7.

Nimitz's first strike against the Japanese came on February 1. Planes from William Halsey's *Enterprise* and Frank Jack Fletcher's *Yorktown* attacked airfields and harbors at Kwajalein, Wotje, and Jaluit in the Marshall Islands and Makin in the Gilberts. The two carrier task forces operated separately, with *Enterprise* striking the north Marshalls and *Yorktown* hitting the south Marshalls and the Gilberts. (American doctrine at this time called for carriers to operate separately rather than in the massed striking forces the Japanese employed.) In addition, Wilson Brown's *Lexington* task force was sent to the southwest Pacific to assist the ANZAC forces operating out of Australia. On February 20, near the Solomon Islands, *Lexington*'s air group engaged Japanese planes in the first substantial air combat of the war—producing the American navy's first ace.

It was "Butch" O'Hare, who shot down five Japanese land-based naval bombers (for which he later received the Congressional Medal of Honor and had the international airport in Chicago named after him). American Wildcat fighters shot down at least thirteen bombers, for a loss of but two fighters (fortunately for the Americans there were no Zeros accompanying the bombers). These results were a tremendous morale-booster for the *Lexington* air group in particular and the Pacific Fleet in general—sorely needed after the recent disasters.

Hit-and-run attacks by these three carriers against targets from Wake Island to the Solomons continued throughout February and March. Not a lot of damage was inflicted—and the Japanese push into the Dutch East Indies proceeded unabated—but American losses were light, and the carrier air crews gained much needed combat experience. Also, the navy learned from these early encounters that the carriers needed a larger fighter squadron than the eighteen Wildcats that were being carried and that the planes needed more protection in the form of self-sealing gas tanks and pilot seat armor. This soon led to the introduction of the folding-wing model of the Wildcat, which had better pilot protection.[6]

THE DOOLITTLE RAID ON TOKYO—
CATALYST FOR MIDWAY OPERATION

On April 18, as the Mobile Force was returning to home waters from the Indian Ocean campaign, a shocking announcement came over *Akagi's* radio: Tokyo had been bombed. The Doolittle Raid, as it was popularly called, was the brain-child of Admiral Ernest J. King, who since mid-March had been the chief of naval operations as well as commander in chief of the United States Fleet. The plan was for sixteen army B-25 Mitchell light bombers to take off from the newly completed *Hornet*, led by the charismatic Colonel "Jimmy" Doolittle—who was already famous as a daredevil racing pilot. *Hornet*, with two cruisers (the heavy cruiser *Vincennes* and the light cruiser *Nashville*) would join Halsey's task force, which included *Enterprise* and two more heavy cruisers—*Northampton* and *Salt Lake City*. The plan was for the Mitchells to drop 500-pound bombs (four from each bomber) on Tokyo, Yokohama, Osaka, Kobe, Nagoya, and the Yokosuka naval yard, and then fly on to China, where it was hoped that they could land safely on one of Chiang Kai-shek's airfields. It was not expected that much damage would be done by only sixty-four medium bombs, but it was hoped that such a daring raid on the Japanese homeland would give a badly needed boost to American morale (and maybe make a dent in Japanese morale).

Bombers that heavy had never flown off a carrier deck before, but because of the Mitchell's powerful engines it had been found that with a strong enough headwind it was possible.[7] The plan called for an approach to within 500 miles of Tokyo and a launch in the late afternoon so that the bombers would be over Japan after nightfall and arrive in China at daybreak. However, on the morning of the 18th, a Japanese picket boat with powerful radio gear was spotted. Halsey, certain of detection and fearing an attack by Japanese bombers if he continued his course toward Japan, decided to launch immediately. He made this decision even though it would mean a daytime raid over Japan and a nighttime landing in China—both adding substantially to the hazards for the bomber crews. Moreover, it would add a critical 170 miles to the total distance, putting the bombers at risk of running out of fuel. At 0820, Doolittle launched. The lead plane had only a little over four hundred feet of flight deck, but a strong headwind combined with *Hornet's* 33-knot speed gave the bomber a wind over deck of 50 miles per hour, which was enough—but barely.

The bombers flew toward their destinations just above the waves and man-aged to evade radar. Although they met resistance over their targets from army interceptors and antiaircraft gunfire from the ground, none was shot down. An aircraft factory in Nagoya was bombed, along with several power plants in the Tokyo and Osaka areas. But the most lucrative target was the Yokosuka naval yard, south of Yokohama. It was Japan's largest, and there they claimed the first

hit of the war on a Japanese aircraft carrier: the *Ryuho*, a new light carrier undergoing conversion from a submarine support ship. It took several hits, and the
damage delayed its completion until November.

When Doolittle's bombers got to China after dark, they had no chance of
finding their airfield. One plane landed at Vladivostok, and the crew was interned by the Russians. The remainder ran out of fuel, and either they crash-
landed or their crews bailed out, all in Japanese-held territory. Four crewmen
were killed and eight were captured by the Japanese; three of them were executed as "war criminals"—(an army hospital and some schools had been accidentally hit along with the military targets; 250 civilians had been killed or injured). But most of the crewmen were found by Chinese guerillas, who helped
them reach friendly territory. Miraculously, seventy-one out of the eighty—
including Doolittle—survived the war. The Chinese were not as lucky. The
Japanese army, in revenge for the help given the downed airmen, rampaged
through the east China countryside, burning towns and villages to the ground
and killing an estimated 250,000 Chinese.

The raid did, however, prove to be a tremendous boost to the morale of the
American people and servicemen, who had endured over four months of hu-
miliation at the hands of the Japanese. It also showed to the Japanese people
that their cities were not immune to American bombs and that their early suc-
cesses at the expense of the Americans would have a price to pay. For a short
while it was a mystery where the bombers came from. (Roosevelt, when asked
by the press, coyly replied that they had flown from "Shangri-La.") Yamamoto
and the Japanese high command soon deduced, however, that the bombers
had come from American carriers—a price paid for not destroying them at the
outset of the war.

The Doolittle raid had a profound affect on Japanese naval strategy: up until
then, although Yamamoto had been toying with a plan to lure the American
carrier fleet into a decisive battle at Midway, the naval high command had
been lukewarm about the idea. After the raid all opposition ceased; only the
details remained to be worked out. But first, there was a more pressing operation to be undertaken far to the south in the Coral Sea.

THE BATTLE OF THE CORAL SEA

While the Japanese had largely destroyed British naval and air power in the
southwest Pacific, General MacArthur had been building up American air
power in Australia since he arrived there from the Philippines in mid-March.
By the end of April, there were 144 bombers of various types and 50 fighters—
mostly P-39s—at bases in north Queensland, and another 50 fighters at Port
Moresby on the south coast of Papua New Guinea. They were being transported there through the chain of Islands that formed the eastern barrier to the

Coral Sea. The Japanese high command decided that something had to be done to block this lifeline to MacArthur's forces. A plan to invade north Australia had been worked out by Yamamoto's staff, but had been vetoed by the army; ten divisions of troops would be required, and the army refused them. (It was optimistic that Hitler's summer offensive in Russia would defeat the Soviet Army and wanted troops on hand to occupy eastern Siberia.)

Yamamoto, therefore, had to devise a plan to eliminate Australia as an American base that would require only minimal participation by the army. (The Japanese navy did not have a sizable marine-type ground force of its own as did the American navy.) He decided to isolate Australia by cutting the American supply lines through the Coral Sea. This would require Japanese naval airbases closer to Australia than those already being built at Rabaul in New Britain and Lae on the north coast of New Guinea. Port Moresby on the southeast coast of New Guinea would be ideal. From it, all of northeast Australia would be in range of naval bombers and Zeros. Also, Tulagi in the Solomon Islands to the west would be taken at the same time and a seaplane base established. After that, Fiji, Samoa, New Hebrides and New Caledonia would be taken—which would effectively cut American supply lines to northeast Australia.

The isolation of Australia was seen as a prerequisite to the broader plan for eliminating American naval and air power in the Pacific: the capture of Midway and the western Aleutians, and the subsequent invasion—or at least neutralization—of Hawaii. (It was expected that the capture of Midway—in addition to eliminating an important American naval forward base—would draw the American carrier fleet into a decisive battle where it could be destroyed, and thus would complete the mission unfulfilled by the Pearl Harbor operation. More about this later.) With this accomplished, Japan would be free of flank attacks on its supply lines from the oil-rich South Seas.

But the first order of business was the capture of Port Moresby—in a campaign code-named "MO." Air attacks from Rabaul would be followed by landings from eleven troop transports. These troop landings would be supported by the light carrier *Shoho* and four heavy cruisers. Prior to landings on Port Moresby, Tulagi in the Solomons would be seized by another invasion group. It was known that *Lexington* (thought to be *Saratoga*) was operating in the area. To dispose of it, the Fifth Carrier Division—the *Shokaku* and *Zuikaku*—supported by two heavy cruisers would be sent as a "striking force," commanded by Vice Admiral Takagi. (The remainder of the Mobile Force needed some upkeep after the Indian Ocean campaign to get ready for the Midway operation.)

Unbeknownst to Yamamoto, Nimitz's code breakers had uncovered the MO operation and its date for the landing at Port Moresby—May 8. Nimitz wanted to send three more carriers—*Yorktown*, *Enterprise*, and *Hornet*—to join *Lexington* in ambushing the invasion force and taking on *Shokaku* and *Zuikaku*. However, *Enterprise* and *Hornet* were returning from the Doolittle raid and could not be made ready in time, so Nimitz was able to send immediately only *York-town* to join *Lexington*. *Enterprise* and *Hornet* would be sent later if still needed.

As the upcoming carrier battle was the first in history, and the warm-up for Midway, it will be described in some detail—especially the Japanese search operations, so they can be compared with those later used at Midway. (One of the dogmas of the standard scenario of Midway is that the Japanese were loath to use carrier-based attack planes for search patrols—which is regarded as a flawed doctrine that was, in large part, responsible for their defeat at Midway.)[8]

When the two opposing carrier forces entered the Coral Sea, they were almost equal in numbers of operational aircraft. *Lexington* and *Yorktown* carried a total of 138 planes (69 each), of which 132 were operational: *Lexington* had available 19 Wildcat fighters, 35 Dauntless dive-bombers, and 12 Devastator torpedo bombers. *Yorktown* had exactly the same complement.[9] *Shokaku, Zuikaku,* and *Shoho* carried a total of 149 planes, of which 127 were operational (*Shokaku* and *Zuikaku* were ferrying nine land-based Zeros to Rabaul, which are not included in the operational tally): *Shokaku* had available 18 Zeros, 19 Val dive-bombers, and 19 Kate torpedo planes. *Zuikaku* had 19 Zeros, 17 dive-bombers, and 17 torpedo planes. *Shoho* had 12 fighters (eight Zeros and four older Claudes) and six torpedo planes.[10]

Yorktown, under Frank Jack Fletcher, and *Lexington,* under Rear Admiral Aubrey Fitch, joined up on May 1, with Fletcher in overall command—but soon became separated because of different refueling schedules. On May 3, Fletcher received a message from MacArthur that the Japanese were commencing landings on Tulagi in the Solomon Islands. This was 500 miles away, so he immediately headed toward it without *Lexington*, which was tied up with refueling operations. At sunrise the next morning, *Yorktown* launched an attack on Tulagi harbor. It did little damage and cost Fletcher a torpedo bomber and two Wildcat fighters; it did not prevent the Japanese from establishing a seaplane base there.

After these preliminaries, each side began in earnest to hunt for the other's carriers. The opposing forces came within 70 miles of each other, but cloud cover made search difficult. On the 6th, four B-17s from Queensland en route to Port Moresby spotted *Shoho* and attempted to bomb her, but without success. (On this same day, General Wainwright surrendered at Corregidor.) On the 7th the search planes of both carrier task forces finally found targets, but not each other. Rear Admiral Hara, commander of the Fifth Carrier Division, had sent out twelve Kates—one of which found the oil tanker *Neosho* and its escort, destroyer *Sims*, at 0722. However, the sighting report did not specify carriers—just "American ships." At 0745, the search plane amplified its report, but erroneously identified the ships as a carrier and a cruiser. Elated, Hara launched a full deckload of planes, beginning at 0800, from each of his carriers, seventy-eight planes in all: nine Zeros, thirteen Kate torpedo planes, and nineteen Val dive-bombers from *Shokaku*; nine Zeros, eleven torpedo planes, and seventeen dive-bombers from *Zuikaku*.

When the strike force reached the reported target area at 0915, no carrier was to be found. The strike leader, Lieutenant Commander Takahashi, searched for another two hours, but when he finally concluded that there was no carrier in the area he ordered his twenty-four Kates and nine of the Zero escorts to return without attacking. As at least a tanker and destroyer had been found, he ordered, at 1115, the thirty-six dive-bombers to attack. Four of them went after the destroyer *Sims* and thirty-two attacked *Neosho*. Three hits—with 250-kilogram bombs—were scored on *Sims*; it exploded and went down almost immediately, taking most of the crew with it. One Val appears to have been hit by *Sims*'s guns and made a flaming suicide crash on *Neosho*. Seven bomb hits were made on *Neosho*. The tanker did not sink but was a total loss; it was scuttled four days later.

Shokaku's nineteen Val dive-bombers sustained no losses and all returned safely. However, *Zuikaku*'s seventeen Vals were not so fortunate. After losing one in the attack, the remainder got lost attempting to return to their carrier because of bad weather. When they finally found *Zuikaku* two Vals crash-landed on the carrier deck, destroying the planes, but the flight crews were uninjured. Also, two of the Kates from *Shokaku* that had been on reconnaissance ran out of fuel and had to make crash landings in the sea. The crews were rescued, but the planes were lost. Thus, Hara lost at least five planes in the *Neosho* and *Sims* venture. Hara admitted that he had made a costly blunder; it was clear that ship identification skills of the search plane crews needed improvement.

Fletcher had better luck that day. At 0815, one of his search planes reported having spotted "two carriers and four heavy cruisers." As their position was 210 miles away—beyond the combat radius of the short-legged Wildcats and Devastator torpedo bombers—there was some discussion whether to launch a strike with just the longer-ranged dive-bombers immediately or to steam closer. It was decided to steam closer so that a full-strength attack could be sent. At around 0930 *Lexington* launched—in a single deckload—ten fighters, twenty-eight dive-bombers, and twelve torpedo bombers. Fifteen minutes later, *Yorktown* launched eight fighters, twenty-five dive-bombers, and ten torpedo bombers—ninety-three planes in all.

After the launch, the scout plane that had discovered the Japanese ships returned, and when the pilot was informed that a strike had been launched against carriers, he was dumbfounded. He thought he had reported finding two cruisers and two destroyers. A quick check of his cipher pad revealed a coding error not of his fault. Fortunately, Fletcher had just received a sighting report from one of MacArthur's search planes locating a carrier, ten transports, and several other ships only 30 miles from the original target. At 1053 he redirected the strike force to the new location. This turned out to be the Port Moresby invasion force with its covering force consisting of the light carrier *Shoho* and four heavy cruisers.

When the *Lexington* air group arrived over the carrier *Shoho* there was a combat air patrol of only three fighters—one Zero and two Claudes. The first dive-bombing attack was made at 1110 by thirteen Dauntlesses, "Scouting Two." *Shoho* maneuvered radically and none of the thirteen 500-pound bombs hit, but near misses may have blown five planes off her flight deck. One Dauntless was shot down by a Zero. *Shoho* then managed to launch three more Zeros for air defense. However, *Shoho*'s number came up when "Bombing Two," with fifteen Dauntlesses carrying 1,000-pound bombs, began its dive at 1118. Two bombs hit, and *Shoho* erupted in flames. These were probably enough to destroy such a small carrier, especially in the vulnerable position she had, with fueled and armed planes in the hangar deck.

Lexington's twelve torpedo bombers then made their run-ups. By that time, although *Shoho* was still steaming under full power, her command center was in shambles and her commander was powerless to make effective evasive maneuvers. At least two torpedoes hit, but it appears that only one actually exploded. But even one effective torpedo hit was enough to finish her off: her engine rooms were destroyed, and she immediately lost all power.

When *Yorktown*'s air group arrived at 1125, *Shoho* was a burning wreck and dead in the water. She was hit again, anyway, and as a sitting duck provided the target for some of the most impressive bombing and torpedoing statistics for American carrier pilots of the first year of the war: the twenty-five dive-bombers scored eleven hits, and the ten torpedo bombers at least two (that exploded). All told, fifty-three Dauntlesses had put thirteen bombs into the little carrier, and twenty-two Devastators may have hit her with as many as seven torpedoes, with at least three exploding. No other ship in *Shoho*'s covering group was hit, but the carrier provided plenty of much-needed practice for the air groups of *Lexington* and *Yorktown*.

Ironically, however, this fortuitous torpedo performance turned out to be unfortunate for the American navy. It postponed realization that the Mark 13 aerial torpedo was virtually useless against a speedily maneuvering ship: it was slow and did not run straight and, even when it hit, often did not detonate because of a defective firing pin. Its deficiencies were not fully realized until after the battle of Midway a month later, when fifty-one torpedo bombers failed to score a single exploding hit against carriers. This dismal record was repeated the remainder of 1942, forcing the navy to make improvements that should have been made before the war. The U.S. Congress's failure to provide sufficient funds for adequate testing of the Mark 13 resulted in many brave men dying while attempting to deliver a torpedo that—except on the already crippled *Shoho*—essentially did not work.

Less than four minutes after the last torpedo hit, *Shoho* went under. Of her crew of around 800, only 204 survived. All the aircraft in her small air group of eighteen planes were lost (ten while still on board) and roughly ten carrier pilots were lost to the Japanese Navy. The Americans lost only three dive-bombers shot down—two from *Lexington* and one from *Yorktown*. On the way back, *Lexington*'s Scouting Two commander, Bob Dixon, radioed his famous announcement: "Scratch one flat top!" With air cover for the invasion force now gone, the Japanese landings at Port Moresby scheduled for the next day were postponed, and the troop transports were ordered to retreat toward Rabaul to get out of the range of American carrier planes.

The grief for the day was not yet over for the Japanese. After the planes that had attacked *Neosho* and *Sims* returned to *Shokaku* and *Zuikaku*, Hara received a message from a bomber flying out of Rabaul, reporting the sighting of American carriers. In fact, what had been sighted was Rear Admiral Crace's support group from "MacArthur's Navy," containing one light and two heavy cruisers, and the bomber's crew had erroneously reported its location as being about 40 miles southwest of where it actually was. At 1600 Hara sent out a small attack force—specially selected for night-flying ability—to find the "carriers" at dusk. Only fifteen torpedo planes and twelve dive-bombers were launched. No Zeros were included because, as they lacked homing receivers, it was feared that they would not be able to find their way back after dark.[11]

The strike force, hampered by an inaccurate sighting report and poor weather, found nothing on their outbound course, and jettisoned its ordnance. On returning, however, they ran smack into *Lexington*'s combat air patrol at 1800. Eight torpedo planes—five from *Zuikaku* and three from *Shokaku*—were shot down, along with one dive-bomber from *Zuikaku*. Another torpedo plane from *Zuikaku* was badly damaged, though it made it back to its carrier. The Americans lost three Wildcats, and another was rendered inoperable. After sunset, the surviving eighteen planes then flew right past *Yorktown*, and some of them, assuming it was their carrier, attempted to land. They were quickly and rudely made aware of their mistake but managed to escape without further damage. All eighteen apparently landed safely on their carriers between 2000 and 2200 (though most accounts have many of them ditching in the water, with fatal consequences for their crews).[12]

The Americans had clearly won the round on the day of May 7. A Japanese light carrier had been sunk in exchange for a destroyer and an oiler. Eighteen of *Shoho*'s planes had been destroyed (along with about ten even harder to replace pilots). The two large Japanese carriers had lost eleven Kate torpedo planes, with eight pilots killed, and four Val dive-bombers, with two pilots killed. Altogether, thirty-three Japanese planes and about twenty pilots were lost, in exchange for just three Dauntless dive-bombers and four Wildcat fighters for the Americans. Even counting prior carrier plane losses at Tulagi of two Wildcats and a torpedo bomber for the Americans against a Zero for the Japanese, the overall margin was heavily in favor of the Americans.

By the end of the day, Hara knew that two American carriers were close by, and looked forward to recouping his losses, and even more, in a decisive carrier battle the next morning. However, he was down to 95 operational planes: 37 Zeros, 33 Vals, and just 25 Kates. Fletcher was in better shape. He had 118 operational planes: 32 Wildcats, 65 Dauntlesses, and 21 Devastators.[13]

THE CARRIER BATTLE OF MAY 8

At first light the next morning both sides sent out search patrols to find each other's carriers. At 0615 Hara launched seven Kate attack planes (four from *Shokaku*, three from *Zuikaku*) to search the southerly sectors of the Coral Sea where the American task force was thought most likely to be. Complementing this to cover the northern Coral Sea were seven more planes that took off from Rabaul and Tulagi. At 0625, *Lexington* launched eighteen Dauntless dive-bombers to search in all directions from Task Force 17. About two hours later each side's search planes found the other's carriers at almost the same time — 0820 for an American Dauntless and 0822 for a Japanese Kate. The first carrier battle of the war, and the first naval battle in history between ships out of sight of each other, was about to begin.

At 0900, *Yorktown* launched its attack group of thirty-nine planes: six Wildcats, twenty-four dive-bombers, and nine torpedo bombers. Seven minutes later *Lexington* launched thirty-six planes: nine Wildcats, fifteen dive-bombers, and twelve torpedo bombers — seventy-five planes in all. At 0910, *Shokaku* and *Zuikaku* together launched a strike force of sixty-nine planes: nine Zeros, nineteen dive-bombers, and ten torpedo planes from *Shokaku*, and nine Zeros, fourteen dive-bombers, and eight torpedo planes from *Zuikaku*.[14] (It might prove interesting to see what happened when *both* sides got their strike forces launched at the outset — unlike at Midway. But it should be noted that at Coral Sea the Japanese sent out their "B-Team" against an American "A-Team.")

The Americans found their target first, with the arrival of *Yorktown*'s attack group at around 1050. It was greeted with a combat air patrol of ten Zeros. Seven Dauntlesses from "Scouting Five" made the first dive on *Shokaku* at 1057, but scored no hits. (*Zuikaku* had separately found refuge under dense cloud cover and would not be seen by the Americans during the attack.) After this attack, six more Zeros were launched for combat air patrol. Seventeen Dauntlesses from "Bombing Five" then came in at 1103 and scored two hits with 1000-pound bombs on *Shokaku*. Together they wrecked the forward part of the flight deck and set off intense fires in the hangar. *Shokaku* would not be able to launch any more planes, though she could still conduct landing operations. Two Dauntlesses were shot down by Zeros in this attack. Also, the dives through the warm, humid Coral Sea air had revealed one serious defect in this otherwise excellent and much-loved plane: the moist air fogged the bomb sight when near the bottom of the dive, making aiming very difficult. (The only way found subsequently to prevent this problem was to make the dive with the canopy open—not very comfortable at 250 mph.)

Yorktown's "Torpedo Five" with nine Devastators made its run-up against *Shokaku* at 1108, but none of the nine torpedoes—some of which ran erratically —hit. Its fighter escort did a fine job, however, protecting the slow old torpedo bombers; all nine returned to the *Yorktown*, and a Wildcat claimed a Zero shot down in the attack.

Lexington's attack group had a rougher time of it. Almost immediately after launch one torpedo bomber had to return because of engine trouble. Three Wildcats then lost contact with the rest of the group because of clouds and returned to the carrier. Then, the eleven Dauntlesses of "Bombing Two" got lost because of poor visibility on the way to the target and did not participate in the attack. This left Commander Bill Ault, the air group commander, with only four dive-bombers and eleven torpedo bombers, with an escort of six fighters, to proceed to the target. Upon arriving shortly after 1130 he encountered a combat air patrol of thirteen Zeros (two Zeros had been shot down in *Yorktown*'s attack and another forced to land with heavy damage). Three of the six Wildcats were shot down during the fray, with no more Zeros shot down (though two were apparently forced to ditch).

The four Dauntlesses made their attack on *Shokaku* at 1140, dropping three 1,000-pounders (one bomb would not release), and scored one hit abaft the island. This put the carrier out of action as no further flight operations were possible. The total of three hits from 1,000-pound bombs might have completely destroyed a smaller carrier such as *Soryu*, but *Shokaku* proved able to absorb a lot of punishment and, though out of action for two months (missing the Battle of Midway), survived to fight again.

Eleven torpedo bombers from "Torpedo Two" then attacked two minutes later; none of the eleven torpedoes hit. (The Japanese commented that they ran so slowly that they were easily evaded.) It might seem curious that none of the twenty torpedoes scored, while the prior day the same Devastators had made several hits on *Shoho*. But it would turn out that the torpedo attack on *Shoho* was the anomaly—the attack on *Shokaku* was just the beginning of a pattern that persisted throughout the year, where no aerial torpedo hits were made on a ship able to maneuver evasively. No Devastators were shot down, though one had been hit and fatally ditched attempting to return.

Meanwhile, Hara's strike force had been proceeding toward the American carrier force. Although it had been launched just minutes after the American launch, and its planes were faster, it had a more difficult time finding its target (and, in fact, had to be led there by the search plane that discovered it) so it arrived in the vicinity of the American carriers several minutes after the American attack on *Shokaku* had begun. When it arrived shortly after 1100 it was confronted with a combat air patrol of seventeen Wildcats (nine from *Lexington* and eight from *Yorktown*) and twenty-three Dauntless dive-bombers. Because of the shortage of fighters, the Dauntless SBDs had been deployed as a low-level anti-torpedo plane patrol. Although unladen Dauntlesses were effective interceptors against torpedo-laden Kates—and shot down three of them as they were approaching the task force—they were no match for Zeros, all eighteen of which had been assigned to protect the Kates. Eight Dauntlesses (from *Yorktown*) were pounced upon by six Zeros, and four were shot down against no losses for the Zeros.

The first to attack were the torpedo planes. Of the fifteen that made it through the defensive screen (three had been lost to SBDs), eleven targeted *Lexington* and four *Yorktown*. Kates usually launched their torpedoes at high speed—over 200 miles per hour—and within five hundred yards of the target. From this short distance, the 42-knot speed of the Type 91 torpedo made it very difficult to evade. (During 1942, one in five, on average, hit and exploded, even against ships maneuvering at battle speed.) The first torpedoes were dropped by the four Kates attacking *Yorktown*. None of the four hit, and two of the Kates were "splashed" by antiaircraft gunfire. The eleven Kates attacking *Lexington* split into two groups for an "anvil" attack on both sides simultaneously. At 1120, at least two torpedoes struck "Lady Lex" on her port side. (Some accounts say three hit, with the third striking the tip of the bow and doing little damage.)[15] The two main hits did substantial damage, rupturing aviation gasoline tanks and water mains and flooding three of the fire rooms; the elevators were also knocked out when the hydraulic system was damaged.

A couple of minutes later the thirty-three Val dive-bombers began their dives. *Shokaku*'s nineteen went after *Lexington*, and *Zuikaku*'s fourteen dove on *Yorktown*. The escorting Zeros had largely drawn off the Wildcats, so the main peril to the bombers was antiaircraft guns—*Lexington* had forty-eight—which shot down one Val. Only two bombs directly hit *Lexington*—one a 242-kilogram high-explosive instant-detonation bomb, which knocked out a 5-inch gun battery (which was the purpose of equipping some dive-bombers with "land" bombs for attacks on ships) and the other a 250-kilogram armor-piercing delay-fuse bomb, which, fortunately for "Lady Lex," hit the huge smoke stack, doing little damage to the ship. The damage sustained from the torpedoes and bombs did not appear fatal; the fires were quickly put out, and the carrier could soon make 24 knots. As for *Yorktown*, at 1127 a 250-kilogram armor-piercing delay-fuse bomb hit the center of her flight deck and penetrated four more decks before exploding in the aviation storeroom, rupturing bulkheads and setting off fires.[16] Several near-misses did almost as much damage as the direct hit, cracking the hull plates in several places. Only one Val was shot down by a Wildcat.

The dive-bombing performance by the Fifth Carrier Division planes was sub-par by usual Japanese standards—just three hits out of thirty-three bombs dropped. Only a month earlier in the Indian Ocean dive-bombers led by *Soryu*'s

Commander Egusa had achieved over 40 percent hits. (And in later battles at Midway and the Solomons the hit ratio would average around 25 percent.) The mediocre performance at the Coral Sea is probably attributable to the "green-ness" of most of the Fifth Carrier Division's pilots, as earlier noted. The experi-ence gained in this battle, however, would later prove to have brought them up to a level at least close to that of the rest of the Mobile Force's dive-bomber pilots.

After the torpedo and bombing attacks were finished, Hara's strike force had to fight its way out of the area to get back to its carriers. The Wildcat combat air patrol had been reinforced by three fighters that originally were sent to escort the attack on Hara's carriers, but that had to return before reaching the target. This was most welcome because all eighteen Zeros were still in the air, and sev-eral Wildcats had been forced to leave the fray because of battle damage (though none had yet been shot down). During the withdrawal three more Kates were shot down—two by Dauntlesses and one by a Wildcat—and one more Val was shot down by a Wildcat. Three more Vals crashed at sea from battle damage—with their crews lost. The most costly loss to the strike force, however, was that of its leader, Lieutenant Commander Takahashi. His Val was shot down halfway back to its carrier by a Wildcat returning from the American strike on Hara's carriers. Throughout all this, none of the escorting Zeros was shot down. (However, one was badly enough damaged that it did not get back to its carrier—it ditched near a Japanese-held island, but its pilot was rescued.) The Americans lost three Wildcats and another Dauntless, shot down by the Zeros, during the attacks on the retiring strike force.

THE ACCOUNTING

By time Hara's strike force got back to its carriers, seven Kates had been shot down and eight Vals had been shot down or were missing. Seven more planes (including the Zero mentioned) were so badly shot up that they ditched—five Vals and a Kate near the carriers, where their crews were rescued. Another Val crash-landed on *Shokaku*'s ravaged flight deck, but its crew survived. Of those that landed on *Zuikaku*—*Shokaku* could not land any of her planes—twelve were so badly damaged that they were jettisoned off the side to make room for the additional planes from *Shokaku*'s air group. (Three Zeros, four Vals, and five Kates were pushed overboard.) In addition to these losses to the strike force, there were losses to the Zeros on combat air patrol and the Kates sent out for search patrol. Two Zeros had been shot down while defending against the American attack—and at least two more had been forced to ditch. The Kate that had found the American carrier force was shot down on its return to its carrier by a Wildcat that was returning from the American attack on *Shokaku*. (This Kate had delayed its return to guide the strike force to the American carriers.)

Thus, in all, about forty Japanese carrier planes had been lost during the day; of the fifty-two that were recovered and retained on board *Zuikaku* (the fate of those on *Shokaku* is unknown), thirteen were damaged and at least temporarily out of action—leaving only thirty-nine operational at the end of the day (and only six were the deadly Kates).[17] But much more costly than the plane losses were the eighteen pilots lost. They were virtually irreplaceable (and this is my main reason for making this account of casualties as detailed as it is): Yamamoto was fighting a war of attrition; he had to destroy the American carrier force in the first year of the war and do it before he ran out of carrier pilots. He had lost over twenty in the Coral Sea prior to May 8, bringing the total pilot losses for the operation to around forty. As he had already lost about sixty carrier pilots in previous operations, he was now down one hundred from the little over four hundred first-line carrier pilots he had at the beginning of the war. He no longer had enough of them to fully man the regular air group complements of his six attack carriers—or even the five he had left with *Shokaku* out of action. He was running out of pilots faster than he was reducing American carrier strength.

Back at the American task force, *Yorktown's* attack group returned at 1240. *Yorktown's* flight deck had been patched up from the bomb hit and her speed was back to normal, so she was ready for landing operations. Of the thirty-nine planes that had been launched, one Wildcat and two Dauntlesses had been shot down in the attack on *Shokaku*. Of those that returned, one Dauntless could not land because of damage to the undercarriage and had to ditch, but the rest of the attack group—thirty-five planes—landed safely by 1300: five Wildcats, twenty-one Dauntlesses, and all nine of the Devastators. Four Dauntlesses that had been on combat air patrol had also landed, and a little later five Wildcats from the CAP were recovered. Of those forty-four planes recovered on *Yorktown* (all that was left of the fifty-five that had seen duty that day) only thirty were found to be still operable: seven fighters, fifteen dive-bombers, and eight torpedo bombers.

Lexington's attack group got back later and found a less seaworthy carrier, but landing operations were still possible; landings began at 1322. *Lexington's* condition had deteriorated shortly before its attack group returned. A series of explosions from gasoline fumes from tanks ruptured by the torpedoes had wracked her in several compartments—including a motor generator room—and fires were becoming increasingly difficult to control because of the loss of water pressure in the fire hoses. The thirty-six planes originally in *Lexington's* attack group had been more severely diminished than *Yorktown's*. Twenty-eight planes were recovered: five Wildcats, twelve Dauntlesses, and eleven Devastators. In addition to the three fighters lost during the attack, another got lost in the clouds, and its pilot radioed that he was ditching. He was never heard from again. A torpedo bomber also failed to make it back and was not heard of again. A group of three dive-bombers, including that of the air group leader, Bill Ault, who had been wounded, had a similar fate. One of them went down near a friendly island, and its crew was rescued, but the other two, including Ault's, were never found.

After the attack group had been landed, two major explosions—the first from gasoline vapor ignited by a generator motor left running—set off fires on *Lexington* that raged out of control and soon engulfed the carrier. By 1500 it was clear that she was doomed. All hands were ordered to abandon ship at 1707, and by 1800 they were all just barely off the carrier when a series of enormous explosions set off an inferno that turned her into a pyre. At 1957 the old "Lady" was sent to the bottom by five torpedoes from the destroyer *Phelps*. Over two hundred of her crew killed by the earlier explosions and fires—along with at least thirty-four planes on board—went down with her. Two thousand seven hundred seventy men had been rescued, and most of her air crew would fight another day—many of them at Midway less than a month later. Even nineteen of her planes were saved; they had been on combat air patrol and found refuge on *Yorktown*.

At least fifty-seven American carrier planes were lost on May 8 (including at least thirty-four that went down with *Lexington*).[18] But only eighteen pilots had been lost—the same number as for the Japanese. The total carrier aircraft losses in the Coral Sea since air operations began on May 4 were as follows: for the Americans, approximately sixty-five planes and twenty-five pilots; for the Japanese, about seventy-five planes and forty pilots. Because of the small number of operational planes left at the end of May 8—forty-nine for the Americans and thirty-nine for the Japanese—both task force commanders decided to terminate the battle and head for home.

Had *Lexington* been saved, even though badly damaged, it would have been a clear victory for the Americans. But she was not, which turned the battle into a tactical victory for the Japanese; one light carrier lost and an attack carrier badly damaged in return for a large American attack carrier lost and another lightly damaged.

As for which side won the strategic victory, things are not as clear-cut—and both sides claimed it with some justification. In favor of the Americans: Nimitz's objective had been to prevent the Japanese from taking Port Moresby, and that was achieved. The Japanese called off the MO operation (though they rescheduled it for the summer after the Midway operation). But, in favor of the Japanese claim is the fact that the MO operation was merely postponed, and had they won at Midway, Port Moresby and all the other islands in the Coral Sea area could have been quickly taken, and American naval and air power eliminated from the resource-rich South Seas area.

But none of this ever transpired. Considering that the main reason for Japan going to war against the United States was to achieve self-sufficiency in oil, and that for this the Imperial Japanese Navy needed to control the sea lanes from the southern islands to Japan, the failure to oust American air power from that vital area in May of 1942 was a serious setback—regardless of what the outcome at Midway might be. Moreover, the loss of carrier planes, and especially carrier pilots, was so severe as to prevent even the undamaged *Zuikaku* from participating in the Midway operation. And, added to this, the combat experience and boost to morale gained by the American carrier pilots (they thought they had won) no doubt gave them the skill and confidence to make a decisive contribution to the pivotal battle a month later at Midway. So, on balance, it must be concluded that the Americans won.

THE MIDWAY OPERATION

The Midway operation (code named "MI") had been hatched by Yamamoto in early April with the objective of engaging the American carrier fleet in a decisive battle. The failure of the Pearl Harbor operation to catch any carriers there had been a bitter disappointment to him because he realized, more than anybody else in the Japanese naval high command, that aircraft carriers had replaced battleships as the dominant capital ships in any war for control of the Pacific Ocean. And he also knew that for Japan to have any chance of winning the war the American carrier fleet had to be destroyed early on. It was now time to make good the unfinished business from the Pearl Harbor operation.

The Naval General Staff had at first been cool to Yamamoto's scheme; as of early April things had been going very well for Japan in the South Seas, and there were hopes that the American carrier force would eventually be taken care of in due course by attrition—without an enormous, costly (in fuel oil), and risky operation such as MI entailed. That complacence had been shattered by the Doolittle raid on April 18. The attack on the home Islands had been a huge embarrassment (and an intolerable affront to the emperor). The Battle of the Coral Sea—which caused a postponement of the Port Moresby operation—had made the need to destroy American carrier air power even more urgent as it had demonstrated that the Japanese navy could not solidify its conquest of the resource-rich South Seas area until all the American carriers had been eliminated.

The Midway operation provided Yamamoto his chance to engage the American carrier fleet in a decisive battle where it—or at least most of it—could be destroyed. A follow-up operation was also envisioned to mop up the remnants of the carrier fleet and capture, or at least neutralize, Hawaii and possibly even destroy the Panama Canal.[19] All this promised to knock the American navy out of the Pacific for at least a year, which would give Japan time to exploit the oil and other resources it acquired by capturing the South Seas islands in the first phase of the war.

Destruction of the American carrier fleet, then, was the strategic objective of the Midway operation. The tactical objective was the capture of the Midway Islands themselves. Not only would this deprive the Americans of an indispensable forward base in the mid-Pacific, but, more importantly, it would entice the American carrier fleet into the area in an attempt to retake such a vital asset. Those carriers could then be drawn into a decisive battle, at a time and place advantageous to the Japanese navy, thereby fulfilling the strategic objective.

A coordinate operation (AF) in the Aleutians got grafted onto the Midway operation at the insistence of the Naval General Staff, as a condition for its support.[20] The Naval General Staff—as well as the army—had long feared an American invasion of the northern Japanese islands launched from the Aleutian Islands. Thus, the western islands of Kiska, Attu, and Adak were to be captured, and Dutch Harbor in the east—the largest naval base in the Aleutians—was to be neutralized by bombing. Although this was not part of Yamamoto's original plan, and was initially opposed by him for spreading his fleet too thin, he decided to make use of it as a diversionary attack that had the potential for dividing the American fleet until Midway had been secured. (However, he certainly did not want any of the American *carriers* diverted—he wanted all of them to rush to Midway.)

The Japanese high command hoped that the attack on Midway would be a surprise to the Americans. The problem for Yamamoto, of course, was that Admiral Chester Nimitz, at Pearl Harbor, had deduced the broad outline of the operation and the approximate time of the attack. Neither Yamamoto nor anyone else in the Japanese navy suspected that the American navy had cracked its JN-25 code.[21] (Like the Germans with their Enigma cipher machine, JN-25 was assumed to be "unbreakable.") However, Yamamoto had accepted the possibility that before the actual attack on Midway the Americans would discover that an attack *somewhere* in the Pacific Ocean was impending. A fleet operation as vast as would be involved in MI and AF could not be completely shielded from submarine surveillance.

But Yamamoto thought it unlikely that the Americans would deduce the fact that Midway was the main target until it was too late for them to prevent its capture. He hoped that even if the Americans discovered that a Japanese naval operation was headed to somewhere in the eastern Pacific, they would regard Hawaii, Alaska, the west coast of the United States, or even the Panama Canal as targets as likely as Midway.[22]

The Battle of the Coral Sea, on May 7 and 8, required an alteration of the Midway operation plan. Originally, all six attack carriers of the Mobile Force were to participate. But the battle took its toll; *Shokaku* was badly damaged and knocked out of action for two months. *Zuikaku* was undamaged, but its air group was decimated and could not be reconstituted in time for the Midway operation. The most serious losses at Coral Sea were not the carriers or the seventy-five planes lost, but the more than forty pilots killed or permanently disabled. Some of the personnel of the air groups of *Shokaku* and *Zuikaku* were reassigned to the remaining four carriers of the Mobile Force and to the newly commissioned *Junyo* (which would be used in the Aleutian campaign).[23] This reduction in resources was not, however, regarded by the Japanese high command as jeopardizing the success of the operation. Japanese losses were believed to have been more than outweighed by the damage inflicted on the American carrier fleet. It was assumed that two fleet carriers—*Saratoga* and *Yorktown*— had been sunk. (Actually, as we have seen, only *Saratoga*'s misidentified sister ship *Lexington* was sunk; *Yorktown* was only damaged and would see action at Midway.)

DEPLOYMENT OF COMBINED FLEET

On May 12, Yamamoto issued his Operation Order to the Combined Fleet for the Midway and Aleutian campaigns. The operation was vast—five fleets containing almost every major ship in the Japanese navy would be involved. Yamamoto would be in overall command from his flagship *Yamato*. He would also directly command the First Fleet containing the seven largest battleships, which two days before the attack on Midway would be divided into the Main Body and the Guard Force.

The Main Body would, on the morning of June 4, be positioned 300 miles behind the carrier striking force, and would be there for the purpose of taking on any American battleships that might show up in the Midway area. It contained the three most powerful battleships in the Japanese navy—the mighty *Yamato* (with its nine 18.1-inch guns) and *Nagato* and *Mutsu* (with 16-inch guns)—which were supported by the light carrier *Hosho*, with eight old biplane torpedo bombers for antisubmarine patrol, two seaplane carriers equipped with miniature submarines, and a screen of nine destroyers led by a light cruiser. The Guard Force was to position itself between Midway and the Aleutians for the purpose of taking on any American battleships that might head for the Aleutians (as Dutch Harbor was to be attacked the day before Midway). It also was to intercept any American forces that might redeploy from the Aleutians to Midway after it was attacked. (The Guard Force contained four old battleships—*Fuso*, *Hyuga*, *Ise*, and *Yamashiro*, and a screen of twelve destroyers led by two light cruisers.)

The "teeth" of the Midway operation was the First Air Fleet, commanded by Admiral Nagumo. (This, as noted, was also called the Striking Force—*Kido Butai* in Japanese—or Mobile Force; I will refer to it as the Mobile Force.) It contained four of Yamamoto's six fleet attack carriers:[24] *Akagi*, *Kaga*, *Hiryu*, and *Soryu*, which carried approximately 225 operational planes (81 torpedo planes, 72 dive-bombers, and 72 fighters) in their air groups, plus 21 land-based fighters of the Sixth Air Group to be used in the defense of Midway after it was captured.[25] The Mobile Force also contained two fast battleships (*Haruna* and *Kirishima*), two heavy cruisers (*Tone* and *Chikuma*) that had been specially designed to carry extra float planes for search duty, and a screen of twelve destroyers led by a light cruiser.

The Midway Invasion Force was the Second Fleet, commanded by Admiral Kondo. It was the largest fleet and consisted of four groups:

1. a Main Body containing two fast battleships, *Kongo* and *Hiei*; four heavy cruisers; the light carrier *Zuiho* carrying twenty-four planes (twelve Kate attack planes and twelve fighters) to support amphibious invasion operations; and a screen of eight destroyers led by a light cruiser;
2. a close support group containing four heavy cruisers and two destroyers;
3. a transport group of twelve troop ships and three troop-carrying patrol boats, carrying 5,000 troops, with a screen of ten destroyers led by a light cruiser (A subgroup with a seaplane carrier and a seaplane tender—together carrying twenty-eight float planes—a troop-carrying patrol boat, and a destroyer accompanied the transport group. Its purpose was to occupy Kure Island, 60 miles west of Midway, and establish a seaplane base);
4. a minesweeper group containing four minesweepers and three submarine chasers.

Troop landings on Midway were scheduled for dawn, June 6.

The Northern (Aleutian) Force was the Fifth Fleet, commanded by Admiral Hosogaya. It consisted of five small groups:

1. a Main Body with a heavy cruiser and two destroyers;
2. the Second Carrier Striking Force, commanded by Admiral Kakuta, which contained *Junyo* and light carrier *Ryujo* (together carrying eighty-eight planes—forty-six fighters, twenty-one torpedo planes, and twenty-one dive-bombers),[26] two heavy cruisers, and three destroyers;
3. the Adak-Attu Invasion Force, consisting of a light cruiser, four destroyers, one seaplane tender with six flying boats, one minesweeper, and a transport carrying 1,200 army troops;
4. the Kiska Invasion Force, consisting of two light cruisers, one auxiliary cruiser, three destroyers, three minesweepers, and two transports carrying 1,250 navy troops;
5. a submarine detachment of six submarines.

The Advance (Submarine) Force was the Sixth Fleet, commanded by Admiral Komatsu, headquartered in the light cruiser *Katori*. The Sixth Fleet, based at Kwajalein in the Marshall Islands, consisted of fifteen submarines and two submarine tenders. In addition to hunting down and attacking American ships, the submarines were to monitor fleet movements west from Pearl Harbor. They also provided most of the intelligence about American activity at Midway. (All the fleets except the Advance Force were also accompanied by supply trains consisting of eighteen oil tankers and seven cargo ships.)

In summary, the major ships used in the MI operation and its Aleutian adjunct were all eleven battleships; eight of the ten aircraft carriers (not counting the two escort carriers, which, unlike their American counterparts, could not land planes and were used only to ferry planes for the shore-based air groups); all five seaplane carriers and tenders; thirteen of eighteen heavy cruisers (four were left behind to escort *Zuikaku* when she sailed later to provide relief in the Aleutian operation, and one was out of action from battle damage); ten of fifteen light cruisers; sixty-six destroyers and twenty-one submarines. The total number of carrier-borne aircraft involved was over 380 (including spares and the thirty-three Zeros of the Sixth Air Group destined to be based on Midway after its capture). In addition to the carrier-borne aircraft, there were about one hundred seaplanes for reconnaissance duty, thirty-four on seaplane carriers and about seventy carried on cruisers and battleships.

SORTIE OF THE FLEETS

The sortie of the fleets from home waters was spread over a four-day period from three staging areas. The first to leave was the Second Carrier Striking Force, which departed from Ominato Harbor at the northern tip of Honshu on May 26. It was part of the Northern Force and was headed for Dutch Harbor in the Aleutians. Next to go, on the 27th, was Nagumo's Mobile Force, which departed from Hashirajima anchorage in Hiroshima Bay in the Inland Sea near the southwestern tip of Honshu. On the 28th, the rest of the Northern Force sortied from Ominato. The same day the Midway Invasion Support Group departed from Guam, and the Transport Group departed from Saipan, both in the Mariana Islands. (Staging from these points cut about 800 nautical miles off the journey, allowing these slower ships to arrive at Midway at about the same time as the faster fleet elements.) The last to leave, on the 29th of May, were the Covering Group of the Midway Invasion Force (with cruisers and fast battleships) and, finally, the Main Body under Yamamoto. They departed from Hashirajima anchorage.[27]

As Yamamoto's Main Body and Guard Force of seven battleships and twenty-five other ships entered the Bungo Strait (connecting the Inland Sea with the Pacific Ocean) American submarines were spotted. They were chased away without incident, but Yamamoto realized that they at least saw that a large battleship fleet was headed for somewhere in the Pacific. The next day, *Yamato*'s radio crew intercepted an urgent message sent by an American submarine to Midway from a position directly ahead of the Transport Group, east of Saipan. Although the text of the coded message could not be deciphered, Yamamoto realized that the Americans might deduce that the purpose of the transport convoy was an invasion of Midway, as that was the general direction of the convoy.

Thus, almost from the beginning of the sortie from Japan Yamamoto became aware of ominous signs that his Midway operation was no longer a secret. But there was more to come.

On May 31, *Yamato's* radio intelligence unit picked up radio traffic indicating at least the possibility of preparations for a sortie of American naval forces from Hawaii. The next day, radio silence was broken when, because of dense fog, the Main Body could not find its tanker train for a scheduled refueling. The tanker train had to radio its position for *Yamato* to make the rendezvous. Yamamoto assumed that the Americans were now aware of the position of the Main Body. Later that day (June 1) *Yamato's* radio intelligence unit noticed sharply increased communications traffic out of Hawaii, further indicating that an American naval sortie from Pearl Harbor might be in progress.[28] A Japanese patrol plane from Wotje in the Marshall Islands encountered an American patrol plane 700 miles west of Midway, indicating that Midway-based patrols had extended the radius of their search efforts far to the west. This caused concern as the transport group would be entering this radius two days hence.

As of the end of June 1—four days before the attack on Midway (which was scheduled for June 5 Tokyo time, June 4 Midway time)—Yamamoto then had ample evidence that his Midway invasion plan might have been discovered by the Americans and that they might be preparing a response to it. However, Yamamoto was not dismayed by the prospect that an American carrier fleet might be rushed to Midway to oppose the invasion. To the contrary, he and his staff probably welcomed it. This would permit the decisive engagement with the American carrier fleet, which was the main objective of the operation, to take place earlier than had been planned. It would allay the thing Yamamoto most feared—that the American carrier fleet would not be drawn to Midway where it could be destroyed.

The problem was that Nagumo knew none of this. His radio crew on *Akagi* had not picked up any of the radio traffic from Hawaii or from the American submarines. The reason they could not receive it, or communications from Tokyo, was because the radio antennae on *Akagi* were not large enough to pick up low-frequency, long-wave (long-distance) signals. This was one of the costs of the small superstructures on the Japanese carriers, which, along with sideways-venting smoke funnels, were designed to minimize obstructions to landing aircraft on the flight decks. Kusaka, Nagumo's chief of staff, had worried about this very problem and, prior to the sortie, had requested that *Yamato* relay important intelligence to *Akagi*; he had been refused in the interests of radio silence.[29] Also, incredibly, no arrangements had been made for the battleships in the Mobile Force—which had ample antennae and could have received the long-distance transmissions—to monitor the radio traffic and relay the information to *Akagi* by visual signals. Yamamoto had not relayed any of this radio intelligence to Nagumo because he assumed—erroneously as it turned out—that

Akagi had picked up all the communications *Yamato* had received, and he did not want to break radio silence unless absolutely necessary.[30]

It is possible, however, that Yamamoto's suspicions (and hopes) that the Americans might be preparing a response to his Midway operation that would include carriers was dampened by a report from the Naval General Staff in Tokyo, also on June 1 (May 31, Midway date). That report stated that it had been concluded from its analysis of American radio traffic from the Solomon Islands area that an American carrier force was still operating there (with the obvious implication that the Americans were not yet concerned about Midway).

Two carriers, *Enterprise* and *Hornet* (in Admiral Halsey's Task Force 16), had indeed been there. They had been sent to the southwest Pacific after their return from the Doolittle Raid to assist *Lexington* and *Yorktown* in the Coral Sea operation. They got there too late to join in the Battle of the Coral Sea, but were still in the eastern Solomons area on May 15, when they were sighted by a Japanese patrol plane. (Their presence had been intentionally brought to the attention of the Japanese on the 15th after Nimitz ordered Halsey to let his force be sighted.)[31] The next day, Nimitz ordered Halsey to return to Pearl Harbor.

Nimitz had become convinced, around the middle of May, that Yamamoto was organizing a massive naval operation against Midway and the Aleutians. This was due to the extraordinary work of his crack code-breaking unit—known as "Hypo"—under the leadership and genius of Joseph J. Rochefort. He did not yet know the date of the invasion, and still needed to convince his superior, Admiral Ernest J. King, commander in chief United States Fleet, that Midway was the target, but he began preparing his response. Among the things he did was to perpetrate a clever, and apparently effective, disinformation scheme using phony radio communications to persuade the Japanese that Halsey's task force was still in the south Pacific for some period after it had, in fact, been called back to Pearl Harbor.[32] *Enterprise* and *Hornet* arrived at Pearl on May 26, the very date Naguno departed the Inland Sea (the 27th in Japan). The crippled *Yorktown*, which the Japanese thought had been sunk (along with *Lexington*) in the Battle of the Coral Sea, arrived the next day.

Other important information known to Yamamoto also failed to reach Nagumo: An operation known as Operation Second K had been planned to provide surveillance over Hawaii on the morning of May 31 (local time). Two long-range "Emily" flying boats were to fly from Wotje in the Marshall Islands to Pearl Harbor to check for carriers. Nagumo knew of this plan before he left Japan. He also had reckoned that two to three American carriers might be at Pearl Harbor.[33] Thus, after his departure, any new information revealing whether or not carriers were at Pearl Harbor on May 31 would have been extremely helpful. But Operation Second K was aborted on May 31. The operation had required that the flying boats be refueled en route by submarines at French Frigate Shoals (between Midway and Hawaii). When the submarines arrived at French Frigate Shoals on the 30th, they found two American sea-plane tenders already there. After a twenty-four-hour postponement to see if the tenders would leave, which they did not, the operation was canceled.

Yamamoto's radio crew on *Yamato* received the report canceling the opera-tion from Kwajalein. He assumed that Nagumo had also received it, and so did not think it necessary to break radio silence to pass this information on to Na-gumo. But Nagumo did not receive it; as mentioned, *Akagi*'s radio gear was in-adequate to pick up the signal from Kwajalein. Thus, Nagumo was left to as-sume that Operation Second K had been performed and had not discovered any change in the status quo—that is, that the carriers were still at Pearl Harbor four days before his scheduled attack on Midway. Had Second K worked, the flying boats would have found no carriers at Pearl. *Enterprise* and *Hornet* departed on the 28th, and *Yorktown*—after being miraculously patched up in forty-eight hours—departed the on morning of the 30th. The absence of the carriers on the 31st would have raised at least a strong possibility that they were headed for Mid-way. But with Second K aborted, Yamamoto did not know where the carriers were, but still could not preclude the possibility that they had left for Midway—and Nagumo did not know that this was a possibility.

There was another operation planned to detect any movement of American carriers from Pearl Harbor to Midway: Two cordons of submarines, from the Ad-vance Force, were to take up station between Hawaii and Midway on June 1 (Midway date). This operation was delayed by two days (in part because some of the submarines had been assigned to the Second K operation, which had also been delayed before it was canceled). By the time the cordons were in place they found nothing because Nimitz's carriers had already passed through. Even had the cordons been on schedule they would have missed *Enterprise* and *Hor-net*, but it is possible that they could have spotted *Yorktown*. Yamamoto knew that the submarines were too late to provide useful information before the battle, but, again, Nagumo was unaware that the last chance to monitor movements of the American carriers from Hawaii had vanished.

On June 2 (June 1, Midway date), the Naval General Staff in Tokyo made a startling about-face, reversing its opinion—reiterated just the day before—that an American carrier force was in the South Pacific and, thus, that the Ameri-cans were unaware of the Midway operation. It sent an urgent radio message addressed to both Yamamoto and Nagumo warning that it now concluded that the Americans were probably aware of the Midway invasion plan, and might be sending carriers to Midway to ambush the Mobile Force. Yamamoto received this warning, but Nagumo did not. Yamamoto was inclined to relay it to Na-gumo but, incredibly, was talked out of it by his senior staff officer—Kameto Kuroshima—on grounds that Nagumo had probably received it and radio si-lence should be maintained.[34]

On the morning of June 4 (June 3 Midway date) Yamamoto received a radio message informing him that the transport group had been sighted by an American patrol plane. This was the first direct evidence he had that at least part of his forces had been discovered by the Americans. Later that day he received another report that the group had been attacked by B-17s, and early the next morning—the day of the battle—a report that a torpedo bomber attack had damaged a tanker at the rear of the column. It appears that *Akagi's* radio did receive these reports and that Nagumo was finally aware that at least elements of the Midway Invasion Force had been discovered.[35]

But the only evidence Nagumo had before the day of the battle that the Americans might have discovered his Mobile Force was an incident that occurred a day earlier, on June 2. Because of heavy fog that made visual signaling impossible, he was forced to break radio silence to communicate a course change to his fleet. Although he used a low-power inter-fleet radio for the signal, he feared that it might be picked up by the Americans and reveal his position. (It was received by *Yamato* 600 miles to the rear, but Nagumo's fears did not materialize because it was not picked up by the Americans.) In any event, Nagumo and his staff were not greatly concerned by the possibility that their presence would be discovered by the Americans at that late date—two days before the battle. They concluded that at that time it was probable that the American carriers were still at Pearl Harbor and thus could not reach the vicinity of Midway until after it was attacked.

It is now apparent that the seeds of the upcoming Japanese debacle at Midway were sown in the form of a massive communications failure, which was Yamamoto's fault, not Nagumo's. Nagumo had been left out of what was really another battle before the Battle of Midway—one of competing intelligence capabilities, with its own thrusts and ripostes: Yamamoto hoped his Midway operation would be a surprise. But Nimitz's intelligence crew had largely broken the Japanese naval code and deduced Yamamoto's plan to attack Midway. Nimitz then prepared his carrier force to set an ambush, hoping that it would not be detected in time for Nagumo to avoid it. Then, just days before the battle, Yamamoto deduced Nimitz's plan—or at least surmised that an American carrier force at Midway was a distinct possibility. Even the Naval General Staff in Tokyo had concluded—three days before the attack—that the Americans had probably discovered the Midway operation and might be sending carriers to ambush Nagumo's Mobile Force.

Thus, three days before the attack on Midway it seems that just about everyone in the Japanese high command suspected that American carriers might be at Midway—everyone except Nagumo. At the end of this intelligence skirmish the Japanese were actually in a position to ambush Nimitz's carriers on June 4, instead of being on the receiving end of Nimitz's ambush. The problem was that nobody shared any of this with Nagumo.[36] Just before he launched his attack on the morning of the battle, Nagumo gave his estimate of the situation to his staff: "The enemy is not aware of our plans. . . . It is not believed that the enemy has any powerful unit, with carriers as its nucleus, in the vicinity."[37]

In actual fact, three American carriers were lurking about 230 nautical miles to the east, poised to ambush Nagumo's Mobile Force. *Enterprise* and *Hornet*, in Admiral Spruance's Task Force 16, had sortied from Pearl Harbor on May 28, and *Yorktown*, in Admiral Fletcher's Task Force 17, left two days later. They effected a rendezvous on June 2 at a point about 325 miles northeast of Midway. *Yorktown*'s air group consisted of a scratch crew hastily assembled to replace the planes and pilots lost at Coral Sea and those pilots sent on medical leave.[38] Most of the replacements came from *Saratoga*, which had been laid up in San Diego for repairs after having been torpedoed on January 11. These three carriers, the nucleus of Nimitz's carrier striking force, were escorted by seven heavy cruisers, one light antiaircraft cruiser, and fifteen destroyers.

AIRCRAFT ON HAND

The Battle of Midway is often depicted as a naval battle in which the Americans were vastly outnumbered in ships and aircraft—a sort of David versus Goliath affair. The scenario is of a puny American carrier striking force pitted against the total array of Japanese fleets and air power that were committed to the MI campaign, including substantial land-based air power based as far away as the Marshall Islands. In reality, the battle that actually took place was between just Nagumo's Mobile Force, containing four carriers, and the American carrier striking force—with three carriers—together with air power based on Midway. The remainder, and bulk, of the Japanese naval forces played no significant part in that battle. Opposing the 229 operational carrier aircraft and 16 cruiser- and battleship-based reconnaissance float planes of the Mobile Force were the 221 operational planes on *Enterprise, Hornet,* and *Yorktown* and 111 planes based at Midway (which can be regarded as a fourth, albeit fixed, aircraft carrier). Thus, in raw numbers, the Americans outnumbered Nagumo's Mobile Force in aircraft by around 332 to 245.

A word is in order here about the difficulty in ascertaining the aircraft complements of the Japanese carriers in the Mobile Force. They have been somewhat of a mystery to American commentators from the beginning. This is because records of the precise complements of aircraft did not survive the battle. Estimates have to be made from other data (which is why there is such a variation in the numbers given by different commentators). It is now, however, possible to deduce the number of operational planes of the various types in the air groups of each of the four carriers from their Action Reports[39] and from Senshi Sosho (the official Japanese history of World War II). Also, the number of Zeros in the Sixth Air Group, carried aboard the carriers for the defense of Midway after its capture, has been uncovered by Hata and Izawa (but this information was not available to the early commentators).[40]

In addition, each squadron contained some "spares," but the number is unknown.[41] Ordinarily, a full-strength Japanese carrier squadron contained eighteen planes plus three spares. Most accounts of the battle (including Senshi Sosho) assume that each squadron on board the four carriers in the Mobile Force at Midway carried three spares. But this was probably not the case at Midway. As the carrier hangar decks were burdened by the additional twenty-one Zeros of the Sixth Air Group, some of the spares ordinarily carried may have been dispensed with when the Mobile Force left Japan. (This seems especially possible for the smaller carriers *Hiryu* and *Soryu*. There is testimony from *Soryu* veterans that there may have been only one or two spares per squadron.)[42]

In the following Orders of Battle it will be assumed that each squadron on the larger carriers—*Akagi* and *Kaga*—carried the usual three, but that the smaller *Hiryu* and *Soryu* carried only two. In addition, each carrier embarked some Zeros of the Sixth Air Group: *Akagi*—six, *Kaga*—nine, *Hiryu*—three, *Soryu*—three. But apparently only three, all on *Akagi*, were operational for carrier duty.

ORDERS OF BATTLE

Japanese
Mobile Force
Vice Admiral Chuichi Nagumo

CarDiv 1, Vice Admiral Nagumo

Akagi	Commanders	Aircraft		
Air Group	Cdr. Mitsuo Fuchida[43]	On board	Operational	
Fighters	Lt. Cdr. Shigeru Itaya	27	21[44]	A6M2
Dive bombers	Lt. Takehiko Chubaya	21	18	D3A1
Attack planes	Lt. Cdr. Shigeharu Murata	21	18	B5N2
		69	57	

Kaga				
Air Group	Lt. Cdr. Tadashi Kusumi			
Fighters	Lt. Masao Sato	30	18[45]	A6M2
Dive bombers	Lt. Shoichi Ogawa	21	18	D3A1
Attack planes	Lt. Ichiro Kitajima	30	27	B5N2
		81	63	

CarDiv 2, Rear Admiral Tamon Yamaguchi

Hiryu				
Air Group	Lt. Joichi Tomonaga			
Fighters	Lt. Shigeru Mori	23	18	A6M2
Dive bombers	Lt. Michio Kobayashi	20	18	D3A1

Attack planes	Lt. Rokuro Kikuchi	20	18	B5N2
		63	54	

Soryu

Air Group	Lt. Cdr. Takashige Egusa			
Fighters	Lt. Masaharu Suganami	23	18	A6M2
Dive bombers	Lt. Masahiro Ikeda	20	18	D3A1
Attack planes	Lt. Heijiro Abe	20	18	B5N2
Reconnaissance[46]		2	2	D4Y1
		65	56	
		278	229	

Close support ships, Rear Admiral Hiroaki Abe
CruDiv 8: CA *Tone*, CA *Chikuma*
BatDiv 3, 2nd Section: BB *Haruna*, BB *Kirishima*
Screen, (DesRon 10), Rear Admiral Susumu Kimura in CL *Nagara*
DesDiv 4: *Arashi, Nowaki, Hagikaze, Maikaze*
DesDiv 10: *Kazagumo, Yugumo, Makigumo, Akigumo*[47]
DesDiv 17: *Isokaze, Urakaze, Hamakaze, Tanikaze*
Supply Unit: Five Oilers

American[48]
Carrier Striking Force
Rear Admiral Frank Jack Fletcher
Task Force 16, Rear Admiral Raymond A. Spruance

Enterprise	Commanders	Aircraft		
Air Group	Lt. Cdr. Wade McClusky	On board	Operational	
Fighting Six	Lt. James S. Gray Jr.	27	27	F4F-4
Bombing Six	Lt. Richard H. Best	18	15	SDB-3
Scouting Six	Lt. W. Earl Gallaher	19	18	SBD-3
Torpedo Six	Lt. Cdr. Eugene E. Lindsey	14	14	TBD-1
		78	74	

Hornet

Air Group	Cdr. Stanhope C. Ring			
Fighting Eight	Lt. Cdr. Samuel G. Mitchell	27	27	F4F-4
Bombing Eight	Lt. Cdr. Robert R. Johnson	19	19	SBD-3
Scouting Eight	Lt. Cdr. Walter F. Rodee	16	15	SBD-3
Torpedo Eight	Lt. Cdr. John C. Waldron	15	15	TBD-1
		77	76	

Cruiser Group, Rear Admiral Thomas C. Kinkaid
CruDiv 6: CA *New Orleans*, CA *Minneapolis*, CA *Vincennes*,
        CA *Northampton*, CA *Pensacola*, CLAA *Atlanta*
Destroyer screen, Captain Alexander R. Early
DesRon 1: *Phelps, Worden, Monaghan, Aylwin*
DesRon 6: *Balch, Conyngham, Benham, Ellet, Maury*
Oiler Group: Two oilers, Two destroyers (*Dewey, Monssen*)

Task Force 17, Rear Admiral Fletcher

Yorktown

Air Group	Lt. Cdr. Oscar Pederson			
Fighting Three	Lt. Cdr. John S. Thach	27	25	F4F-4
Bombing Three	Lt. Cdr. Maxwell F. Leslie	18	17	SBD-3
Scouting Five	Lt. Wallace C. Short	19	17	SDB-3
Torpedo Three	Lt. Cdr. Lance E. Massey	15	12	TBD-1
		79	71	
		234	221	

Cruiser Group, Rear Admiral William W. Smith
CA *Astoria*, CA *Portland*
Destroyer screen, Captain Gilbert C. Hoover
DesRon 2: *Hammann, Hughes, Morris, Anderson, Russell, Gwin*[49]

Aircraft based on Midway[50]

Naval Air Station, Midway, Captain Cyril T. Simard

Navy		On hand	Operational	
Search planes[51]	Cdr. Logan Ramsey	32	30	PBY-5
Torpedo Eight	Lt. L. K. Fieberling	6	6	TBF
Marine				
Aircraft Group	Lt. Col. Ira E. Kimes			
VMF-221	Maj. Floyd B. Parks			
Buffaloes		21	20	F2A-3
Wildcats		7	6	F4F-3
VMSB-241	Maj. Lofton R. Henderson			
Vindicators		17	12	SB2U
Dauntlesses		19	16	SBD-2
Army				
Air Force Group	Maj. Gen. Willis H. Hale			
Marauders	Capt. James F. Collins	4	4	B-26
Heavy bombers	Lt. Col. Walter C. Sweeney	19	17	B-17
		125	111	

CHAPTER FOUR

THE FATAL DECISION

A T 0715 ON THE MORNING of the battle, Admiral Nagumo made the fatal decision to rearm his torpedo planes with land bombs for a second strike on Midway. It was the first of three crucial decisions Nagumo made during the three critical hours before most of his carriers were destroyed at 1025. In this chapter I analyze that decision—and the events immediately preceding it—and give a judgment of its reasonableness. Nagumo's second crucial decision—his decision countermanding the rearming order—will be discussed in chapter 5, along with the controversies surrounding *Tone* 4's sighting reports. The third decision by Nagumo—to postpone his attack—made at around 0830 is his most controversial decision; it will be covered in chapter 6. But first, the events preceding the decision to rearm: the attack on Midway and the search effort.

OPENING MOVES

The attack on Midway was launched at 0430—just as dawn broke on the morning of June 4. It was still a half-hour before sunrise, but the engine and weapons mechanics of the air groups on the four carriers of Nagumo's First Air Fleet (Mobile Force) had been up since 0130 preparing the planes for the strike on Midway. The Midway strike force consisted of 108 planes. Launched first were thirty-six Zero fighters, nine from each carrier. They would take on the Midway-based fighters and strafe the ground defenses. Following them on *Hiryu* and *Soryu* were thirty-six Kate torpedo planes (eighteen from each carrier) that had been armed with 805-kilogram instant-detonation fragmentation land bombs. Following the Zeros on *Akagi* and *Kaga* were thirty-six Val dive-bombers (eighteen from each carrier) that had been armed with 242-kilogram high-explosive land bombs. The strike force was led by Lt. Joichi Tomonaga of *Hiryu*, who had replaced Mitsuo Fuchida as strike force commander when Fuchida became disabled from an appendicitis operation.

The launch took less than fifteen minutes. In addition to the Midway strike force planes, twelve Zeros—three from each carrier—were launched, along with the strike force, for combat air patrol.[1] Also, an additional Kate torpedo plane each from *Akagi* and *Kaga* was launched as part of the search patrol. Thus, thirty planes each were launched from *Hiryu* and *Soryu*, and thirty-one each from *Akagi* and *Kaga*, for a total of 122 aircraft. By 0445 the Midway strike force had formed up and headed for Midway—about 210 nautical miles away. (One Kate from *Hiryu* developed engine trouble and returned—making an emergency landing on *Soryu*, apparently the closest carrier.)

At the same time the carrier planes were being launched, catapult launches of float planes were taking place on the cruisers *Tone* and *Chikuma* and on the battleship *Haruna*. One plane each from *Tone* and *Chikuma* was launched for antisubmarine patrol and five planes, two each from *Tone* and *Chikuma* and one from *Haruna*, were launched for the surface ship search patrol. At the last moment launch priority had been given to the antisubmarine patrol over the surface ship search (as Nagumo considered American submarines to be the greater threat). Last to be launched was the *Tone* 4 search plane. It had been scheduled for 0440 after the antisubmarine patrol plane had been launched, but was delayed until 0500.[2] (The cause of the delay is disputed—some say engine trouble, others say catapult trouble.)

Nagumo had issued his search plan two days earlier. He had not seen fit to alter it—even after he learned that the transport group of the Midway Invasion Force had been discovered. This was because, as we have seen, he had been given no reason to suspect that American carriers might be in the area. The search plan consisted of seven lines, six of them extending 300 nautical miles from the Mobile Force, the seventh—to the north—extending 150 miles (it was covered by an older-type float plane from *Haruna* and was considered to be a much less likely place to find American ships). Altogether, the search paths covered an arc from 20° to 180°. At the end of each search line the planes would make a dogleg to the left for 60 miles before returning to their mother ships.

After the planes of the Midway strike force had been launched, Nagumo had the following left onboard his carriers, excluding spares and Zeros from the Sixth Air Group: forty-three torpedo planes, with twenty-six on *Kaga* and seventeen on *Akagi*[3] (there had been forty-five operational Kates on those two carriers, but two had been used for search duty); thirty-six dive-bombers, with eighteen each on *Hiryu* and *Soryu* (this does not include the two experimental Judy dive-bombers on *Soryu* intended for supplemental reconnaissance); twenty-four Zeros, with six on each carrier (in addition, as already noted, three of the Zero pilots from the Sixth Air Group, all from *Akagi*, were carrier-qualified and later participated in the combat air patrol). The torpedo planes and dive-bombers left on board, along with some Zeros, constituted the second-wave strike force.

The second-wave planes were armed to attack ships and on standby in case American carriers showed up. About two-thirds of the 36 dive-bombers on *Hiryu* and *Soryu* were armed with 251-kilogram armor-piercing antiship bombs with a ⅒-second delay fuse; the remainder were armed with 242-kilogram instant-detonation high-explosive bombs. (Although these are usually called "land" bombs, some were intentionally used for attacks against ships—to neutralize antiaircraft gun batteries and, in the case of aircraft carriers, to hole flight decks.) Seventeen torpedo planes on *Akagi* and probably eighteen on *Kaga* were armed with torpedoes. (It appears that the other eight torpedo planes on *Kaga* were unarmed and, with less experienced crews, were treated as a reserve.) The twenty-four operational Zeros of the carrier air groups remaining after the combat air patrol was launched were originally assigned to escort these dive-bombers and torpedo planes. However, twelve of those Zeros were soon allocated to the combat air patrol to supplement the twelve already aloft when the threat of bomber attacks from Midway became obvious. This left only twelve to serve as escorts for the second-wave bombers—and they would eventually be deployed for combat air patrol (CAP) by soon after 0800, leaving none for escort.

Most American accounts of the battle, beginning with Morison's—and some Japanese accounts, including Fuchida's—have the second-wave planes raised to the flight decks and spotted for launch soon after the Midway strike force departed. The usual Japanese practice, however, was to keep the attack aircraft in the hangars until a decision to launch a strike was made, so as to leave the flight decks clear for CAP operations. It is not known for certain what was done to the second-wave planes in this case after the first wave was launched. (One of the *Kaga* torpedo plane pilots interviewed—Takeshi Maeda—was insistent that *Kaga*'s torpedo planes remained in the hangar. But one of *Akagi*'s torpedo plane pilots—Fukuji Inoue—was equally certain that his plane had been brought up to the flight deck, and the others from those two carriers had no recollection either way. As for the dive-bombers on *Hiryu* and *Soryu*, most of the veterans from those carriers recalled that they had been raised to the flight decks, but memories were dim.)

But even if the usual practice was to leave attack aircraft in the hangars until a launch had been ordered, it may have been different on the morning of June 4 at Midway. Yamamoto had given Nagumo a standing order to keep half the torpedo planes on standby equipped to attack ships in case American carriers were suddenly discovered. It would seem that full compliance with this directive would have required that the torpedo planes be spotted on the flight decks, as it was very time-consuming to raise and spot a squadron of torpedo planes for launch. Also, as the CAP Zeros launched at 0430 were expected to be in the air for three hours before requiring refueling,[4] clear flight decks would not be required for awhile. (And at the time it was expected that the attack on Midway would catch and destroy the bombers based there on the ground, eliminating any attacks on the Mobile Force from Midway.)

Therefore, it seems reasonable that the second-wave planes would have been spotted on the flight decks soon after the Midway strike force departed. It certainly seems that the offensive-minded Yamaguchi, commander of the carrier division containing *Hiryu* and *Soryu*, would have wanted his dive-bombers on hair-trigger standby. Also, Fuchida's account of the spotting of the second attack wave on the flight decks must be given credence.[5] He obviously was familiar with Japanese carrier operations doctrine. Although there are details in his account of the morning's activities that are questionable (he was in sick bay much of that time and learned of some of them secondhand), the fact that he *assumed* that the second-wave planes were raised to the flight deck immediately after the Midway strike force departed indicates that such an operation would not have been considered unusual, given the circumstances of that morning. I conclude that it was done.

*   *   *

As of 0530 on the morning of the battle things were going well for Nagumo. His Midway strike force was heading to its target. There was no indication that American headquarters at Midway was aware of his impending attack. His search planes were combing the area on the off-chance that the Americans had somehow managed to get ships to the vicinity of Midway. His second-wave planes were on standby armed to attack any American carriers that might be discovered. There had been only one minor hitch in operations that morning—the late launch of the *Tone* 4 search plane.

But one hour after the Midway strike force was launched, the wheels began to come off Nagumo's well-oiled machine. At 0532 an American Catalina PBY flying boat was spotted surveying the Mobile Force. Nagumo now knew that his attack on Midway would no longer be a surprise. That meant that the Americans would have time to get their planes off the ground before his strike force arrived there at about 0630. He also realized that his Mobile Force was now a target for Midway-based bombers. Six Zeros were scrambled for combat air patrol (three each from *Hiryu* and *Akagi*) to reinforce the dozen already aloft.

The Catalina PBY was one of twenty-two that had left Midway before dawn for search patrol. At 0534 it reported back to Midway that it had found "enemy carriers," but no location was given. At 0540 it reported the location as bearing 320°, distance 180 miles from Midway. At 0552 it gave the number of carriers as two, and added their course (135°) and speed (25 knots). This was the only information the Americans received about Nagumo's carriers from the PBYs—and it was off by two carriers and 40 miles.[6] But it was enough.

A little over 200 miles east of the Mobile Force there was another recipient of this report as of yet unknown to Nagumo. Rear Admiral Frank Jack Fletcher, the commander of the American carrier forces on *Yorktown*, received this information at 0603 and signaled it to Rear Admiral Raymond A. Spruance on *Enterprise* at 0607, with orders to "attack enemy carriers when definitely located." Fletcher had his doubts about the accuracy of the report because he had been informed by Nimitz that there would be at least four Japanese carriers in the Mobile Force. Although he authorized Spruance to attack right away, he decided to withhold his own attack until he got better information. He never got it.

At 0545 another PBY had reported that "many planes" were heading toward Midway, and at 0553 Midway radar picked them up when they were 93 miles away. The Midway air groups were now safe from surprise attack. At 0600, twenty-four fighters (twenty Buffaloes and four Wildcats) began taking off, then six TBF torpedo bombers, followed by four B-26s, then twelve Vindicator dive-bombers, and finally, sixteen Dauntless dive-bombers. They were all off the ground by 0616, with the Japanese planes just 29 miles away. (Earlier, sixteen B-17s had left at dawn—to find and bomb the invasion force spotted the day before—but two later returned because of engine trouble.) One Vindicator and one Buffalo had to return immediately after takeoff because of engine trouble. Two Wildcats that had been on dawn patrol, and had landed for refueling, took off at 0625, bringing the total number of fighters in the air to defend against the Japanese attack to twenty-five. All that was left on the ground were a few inoperable planes, along with the fighter and dive-bomber that had returned, and two SBD Dauntlesses that did not take off because of balky engines.

Back on board Nagumo's carriers, at 0555—according to Senshi Sosho—the *Tone* search plane on search line #3 radioed that "15 enemy planes are heading toward you."[7] Although the time of this sighting report was almost certainly mislogged—it had to have come at least fifteen minutes later than 0555—at whatever time it was received it was assumed that these planes were from Midway. In response, six more Zeros (three each from *Hiryu* and *Soryu*) were scrambled for combat air patrol. Now the only operational Zeros left onboard (apart from the Sixth Air Group Zeros) were the twelve assigned to escort the second wave on standby in case American ships were discovered. At 0609 the Mobile Force increased its speed to 28 knots and prepared for the expected American attack from Midway.

ATTACK ON MIDWAY

At 0616 the Japanese attack force was intercepted about 30 miles out by the Marine fighters. Although they inflicted some damage, almost all were wiped out by Zeros. It was an unequal contest. The nineteen obsolete Buffalo fighters were hopelessly outclassed, and even the F4F-3 Wildcats (which were more agile than the F4F-4s that replaced them) were outrun, outclimbed, and worst of all, outmaneuvered, by the Zeros. Of the twenty-five fighters that engaged the enemy, fifteen were shot down and two more crashed from battle damage. Of the eight that landed, only three (two Buffaloes and a Wildcat) were operable. Two Zeros were shot down and five were damaged—some by ground fire over Midway. Also, some of the Kate torpedo planes—being used as horizontal bombers—were hit before they reached Midway (but most of the losses would be from antiaircraft ground fire).[8]

At 0634 the attack on Midway began. The Kates attacked first as high-level bombers with their 805-kilogram bombs. The First *Chutai* of six planes from *Soryu* came in at 2,700 meters and dropped their bombs on the dual-purpose gun emplacements on Sand Island. The Second and Third *Chutais*—twelve planes—from *Soryu* came in at 3,400 meters (11,200 feet) and hit the runways on Eastern Island. The seventeen Kates from *Hiryu* also came in at 3,400 meters and bombed fuel tanks, gun emplacements, and the flying boat ramp, all on Sand Island. Then the Val dive-bombers followed at 0640 with their 242-kilogram bombs. The eighteen dive-bombers from *Kaga* hit various targets on Sand Island, and the eighteen from *Akagi* hit the runways on Eastern Island. In addition to damaging the runways, the attacks destroyed the marines' command post and mess hall, the powerhouse, the seaplane hangars, and the oil tank farm. Some antiaircraft (AA) gun batteries were damaged, but none was completely knocked out.

Probably the most serious damage, however, was to the aircraft gasoline pumping system. The electric pump had been destroyed, the consequence of which was that thereafter planes could be refueled only by hand-pumping from gasoline drums. (This meant that if the American carriers were to be destroyed, Midway could not effectively serve as a substitute base for any carrier aircraft that survived.) However, the attack failed in its most important objective: that of destroying Midway's bomber strength on the ground; all operational planes were in the air. It also failed to make the runways unusable. Casualties were light amongst the ground crews—only eleven killed and eighteen wounded. But about fifteen marine fighter pilots had been killed in the defense of Midway. Though battered, Midway was still in business.

The bombing attack was over by 0645, and some of the torpedo planes (twelve from *Soryu*) headed back to their carriers at 0650. Most of the Zeros, however, continued strafing installations on Midway, while most of the dive-bombers and torpedo planes orbited out of range of ground fire, waiting for the

Zeros to finish up before joining them for the return. The bulk of the strike force assembled and began their return to the carriers between 0720 and 0730.[9] The commander of the Midway strike force, Lieutenant Tomonaga from *Hiryu*, had seen that the attack had not accomplished its objectives. Accordingly, at 0700 he radioed First Fleet Headquarters: "There is need for a second attack wave." Nagumo received this report at around 0705.[10]

The limited success of the attack was not without its costs for the Japanese: almost half of *Hiryu* and *Soryu*'s torpedo planes had been shot down, crash-landed in the ocean, or returned to the carriers inoperable (five had been shot down). *Hiryu* was left with only nine that could be used in another attack that day; *Soryu*, ten. Dive-bomber and Zero losses were much lighter—one Val shot down and six damaged (leaving twenty-nine operable); two Zeros shot down and five damaged (leaving twenty-nine operable). But the most costly loss was eight pilots killed and at least three seriously wounded.[11]

MIDWAY'S FIRST ATTACK ON THE MOBILE FORCE

Now it was Midway's turn to attack. The first to go in were six Navy TBF Avenger torpedo bombers, making their debut in this battle. They were intercepted at 0705, and those that got through began dropping their torpedoes at 0710. There were no hits, and five of the six were shot down by Zeros. The one that returned to Midway had been rendered inoperable. This was not an auspicious beginning for a plane that would eventually become the best torpedo bomber in the war.

Next came four army B-26s that had been specially rigged to carry torpedoes. There had been no coordination between the two groups. There were no hits, and two of the B-26s were shot down—with the other two returning so shot up as to be of no further use. The Mark 13 aerial torpedoes that were dropped proved to be practically worthless. (They were so slow—33.5 knots—that they were easily evaded—one was even picked off by a machine gun.) The torpedo attacks were over by 0715.

While this was going on, according to the log in the Official Report, Nagumo's carriers were also being subjected to high-level bombing. The planes doing it were recorded variously as "heavy bombers," B-17s, B-26s, or PBYs, and nine or ten were counted. Two to five were recorded as having been shot down. It is a mystery what these planes were. The American accounts make no mention of any high-level bombing at this time. They clearly could not have been B-17s or B-26s—the fourteen B-17s did not reach the area until after 0730 and did not begin bombing until after 0810.[12] And all four of the B-26s had made low-level torpedo attacks. The Japanese appear to have been confused while undergoing attacks from ten torpedo-bearing bombers (including four B-26s), with also at least two PBYs in the area.

It is possible that these mystery planes were Catalina PBYs—as many as a

Chester W. Nimitz, Admiral, Commander in Chief, United States Pacific Fleet. Naval Historical Center.

Raymond A. Spruance, Admiral, United States Navy, Commander Central Pacific Force, U.S. Pacific Fleet in 1944. National Archives.

Frank Jack Fletcher, Vice Admiral, United States Navy. Naval Historical Center.

Captain Clarence Wade McClusky.
Naval Historical Center.

USS *Enterprise*. Naval Historical Center.

USS *Yorktown*, during builder's trials. Naval Historical Center.

SBD Dauntless dive-bombers during the battle. The burning ship may be the cruiser *Mikuma*. National Archives.

Grumman F4F-3 Wildcat on flight deck during machine-gun testing. National Archives.

TBD-1 Devastator torpedo bomber. National Archives.

Isoroku Yamamoto, Admiral, Commander in Chief, Combined Fleet, Imperial Japanese Navy. Naval Historical Center.

Chuichi Nagumo, Vice Admiral, Commander in Chief, First Air Fleet, Imperial Japanese Navy. Naval Historical Center.

Lieutenant Joichi Tomonaga, Commander of the *Hiryu* air group. Killed during a torpedo strike on the *Yorktown*. Naval Historical Center.

Akagi, Japanese aircraft carrier. Naval Historical Center.

Kaga, Japanese aircraft carrier, following modernization in 1936. Naval Historical Center.

Hiryu, Japanese aircraft carrier, during trials in 1939. Naval Historical Center.

Mitsubishi A6M2 Zero fighter plane. Official U.S. Navy Photograph, now in the collections of the National Archives.

Aichi D3A1 Val dive-bomber. Official U.S. Navy Photograph, now in the collections of the National Archives.

Nakajima B5N2 Kate torpedo plane. Official U.S. Navy Photograph, now in the collections of the National Archives.

half-dozen—which had been drawn to the area after discovery of the Japanese carriers. They were equipped for high-level bombing, but there is no record of any concerted bombing activity by them. (However, it should be noted that the records of PBY activity on June 4 are spotty, and most of the PBYs did not return to Midway. They had been ordered to fly to the safer havens of Laysan and Lisianski Islands after completing their search patrols.) A more likely explanation for this little mystery is that the high-level bombing incident was mislogged in the confusion attending the torpedo bomber attacks; that bombing by B-17s actually happened an hour later than recorded—beginning at 0814, not 0714.

At any case, it was during this period that Nagumo ran out of Zeros for his second-wave strike force. As the American torpedo bombers were spotted coming in, most of the remaining twelve Zeros—those assigned to escort the second wave—were launched to reinforce the air defense. One Zero already on combat air patrol had been shot down, and another had returned with engine trouble. To make up those losses so as to have thirty-six in the combat air patrol until the Midway strike Zeros returned, Nagumo dipped into the Zeros of the Sixth Air Group (which were being ferried for the Midway occupation defense). Two of them were launched from *Akagi* at 0710 to help intercept the B-26s that were coming in for attack.[13]

Also at around 0700, just before the torpedo bombers attacked, some of the Zeros on combat air patrol had to be landed for reservicing—three from *Akagi* and two from *Hiryu*.[14] (They had tangled with the American PBY search planes and had probably exhausted their 20-mm cannon ammunition as well as running low on fuel.) This meant that the flight decks of those carriers needed to be cleared of any planes spotted aft before the Zeros could be recovered. (The flight decks on Japanese carriers were relatively smaller—especially at the front—than their American counterparts, so there was not as much room to allow planes to be parked out of the way on the flight deck while CAP operations were taking place.) Therefore, even if the second-wave strike planes had been spotted on the flight decks after the Midway strike force departed, they probably would have been stricken below before 0700. (On *Hiryu* and *Soryu*, however, it appears that only half the dive-bombers were taken below to the hangar, with the other half being merely pushed forward on the flight deck.)

WHEN AND WHY THE DECISION
TO REARM WAS MADE

It was while the torpedo bomber attacks were beginning that Nagumo received Tomonaga's recommendation for a second strike against Midway—a recommendation no doubt given added weight by the attacks from Midway. Actually, Nagumo had foreseen that a second strike might be necessary and earlier that morning, at 0520, had advised the commanders of his second-wave attack planes to be prepared to change the armament to land bombs for a second strike on Midway "if no changes are observed in the enemy situation."[15] (By this, I assume that he meant that if there still was no evidence of American carriers in the area.) Now, the torpedo bomber attacks graphically confirmed the earlier fear that the American Midway-based bombers would not be destroyed on the ground, which had been the principal objective of the attack on Midway. At 0715 Nagumo made his fateful decision to rearm his second-wave torpedo planes and dive-bombers with land bombs.

As discussed in chapter 1, Hisae Sawachi contends that the change from torpedoes to land bombs on the torpedo planes on *Akagi* and *Kaga* actually began at 0520, and that the rearming order logged at 0715 in Nagumo's Official Report was a fabrication.[16] (This fabrication, allegedly, was for the purpose of making Nagumo's disregard of Yamamoto's standing order—to keep half the torpedo planes on standby armed to attack ships—appear less flagrant.) While I reject Sawachi's contention, it is reasonable to conclude that preparations for a rearming operation began soon after 0520 by bringing up 800-kilogram land bombs from the magazines to the hangar decks on *Akagi* and *Kaga*.[17] In the event a second strike became necessary, a great deal of time could be saved in the rearming procedure if the land bombs were already in the hangar deck.

The decision to rearm could not have been an easy one for Nagumo. It would contravene Yamamoto's standing order to keep half his torpedo planes in a state of readiness to attack any American carriers that might show up. But it appears that Nagumo's thinking was that, as of 0715, Midway was still operational as an airbase—and a clear and present threat to his carriers. Moreover, the invasion of the atoll, scheduled for June 6, could not take place until it was neutralized. He therefore concluded that another attack was necessary, and it could not wait until the first-wave planes returning from Midway could be landed, rearmed, and launched for a second attack. The second-wave torpedo planes and dive-bombers on standby would have to be rearmed with land bombs to do the job.

Yamamoto's standing order to Nagumo to keep half the Mobile Force's torpedo planes armed for ships was premised on priority being given to the objective of destroying American carriers over the objective of supporting an invasion of Midway. Nagumo concluded at 0715 that it was necessary to reverse those priorities. His reasoning appears to have been that as the search planes were over two and one-half hours into their search, and had reached the end of their search lines without discovering any American ships, the possibility of American carriers being in the area was even more remote than he had earlier believed. On the other hand, the need to finish off Midway as soon as possible seemed obvious.

We now know that fifteen minutes later American carriers would show up, despite Nagumo's confidence to the contrary. It has often been alleged that a better search effort by Nagumo on the morning of the battle would have led to an earlier discovery of those carriers and would have forestalled his decision to rearm his torpedo planes at 0715. A "perfunctory" and inadequate search plan has thus been cited as one of the chief causes of the Japanese defeat. While, with the benefit of hindsight, a more thorough search plan can certainly be devised, if we are to be fair with Nagumo the question is whether his plan was inadequate under the circumstances of his situation at the time. But apart from that, the real question is whether a more timely and higher-density search would have found the American fleet, thus preventing the fatal decision to rearm.

ADEQUACY OF THE SEARCH PLAN

For a precautionary search where enemy carriers were not expected, Nagumo's search plan was actually fairly extensive, at least in comparison with other searches by both sides in the first year of the Pacific War. As previously described, it consisted of seven lines covering an arc of 160° to a distance of 300 nautical miles. (The attack path to Midway served as an eighth line.) However, this meant that at the extremities the outbound lines were 120 miles apart, which would not be of sufficient density to provide complete coverage—considering that maximum visibility was about 50 miles in clear weather. (It may have been that the return paths—which were offset to the left by a 60-mile dogleg—were counted on the cover the gaps at the extremities.)

By comparison, the American search plan at Midway on the morning of the battle—where enemy carriers *were* expected—consisted of twenty-two lines covering an arc of 180° to a distance of 425 nautical miles. (There was no dogleg to a different return path.) In terms of density at the critical distances—200 miles out for the Japanese plan, 300 out for the American plan—the search lines were 80 miles apart for the Japanese and 43 miles apart for the Americans. The Japanese search density was clearly very thin at the critical points in the search.

In terms of timeliness, Nagumo's plan called for a launch of the search planes at 0430, the American plan at 0415.[18] In actual execution, however, none of Nagumo's search planes were launched on schedule. Three of the four cruiser float planes were launched about ten minutes later than 0430 because priority was given to launching the antisubmarine patrol, and the fourth—*Tone* 4—was not launched until 0500 because of catapult or engine problems. (On the other hand, at least some of the American PBYs appear to have been launched even earlier than the scheduled 0415; the one that first found the Mobile Force at 0534 would had to have departed Midway at around 0400.)[19] Thus, Nagumo's search effort was less thorough and less timely than the American one. But considering that, unlike the Americans, Nagumo was not expecting enemy carriers to be in the area, it was not all that bad for a routine, merely precautionary search.[20]

On the other hand, had Nagumo been advised by Yamamoto on the eve of the battle that there was a distinct possibility that American carriers might be in the area, he clearly could have mounted a much more intensive search effort. The eight reserve Kates on *Kaga* could have been dispatched for armed reconnaissance, as had been done by Hara at Coral Sea. (There were also four high-performance "Jakes" remaining on board the cruisers *Tone* and *Chikuma*, and several older-type float planes on the battleships *Haruna* and *Kirishima* that could have been launched an hour later for a second-phase search to reinforce the search lines.) It should not be assumed that Nagumo would not have beefed up his search effort had he been better informed of a possible American carrier threat.

Would a more thorough search have found the American carriers before 0715? Surprisingly, perhaps, the answer is probably no. In point of fact, one of the Japanese search planes—*Chikuma* 5—flew almost right over Fletcher's Task Force 17 at 0630 (see Search & Course Chart). It saw nothing because of low-level clouds.[21] (Weather on the search line to the north was even worse—another *Chikuma* search plane had to abandon the search at 0635 and turn back because of a storm in the area.) Had Nagumo covered the sky with search planes, none would have been in a better position to discover the American carriers than *Chikuma* 5 was. Nimitz had been aware of the weather forecast for the Midway area and chose the rendezvous point for his carrier task forces with concealment in mind—as any smart admiral would have done. Thus, the low search-line density was *not* responsible for the failure to discover the American fleet earlier.

Cloud cover over the American carriers did not begin to break up until almost 0730.[22] Therefore, whether there had been fourteen search lines or twenty-two, armed reconnaissance with Kates or earlier launches by the search planes, because of cloud cover over the American fleet it is very unlikely that the American ships would have been seen much before 0728, when *Tone* 4 spotted them. As Nagumo lamented, with some justification, in his Official Report, "The weather of the day certainly was not a friend of our search planes."[23] In any case, Nagumo's search plan made absolutely no difference in the outcome of the battle.

THE LATE LAUNCH OF *TONE* 4

Much has been made of the fact that the *Tone* 4 search plane (which discovered the American fleet at 0728) was launched thirty minutes late—0500 instead of the originally scheduled 0430. The assumption, widely held, is that had it been launched on time, the American fleet would have been discovered 30 minutes earlier—at 0700 rather than 0728. This, too, would supposedly have avoided the debacle that resulted from the decision to rearm at 0715. If we ignore the fact that cloud cover would probably have prevented a sighting at 0700, there is a simple and appealing logic to this assumption (which has made it one of the most enduring myths of Midway). But it is not true. One of the more stunning ironies of Midway is that had *Tone* 4 been launched on time it most likely would not have discovered the American fleet as early as it did! Had it been on schedule and stayed on course, it could not have arrived in the vicinity of the American fleet until a little after 0800.

How is this so? It now appears certain that the reason *Tone* 4 reached the area of the American fleet as early as it did is because it shortened its course.[24] It turned north on its dogleg about 60 nautical miles short of the scheduled course change—at about 240 miles out from the Mobile Force instead of the scheduled 300 (see Search & Course Chart). After proceeding north for about 40 miles, it then turned west to return to its mother ship. It appears that shortly after turning west it found the American fleet. By cutting its course short, *Tone* 4 saved a little over one hour of flying time to reach the same point. (The scheduled course would have been 60 nautical miles longer outbound and 60 more inbound, along with a 20 mile longer dogleg; *Tone* 4's cruising speed was 120 knots.) Thus, had it been launched a half hour earlier and not shortened its course, it would not have arrived at the point it did until a little over a half hour later—at around 0810.

It is not known why *Tone* 4 shortened its course. It was not instructed to do so, and there is no recorded explanation by its crew after they returned. As none of the crew survived the war, it will remain a mystery. It has been suggested by Yoshiji Doi, who was a member of the staff in charge of the search planes on the cruiser *Tone*, that it was accidental. He speculates that *Tone* 4, because it was launched late, had increased its speed to 150 knots so as to reach the end of its outbound path at the originally scheduled time. But, because of a miscalibration of its air speed indicator, it was actually flying at a much lower speed—120 to 130 knots—than assumed by its pilot. Thus, under this theory, when it turned north on its dogleg, the pilot thought he had flown 300 miles, but actually had flown only about 250 miles.[25]

Although this is an interesting theory by someone who was at the scene, I must reject it on the basis of the known record. Had the crew of *Tone* 4 thought they were 50–60 miles further east than they actually were, then they would have reported the position of the American fleet that much further east of its actual position. But they did not. Although the position of the American fleet as reported by *Tone* 4 was in error by about 55 miles, this error was almost entirely on the north-south axis, not the east-west one. The reported and actual positions were, in fact, about the same number of degrees east of the Mobile Force (see Search & Course Chart). Thus, while the crew of *Tone* 4 obviously did not know how far north of Midway the American fleet was (being only about 185 miles north instead of the 240 they reported) they judged its position on the east-west axis fairly accurately. From this it can be inferred that their air speed indicator was fairly accurate—giving them a pretty good estimate of how far east they were at the time of the sighting.

From this I conclude that the crew of *Tone* 4 intentionally shortened its eastward outbound course. They probably turned north on their dogleg at exactly the time (a little before 0700) that they would have done had they been launched on time at 0430. Thus, it now appears that this much-maligned crew of *Tone* undertook a decision that actually exhibited bold and risky initiative. In any case, whether the shortened course was accidental—as Doi has theorized—or intentional, it appears that the pilot of *Tone* 4 was, indeed, trying to make up for lost time. The premature turn north that resulted in the discovery of the American fleet at 0728 almost certainly would not have happened had *Tone* 4 been launched on time. Ironically, then, the late launch of *Tone* 4—rather than being the cause of a belated discovery of the American fleet as is widely assumed—actually resulted in a fortuitous early discovery. It was the only lucky break Nagumo got that morning. But, alas for the Japanese, he was not able to take advantage of it.

NATURE OF THE DECISION TO REARM

The text of Nagumo's infamous rearming order at 0715 is ambiguous, and its meaning has long been in dispute. The only record of it is in Nagumo's Official Report. All it says is: "Planes in second attack wave stand by to carry out attack today. Re-equip yourselves with bombs."[26] It does not say when that attack will be launched—whether before or after the first wave has been landed. Nor does it specify the types of planes to be reequipped—whether the dive-bombers were to be rearmed with land bombs along with the torpedo planes. The ambiguity is perpetuated by the order from Nagumo recorded thirty minutes later in the Official Report countermanding the rearming order. It says: "Prepare to carry out attacks on enemy fleet units. Leave torpedoes on those attack planes which have not as yet been changed to bombs." This has led some commentators to conclude that only the torpedo planes were rearmed pursuant to the 0715 order.[27]

I conclude, based primarily on the authority of Senshi Sosho—and supported by the testimony from the veterans—that the dive-bombers on *Hiryu* and *Soryu* were rearmed with land bombs, along with the torpedo planes on *Akagi* and *Kaga*. I believe that, despite the vagueness of his order, Nagumo intended the dive-bombers to be included, but left the responsibility for implementing the rearming order on *Hiryu* and *Soryu* to the commander of the Second Carrier Division—Tamon Yamaguchi. This conclusion is also supported by the simple observation that it would have been irrational not to have attacked Midway with the dive-bombers, as dive-bombers were especially effective for destroying airplanes on the ground—one of the main purposes of the second strike. And to be effective for this purpose, they had to be rearmed with high-explosive land bombs.

I also conclude that Nagumo intended the second-strike planes to be launched before the first wave back from Midway was landed. This is because it would have been foolhardy to disable his standby torpedo planes before the search was completed unless they could be rearmed and launched before the first wave was landed. Although I have found that Nagumo and his staff made some serious errors of judgment that contributed to their defeat, I have seen no credible evidence that they were stupid. (However, a less charitable view was expressed by Katutaro Akimoto, a torpedo mechanic on *Akagi*, who opined that he doubted that the "honchos" in headquarters had any idea how long the rearming operation would take when they made the decision to rearm, or whether the second strike on Midway could be launched before the first-strike planes returned. "That is why we lost the battle.")[28]

REASONABLENESS OF THE DECISION TO REARM

The decision to rearm for a second strike on Midway has generally been deemed a reasonable one by most commentators in the United States as well as in Japan—this, despite the fact that Yamamoto was appalled when he learned that Nagumo had disobeyed his "standing order" by rearming the second-wave torpedo planes.[29] Yet, considering that it was the most fateful decision of the battle, there has been surprising little analysis devoted to it. Even Senshi Sosho, which deals extensively with the decision to countermand the rearming order and especially the decision to postpone the attack, devotes little comment to it.

In retrospect, it was the most ironical decision made by Nagumo. The main purpose of it was to eliminate the Midway-based air power, but most of that air power had already been destroyed, or soon would be, without a second strike. The Midway fighters had been destroyed in the first attack (of the twenty-six that saw action only four remained serviceable), and most of the ten Midway torpedo bombers were destroyed in the first attack from Midway (none remained serviceable). Most of the dive-bombers yet to attack were later destroyed (only eleven of the twenty-seven remained serviceable). Even the PBY flying boats used for reconnaissance were being diverted out of the area. Only the B-17s, yet to attack, were left largely unscathed, and they were virtually worthless against moving ships.

However, Nagumo did not know any of this at 0715, and had to assume that Midway-based air power remained a threat. Still, serious questions are raised concerning the timing of the decision and whether there were any alternatives available to Nagumo that would have accomplished the main purposes of a second strike on Midway without forfeiting the ability to respond to the sudden appearance of American carriers.

COULD NAGUMO HAVE WAITED UNTIL
THE SEARCH WAS CLOSER TO COMPLETION?
Even if it is conceded that the decision to rearm for a second strike was a reasonable one, a question that still lingers is why the rearming had to begin at 0715;
why Nagumo could not have waited at least a few more minutes until all the
search planes—including *Tone* 4—had completed their scheduled outbound
courses. With the benefit of hindsight we know that *Tone* 4 discovered the
American fleet at 0728 (but only because the pilot of *Tone* 4 shortened its
course). But Nagumo knew none of this. However, Nagumo did know that
Tone 4 had not been launched until 0500 and, thus, would not reach the end of
its scheduled search line until 0730. Why did Nagumo not wait until then? Actually, there was a good reason for not waiting—even until 0730.

It turns out that at 0715 Nagumo faced serious time constraints: for a second
strike to reach Midway after the American planes had returned and landed, but
before they could be refueled and rearmed for another take off, the second
wave had to be launched before the first wave back from Midway was landed. If
the second wave was not launched before then, it could not be launched until
about 1000[30]—and would not reach Midway until after 1100—making it very
unlikely that the American planes would be caught on the ground.[31] The dive-
bombers in the first wave were due back around 0830 and had to begin landing
on *Akagi* and *Kaga* before 0900 or they would start running out of fuel. Therefore, the second wave had to be launched by 0900 at the latest.

The problem was that it would take at least one and one-half hours to change
the torpedo planes on *Akagi* and *Kaga* from torpedoes to 800-kilogram land
bombs.[32] This is a half-hour longer for the operation than the one hour given by
most commentators. (One hour was the time it usually took to arm a squadron
of *empty* torpedo planes, which was the usual situation. Rearming from torpedoes to land bombs was highly unusual and, in fact, had been done only once
before—in the Indian Ocean campaign.) Added to this one hour and thirty
minutes was the time it would take to raise the last rearmed plane back up to
the flight deck, spot it for launch, and warm up its engine—at least another ten
minutes. (The raising, spotting, and warming up for most of the planes could
be done while the last planes were being rearmed.) Thus, for a launch to begin
by 0900, the rearming operation had to begin by 0715, at the latest. Even this
would be an extremely tight fit—especially if the carriers came under further
attacks—and would be impossible unless the 800-kilogram land bombs had already been brought up from the magazines to the hangar decks of *Akagi* and
Kaga.

One would expect that, at 0715, Nagumo and his staff had been engaging in
some sort of risk-benefit analysis since receiving Tomonaga's admonition for a
second strike on Midway at 0705. In such a case, the advantages of beginning
the rearming operation immediately would have been balanced against the

likelihood of American carriers being discovered after the rearming operation began. We have seen why Nagumo thought a second strike against Midway was necessary (even though it turned out to be much less urgent than he thought). We have also seen that such a strike would have to be launched by 0900 to accomplish its purpose—which would require that the rearming begin immediately. (Indeed, if the strike could not be launched before the first wave back from Midway had to be landed—by around 0900 at the latest—there would be virtually nothing to be gained by beginning the rearming of the torpedo planes before the search was closer to completion. Thus, it is probably fair to say that the very rationality of the decision to rearm at 0715 hinged on a launch being possible before the first wave landed.)

The other side of the equation was the likelihood of American carriers being discovered after the rearming operation was underway. We have seen that when the search effort began, Nagumo believed that it was very unlikely that American carriers were in the area. At 0715, Nagumo's original belief was no doubt reinforced by the fact that no American ships had been found during the two and one-half hours since the search began. Moreover, all but one of the search planes had completed their outbound search lines. The search plane that had not completed its outbound line was, of course, *Tone* 4. As it had not been launched until 0500, it could only have flown only about 270 miles of its easterly path by 0715, and would not reach the end of its *scheduled* line until 0730. Should Nagumo have waited another fifteen minutes—until *Tone* 4 completed the last 30 miles of its search line before rearming?

Actually, it is easy to see that from Nagumo's perspective at 0715, there was little to be gained by waiting even another fifteen minutes. American carriers beyond 250 miles from the Mobile Force presented little immediate threat. The reason for this is that they would be too far away to launch an escorted, coordinated attack against the Mobile Force with planes capable of returning to their carriers. The combat radius of the American Wildcat fighter was considered by Nagumo's staff to be less than 200 miles.[33] (And that of the Devastator torpedo bomber was even less.) Therefore, while Dauntless dive-bombers could attack and return from more than 250 miles, it was believed that without fighter escorts to protect them, the dive-bombers would be extremely vulnerable and could be easily repelled by the air defense Zeros of the Mobile Force. Thus, if a second strike were to be made at all, the decision to begin the rearming operation immediately at 0715 appears to have been an easy one to make.

WERE THERE ALTERNATIVES?
If launching a second strike on Midway and maintaining the capability to attack American carriers were mutually exclusive options—as most commentators have assumed—I would conclude that Nagumo's decision to rearm at 0715 was a reasonable one under the circumstances. However, I suggest that they

were not mutually exclusive options—Nagumo could have done both. This is because a reasonably effective second strike could have been made against Midway with just dive-bombers rearmed with land bombs—along with Zero fighters. (It should be noted that in the first-wave attack at Pearl Harbor the airfields were attacked by only dive-bombers and Zeros; almost all the aircraft destroyed on the ground at Hawaii were hit in that attack.) The second-wave torpedo planes were not necessary; they could have remained armed with torpedoes.

This suggested alternative may seem radical, and it has not been mentioned in any of the leading accounts of the battle. But it seems a reasonable solution to Nagumo's dilemma at 0715. On the one hand, he was under a standing order from Yamamoto to keep his second-wave torpedo planes in a state of readiness to attack any American carriers that might be discovered. His search operation was not yet completed, and it clearly remained possible that American carriers would be discovered—within striking distance of the Mobile Force—by a search plane on its return course. Rearming the torpedo planes with land bombs would incapacitate them for a considerable period and was not quickly reversible if American carriers suddenly appeared. On the other hand, a second strike on Midway seemed necessary, and for it to be effective it had to be launched before the first wave back from Midway was landed. Dive-bombers could quickly be rearmed with land bombs—much more quickly than torpedo planes as we will see—and the armament could be quickly reversed if need be. Moreover, they could be launched well before the first wave had to be landed.

Given the objectives of the second strike, is this "dive-bombers and Zeros only" option one that would make sense from Nagumo's perspective at 0715, or is it just another "20–20 hindsight" observation? According to the accounts by Nagumo's staff officers who survived the war, there were several purposes of a second strike, but the paramount one was to destroy the American Midway-based airplanes on the ground after they returned from their first attack on the Mobile Force. This could clearly have been done with dive-bombing and strafing by Zeros (and, in fact, done better than by bombing from high level by torpedo planes). Other stated targets were the dual-purpose gun emplacements and the runways. The gun batteries also could have been taken out with dive-bombers.

Only the runways could not have been effectively damaged by the smaller bombs the dive-bombers carried. The 805-kilogram bombs, which could be carried only by the torpedo planes, would have been required to effectively "crater" the runways. (Nagumo's staff appear, however, to have been somewhat ambivalent about destroying the runways at Midway. While they wanted to deprive the Americans of their use, and were especially concerned that Midway's air strength might be reinforced by bombers flown in from Hawaii, they also hoped to use the runways themselves after Midway was captured.) But even under the "dive-bombers and Zeros only" option, if it later became clear that torpedo planes were required to knock out the runways they could be sent in a third strike made up from first-wave planes rearmed after their return from Midway. (Once Midway's aircraft were destroyed there would be no urgency to destroy the runways right away.)

Although a scaled-down attack of this kind would not have been quite as effective as a full-scale attack that included the torpedo planes, preparing for it would have carried almost no risk for Nagumo. The rearming of the thirty-six dive-bombers on *Hiryu* and *Soryu* with land bombs was a quickly reversible procedure, and even if there would not be time to switch the dive-bombers back to armor-piercing bombs, land bombs were a highly effective weapon against aircraft carriers. (Indeed, American dive-bombers later destroyed the Japanese carriers with what were essentially land bombs.) By contrast, once torpedoes were removed from the torpedo planes it was a very time-consuming procedure to change back to torpedoes—and, as we will see, close to impossible to do it while the carriers were under attack.

Thus, the nub of the case against rearming the torpedo planes is that the decision was, essentially, irreversible in the event American carriers appeared on the scene. Moreover, if the torpedo planes could not be changed back in time, land bombs on torpedo planes were practically worthless against moving ships; Kate torpedo planes could not do dive-bombing, and it was next to impossible to hit a fast-moving target with horizontal or glide bombing. I conclude, therefore, that the fatal blunder by Nagumo was not his decision to rearm for a second strike on Midway at 0715, but rather his decision to include the torpedo planes.

WHY WAS A LESS RISKY OPTION NOT TAKEN?

It does not appear that Nagumo considered the option of making the second strike with just dive-bombers and Zeros. Had it been necessary to make the decision immediately at 0715, this might be understandable, especially in view of the fact that he was undergoing the first attack from Midway at that time. But we now know that he had been considering the second strike since 0520. I was unable to get a satisfactory explanation from the veterans for why it was believed necessary to use torpedo planes for the second strike. The best reason ventured was the following.

The doctrine of coordinated attack—using all three types of carrier aircraft—was so deeply ingrained in the Japanese carrier commanders that where there was time to prepare such an attack, nothing less would be considered. (This tactic of using one's full strength in a single stroke has its basis in a form of swordplay known as *Kinshicho-Oken*.)[34] A coordinated attack had the obvious and proven advantages of being more effective and incurring fewer losses. An attack with torpedo planes as well as dive-bombers was more effective because some targets (such as the runway at Midway) were more likely to be destroyed by 800-

kilogram bombs carried by the torpedo planes, while others (such as planes on the ground) were more likely to be destroyed by 250-kilogram bombs delivered accurately from low altitude by dive-bombers. Moreover, these superior results could be achieved with fewer losses to the attacking planes. This is because in an attack from different altitudes, defenses from both fighter planes and anti-aircraft ground fire were divided and confused, making them less efficient. (And, as we will see later, minimizing pilot losses was probably a higher priority for the Japanese than for the Americans because of their more limited pool of carrier plane pilots.)

The virtues of a coordinated attack, as a general proposition, are undeniable. But in the special circumstances pertaining to Midway at 0715—where Nagumo's first priority was supposed to be the destruction of the American carrier fleet—the superiority of an attack that included torpedo planes over one using just dive-bombers and Zeros seems marginal. And as that added margin was gained at the cost of incapacitating the Mobile Force against a possible American carrier threat for a considerable length of time after 0715, it seems fair to criticize Nagumo's decision even with the benefit of hindsight.

The risk Nagumo took is what I would characterize as a "reverse lottery" gamble: instead of risking a little for a chance of gaining a lot, he risked a great deal in order to gain very little. The additional margin of effectiveness he gained by rearming the torpedo planes seems slight when compared with what could have been had for minimal risk by rearming only the dive-bombers. (There is reason to believe that Yamaguchi—had the decision been his—would have opted for a scaled-down second strike that would have preserved the Mobile Force's capability to quickly respond to any American carrier threat that might emerge: in addition to his being more apprehensive of American carriers being in the area than was Nagumo, we will see that at 0830—after an American carrier had been identified—he was willing to abandon preparations for a coordinated attack in favor of sending just the dive-bombers to attack the carrier.)[35]

Why, then, did Nagumo not consider a less risky option? There seem to be only two explanations for why he opted to commit everything he had to the second strike: The first is that he totally discounted the possibility of American carriers being in the area, in which case he did not acknowledge any risk. This is the explanation accepted by most commentators, and was given by Nagumo himself.[36]

The other explanation, more plausible to me, is that even if he had some nagging doubts as of 0715 about whether the Americans had been tipped off—the apparent readiness of Midway to engage his forces, and the discovery and attack on the Transport Group the day before must have bothered him—Nagumo was simply loath to deviate from the tried and trusted doctrine of coordinated attack. The coordinated attack was a specialty of the Japanese navy carrier forces, and it had served them well. Nagumo may, in a sense, have been a victim not of "victory disease"—as has been alleged—but of his own rigid professionalism.

There is one last possibility: that Nagumo opted for a bold, all-out second strike because he was still smarting from criticism that he had been too conservative at Pearl Harbor. There he had faced a similar dilemma when he was urged by some of his subordinates to make a third strike to knock out the oil tank farms and dry docks at Pearl Harbor. He had rejected this on the ground that American carriers might be in the area, posing a threat to his Mobile Force. He had thought it more prudent to retire from Pearl Harbor to avoid detection, and to arm his carrier attack planes with antiship weapons in case his search planes located those carriers. As it turned out, those carriers never appeared, and the failure to destroy the oil tank farms and other facilities at Pearl Harbor later caused enormous grief to the Japanese navy. At 0715, Nagumo may have feared that if he did not hit Midway with everything he had in an attempt to finish it off, he would look foolish if no American carriers appeared and then his Mobile Force or the invasion force later sustained damage from Midway-based air power.

*   *   *

Nagumo's decision at 0715 to rearm his standby torpedo planes was an improvident gamble. But he and his staff were not alone to blame. As we saw in the last chapter, he did not receive much help from Yamamoto before the day of the battle. He did not get crucial intelligence that would have helped him better assess the American carrier threat. Had he known what Yamamoto knew, Nagumo might have made a very different decision at 0715. He later lamented in his Official Report, "we had practically no intelligence concerning the enemy. We never knew to the end where or how many enemy carriers there were. In other words, we participated in this operation with meager training and without knowing the enemy."[37]

The bitterness here is palpable. One cannot help feeling some sympathy for poor Nagumo. He got most of the blame for the debacle at Midway—largely because of his decision to rearm—but he had been badly let down by Yamamoto. Two years later at Saipan—after the island had fallen to the Americans, when it was clear that Japan would lose the war—he unsheathed his sword and committed suicide.

EXECUTION OF THE REARMING ORDER

At 0715, when the order to rearm for a second strike on Midway was issued by Nagumo, the Mobile Force was under attack by four torpedo-carrying B-26s from Midway. All the carriers were maneuvering radically at high speed to avoid torpedoes. The last torpedo from that attack was dropped at 0715, but it probably took several minutes for the carriers to straighten out and slow down so torpedoes could safely be removed from the torpedo planes in the hangars of *Akagi* and *Kaga*. Thus, the rearming operation for the torpedo planes probably did not begin until around 0720.

PROCEDURES FOR REARMING TORPEDO PLANES[*]

We have seen that it took one and one-half hours—not one hour as has been generally assumed—to change a squadron of eighteen torpedo planes from torpedoes to 800-kilogram land bombs (assuming that the planes and bombs were already in the hangars). As for how many torpedo planes had to be rearmed, there were seventeen torpedo planes on *Akagi* and twenty-six on *Kaga* after the first wave departed (with one plane from each squadron having been used for search patrol). However, it appears that only eighteen of *Kaga*'s planes had been armed with torpedoes—with the remaining eight, with less experienced crews, serving as a reserve unarmed with any weapons.[38]

If the torpedo planes were spotted on the flight decks of *Akagi* and *Kaga* at 0715, as conventionally assumed, the first step in the rearming procedure would be to strike them below to the hangars.[39] It is more likely, however—as discussed earlier—that the torpedo planes had already been stricken below in order to land Zeros on combat air patrol for reservicing just prior to the American torpedo bomber attacks from Midway. Assuming that the torpedo planes were already in the hangars at 0715, the following scenario for rearming them can be constructed from the testimony of the veterans involved in the procedure.[40]

The first step was to roll the heavy weapons "carrier cars" to the planes and position them under the torpedoes. There were double jacks on the carrier cars, which were cranked up to the torpedo by hand (there being no motors to assist the operation). A torpedo mechanic disarmed the torpedo (by removing its detonator) and then disengaged it from its release mechanism on the belly of the plane. The torpedo was then cranked down to the bed of the carrier car. These operations took five to ten minutes—let us say seven minutes. The loaded carrier car was then rolled to the heavy weapons rack where the torpedo was deposited. This required at least five men to manipulate the torpedo off the carrier car—as the Type 91 aerial torpedo weighed 1,872 pounds—and took about five minutes.

These operations were performed neither on all the planes in the squadron simultaneously nor on them one at a time, as has respectively been stated by various commentators. Rather, the torpedo planes were rearmed in shifts—by *chutais* (divisions) of probably six planes on *Akagi* and possibly nine on *Kaga*. There were only enough heavy weapons carrier cars and weapons mechanics on those carriers to rearm a division of torpedo planes simultaneously.[41] (*Kaga*,

---

[*]A summary of this procedure was given in chapter 1, but here more detail is called for in order to fix the chronology during this crucial period.

with its larger squadron of twenty-seven planes, had more carrier cars and weapons mechanics than *Akagi*.) Assuming that six planes could be processed at a
time on *Akagi*, and nine at a time on *Kaga*, the torpedoes on the first *chutai* of
planes in each squadron were removed at about 0727 and deposited on the heavy
weapons rack by about 0732. (This assumes that the operation began at 0720,
when the American torpedo attacks were over.)

After a torpedo was removed, but before a bomb could be attached, it was
necessary to change the "launcher."[42] This was the ribbed rack on the belly of
the plane to which torpedoes or bombs were attached. (Japanese torpedoes
were long and slender, but 800-kilogram land bombs were short and stubby.)
The torpedo launcher had to be unbolted and replaced by a bomb launcher,
a procedure that took a surprisingly long time—at least twenty minutes, and
perhaps as long as thirty minutes.[43] It was done by two engine-body mechanics—weapons mechanics were not required—so the procedure could begin as
soon as the torpedo was removed (which would be at around 0727 under this
scenario). Changing the launchers was the most time-consuming procedure
in the entire rearming operation—accounting for a substantial portion of the
total one and a half hours required for the operation. By about 0742 the torpedo launchers would have been removed from the planes in the first division,
and work to install the bomb launchers would have then proceeded.

In the meantime, after the torpedoes removed from the first division had
been deposited on the heavy weapons rack at about 0732 (they were not taken
to the torpedo magazine on this occasion) the carrier cars were used to remove
the torpedoes from the second division. It took about one minute to roll the
empty carrier cars to the planes, and about twelve minutes to remove the torpedoes, crank them down, and cart them to the heavy weapons rack. This would
have been done by around 0745. As the bomb launchers would not have yet
been installed on the first division planes, the carrier cars were then most likely
used to remove the torpedoes from the third division of planes on *Akagi*. (On
Kaga, if torpedoes were removed from only eighteen planes, nine at a time,
800-kilogram bombs could have been loaded onto the carrier cars at this time.)

According to the standard scenario of Japanese carrier operations at Midway,
as discussed in chapter 1, things would have come to an abrupt halt in the hangar decks of *Akagi* and *Kaga* at this time—0745. That is when Nagumo supposedly issued his order countermanding the rearming operation after learning of
the discovery of the American task force by *Tone* 4. But as will be seen in the
next chapter, Nagumo most probably did not learn of the presence of American
ships until about 0800, and thus his countermand order would not have been
given until shortly after that time. That being the case, the rearming operation
would have continued past 0745. After the torpedoes were removed from the
second division of planes on *Akagi* and deposited on the heavy weapons rack
at 0745, the torpedoes from the third, and last, division on *Akagi* would have

been removed and deposited on the rack about thirteen minutes later, at around 0758.

Thus, at this time—around 0800—all the torpedoes would have been removed from *Akagi*'s torpedo planes (probably earlier on *Kaga*), the launchers would have been changed for bombs on the first division, and the carrier cars and weapons mechanics would have been available to begin installing the land bombs on *Akagi*'s six first-division planes.[44] The 800-kilogram land bombs were already in the hangars of *Akagi* and *Kaga* when the order to rearm was given (having been brought up from the magazines pursuant to Nagumo's precautionary order at 0520). But, as we will see in the next chapter, only a few, if any, land bombs ever got installed on any of *Akagi*'s torpedo planes—though as many as nine may have got put on *Kaga*'s.

PROCEDURE FOR REARMING DIVE-BOMBERS

As already mentioned, the rearming of the dive-bombers on *Hiryu* and *Soryu* was a much easier and quicker operation than for the torpedo planes. This probably explains why there is no reference to dive-bombers in Nagumo's 0715 rearming order—or in the subsequent order countermanding the rearming operation. It is even possible that the dive-bombers were not even armed with antiship bombs—or any other bombs—at 0715. Bombs were often installed on the flight deck during spotting and engine warm-up operations just before launch.[45] However, the morning of June 4 was a special case, and it appears (from the testimony of the veterans) that on that morning they had, in fact, been armed with antiship bombs. Yamaguchi was much more concerned than Nagumo about the possibility of American carriers being in the area, so it seems likely that he would have ensured that his standby dive-bombers were in the highest possible state of readiness. Thus, the dive-bombers had to be changed from antiship bombs (armor-piercing) to land bombs after Nagumo's order—but still, it was a fairly simple process compared with the rearming of torpedo planes.

It took only about thirty minutes to rearm the dive-bombers—a third the time required for the torpedo planes. There were several reasons for this. Only two-thirds had to be rearmed, as one-third already had land bombs on. (As previously explained, even when dive-bombers were armed for ships, some were equipped with high-explosive instant-detonation—"land"—bombs to knock out AA gun batteries and, against aircraft carriers, to blast holes in wooden flight decks.) It was not necessary to change launchers as the same launcher accommodated both types of bombs. Also, the smaller bombs (at 250 kilograms—less than a third the weight of torpedoes or 800-kilogram bombs) were more easily moved and manipulated into position. And dive-bombers could be rearmed on the flight decks as well as in the hangars, saving elevator time.

As for where the dive-bombers were rearmed on this occasion, the recollections of the veterans are a bit murky. We have seen that the torpedo planes on *Akagi* and *Kaga* were already in the hangars at 0715 when Nagumo's rearming order was issued; they had been stricken below before 0700 to clear the flight decks for combat air patrol operations. But as for the dive-bombers on *Hiryu* and *Soryu*, things appear more complicated. It is known that *Hiryu* landed two Zeros at about the same time *Akagi* landed three—at around 0700 (though none were landed on *Soryu* until 0730). Accordingly, one might assume that any dive-bombers on the flight decks of *Hiryu*, and probably *Soryu* as well, would also have been lowered to the hangars before that time. However, it appears from the testimony of the veterans from those carriers involved with rearming the dive-bombers that all the dive-bombers had been spotted on the flight decks after the Midway strike force departed—and that only *half* the dive-bombers (nine) on each carrier had been lowered to the hangars prior to Nagumo's 0715 rearming order. Those dive-bombers were rearmed in the hangars, but the remaining half—according to the weight of the testimony—remained on the flight decks and were rearmed there.[46]

But if half the dive-bombers remained on the flight decks of *Hiryu* and *Soryu*, how were the two Zeros landed on *Hiryu* at 0700? Those landings were accommodated by moving the *Hiryu* dive-bombers forward beyond the crash barrier.[47] This would not have been practical for all eighteen dive-bombers, but could be done with only nine of them. It would have been inconvenient, but it seems credible that the aggressive Yamaguchi would have tolerated this inconvenience for the trade-off of being able to make launches more quickly should the need suddenly arise, as only half his dive-bombers would have to be raised from the hangars and spotted.

As for the rearming schedule with the dive-bombers: When the rearming order was given at 0715, the six planes in the hangar with armor-piercing bombs were probably rearmed first. Four men were required to manhandle the 550-pound bombs, so there were only enough mechanics to rearm half the squadron at a time. After the bomb carts were positioned under the bombers, the bombs were defused, detached from the launcher, and manually lowered to the carts. This took less than five minutes. The bombs were then hauled to a rack, deposited, and replaced by high-explosive land bombs—which were then hauled back to the planes. This took about another five minutes. (The 242-kilogram land bombs appear to have already been in the hangar—as with the 800-kilogram bombs on *Akagi* and *Kaga*; they probably had also been brought up from the magazine after Nagumo had issued his precautionary order at 0520.) The land bombs were manually lifted and attached to the launcher, which took about another five minutes. The fuse was then armed, and fine adjustments made to ensure proper clearances, which took only about another two to three minutes. While this last procedure was being done the bomb carts were used to take the remaining bombs up to the flight deck by elevator.

Thus, by around 0730, the half-squadrons of dive-bombers in the hangars of the two carriers were rearmed, and the bomb carts and rearming crews were on the flight decks ready to repeat the same procedures on the remaining half of the squadrons. However, at 0730, there was an interruption: *Soryu* landed six Zeros on CAP (and *Hiryu* may have landed a couple), which would have required that the dive-bombers be moved forward. This would have caused a delay of several minutes until the bombers could be moved back, after some jockeying to get the Zeros around them to their forward elevator. But, it appears that soon after 0745 all the dive-bombers on *Hiryu* and *Soryu* had been rearmed with land bombs. Half were on the flight decks; the other half remained in the hangars.

However, soon after the dive-bombers on the flight decks were rearmed, American dive-bombers from Midway were spotted approaching the Mobile Force shortly before 0800. At about this time it appears that even the aggressive Yamaguchi finally relented and, to free up his flight decks for unfettered CAP operations, began striking below the nine Vals still on the flight decks of each of his carriers.[48]

*   *   *

When Nagumo decided—at 0715—to rearm his attack planes for a second strike on Midway, he made one of the greatest tactical gambles in naval history. He bet that no American carriers were in the area. In actual fact, even before his rearming operation commenced, at 0705 Raymond Spruance was beginning his launch operations on *Enterprise* and *Hornet*. By the time his launch was completed shortly after 0800, and the American carrier bombers began heading for the Mobile Force, Nagumo's own carrier bombers and torpedo planes had been stripped of their antiship weapons. The dive-bombers, as we have seen, could be fairly quickly switched back to armor-piercing bombs. But by 0800, the rearming operation on the torpedo planes had reached the point where it was no longer quickly reversible. Nagumo had become, in Commodore Richard Bates's words, "a victim of the mechanics of carrier operations."

CHAPTER FIVE

GAMBLE LOST

L ESS THAN FIFTEEN MINUTES after Nagumo gave the order to rearm his standby torpedo planes and dive-bombers for a second strike on Midway, the *Tone* 4 search plane discovered the American fleet. As we have seen, this discovery was fortuitous and could not have been made by *Tone* 4 this early had it not shortened its scheduled course substantially. It radioed its report at 0728, which said "Sight what appears to be 10 enemy surface ships, in position bearing 10 degrees distance 240 miles from Midway. Course 150 degrees, speed over 20 knots." Nagumo had gambled everything on his belief that no American carriers were in the Midway area. Although he would not know it for a while, he had lost his gamble.

WHEN DID NAGUMO RECEIVE
THE SIGHTING REPORT?

The question that has baffled commentators on the battle from Morison's time to the present is when did Nagumo receive this report. Its resolution provides the key to cracking the most puzzling mystery of Midway: why was Nagumo unable to get a strike force launched before his carriers were bombed at around 1025? Three different times for receipt by Nagumo have been suggested by the authorities: 0728, 0740, and 0800.[1] The determination of what time it was is essential not only for understanding the armament status of Nagumo's torpedo planes at the crucial times, such as 0830 and 1000—when a strike force could have been launched—but also for evaluating the reasonableness of Nagumo's response to the sighting report: whether he was indecisive and "dithering" as often charged, or was actually appropriately responsive. Had he received it almost immediately at 0728–0730, as the earliest commentators assumed, there would be no good excuse for failing to quickly reverse the rearming operation. As very little progress would have been made in rearming the torpedo planes by that time, the operation would have been easily and quickly reversible.

But if he received the sighting report at around 0740—as is widely assumed— then his ability to quickly reverse the rearming procedure is more problematic. However, it is still likely that the torpedoes would have been restored to the torpedo planes by around 0920—even with all the disruptions caused by American attacks between 0800 and 0830. If, on the other hand, he did not receive the sighting report until about 0800—as he claimed—his hands would then have been tied; as seen in the last chapter, all the torpedoes would have been removed from the torpedo planes, and work to reattach them could not have begun in earnest until the American attacks from Midway were over after 0830. Then, because of the disruptions caused by the operations to land the Midway strike force and, especially, by the American carrier-launched torpedo bomber attacks between 0930 and 1000, it would have been next to impossible, as we will see, for those torpedoes to have been restored to all the torpedo planes before 1000. This would mean that those planes could not be spotted on the flight decks, let alone launched, before Nagumo's carriers were bombed at 1025.

It is now certain that Nagumo did not receive the sighting report directly from *Tone* 4 at 0728. *Akagi*'s radio was not, at that time, tuned to the frequency used by the search planes. The report was sent by *Tone* 4 in code and received by its mother ship—the cruiser *Tone*. It was then deciphered and relayed to *Akagi* by visual signals. Accordingly, most authorities conclude that Nagumo received it around 0740. This conclusion is based primarily on inferences drawn from certain entries in the composite log of the Official Report: the first is an order from Nagumo, logged at 0745, countermanding the rearming operation; the second is an order, logged at 0747, to *Tone* 4 to "ascertain ship types." Of course, neither of these orders would make sense if Nagumo had not already received the sighting report. Thus, Nagumo's claim in the narrative portion of the Official Report that the sighting report was not received until about 0800 has generally been disregarded. As Morison observed, back in 1949, this statement was "belied" by the record of the countermand order at 0745.[2] There is other circumstantial evidence—some of a statistical nature—that has been cited by American commentators in support for a pre-0745 receipt time: an analysis of other radio messages noted in the composite message log of the Official Report—where both the times of transmission and receipt are indicated—shows that the average interval is only about ten minutes. Indeed, a thirty-minute delay in getting the *Tone* 4 sighting report to Nagumo does, at first blush, seem extreme.

Despite this apparently compelling circumstantial evidence of a pre-0745 receipt time, especially the countermand order, we still have Nagumo's claim in his Official Report that the sighting report was not delivered until "about 0800." This is not mentioned in a merely cursory manner, or in a general rounded-off sort of way. It is stated (twice) very explicitly; Nagumo goes on to complain that the delay in getting the report to him "greatly affected our subsequent attack preparations."[3] It is curious that such an explicit complaint was disregarded by early American commentators such as Morison. One would think that it would have at least raised a question about the reliability of the log entries indicating a pre-0745 receipt time for the report. Perhaps his complaint was deemed self-serving—as just providing an excuse for his failure to respond quickly to the unexpected American carrier threat. However, had that been his purpose, it would seem that he would have altered the times given in the composite message log—of his *own* battle report—for his countermand order and request to *Tone* 4 for details of "ship types" so they would not be inconsistent with his claim of an 0800 receipt time. As we will see, however, there are reasons why entries in the composite log inconsistent with statements in the narrative of his Official Report would not have been of particular concern to him.

Before getting into my evaluation of those conflicting entries in the composite log, it should be noted that the first report on the Battle of Midway written by Japanese officers after the war (Japanese Monograph No. 93—"Midway Operations May–June 1942")[4] says that the sighting report was received at about 0800 and that at 0800 a request for details as to the type of ships discovered was sent to *Tone* 4. Although the monograph is very detailed and tracks the Official Report very closely, it does not mention any countermand order being issued, and certainly none being given before 0800. It should also be noted that the original book by Fuchida and Okumiya, *Midway: The Battle That Doomed Japan*, published in Japan in 1951, also states that the sighting report was received by Nagumo at 0800.[5] This may be surprising to those familiar with only the English-language literature on the battle; the Fuchida book is generally cited in support of an 0740 receipt time.

However, as earlier mentioned, when this book was translated into English, and edited by Roger Pineau and Clarke K. Kawakami, the 0800 receipt time was omitted and an editors' note was added to point out that Nagumo's claim of an 0800 time "is clearly shown to be inaccurate" by the two entries in the composite log indicating a pre-0745 receipt time.[6] (Pineau had assisted Morison with the writing of the chapters on the Battle of Midway in volume 4 of his *History of United States Naval Operations in World War II*, first published in 1949. He probably meant only to "correct" what he believed was an obvious

error—in view of Morison's observation.) The Fuchida-Pineau book was published in 1955, and, as it was the first full-length account of the Battle of Midway
made available to the American public—and one written by Japanese naval
officers—it was tremendously influential. It was the principal source of the
American standard scenario of the battle.

Thus, the notion of a pre-0745 receipt time became imbedded in stone and
accepted as irrefutable fact by all subsequent American authorities on the battle.
However, in Japan the issue is not so open and shut: although Senshi Sosho, the
"official" Japanese government history of the war, takes the position that Nagumo received the *Tone* 4 sighting report before 0745—a stance that departed
from previous accounts of the battle—subsequent commentators, most prominently Hisae Sawachi,[7] have disputed Senshi Sosho's chronology of a number
of key events, including time of receipt of the sighting report. Most Japanese
historians of the battle adhere to the 0800 time claimed by Nagumo.[8]

The case for an 0800 receipt time for the sighting report is, indeed, strong:
Nagumo's claim for that time was corroborated after the war by Rear Admiral
Kusaka, Nagumo's chief of staff, and by Minoru Genda, his air officer.[9] They
were on the bridge with Nagumo when the sighting report was received, and, in
view of its shocking nature, it would seem that they would have made particular
notice of the time it came in and remembered it with a fair degree of clarity.
They never wavered in their contention that the sighting report was not received
until 0800. (As late as 1969, when they were interviewed by Tsunoda, who wrote
the Senshi Sosho volume on Midway, they reiterated that contention.)[10]

Even if Nagumo's credibility can be questioned—and he did not survive the
war to be interrogated—no one has challenged the veracity of Kusaka or
Genda (though some have questioned the reliability of their recollections).
Both earned reputations for candor and objectivity with American authorities
who interviewed them. (Genda was generally regarded as the "brains" of Nagumo's staff, and later served a long tenure as head of Japan's Self-Defense Air
Force.) Their insistence on an 0800 receipt time for the sighting report deserves far more credence than has been accorded them.

As I have admitted (with some trepidation), the establishment of an 0800 receipt time is absolutely critical to my new scenario for explaining why Nagumo
could not launch a strike against the American carriers before the destruction
of most of his own carriers at 1025. We have seen that *only* if the rearming operation continued until 0800 would all the torpedoes have been removed from
the torpedo plane squadrons. And in such a case, we will see that they could not
have been restored in time for the torpedo planes to be launched before 1025.
But as American historians have been unanimous for over fifty years in assuming that Nagumo received the sighting report before 0745, I am aware that a
high burden of persuasion is placed on me when I challenge such a venerable
pillar of the standard scenario. This burden will not be an easy one because, like

many events that occurred in the fog of war over sixty years ago, the exact time Nagumo received that crucial report can never be known with certainty. It is possible only to draw inferences from what evidence is available.

THE EVIDENCE FAVORS 0800

We have seen that the clear weight of direct evidence—the eyewitness testimony of Nagumo, Kusaka, and Genda—points to an 0800 receipt time for the *Tone* 4 sighting report. It should stand unless it can be impeached by credible evidence showing that those officers were mistaken. The strongest evidence for a pre-0745 receipt time remains, of course, the countermand order logged at 0745 and the request for identification of ship types logged at 0747. But they have weight to contradict the eyewitness testimony of Nagumo, Kusaka, and Genda only if the times given for those entries in the composite log can be presumed accurate. What if those times were erroneously logged—with the two orders actually having been issued at 0800 or later? As will be seen, there are substantial grounds for doubting the accuracy of those entries.

In fairness, however, to early commentators who placed great stock in the time given for the countermand order, certain telling insights casting doubt on the reliability of entries in the composite log did not come to light until 1971, when Senshi Sosho was published in Japan. The compiler of the composite log of the Official Report, and sections containing the battle charts and tables, was Chuichi Yoshioka, a junior staff officer on Nagumo's flagship *Akagi*. In Senshi Sosho, he explains the difficulties he had in compiling those portions of the report: *Akagi*'s headquarters log (which contained the record of communications to and from Nagumo) had been lost in the battle; the record had to be gleaned from other logs and diaries, including the radio logs of the supporting ships in the Mobile Force. He noted that entries from these various logs were fragmentary and often inconsistent; he cautioned against placing too much reliance on their accuracy.[11]

This means that there is no primary record of the exact text of any of Nagumo's orders, or of the time they were issued. Particularly, the only evidence of the countermand order was in the message log of a ship other than *Akagi*. Early American scholarship on Midway lacked the benefit of Yoshioka's caveat about the reliability of the entries in the composite log, and assumed that the times indicated for certain entries, such as the countermand order, were accurate.

This was an easy assumption to make: in the American translation of the original Official Report the headings for some of the sections were somewhat misleading. What has been referred to as the "composite log" is actually a section entitled "Outline of Events (Excerpts)." However, it is not actually an "outline" of events in the usual meaning of the term—which would indicate a chronological summary of the key events during the battle, with the times indicated assumed to be accurate. Rather, the Japanese words for the title are *Keika gaiyo (Bassui)*, which connotes a description of the evolution of the battle *by excerpts* of radio and signal messages.[12] Accordingly, instead of being an "outline" or summary of events, the entries actually consist of very detailed, minute-by-minute reports compiled from the message logs and other records from several ships in the Mobile Force.

But, as will be seen, there are multiple entries of the same message, logged at different times, and often inconsistent—just as one would expect from such a compilation. This is why I refer to it as a "composite log." All this is understood in Japan, and Japanese scholars are less inclined to assume that the times given in the log entries are the exact time the events referred to actually occurred—especially when they are inconsistent with times given in the narrative portion of the report.[13] This may also explain why Nagumo left those log entries alone—even though some were inconsistent with his statement of an 0800 receipt time for the sighting report. He understood that they were a hodgepodge collected from multiple logs of various ships.

As Nagumo's Official Report is referred to extensively in this work—especially this chapter—it is set out in an appendix, and I invite readers to look at it. It will be noted that while the composite log entries are often redundant and inconsistent, the narrative portion of the report, in contrast, is tightly written and internally consistent. (It was probably written by Nagumo's senior staff officers—Kusaka appears to have had a major role.)[14] Accordingly, the times given in the narrative for key events—such as the time the *Tone* 4 sighting report was received—also deserve much more credence than they have been given.

PROBLEMS WITH THE LOG ENTRIES
In view of the foregoing context, we can now turn to the two log entries cited as "proof" of a pre-0745 receipt time for the sighting report, and assess their reliability as evidence to impeach the direct evidence for an 0800 receipt time. Let us first examine Nagumo's order to *Tone* 4, logged at 0747, for identification of ship types. It is almost identical to an order logged at 0800 to "advise ship types." American commentators have assumed that this was a repeat order, and some have even portrayed Nagumo as being extremely irritated by the lack of response from *Tone* 4.[15] (It is considered to be evidence of lackadaisical performance by the search plane's crew.) *Tone* 4 did not respond to Nagumo's request for details until 0809, when it reported back that the "10 surface ships" consisted of five cruisers and five destroyers. Now, twenty-two minutes—from 0747 to 0809—is a long time to take in responding to an admiral's request in any navy, and by itself casts doubt on whether the request for details was sent as early as 0747. However, a nine-minute turnaround time for such radio messages (from 0800 to 0809) would be more normal.

Could it be that the two orders to *Tone* 4 to identify ship types were one and the same and that the order was actually sent at 0800? If so, this would not be inconsistent with Nagumo's claim that he did not receive the sighting report until around 0800; indeed, it would tend to support that claim.

In the composite log there are numerous examples of messages logged more than once, and in which the earliest of two or more entries is clearly not the correct one. Among them: Nagumo's message to his Mobile Force advising them to "Proceed northward after taking on planes. We plan to contact and destroy the enemy task force." This is logged as having been sent at 0855 and again at 0905. However, in the narrative portion of the report Nagumo states that he sent the message at 0905.[16] Likewise, the report by *Tone* 4 sighting two additional cruisers in the American task force is stated in the narrative as having been received at 0840, but is logged in the composite log at 0830, at 0845, and again at 0850.

An examination of the composite log will reveal about a dozen more examples of the same message logged more than once (which is what one would expect if the entries came from the message logs of several ships). Thus, it is likely that the 0747 entry for Nagumo's order for *Tone* 4 to "ascertain ship types" is erroneous and that the 0800 entry for essentially the same request—which is consistent with Nagumo's claim of an 0800 receipt time—is actually the correct time the order was sent.

It must be noted, however, that a recent book cites to what, at first blush, purports to be independent (and conclusive) evidence that Nagumo sent a message to *Tone* 4 at 0747 in response to the sighting report: "More important, American signals intelligence on Hawaii also noted a return transmission from *Akagi* at 0747, requesting that *Tone* 4 'retain contact.'"[17] The supporting note cites "HYPO Log, p. 500." On closer examination, however, it turns out that the source is not the original HYPO log—or any other log—but rather a *summary* of radio intelligence log entries prepared after the war and released to the public in 1979 (the original logs are unavailable).[18]

Although most of the summaries contain the time the message was sent—taken from the text of the message and in Tokyo time (which is self-authenticating as to time sent)—the summary in question contains no such time. Rather, the only time given for this message summary is in the left margin of the page and appears to have been added when the summary was prepared. Who knows where it came from? It could have been derived from Japanese documents translated after the war—very possibly Nagumo's official report itself![19] Therefore, this citation is not probative as an independent confirmation of an 0747 time for Nagumo's reply to *Tone* 4's sighting report. It still remains likely that there was only one request for details as to ship types made by Nagumo to *Tone* 4 and that it was at 0800—consistent with Nagumo's claim that he did not receive the sighting report until about 0800.

But what about the troublesome order countermanding the rearming operation, which is logged only once and at 0745? There are also several examples in the composite log of events being logged at the wrong time, where the correct time can be established independently by American records of undisputed reliability. In particular, a Japanese search plane on a southeastern course that took it near Midway radioed a report to the Mobile Force—logged at 0555—that "15 enemy planes are heading towards you."[20] Those planes were almost certainly a squadron of sixteen Dauntless dive-bombers from Midway. But they did not take off from Midway until after 0600 and did not form up into a group until around 0615.[21] Nor did any other group of planes—Vindicator dive-bombers, torpedo bombers, or fighters—take off before 0600 in response to the air raid warning sounded at 0555. The only American planes from Midway that were in the air as a group at 0555 were a squadron of B-17s, which was over 200 miles west of Midway. No group of planes could have been seen by that search plane until at least fifteen minutes after 0555.

Other events involving American planes were also logged at the wrong time in the composite log—cases where the correct time is established by American records. Among them: fourteen bombers were reported to have flown over *Soryu* at high altitude at 0755 and to have dropped "9 or 10 bombs" at that time.[22] The only American bombers fitting that description were fourteen B-17s, which American records show did not drop any bombs on the Mobile Force until after 0810. (It is also reported that *Akagi* was subjected to dive-bombing at 1014—about ten minutes before it actually happened.)

Thus, it is apparent that the times given in many of the entries in the composite log are unreliable; we cannot determine from the composite log alone the precise time the countermand order was issued. And this means that we cannot infer merely from the 0745 entry that Nagumo must have received the 0728 sighting report before 0745. I believe it much more likely that the countermand order was given after 0800—after Nagumo received the *Tone* 4 sighting report at "about 0800."

OTHER EVIDENCE

While the inferences that have been drawn from those two entries in the composite log now appear to be unjustified, it must be noted—in fairness to the early American commentators—that there is other circumstantial evidence at least suggesting an earlier receipt time. The *Tone* 4 sighting report was picked up by Yamamoto's flagship *Yamato*—about 500 miles to the rear. It was decoded and relayed to Yamamoto's headquarters at 0740.[23] There is also evidence in *Soryu*'s records that an order countermanding the rearming operation was received by blinker at 0750.[24] It is not clear where that communication originated. Although Tsunoda, who wrote the Senshi Sosho volume on Midway, assumes that it came from Nagumo, it could have come from Yamaguchi's headquarters on *Hiryu*. The implication is that if Yamamoto (and possibly Yamaguchi) received the sighting report this early, so must have Nagumo.

But, just because Yamamoto, and perhaps Yamaguchi, got the sighting report before 0745 does not mean that Nagumo did as well. Yamamoto and Yamaguchi, unlike Nagumo, were worried about the possibility of American carriers being in the Midway area, and appear to have had their radio rooms on alert to receive reports from the search planes. However, we have seen that *Akagi*'s radio was not tuned to the search plane radio frequency, so *Akagi* did not directly receive the report; it was relayed from cruiser *Tone*. Even so, unless there is an explanation for how it could have taken thirty minutes for the sighting report to reach Nagumo from cruiser *Tone*, it is not unreasonable to suppose that he received it earlier than 0800.

WHY IT TOOK SO LONG TO RELAY SIGHTING REPORT

Thirty minutes does seem an inordinate time for *Tone* 4's report to get to Nagumo. The composite log shows that reports from that search plane, after the initial sighting report, typically took only about ten minutes to reach *Akagi*'s headquarters (and this has been cited as evidence that the 0728 report was probably received around 0740). However, initial sighting reports are not typical. They are often unexpected, as was the case with this one, and if communications personnel are not on alert to receive and expedite the decoding and delivery of these messages, the procedure can easily take much longer than ten minutes. To see how, let us look at the various operations involved in getting the report to Nagumo's headquarters. We have seen that the 0728 sighting report received by the cruiser *Tone* was not sent in plain language, but in encrypted Morse code.[25] It would appear that the radioman was caught not fully prepared to decipher it, and, although the code was a fairly simple one, it probably took several minutes to decipher it. Moreover, at 0740, a second report was received from *Tone* 4 commenting on the weather conditions in the vicinity of the American ships.[26] As this was received at about the time the first message was being deciphered, there may have been a further delay in processing the two messages.

The sighting report was transcribed and then taken to the bridge on *Tone*, which took a few more minutes. *Tone*'s signalman then had to get the attention of the signal crew on *Akagi*—some distance away—who also were not expecting an urgent communication. (Messages between ships in the same formation were usually sent by visual signals such as blinkers or flag semaphores—"wigwags.") The message was then transcribed and hand-delivered to Nagumo's headquarters. Altogether, this could easily have added up to thirty minutes.

Subsequent messages from *Tone* 4 took much less time to reach Nagumo's headquarters because they were expected; communications crews were standing by to speed their delivery. Some were in plain language, and even those sent in code were more quickly decoded. All were sent without delay, by blinker or wigwag, from cruiser *Tone* to *Akagi*'s now alerted signalmen. Thus, the time it took for those messages to get to Nagumo is not indicative of the time it took the *initial*, unexpected, sighting report to reach him.

In point of fact, it turns out that a thirty-minute delay was not unusual for initial sighting reports at this time in the war. An earlier report from *Tone* 4 sighting American submarines is recorded in the log of the Official Report as having been sent at 0520 (0220 Japanese time) and received by *Akagi* at 0545— a delay of twenty-five minutes. And lest one conclude that all this shows is that the communications crew on cruiser *Tone* was not "up to speed," it should be noted that the American communications personnel also had difficulties that morning in relaying the initial report sighting the Japanese carrier force. It was sent in code by a PBY Catalina search plane at 0530, and received at Midway headquarters, but was not forwarded on to *Enterprise* or *Yorktown*. A subsequent amplifying report was sent in plain English by the PBY at 0552, but not relayed to Fletcher's flag bridge on *Yorktown* until 0603. A total of thirty-three minutes had elapsed since the first sighting—and American commanders, unlike Nagumo, were expecting to find enemy carriers in the area.

Commodore Richard Bates, in his Naval War College Midway analysis, commented: "Delays of this nature in the decoding and delivering of important messages are serious at any time, but in air warfare where minutes and seconds have such a vital effect on relative position, they can be an important contributing factor to the defeat or victory of any force. Plain English, authenticated, would have saved vital minutes in this case."[27] Although Bates was criticizing the delay in forwarding the American sighting report, Nagumo, no doubt, would have heartily endorsed this criticism. Fortunately, however, the delay on the American side did not have serious consequences; the delay in getting the sighting report to Nagumo probably cost him the battle.

This comparison does not excuse the lengthy delay that appears to have occurred with the 0728 *Tone* 4 sighting report, but shows that a thirty-minute delay in getting it to Nagumo is not as anomalous as it first appears. This being the case, it does not serve to negate Nagumo's claim of an 0800 receipt time. In fairness, the blame for the delay rests not with Nagumo, or even with the communications personnel of cruiser *Tone*; it lies with Yamamoto. Had Nagumo been made aware of the possibility that American carriers might be in the Midway area he most likely would have ensured that the communications crews on *Tone* and *Akagi* were on a higher state of readiness to receive sighting reports—and may even have had *Akagi*'s radio room on standby to receive search plane reports directly.

In conclusion, based on all the evidence—direct and circumstantial—on both sides of the issue, it now seems that the following inferences can be drawn: Nagumo did not receive the *Tone* 4 sighting report until "about 0800," as he claimed; his request for identification of "ship types" (there was only one) was sent at 0800; and the order countermanding the rearming operation was issued after 0800.

We will see that the delay in getting the sighting report to Nagumo, indeed, "greatly affected [his] subsequent attack preparations." In some cases, the difference between a ten-minute delay and a thirty-minute one would not be critical. However, at the time in question—when torpedoes were being stripped off the torpedo planes and replaced by bombs virtually worthless against aircraft carriers—a twenty-minute difference would turn out to be crucial. It meant that twenty minutes' more work had to be done to restore the torpedoes in twenty minutes *less* time for a launch to begin at 1000—a forty-minute swing. Had Nagumo received the sighting report at around 0740—as most commentators believe—the torpedoes probably would have been restored well before 0930, and the torpedo planes would probably have been on the flight decks ready for launch by 1000. As it was, those planes were not ready to go when time ran out for Nagumo at 1025.

THE DECISION TO COUNTERMAND

When Nagumo received the *Tone* 4 sighting report at about 0800, it could not have come at a worse time. His carriers were coming under attack from sixteen Dauntless dive-bombers from Midway, and the first of his Midway strike planes were back—their pilots eager to land as soon as possible.[28] The sighting report was not very specific and made no mention of carriers—just "10 enemy surface ships." Senshi Sosho states that Nagumo's first reaction was skepticism (more likely shock) but that he became convinced of the report's validity when it was quickly followed by another report from *Tone* 4 commenting on the weather in the vicinity of the ships.[29] Nagumo immediately sent an order to the search plane to identify ship types—but it seems very likely that he realized that carriers were probably among the ships sighted.

NATURE OF THE COUNTERMAND ORDER
Soon after receiving the shocking news of the sighting report, Nagumo made his second crucial decision of the morning: to countermand the rearming order that he had issued at 0715. However, the nature of that order is the subject of some controversy. Most American commentators take the position that the "countermand order" merely suspended rearming operations—that it did not actually reverse them.[30] (It is said that he wanted to leave his options open pending more precise information on the composition of the American force.) Senshi Sosho, on the other hand, takes the position that the order was interpreted by the arming crews as meaning that the rearming operation was to be reversed; that the torpedoes that had been removed were to be immediately restored to the torpedo planes.[31]

The only surviving record of that order is the entry in the composite log—logged erroneously, I have concluded, at 0745. It is recorded as a "Message from

Commander, Mobile Force, to Mobile Force" and, somewhat ambiguously, says "Prepare to carry out attacks on enemy fleet units. Leave torpedoes on those attack planes which have not as yet been changed to bombs."[32] While the second sentence gives rise to the notion that the rearming operation was to merely be suspended, the first sentence of the order could be effectively carried out only by reversing the armament of the torpedo planes back to torpedoes.

The assumption under the American standard scenario that the counter-mand order was given at 0745—and merely suspended the rearming operation—is the basis of the scornful charge that Nagumo was indecisive and "dithering" in his response to the sighting report. Had such an order been given at that time—only thirty minutes into the rearming operation—it indeed would have been a tepid response to the American threat. This is because, as we have seen, not a great deal had been done by then to rearm the torpedo planes with land bombs; although torpedoes had been stripped off at least half the planes, the "launchers" had not been converted to accommodate bombs. It would have ap-peared possible—at 0745—to get the torpedoes back on well before 0830. (As things turned out there would not have been time, because of the disruptions caused by American bombing attacks between 0805 and 0830, to restore the tor-pedoes by 0830, but they could have been restored soon after 0900—had the op-eration been reversed at 0745.) Thus, a mere suspension of the rearming opera-tion at 0745 would have resulted in squandering twenty minutes of unfettered time.

It has been suggested, however, that Nagumo was skeptical about whether there were any carriers among the "10 surface ships" reported by *Tone* 4 and preferred to merely suspend the rearming operation until he received an an-swer to his request for identification of ship types. This is dubious. The Japa-nese record indicates that Nagumo and most of his staff almost immediately suspected the presence of carriers, and the main concern was how many. In fact, when *Tone* 4 responded to the request for details and identified the ships as five cruisers and five destroyers Nagumo's chief of staff Kusaka was puzzled: what were those ships doing there, he asked, if not to escort carriers?[33] In such circumstances it clearly would have been irresponsible to have merely sus-pended—instead of reversing—the rearming operation at 0745. But if the order was not issued until a little after 0800—when the Mobile Force was under air attacks—suspension of the rearming operation until the attacks were over would have been a reasonable, perhaps the only practical, option.

There are also problems with Senshi Sosho's interpretation of the counter-mand order as *reversing* the rearming operation at 0745. While it makes Na-gumo appear much more decisive in his response to the sudden American threat, its scenario is puzzling: Senshi Sosho suggests that after receipt of the sighting report, but before the countermand order was issued, there was a de-liberation by Nagumo as to whether the rearming of the torpedo planes with land bombs should continue to completion, and the attack against the American ships be made by bomb-laden torpedo planes, or whether the operation should be reversed—restoring the torpedoes. In the end, the decision was fairly quickly made to restore the torpedoes, as level bombing by torpedo planes against moving ships had proved very ineffective in comparison with torpedo attacks.[34]

It seems doubtful that such a quandary would have arisen prior to 0745, when about half the torpedo planes still had torpedoes attached, and when it would have taken much less time to restore the torpedoes to the remaining planes than it would to rearm the entire squadron with land bombs. If, on the other hand, Nagumo did not get the sighting report until 0800, his options would have been much more complicated: all the torpedo planes would have been stripped of torpedoes, and some of them would have had land bombs attached. It probably would have taken longer to change back to torpedoes than to complete the rearming with land bombs. A deliberation at that time over which option to pursue would seem much more reasonable.

Even assuming a brief deliberation (there really was not much of a choice), it is very unlikely, as we have seen, that any countermand order was issued before about 0805. As the Mobile Force had come under a dive-bombing attack by then, very little could be done to change back to torpedoes until the American attacks were over. Thus, as a practical matter there would have been little difference between suspending and reversing the operation, so that controversy is largely a moot point. It is even possible that the countermand order was implemented in two stages: an interim suspension at around 0805 ("Leave torpedoes on those attack planes which have not as yet been changed to bombs"),[35] with a full reversal of the rearming operation ("Prepare to carry out attacks on enemy fleet units") ordered at around 0835–0840, after the American bombing attacks had ceased, and after Nagumo received the *Tone* 4 report identifying an American carrier.[36]

It should be noted that the foregoing scenario for the timing and nature of the countermand order applies only to the torpedo planes on *Akagi* and *Kaga*. As for the dive-bombers on *Hiryu* and *Soryu*, it appears that events were more in accordance with those conventionally assumed to have applied to the entire Mobile Force. Yamaguchi, on *Hiryu*, may in fact have received the *Tone* 4 sighting report before 0745. Moreover, as noted, there is evidence that *Soryu* received an order—by blinker—countermanding the rearming operation at 0750—which may have been issued by Yamaguchi at 0745. It further appears that pursuant to that order, the armament of the dive-bombers was changed back to antiship bombs. (This would explain why the dive-bombers were ready, as we will see, for a launch to attack the American fleet soon after 0835.)

As for the armament status of the torpedo planes on *Akagi* at 0805—when the rearming operation was probably suspended (or reversed): it was, approximately, as follows. The torpedoes had been removed from *all* the planes. The launchers on the planes of the first division of each squadron had been changed for bombs, and 800-kilogram land bombs were being jacked up and attached to the launchers. On *Kaga* the procedure may have been more advanced, and the installation of as many as nine bombs could have been completed by 0805.[37]

It should be noted that even without an order suspending or reversing the rearming operation at 0805, things would have been brought to an abrupt halt at that time by the American dive-bomber attacks. The radical, battle-speed maneuvering of the carriers—making sharp deck-heeling turns to avoid the bombs—would have made it impossible to jack up and attach any more 800-kilogram bombs. For the same reason, no torpedoes could have been reinstalled. The only operations feasible during the period of the bombing attacks would have been the conversion of the launchers back for torpedoes. (But it appears that not even this was done, as will be seen in the next chapter.)

This means that the armament status of the torpedo planes at 0805 is pretty much what it would still be at 0830—when Nagumo would be faced with having to make a decision whether or not to launch an immediate attack against the American force. This status—none of the torpedo planes having torpedoes attached, but a few of them having 800-kilogram land bombs—is the very status that has been described by some commentators for the torpedo planes at 0830. Had the rearming operation on *Akagi* and *Kaga* been reversed at 0745—as contended by Senshi Sosho—there almost certainly would have been some torpedo planes equipped with torpedoes, and none with bombs attached. Thus, it should be apparent that the reported armament status of those planes at 0830 is consistent only with a rearming operation that continued until a little after 0800.

In conclusion, the image of a "dithering" Nagumo at 0745 is a myth. Instead, it appears that when he received the sighting report from *Tone* 4 at around 0800 his response was reasonably quick and appropriate (though because of the American attacks there was not a lot he could do). His countermand order—even if it only suspended the rearming operation—was, therefore, was not one of the causes of the disaster that befell his Mobile Force at 1025.

ATTACKS FROM MIDWAY
The attack that caused the disruption in the rearming operation at around 0805 was by sixteen Douglas Dauntless dive-bombers that had taken off from Midway at 0605 and departed in formation at approximately 0615. When the squadron approached the Mobile Force, the squadron leader—Major Henderson—decided to attempt a glide-bombing attack, as none of his pilots had experience with dive-bombing. None of the bombs hit, and eight dive-bombers were shot down (with two more too shot up to be of further service). The attack was over at around 0812.

But there was no relief for the arming crews in the hangar decks of *Akagi* and

Kaga, because a second attack began almost immediately. This was from fourteen B-17s, led by Lieutenant Colonel Walter Sweeney, which had arrived over
the carriers and began dropping 500-pound bombs from 20,000 feet at 0814.
They had taken off from Midway at about 0430 to attack the transports of the
Occupation Force, but had been diverted to attack the Mobile Force instead.
None of the bombs hit, and none of the bombers was shot down. This attack
lasted until around 0820.[38]

The B-17s were followed by another wave of dive-bombers from Midway.
They were eleven obsolete SB2U "Vindicators" that had taken off immediately after the Dauntlesses. Led by Major Benjamin Norris, they first attacked
the battleship *Haruna* at 0827, but it appears that several switched to *Akagi*
and *Kaga.*[39] There were no bombs hits, and three were shot down (three more
were too badly damaged to be of further use).[40] The fact that only three of
these slow, poorly armored planes were shot down is odd; it indicates that the
Zeros on combat air patrol were out of 20-mm ammunition by this time. This
final attack from Midway was over by 0839.

It was during this chaotic time that Nagumo received (at 0830) a further report from *Tone* 4, sent at 0820: "the enemy is accompanied by what appears to
be a carrier in a position to the rear of the others."[41] Although carriers had been
suspected, this confirmation dispelled the last glimmer of optimism—held by
some on his staff—that there were no American carriers in the area. (These few
optimists had hoped that the cruisers and destroyers reported by *Tone* 4 at 0809
could be disposed of later—perhaps after the scheduled second strike on Midway had been carried out.) It was now clear to Nagumo that an attack on the
American carrier force had to be made as soon as an effective strike force could
be organized. But what was available, and what to do about the Midway strike
force that had now returned, desperate to land? This will be dealt with in the
next chapter. For now, we will explore some of the issues that have been raised
concerning the performance of *Tone* 4's crew in ascertaining and reporting the
composition of the American naval force.

PERFORMANCE OF *TONE* 4'S CREW

Tone 4 did not identify a carrier until 0820—fifty-two minutes after the first
sighting of the American ships. And even then, its crew saw only one of the three
carriers in the area. The crew of *Tone* 4 has been subjected to much criticism—
even ridicule—for taking so long to identify a carrier. As one commentator put
it "nobody could miss anything that big for so long."[42] This is, indeed, a perplexing mystery—and the crew of *Tone* 4 did not survive the war to explain it.

Most American commentators have assumed that *Tone* 4 was a considerable
distance—at least 30 miles—from the American fleet when the first sighting
was made at 0728, which would seem a likely explanation for why no specific

ship types were identified. It is then assumed that, in an overly cautious effort to evade detection, the search plane took fifty-two minutes to get close enough to clearly see a carrier—which is further assumed to have been with the "ten ships" all along. It now appears that all of these assumptions are unjustified. Senshi Sosho reveals that *Tone* 4 was actually quite close to the American ships when it first sighted them at 0728.[43] Under this scenario the ships were not seen earlier because they were obscured by cloud cover.[44] But at 0728 *Tone* 4 happened upon a hole in the clouds, giving its crew a partial view of what appears to have been Spruance's Task Force 16.

The reason Senshi Sosho gives for concluding that *Tone* 4 was fairly close to the American ships, apart from the fact that clouds in the area made it impossible for its crew to see those ships from a distance, is that *Tone* 4's observer was able to give quite precise information about the ships' course and speed: 150° at 20 knots. Even if he could have seen the ships from a distance of 30 miles, he would have been unable to discern their precise course. He could have estimated the course of the ships only in terms of general direction—such as "southeasterly."[45] Given the degree of precision of the *Tone* 4 report, it is likely that *Tone* 4 was no more than about 10 miles from the American ships when its crew first saw them at 0728. At that distance, ship types would have been clearly discernable. Why were no carriers seen?

WHY IT TOOK SO LONG TO IDENTIFY A CARRIER

It is just possible that the reason the crew of *Tone* 4 did not see a carrier at 0728, and again at 0755 when it reported a course change for the American ships, is because no carrier was in the group of ships seen by the *Tone* 4 crewmen at those times. It is almost certain that the ten ships in the formation they saw belonged to Task Force 16. That task force consisted of two carriers (*Enterprise* and *Hornet*), five heavy cruisers, one light antiaircraft cruiser, and nine destroyers.[46] (Task Force 17, with *Yorktown*, had only two heavy cruisers and five destroyers—so *Tone* 4 saw too many ships, especially cruisers, for them to be TF 17.) But if it was TF 16 that was spotted, why did *Tone* 4 see only ten of the seventeen ships in that task force?

This is a mystery, but there is a possible explanation: as of 0728, Task Force 16 could have become spread out over a considerable area during launch operations for the strike force, which began at 0705. In such a case, as there was a lot of cloudiness in the area, it is likely that partial cloud cover obscured a view of the entire task force. It is known that shortly before launch operations began the task force separated into two groups—one for each carrier. (By 0738, the *Enterprise* and *Hornet* groups were reported to be about 8 miles apart.)[47] This would explain why not all the ships in TF 16 were seen, but the question remains: why was not at least one carrier seen?

Ordinarily, carriers were surrounded by their escorts—cruisers close to the carriers and destroyers further out, forming an outer screen.[48] When the task force separated into two smaller groups, one would expect that each carrier would still be surrounded by its escorts. The larger of the two groups would have been *Enterprise* accompanied by three heavy cruisers and five destroyers. (The *Hornet* group had two heavy cruisers, one light cruiser, and four destroyers.) It appears to be assumed — by those who believe that a carrier was among the "ten ships" all along — that the *Tone* 4 crew mistook the carrier *Enterprise* for a cruiser, and then miscounted the cruisers to come up with the five cruisers and five destroyers it reported at 0809 in response to Nagumo's request for clarification of the types of ships seen at 0728.

If the ships were sighted at a great distance — 30 miles or more, as most American commentators assume — this would be a reasonable supposition. If, however, *Tone* 4 was fairly close — as now appears to be the case — then this is not a satisfactory explanation. If the aircraft's crew was close enough to distinguish cruisers from destroyers then, surely, they could have distinguished a carrier from a cruiser — which was about as much larger than a cruiser as a cruiser was a destroyer. (Incidentally, the reason the aircrew did not report the ship types in the first place is probably because they were in a great hurry to encode and transmit the essentials of their discovery, and, as no carriers were seen, they did not think it important to distinguish between cruisers and destroyers.)

In regard to the *Tone* 4 crew's ability to distinguish ship types, the wording of the 0820 report finally identifying a carrier is revealing — and indicates that the aircrew was capable of distinguishing a carrier from a cruiser even at a distance considerably greater than with the initial sighting report. In the narrative of the Official Report — not the log — the *Tone* 4 message is recorded as saying that the ships previously mentioned were "accompanied by what appears to be a carrier in a position *to the rear* of the others." (Emphasis added.) This strongly suggests that a carrier not with the group originally spotted was now rejoining its main escorts. (It will be noted that the message log entry in the Official Report merely says "The enemy is accompanied by what appears to be a carrier," omitting the last phrase "in a position to the rear of the others." This is the version to which most commentators refer, and it conveys the idea that the carrier had been with the other ships all along.)

But what was a carrier doing in a position to the rear of its main body of escorts? Is it possible that the carriers gradually became separated from most of their escorts during launch operations? There is no evidence in the American record for this, but that record is sketchy and does not preclude such a possibility. What is known is that during those launch operations it was necessary for the carriers to make adjustments for changes in wind direction (*Hornet*'s course changed from 155° to 145, and finally to 135° at the end of the launch).[49] On the other hand, most of the escorts may have maintained a steady course (such as the 150° *Tone* 4 reported at 0728), instead of attempting to track every twist and turn of the carriers. Moreover, as the carriers were launching full deckloads, they had to temporarily increase speed to very close to their maximum of 33 knots—while it appears that the escorts maintained a steady 30 knots, causing them to have lagged behind somewhat.

Such a scenario is admittedly speculative, but a combination of slightly different courses and speeds *could*, over a thirty-minute time span, have resulted in a separation of several miles between the carriers and most of their escorts. (The commander of the cruiser division sent a message to *Hornet* at 0757—*Hornet* had completed its launch at 0755—"screen will conform to your movements."[50] This at least suggests the possibility that courses had not been tightly synchronized during launch operations.) Thus, it is possible that what *Tone* 4's crew saw through the gap in the clouds were elements of both carrier subgroups—five cruisers and five destroyers—but that clouds obscured the carriers, which may have steamed ahead on slightly different courses—taking them outside the restricted field of view. It should be noted that some of the escorts—one heavy cruiser and four destroyers—were not seen either; they may have stayed closer to the carriers. (*Minneapolis*, the flagship of the cruiser division, is reported to have been 2,500 yards from *Hornet* at 0730.)[51]

Another report from *Tone* 4 also lends support to the theory that the carriers had become separated from their escorts during launch operations. At 0755 the search plane radioed that the American ships had changed course to 080° (from the original 150). This would make no sense for the carriers; planes were still being launched from *Enterprise* (and *Hornet*, which completed its launch at 0755, immediately began recovering fighters on combat air patrol). It is almost certain that those carriers remained steered into the wind—around 135° at that time—until launch and recovery operations were completed at 0806. If, however, the ten cruisers and destroyers seen by *Tone* 4 at 0728 had been diverging from the carriers during launch operations, it would make sense for them to make a course correction to close formation with the carriers near the end of flight operations.[52] It is known from the track charts of Task Force 16 that after launch operations were completed the entire task force changed course to 240° (from southeasterly to southwesterly). If *Hornet* had, by the end of its flight operations, strayed ahead of most of its escorts, it would after its course change indeed be joining them from the rear. I think it likely that this carrier emerged from under cloud cover at around 0820, which was why it was not seen earlier.

Therefore, it is possible—even likely—that the carriers steered a course somewhat independent of the escorts for approximately an hour between 0705 and 0806. During this period the carriers could easily have become separated from the main body of escorts by a few miles as of 0728, when *Tone* 4 made its initial sighting. Given the cloud conditions in the area at the time, this could explain why no carriers were seen. (The extent of the cloudiness over the area

of Task Force 16, until after 0820,[53] has been underappreciated by most American commentators.)

Immediately after sending its report at 0820, *Tone* 4 was pursued into clouds
by fighters from *Enterprise*. Had the search plane been able to stay in the clear
for a few more minutes its crew probably would have also seen *Enterprise*
emerging from under cloud cover. It should be noted that by this time, *Tone*
4 had retreated to about 30 miles south of Task Force 16, where it had been
detected on radar at 0815. (Its distance at this time appears to be the main basis
of the assumption that it was this far away at 0728 when it first sighted the
American fleet.)

The question of why no carrier was seen until 0820 will probably never be
satisfactorily answered; my speculative scenario certainly leaves a lot of loose
ends hanging. But all this does at least raise the possibility that the crew of *Tone*
4 may not have been as poor observers as they have been made out to be (even
by the official Japanese government history, *Senshi Sosho*). It is just possible
that they saw what was visible and accurately reported what they saw. They can,
however, be faulted for not being more persistent in developing the initial contact by getting beneath the clouds to survey the entire task force—even at the
risk of being shot down.

In the larger scheme of things, though, this would not have made much difference. We have seen that Nagumo still would not have received the sighting
report until about 0800, just as he was coming under attack by dive-bombers
from Midway. Even had two carriers been reported, there was little that could
have been done to prepare an attack against them until the American bombing
attacks were over. Thus, the failure of the *Tone* 4 crew to identify a carrier until
0820—which has been roundly criticized—turns out also not to have been a
cause of the disaster that befell the Mobile Force.

MISLOCATING THE POSITION OF THE AMERICAN FLEET
The crew of *Tone* 4 did, however, make one fairly serious mistake. Their 0728
report had the position of the American ships about 55 miles north of where
they actually were. Had a strike been launched against these ships soon after
that time, the error in position could have resulted in the attacking planes' failure to find their target. But by the time an attack was finally launched, hours
later, the true location of the American fleet had been determined by other
reconnaissance.[54] As we will see in the next chapter, the error did, however,
mislead Nagumo into believing that the American carriers were further from
his Mobile Force (by about 30 miles) than they actually were when he was
considering his decision, at 0830, whether to launch an attack immediately or
postpone until after the Midway strike force had been recovered.

Why *Tone* 4's crew reckoned the position of the American fleet so far north
of its actual position remains a mystery. It has been suggested that because of

a compass error *Tone* 4 flew a course more southeasterly than the 100° scheduled.[55] Under this theory, at 240 miles out *Tone* 4 was about 55 miles further south than its navigator thought it was. This supposition must be rejected for the simple reason that *Tone* 4 could not have found the fleet had its outbound course taken it that far south before it turned north on its dogleg. Such a course would have put it in a position requiring over 60 miles of visibility— which is too far even in clear weather to make out ships, and there was substantial cloudiness in the area at 0728.

Actually, *Tone* 4 found the American task force almost exactly where it should have found it had the search plane flown an outbound course of 100°, as scheduled, but made its dogleg to the north about 65 miles earlier than scheduled. As it now appears that *Tone* 4 was quite close to the American ships at 0728, the crew must have thought they were about 240 miles north of Midway, instead of the 185 miles they actually were. There has been no satisfactory explanation advanced for why they thought they were 55 miles further north of Midway than they actually were. The only possibilities seem to be either that they had a defective chart showing Midway 55 miles south of its true position, or they erroneously thought that the Mobile Force was 55 miles north of where it was when they were launched at 0500. (Senshi Sosho could find no evidence to support either possibility, and neither have I.)

Although the miscalculation by *Tone* 4's navigator cannot be excused, this kind of navigational error was not unusual in the first year of the Pacific War. Aerial reconnaissance at sea was not very accurate for either side. In fact, it is hard to find a case where ships actually were within 30 miles of where they were reported to be by search planes. (The American sighting report of the Japanese carriers at Midway mislocated those carriers by about 40 miles, and, as a result, some of the American dive-bombers were unable to find the Mobile Force.) Even though the error made by *Tone* 4's crew in reckoning position was greater than average, they were not alone to blame for any consequences that may have resulted from it. The error should have been noticed back in *Tone* headquarters —because it clearly was impossible for *Tone* 4's crew to have seen ships as far north of Midway as they reported, had they been on course. A request to *Tone* 4 for a direction-finding radio transmission would have revealed her approximate distance north of Midway. (This was, indeed, done later at 0855, but after Nagumo has already made the decision to postpone.)

VERDICT ON THE PERFORMANCE OF *TONE* 4 CREW

The crewmen of the *Tone* 4 have generally been portrayed by the standard scenario as sloppy, myopic incompetents who bear a major responsibility for the Japanese disaster at Midway. (As one popular author put it: "Having turned in this sorry performance, he vanished from history; like the asp that bit Cleopatra, a small creature on whom the fortunes of an empire had briefly and sadly turned.")[56] Actually, however, they appear to have been reasonably observant and even resourceful aviators. Although their navigation was faulty, we have seen that without their shortcut some 65 miles before the end of their prescribed search path, the American ships would not have been discovered as early as they were.

This fortuitous turn to the north cannot be attributed to mere navigational error; it was almost certainly intentional. When they found the American ships, they not only reported what was visible to them but stayed in the area monitoring their discovery for almost one and a half hours—at considerable risk to their safety. (Though had they been a bit more adventurous they could have maneuvered to get a better view of the American task force.) They also sent back seven reports during that time, which, while not identifying additional carriers, did report two more cruisers—and they gave the first warning of a carrier plane strike group heading toward the Mobile Force. Compared with most other naval reconnaissance of that time in the war (including the American effort that same morning), this was quite a diligent performance. All in all, rather than being condemned, the *Tone* 4 crew deserved to be commended.

NIMITZ ALSO LOSES GAMBLE

When Admiral Nimitz sent his carriers to Midway, Nagumo lost the gamble he made that there would be none in the area when he decided to rearm his carrier attack planes for a second strike on Midway. But things did not go as planned for Nimitz either. His tactical plan was based on ambush. He knew that his carriers would be outnumbered and that the Japanese possessed—especially with their aerial torpedoes—more ship-sinking firepower than he could muster. To counter this disadvantage he did what all resourceful commanders who were outnumbered would do: he planned to neutralize Nagumo's superior firepower by getting in the first strike.

The details of the tactical plan Nimitz envisioned for achieving ambush are unknown; he was a reserved, modest man who did not reveal very much after the war. However, a few of its likely premises can be deduced from the sparse record. It appears that Nimitz knew that the weather to the northeast of Midway would probably be stormy and counted on cloud cover to shield his carriers from view by Japanese search planes, for at least the early hours of the morning of June 4. He had picked the spot for the rendezvous of Spruance's and Fletcher's task forces for that reason.

It also appears that he—or at least Spruance—expected that Nagumo would attack Midway in the early morning with all his strike planes—launched in two deckloads[57]—as had been done at Pearl Harbor. This would mean that if the American carriers could remain undiscovered until both waves of those planes had attacked Midway there would be nothing left in reserve on Nagumo's

carriers with which to attack the American carriers—even if they were then discovered. In such a case, Nimitz's carrier commanders would have ample time
to hit the Japanese carrier force before Nagumo's Midway strike force could be
rearmed and relaunched after its return to the carriers. Nimitz's tactical plan
appears to have been based largely on these two critical assumptions: that his
carriers would not be discovered early and that all of Nagumo's dive-bombers
and torpedo planes would be used in the attack on Midway.

Accordingly, Spruance's plan was to launch his strike force at a time calculated to hit Nagumo's carriers while the planes that had returned from Midway
were being rearmed and refueled. The decision-making process in his command center that led to the exact launch-time was, however, fraught with anx-
ieties. When Spruance received the PBY report at 0603 sighting elements of
the Japanese carrier force, calculated to be 175 miles away, his first inclination
was to delay his launch until he had steamed closer to the Mobile Force, to give
his short-legged Wildcat fighters and Devastator torpedo bombers a better
chance of returning to their carriers. But he soon began to worry that his task
force might be discovered by the Japanese (and "bogeys" were being picked up
on his radar screen) and that the Japanese Midway strike force might then be
diverted to attack his carriers before he could complete his launch.

To forestall this possibility he contemplated an immediate launch. But the
problems with this option were that the reported position of the Japanese carrier
force was beyond the combat radius of his torpedo bombers and also that his
strike force might reach the Mobile Force before its Midway strike force had returned to the carriers. In the end, Spruance resisted the temptation for an immediate launch and took a calculated risk: gambling that cloud cover would prevent his task force from being spotted by Japanese search planes until all of
Nagumo's strike force had reached Midway, he scheduled his launch to begin
around 0700 (and be completed by around 0800). This not only would give his
torpedo bombers a better chance of returning, but also would enable his strike
force to reach the projected location of the Mobile Force at around 0920. This
could be expected to catch the second wave of Nagumo's strike force (which was
assumed to have been sent to Midway) just after it had returned and landed, but
well before the first wave—which would have landed about an hour earlier—
could be rearmed and launched.

The gamble paid off. As things worked out, his dive-bombers—though their
arrival over the Mobile Force had been delayed an hour because of a faulty
sighting report—did indeed hit Nagumo's carriers while they were still rearming their strike planes. But that it actually worked out this way was more the
product of sheer luck than of planning. If Nimitz had counted on Nagumo attacking Midway with his full strength, he lost that gamble. We have seen that
Yamamoto had anticipated the very vulnerability that Nimitz may have hoped
to exploit by ordering that one-half of Nagumo's offensive strength be held in

reserve during the attack on Midway—just in case American carriers showed up. As a result, there remained enough ship-sinking firepower on board even after the Midway strike force departed to deal a crippling blow to the American carriers *if* they were discovered in time. Nimitz had also counted on his carriers' not being discovered until it was too late for the Japanese to launch a strike against them. In a sense, he lost that gamble as well when Spruance's task force was sighted at 0728 by *Tone* 4. Ordinarily, there would have been time for Nagumo's second-wave planes to be launched, but Nimitz was—most fortuitously—bailed out of that lost gamble by an astonishing series of blunders on the Japanese side.

The main blunder was, of course, the rearming of the torpedo planes. Had Nagumo not contravened Yamamoto's "standing order" by incapacitating his standby strike force, he could have launched a deadly attack against the American carriers—probably before the returning Midway strike force had to be landed. Then, even with Nagumo having issued the rearming order, had his communications personnel been more efficient he would have received the *Tone* 4 sighting report earlier, and could have reversed the rearming operation before it had proceeded too far. In such a case, we have seen that he could still have launched his strike force well before the American carrier dive-bombers arrived over the Mobile Force. Thus, rather than Nimitz being the ambusher, it was his carriers that came perilously close to being on the receiving end of an ambush.

However, while some of Nimitz's expectations had been thwarted, there was one element of his tactical plan for which the Japanese had no effective countermeasures, and which saved the day for the Americans: Nimitz had beefed up the air power on Midway so it could attack the Mobile Force pending the arrival of strike planes from his lurking carrier force. These measures paid off handsomely, though perhaps not in the way Nimitz intended.

While the mostly green aircrews Nimitz had rushed to Midway were unable to score any bomb or torpedo hits on the Mobile Force, their relentless series of attacks did manage to seriously disrupt operations on Nagumo's carriers in several crucial ways. First, we saw that the initial torpedo bomber attacks around 0700 probably influenced Nagumo's decision to rearm his standby planes for a second strike on Midway—thereby ruining Yamamoto's trump card against Nimitz's ambush plans. Second, the series of attacks from Midway forced Nagumo to use up all his Zeros for air defense, including those assigned to escort the second wave. Even though the armament of the dive-bombers on *Hiryu* and *Soryu* had been reversed back to antiship bombs by 0830, there were no Zeros available to escort them—which (as we will see in the next chapter) was one of the reasons why Nagumo decided against launching an attack before the Midway strike force was recovered.

Lastly, and most critically, when the rearming operation on the torpedo planes was countermanded, the bombing attacks by dive-bombers and B-17s between 0800 and 0840 prevented any substantial operations to restore the torpedoes to the torpedo planes. This was largely responsible for those planes not being ready for launch before most of Nagumo's carriers were destroyed at 1025. The dive-bomber aircrews from *Enterprise* and *Yorktown* got most of the glory for the spectacular American victory at Midway, but it was the green aircrews that Nimitz had rushed to Midway that helped set up Nagumo's carriers for the kill.

*   *   *

There is an enduring notion that the breaking of the Japanese naval code by Nimitz's HYPO operation made an American victory at Midway almost inevitable. But, as we have seen, that most certainly was not the case. While HYPO's early discovery of Yamamoto's Midway plans certainly made the American victory possible, without some incredibly bad luck for Nagumo—and some very good fortune for the Americans—the code-breaking triumph could have had the ironical result of leading Nimitz's carriers into Yamamoto's trap. The Americans could easily have lost that battle. The probable dimensions of the disaster that would have befallen Nimitz had Nagumo's second-wave planes gotten launched will be explored in detail in the final chapter ("Postmortem"). However, to put in perspective what the Americans stood to lose had that happened, a brief preview may be in order at this point.

The Japanese, instead of losing four fleet carriers, would probably have lost only two, with a third badly damaged. (*Hiryu* most likely would have escaped untouched.) *Hiryu* would have been joined by *Zuikaku* and the soon to be repaired *Shokaku*. Therefore, after the damaged carrier—let us say *Akagi*—was repaired, Yamamoto would have had four fleet attack carriers (along with two light carriers and two heavy "support" carriers—after *Hiyo* came on line in August) with which to prosecute further offensive operations.[58]

The Americans, on the other hand, would probably have ended up losing all three carriers sent to Midway—along with the Midway base. The American navy would have been reduced to two fleet carriers—*Saratoga* and *Wasp*.[59] Without carrier air supremacy in the Pacific, the American naval operations planned for the second half of 1942—the most important being the Guadalcanal campaign to secure a foothold in the South Pacific—would have been postponed for at least a year. Indeed, the whole theater of Pacific operations would have been shifted thousands of miles east to the American side of the Pacific, as Hawaii and the Panama Canal would have been threatened after Midway fell into Japanese hands. The two remaining American fleet carriers most likely would have been lost defending a carrier attack on Hawaii a couple of months later.

This, then, is what Nimitz stood to lose when he made his bold gamble at Midway. Had Nagumo's second-wave planes been launched before 1025, Yamamoto not only would have won the Battle of Midway, but would have gone on to achieve his strategic objective for the first year of the war: knocking the American carrier fleet out of the Pacific. Although America would eventually have regained carrier air supremacy—by the end of 1943—the Pacific War would have been a much longer and much costlier ordeal for the United States. The next chapter will further explore the most baffling mystery of Midway: why Nagumo could not get an attack launched before 1025.

CHAPTER SIX

TO LAUNCH OR NOT TO LAUNCH

THE DECISION TO POSTPONE

We have seen that at 0820 *Tone* 4 spotted an American carrier "to the rear" of the cruisers and destroyers earlier reported. Nagumo received this report at 0830.[1] It is doubtful that he was shocked by this discovery—as already mentioned, he probably had suspected the presence of carriers since 0800. In fact, he should have suspected that there were two carriers—he knew that there were at least two operational American carriers in the Pacific, and was probably aware that American carriers had been deployed in pairs since April. But rather than launching an immediate attack, Nagumo made—at around 0835—his second fateful decision of the morning: he postponed his attack on the American carrier force until after the Midway strike force, waiting to land, had been recovered. This has been the most severely criticized decision Nagumo made during the battle.

All commentators concede that this was an especially stressful time for Nagumo. His Mobile Force had been under attack continuously since 0800, an enemy submarine had just been spotted shadowing his fleet, and the commander of the Midway strike force was urgently requesting permission for an immediate landing. While Nagumo had two squadrons of dive-bombers available and properly armed by 0830, the armament status of his torpedo planes—by far his most effective weapon—was in shambles because of his 0715 rearming order. Also, there were no Zeros available to escort the dive-bombers. In the circumstances he decided against launching an immediate attack and, instead, ordered that the Midway strike force be landed.

Recovery operations for the Midway strike force began at 0837 on *Akagi* and *Kaga* (though halted at 0839, when an American dive-bomber suddenly appeared heading for *Akagi*, but resumed at 0840). On *Hiryu* and *Soryu*, it appears that landings did not begin until around 0850. (As we will see, Yamaguchi had been hoping for an immediate launch of his dive-bombers against the American carrier, and may even have been in the process of raising those dive-bombers to the flight decks when Nagumo made his decision to land the Midway strike force.)

A number of reasons for postponing the attack have been given, but the main ones appear to be that Nagumo did not think an effective strike could be made with what he had available at 0830—just the dive-bombers—and that he thought he had the time to land the Midway strike force and then organize a much more effective coordinated attack, one that would include rearmed torpedo planes and thus be capable of inflicting decisive damage on the enemy while resulting in fewer losses to his own pilots.[2]

As it turned out, he did not have the time, and the failure to get his planes off his carriers before being attacked by American carrier bombers was the root cause of his defeat. Because of the obviously fatal consequences of that failure —and the almost universal condemnation that has been heaped on Nagumo because of it—one of the main purposes of this inquest has been to determine the reasonableness of his decision to postpone.

This analysis will proceed through four stages: First, we must determine what carrier striking power was actually available to Nagumo at 0830 and what could have been made available for an attack in the following thirty minutes before the Midway strike force absolutely had to be landed to avoid unacceptable losses from ditching. Then we must attempt to understand why what was available for an immediate attack was not a palatable option for Nagumo at 0830. Third, we must determine whether it was reasonable for him to think that he had the time to organize a superior option. Finally, we must try to solve the central mystery of this inquest: why an attack could not be organized and launched in less than two hours after 0830—before the American dive-bombers from *Enterprise* and *Yorktown* showed up at 1020.

WHAT NAGUMO HAD AVAILABLE AT 0830

There is disagreement among the authorities as to what carrier striking power was available to Nagumo at 0830. The various estimates cover a broad range. At the high end we have: all the second-wave dive-bombers armed with antiship bombs, and all on the flight decks of *Hiryu* and *Soryu*;[3] half the second-wave torpedo planes armed with 800-kilogram land bombs and also on the flight decks of *Akagi* and *Kaga*, with the other half armed with torpedoes in the hangar decks;[4] and about a half dozen Zeros available for escort.[5] At the low end we have: no dive-bombers armed with anti-ship bombs, and all in the hangar decks;[6] no torpedo planes armed with torpedoes, and all in the hangar decks; and no Zeros available for escort.[7] What did Nagumo actually have readily available?

STATUS OF THE TORPEDO PLANES AT 0830

As torpedoes were the most deadly antiship weapons Nagumo had, the status of the torpedo planes at 0830 is paramount and will be dealt with first. The Japanese record is vague; Senshi Sosho says only the torpedo planes on *Akagi* and *Kaga* "were not rearmed for ships."[8] What were they armed with, if anything? We saw in the last chapter that shortly after 0800, when the rearming of the torpedo planes probably ceased, the rearming operation was at about its halfway point. It appears that very little, if anything, was done to reverse the procedure between 0800 and 0830. This is because the Mobile Force was under constant attack during that period and the battle-speed evasive maneuvering of the carriers made it virtually impossible to install torpedoes on the torpedo planes. Thus, the armament status of those planes at 0830 was pretty much what it was at 0805, when Nagumo countermanded his rearming order.

What, then, was the status at 0805? This was not recorded and can be deduced only by determining what probably had been done to the torpedo planes in the forty-five minutes since the rearming order began to be implemented at around 0720. The various procedures of the rearming operation, as reconstructed from the testimony of the veterans, were described in detail in chapter 4, but to summarize: The torpedo planes were probably already in the hangars when the rearming order was given. The procedures were performed on the planes one *chutai* (division) at a time—because of the limited number of torpedo mechanics and, especially, heavy-weapons carrier cars. It took around seven minutes to crank up the jacks on the carrier cars, release the torpedo from the plane, and crank it down, and another five minutes to roll it to the heavy-weapons rack, where it was deposited. After the torpedoes were removed from the planes, but before land bombs could be attached, the "launcher" (the ribbed rack on the belly of the plane to which ordnance was attached) had to be changed. This was the most time-consuming procedure in the entire operation, taking as much as thirty minutes.

While the launchers were being changed on the first division, the carrier cars were used to remove the torpedoes from the next division of planes. It took about one minute to move the empty carrier cars and position them under the planes, and then the procedures (taking a total of about twelve minutes) were repeated on the last division. On *Akagi*, these operations would have resulted in six torpedoes having been removed by around 0727, twelve by around 0740, and all seventeen by about 0753. By about 0758, the last torpedo would have been deposited on the heavy-weapons rack and the carrier cars would have been available to transport 800-kilogram land bombs to the planes of the first division. (The launchers would have been converted for bombs on that division by that time.)

On *Kaga* the rearming procedure probably moved at a quicker pace. This is because its more numerous carrier cars and weapons mechanics made it possible for nine planes to be processed at a time. And, while *Kaga* had a larger squadron of twenty-six torpedo planes, it is likely that only eighteen of its planes were armed with torpedoes in the first place—with the remainder held in reserve unarmed as of 0715. In such a case, all eighteen of the torpedoes on the planes of the first and second divisions would have been removed well before 0800. Moreover, as it was not necessary to remove torpedoes from the third division, by 0805 the nine planes in the first division could have had bombs attached. (We have seen that the 800-kilogram land bombs were already in hangars—they had been brought up from the magazine pursuant to an order by Nagumo at 0520 to prepare for the possibility of a second strike on Midway.)[9]

By 0805, rearming operations on both carriers would have ceased—probably before installation of the first six land bombs on *Akagi* had been completed. We have seen that, even had the rearming operation not been countermanded by then, further operations with 800-kilogram ordnance would have been difficult if not impossible; the first dive-bomber attack from Midway began at that time, causing the carriers to undertake radical evasive maneuvers. Thus, at 0830, the armament status of the torpedo planes appears to have been as follows: None of the planes on *Akagi* and *Kaga* had torpedoes on them. A few torpedo planes, perhaps as many as nine on *Kaga*, had 800-kilogram land bombs attached. All the torpedo planes were in the hangar decks.[10]

STATUS OF THE DIVE-BOMBERS

Unlike the case with with the torpedo planes, there is ample evidence in the Japanese record—and from the veterans—of the armament status of the dive-bombers on *Hiryu* and *Soryu*. At 0830, all thirty-six of them were "appropriately armed" to attack carriers. Senshi Sosho states that they "had finished changing back to anti-ship bombs."[11] The dive-bombers had all been rearmed with land bombs pursuant to the 0715 rearming order, and that operation had most likely been completed very soon after 0745. After the order to reverse the rearming operation was given, whether given at around 0750 by Yamaguchi (who, we saw, may have received *Tone* 4's sighting report directly), or after 0800 by Nagumo, the two-thirds of the dive-bombers that had been changed to land bombs

were changed back to antiship bombs by 0830. (Even with the evasive maneuvering of Hiryu and Soryu between 0805 and 0830, rearming could still be done
with the much smaller bombs, though at a slower pace.)

Thus, at 0830, around two-thirds of the dive-bombers had armor-piercing,
delay-fuse ("antiship") bombs on. The remaining third had high-explosive,
instant-detonation fragmentation ("land") bombs on—which, as has been explained, were intentionally installed even for attacks on ships (and were useful
for holing carrier flight decks).

It also appears that as of 0830 a few dive-bombers may have been brought
back up to the flight decks of each of the carriers in Yamaguchi's Second Carrier Division. The majority of the dive-bombers of each carrier that were still in
the hangars at 0830 could have been raised and spotted for launch on the flight
decks in about twenty minutes as both the midship and aft elevators could be
used (because there were no torpedo planes in the hangar). Thus, had Nagumo
opted to attack with just dive-bombers, the launch probably could have commenced at around 0850, with the planes off the flight decks by 0900. As for the
torpedo planes and Zeros back from Midway waiting to land on Hiryu and Soryu, they had sufficient fuel left to wait that long. (In the actual event, they did
not begin landing until around 0850 and, as we will see, some of Soryu's torpedo planes did not land until 0950.)

STATUS OF THE ZEROS

One of the main reasons why Nagumo did not think that an effective attack
could be launched soon after 0830 was the lack of Zeros to escort the dive-
bombers. According to Senshi Sosho all the second-wave Zeros had been committed to combat air patrol.[12] Nagumo believed that without escorts, the dive-
bombers would not be able to inflict sufficient damage on the American carriers to justify the cost in planes and, more importantly, pilots.

Why were there not enough Zeros on hand to provide an escort for the dive-
bombers while, at the same time, maintaining an adequate combat air patrol?
There has been considerable confusion over the number of Zeros available to
Nagumo on the morning of the battle. Some of the early commentators on
Midway placed the number at ninety or more,[13] which made it difficult to understand how the Japanese could have run short of them so early. Actually,
Nagumo entered the Battle with only seventy-two operational Zeros in the carrier air groups—eighteen on each carrier.[14] As mentioned earlier, there were
twenty-one other Zeros, part of the land-based Sixth Air Group, being carried
for use in the defense of Midway after its expected capture (nine on Kaga, six
on Akagi, and three each on Hiryu and Soryu). However, very few of the pilots
in that air group were carrier-qualified; there is record of only two of those
Zeros being used for carrier defense.[15] There were also an undetermined number of "spares"—perhaps only about a half-dozen. On the morning of the battle

most of these can be regarded as culls that were inoperable; in any event they had no pilots and can be disregarded.

Thus, it appears that there were only seventy-four Zeros actually available to Nagumo on the morning of the battle. Thirty-six (nine from each carrier) were sent in the first wave to attack Midway at 0430, leaving thirty-eight on board (including two in the Sixth Air Group). To better understand why *none* of these was available for escort duty at 0830, a summary of the combat air patrol activity (gleaned from Senshi Sosho and the Action Reports of the four carriers) might be helpful.[16]

COMBAT AIR PATROL ACTIVITY

According to Senshi Sosho, twelve Zeros were launched for combat air patrol at 0430—three from each carrier. However, it appears from *Kaga*'s Action Report that she launched only two in that first patrol. (One intended for launch may have had engine trouble.) I accept the data from the Action Reports indicating that only eleven were launched for combat air patrol at 0430. This left twenty-four operational Zeros in the carrier air groups available to escort the second wave in the event an American carrier force turned up. In addition, one from *Kaga* being worked on, and two from the Sixth Air Group, would later be available for combat air patrol—for a total of twenty-seven still on board.

It had been hoped that the attack on Midway would destroy on the ground most of the bombers based there, eliminating the need for very many additional Zeros in the combat air patrol to ward off an attack from Midway. But the American bombers were not destroyed on the ground, and, as things turned out, twelve more Zeros (six from *Hiryu*, and three each from *Akagi* and *Soryu*) were launched for combat air patrol between 0515 and 0615. Most took off after Catalina PBY reconnaissance planes from Midway had been sighted beginning at 0530. There were now twenty-three in the air, leaving just fifteen Zeros on board, including two from the Sixth Air group. Around 0700, when torpedo bombers (six of the newly deployed TBF Avengers) from Midway attacked, eight more Zeros were launched for air defense. This left seven on board. Six Zeros then landed for reservicing, and one Zero from *Hiryu* had been shot down—apparently by an Avenger torpedo bomber. Thus, at 0700, there were twenty-four Zeros aloft—leaving on board only seven not yet launched—along with six that had landed and were being serviced for relaunch. Shortly after 0700, more bombers were sighted—these were four Army B-26s that had been specially rigged with torpedoes. Eight more Zeros were launched (including three that were being launched for a second time after refueling).[17]

Thus, as of about 0715—when, incidentally, Nagumo made his fatal decision to rearm—thirty-two Zeros were aloft on combat air patrol. Of the remaining six from the original stock, one had been shot down, one was having its engine worked on, and two were having their guns reloaded in the hangar of *Hiryu* for relaunch. This left only two Zeros from the second-wave that had not yet been used for combat air patrol. In the next forty-five minutes, twenty-three Zeros were brought down for refueling and rearming—leaving only nine in the air. This meant that as of 0800—when *Tone 4*'s report sighting the American ships was received in *Akagi*'s headquarters—Nagumo was in pretty good shape for Zeros. What happened between then and 0830, when he had to make his decision whether or not to launch a strike against the American task force?

What happened was that Major Lofton Henderson and his sixteen Marine Corps SBD Dauntless dive-bombers from Midway showed up. When that first wave of dive-bombers arrived at 0800 it appears that fourteen Zeros were re-launched to reinforce the meager combat air patrol.[18] Then at about 0815 four-teen B-17s, led by Walter Sweeney, began dropping bombs on the Mobile Force. To attack them five Zeros were launched from *Kaga*, which included the *last* two Zeros in the second wave. Seven Zeros (three from *Kaga*, four from *Akagi*) that had landed for refueling and gun reloading were relaunched at around 0830 when the second wave of dive-bombers from Midway—eleven Ma-rine Corps Vindicators led by Benjamin Norris—attacked.[19] There were now thirty-two Zeros on combat air patrol—all the operational fighters Nagumo had. (Three more Zeros had been shot down since 0800, bringing the total to four; two were having their engines worked on.)

*   *   *

Thus, it can be seen that at 0830, when Nagumo had to make a decision whether to launch the dive-bombers immediately or postpone his attack, there were no Zeros available to escort the dive-bombers. All thirty-eight left on board after the Midway strike force had departed had been used for air defense. Two had become inoperable, and four had been shot down. Most of the thirty-two remaining on combat air patrol were out of ammunition; they needed to be landed as soon as possible and rearmed in order to provide a fresh combat air patrol against expected attacks from American carriers. None of them would be available for escort duty, either immediately or later. Moreover, even those thirty-two would not be enough to provide an adequate air defense. At least forty-eight would be required to protect against the dive-bombers and torpedo planes that could be expected from two carriers—especially if they attacked in waves and the Mobile Force became dispersed. These additional Zeros needed to bolster the air defense would have to come from the first wave back from Midway.

But a problem for Nagumo was that there would not be very many Zeros available for escort duty later in the morning even after the Midway strike force Zeros had been recovered and reserviced. Of the thirty-six that had been launched at 0430 for the strike on Midway, two had been shot down over Midway, and five more had been damaged badly enough to keep them out of action for the rest of the day. This left twenty-nine, which when added to the thirty-two on combat air patrol gave Nagumo a stock of sixty-one serviceable Zeros as of 0830. This meant that only about a dozen could be used for escort duty if an adequate air defense was to be maintained. (And this, indeed, was the number that would be assigned to escort the strike force that was later organized.)

The fact of the matter is that Yamamoto had not provided Nagumo with enough Zeros on his four carriers to provide both an adequate air defense against an American carrier bomber attack and an adequate escort for an attack of his own against the American carriers. He was about a dozen Zeros short. This shortage of Zeros would prove to severely limit his options for handling the American carrier threat. Had there been anything close to the ninety Zeros assumed by early American scholars of the battle to be available to Nagumo, there probably would have been at least a dozen available for escort duty at 0830, as well as an adequate number to escort another attack later on. But, alas, he had only a little over seventy-two. (This was the real cost of the Aleutian campaign foisted on Yamamoto—the Zeros squandered there were sorely missed at Midway.)

THE "ORBIT AND COBBLE" OPTION

It has been suggested that Nagumo could have ordered the launch of the dive-bombers at 0830, and then had them orbit in a fuel-conserving pattern until an adequate escort could have been cobbled together from the Zeros back from Midway.[20] (Spruance did something similar to this an hour and a half earlier when he launched his dive-bombers and had them orbit for almost an hour while the fighter escorts and torpedo bombers were brought up from the hangar decks and launched.)

Under this idea, the nearly out-of-gas dive-bombers back from Midway could have been immediately landed on *Akagi* and *Kaga*, along with enough Zeros to serve as escorts for the dive-bombers launched from *Hiryu* and *Soryu*. (The torpedo planes back from Midway expecting to land on *Hiryu* and *Soryu* could have waited long enough not only for the dive-bombers to be launched from those carriers, but for some Zeros to be landed as well.)[21] Twelve refueled and rearmed Zeros, three from each of the four carriers, would, under this scheme, have provided an adequate escort for thirty-six dive-bombers.

This would seem an attractive option—and it should not be assumed that Nagumo did not consider it. The problem with it, however, is that it would have taken at least forty-five minutes to land and lower to the hangar decks three Zeros on each carrier, reload their guns, refuel them, raise them to the flight decks, and launch them. Although forty-five minutes might seem an inordinate length of time for such an operation, that was the evidence from the Zero mechanic veterans[22]—and it is consistent with the entries in the log of the Official Report indicating the turn-around time for Zeros.

The main reason it took so long to rearm a Zero is that its four guns were reloaded at a special station in the forward part of the upper hangar deck, and the reloading operation took twenty minutes once the Zero was in the hangar. The most time-consuming part of this operation was reloading the 20-mm cannons. As they were in the wings, the wings had to be opened up—a more cumbersome procedure than reloading the 7.7-mm machine guns, which could be accessed from the cockpit.

The landing of the Zeros, under this "orbit and cobble" option, could not have begun until about 0900. It would have taken until about then to launch the second-wave dive-bombers on *Hiryu* and *Soryu* and land the first-wave dive-bombers back from Midway on *Akagi* and *Kaga*. This means that the Zeros thus cobbled together for escort duty could not have been launched before 0945. But, as we will see, when Nagumo made his decision to postpone at 0835, he probably expected to be able to launch a full-scale coordinated attack soon after then. This option, then, would not have offered a quick fix to Nagumo's dilemma at 0830.

WHY AN ATTACK WITH WHAT WAS AVAILABLE AT 0830 WAS UNPALATABLE TO NAGUMO

We have seen that the only attack option immediately available to Nagumo at 0830 was to launch the dive-bombers on *Hiryu* and *Soryu*, and to do it without escorts. This was the option urged by Rear Admiral Tamon Yamaguchi, commander of the Second Carrier Division (containing *Hiryu* and *Soryu*). He was fearful of an American carrier plane attack if the launch was postponed and believed that a limited attack was better than the possibility of none at all. We have seen that there were also a few torpedo planes on *Kaga* that probably had 800-kilogram land bombs attached, but they were in the hangars and could not be quickly launched. To have delayed the recovery of the dive-bombers back from Midway while the torpedo planes were raised to the flight decks and launched would most likely have resulted in many dive-bombers ditching, as most were almost out of fuel and some were badly damaged. In any case, level bombing by torpedo planes was considered virtually worthless against moving ships,[23] and sending them without escorts would have merely wasted more irreplaceable pilots.

Thus, at 0830 the only attack option immediately available was the "Yamaguchi" option of sending the dive-bombers alone. With the benefit of hindsight, the universal opinion is that this option should have been taken. And it would seem even at the time that thirty-six dive-bombers—though many would not get through the American air defenses without escorts—would still have been reckoned to constitute a significant strike force that could, with a little luck, cause serious damage to the American carriers. Nagumo's decision to forego this option, therefore, needs to be examined with particular scrutiny.

Senshi Sosho gives as the main reasons Nagumo decided against an immediate attack: that he did not think that an attack with dive-bombers alone would inflict sufficient damage to justify the pilot losses and that he thought he had time (for reasons that will be explained later) to organize a coordinated attack that would do far more damage with fewer pilot losses. Accordingly, at 0830, the Yamaguchi option had to compete with the alternative of a coordinated attack launched after landing the Midway strike force, and after the torpedoes had been restored to the torpedo planes and some of the Zeros back from Midway had been refueled and rearmed for escort duty. This alternative was clearly risky—an awful lot of things could go wrong, the worst being the arrival of American carrier bombers before the grand-scale strike got launched.

A grim cost-benefit analysis of the two options had to be quickly made by Genda and others in Nagumo's headquarters. The main cost of the Yamaguchi option was pilot losses. Without Zero escorts for the dive-bombers Nagumo faced the prospect of horrendous losses—probably at least three-quarters shot down. (Such an estimate would not be exaggerated; when *Hiryu* later did send its eighteen dive-bombers to attack *Yorktown* with an insufficient number of escorts—only six—thirteen dive-bombers did not make it back, and the three hits scored did not inflict fatal damage.)

But the sacrifice of dive-bombers and their crews was not the only problem: the torpedo planes, when rearmed and sent to attack later, even if they had escorts, would be much more vulnerable to enemy air defense fighters and ship AA gunfire than if accompanied by dive-bombers. This is because dive-bombers attacking from high altitude could be expected to divert a good portion of the enemy fighters and AA fire from the low-flying torpedo planes, which were extremely vulnerable because they had to hold a straight and level course for a considerable distance to accurately launch their torpedoes. If the torpedo planes later attacked without dive-bombers, they could be expected to attract the full fury of the American fighter force. It could be expected that at least half would be shot down (and, again, such a loss rate would not be far-fetched; that was what was sustained by *Hiryu*'s torpedo planes when they were later sent against *Yorktown* without being accompanied by dive-bombers). Thus, Nagumo had to be concerned not only about wasting dive-bomber crews for modest gain, but also about wasting torpedo plane crews later on.

A variety of game-modeling exercises—of the kind routinely practiced by carrier tacticians such as Genda—show that an adequately escorted coordinated attack can be expected to inflict around twice as much damage for about half the cost in planes and crew than can be expected from separate unescorted attacks by dive-bombers and torpedo planes. Put another way: a later coordinated attack could be expected to inflict about *four* times as much damage on American carriers for each plane and pilot lost than could be expected with separate attacks by dive-bombers and torpedo planes (with the dive-bombers unescorted) under the immediately available Yamaguchi option.

It was for this reason—conservation of carrier pilots—that Japanese escort doctrine was more rigorous than American. Japanese dive-bombers and torpedo planes were less robust and more lightly armed than their American counterparts and, thus, more dependent on fighter escorts for survival. And the Japanese had a more limited pool of carrier plane pilots than did the Americans, meaning that they were less able to afford pilot losses. (It should also be noted that they had had more extensive—and more bitter—experience with the consequences of unescorted carrier bomber attacks than had the Americans.)

Thus, the advantages of a coordinated attack by dive-bombers and torpedo planes, with Zero escorts, were deeply ingrained in practitioners of Japanese naval air tactics. As has been mentioned, this tactic—all three types of carrier planes attacking in a concentrated single stroke—was followed almost religiously by the time of the Midway operation, and was described in terms borrowed from the form of swordplay known as *Kinshicho-Oken*.[24] We have seen that the failure to deviate from this dogma in the decision for the second strike on Midway was a serious blunder (the torpedo planes should have been withheld), but we will see that for an attack against American carriers it was an eminently sound doctrine.

THE PILOT SHORTAGE PROBLEM

To better understand Nagumo's concern for pilot losses, it might be useful to digress and deal with a serious problem that the Japanese navy had at the beginning of the Pacific War—one that has not received the attention it deserves from American commentators: a severely limited pool of experienced carrier pilots. This problem pervaded the strategic and tactical decision-making process of Japanese naval commanders, especially in the carrier battles of the first six months of the war. It limited the options available to Nagumo at Midway. In particular, conservation of carrier pilots was a paramount concern of Nagumo (and especially Genda) in weighing the attack options at 0830. And for good reason: if the Japanese navy lost too many pilots at Midway, even if it "won" the battle in the sense of sinking more American carriers than it lost, Japan could still fail to achieve its main objective of the first year of the war—which was to knock the United States Navy out of the Pacific. Thus, Nagumo's decision at 0835 to reject the Yamaguchi option must be viewed in this broader context.

For Japan to have a decent chance of clearing the American navy out of the Pacific in the first year of the war, enough carrier pilots had to survive the Battle of Midway to complete the next phase of the campaign.[25] In the next and final phase of the first year's campaign, American military presence in the entire Pacific theater was to be eliminated. This would require at least one more big carrier battle to wipe out the remaining American fleet carriers (including those brought in from the Atlantic), and then there had to be enough carrier pilots left to capture, or at least neutralize, Pearl Harbor and put the Panama Canal out of operation. All this had to be done in the first year—before the new American *Essex*-class carriers came on line in 1943, with improved carrier fighter planes and torpedo bombers, and the hordes of American carrier pilots being trained at the navy flight school at Pensacola, Florida, and other new flight schools set up around the country. This urgency is what Yamamoto was referring to when he said to Prime Minister Konoye in 1940, "In the first six to twelve months of a war with the United States and Great Britain I will run wild and win victory upon victory. But then, if the war continues after that, I have no expectation of success."[26]

It was understood by Yamamoto, and others in the Japanese naval high command, that only by eliminating the American carrier force from the Pacific in the first year did Japan have a chance of surviving the war with its empire mostly intact. Only by forcing the American navy—after it rebuilt its carrier force in 1943–44—to start its offensive push on America's side of the Pacific could Japan make the road to victory over Japan so lengthy and costly that America just might settle for less than total victory. In the meantime, Japan would have the breathing space it needed to exploit its newly acquired oil resources in the Dutch East Indies and get them back to Japan to fuel its war machine, strengthen defensive positions in its expanded perimeter, and build up reserves for the ordeal ahead.

Japan's hopes for a quick victory over the American navy rested, to a large and precarious extent, on a highly skilled but small cadre of carrier pilots. She entered the Pacific War with only about 400 first-line carrier pilots: 250, mostly in the First and Second Carrier Divisions (*Akagi, Kaga, Hiryu,* and *Soryu*), were veterans with at least two years of carrier experience—many with combat experience in China; 150, mostly in the Fifth Carrier Division (on the newly commissioned *Shokaku* and *Zuikaku*), were less experienced. They were derided as second-rate by the veterans of the First and Second Carrier Divisions, but were nevertheless quite skilled by world standards and would become even better by the time of the Battle of the Coral Sea.

As of December 1941, there were about another seventy carrier-qualified pilots, mostly on the light carriers *Ryujo* and *Zuiho* (and awaiting the soon to be completed *Shoho*). Most of these were second-line carrier pilots at the beginning of the war. Although some of them would improve enough to become "attack" carrier replacements later in the first year, most would be limited to light-carrier duty such as supporting amphibious invasion operations. The Japanese navy had about another one thousand pilots in land-based air groups and seaplane squadrons, but very few would become carrier-qualified in the first year of the war. The naval pilot training program would add only about a hundred carrier-qualified aviators in the first year of the war. As those showing the most promise had already been skimmed off and accelerated into the newly commissioned Fifth Carrier Division in late 1941, the cohort scheduled to come on line in 1942 was smaller than might be expected, and most would not be ready for attack carrier duty until later in the year.

For all practical purposes, then, Japan's hopes for a quick victory in the Pacific rode on the skills of the four hundred pilots who took part in the attack on Pearl Harbor. They were the most elite cadre of carrier pilots in the world, averaging over 700 hours of flight time—an incredible amount considering that most American carrier pilots had less than 300 hours at the time. (This also contrasts sharply with the 150-hour average for the Japanese carrier pilots who had to replace the original cadre after the first year.) There were only enough of these elite pilots for about a half-dozen naval battles—about one year's worth. If the Japanese navy could not knock the American navy out of the Pacific before they were used up, Japan had no realistic chance of avoiding a crushing defeat.

Thus, Japan's predicament at the start of the Pacific War was that, unlike America, its carrier pilots on hand at the beginning of the war, essentially, could not be replaced. There were several reasons for this. The most obvious are that Japan's population was only about half that of the United States, it was far less industrialized, and it had a severely limited supply of aviation gasoline to expend on flight training. Less well known is the fact that it took much longer to train Japanese carrier pilots—especially Zero pilots—than it did to train their American counterparts. This is because more skill was required to survive aerial combat in the agile but lightly protected Zero.

The Zero was a superior dogfighting plane only in the hands of a highly skilled pilot. In the hands of a green pilot it was a death trap. And as the dive-bombers and torpedo planes were also lightly armored, without Zeros to protect them they also were death traps. Much has been made of the fact that Zeros lacked pilot armor and self-sealing gas tanks—as if the Japanese high command were not concerned about protecting their pilots. The fact of the matter is that the pilots strongly preferred this lack of protection and resisted adding it because the extra weight degraded the Zero's performance. Skilled pilots fervently believed that they had a better chance of surviving aerial combat in a lighter and more maneuverable plane. (Pilot armor and self-sealing gas tanks were added to the A6M5 Zero model in 1944 when green pilots had to replace the veterans killed in 1942, but the additional seven hundred pounds reduced performance so badly that it was discontinued.)[27]

American carrier planes, on the other hand, were more ruggedly built and, thus, could take more punishment in combat. Accordingly, less training was required to fly them and survive combat. The American philosophy for waging aerial warfare in the Pacific was to exploit its superior resources by producing overwhelming numbers of planes and pilots and win by attrition. All America had to do to guaranty a victory over Japan was for its navy to survive in the Pacific for one year after Pearl Harbor. This would provide enough time for its potentially colossal armaments industry to get geared up and come on line.

The key Japanese military planners—especially Yamamoto—were well aware of this and knew that they could not win a long war of attrition with the United States because of Japan's much more limited resources. (Industrial production was only about one-eighth that of America's.)[28] Most critically, Japan had only enough oil and gasoline on hand at the beginning of the war for only a little more than year's worth of full-scale offensive naval and air warfare.[29] Therefore, if it was to win the Pacific War, it had to win quickly—and do so with the carrier planes and pilots on hand at the outset. This very different philosophy of warfare—stressing fast, agile planes flown by a small elite of highly trained pilots—was not a matter of choice but of necessity, dictated by limited industrial capacity and even more limited fuel.

Because of Japan's shortage of fuel oil and aviation gasoline, her naval pilot training program was not designed to replace more than a fraction of the original four hundred carrier pilots during the first year of the war. Even when the need for more pilots became obvious after Midway, there simply was not time to train a new cadre of highly skilled carrier pilots. Although Japan had greatly expanded her pilot training program in 1941 in anticipation of war with the United States, the several thousand naval pilots produced after 1941 were mostly intended for land-based defensive action to hold the territorial gains expected to be captured in the first year of the war. (Interesting evidence of Japan's strategic plan for a short offensive war in the Pacific is the fact that Japanese war plans contained no provisions to replace the six attack carriers that were to be the spearhead in sweeping the American navy from the Pacific. No new attack carriers joined the fleet until mid-1944.)[30]

I have made this digression to explain a factor generally overlooked, or at least underappreciated by American analysts of Japanese naval strategy and tactics in the first year of the war: the need to use in the most efficient way possible the limited and irreplaceable cadre of carrier pilots. This stark imperative was an essential part of the context of Nagumo's decision to postpone his attack against the American carriers. Simply put, Nagumo had to destroy the most American carriers possible with the fewest of his own pilots lost—lest any victory at Midway turn out to be a Pyrrhic one.

THE TIME FACTOR

Let us concede that the advantages of a coordinated attack were so substantial that a postponement in order launch one, even at some risk, can be justified.

But, in view of the fact that Nagumo knew by 0600 that his Mobile Force had been discovered by the Americans, a question that has bedeviled many scholars of the battle is: what made him think he had the time to organize such an attack? It is known from his Official Report that the launch was scheduled for 1030—almost two hours after the decision to postpone was made. Accordingly, it is widely assumed that the 1030 launch time was scheduled at—or soon after—the time the decision to postpone was made at 0835.[31] As it would seem that, at that time, an American carrier bomber attack was imminent (and in fact it arrived at 0930 with the first wave of torpedo bombers), such a postponement strikes many as evidencing a reckless, and even arrogant, disregard for the American threat. This is one of the cornerstones of the theory that by 0830 Nagumo had become, under the stress of battle, irrational or at least incompetent.

WHEN WAS THE 1030 LAUNCH TIME SET?
The assumption by many commentators that the 1030 launch time was set at 0835 when the decision to postpone was made turns out to be erroneous. It is now clear that the 1030 launch time was not scheduled until around 0920.[32] At 0835, Nagumo assumed that his torpedo planes, rearmed with torpedoes, could be raised to the flight decks as soon as the Midway strike force had been landed,[33] and be ready to launch before 1000.

The facts of the 1030 scheduling appear to be: at around 0910, after Nagumo had advised his Mobile Force that "after taking on the returning planes, we shall proceed north to contact and destroy the enemy task force," he inquired of his carrier air group commanders when the planes would be ready for launch. A few minutes later, he received back what must have been very bad news to him: he was informed that the torpedo planes on *Akagi* and *Kaga* would not be ready for launch until 1030. This appears to have been the first inkling he had that he would not get an attack off until 1030. (It may also have been when he first became aware of the difficulties in the hangar decks with getting the torpedoes back on the torpedo planes.)

It was at this time that Nagumo had to have realized that his Mobile Force was in serious trouble. At 0920 reports reached him that sixteen American carrier torpedo bombers were approaching from 22 miles out, and at 0930, a second wave had been spotted. This meant that he could also expect that at least two carriers' worth of dive-bombers would be arriving momentarily. It would then have appeared very unlikely that he would get his coordinated attack off before absorbing an American dive-bomber attack. His only hope was that his combat air patrol would minimize the damage sufficiently to permit most of his own planes to be launched soon after 1030.

It is not known whether at that time Nagumo regretted his decision not to launch an attack at 0835. It was clear that he had lost his gamble that he had sufficient time to organize a grand-scale attack and that the very survival of his

Mobile Force was at stake. But despite the unexpected impediments that later arose, what is relevant to our inquiry is the reasonableness of the gamble he made at 0835 that he had a good chance of launching a coordinated attack—after landing the Midway strike force—before being attacked by American carrier bombers.

When Nagumo made his decision to postpone, it could be expected to take about thirty minutes to land and strike below the planes that had returned from Midway. In fact, the landing commenced on *Akagi* at 0837 (and after a brief suspension resumed at 0840), and the dive-bombers were landed by 0859. The landings of Zeros, including some on combat air patrol, were completed at 0910 on *Akagi* (but not until 0918 on some of the carriers). If the torpedo planes were rearmed with torpedoes by then—which Nagumo counted on at 0835—it would then take another forty-minutes to raise and spot on the flight deck, and warm up the engines, on a squadron of torpedo planes on *Akagi*, and ten more minutes to launch them. (Zeros for escort could be launched ahead of the torpedo planes.) Thus, at 0835, Nagumo expected to be able to begin launching his attack by about 0950 and to have his planes off the flight decks by 1000.

WHAT MADE NAGUMO THINK HE HAD THE TIME?

Even accepting that when Nagumo made his decision to postpone the attack—at 0835—he expected a launch before 1000, not 1030, in view of the fact that the first wave of the American attack actually arrived in the vicinity of the Mobile Force at 0920, what made Nagumo think that he had even until 1000 to get a grand-scale attack off his carriers before being attacked? Well, according to the Japanese official history, there was, in fact, good reason for him to think he had the time. Senshi Sosho states that the most crucial piece of information that influenced Nagumo's decision to postpone was the reported position of the American ships in the 0728 sighting report from *Tone* 4: "bearing 10 degrees, distance 240 miles from Midway." This was quickly calculated to put the American fleet approximately 205 nautical miles from the Mobile Force.[34]

This assumption was critical because it led Nagumo and his staff to conclude that the American carrier force was too far away to launch an effective attack against the Mobile Force. According to Senshi Sosho, although this distance was regarded by Nagumo's staff as putting the Mobile Force within range of the American carrier bombers, it was judged to be beyond the combat radius of the American Wildcat fighter plane—which was apparently assumed to be about 175 miles.

Senshi Sosho goes on the state that Nagumo's staff concluded, therefore, that the American carrier task force commander had two options—both favorable to the Japanese: either the American carriers would have to move closer to the Mobile Force before launching their attack, giving Nagumo time to organize and launch his coordinated attack before being attacked himself; or an earlier attack from over 200 miles would have to be made without fighter escorts, making the bombers easy to shoot down by air defense Zeros and giving the Mobile Force a good chance of surviving the attack and getting off its own.[35] It appears that Nagumo's staff judged the most likely option to be a delay in the American launch until the American carriers got to within 175 miles.

The assumption then appears to have been that it would take at least an hour—after 0728—for the American fleet to get close enough to launch the Wildcat fighters for an escorted attack. (Assuming those ships would be steaming at 25–30 knots toward the Mobile Force, this would bring them to within about 175 nautical miles after one hour.) It was, therefore, assumed that an escorted attack would not depart from the vicinity of the carriers until around 0845 and, as it would take around one and a half hours to fly 175 miles to the Mobile force, would not arrive before 1015. This would allow time (though it would be cutting it pretty close) for a coordinated attack to get launched from Nagumo's carriers.

At first glance, this is a stunning explanation for Nagumo's decision to postpone his attack. It is not mentioned in any of the English-language accounts of the battle. Nevertheless, a quick reference to the Search & Course Chart showing the position of the Mobile Force at 0728 and the position of the American fleet, with respect to Midway, reported by *Tone* 4 will enable one to easily calculate that the distance between them was, indeed, about 205 miles. And the reported effective combat radius of the Wildcat fighter was, indeed, only about 175 miles. Thus, it is not as outlandish an explanation as it first seems.

However, there was one horrendous problem with Nagumo's calculation: *Tone* 4's navigator had mislocated the position of the American task force. It was, as we have seen, actually about 55 miles further south than reported and 30 miles closer to the Mobile Force—only about 175 miles away at 0728.

The position of the American fleet reported by *Tone* 4 was not only erroneous; in fact, it was impossible for that fleet to be seen at its reported position— 240 miles north of Midway—by *Tone* 4 if that plane had been on course. The fleet would have been 140 miles away from *Tone* 4's scheduled position at 0728. (See Search & Course Chart.) Yet, incredibly, according to Senshi Sosho, nobody in Nagumo's headquarters noticed this anomaly when the sighting report was received; the report was assumed to be accurate.

Is there a reasonable excuse for this oversight? It has to be granted that at the time the sighting report was received—at about 0800—the Mobile Force was coming under attack by dive-bombers from Midway, so protecting the carriers was Nagumo's first priority. Also, there was shock and disbelief that enemy ships would be in the Midway area at that time. Nagumo and his staff were kept very busy the next thirty minutes evading bombing attacks from the first wave of dive-bombers and then from B-17s. In the meantime, at 0811, Nagumo received another report from *Tone* 4 identifying the enemy ships as five cruisers and five destroyers—which raised the possibility, at least, that there was no threat from carriers.

While it might be understandable why nobody in Nagumo's headquarters would have checked the search charts during this period to ascertain *Tone* 4's search path, it is much less understandable why nobody in cruiser *Tone*'s headquarters noticed the anomaly. *Tone* 4 was under their direct command, and they had more details concerning *Tone* 4's launch time and search path than did Nagumo's staff. (When this is added to the lengthy delay in forwarding the sighting report, it is difficult to avoid the conclusion that Nagumo was sorely let down by the personnel on cruiser *Tone* in charge of *Tone* 4's search operations.)

In any event, at 0830 when Nagumo received the *Tone* 4 report identifying a carrier, and a decision had to be made whether to launch an immediate attack or postpone, it was clearly necessary at that time to consult the navigational charts. This had to be done in order to determine where the American fleet was in relation to the Mobile Force. It was probably then that the distance between the fleets was calculated to have been 205 miles at 0728. Even if it is understandable why the anomaly was not noticed thirty minutes earlier, why was it not noticed at 0830? The only apparent explanation is that at that time a decision had to be made quickly; the dive-bombers back from Midway were waiting to land, some in distress. And, as there were no torpedo planes or fighter escorts available to launch, there was probably a strong predisposition to immediately land the Midway strike force. One cannot help but suspect that Nagumo's staff were looking for data to support a decision they already wanted to make—to postpone the attack. According to Yoshioka's recollection in Senshi Sosho, the decision "was easily made."[36]

However, it appears that about twenty minutes after the decision was made somebody finally noticed that the position of the American fleet reported by *Tone* 4 was too far north to be seen by *Tone* 4's crew if their plane was on course. The log of the Official Report shows a message from Nagumo to *Tone* 4 at 0854 ordering it to "go on the air with transmitter for DF [direction-finding] purposes." (A minute later a similar request was made by cruiser *Tone*'s headquarters.) *Tone* 4's transmission in response to this order was not received by *Akagi*'s radio, and there is no evidence that Nagumo learned of *Tone* 4's true course until well after the battle. In any case it would have been too late to change the decision: the dive-bombers on *Hiryu* and *Soryu* had been stricken below, and all four carriers were in the process of recovering the Midway strike force.

One can only speculate what Nagumo's decision at 0835 would have been had he known that the American fleet was actually only 175 miles away at 0728 (instead of the over 200 miles assumed). He would have been forced to assume that his Mobile Force had been within the combat radius of the Wildcat fighter for over an hour and that thus he was subject to an *escorted* carrier bomber attack at any moment. Even worse, most of his Zeros on combat air patrol were low on ammunition—especially the plane-killing 20-mm cannon shells—and could not be relied on to protect his carriers until they had been landed and rearmed. This would take the better part of an hour, to perhaps 0930. It would seem that pressure to immediately launch Yamaguchi's dive-bombers would have been well nigh irresistible. (And it is unlikely that anyone on Nagumo's staff would have recalled—as Yoshioka later did—that the decision was "easily made.")

Be that as it may, at 0835 Nagumo assumed that the American carrier force was over 200 miles away. He, therefore, had reason to believe that he had time to organize a coordinated attack to be launched after the Midway strike force had been recovered. Postponement clearly posed a risk that he would be attacked before he got his own attack launched, but the likelihood of an escorted American attack in such a case appeared slim. The prospects envisioned by a grand-scale attack were so clearly superior to what the Yamaguchi option offered that the risk appeared worth taking. It was the only hope for a decisive victory at a cost that could be afforded. Kusaka's retrospective is apt: "the seeds of our defeat were also the seeds of our victory."[37]

In the end, at 0835 Nagumo rolled the dice. It would be the second big gamble he lost that morning. Was it a reasonable gamble? As it was based on two erroneous assumptions that could have been called into question with a little checking out—that the Mobile Force was out of range of an escorted American strike and that the torpedo planes would be rearmed with torpedoes when the Midway strike force was landed—one well might question its reasonableness. But given the chaotic circumstances in Nagumo's headquarters between 0800 and 0830, his failure to better comprehend what was going on is at least understandable. I am inclined to view his decision to postpone as a classic example of the "fog of war."

In any case, in the final analysis, Nagumo's failure to order an immediate attack at 0835 probably did not make much difference in the outcome of the battle, as is commonly supposed. An attack by thirty-six unescorted dive-bombers is not likely to have inflicted much more damage on the American carriers than was inflicted by the later actual attack on *Yorktown* by *Hiryu*'s eighteen dive-bombers with minimal escorts, and the cost in pilots is likely to have been much higher.

Moreover, the absence of those dive-bombers from Nagumo's carriers when the American dive-bomber attacks came at 1020 probably would not have substantially reduced the damage sustained by the Mobile Force, as is also often assumed. If we, instead, assume that the same three carriers would have been hit by the same number of bombs, *Akagi* and *Kaga* would still have been caught with all their torpedo planes on board—fully fueled and with 800-kilogram bombs still in the hangar—and would have been destroyed. As for *Soryu* and *Hiryu*, the smaller *Soryu* would probably have been destroyed by the three 1,000-pounders that hit her at 1025 *even* had the dive-bombers not been on board. *Hiryu*, not hit until later in the day, would have had about the same number of planes on board as she actually had after launching two attacks on *Yorktown*—and in any case would surely have been destroyed by the four 1,000-pounders that hit her.

Therefore, I suggest that it was not Nagumo's failure to launch an attack immediately after 0830 that doomed the Mobile Force. It was the failure to get his coordinated attack off his carriers before 1020 that was the real cause of the Japanese debacle at Midway. The central focus of this inquest is to explain that failure, without resort to theories predicated on incredible stupidity on the part of Nagumo and his staff.

WHY NAGUMO'S LAUNCH NEVER GOT READY

We now come to the most baffling mystery of Midway: why no launch ever got made before the American dive-bombers arrived at 1020. Nagumo had been given a big break with his launch-time problem because, as we will see in the next chapter, the American dive-bombers from *Enterprise* got lost en route because of a faulty PBY search plane sighting report; otherwise, they would have arrived at 0920. Thus, as it turned out, Nagumo had a fifteen-minute window—between 1000, when the second torpedo bomber attack from *Enterprise* ended, and 1015, when the third torpedo bomber attack from *Yorktown* began—during which a grand-scale attack could have been launched. This, provided that all his second-wave planes had been on the flight decks ready for launch at 1000. Why was Nagumo unable to get his planes ready for launch by 1000? This is an especially perplexing question in view of the fact that he had received notice of a probable American carrier threat two hours before then. But, as we have seen, when the launch was scheduled—at around 0920—it was not expected to be made until 1030. The reasons for the delay until 1030 have never been adequately explained.

We saw that when Nagumo made his decision, at 0835, to postpone his attack until after the Midway strike force had been recovered, his apparent assumption was that the all the torpedoes would be restored to the torpedo planes by time those planes were landed (at soon after 0900). This was overly optimistic. (Actually, it appears that Nagumo and his staff were totally oblivious of the real armament status of the torpedo planes when the decision to postpone was made.)[38] When the rearming operation was suspended at about 0805, all the torpedoes had been removed from the torpedo planes on both *Akagi* and *Kaga* (and a few 800-kilogram land bombs probably installed on *Kaga*'s planes). Moreover, the launchers for torpedoes had mostly been removed from these planes. And it now appears that after rearming was suspended nothing was done to convert the launchers back for torpedoes between then and 0840.

This, though perhaps surprising, is understandable. The carriers had been under attack by bombers from Midway during most of that time, and the head-quarters staff appears to have been too preoccupied by those attacks, and by additional reports from *Tone* 4 on the composition of the American naval force, to issue further instructions to the arming crews. There is evidence that the order to reverse the rearming operation and "prepare to carry out attacks on enemy fleet units" was not actually issued until 0840 — just after the decision to postpone the launch had been made.[39] Although this contradicts the contention in Senshi Sosho that the rearming operation was reversed at 0745, it is — as we will see — the only way that the later scheduling of the launch for 1030 can be explained.

After the last attack from Midway ceased just before 0840, operations to restore the torpedoes to the torpedo planes resumed. The first procedure was to get the torpedo launchers back on — and on *Kaga*, to remove the 800-kilogram bombs that probably had been installed on as many as nine of her planes. About thirty minutes would be required to change back the launchers on those planes that had been completely converted for bombs. (While less time would be required for those launchers still in the process of being converted, it appears that some of the mechanics in the torpedo plane squadrons had been diverted to assist in emergency repairs on some of the dive-bombers that arrived in the hangars badly shot up, some with leaking fuel tanks.) Work on the torpedo planes also would have been slowed somewhat until about 0910 by the recovery of those dive-bombers, which landed between 0840 and 0900 and had to be lowered to the hangar decks. Thus, it appears that the torpedo mechanics did not begin to reinstall torpedoes on the planes until about 0910.

This was the likely armament status of the torpedo planes — no torpedoes yet reattached — when Nagumo's air group commanders were asked, at around 0910, when those planes would be ready for launch. They reported back a few minutes later that the torpedo planes on *Akagi* and *Kaga* would not be ready for launch until 1030. Let us now see how could it take an hour and twenty minutes — after 0910 — to get the torpedo planes ready for launch (even if there were no disruptions from American carrier-plane attacks, which had not yet occurred at the time the estimate was made).

When work on the torpedoes began, the procedures for installing a torpedo took longer than those for removing it. (The rearming experiment conducted on *Hiryu* in the Indian Ocean campaign showed that while a squadron of torpedo planes could be changed from torpedoes to 800-kilogram land bombs in one and one-half hours, it took two hours to change back to torpedoes; the two operations were not symmetrical.) The main reason appears to be that more time was required to install the firing pin and detonator — and set the fuse — than to remove them. We saw in chapter 4 that it took around seven minutes to crank up the jacks on a carrier car, disarm a torpedo, release it from the launcher, and crank it down, and another five minutes to cart the torpedo to the heavy-weapons rack. However, it took a little longer to load a torpedo on to the carrier car and move it to the plane (perhaps six to seven minutes), and at least ten minutes to crank it up to the launcher, attach it to the release mechanism, and install the firing pin and detonator. After this was done, the carrier car would be moved to the next torpedo—which took about one minute. Thus, it took close to twenty minutes to reinstall the torpedoes on a division of six planes on *Akagi*—as compared with twelve to thirteen minutes to remove them (about one hour to restore the torpedoes on the entire squadron as compared to around forty minutes to remove them).

Under this timetable—with restoration beginning at around 0910—torpedoes would have been restored to one division of torpedo planes on *Akagi* by around 0930, on a second by 0950, and on all three by about 1010. Although the torpedo planes could have been raised to the flight deck as soon as they were rearmed with torpedoes, the need to keep the flight deck clear for landings of Zeros on combat air patrol would have dictated that this not be done until absolutely necessary. As it had probably been estimated that the last division of *Akagi*'s torpedo planes would not have their torpedoes restored until around 1010, it seems that operations to raise torpedo planes on *Akagi* to the flight deck would have been expected to begin at around 0950. This is because if the launch was expected to begin at 1030, it would take about forty minutes to raise (using just the aft elevator), spot on the flight deck, and warm up the engines of *Akagi*'s seventeen torpedo planes.[40]

This schedule is what would have been projected just prior to 0920. But it did not come to be. At 0930 the American torpedo bombers from the carrier *Hornet* began their attack on the Mobile Force. Rearming operations came to a halt as the carriers maneuvered radically to avoid torpedoes. Operations to complete the restoration of torpedoes could not resume at full pace until around 1000, when the second torpedo bomber attack (from *Enterprise*) ceased. These interruptions probably added about a half-hour to the time. It now appears that no torpedo planes were spotted on *Akagi*'s flight deck until after 1010 (three Zeros on combat air patrol were landed at that time). Thus, when the American dive-bombers arrived over the Mobile Force at 1020, there was still at least twenty minutes more rearming work to be done on Nagumo's torpedo planes. Most of them were still in the hangars,[41] and would not have been ready for launch until close to 1100.

Thus, contrary to widely held belief, Nagumo was nowhere near being able to launch his strike force when American bombs began raining down on his carriers at 1022. Reports from American dive-bomber pilots that a launch was under way at that time—Zeros were seen taking off—are erroneous. The Zeros seen taking off from *Akagi* were, in fact, reinforcements to the combat air patrol.[42]

The fact that most, if not all, the torpedo planes were still in the hangars when the carriers were bombed between 1022 and 1027—as revealed by Senshi

Sosho—has led some Japanese commentators, such as Hisae Sawachi, to pos-
tulate that the original rearming operation must have begun well before the
0715 time claimed by Nagumo in his Official Report.[43] If the rearming operation began before 0600, as Sawachi speculates, *all* the torpedo planes would
have had 800-kilogram bombs on by 0800, requiring at least two hours—after
0840—to restore the torpedoes. (We saw in chapter 1 that according to her the
0715 time was fabricated to make Nagumo's decision to rearm his second-wave
attack planes appear more reasonable.)

However, as can be seen from the scenario I have constructed, even if the
rearming operation did not begin until 0715 (or 0720), if it was not suspended
until about 0805—instead of the 0745 time generally believed—the status of
the torpedo planes at 1022 can still satisfactorily be accounted for without resort
to fabrication or conspiracy theories. While it may seem astonishing that forty-
five minutes of rearming work could not be reversed in less than two and one-
half hours, that was, in fact, the case. We have seen that the nature of the rearming procedures and the timing of the various disruptions—especially the
American attacks—after 0805, did, indeed, make it impossible to undo the neu-
tering of the torpedo planes that resulted from Nagumo's fatal rearming decision at 0715.

The key, then, to solving the mystery of why Nagumo could not get an attack
launched before his carriers were bombed at 1022 is acceptance of his claim that
he did not receive the *Tone* 4 sighting report until around 0800, rather than
prior to 0745 as generally assumed. This twenty-minute difference in receipt
time meant that twenty minutes' more rearming work on the torpedo planes
had to be undone in twenty minutes' less time—a forty-minute swing.

WHAT IF REARMING REALLY HAD
BEEN REVERSED AT 0745?

I have previously contended that had the rearming operations been reversed at
0745—as claimed by Senshi Sosho—it would have been possible for Nagumo
to get his strike force launched before the fatal bombing of his carriers by dive-
bombers from *Enterprise* and *Yorktown*. (And, had this happened, it almost certainly would have changed the outcome of the Battle of Midway and altered the
course of the Pacific War, as will be seen in chapter 10.) It is now time for that
general assertion to be backed up by some particulars; to show how there would
have been time, even with all the disruptions, to have restored the torpedoes to
the torpedo planes on *Akagi* and *Kaga* and get the strike force up to the flight
decks and launched before 1020—had Nagumo reversed the rearming operation at 0745.

We saw in chapter 4 that the status of the torpedo planes on *Akagi*, as of 0745,
was approximately as follows: the torpedoes had been removed from the first

two divisions (eleven or twelve planes), but the six planes in the third division would still have had their torpedoes attached. The torpedo launchers on the first division would have been removed, but work to remove the launchers on the second division would only just have begun. Had the rearming operation been reversed at 0745, there would have been roughly twenty minutes—till 0805—to begin restoring the torpedoes before the American dive-bomber attack from Midway would have brought proceedings to a halt. What could have been done in twenty minutes?

Even though procedures to restore torpedoes took longer than those to remove them, there still would have been time to do the following: the torpedoes from the second division planes could have been loaded back on the carrier cars and carted back to the planes in about seven minutes. By time the torpedoes arrived under the planes, the torpedo launchers would have been ready for them (about five minutes of unbolting work since 0740 would have been reversed). It would then have taken about ten minutes to crank up the torpedoes, attach them to the release gear and reinstall the detonators and firing-pins. All this would have taken around seventeen to twenty minutes. In the meantime, the torpedo launchers on the first-division planes would have been restored. Thus, by 0805—when rearming operations would have been halted—it could reasonably be expected that two-thirds of the torpedo planes in *Akagi*'s squadron would have had their torpedoes attached (including those from which they had not been removed), and the remaining six planes would have been ready to have their torpedoes put back on as soon as rearming could resume. (All this providing that the rearming operation had been reversed at 0745.)

In such a case, after resumption of the rearming operation, there would have been only about twenty minutes' worth of work left to be done to completely restore the torpedoes to *Akagi*'s torpedo planes. Even if rearming operations would not have resumed until 0840—when the series of attacks from Midway finally ceased—and even if operations were slowed somewhat by the recovery of the Midway strike force dive-bombers, it would still have been possible for all the torpedo planes on both *Akagi* and *Kaga* to have had their torpedoes put back on by around 0910. This is the likely scenario had the rearming operation actually been reversed at 0745, as contended by Senshi Sosho.

Operations could then have begun to raise the rearmed strike planes to the flight decks as soon as the Midway strike force had been recovered. But this brings us to the question of when the Midway strike force was actually recovered—because deck-spotting operations could not have begun until those planes (and any Zeros on combat air patrol requiring reservicing) had been landed. The time usually given for the end of recovery operations is 0918—the time stated in the composite log of the Official Report. However, it turns out that the issue is more complicated; the actual time varied among the four carriers of the Mobile Force.

Akagi's action report states that her Midway strike planes were recovered at 0910 and that the last Zero on combat air patrol landed for reservicing during this period also came down at 0910.[44] As only twelve Zeros (eight in the Midway strike force—one having been shot down—and four on combat air patrol) needed to be landed, it does seem likely that they all could have come down between 0859 and 0910. (Eighteen dive-bombers—requiring more time per plane to recover than Zeros—had been landed in twenty minutes.) *Kaga's* action report says that her Midway strike planes were recovered between 0840 and 0850 (but probably took a few minutes longer) and that her Zeros on combat air patrol requiring reservicing were also landed at 0910.[45] Thus, it appears that operations to raise the torpedo planes on both *Akagi* and *Kaga* could have begun at 0910.

As for when the Midway strike planes were recovered on *Hiryu* and *Soryu*, the record is more confusing.[46] It appears that the recovery of *Hiryu's* planes was delayed—probably until 0850 because of Yamaguchi's reluctance to abandon a strike with his dive-bombers—and they were probably not finally recovered until 0918 (the time given the Official Report for completion of the Midway strike force recovery operation). Thus, deck-spotting operations for *Hiryu's* dive-bombers could not have commenced until about 0918.

The record is even murkier as to *Soryu's* recovery operation. It appears from *Soryu's* Action Report and testimony from one of her torpedo-plane pilots that at least some of the Midway strike planes did not get recovered until 0950![47] It seems that two of the three *chutais* of torpedo planes returned early—at around 0750—and when American dive-bombers were seen approaching the Mobile Force, they fled from the vicinity to seek the safety of clouds. For reasons unexplained their landings were delayed—not completed until around 0920[48]—and the last torpedo plane did not get recovered until 0950 (apparently because the American torpedo bomber attacks disrupted landings). The recovery of *Soryu's* Midway strike Zeros was also delayed. Although six landed at 0850, the other three did not land until 0945.[49] On their return they sighted the B-17s that were returning to Midway after their bombing run. They gave chase to attack them (unsuccessfully) and did not get back to the vicinity of the carriers until after 0920.

Though it would appear that because of those delayed landings no deck-spotting operations for *Soryu's* dive-bombers could have begun until 0950, that is not necessarily the case. Had Nagumo made the decision to spot a strike force on the flight decks as soon as possible after 0910, we can assume that the aggressive Yamaguchi would not have countenanced a serious delay in the deployment of his dive-bombers because of a few Midway strike force stragglers. They most likely would have been required to stay aloft—even at the risk of ditching—until the strike force was launched.

But, as we have seen under this hypothetical scenario (premised on a supposed reversal of the rearming operation at 0745), operations to deploy the all-important torpedo planes to the flight decks on *Akagi* and *Kaga* could have commenced at around 0910. As it took about forty minutes to raise, spot on the flight deck, and finish preparations for a launch of eighteen torpedo planes, a launch of those planes would appear possible beginning at around 0950. However, this would not have been an ordinary deck-spotting operation. *Hornet*'s sixteen torpedo bombers arrived and began their run-up to the Mobile Force at 0925. At that time *Akagi* swerved around to the west to present its stern to the planes. *Akagi* and the other carriers were required to make evasive maneuvers until 0958 in order to minimize the danger of being hit by torpedoes launched by two waves of torpedo bombers (fifteen from *Enterprise* had begun attacking at 0940).

What impact would this have had on the deck-spotting operations? We have seen that operations to rearm torpedo planes with torpedoes were severely constrained during this period, but that does not mean that torpedo planes could not be raised in the elevators and spotted on the flight decks while the carrier was swerving to avoid torpedoes. The evidence from the veterans was that they could, but that the pace would be slowed somewhat; it may have added ten minutes to the procedure. (An 1,872-pound torpedo raised on the jacks of the narrow carrier car is obviously unstable, but a torpedo plane—with its wide landing-gear stance—is very stable.) Thus, if the deck-spotting operation for *Akagi*'s torpedo planes began at 0910, those planes still could have been ready for launch by 1000—when the fifteen-minute window of opportunity between the second and third torpedo-bomber attacks presented itself.

There would, however, have been another complication to the deck-spotting procedure caused by the arrival of the American torpedo bombers: flight operations for the combat air patrol. It would be impossible to land Zeros needing reservicing during the extended period when the torpedo planes were being deployed to the flight decks for launch. Would this have compelled Nagumo to postpone deployment of his strike force until the American attacks were over? Probably not.

As many as fourteen Zeros on combat air patrol had already been landed for reservicing between 0859 and 0910. This provided a large supply of reinforcements, and when rearmed they could be relaunched even with planes spotted aft on the flight decks (there were, in fact, over thirty takeoffs of Zeros between 0915 and 1015). Nagumo's official report shows that only four Zeros were landed between 0910 and 1010, two from *Soryu* at 0930 and two from *Akagi* at 0951. *Soryu*'s two Zeros probably could have landed before 0920, and it can be assumed that the landings of *Akagi*'s two would have been deferred.

Therefore, had deck-spotting operations for the torpedo planes been commenced at 0910 (which would have been possible had the rearming operation been reversed at 0745), the combat air patrol activity required to defend against the subsequent American attacks would not have impelled Nagumo to cancel them. To the contrary, it would seem that the need to get the strike force off the carriers as soon as possible would have become even more imperative.

Under this scenario, *Akagi*'s seventeen torpedo planes would have been on the flight deck ready for launch at 1000. *Hiryu*'s dive-bombers (and probably *Soryu*'s) would also have been ready. (Even though *Hiryu*'s and *Soryu*'s deck-spotting operations could not have begun until a few minutes after *Akagi*'s, the newer elevators on those carriers were faster than those of *Akagi*.) All this would appear to have made things look very promising for the grand-scale attack envisioned by Nagumo to be launched during the fifteen-minute window that presented itself at 1000. There would, however, have still been one fairly serious problem.

This problem was with *Kaga*'s torpedo plane squadron. It had twenty-six planes, and although they could have been rearmed with torpedoes by 0910, there would not have been time to get all of them up to the flight deck by 1000. Eighteen or nineteen could have been brought up, but because of the delay due to the American attacks, another fifteen to twenty minutes would have been required to get the last seven or eight up and prepared for launch.

Would Nagumo have been inclined to postpone the launch of his strike force until all of *Kaga*'s planes were ready to go? Nobody, of course, knows. Although he postponed a launch at 0835 in order to launch a grand-scale attack later, it seems most unlikely that he would have delayed this time. At 1000, Nagumo would have had available for immediate launch about thirty-six torpedo planes (seventeen on *Akagi*, nineteen on *Kaga*), thirty-six dive-bombers, and twelve Zeros (three from each carrier). Though less than the full second wave, such an array would still, unlike what was available at 0835, have been a very formidable strike force. Moreover, at 1000 the skies would finally have been clear of American torpedo planes, but dive-bombers were expected soon. In fact, as more American torpedo planes had been detected 25 miles out, Nagumo would have realized that he had only about fifteen minutes to get his strike force launched. It would have been "now or never."

Assuming that Nagumo opted for a launch at 1000, it could have been completed in about ten minutes.[50] The last plane would have got off its carrier at around 1010—just five minutes before the third wave of American torpedo bombers, this time from *Yorktown*, bore down on Nagumo's carriers.

Had a launch been made before the fatal American dive-bombing attack, Nagumo would in all likelihood have won the battle. The probable results of a Japanese attack made with substantial strength against the American carriers are detailed in chapter 10. It will be seen that while this initial attack probably would not have knocked out the American carrier force, it very likely would have badly crippled two of the three carriers. And because most of the second-wave planes—with their inflammable fuel and ordnance—would have been off Nagumo's carriers, those carriers (especially *Akagi*) would have sustained much less damage from the American dive-bombing attack that came at 1022. As will be seen, this would have permitted subsequent Japanese attacks with sufficient strength to probably have finished off the American carriers—and forestalled the second American attack in the afternoon that destroyed *Hiryu*.

*   *   *

But, of course, the foregoing nightmare scenario never happened. It did not happen because the rearming operation on Nagumo's carriers did not get reversed at 0745—and this because Nagumo did not receive the *Tone* 4 sighting report until 0800. It may seem incredible that such a momentous swing in the fortunes of war could have resulted from a mere twenty-minute difference in time of receipt of a sighting report. But, as we have seen, because of the mechanics involved in reversing a rearming operation with torpedoes, this twenty-minute difference compounded into a forty-minute swing in the time it took to restore the torpedoes to Nagumo's torpedo plane squadrons. Other famous battles in history have turned on fortuities far more trivial than this.

CHAPTER SEVEN

IRONIES

Iᴎ ᴛʜᴇ ᴘʀɪᴏʀ ᴛʜʀᴇᴇ ᴄʜᴀᴘᴛᴇʀs, Nagumo's fateful decisions on the morning of June 4, 1942, have been analyzed from the perspective of the Japanese side of the battle. In this chapter I will attempt to put those decisions into the broader context that takes into account what happened on the American side of that battle during the three critical hours between 0715 and 1020. While Nagumo was undergoing his ordeals, which began with his decision to rearm his torpedo planes for a second strike on Midway, the American carrier force commanders Raymond Spruance and Jack Fletcher were having problems of their own getting their strike forces launched and to their target. As will be seen, the miscalculations and blunders on the American side very nearly bailed Nagumo out of the blunders he and his subordinates made.

IRONIES IN NAGUMO'S ASSUMPTIONS

Of the decisions made by Nagumo that morning, the most controversial one was his decision, at 0835, to postpone his attack on the American carrier force. As we saw in the previous chapter, that decision was based, in large part, on his conclusion that he had enough time to organize and launch a grand-scale attack before being attacked himself by an American carrier bomber force capable of destroying a significant number of his carriers. This conclusion was based on the sighting report sent by *Tone* 4 at 0728, which erroneously placed the American fleet 30 miles further away from Nagumo's Mobile Force than it actually was (about 205 nautical miles rather than 175).

This error in the sighting report was critical because it misled Nagumo into believing that the American carrier force was too far away to make an *escorted* bomber attack against the Mobile Force; the combat radius of the Wildcat fighter was reckoned to be less than 200 miles. It was therefore concluded that either the American carrier bombers would have to attack without fighter escorts—which would make them easy prey for his combat air patrol—or that the carriers would have to delay launching an attack until they moved closer. Both options favored Nagumo's chances of getting his strike force launched. The assumptions Nagumo made from the erroneous sighting report are satiate with irony and paradox.

While the assumption by Nagumo's staff about the Wildcat's limited range was correct, the more serious concern in Spruance's command center on the carrier *Enterprise* was the range of the Devastator torpedo bomber; it had a combat radius even less than that of the Wildcat—only about 175 miles.[1] This concern did, in fact, lead Spruance to delay the launch of his attack against the Mobile Force until he got close enough to give the Devastators a decent chance of returning to their carriers.

SPRUANCE ALSO MISLED BY A FAULTY SIGHTING REPORT

Perhaps the greatest irony in Nagumo's assumptions based on the erroneous *Tone* 4 sighting report is that Spruance was also misled in his launch-time decision by an American PBY search plane sighting report almost as inaccurate as that of *Tone* 4. This sighting report placed the Mobile Force 27 miles closer to Spruance's carrier force than it actually was. Had the report been accurate, Spruance might, indeed, have further delayed his launch to steam closer so his torpedo bombers would have a better chance of returning—perhaps to as late as Nagumo hoped (completing it after 0830 instead of at 806).

The sighting report Spruance relied on was sent by a Catalina PBY at 0552 and received on *Enterprise* at 0603. (As we saw in an earlier chapter, it was an amplification of a report sent at 0530 that never reached the American task force commanders.) It gave the location of the Japanese carriers as "bearing 320 degrees, distance 180 miles" from Midway.[2] This placed the Mobile Force about 40 miles southeast of its actual location, which put it 175 miles from Spruance's Task Force 16 while, in fact, it was 202 miles away. This 27-mile error was of about the same magnitude as the 30-mile error in *Tone* 4's 0728 sighting report. (Moreover, only two Japanese carriers were reported, instead of the four actually in the Mobile Force—further paralleling the Japanese report of but one of the three carriers in the American force.)

We have already seen that after receiving the sighting report, Spruance and his staff were thrown into a quandary: should he launch a strike immediately (his planes were already on the flight decks of *Enterprise* and *Hornet*) or delay for one hour to give him time to move closer to the Mobile Force, and possibly receive confirmation of its location. The case for an immediate launch was that he may already have been discovered by Japanese reconnaissance planes — several "bogeys" (which turned out not to be Japanese planes) had been picked up on *Enterprise*'s radar screen. If he had been discovered, he feared, there was a possibility that Nagumo's Midway strike force — which Spruance knew was heading toward Midway from another PBY report — could be diverted to attack him before he got his own planes off his carriers.

But the case for postponing his launch until 0700 was strong: it had been calculated by Spruance's chief of staff, Captain Miles Browning, that the optimum time to hit the Japanese carriers was after the Midway strike force had returned to its carriers and was being refueled and rearmed. That time was estimated to be a little after 0900. (As discussed earlier, Spruance appears to have assumed that the entire bomber complements of the Japanese carriers had been sent — in two waves — to attack Midway.) Also, he should wait, if feasible, until he had received confirmation of the location of the Mobile Force and the number of carriers actually present. (Fletcher had advised this in a directive sent at 0607 "to proceed southwesterly and attack enemy carriers when definitely located" — most likely because of his experience in the Battle of the Coral Sea, where inaccurate sighting reports had resulted in wasteful deployment of strike forces.) The final consideration for Spruance was that the 175-mile distance from the Mobile Force indicated by the 0603 report was at the extreme limit of the combat radius of his torpedo bombers. If he could close the distance by another 20 miles it would provide a margin of safety for those torpedo bombers.

Spruance took a calculated risk and decided to postpone. It appears that the range of the TBD Devastator torpedo bomber was the controlling factor in this decision.[3] The launch of the strike force was then scheduled for 0700, when, it was estimated, the distance to the Mobile Force would be 155 miles. In actual fact — unknown to Spruance at the time — the actual distance to the Mobile Force at 0700 was not 155 miles, but 182.

Thus, had Spruance known that the true distance to the Mobile Force was over 180 miles, there is a distinct possibility that he would have delayed his launch for perhaps another thirty minutes — until after 0730 — in order to get within 170 miles.[4] How might this have affected the outcome of the American attack on the Mobile Force? At first blush, it might seem that a thirty-minute delay in the launch of the *Enterprise* dive-bombers would have resulted in those dive-bombers arriving over the Mobile Force thirty minutes later than they actually did — at around 1050 instead of 1020. In such a case, Nagumo would have had some chance of getting most of his strike force off his carriers before being bombed by the *Enterprise* dive-bombers.

But, paradoxically, a later launch of those dive-bombers—based on an accurate American sighting report—would almost certainly have resulted in those planes reaching the Mobile Force much earlier than they actually did. How can this be so? As will be explained in more detail later, the inaccurate sighting report not only misled Spruance in his launch-time decision, it also misled the commander of the *Enterprise* dive-bombers as to the likely location of the Mobile Force: the projected "interception point" for the Mobile Force—at which the dive-bombers arrived at 0920—was over 30 miles southeast of where the Japanese carriers actually were. This resulted in the *Enterprise* dive-bombers' missing those carriers where they were expected to be, which delayed their arrival over the Mobile Force by about an hour. But in a bizarre twist of fate, this delay provided the key to the American victory: it allowed the *Enterprise* dive-bombers to arrive at exactly the same time as the *Yorktown* dive-bombers and, more critically, just after the third wave of torpedo bombers (also from *Yorktown*) had drawn down the high-level Japanese combat air patrol.

On the other hand, had the American sighting report been accurate, the projected interception point for the later arrival of the *Enterprise* dive-bombers (at 0950 instead of 0920) would have been much closer to the actual location of the Mobile Force. Although the Mobile Force would have changed course to the northeast at 0920, Nagumo's carriers would, almost certainly, have been visible to the dive-bombers—probably a few minutes before they even reached the interception point.[5] Most crucially, however, the *Enterprise* dive-bombers would, undoubtedly, have arrived over the Mobile Force several minutes *before* the first wave of torpedo bombers (from *Hornet*)—whose launch would have been similarly delayed—reached it.[6] In such a case, the dive-bombers would have been confronted by a Japanese high-level combat air patrol not yet distracted by the American torpedo bombers.

One can only speculate how those dive-bombers would have fared. Some, most likely, would have been shot down, and many others would have been deflected from their bombing targets. It is entirely possible that one or both of the two carriers actually destroyed by *Enterprise*'s dive-bombers—*Akagi* and *Kaga*—would have survived to get their strike forces launched—just as Nagumo had hoped when he gambled on a postponement of his attack at 0835. (*Yorktown*'s dive-bombers would still have arrived when they did at 1024, but there is no reason to believe that they would have destroyed more than the one carrier they actually targeted—*Soryu*.)

Although they were not aware of it, Nagumo and Spruance were—in effect—playing a game of "blind man's bluff," each of them planning to strike at where they erroneously thought the other to be. However, Spruance had much better luck than Nagumo with this murky game: the error in the sighting report he received not only led him to strike earlier than he otherwise might have, but also—most fortuitously—misdirected the commander of the *Enterprise* dive-bombers, resulting in a delay in arriving over the Mobile Force, which produced an almost perfect, though completely accidental, coordinated attack. On the other hand, the error in the sighting report Nagumo got influenced him to schedule the launch of his strike later than he otherwise might have—with disastrous consequences. There is, indeed, great irony here.

NAGUMO'S EXPECTATION OF AN UNESCORTED AMERICAN ATTACK
Another irony, perhaps not as bizarre but nevertheless odd, arose from Nagumo's assumption that if the Americans attacked before he was able to get his own grand-scale attack off his carriers, the American attack would be by unescorted bombers—which would make them easy for his combat air patrol to fend off. Well, as it happened, the dive-bombers that destroyed three of Nagumo's carriers before 1030 were, indeed, unescorted when they arrived over the Mobile Force. But this did not save his carriers because the vaunted Zeros he counted on to protect him in such an event were not there to meet them.

The reasons for the lack of fighter escorts for the *Enterprise* dive-bombers, as well as the *Enterprise* torpedo bombers, are so curious, and the potential consequences so grave, that they deserve an explanation in some detail. The absence of escorts was not for the reason Nagumo assumed—lack of range of the Wildcat fighters. Though the distance to the Mobile Force—which was further than Spruance had calculated—made things tight, *Enterprise*'s Wildcats actually made it back to their carrier. After launch the American carriers had turned southwest to close with the Mobile Force—making the return leg for *Enterprise*'s fighters considerably less than 180 miles. (Even the shorter-ranged Devastators—the few that survived—were able to make it back, though barely.) Spruance had sent twenty Wildcats to escort the sixty-seven dive-bombers and twenty-nine torpedo bombers launched from *Enterprise* and *Hornet*. Yet, because of a fairly incredible series of mishaps, none fired a shot in defense of their charges during the attack on the Mobile Force.

WHY WERE THE AMERICAN DIVE-BOMBERS UNESCORTED?

At the root of this failure of fighter protection was the vagueness and impracticality of the escort assignments. The fighters of each carrier air group were supposed to protect both the dive-bombers and the torpedo bombers in their air group. This was a virtual impossibility, especially when skies were cloudy, because of the vastly different altitudes the two plane-types flew at when loaded with ordnance—20,000 feet for the dive-bombers, 1,500 feet for the torpedo bombers. When this impracticality became obvious to the fighter squadron leaders soon after the launch, they apparently improvised new escort tactics: the *Hornet* fighters (Fighting Eight) joined up with the *Hornet* dive-bombers

(Bombing Eight and Scouting Eight), forsaking the *Hornet* torpedo bombers, and the *Enterprise* fighters (Fighting Six) covered a squadron of torpedo bombers they *thought* were their own — leaving the *Enterprise* dive-bombers to fend for themselves.

There had been no plan to coordinate the air groups of *Enterprise* and *Hornet.*[7] It would have made sense for one fighter squadron from Task Force 16 to protect the dive-bombers of both carriers and for the other to protect the torpedo bombers of both. But this was not done. Moreover, the dive-bombers and torpedo planes of *Enterprise* and *Hornet* departed at different times, and on different courses, making such an arrangement — even on an ad hoc basis — impossible.

THE LAUNCH OF SPRUANCE'S STRIKE FORCE

The launch of Task Force 16's two air groups commenced at 0705. First off the flight decks were eight Wildcats from each carrier for combat air patrol, followed by the strike force dive-bombers. There were thirty-three dive-bombers in Bombing Six and Scouting Six from *Enterprise*, and thirty-four in Bombing Eight and Scouting Eight from *Hornet*. The second deckloads consisted of fighters for escort, ten from each carrier, and then the torpedo bombers — fourteen in Torpedo Six from *Enterprise* and fifteen in Torpedo Eight from *Hornet*.[8] The launch was completed at 0806 on *Enterprise*, though *Hornet*'s launch appears to have been completed a few minutes earlier, at around 0755.[9]

The launch plan was for a "deferred departure," which meant that the Dauntless dive-bombers did not proceed directly to the target but orbited above the carriers while the remaining planes were brought up from the hangars and made ready for launch. The purpose of a deferred departure was to ensure that all the squadrons of the air group would form up and depart at the same time. Thus, a deferred departure (in which it was the departure of the dive-bombers that was actually deferred) was an essential prerequisite for a coordinated attack when two deckloads of planes had to be launched and, because of their short range, the escort fighters and torpedo bombers had to be in the second deckload. (The Dauntlesses could afford the gasoline to wait because they had, by far, the longest range of the three plane types.)

As things turned out, however, Spruance got impatient with the length of time it was taking to launch the second deckload. At 0745, he ordered the *Enterprise* dive-bombers to proceed to the target without waiting for the remainder of the air group. Led by Lieutenant Commander Clarence "Wade" McClusky, they departed at 0752. Thus, the planned coordinated attack — with fighter escorts — was abandoned. Although Fighting Six had been assigned the task of protecting both the dive-bombers and torpedo planes in the *Enterprise* air group, when the dive-bombers departed prematurely, the commander of Fighting Six, Lieutenant James S. Gray, decided to accompany the torpedo bombers.

But he mistook Torpedo Eight for Torpedo Six. This, as we will see, resulted in neither torpedo squadron having any fighter protection.

As for the ten Wildcats from *Hornet*, their fate was even worse: as mentioned, they attached themselves to the *Hornet* dive-bomber squadrons. When the *Hornet* air group leader, Commander Stanhope C. Ring, was unable to find the Mobile Force at the expected interception point at 0920 he turned southeast toward Midway in an effort to find it. He never found it, and the *Hornet* dive-bombers and fighters missed the battle altogether (as will be discussed in more detail later). The ten escorting fighters followed the dive-bombers until shortage of fuel forced them to break away and head back to their carrier. They eventually ran out of gas and ditched in the ocean. Thus, one-half the fighters Spruance sent to escort the attack on the Mobile Force never made it to the battle.

Though the ten fighters from *Enterprise*'s Fighting Six made it to the target, the misadventures that befell them border on farce. We have seen that though intending to accompany the *Enterprise* torpedo bombers, they mistakenly joined up with the *Hornet* torpedo bombers. This might seem inexcusable, but odd as it may seem, there were no markings on the torpedo bombers that distinguished Torpedo Six from Torpedo Eight,[10] making it easy to confuse the two squadrons of torpedo bombers. The only way for Fighting Six to identify a torpedo bomber squadron for certain was through radio contact, but a policy of strict radio silence precluded this.[11]

Nevertheless, one might think that the torpedo bomber squadrons of both carriers would stay together for the flight to the Mobile Force, thereby making it unimportant which squadron the *Enterprise* fighters joined up with. However, that was not the case. As mentioned, there was no plan for the *Hornet* and *Enterprise* air groups to coordinate their attacks. Lieutenant Commander John C. Waldron, leading Torpedo Eight, had his own ideas about where the Mobile Force was; part way out he broke away from the rest of the *Hornet* air group—and the *Enterprise* torpedo bombers—and independently set his course to the target. (Waldron, who proudly claimed to be one-eighth Sioux, was well known for following his own intuition despite orders from his superiors.) The *Enterprise* fighter group followed Waldron's Torpedo Eight.

ARRIVAL AT THE TARGET—MORE CONFUSION

One might also think that after the two torpedo bomber squadrons reached the Mobile Force, even though arriving separately, the *Enterprise* fighters would see the torpedo planes and be able to protect at least some of them from attacking Zeros. That did not happen. Soon after departure from *Enterprise*, Fighting Six—though intending to cover the *Hornet* torpedo bombers to which it had become mistakenly attached—climbed to 22,000 feet, while Torpedo Eight climbed only to 1,500 feet. Fighting Six was able to maintain visual contact with

Torpedo Eight until they got near the target, when intervening clouds then obscured the view.

But Gray, leading Fighting Six, probably was not too concerned about losing visual contact with the torpedo bombers after reaching the area above the Mobile Force at about 0930 because he had previously arranged with Lieutenant Commander Eugene E. Lindsey, leading Torpedo Six, that when fighter support was needed Lindsey would signal by radio for help. Until then, Gray believed that he would be in the best position to spot and engage enemy combat air patrol if he stayed at above 20,000 feet.

When Torpedo Eight—the first to arrive—came under attack at 0928, Fighting Six could not see the torpedo bombers because of intervening clouds. If Waldron of Torpedo Eight radioed for help, Gray of Fighting Six did not receive the call because the radios of the *Enterprise* air group were tuned to a different frequency than those of the *Hornet* air group.[12] As they were without fighter escorts to defend them, all fifteen planes of Torpedo Eight were shot down—all but one before releasing their torpedoes—and no hits were scored, just as Nagumo had hoped.

As for the torpedo bombers of *Enterprise*'s Torpedo Six—the ones Fighting Six was suppose to cover—the reasons why they did not receive any help are even more unfortunate. After departing from *Enterprise*, Lindsey of Torpedo Six noticed that Fighting Six did not join up as expected, so he proceeded independently toward the target at 1,500 feet. When he reached the target and came under attack at about 0940, he could not see Fighting Six because of intervening clouds and did not know it was in the vicinity. Even if Lindsey had intended to make the prearranged call to Fighting Six for help, he might not have had time to do so, as it appears that he was one of the first to be shot down. (Nine more of Torpedo Six's planes would soon follow him into the water.) Thus, during the carnage inflicted on the torpedo bombers of Torpedo Eight and Torpedo Six, the fighters of Fighting Six remained circling above the clouds at 20,000 feet—oblivious to what was going on down below.

As for the *Enterprise* dive-bombers, when they finally arrived at 1020—an hour late—Fighting Six was no longer in the vicinity. After having orbited high over the Mobile Force for a half-hour, the fighters ran low on gas and headed back to the *Enterprise* at 1000, not having engaged any Zeros. In the end, although Spruance sent twenty fighters for escort, only half made it to the Mobile Force, and of them not one fired a shot at a Japanese Zero. Had more effort been made to coordinate the flights of TF 16's squadrons to the target, the Wildcats might have played a more productive role in the battle—especially in protecting the pitifully vulnerable torpedo bombers. But when the *Enterprise* dive-bombers arrived it turned out that they did not need any protection from the fighters because there was no Japanese combat air patrol at high level to meet them.

WHY WAS THERE NO JAPANESE
COMBAT AIR PATROL?

When the dive-bombers from *Enterprise*—and those from *Yorktown* as well—
arrived over the Mobile Force, the Zeros that were supposed to be on high-level
combat air patrol had been drawn down to sea level to attack the torpedo bombers that preceded the dive-bombers to the target. It is commonly misunder-
stood, however, when and why the high-level patrol had been drawn down to
sea level. It is often implied that the Japanese did not station Zeros at high altitude to defend against dive-bombers, that they kept their combat air patrol at
lower altitude so as to make it easier to spot and quickly confront torpedo bombers. The reason sometimes given is that the Japanese feared torpedoes much
more than bombs.[13]

But this was not the case. Although they would have feared their own aerial
torpedoes more than they would have feared their own 250-kilogram bombs,
the Japanese had begun to suspect after the Battle of the Coral Sea that American aerial torpedoes were much less effective than their own. But they also had
learned that American 1,000-pound bombs appeared to be deadlier than their
own bombs. Thus, in fact, they feared the Dauntless dive-bomber at least as
much as, and probably more than, they feared the Devastator torpedo
bomber.[14] Accordingly, Japanese policy was to keep a substantial part of their
combat air patrol at high level when anticipating a dive-bomber attack.[15] That
appears to have been the status of Nagumo's fighter air cover when *Hornet*'s torpedo bombers were first detected at 0918 about 20 miles out; of the seventeen
Zeros in the air at that time, at least a half-dozen were at high altitude. Had
McClusky's dive-bombers arrived when they were supposed to at 0920 they
would have been intercepted.

As it turned out, Torpedo Eight was attacked at 0928 by eleven Zeros already
on low- and mid-level patrol, soon joined by six reinforcements that had been
launched from *Kaga*. It was at about this time that the half-dozen or so Zeros
that had been maintaining high-level patrol at around 20,000 feet probably
dove down to help out with the torpedo bombers.[16] This assistance was necessary because most of the eleven Zeros on lower-level patrol, before *Kaga*
launched fresh reinforcements at 0920, were probably out of cannon ammunition—having expended it fending off the attacks from Midway between 0800
and 0840.[17] Five of those Zeros were landed on *Soryu* for reservicing at 0930,
and two more had been shot down. To help replace them five Zeros were
launched from *Akagi* at 0932. This gave a total of twenty-one in the air to take
on the defenseless Torpedo Eight; all fifteen torpedo planes were shot down by
about 0940. (Only one of the thirty crewmen survived—Ensign George Gay
piloting the last Devastator shot down—who witnessed the entire carrier battle
while clinging to a rubber boat.)

But there was not any time for the Zeros to reestablish a high-level patrol be-cause, at 0940, the second wave of torpedo bombers—fourteen from *Enterprise* —showed up. Twenty-five Zeros were in the air to greet them (four having been launched from *Hiryu* at 0937). Then seven more Zeros were launched at 0945, which were needed because many of those already aloft had run out of ammunition—especially the plane-killing 20-mm shells, which had been ex-pended on Torpedo Eight. Nine of the fourteen torpedo bombers from *Enter-prise* were shot down during the attack, but the lower total than for *Hornet* in-dicates an ammunition exhaustion problem. Although at least a half-dozen torpedoes were launched—a much more threatening performance than from Torpedo Eight—there were no hits. The attack of Torpedo Six was over by 0958, but about a dozen Zeros continued to pursue the remnants of it for about another ten minutes, downing another torpedo bomber—for a total of ten.

Beginning at this time, as we have seen, there was a fifteen- to eighteen-minute respite for Nagumo between the end of the second-wave torpedo bomber attack and arrival of the third wave of twelve torpedo bombers from *Yorktown*, which began its attack at 1016. During this interlude, nine Zeros were launched to reestablish the high-level patrol, and a few of the Zeros already aloft that still had cannon ammunition were able to join them at high altitude, as dive-bombers were expected momentarily. It thus appears that there were at least a dozen Zeros at high level by 1010 when *Yorktown*'s Torpedo Three began its approach.

Had Nimitz deployed only two carriers to Midway—the number Japanese intelligence thought the most likely available to him—Nagumo would have been in pretty good shape when the dive-bombers arrived. Most of the Zeros on combat air patrol that still had cannon ammunition were in position at high altitude to intercept dive-bombers as of 1010—and another six rearmed Zeros were launched by 1015. But, alas for the Japanese, there were three American carriers. And it was the torpedo bombers of *Yorktown*—a carrier that would not have been there but for a miracle repair job after the Battle of the Coral Sea— that broke Nagumo's back.

FLETCHER'S LAUNCH

Because of the pivotal role the *Yorktown* air group played in the success of the American dive-bomber attack on the Mobile Force, a more detailed account of its participation is called for at this point. Frank Jack Fletcher had com-menced his launch on *Yorktown* at 0838. He had delayed launching until then because the 0552 sighting report had reported finding only two Japanese car-riers. As Fletcher knew there were at least four in the Mobile Force, he was waiting for the remaining carriers to be found so they could be attacked as well. When no more were reported, he decided to supplement Spruance's at-tack, but held back his second squadron of dive-bombers—Scouting Five—

along with six fighters as a reserve in case more Japanese carriers were found later on.

In contrast to the lack of coordination, difficulty in finding the target, and failure of the escort assignments that bedeviled Spruance's strike force from *Enterprise* and *Hornet*, the deployment of *Yorktown*'s air group was a model of precision. And its fighter escorts performed even better than would be expected for such a small number — just six — largely due to the extraordinary skill of their commander, Lieutenant Commander John S. Thach. (I stated in the previous chapter that Japanese carrier fighter plane pilots were generally more experienced and skilled than their American counterparts at the beginning of the war. A clear exception to this was John Thach. He was quite possibly the most gifted carrier fighter pilot in the world, and inventor of the "Thach weave" — a maneuver that enabled clumsy Wildcats working together to, in effect, trap and shoot down a much more agile Zero.)[18]

By extolling the deployment of Fletcher's air group, I do not mean to denigrate Spruance. His task was immensely more difficult than Fletcher's: he had two carriers worth of planes to deploy to Fletcher's one, and he had to launch two deckloads from each of his carriers to Fletcher's one. Moreover, Fletcher's air group — though hastily reorganized when most of the pilots who fought at Coral Sea were sent shoreside for much needed rest and rehabilitation — were largely veterans. Most of the replacement pilots were from the venerable and seasoned *Saratoga*, which was still not back in service after having been torpedoed January 11.[19] On the other hand, *Hornet*, in Spruance's TF 16, was only recently commissioned, and most of the pilots in her air group were rookies.

Fletcher also had the advantage of having already been through one carrier battle — at Coral Sea — while Spruance had never commanded a carrier task force. Although he had inherited Halsey's very capable staff (most prominently the brilliant but irascible Captain Miles Browning, his chief of staff), they had not been through a carrier battle either. Fletcher's air group had some other advantages: when they launched at 0838 the cloud cover was clearing, making it easier to stay together en route to the target — and easier to see the Mobile Force when they got near it. Fletcher's staff also counted on the likelihood that the Mobile Force would have been impeded by the attacks from TF 16, in addition to those from Midway, and thus would have had its southeasterly course substantially shortened. This assumption proved crucial because it resulted in the squadron leaders being clearly instructed that if the Mobile Force was not at the interception point expected on the basis of the early morning PBY sighting report, they were to turn *northwest* and proceed in that direction until they found it.[20]

Yorktown's launch was completed at 0906. It consisted of seventeen dive-bombers (Bombing Three), followed by twelve torpedo bombers (Torpedo Three), and last to be launched, the six fighters of Thach's Fighting Three.[21]

The dive-bombers deferred their departure until the torpedo planes—with their loaded speed of only about 100 knots—got a head start toward the target. The faster dive-bombers and fighters, which cruised at 120 and 140 knots, respectively, were left to catch up en route.

The fighters and dive-bombers soon caught up with the torpedo bombers, and the three groups stayed in contact with each other for most of the flight. The plan was for the fighters to escort only the torpedo bombers, and for the dive-bombers to attack first, unescorted, when they reached the target. At 1000, just before reaching the expected interception point with the Mobile Force, the air group encountered clouds at the 2,000-foot level, causing visual contact between the dive-bombers and torpedo planes to be lost. This, ironically as will be seen, turned out to be a very lucky break for the Americans (and yet another unlucky break for the Japanese).

FIGHTING THREE AND TORPEDO THREE PRE-DOOM MOBILE FORCE

Lieutenant Commander Lance Massey, commander of Torpedo Three, was flying at 1,500 feet when, at 1003, he sighted smoke on the horizon about 30 miles to the northwest. Suspecting it to be the Mobile Force, he changed course to approach it. The six fighters of Thach's Fighting Three noticed the course change and followed the torpedo bombers. Lieutenant Commander Maxwell Leslie, leading Bombing Three, did not see the smoke because of clouds, nor did he see (from 15,000 feet) the torpedo bombers or fighters change course. Bombing Three continued on toward the expected interception point for another few minutes before turning north.[22]

This would result in the *Yorktown* dive-bombers arriving over the Mobile Force several minutes after the torpedo planes had attacked—and, most important, several minutes after the Japanese combat air patrol had been drawn down from high altitude to attack the torpedo bombers.[23] Although a more detailed treatment of the ordeal of *Yorktown*'s Torpedo Three will be given in the next chapter, because of the critical role it played in setting up the Mobile Force for the kill by clearing the sky of Zeros, a brief discussion of the aerial combat between Torpedo Three, Fighting Three, and the Japanese combat air patrol is in order at this point.

At 1010, about 14 miles from the Mobile Force, the twelve torpedo bombers of Torpedo Three were spotted coming in low from the southeast by eleven Zeros that had been chasing the fleeing survivors of *Enterprise*'s Torpedo Six. Also spotted were Thach's six Wildcats stacked above them. A minute or two later those Zeros plunged into the intruders; most of them—perhaps nine— went after Thach's Wildcats, with only two attacking Massey's torpedo bombers. Just minutes later another group of ten Zeros on low-level patrol in the southeast sector plunged into the fray—but split evenly against the torpedo bombers and the fighters.

In the melee that ensued with Fighting Three, one Wildcat was shot down, but four Zeros were also destroyed—three by squadron commander Thach.[24] This was a remarkable performance by American fighter pilots at this point in the war. Ordinarily, in a dogfight between equal numbers of fighters on both sides at that time it could be expected that more Wildcats would be shot down than Zeros—perhaps two to one. But here, although the Wildcats were out-numbered at least two to one, they more than reversed the expected kill ratio.

The attack on the torpedo bombers was even more disappointing for the Japanese. At least seven Zeros had attacked the twelve lumbering Devastators of Torpedo Three. It could be expected, based on the prior performance against Torpedo Eight and Torpedo Six, that at least a half-dozen torpedo bombers would have been shot down with little or no losses for the Zeros. In fact, although several torpedo bombers were hit, it appears that no more than one was shot down in its approach to the Mobile Force, and one Zero was shot down by rear-gunner fire.[25] In all, at this point in the skirmishes, twenty-one Zeros had attacked eighteen American planes; five Zeros had been shot down or crashed while knocking out but one Wildcat and one torpedo bomber. What can explain this abysmal performance by the Zeros? The loss of the three Zeros to Thach is not surprising—given that he was a dogfighting genius. What was incredible, however, is that these Zeros were unable to shoot down any more than one of the Devastators.

There is an explanation for this apparent anomaly: most of the twenty-one Zeros in this fray were out of 20-mm cannon ammunition. They had been launched between 0920 and 0945 to attack Torpedo Eight and Torpedo Six, and it was those planes that had sacrificially absorbed most of the plane-killing cannon shells. While the Zeros still had machine-gun ammunition left, the 7.7-mm bullets, by themselves, were too light to do much damage to the relatively well-armored American planes. (Zero machine-gun fire, especially tracer rounds, was best used to get a fix on the target so that short bursts of explosive cannon shells could inflict the lethal damage.) At this point in the battle most of the fully armed Zeros in the air—around fourteen—were still stationed at high altitude awaiting dive-bombers.

At 1015, the remaining eleven torpedo bombers of Torpedo Three broke through the depleted defenses and headed toward Nagumo's carriers. Thach's escorts had done their job well, tying up over twice their number of Zeros. Six rearmed Zeros were quickly launched to bolster the air defense against the torpedo bombers, but were too few. With twenty-one Zeros now effectively out of the picture, those six were all that were available to take on eleven torpedo bombers *if* a high-level patrol was to be maintained to guard against a dive-bomber attack that was expected momentarily.

At 1016, Massey's torpedo squadron began its run-up at *Akagi, Kaga,* and *Soryu*. At that moment things must have looked pretty desperate to the Japanese. This, apparently, is when the Zeros on high-level patrol were forced to abandon their vigil against the anticipated dive-bombers and dive down to help out with this more immediate threat to the Mobile Force. Apart from the six fresh Zeros just launched, the Zeros on high-level patrol were the only Zeros in the air with any cannon ammunition left. At almost the last second before releasing torpedoes, Massey found the targets unpromising because of evasive maneuvers and decided to bypass them and go after *Hiryu*—about 10 miles away. During this protracted run, six torpedo bombers were shot down by the last group of about twenty fully armed Zeros, leaving only five Devastators to release their torpedoes at *Hiryu* (none of which hit). Three more of *Yorktown*'s Devastators were shot down after releasing their torpedoes, for a total of ten torpedo bombers lost in the attack. (Only two survived, and they later ditched because of battle damage and fuel exhaustion.)

This, then, is why when the dive-bombers from *Enterprise* and *Yorktown* arrived high over the Mobile Force at 1022 there were no longer any Zeros at high level to meet them: all of Nagumo's combat air patrol was still down at sea level engaged with the *Yorktown* torpedo bombers and fighters. (These air battles will be covered in more detail in the next chapter, but a summary is given here to show what happened to the Japanese combat air patrol.)

Meanwhile, *Yorktown*'s Bombing Three had continued on to the assumed interception point, and not finding the Mobile Force there, turned northwest as instructed. At 1005, the clouds had mostly dissipated, and Leslie spotted smoke from the Mobile Force. Although the plan had been for the dive-bombers to attack the Mobile Force ahead of the torpedo bombers, fortunately for the Americans—as we have seen—the torpedo bombers and their escorts had arrived first, and had cleared the skies for *Yorktown*'s dive-bombers. At 1024, Leslie's seventeen dive-bombers attacked the closest carrier—which happened to be *Soryu*. At exactly the same time, and unbeknownst to Leslie, McClusky's two squadrons of dive-bombers from *Enterprise* attacked *Akagi* and *Kaga*. Although *Yorktown*'s dive-bombers had departed over one hour later than *Enterprise*'s, we have seen how—by sheerest accident—the two groups managed to combine for a perfectly coordinated dive-bomber attack.

Thus, paradoxically, Nagumo got part of what he hoped for when he had earlier contemplated the possibility that he might be attacked before he got his own strike force launched—an attack by unescorted American dive-bombers. But what he did not get was the part most vital—a Zero combat air patrol to neutralize them. The irony of it all must have haunted him until his suicide on Saipan two years later.

THE ELEMENT OF LUCK

In many of the famous battles of history—be it Waterloo, Trafalgar, or Gettysburg—sheer luck played a prominent role in the outcome, and Midway is

certainly another example. There may be those who are more comfortable with
the belief that the American victory at Midway was inevitable because of the
general superiority of America's intelligence, machinery of war, and fighting
spirit—and even because of divine providence. There are a great number of
books already available that nourish such a myth, but—as readers who have
read this far are well aware—this is not one of them. Rather, this book was written from a more detached—and I believe more objective—perspective. America really could have lost that battle, and probably would have, without a great
deal of good luck on the part of the American commanders (to go with all the
ingenuity and heroism)—coupled with some incredibly bad luck (to go with all
the blunders) on the part of the Japanese.

We have already seen some of that luck—good for the Americans, bad for the
Japanese: the cloud cover on the morning of June 4 that obscured the American
carrier fleet from view by the Japanese search plane from *Chikuma*; the erroneous sighting reports on both sides that misled the respective commanders in their
launch-time decisions (favorably for Spruance and unfavorably for Nagumo);
intervening clouds near the Mobile Force that delayed the arrival of *Yorktown*'s
dive-bombers over Nagumo's carriers until after the *Yorktown* torpedo bombers
had attacked. But we saw that the luckiest break of the entire day for the Americans came out of what could have been a disastrous blunder: an inaccurately
plotted "interception point" based on the erroneous PBY sighting report.

This contributed to *Hornet*'s dive-bombers missing the Mobile Force altogether, but resulted in *Enterprise*'s dive-bombers merely being delayed in finding the Japanese carriers—but, miraculously, being delayed by just the right
length of time to allow them to arrive over the target at the precise moment to
join the *Yorktown* dive-bombers in producing—albeit accidentally—an almost
perfect coordinated attack. But they were helped in this fortuitous arrival time
by another piece of good fortune: having one of Nagumo's own destroyers point
the way to the Mobile Force.

ARASHI, NAUTILUS, AND MCCLUSKY

We have seen that the 0552 PBY sighting report received by Spruance at 0603
placed the Mobile Force about 40 miles southeast of its actual position. Before
the launch of Spruance's two air groups, a projected interception point with the
Mobile Force had been plotted based on this report. Its course of 135° had been
projected forward from the reported position at 0552, with some allowance
made for the likelihood that its progress toward Midway after 0552 would be impeded by attacks from Midway. That interception point was—at 0920 when the
air groups were expected to arrive—about 111 miles, bearing 323°, from Midway.[26] To reach the expected interception point, when McClusky departed
from *Enterprise* with his two squadrons of dive-bombers at 0752 he set his course
southwesterly on 231°.

When McClusky arrived at that point, at 0920, the actual position of the Mobile Force, however, was about 32 miles away to the northwest. And at that very
moment, the Mobile Force had just completed a course change from southeasterly to the northeast—a change Nagumo had ordered so as to close with the
American carrier force as soon as the Midway strike force had been recovered.
Clouds in the area between McClusky and the target limited his visibility to
less than 25 miles and thus prevented him from seeing the Mobile Force. (*Enterprise*'s torpedo bombers flew a slightly more westerly course—240°—when they
departed at 0806 and, therefore, though arriving later at the interception point
were in a better position to see the Mobile Force. Also, being beneath the
clouds they had better visibility than the dive-bombers, which enabled the
commander of Torpedo Six to see the target at 0930.)

When the Mobile Force was nowhere to be seen at the expected interception
point, McClusky continued southwesterly on his 231° course for another fifteen
minutes until 0935. Then, employing an "expanding square" method of search,
he turned northwest to 315° to track the reciprocal of the course the Mobile
Force had been on according to the 0552 sighting report. He intended to stay
on that course for 50 miles until 1000, when he would then turn northeast to
return to *Enterprise*. But at 0955 he got a big break: he spotted the wake of a ship
steaming at high speed in a northeasterly direction. He correctly surmised that
it was a destroyer headed for the Mobile Force and turned right to follow its
track. Ten minutes later he sighted the Mobile Force some 25 miles away.

That ship was the destroyer *Arashi*. It had been diverted around 0830 to go
after an American submarine that had been spotted at 0824 threatening the
Mobile Force. That submarine was the *Nautilus*. It had penetrated the outer
destroyer screen and fired a torpedo at one of the two fast battleships escorting
Nagumo's carriers. Then at 910 *Nautilus* fired torpedoes at the light cruiser *Nagara* and then at *Arashi*, which was closing to drop depth charges. *Nautilus* escaped without sustaining serious damage. Although none of its torpedoes
struck, it played a possibly crucial role in the battle: by drawing *Arashi* to its lair
it was indirectly responsible for McClusky's two squadrons of dive-bombers arriving over the Mobile Force at the same time as *Yorktown*'s seventeen dive-
bombers.

It cannot be concluded, however, that McClusky would not have found the
Mobile Force but for the fortuitous spotting of the *Arashi* at 0955. McClusky
had planned to turn northeast in any event at 1000, and probably would have
run into the Mobile Force. But he would have arrived at least five minutes
later. The consequences of such a seemingly insignificant delay in arrival time
could have been more serious than one might expect. We know that the success of McClusky's dive-bombers in destroying two of Nagumo's carriers in
those fateful minutes around 1024 was due, in large part, to the fortunate fact
that there were no Zeros on high-level Japanese combat air patrol to intercept

them when they arrived over the Mobile Force. (They were still pursuing *York-town*'s torpedo bombers — which had finished their attack on *Hiryu* at around 1022 — almost the very moment the dive-bombers began their dives.)

While those Zeros had not had time to regain high-level altitude when the dive-bombers arrived, had McClusky's dive-bombers arrived five minutes *after* the *Yorktown* dive-bombers attacked, things might well have been different: at least several Zeros — having been alerted to a dive-bomber threat and broken off from pursuing the remnants of Torpedo Three — might have had time to regain sufficient altitude to take on the dive-bombers.[27] One can only speculate what this would have done to McClusky's dive-bombers. As he had no fighter escorts to engage any Zeros that might have attacked, casualties and disruptions to his dive-bombers from just a few Zeros could have been substantial. It is likely, at the least, that they would have scored fewer hits on *Akagi* and *Kaga* (and as *Akagi* was hit by only two bombs in the actual event, with one fewer she could have survived to launch her strike planes). We have seen that in carrier warfare just a few minutes can make a huge difference in the outcome of a battle.

But as far as luck goes, McClusky's spotting the *Arashi* pales into insignificance compared with the incredible fortuity of his dive-bombers arriving on the scene just after the last of three waves of torpedo bombers had attacked the Mobile Force. And this — as we have seen — would not have happened *but for an inaccurate sighting report* from an American PBY crew in the early hours of the morning.

HORNET'S LOST SQUADRONS

Nagumo did catch one lucky break in all this, which probably prevented an even more lopsided American victory. The erroneous American search plane report was at least partly responsible for *Hornet*'s dive-bomber squadrons failing to find Nagumo's carriers. Had these thirty-four dive-bombers — 40 percent of the total sent by Spruance and Fletcher — found the Mobile Force, they could have targeted its fourth carrier — *Hiryu* — in the morning attack.[28] In such a case, there would have been no launch of the two Japanese attacks against the American carrier force later in the day, and *Yorktown* would have been spared.

What actually happened to *Hornet*'s dive-bombers has been a mystery. *Hornet*'s records are fragmentary, and the testimony from her air group veterans has been inconsistent. Early commentators assumed the following scenario: that after launch, *Hornet*'s air group — led by Commander Stanhope Ring — proceeded on a course toward the expected interception point similar to that of *Enterprise*'s dive-bombers — southwest at around 230–240°.[29] Part way out, Waldron's Torpedo Eight broke away and proceeded independently on a more westerly course, and was rewarded in this initiative by finding the Mobile Force. When Ring reached the expected interception point at around 0920 and found nothing, instead of turning northwest—as McClusky did—he turned southeast toward Midway (judging that the Mobile Force had proceeded further in that direction than expected). At that time, however, Nagumo's carriers were over 30 miles to the northwest.

A radically different scenario for *Hornet*'s air group has been advanced that has gained considerable currency in recent years: that Ring proceeded not on a course of 230–240°, but on a course of 265° (almost due west).[30] This took his dive-bombers and fighter escorts to the *north* of the Mobile Force, rather than to the south of it. (When Waldron's torpedo bombers broke away, under this scenario, they veered off to the left and flew in a southwesterly course, instead of to the right in a more westerly direction as previously assumed.)[31] Then, when Ring reached what he thought was the interception point he continued west for about another 50 miles and then turned back toward his carrier— again taking him north of the Mobile Force. However, his Bombing Eight squadron turned southeast, and most of its dive-bombers reached Midway.

While there is some fairly impressive evidence for this scenario, it is contradicted by Ring himself. A letter he wrote in 1946 was found and published in 1999.[32] In it he states that he flew the "pre-estimated interception course," which took him to a point "between the last reported position of the enemy and Midway Island." While he does not specify the course in degrees, he goes on to say that "VT-8 and *Enterprise* Group made contact with the enemy, north of the point at which I turned south." The interception course had been calculated by Spruance's staff to be 231°, so this appears to be the approximate course Ring *thought* he had flown. (He admits in his letter that when he reached the expected interception point, he made a serious mistake in turning south rather than north.)

The actual course Ring flew may never be known with certainty. It is extremely doubtful that he would have been briefed by Rear Admiral Marc Mitscher's staff on *Hornet* to fly a course of 265°; such a course would have taken Ring's air group not only north of where the Mobile Force actually was at 0920, but north of where it was *reported to be* three and one-half hours earlier in the American sighting report sent at 0552. (It is difficult to imagine that anyone would have thought that it had gone backward since then.) But it is possible that Ring got disoriented and flew a course of 265° in error rather than the course to the projected interception point (230–240°) that he thought he had flown. (The record of the first year of the war is replete with navigational errors at sea on both sides, and Ring was very inexperienced with Dauntless dive-bombers.) Therefore, his recollection in his letter may have been sincere, but mistaken.[33] In any event, what is absolutely clear and undisputed is that the *Hornet* dive-bombers failed to find the Mobile Force and that the Americans thereby lost an opportunity to finish off Nagumo's carriers all at once in the morning attacks.

TACTICAL DOCTRINE TURNED ON ITS HEAD

We have seen that the key to the American victory was the absence of any Zeros on combat patrol at high level over the Mobile Force when McClusky and Leslie's dive-bombers arrived. This was a circumstance totally unforeseen by Nagumo when he made his decision to postpone at 0835. But it would not have happened had things gone as planned by Spruance and Fletcher. Tactical doctrine in the American navy, as well as the Japanese, held that a coordinated attack with all the dive-bombers and torpedo planes arriving over the target together, rather than attacking piecemeal, was the most effective and least costly method of attack.[34] Ironically, however, had Spruance and Fletcher managed to mount such an attack, the Americans might well have lost the battle; it turned out to be absolutely essential that the torpedo bombers arrive first.

The reason for this counterintuitive tactic lies in the differences between the ordnance of the two sides. A coordinated attack was essential for Japanese success because of the marked superiority of Japanese aerial torpedoes over Japanese bombs in sinking large ships. But for those torpedoes to be delivered, the lightly armored Kate torpedo planes needed all the protection they could get, not only from Zero escorts but also from Val dive-bombers participating in the attack to draw off American fighters. On the other hand, because the big punch for the Americans was 1,000-pound bombs, not torpedoes, the key to American success was in getting as many Dauntless dive-bombers through Japanese air defenses as possible. Zeros on high-level patrol had to be drawn down to sea level in advance. This was best done when the American torpedo bombers arrived first, preferably in a series of attacks that would exhaust the Zero's limited cannon ammunition, and preferably with the last wave arriving just before the dive-bombers so that Zeros would not have time to regain altitude (just as actually happened, albeit accidentally).

Though this resulted in the sacrifice of the Devastator torpedo bombers—and would not have been deliberately planned by Spruance or Fletcher—it cleared the skies, at high level, of Zeros. But had the American torpedo bombers and dive-bombers arrived at the same time—in a coordinated attack—we have seen that part of Nagumo's combat air patrol most likely would have been stationed at high altitude to take on at least some of the dive-bombers. There almost certainly would have been substantial dive-bomber losses, and disruptions even to those bombers not hit would probably have significantly affected the accuracy of their bomb drops. Again, one can only speculate how many bombs would have hit the Japanese carriers—almost certainly fewer than actually did.

It would have been even worse for the Americans had the dive-bombers arrived first as was, in fact, intended by Spruance at the last minute when he aborted the planned coordinated attack by sending McClusky's dive-bombers ahead before the torpedo planes were launched. (And this would have happened, as we have seen, had McClusky not got lost due to a faulty sighting report.) Even more Zeros would have been in a position to go after the dive-bombers. Even if Fighting Six's ten Wildcats had been on hand to take on the Zeros, the results of the dive-bombing attack most likely still would have been much less satisfactory than was actually achieved in the later attack by dive-bombers without escorts—but after the torpedo bombers had been decimated. Thus, it was the series of attacks by torpedo bombers proceeding the dive-bombers that proved to be the sine qua non for the American victory.

LIMITED ZERO CANNON ROUNDS

The piecemeal attacks by American torpedo bombers were effective, in large part, because they were able to take advantage of perhaps the greatest weakness of the Zero fighter: a very limited supply of its deadly 20-mm cannon ammunition—only 60 rounds per gun. At a firing rate of 520 rounds per minute, this gave it only about seven seconds' worth of cannon fire. Zero pilots tried to be as economical as possible with cannon ammunition, using the much lighter 7.7-mm machine guns (for which there were 660 rounds per gun—some of them tracer rounds) to pinpoint the target, and then giving short bursts of cannon fire to finish it off. But the cannon ammunition was usually exhausted after a couple of encounters, and the light machine-gun rounds did not do much damage to the beefy American planes. This is why even a large low-level combat air patrol could not last long in attacking the successive waves of torpedo bombers, and why the Zeros at high level almost inevitably had to soon drop down to help out.

Thus, although the Zero's 20-mm cannon was, round for round, deadlier than the 50-caliber machine gun on the Wildcat,[35] the short duration of its cannon fire at Midway was so extreme as to render the Zero almost impotent against all but the first wave of a series of American attacks. To correct this weakness, the number of rounds per gun was increased to 100 in later Zero models.[36] But had the cannon magazines been enlarged before Midway, the Americans most certainly would have paid a heavier price for making piecemeal attacks. (It should be noted that American fighter pilots at Midway also complained about running out of ammunition too soon with the new F4F-4 model Wildcat. When the number of 50-caliber guns was increased from four to six, the number of rounds in each magazine had been reduced from 450 to 240.)

It, therefore, turned out that piecemeal attacks, in rapid succession—so there was not time for the Zeros to land and reload their guns—were the perfect American tactic for taking advantage of the Zero's limited supply of cannon ammunition. (We have already seen that successive attacks from Midway earlier in the morning were responsible for the fact that no Zeros were left for escort duty at 0830.) This reversal of textbook tactical doctrine is yet another of the many ironies of Midway.

DEFECTIVE TORPEDOES

The reason American torpedo bombers could be sacrificed in piecemeal attacks without actually diminishing overall firepower very much was—as we have already seen—because American aerial torpedoes were practically worthless at this time in the war. In addition to being slow and inaccurate, they often did not explode even when they hit because of a defective firing-pin. The Japanese may have discovered before the battle that American aerial torpedoes were not as good as theirs, but appear not to have realized just how bad they really were. They still feared them enough to take very aggressive measures to fend them off—even at the expense of weakening defenses against the more deadly American dive-bombers. Therefore, because of the defects of the American torpedoes, the optimum tactic for the Americans—if one were to be cold-blooded about it—would have been to use the Devastator torpedo bombers as decoys for the Japanese combat air patrol so that the Dauntless dive-bombers would have a better chance of getting through unscathed.

It is not clear whether at the time of Midway Spruance and Fletcher realized how defective the Mark 13 torpedo actually was. There had been complaints about it, but it would take until the end of the war before it was discovered that no Japanese fleet carrier was even hit, let alone sunk, by a Mark 13 aerial torpedo in the first year of the war. (In the Battle of the Coral Sea the light carrier *Shoho* was hit by at least one Mark 13, but only after having been immobilized by several bomb hits.) In any case, even if Spruance and Fletcher did not have much faith in the Mark 13 torpedoes, they did not regard the torpedo bombers and their crews as expendable; they took considerable pains to give them a fighting chance to survive the battle and return home.

BUT NOT IN VAIN

Although three waves of American torpedo bombers—forty-one planes in all—attacked without scoring a single torpedo hit, we have seen that their contribution to the American victory was, arguably, just as important as that of the dive-bombers that delivered the fatal bombs—and whose airmen received most of the glory. Without the skies at high level having been cleared of Zeros by the torpedo bombers, it is doubtful that very many bombs from McClusky and Leslie's dive-bombers would have hit Nagumo's carriers—almost certainly fewer than the nine that actually scored.

And, though the last wave of torpedo bombers, those from *Yorktown*, have been given most of the credit for clearing the skies of Zeros—as they immediately preceded the dive-bombers and drew down to sea level the last Zeros remaining at high altitude—it was the first two torpedo bomber squadrons from

Hornet and *Enterprise*, attacking between 0930 and 1000, that set the stage for that last wave. They had used up the 20-mm cannon ammunition of most of the Zeros on combat air patrol, which is why when *Yorktown*'s torpedo bombers arrived there were only about a dozen and a half Zeros with any cannon ammunition left—and most of these were the ones at high altitude. It was when they dove down to go after that last wave of torpedo bombers that the Mobile Force was set up for the kill by the three squadrons of dive-bombers.[37]

Thus, the crews of the thirty-five torpedo bombers that were shot down did not lose their lives in vain. But for their contributions making it possible for the dive-bombers to attack unhindered, most of Nagumo's carriers would probably have survived to get a good part of their grand-scale attack launched. In such a case the Americans probably would have lost the battle. There was luck and there were ironies in all this, but there was also an uncommon measure of valor.

CHAPTER EIGHT

DENOUEMENT

BEFORE THE DELUGE

After three hours of almost unremitting attacks on the Mobile Force, at 1000 a moment of calm finally arrived in Nagumo's headquarters on *Akagi*. The last torpedo from the second wave of American carrier-launched torpedo bombers had just been dropped at 0958, and there were no other American planes in sight. It had been a most harrowing three hours for Nagumo and his staff, but the Mobile Force had come through it unscathed. In all, seven groups of planes had attacked during three periods. First, between 0700 and 0720, six TBF Avenger torpedo bombers from Midway, followed by four torpedo-equipped B-26s, attacked with torpedoes. None of their torpedoes had hit, and seven planes had been shot down, with the loss of only one Zero. Then between 0805 and 0839 three waves of bombers from Midway came in—sixteen Marine SBD Dauntless dive-bombers, followed immediately, at 0814, by fourteen B-17s, then by eleven SB2U Vindicator dive-bombers at 0828. No hits had been scored by any of them either, and eleven Marine dive-bombers had been shot down, for a loss of three Zeros.

Finally, after a fifty-minute pause during which the Midway strike force was landed—and the discovery of the American carrier force had intensified the urgency to get the second-wave strike force rearmed and launched—the latest and most nerve-wracking period had begun: between 0928 and 0958 twenty-nine carrier-based torpedo planes attacked—first fifteen TBD Devastators from *Hornet* and then, at 0940, fourteen more from *Enterprise*. None of those torpe-does had hit either, and twenty-five torpedo planes had been shot down, for a loss of only three more Zeros.

In all, fifty-one dive-bombers, B-17s, and torpedo planes had attacked from Midway, and twenty-nine torpedo planes from American carriers. Forty-three of the eighty planes had been shot down, with a loss of only seven Zeros from the combat air patrol. This was a most heartening kill ratio and further bolstered the confidence of Nagumo's staff in the superiority of Japanese aircraft and aircrews over their American counterparts. Even the attack on Midway, though not a complete success, had substantially degraded its ability to function as an air base, and had cost only eleven planes—while destroying seventeen American fighter planes. (Two PBY Catalina search planes from Midway had also been shot down.) Thus, in the accounting as of 1000, the tally of planes shot down favored Nagumo 62 to 18.[1] However, as we have seen, the American attacks had managed to make one troublesome impact on the Japanese: they had seriously disrupted rearming operations on Nagumo's second-wave torpedo planes.

Now, with the desperately needed respite at 1000, it would be possible to finish the rearming of the torpedo planes on *Akagi* and *Kaga* and get them, along with the dive-bombers on *Hiryu* and *Soryu*, up to the flight decks so that the grand-scale attack envisioned an hour and a half earlier could finally be launched against the American carrier force. The originally scheduled 1030 launch time would be delayed, but—it was hoped—not by much. In the mean-time, the defense posture of the Mobile Force could also be improved. Several Zeros on combat air patrol were about to come down for rearming, and nine were being relaunched to replace them and others whose 20-mm cannon am-munition had been exhausted in defending against the torpedo bomber attacks of the past half-hour. This would enable a high-level patrol to be reestablished. The carriers of the Mobile Force could also begin tightening up their forma-tion so that the combat air patrol could more efficiently protect them against any further attack. (They had become widely dispersed because of their high-speed evasive maneuvers since 0930, and *Hiryu* had steamed almost beyond the horizon from the three other carriers.)

Yes, at 1000, things were finally looking much better to Nagumo and his staff. Optimism revived that the gamble made at 0835—when the decision to post-pone attack was made—might still be won. Nagumo needed about another fifty minutes—because of the disruptions—to finish rearming his torpedo planes and get them up to the flight decks. The dive-bombers on *Hiryu* and *Soryu* had been properly armed for attacking carriers since before 0830 but were mostly still in the hangars.

The fact that two waves of carrier-based torpedo bombers had finished their attack posed some good and some bad news for Nagumo's staff: it appeared that there were only two American carriers, which meant that there should be no further torpedo bomber attacks. The bad news was that no carrier-based dive-bombers had yet attacked; they normally would be expected to accompany the torpedo bombers. Where were they? It thus appeared that the carriers of the Mobile Force might still have to survive a dive-bomber attack before they could launch their own strike force. There was, however, great confidence that the high-level combat air patrol being reestablished could take care of most of the attacking dive-bombers so that the damage to the carriers would be minimal. These were the concerns that occupied the minds of the headquarters staff between 1000 and 1010. Still, as of 1010 on the morning of June 4, Nagumo and his staff had reason for optimism. And, had Nimitz sent only two carriers to Midway, Nagumo almost certainly would have won his gamble. But, as we have seen, there was a third carrier—the miraculously repaired USS *Yorktown*.

THE FATAL ATTACKS

THE SAGA OF TORPEDO THREE

At 1010, Nagumo's quietude was rudely shattered when some Zeros that had been chasing the fleeing survivors of Torpedo Six from *Enterprise* spotted Lieutenant Commander Lance Massey's twelve-plane torpedo squadron from *Yorktown* coming in low from the southeast. This was especially disquieting because it meant that there were *three* American carriers—not two. The torpedo bombers were about 14 miles from the Mobile Force, and were accompanied by Lieutenant Commander John Thach's six-plane fighter group.

As we saw in the last chapter, Massey and Thach's intruders were then attacked by two groups of Zeros on low- and mid-level patrol—twenty-one in all. Of these, about fourteen tangled with the six Wildcats, and the other seven went after the torpedo bombers. The results were extremely disappointing for the Japanese: only one torpedo bomber and one Wildcat were shot down, while five Zeros were lost. We saw that this poor performance of the Zeros was attributable to two things: Thach's extraordinary skill and the fact that most of the twenty-one Zeros were out of 20-mm cannon ammunition. (Credit for rendering those Zeros largely impotent must be given to the two prior waves of torpedo bombers— Torpedo Six and Eight—which had sacrificially absorbed most of the cannon ammunition.) There were, however, also about fourteen Zeros yet to be heard from; they were on high-level patrol directly above the carriers of the Mobile Force, still maintaining a vigil against the anticipated dive-bombers. And most of them had just been launched and had a full load of cannon ammunition.

At about 1015, Massey's largely intact Torpedo Three had completed its descent through scattered clouds and leveled out about 150 feet above the water to make its torpedo run on the main group of carriers. That group—*Akagi, Kaga,* and *Soryu*—then swung around to the northwest to present their sterns to the attackers while steaming at top speed. Massey, judging this to present an unfavorable target, then decided to turn north and go after the lone *Hiryu.* This was at 1016, and as *Hiryu* was about 10 miles away it would take about five minutes to reach her at the 100 knots speed the planes were flying. But this was, as we have seen, also the moment when Nagumo's fate was sealed: the fourteen Zeros maintaining a high-level patrol—at least a dozen of which had a fresh load of cannon ammunition—dove down to take up the attack. While this would doom Nagumo, it also doomed Torpedo Three. To make matters worse *Hiryu* had just launched three Zeros at 1013 and *Soryu* three at 1015, and they were now also in a position to attack Torpedo Three. Massey's luck had just run out.

During Torpedo Three's desperate run toward *Hiryu*, these twenty Zeros proved to be far more effective against the vulnerable Devastators than had the previous patrols. Massey had separated the squadron's two divisions so as to make a split attack on *Hiryu* from both sides simultaneously. He led the First Division, which was to attack straight in, and Lieutenant Patrick Hart led the Second Division, which was to swing around to the other side of the carrier. Hart's division took the first blows, and all five planes still in it were sent into the ocean before releasing their torpedoes. At about 1020, Massey frantically radioed Thach for help. Thach's Wildcats were still tied up with the Zeros and could not break away to help out with this new, and much deadlier, swarm of Zeros decimating Torpedo Three. Up to this time Thach's fighters had done exactly what an escort was supposed to do—they had kept more than twice their number of Zeros away from the torpedo bombers, and before the battle was over they shot down at least four Zeros. But they were too few to take on the entire Japanese combat air patrol.

About a mile from the torpedo release point, Massey's plane was shot down. The remaining five planes of his division dropped their torpedoes. None hit, and three more torpedo bombers were sent into the ocean. Two planes survived the battle and got back to *Yorktown*, but as the carrier was coming under attack they were directed to *Enterprise*—where they ditched after having run out of fuel (both crews were rescued). Of Thach's six Wildcats, miraculously, only one was shot down; five made it back to the carriers—though most were badly shot up and three of the pilots were wounded. (Only four landed on *Yorktown*, leading some commentators to assume two had been shot down. The fifth, flown by Ensign Daniel Sheedy, had become separated from the others on the flight back and mistakenly landed on *Hornet*, with tragic consequences. While landing, the damaged plane dipped a wing into the carrier deck, causing all six machine guns to fire, killing six *Hornet* crewmen.)[2]

Although none of Torpedo Three's torpedoes hit, and ten of the twelve planes were shot down, by surviving the initial attacks from the low-level combat air patrol they accomplished one thing that would turn out to be indispensable for the American victory: they had forced the high-level patrol to abandon its vigil against dive-bombers. This, as we saw in the last chapter, is what ruined Nagumo's plans. He had counted on his Zeros being able to protect his carriers until he could get his grand-scale attack launched. As things turned out, however, while all his Zeros with any cannon ammunition left were occupied down at water level with Torpedo Three between 1016 and 1024, the skies were clear for three squadrons of dive-bombers to sneak in from high altitude, unchallenged, to deliver the fatal attacks on the Mobile Force.

The Japanese pilots have been roundly criticized—even ridiculed—for abandoning the high-level patrol at this point to go after the torpedo planes; surely, dive-bombers must have been expected momentarily. It has been said that the Japanese at Midway were obsessed with attacking torpedo bombers to the point of utterly disregarding dive-bombers. This criticism is not supported by the Japanese record, and is unjustified. Nagumo's staff knew what American dive-bombers with 1,000-pound bombs could do to carriers and greatly feared them.[3] Generally, it was the practice of the air defense director to maintain a high-level patrol,[4] and, indeed, this had been done until about 1015. But when the eleven torpedo bombers of Torpedo Three broke clear of the low-level patrol—which was out of cannon ammunition by that time in any case—and headed for the carriers, only the high-level patrol was left to defend the Mobile Force against Massey's torpedo bombers. However, it just so happened that as the last torpedo was being dropped by Torpedo Three at 1022, Wade McClusky's dive-bomber was pushing over at 19,000 feet for his dive on *Kaga*.

THE HELL DIVERS

As the American dive-bombing attack on Nagumo's carriers was the single most fateful episode in the Pacific War, it deserves to be treated in some detail. We have seen that Wade McClusky's path to the Mobile Force had been a most circuitous one, but he finally found it at 1005, with some help from the Japanese destroyer *Arashi*. Thirty-three of his SBD dive-bombers had departed from *Enterprise* at 0752, ahead of the fighters and torpedo bombers. There had been eighteen planes in Scouting Six (including McClusky's plane), carrying 500-pound bombs, and fifteen in Bombing Six, carrying 1,000-pounders. One plane from Scouting Six had aborted its flight because of engine trouble soon after takeoff and returned to the carrier. Two more planes (those of Tony Schneider and Eugene Greene), both from Bombing Six, also developed engine trouble near the target area, had to drop out of the formation, and ditched in the ocean. (Schneider and his gunner were later rescued; Greene and his gunner were never found.)[5] This left thirty dive-bombers—seventeen planes in Scouting Six (including McClusky's) and thirteen in Bombing Six—to deliver the attack on the Mobile Force.

Approaching from the southwest at 19,000 feet, McClusky picked the two closest carriers. The one on the left, which happened to be *Kaga*, he took for himself and Lieutenant Earl Gallaher's Scouting Six. The one on the right, a little further away to the east, he assigned to Lieutenant Richard Best's Bombing Six. That happened to be Nagumo's flagship *Akagi*.[6] Best did not get word of the target assignment from McClusky. Since his was the trailing squadron, he assumed that the closest carrier would be his—that had been the practice. But at 1022 McClusky pushed over on *Kaga* and was followed down, in ten-second intervals, by his two wingmen, Pittman and Jaccard, and then by the remaining fourteen SBDs of Gallaher's Scouting Six. Best was surprised to see Scouting Six diving in front of him—and taking his target—but he quickly changed plans and went for *Akagi*. Although the other four planes in his First Division followed him, the eight planes remaining in Divisions Two and Three of his squadron did not see him move on to the next carrier. Those planes apparently pushed over and followed Scouting Six down. Thus, it appears that twenty-five SDBs dove on *Kaga*. There were no Zeros in sight, and not even any antiaircraft gunfire from the ships at the beginning of the dives.

McClusky released his bomb at 1,800 feet, about a minute into the dive. It missed, as did the next two dropped by his wingmen. The fourth bomb dropped, by Gallaher, scored a direct hit starboard aft. (There is confusion over exactly when the first bomb hit *Kaga*, but it appears that it was at 1023.)[7] The next two bombs (dropped by Reid Stone and John Roberts) missed, but the seventh and eighth bombs, dropped by Norman Kleiss and James Dexter, hit. The third bomb to hit (Dexter's) struck just in front of the bridge, detonating a gasoline cart and killing everyone on the bridge. These were all 500-pounders by Scouting Six. It is not known what happened to the last nine planes of Scouting Six because, after an interval, the ninth bomb dropped on target—which scored the fourth and last hit—was a 1,000-pounder by George Goldsmith of Bombing Six. He was apparently the last of the twenty-five to dive. That bomb hit right in the middle of the flight deck and probably administered the coup de grace. The bombs were fused to detonate 1/100 of a second after impact and exploded about four feet into the hangar, where most of the planes and ordnance still were. The four hits set off an inferno on *Kaga*, which soon raged out of control—with most of the damage done by secondary explosions from bombs, torpedoes, and ruptured airplane fuel tanks of *Kaga*'s own air group. *Kaga* was obviously doomed.

A minute later, at 1024, the five planes of Richard Best's First Division of Bombing Six attacked *Akagi*. Two of the trailing planes appear to have released their bombs prematurely—missing widely. But of the three that released their 1,000-pounders on target, two hit *Akagi* (a remarkable hit ratio compared with other American dive-bombing attacks in the first year of the war). The first bomb hit squarely in the middle of the flight deck, knocking out the midship elevator and destroying several Val dive-bombers nearby in the hangar (fortunately they had not yet been rearmed and refueled). The second hit the port edge of the flight deck near the rear, and exploded in the corner of the hangar close to where most of the seventeen rearmed and fueled torpedo planes were waiting to be raised to the flight deck. Gas tanks of the blasted planes ruptured, setting off a conflagration and probably detonating some of the torpedoes. (This was recorded in *Akagi*'s damage report as being the "fatal hit.")[8]

It is not absolutely clear whose bombs hit, but most authorities agree with Dick Best that his bomb scored the first hit. The second hit was by one of his wingmen—either Bud Kroeger or Fred Weber. Without the induced explosions from the loaded torpedo planes in the hangar, the two hits probably would not have done fatal damage to *Akagi*. As it was, however, flames from gasoline began to spread. At first the fires advanced slowly, and for a while it looked like the vessel might be saved. But eventually the damage control systems were overwhelmed, and by 1046 it became apparent that the carrier, like her sister *Kaga*, was also doomed. At that time, Nagumo and most of his staff evacuated; they boarded a launch, and Nagumo shifted his flag to the light cruiser *Nagara*.

Curiously, of the thirty SBDs from *Enterprise* that are reported to have dived on *Kaga* and *Akagi*, it appears that only twelve dropped bombs at or near those carriers. Six of them scored direct hits, and most of the six bombs that missed struck the water close enough to cause damage to the carrier's hull. But what of the other eighteen dive-bombers that appear not to have released their bombs on target—what happened to them? Especially puzzling is the attack on *Kaga*. Twenty-five SBDs supposedly participated in the attack, but there is firm record of only nine bombs being dropped.[9] It would appear that no bombs were dropped by the last nine planes of Scouting Six or the first seven planes of Bombing Six. (Or, if dropped, none hit close enough to the carrier to be noticed by the Japanese.) The available records offer no satisfactory explanation for this. There has been an assumption by commentators that during the dives the sky was clear of Zeros and that even the AA gunfire was late and light. McClusky and other pilots from Scouting Six reported after their return that no Zeros attacked them on the way down (though some did report that their planes were attacked by Zeros immediately after pulling up from their dives).[10] It is possible, of course, that the Japanese observers on *Kaga* who reported the bombing missed some of the bombs, but it seems unlikely that they would have missed any that hit the ship.[11]

There is a possible explanation: although AA gunfire was initially light, it appears that *Kaga*'s antiaircraft gun batteries became very active after the first few bombs were released by Scouting Six; thus, it is very likely that flak disturbed the dives of the last dozen or so planes. The seventh SBD to dive (that of John Roberts of Scouting Six) was, in fact, shot down;[12] so AA gunfire could have become quite fierce by then. As for why this was not reported by the dive-bomber pilots, it should be noted that nine of the planes in that last group to dive either were shot down soon after their attack or ditched during their return with their crews never found.[13] Therefore, we have a wholly incomplete record from most of the pilots in a position to tell us what happened during those dives. It is likely that they were buffeted by flak before they were ready to release their bombs, which resulted in some of the bombs' not being dropped—or being dropped prematurely and far off target.

Also, regarding the planes in the Second and Third Divisions of Richard Best's Bombing Six, there is another problem that may have contributed to their low bomb-drop tally: there was confusion regarding which carrier they were to attack—whether to follow their squadron leader after he changed targets to attack *Akagi* or proceed with the attack on *Kaga*. This may have resulted in some of them attacking neither carrier or, at least, being thrown out of alignment in their dives on *Kaga*. One commentator has stated that the planes in the Third Division of Bombing Six split up and attacked both carriers.[14] If so, this would be a recipe for success against neither. As for Best's First Division of five planes, which attacked *Akagi*, there is also no record of the two planes in the trailing section dropping bombs. There is evidence that at least one of them released prematurely, and the other may have done as well.[15] (To confuse matters even more, one commentator has those two planes joining in the attack on *Kaga*.)[16]

All in all, it appears that—because of all the confusion over targets and damage from flak—eighteen of the thirty planes in McClusky's two squadrons either did not drop their bombs or, if they did, dropped them far from the mark. Giving them the benefit of the doubt, let us assume that most of those eighteen dive-bombers—perhaps a dozen—did release their bombs but missed badly. In such a case, roughly twenty-four bombs would have been dropped—for six hits. (Despite all the problems, this would be a hit ratio fairly close to that recorded by American dive-bombers in other carrier battles of 1942, so perhaps too much fuss has been made over the misses.) In the end, however, McClusky's dive-bombers—even with the communications problems and confusion—did manage to destroy two carriers and change the course of history. Yet, considering the problems those dive-bombers had even without any Zeros to harass them, one can only speculate what might have happened had a high-level combat air patrol been in place. It seems very likely that fewer bombs would have hit *Kaga*—and it is difficult to imagine that the three planes in Best's section of Bombing Six would have gotten through to destroy *Akagi*. In such a case, Nagumo just might have managed to get most of his torpedo bombers launched after all. For the Americans, God bless Torpedo Three.

The grief was not over for Nagumo after McClusky's dive-bombers had finished their work. At almost the same time Best's planes of Bombing Six were attacking *Akagi*, Lieutenant Commander Maxwell Leslie's Bombing Three from *Yorktown* made its dive on *Soryu*. Bombing Three had completed its launch at 0906, over an hour after McClusky's dive-bombers departed from *En-*

terprise. Yet, by sheerest coincidence, they arrived at just the precise time to pull off a perfectly coordinated attack with McClusky's planes. Leslie was unaware of the presence of McClusky's dive-bombers, and McClusky was unaware of his. There were no Zeros anywhere near Bombing Three; all of them were either attacking McClusky's planes or chasing Torpedo Three.

Seventeen SBD Dauntlesses of Bombing Three had left *Yorktown*, but four of them—including that of squadron leader Leslie—lost their bombs en route because of a malfunction in the new electrical arming device. Those planes continued on to the target, however, so as not to disrupt the dive-bombing routine that Leslie had worked out. When Bombing Three reached the Mobile Force, Leslie picked the closest carrier as the target, which happened to be *Soryu*. (Although there has been confusion and controversy over whether the carrier was *Soryu* or *Kaga*—nobody wanted to claim the smaller *Soryu*—it has now been settled that the carrier was indeed *Soryu*.)[17]

At 1025, and from 14,500 feet, Leslie pushed over. All seventeen planes made the dive, though only thirteen had bombs. Nine bombs were dropped at the carrier, and three hit *Soryu* in a row right down the center line of the flight deck. All of them were 1,000-pounders, and fused to explode 1/100 of a second after impact. The carrier immediately erupted in flames. The damage was so obviously fatal that the last four planes switched to other targets, which turned out to be the battleship *Haruna* and a destroyer. These additional four bombs dropped all missed their targets.

Not only were there no Zeros around to bother the planes of Bombing Three during their dives on *Soryu*, there was no AA gunfire until near the end of the dives. Even then the flak was not heavy enough to deflect any of the planes from their targets—all planes with bombs dropped them at their targets (and even the misses were near misses). Unlike the *Enterprise* dive-bombers, *Yorktown*'s were totally unimpeded in their bombing runs. When they were finished, it had taken less than five minutes—between 1023 and 1028—for three of Nagumo's carriers to be reduced to burning wrecks. Although it was not clear until later, at 1028 the Japanese had lost the Battle of Midway.

THE HEROES RETURN

For planes attacking carriers, the withdrawal can often be more hazardous than the approach; the combat air patrol is fully aroused by then. However, for Bombing Three—unlike with the *Enterprise* dive-bombers—there were no Zeros around even to contest its withdrawal from the Mobile Force; all seventeen made it back virtually unscathed. (The only fighter planes they ran into were American Wildcats near *Yorktown* that mistook them for Japanese planes but, fortunately, realized their error before inflicting any damage.) When Bombing Three reached *Yorktown* at 1115, they were ordered to orbit above the carrier until ten SBDs of Scouting Five were launched for search patrol and a dozen Wildcats were launched for CAP. At 1152, just after the last Wildcat had been launched, and just as Bombing Three's planes were coming in to land, "bogeys" were detected on radar. A few minutes later, when Japanese bombers were identified, Leslie's dive-bombers were waived off and ordered to land on *Enterprise*. Two SBDs, including Leslie's, ran out of gas and ditched near the cruiser *Astoria*, where the crews were quickly rescued. The remaining fifteen landed on *Enterprise* shortly after noon, and fourteen of them were later able to join in the attack on *Hiryu*.

McClusky's dive-bombers from *Enterprise* did not fare nearly so well. Of the thirty-two that had made it to the vicinity of the Mobile Force, we saw that two had dropped out of formation because of engine trouble before the attack began, and soon ditched. Of the remaining thirty, one was shot down during its dive, and it appears that three more were fatally hit by AA flak, or by Zeros, almost immediately after making their attacks, and ditched in the vicinity of the Mobile Force; they can be regarded as having been "shot down."[18] This makes a surprisingly low total of only four dive-bombers lost directly to enemy action. (In partial recompense one Zero had been shot down by one of the Dauntlesses).[19] Of the twenty-six SBDs that remained to head toward home, several were badly shot up, including McClusky's, and some of them would later ditch when they ran out of gas from holed fuel tanks.

When McClusky's Dauntlesses returned, in several groups, to where *Enterprise* was supposed to be ("Point Option"), Task Force 16 was nowhere in sight. Its two carriers had been delayed longer than expected by the launches of the strike forces, and they were over 40 miles northeast of Point Option. This was the last thing McClusky's pilots needed when they were almost out of gas. While attempting to find a friendly carrier on which to land, ten SBDs ditched; the crews of six of them were never found.[20] (Thus, the total pilot losses for *Enterprise*'s dive-bomber squadrons were eleven: four shot down, six lost after ditching during the return, and one who dropped out of formation before the attack and was never found.) Of the sixteen dive-bombers that were recovered on the carriers, two, from Bombing Six, found *Yorktown* and landed on her around 1150, just before landings were halted because of the imminent attack by dive-bombers from *Hiryu*. The remaining fourteen dive-bombers—including McClusky's—finally found *Enterprise* and were taken aboard, in a nick of time, beginning around 1150. Of the fourteen Dauntlesses recovered on *Enterprise*, five were from Bombing Six, but one had been badly damaged; nine were from Scouting Six, but two, including McClusky's, were out of action.[21] Eleven of the fourteen would be available later for the attack on *Hiryu*.

YAMAGUCHI'S REVENGE

Back on *Hiryu*, the headquarters staff and many of the aircrew on the flight deck had watched in horror as the other three carriers of the Mobile Force erupted in flames between 1023 and 1028. The apocalyptic panorama was all the more shocking because they had come to believe that the Mobile Force was invincible. Years of training and sacrifice, and the string of spectacular victories from Pearl Harbor to the Indian Ocean to the Coral Sea, had fostered this conviction. But now the Mobile Force was down to one carrier—and only *Hiryu*'s air group remained to carry the battle to the American carriers.

As of the time of the bombing, *Hiryu*'s strike force was not yet ready. There may have been as many as half of its eighteen second-wave dive-bombers on the flight deck, but the rest were in the hangar. Three Zeros (from the returned Midway strike force) had been scheduled for escort duty for the planned grand-scale attack and were on the flight deck. But with the escorts on the other carriers now gone, three Zeros in the hangar that had also returned from the attack on Midway—and that had been intended for the combat air patrol—would now also have to be pressed into service to escort the dive-bombers.

Also in the hangar were nine torpedo planes that had returned from the Midway strike and were being armed with torpedoes. Of the original eighteen in *Hiryu*'s squadron, three had failed to return from Midway, two had crash-landed in the water near the carrier because of battle damage, and four more had returned too badly damaged to be put back into service.[22] There was one more torpedo plane—an orphan from *Akagi*—that would join *Hiryu*'s air group. It had been sent out at 0430 as one of the seven search planes, and on returning around 1030, was unable to land on *Akagi*; *Hiryu* was the only carrier available. Apart from the Zeros on combat air patrol, these thirty-four planes (eighteen dive-bombers, ten torpedo planes, and six Zeros) were the only operational aircraft left in the Mobile Force.

HIRYU'S FIRST STRIKE

Yamaguchi had been impatiently waiting since 0830 to launch the dive-bombers of his Second Carrier Division to attack the American carrier force. Now, at 1030, he would have to do it with the planes of a single carrier. He exhorted the crews of his small attack group of eighteen dive-bombers and six Zeros to quickly complete preparations for a launch, but several dive-bombers still had to be brought up to the flight deck, along with three more Zeros. He told the pilots that they were Japan's last hope, but he also told them not to be rash, advice to which several of the pilots paid no heed, as will be seen shortly. Lieutenant Michio Kobayashi, commander of the dive-bomber squadron, was made strike leader. At 1050, Yamaguchi began his launch, which was completed at 1058. Kobayashi led the twenty-four planes east in the general direction of the American carrier force, which by then was just a little over 90 miles away.

At the time of his launch, Kobayashi did not know exactly where the American carriers were. Search plane data was a couple of hours old (and inaccurate). There is a persistent myth that Kobayashi's strike force was led to *Yorktown* by following some of the American dive-bombers back home. This is without foundation. Leslie, who led Bombing Three back to *Yorktown*, hotly denied the rumor, and with justification. He had left the vicinity of the Mobile Force about thirty minutes before the *Hiryu* attack unit did, and was too far away to be seen by it. Moreover, Kobayashi did not need American planes to lead him to *Yorktown*. Two supplemental search planes from Cruiser Division Eight had earlier been dispatched to relieve *Tone* 4. One of them, *Chikuma* 5, had found the American carriers and radioed back updated—and accurate—location co-ordinates at 1110. At 1132 *Chikuma* 5 radioed an offer to lead Kobayashi to the American carrier force. It was at about this time, however, that the attack unit did run into some American planes: six stragglers of *Enterprise*'s dive-bomber group on their way back home (and this may be the source of the myth). They were a faction from Scouting Six that had become separated from the rest of the squadron and were being led back by Lieutenant Charles Ware.

The escort unit of six Zeros led by Lieutenant Shigematsu could not resist what appeared to be easy meat. They dropped out of formation and attacked the low-flying Dauntlesses (which they mistook for torpedo bombers). This turned out to be a rash and foolish move. Two of the Zeros got shot up and had to return to *Hiryu*; one of them crash-landed in the water near the carrier. This reduced the already inadequate escort to four planes, and probably doomed several dive-bombers to later destruction by *Yorktown*'s combat air patrol. (This lack of discipline was uncharacteristic for such experienced carrier pilots; perhaps the destruction of three Mobile Force carriers they had witnessed barely an hour before fueled an overpowering thirst for immediate vengeance.) None of the SBDs were shot down, but the encounter may have doomed them as well. Some probably took crippling hits, and all expended extra fuel they could not afford in attempting to evade the attackers. All six ran out of gas before finding *Enterprise* and ditched, and five of their crews were never heard of again. They, certainly, did not lead Kobayashi to *Yorktown*.

Shortly before noon, Kobayashi spotted a carrier task force about 30 miles away, which turned out to be *Yorktown*'s Task Force 17. A few minutes before, at 1152, *Yorktown*'s radar detected "bogeys" bearing 255° to the west, distance 32 miles. *Yorktown*'s fighter director ordered Lieutenant Arthur Brassfield's fighter division to investigate the intruders. At that time *Yorktown* had twelve Wildcats on combat air patrol, but they had just been launched and had not yet formed up or gained patrol altitude. The two of them launched last never did get in position to see the Japanese planes and did not participate in the upcoming aerial combat. The remaining ten, after some difficulties with communication, headed for the attacking force. Thirty miles to the southeast, *Enterprise*'s radar also tracked the incoming bogeys. There were nineteen Wildcats on combat air patrol over *Enterprise* and *Hornet*. At 1158 eight of them (four from each carrier) were dispatched to help defend *Yorktown*. The remainder were retained to defend Task Force 16, as both carriers were tied up recovering planes returning from battle and would not be able to launch more fighters to reinforce the patrol for at least another half-hour.

The air battle commenced at 1202 when *Yorktown*'s ten Wildcats plunged into Kobayashi's dive-bomber formation at about 10,000 feet.[23] Initially, there were no Zeros to contend with; incredibly, the rump four-plane escort had not yet caught up with the Val dive-bombers after the ill-fated diversion with the SBDs some thirty minutes earlier. Seven Vals were shot down almost immediately. Three more were forced out of formation, and then dumped their bombs and counterattacked two of the Wildcats. One of these dive-bombers was shot down, but the fighters were driven away from the main formation—at least temporarily. (Without bomb loads, Vals were remarkably maneuverable, and because there were no Zero escorts to do the job, these dive-bomber pilots apparently figured somebody had to help fend off Wildcats in order that some Vals might survive to dive-bomb the carrier.) Eight dive-bombers did manage to break through the melee and headed for *Yorktown*. The two surviving Vals without bombs retired to the sidelines to act as observers; one of them may have been the attack leader Kobayashi.

By this time, about 1205, Shigematsu's four Zeros finally joined the fray. They took on four Wildcats, but one Zero got shot down. None of the Wildcats was seriously damaged, but they ran out of ammunition and retired from action. Two more Wildcats—possibly the only *Yorktown* fighters with ammunition left—swooped in to tangle with the Zeros and shot another one down. Then, four Wildcats from *Hornet* arrived to replace the ammunition-depleted *Yorktown* contingent. In rapid succession, a third Zero was shot down, a *Hornet* Wildcat was shot down by a Zero (the only American loss in the battle), and another Val dive-bomber was shot down by a *Hornet* fighter. This left nine Vals—only seven with bombs—and only one Zero to protect them. However, most of the Wildcats were now out of ammunition.

While the lone remaining Zero occupied the three *Hornet* fighters, seven Vals continued on toward *Yorktown* temporarily free of harassment. Then, at about 1209, *Enterprise*'s four Wildcats arrived over *Yorktown*—just as four of the Vals were about to push over. The leader of the *Enterprise* Division, Lieutenant Roger Mehle, dove on the leading Val, but his guns failed to fire because of an electrical malfunction. He veered off and radioed the other three pilots to continue the attack, but his radio apparently also malfunctioned. As antiaircraft flak intended for the Vals exploded perilously close to the Wildcats, they broke off their dives and followed Mehle. The only obstacle now left for the Vals was AA gunfire from *Yorktown* and her escorting cruisers.

The seven Vals with bombs divided into two groups; three approached from the west and four from the southwest. The westerly three attacked first. At 1210, the first bomber pushed over. Just before the bomb was released at 1211, AA shellfire blew the plane to pieces, but the bomb fell free and hit *Yorktown* near its island. It was a 242-kilogram instant-detonation high-explosive land bomb. (Six of the eighteen Vals had intentionally been equipped with land bombs for purposes of neutralizing AA gun batteries and holing the carrier flight deck; it was intended that those bombers attack first.) The blast knocked out an AA gun battery aft of the island, killing most of its crew. It also blew a hole eleven feet in diameter in the flight deck. (Luckily, ten SBDs of Scouting Five, armed with 1,000-pound bombs, had been launched just before *Hiryu*'s dive-bombers approached.) The second Val to dive was also destroyed by AA gunfire, but its bomb, also a land bomb, missed. The third Val in the group missed with its bomb, but escaped undamaged.

A couple of minutes later the second group, consisting of four Vals, attacked. The fourth bomb to be dropped missed, but the fifth hit. It was an armor-piercing 251-kilogram bomb, fused for ⅒ of a second, which penetrated to the engine fireroom, where it damaged two boilers and extinguished the fires in three more. This left the ship with only one of its six boilers operating, which reduced the *Yorktown*'s speed to 6 knots. The sixth bomb dropped, also armor-piercing, hit as well and set off fires deep within the ship. The seventh and last bomb, dropped at 1215, missed. Seven bombs had been dropped, and three of them hit. The three bomb hits, though damaging, were not fatal. (As the Japanese bombs were not fused to explode in the hangar, as were the American bombs that hit the Japanese carriers, there were no secondary explosions from ordnance and airplane fuel tanks from the seven armed and fueled SBDs in *Yorktown*'s hangar.) The flight deck could have been patched up in about an hour, most of the boilers could have been refired, and the carrier could have recovered to resume full flight operations.

It could have been much worse. The Americans had been the lucky beneficiaries of the poor discipline shown by Shigematsu's escort unit. With an efficient performance by the Japanese escorts—with even just the six Zeros originally dispatched—it is very likely that at least one more bomb could have been delivered by the Vals. In such a case, *Yorktown* most likely would have been knocked out of action and possibly left a smoldering wreck. (And had that happened, we will see that *Enterprise* or *Hornet* would probably have been the target of the second attack from *Hiryu*—which would have substantially altered the subsequent course of events.) But instead, it had been a pitiful performance by the Zero escorts. After having lost two planes going after the SBDs on the way out and getting to the air battle late, they managed to shoot down only one Wildcat while losing three more of their own planes. When combined with the four-to-one drubbing Zeros had earlier taken against Fighting Three over the Mobile Force, this was a most dramatic reversal of the previous superiority Zeros had enjoyed over Wildcats in dogfights.

But as for Kobayashi's dive-bombers, three bomb hits from seven drops was a remarkable performance for the Vals. Even the *Yorktown* veterans of the Coral Sea battle were impressed. There, they had seen rather sloppy dives by the pilots of *Shokaku* and *Zuikaku*'s dive-bombers. Here, the dives had been much more crisp and resolute. Most were nearly vertical and were held steady through intense AA shellfire. And while American dive-bomber pilots usually dropped their bombs and pulled up at around 2,000 feet, the Vals continued their dives to below 1,000 feet. As one *Yorktown* AA gunner commented, the *Hiryu* dive-bomber unit was clearly the "varsity team."[24]

The success of the Vals, however, came with a heavy cost—due in large part to the ineptitude of Shigematsu's Zeros: nine (of the eighteen) had been shot down by the Wildcats during their approach, and two by AA shellfire while attacking *Yorktown*. The final two were shot down by Wildcats afterward under somewhat fluky circumstances. One was a Val that had jettisoned its bomb during an earlier dogfight with a Wildcat. After the bombing attack it was spotted flying at a leisurely speed off to the side, and its crew appeared to be photographing the damage to *Yorktown*. The *Enterprise* fighter contingent, which had earlier aborted their interception because of Mehle's malfunctioning guns, noticed this lone Val lingering about and shot it down. It is believed to have been Kobayashi's plane. The last casualty was shot down during its return to *Hiryu*. It had dropped out of formation to investigate (some say strafe) a ditched TBD from Torpedo Three. A *Yorktown* fighter happened to be in the area and shot down this second lingering Val. This made a total of thirteen Vals shot down, with all crews lost.

Thus, only five of the eighteen Vals made it back to *Hiryu*. They landed shortly after 1330. Most had sustained damage, but four could be patched up for further service. Only two of the six Zeros returned (and only one from the four that had seen battle over *Yorktown*). Three had been shot down and one had ditched after a premature return; only one could be made serviceable.[25] Two of the dive-bomber pilots who returned claimed, overoptimistically as it turned out, that one *Yorktown*-class carrier had definitely been destroyed.

HIRYU'S SECOND STRIKE
After Kobayashi's strike force had departed at 1100, *Hiryu* took aboard over twenty Zeros from all four carriers that had been on combat air patrol (leaving around nine in the air as of 1130).[26] Also landed was the torpedo plane from *Akagi* that had been on search patrol. Yamaguchi then made plans for a second strike on the American carrier force, using the ten operational torpedo planes remaining in the Mobile Force. Six Zeros from those that had landed from the combat air patrol were detailed to escort them. The strike force was to be led by Lieutenant Joichi Tomonaga, *Hiryu*'s air group commander who had led the Midway strike force.

The planes were ready to go at 1245, but Yamaguchi delayed the launch until he could get more accurate information on the status of the American carriers after the first attack. An experimental high-speed dive-bomber (later known to the Americans as "Judy") had been launched from *Soryu* at 0830 to establish close contact with the American carrier force. (At a top speed of 341 mph, it was the fastest plane at Midway and could easily outrun any Wildcat that might pester it.)[27] But after sending an initial report sighting the carriers at 1110, its radio ceased to function—so Yamaguchi had not been getting the kind of last-minute information he hoped for. At 1250 it returned and dropped a message on *Hiryu*'s flight deck informing Yamaguchi that there were three American carriers, and identified them as *Yorktown, Enterprise,* and *Hornet.* This was the first confirmation that there were three carriers (though after the third American torpedo bomber attack an hour and a half earlier it had dawned on the Japanese that there were probably that many).[28]

By 1315, Yamaguchi had also received radio messages from the *Chikuma* 5 search plane reporting that one American carrier—the northernmost one— had been destroyed (and this was soon corroborated by pilots from the first strike). This was good news for Yamaguchi and Nagumo, but it meant that there were still two more carriers to the south of the one attacked by Kobayashi's dive-bombers. Yamaguchi instructed Tomonaga to seek out and attack an undamaged carrier, and then ordered the launch to begin. Tomonaga's plane had returned from Midway with holes in its wing fuel tank, and his mechanics were unable to completely repair it. So it was with knowledge that he probably would not have enough fuel to return that he got into his plane to lead the strike force to a second American carrier. There was optimism all around on *Hiryu* and in Nagumo's new headquarters on *Nagara*. It was thought that if a second American carrier could be knocked out—leaving each side with one apiece—the Midway invasion might still take place, thus salvaging at least a partial victory.

The launch was completed at 1331, and the strike force formed up and headed for the American carrier force, now a little over 100 miles away. The group was a motley assortment consisting of ten Kate torpedo planes, nine from *Hiryu* and one from *Akagi*, accompanied by six Zeros, four from *Hiryu* and two from *Kaga*. The escort unit was led by Lieutenant Shigeru Mori from *Hiryu*. The Kates carried the accurate and deadly Type 91, Modification 3, torpedo that could be dropped at a speed of 200 knots from over 250 feet above the water.[29] Kates had the performance to take advantage of the unique characteristics of the Type 91; they had a top speed of 235 knots, and flew at almost 200 knots during their run-ups, which was almost twice the speed Devastators were limited to when delivering their slow and defective Mark 13 torpedoes. (As we have seen, the Type 91 aerial torpedoes—delivered by Kates—were the secret ship-killing weapons Japan counted on to give it a chance to win the Pacific War.) There were not very many of them on this mission, and there were no dive-bombers to divert part of the American air defense capability and also add synergy to the attack, but they were all Nagumo had left.

At 1430 an American carrier was sighted about 35 miles away. As it showed no signs of damage, Tomonaga assumed it was not the carrier attacked by the dive-bombers and gave the order to attack it. He then divided his ten torpedo planes into two groups for a split ("anvil") attack. He took the First *Chutai* of five planes straight in, and directed the Second *Chutai*, led by Lieutenant Toshio Hashimoto, to swing around to the left and come in on the other side of the carrier—which happened to be *Yorktown* again. By that time *Yorktown*'s radar had picked up the strike force. There were only six Wildcats on combat air patrol over the carrier at that time, and they were ordered by *Yorktown*'s fighter director to intercept. Help from Task Force 16's combat air patrol—40 miles to the southeast—was urgently requested, for the second time that afternoon, and soon eight more Wildcats (five from *Enterprise*, three from *Hornet*) were rushing toward *Yorktown*.

The first interception took place at 1438, about 10 miles out, against Tomonaga's First *Chutai*. One torpedo plane was shot down by two of the *Yorktown* fighters. But this time, unlike the situation with Kobayashi's dive-bomber attack, the Zero escorts were in position and shot down the two attacking Wildcats. The other four Wildcats had overflown the interception point and were temporarily out of position to the west. This left the path clear for the four surviving Kates of Tomonaga's *chutai* to continue on to the target. They began their run-up on *Yorktown* at 1440. At that time, eight more Wildcats, led by the irrepressible Thach, were launched from *Yorktown*. These reinforcements were most welcome because the eight Wildcats from TF 16 had not yet arrived. About this time, the four fighters from *Yorktown*'s original combat air patrol unit that had overflown the interception point had swung back toward *Yorktown* to go after the Kates. On their way back, two Zeros were spotted tangling with a Wildcat near sea level. The four Wildcats dove to the rescue and shot both Zeros down.

The first Kate to release a torpedo—at about 1441—was Tomonaga's. The torpedo missed, and Tomonaga's plane was shot down by Thach, who had just taken off from *Yorktown*. The second torpedo dropped also missed, but the plane evaded Thach's fighters and escaped through the screen—only to be shot down a few minutes later by a Wildcat that had arrived from *Enterprise*. The third torpedo dropped was actually jettisoned as its plane was being shot down by another Wildcat that had just taken off from *Yorktown*. The torpedo ran harmlessly way off target. The fourth and last torpedo to be dropped by Tomonaga's First *Chutai* also missed, and the plane was shot down by *Yorktown*'s AA gunfire. Thus, all five torpedo planes of Tomonaga's *chutai* were shot down with no hits from the three torpedoes that were released on target.

Hashimoto's Second *Chutai* had better luck. As almost all the Wildcats on CAP were engaged with Tomonaga's Kates or Mori's Zeros, the new arrivals faced little opposition. Hashimoto's planes came in from the northeast five abreast at 1443, and four released torpedoes. (The fifth plane, the one from *Akagi*, had a malfunction in its release gear and could not drop its torpedo.) Two of the four hit *Yorktown*. As they were dropped almost simultaneously, it is not known which of the four hit, but the two that struck home inflicted mortal damage. The blasts from the 530 pounds of explosive charge in each of the warheads ripped open *Yorktown*'s hull, flooded the fire rooms, destroyed the generator room, and knocked out all power. She came to a stop and began to list almost immediately.

During the escape of Hashimoto's *chutai* from Task Force 17, one of the Kates shot down a pursuing *Yorktown* Wildcat, and one of the four Zeros remaining shot down another Wildcat. The performance of Mori's escort unit was a far cry from that of the escort that had accompanied Kobayashi's dive-bombers. Eight of the ten torpedo planes got through, and seven dropped their torpedoes—for two hits. Four Wildcats were shot down, three by Zeros, for a loss of but two Zeros. Although five torpedo planes had been shot down—four by Wildcats and one by AA flak—three of them were downed after they had attacked *Yorktown*. Though Tomonaga did not live to see it, the attack had been classically executed; he would have been proud of it.

All five of Hashimoto's Kates made it back to *Hiryu* at 1530, but only one remained serviceable. Three of the four Zero escorts also landed, but the fourth arrived late and had to ditch near *Hiryu*. Of the two Zeros that failed to return, one was Mori's; Japan had lost one of her finest fighter pilots. On the American side, *Yorktown* had been knocked out of action, and flight operations were no longer possible; her surviving Wildcats involved in the air battle all had to land on *Enterprise* and *Hornet*. It was apparent that *Yorktown* was doomed, and she was ordered abandoned at 1455. However, the hardy vessel did not sink until three days later—it took two torpedoes from a Japanese submarine to finish her off.

HIRYU'S SWAN SONG

At 1445, just after the second torpedo hit *Yorktown*, Hashimoto sent a radio message back to Yamaguchi informing him that the attack had been carried out with at least two hits scored against an American carrier. Yamamoto on *Yamato* 300 miles to the rear, and Nagumo now ensconced on *Nagara*, were exultant. They assumed that a second carrier had been knocked out, leaving the two sides even with one carrier apiece. But it was not to be; Spruance still had two undamaged carriers. At that very moment the pilots of two SBDs of *Yorktown*'s Scouting Five—sent out just before Tomonaga's attack—finally spotted *Hiryu*. Ever since 1030 Fletcher and Spruance had been itching to fulfill Nimitz's exhortation from Pearl Harbor to find and "get that fourth carrier." Now they quickly made plans to launch a second strike to do just that.

There were twenty-five operational dive-bombers on *Enterprise*; seven from Scouting Six, four from Bombing Six, and fourteen refugees from *Yorktown*'s Bombing Three. About half had been rearmed with 1,000-pound bombs, the other half with 500-pounders. There were also eight fighters on board ready to go, but, curiously, Spruance's staff decided that none of them could be spared for escort. This is a difficult decision to fathom; Task Force 16 was crawling with fighters. Fighter losses had been surprisingly light: only one had been shot down while attacking the Mobile Force (though four more had been rendered inoperable), and only five more were lost defending *Yorktown* (though two more made water landings) for a total of a dozen unavailable because of combat. Another ten from *Hornet*'s Fighting Eight never made it back from the ill-fated morning sortie, and about a half-dozen were trapped on *Yorktown* (making, in all, about twenty-eight unavailable). But as the Americans began the day with seventy-nine operational Wildcats, this left—counting those inherited from *Yorktown*—over fifty operational Wildcats available to Spruance.[30]

Although *Hiryu* was considered capable of launching another strike, in view of the bomber losses already suffered in the first two strikes it is difficult to see how Spruance could have imagined *Hiryu* being able to cobble together more than a handful of bombers for a third strike. On the other hand, it would seem that the one thing *Hiryu* could be counted on to have a lot of was Zeros for combat air patrol (most of them refugees from the destroyed carriers). Thus, one must wonder why Spruance decided to send the dive-bombers out without escorts.

In addition to the twenty-five dive-bombers on *Enterprise*, *Hornet* also had sixteen ready to launch, but Spruance's staff did not seem much interested in them. Those dive-bombers were from the twenty that had returned between 1118 and 1145 after having failed to find the Mobile Force. We saw in the previous chapter that thirty-four dive-bombers had been launched from *Hornet* (nineteen in Bombing Eight and fifteen in Scouting Eight). All fifteen from Scouting Eight had returned, along with five from Bombing Eight (including air group commander Ring's SBD). The remaining fourteen SBDs from Bombing Eight were not available due to misadventure: after the futile attempt to find the Japanese carrier force, they had gone to Midway, where two ran out of gas and ditched, and another was shot down in the lagoon by "friendly" AA gunfire, having been mistaken for a Japanese plane. (All the crews were later rescued.) Eleven landed on Midway's beat-up air strip at 1135 and were eventually refueled after some difficulty because Midway's gasoline pumping system had been knocked out in the Japanese attack.[31] They had returned to *Hornet* and landed soon after 1510, but would not be fit for further duty until much later in the day.

On *Enterprise*, the twenty-five dive-bombers—led by Earl Gallaher (who had scored the first hit on *Kaga* in the morning attack)—were launched for the strike on *Hiryu* at 1530. During that launch *Hornet* was belatedly ordered by Spruance to launch its dive-bombers. But the delay in getting the word to *Hornet*'s air officer meant that *Hornet*'s air group would not be able to coordinate its attack with the *Enterprise* group's. Also, as *Hornet*'s flight deck had been cleared to land the late arrivals of Bombing Eight from Midway, the sixteen SBDs in its strike force were still in the process of being brought up from the hangar deck. They were finally launched shortly after 1600—also without any fighter escorts.

About 130 miles away on *Hiryu*, Yamaguchi was making plans for a third strike against what he assumed was the last remaining American carrier. He did not have much left with which to do it: four dive-bombers and one torpedo plane were all that could be made serviceable after their return from the first two strikes.[32] There were about twenty-three Zeros still operational, as well as *Soryu*'s high-performance experimental dive-bomber. The Judy would be launched ahead of the attack unit to find the American carrier and guide the strike planes to it. This remnant of a strike force was to be led by Hashimoto (the hero of the torpedo plane attack on *Yorktown*), and nine Zeros were assigned for escort. At 1550 Yamaguchi received some disquieting news from *Tone* 4, which had been relaunched for search duty at 1400 after its fateful service that morning: there were still two American carriers apparently fully operational.

Meanwhile, Gallaher was leading his dive-bombers toward *Hiryu*. One, from Scouting Six, had aborted with engine trouble soon after takeoff—leaving twenty-four. At around 1630 Gallaher sighted *Hiryu*'s task force about 30 miles away. He then swung his dive-bombers around to the southwest so he could attack from the sun. This tactic to catch the Japanese by surprise proved highly successful; his bombers were not spotted until they had almost reached their push-over point at 1701. There were fourteen Zeros on CAP, all at high level, but most were several miles to the east.[33] Apparently, only one SBD was intercepted before the dives began—one of the four from Richard Best's Bombing Six. It was shot down.

At 1705, Gallaher pushed over—followed immediately by the other five planes of Scouting Six. They were pounced on by several Zeros, and it appears that only two managed to drop bombs, which missed the sharply swerving *Hiryu*. Next came the planes of *Yorktown*'s Bombing Three. Just before Gallaher's dive they had been assigned to attack a battleship—which turned out to be *Haruna*—but when their squadron leader Lieutenant Dewitt Shumway saw that none of Scouting Six's bombs had hit the carrier he changed targets to take twelve of his dive-bombers down to attack *Hiryu*. Several more Zeros jumped in, peppering Shumway's bombers with bullets all the way down. Although two more Dauntlesses were shot down, at least eight released their bombs, and three hit *Hiryu* in rapid succession forward of her island. (Two planes of Bombing Three went after the original target, *Haruna*, but their bombs missed.) The last to dive on *Hiryu* were the remaining three planes of Bombing Six. Three bombs were dropped, and one hit the already blazing carrier.

It is not known how many of the four bombs that hit were 1,000-pounders;

some of the planes of Bombing Three, which would normally carry 1,000-pound bombs, were armed with 500-pounders (along with Scouting Six's planes). Chances are that three of the four bombs were 1,000-pounders. This was more than enough to destroy a carrier as light as *Hiryu* even though she was not in a "vulnerable" condition—as the first three carriers of the Mobile force had been. (Only a few planes laden with ordnance were parked at the rear of her flight deck.) It appears that perhaps only thirteen dive-bombers—of the twenty-one diving on *Hiryu*—actually dropped bombs.[34] If so, it would appear that Zeros and AA gunfire kept eight SBDs either from dropping bombs or from dropping them near enough *Hiryu* to be recorded.

Four hits was an impressive performance for Gallaher's dive-bombers, considering that the attack was made without escorts and in the face of at least some Zeros in a position to oppose it at the outset. Equally remarkable was the loss of only three SBDs, even after all fourteen Zeros had joined in the fray; no Dauntlesses appear to have been shot down during the withdrawal. The failure of most of the Zeros on CAP to get into position to attack the dive-bombers before they began their dives highlighted perhaps the greatest weakness of the Japanese in carrier warfare: lack of radar. While *Yorktown* had been able to pick up Japanese dive-bombers on radar when they were over 30 miles out, the Mobile Force had to depend on visual sightings by observers in the ships of the outer screen and Zero pilots on CAP.

This had worked most of the time earlier in the day, when dive-bomber attacks from Midway had come from the south and carrier torpedo bombers had come from the southeast and the sun was high in the morning sky. (It had not worked for the fatal dive-bomber attacks at 1025 because of clouds and preoccupation with torpedo bombers.) But when Gallaher cannily chose to swing around to the southwest, while still out of visual range, the sun was relatively low in the sky, and this made sighting very difficult. His dive-bombers were not seen until they were almost on top of *Hiryu*'s task force. The Japanese were surprised, for the second time that day, by American dive-bombers. Therefore, when Spruance opted not to send escorts he won yet another gamble, and Nagumo's vaunted Zeros had yet another failure. This certainly was not the day for Zero pilots.

The carrier battle of June 4 was now over. Though it would take a while for them to finally sink, in the end Nagumo lost all four of his carriers against just one for the Americans. It was, as Nimitz later said, "a glorious page in our history." It was also the most spectacular naval victory in history, and the pivotal battle of the Pacific War.

AFTER THE DELUGE

For Yamamoto, the eagles had fallen. The loss of four carriers from the Mobile Force was a catastrophe from which Japan would never recover. With only one carrier lost in the battle, the Americans now outnumbered the Japanese in fleet attack carriers four to two (*Enterprise, Hornet, Saratoga,* and *Wasp* versus *Shokaku* and *Zuikaku*). But it had been a day of dramatic swings in the fortunes of battle. We have seen that up until 1000 the scorecard of planes lost heavily favored Nagumo's Mobile Force, by a count of 62 to 18. Since 1000, not even counting the planes lost on board the bombed carriers, the tally was reversed and favored the Americans 38 to 26 in planes shot down or forced down because of battle damage.

To summarize the plane losses in battle after 1000 on June 4: The Japanese lost eleven Zeros in air battles over the Mobile Force between 1015 and 1045 (nine shot down, two crashed from battle damage), seven Zeros while escorting the two attacks against *Yorktown* (five shot down, two ditched). Thirteen dive-bombers and five torpedo planes had been shot down in the attacks on *Yorktown*. There had also been two cruiser-based search planes shot down after 1000. The Americans lost one *Yorktown* fighter escorting Torpedo Three's morning attack on the Mobile Force and seven in air battles over *Yorktown* (five shot down, two crashed). Ten *Yorktown* torpedo bombers had been shot down in the morning attack. Eight dive-bombers had been shot down—four from *Enterprise* in the morning attack, three in the afternoon attack, and one Marine Vindicator dive-bomber from Midway in a late afternoon attack.

In addition to the 56 Japanese and 88 American planes lost in combat for the whole of June 4, a number of planes on both sides crash-landed in the water because of fuel exhaustion—fifteen Japanese and twenty-nine American. (Most of the Japanese planes ditching were the fourteen Zeros on CAP when *Hiryu* was bombed; most of the American planes ditching from fuel exhaustion were the ten fighters from *Hornet* after they failed to find the Mobile Force and twelve dive-bombers from *Enterprise* returning from the morning attack.) Therefore, the grand total of planes lost in battle and from ditching out of gas on June 4 was 71 for the Japanese (including two cruiser float planes) and 117 for the Americans (38 from Midway and 79 from the carriers.)[35] But in the final accounting of Japanese plane and pilot losses that day, far more planes were lost when the four carriers were bombed and later sunk than were shot down. That tally will be given at the end of this section.

JAPANESE ATTEMPTS TO REGROUP

Although with the destruction of the carriers the Battle of Midway was essentially over, several feints and skirmishes remained to be played out before the two fleets headed home. When Nagumo reestablished his command on *Nagara* around noon he ordered his battleships, heavy cruisers, and some destroyers to assemble and go after the American carrier force in a daylight engagement. At the same time, Admiral Kondo, commanding the Second Fleet, which was supporting the occupation force some 200 miles to the southwest,

volunteered to bring his two battleships, four heavy cruisers, and some destroyers up to join the Mobile Force.

Meanwhile, Yamamoto, in his headquarters on *Yamato* 300 miles to the west,
also sprang into action. At 1050 he had been informed by the commander of
Cruiser Division 8 (Nagumo being temporarily without a communications facility) of the bombing of the three Mobile Force carriers. But by 1215 he had also
learned that *Hiryu*'s dive-bombers had bombed an American carrier. Based on
an earlier report from Nagumo that there was apparently only one carrier in the
American force, the situation did not look so grim. At 1220 he ordered the carriers *Junyo* and *Ryujo* in the Aleutian campaign to rush south to join *Hiryu*. He
also ordered the Aleutian Screening Force of four battleships to rendezvous
with his Main Body (consisting of *Yamato*, *Nagato*, and *Mutsu*) by noon the
next day to join in a fleet action against the cruisers of the American task force.
With all this naval power still at his disposal Yamamoto entertained the prospect
that the American force could yet be destroyed and Midway could still be taken.

On the light cruiser *Nagara*, when Nagumo learned—at around 1300—that
there were three American carriers opposing him (he had not yet heard of *Yorktown*'s demise) he suddenly lost his enthusiasm for a daylight engagement.
When Yamamoto learned the same thing his enthusiasm also dampened. But
a little while later when word reached him that a *second* American carrier had
been hit at 1445, his optimism was renewed. However, after 1700 he got two
pieces of news that made clear to him the final dimensions of the disaster: his
last Mobile Force carrier was gone, and the Americans still had at least two undamaged carriers. The only hope left now was for a night action between his
battleships and heavy cruisers and the American force of carriers and cruisers.
He still possessed an overwhelming advantage in firepower in a night action,
where aircraft would not be a factor. For this, Yamamoto ordered his powerful
Main Body of three battleships to move east at top speed to support the two
battleships and two heavy cruisers of the Mobile Force. Kondo was also making
a high-speed run to the northeast with two battleships, four heavy cruisers, a
squadron of destroyers, and the light carrier *Zuiho*.

While this immense armada, which included seven battleships (soon to be
joined by four more)—the largest collection of battleships since the Battle of
Jutland in World War I—was moving into position, Spruance made a decision
that was hotly criticized at the time but proved to be a wise one. After he had
recovered the dive-bombers from his strike on *Hiryu* at 1907, he had been urged
by some of his staff to turn west with his task force—which now contained
seven heavy cruisers—and pursue the crippled Mobile Force. It was not known
in Spruance's headquarters at that time whether the four Japanese carriers that
had been hit were actually destroyed. But it was believed, by those favoring the
move, that a night action could certainly finish them off and possibly destroy or
damage the two battleships and two heavy cruisers accompanying them.

Instead of heeding the battle cries of the more aggressive members of his staff, Spruance decided to retire eastward and wait until morning before resuming the attack. Had he continued west after 1900, shortly after midnight he would have run smack into the four battleships and six heavy cruisers of the Mobile Force and Kondo's Second Fleet. Besides Spruance being outnumbered in big guns, the Japanese were better trained for night actions. Moreover, Yamamoto's Main Body would have arrived on the scene in the morning and added the 16-inch guns of *Nagato* and *Mutsu* and the mammoth 18.1-inch guns of *Yamato* to the slugfest. Spruance's caution avoided yet another trap set by Yamamoto.

While Yamamoto's Main Body and Kondo's Second Fleet were moving into position the night of June 4, Yamamoto was also making plans to proceed with the capture of Midway. At 2030 he ordered Admiral Kurita's Close Support Group of four heavy cruisers to advance to Midway and bombard it. In the meantime, he ordered the only Japanese vessel near the atoll, the submarine I-168, to shell the air base until the cruisers arrived. At around 2300, after a series of communications with the nearly hysterical Nagumo convinced Yamamoto that Nagumo had lost his nerve, Yamamoto relieved Nagumo of command and put Kondo on charge of the heavy ships of the Mobile Force.[36] Nagumo was ordered to tend to his crippled carriers. At 2340, Kondo ordered all the ships under his command to prepare for a night action.

Then, at around twenty minutes after midnight, it began to sink in with Yamamoto and his staff that the game was up. They realized that if their forces continued east and did not make close contact with the American carrier force before morning, their battleships and cruisers would be sitting ducks for an air attack at daybreak by the planes of two carriers. Yamamoto began to resign himself to defeat. He canceled the bombardment of Midway and ordered Kurita to change course to the northwest and join up with the Main Body. At 0255 he ordered a general retirement of all his forces. As far as Yamamoto was concerned, the Battle of Midway was over.

But it was not quite over. While Kurita's cruisers were retiring to the northwest an American submarine, the *Tambor*, was sighted. During an emergency turn at 0342 to escape from the submarine, the cruiser *Mogami* accidently rammed its sister *Mikuma*, badly damaging both cruisers. The *Tambor* radioed a report of the incident to Midway, and at daybreak Catalina flying boats were sent out to find the crippled ships. When they were located, the ten operational dive-bombers remaining at Midway were sent to attack them. There were no bomb hits, and one of the dive-bombers was shot down. However, its pilot, rather than crashing into the sea, chose to crash into *Mikuma*, further damaging the cruiser.[37] A little later, at 0830, eight B-17s attacked. None of their bombs hit either, and the damaged cruisers shot down two of the B-17s, the only B-17s shot down during the battle.

After retiring eastward in the evening of June 4, Spruance had reversed his course shortly after midnight to be in a position to attack the Mobile Force in the morning. Around 0600 on June 5, he received search plane reports of a large Japanese disposition about 200 miles to the northwest moving west, and decided to chase after them. But because "a stern chase is a long chase" it took until 1500 in the afternoon before he was in a position to launch an attack. Fifty-eight Dauntless dive-bombers from *Enterprise* and *Hornet* took off to find and attack what was assumed to be the Mobile Force. They did not find it, but on their return trip sighted a lone destroyer that had been detached to look after *Hiryu*. They attacked it, but the difficulty of dive-bombing a speedy, wriggling destroyer was illustrated by the fact that none of the more than fifty bombs dropped scored a hit. Even worse, one of SBDs (originally from *Yorktown*) was shot down by the destroyer. The remaining 57 SBDs had to make a hazardous night landing on *Enterprise* and *Hornet*. One of *Hornet*'s dive-bombers ditched near the carriers, but its crew was rescued. June 5, thus, ended as a day of almost utter futility for both sides. Most of the damage to Japanese ships was self-inflicted, and four American bombers got shot down attacking ships without any air defenses, and failed to score a single bomb hit.

The next morning the search for *Mogami* and *Mikuma* resumed and they were found by a reconnaissance flight from *Enterprise*. During the day of June 6, beginning at 0800, Spruance launched three attack groups from *Enterprise* and *Hornet* — consisting of eighty-one SBDs (some launched twice), three torpedo bombers, and twenty-eight Wildcats, 112 planes in all — in an effort to finish off the two cruisers. *Mogami* took five bomb hits in the first two attacks but did not sink. *Mikuma* was less fortunate. She took at least three hits and the last, dropped at 1445 in the third attack, finished her off. She went down later in the day, taking most of her complement of almost 1,000 crewmen with her. During the first attack, two SBDs — one each from *Enterprise* and *Hornet* — had been shot down. That evening, Spruance decided that he had pushed his luck far enough and that his pilots had been through enough. He retired east and awaited orders from Nimitz to return to Pearl Harbor.

THE DEATH-AGONY OF THE CARRIERS

In the meantime, the four Mobile Force carriers and *Yorktown* that had been bombed on June 4 took a while to die. The first to sink was *Soryu*. It blew up and went down at 1913 on June 4, taking 718 hands with it.[38] Minutes later an explosion ripped *Kaga* in two, and it went under at 1925 — taking over 800 of its crew with it. (Earlier a torpedo fired by the submarine *Nautilus* had hit *Kaga*, but it was a dud and — contrary to popular belief — did not contribute to its sinking.) The next to go was *Akagi*. It did not go under by itself and probably could have been towed back to Japan. Rather than risk its capture, however, Yamamoto ordered it scuttled. Several torpedoes from four Japanese destroyers were fired into her at sunrise, June 5, and at 0455 she sank. All the surviving crew had been evacuated, but 221 were listed in Nagumo's Official Report as dead or missing.[39]

A few minutes later at 0510 a Japanese destroyer attempted to scuttle *Hiryu*. A torpedo hit, but the ship did not go down for another four hours. It finally sank at 0907 with 416 of its crew listed as dead or missing. Among those on board who were still alive and went down voluntarily with the ship was Rear Admiral Yamaguchi; his advice to launch an attack almost two hours before the Mobile Force was bombed had been rejected by Nagumo, and apparently he could not bear the thought of having to explain the disaster. The Japanese navy thereby lost its "Halsey," and the loss of such an offensive-minded carrier commander may have been almost as grievous to the Japanese navy as that of the carrier.

On the American side, *Yorktown* was still afloat two days after she was hit, and plans were being made to tow her back to Pearl Harbor. However, the Japanese submarine that had shelled Midway on the night of the 4th, I-168, found *Yorktown* and, at 1330 on June 6, put two torpedoes into her. (The destroyer *Hammann* was also hit at that time and sank in four minutes with a loss of over 80 crewmen.) The seemingly indestructible *Yorktown* did not finally go under until about 0600 the next morning. All her surviving crew, as well as most of the dead, had been evacuated.

As for the number of American sailors, marines, and air crewmen killed in the battle, Admiral Nimitz's Action Report states 307. Of these, about 20 were killed on *Yorktown* when she was bombed and torpedoed on June 4; 81 were killed on DD *Hammann*. Only 11 were killed on the ground at Midway in the attack that began the battle.[40] The remainder—about 195—were navy and marine aviators —as will be detailed in the next section. Japanese losses in personnel were very much greater. Nagumo's Official Report states that 2,155 personnel were lost with the four carriers, but this does not necessarily include all the aviators who died. In addition to Mobile Force losses, over 800 went down with cruiser *Mikuma*, and about 90 were killed on cruiser *Mogami*. The total number of Japanese killed at Midway will never be known for certain, but it probably exceeded 3,100—ten times the number the Americans lost.

PLANES AND PILOTS LOST—THE RECKONING

We saw that up to late afternoon on June 4, 117 American planes had been lost from combat and by ditching from fuel exhaustion. After then, plane losses from combat were relatively light but still numbered another seven. Also, when *Yorktown* finally sank on June 7, it appears that twenty planes went down with her—five Wildcat fighters, ten Dauntless dive-bombers, and three Devastator torpedo bombers of her own, plus two dive-bombers from *Enterprise*.[41] This

TABLE 8.1
Summary of American Plane and Pilot Losses, June 4–6

		Launched	Shot down	Crashed	Recovered	Operational	Pilots lost
CAP—							
Midway:	Fighters	26	15	2	9	3	14
Midway search:	PBYs	22	2	0	20	20	2
Midway attacks on MF:	Torpedo planes	6	5	0	1	0	5
	B-26s	4	2	0	2	0	2
	B-17s	17	0	0	17	15	0
	Dive-bombers	27	11	0	16	11	11
		(54)	(18)	0	(36)	(26)	(18)
Morning carrier attacks on MF:	Fighters	26	1	10	15	12	3
	Torpedo planes	41	35	2	4	3	33
	Dive-bombers	84	4	17	63	56	11
		(151)	(40)	(29)	(82)	(71)	(47)
CAP— Fleet:	Fighters	42*	5	2	35	33	3
Afternoon attacks on MF:	Dive-bombers	41	3	0	38	36	3
	B-17s	12	0	0	12	12	0
	MW Dive-bombers	11	0	1	10	10	1
Later attacks on MF:	Dive-bombers	139*	3	1	135	56	3
	B-17s	12	2	0	10	10	2
	MW Dive-bombers	10	1	0	9	9	1
			89	35			94

* Some planes launched more than once

Planes lost in battle: 124
On *Yorktown*:   20
On ground at Midway: 4
Total of planes lost: 148

made a grand total for the entire battle of 144 planes (plus a few inoperable planes destroyed on the ground at Midway—perhaps four). Of the approximately 194 air crewmen killed, the number of pilots killed appears to be around ninety-four, with sixty-one of them carrier pilots (including the five torpedo bomber pilots of "Torpedo Eight," which had been deployed from Midway).

JAPANESE LOSSES

While American plane and pilot losses are known with a fair degree of accuracy from surviving records, that is not the case for Japanese casualties. Although the total number of operational planes on board the four carriers has been determined, and although the number of pilots killed in combat is reported in the surviving the carrier Action Reports, what is not known is the number of pilots killed when the carriers were bombed and sunk. That number can only be estimated based on the number of pilots on board each carrier, the severity of the bombing, and, most important, the testimony of officers from each carrier given after the war. (As will be seen, the estimate I come up with is higher than given in other American accounts.)

As the Battle of Midway was as much a battle of attrition between each side's carrier pilots as it was between carriers, it is important to attempt to determine the total number of Japanese carrier pilots lost at Midway. Only then can the true magnitude of the Japanese defeat be realized. We saw in an earlier chapter that Japan began the war with only about four hundred first-line carrier pilots — and that, unlike the American pilots, they were essentially irreplaceable. About one hundred had been lost in battles prior to Midway, leaving about three hundred first-line pilots (along with another seventy or so second-line pilots on the light carriers). We also saw that conservation of pilots was a paramount concern of Nagumo in his decision-making process during the battle; unless a sufficient number of carrier pilots survived to carry out subsequent operations planned for the first year of the war, any victory at Midway could turn out to be a Pyrrhic one. But, alas for Nagumo, there was no victory, and Japanese pilot losses were much worse than his worst fears. It is now apparent from the subsequent carrier battles in 1942 that the most grievous losses for the Japanese at Midway were not the four carriers, but the elite carrier pilots. Just how many of them were lost in the battle?

It is known that of the approximately 230 carrier pilots who began the battle, forty-four were killed in combat (three from *Akagi*, five from *Kaga*, four from *Soryu*, and thirty-two from *Hiryu*). The unknown quantity is the number lost when the four carriers were bombed and later sunk. To arrive at an estimate of this we must first determine the number of pilots on board each carrier at the time it was bombed. That can be done. (However, as the computations are somewhat laborious, readers not interested in plodding through the details may want to skip to the summary at the end of the section.)

From the original 230 pilots, we subtract the 44 lost in combat and 10 more who were shot down but rescued by destroyers (leaving 176), then subtract the number in the air on combat air patrol or search duty at the time of the bombings. When *Akagi*, *Kaga*, and *Soryu* were bombed at around 1025, most of their Zeros were aloft on combat air patrol: nine from *Akagi*, twelve from *Kaga*, and nine from *Soryu*. In addition, each of those carriers also had a plane on search patrol—one Kate each from *Akagi* and *Kaga*, and a Judy dive-bomber from *Soryu*. This makes a total of 33 planes that were not on board those three carriers at the time of the bombing. (We will deal with *Hiryu* later, as she had inherited a large number of planes from the other carriers by time she was bombed later in the day.) How many pilots did that leave on board the first three carriers when they were bombed?

Taking each carrier in order: From *Akagi*'s original 57 pilots, three had been killed in combat and one had been downed but rescued by a destroyer, leaving 53 still remaining in her air group. Nine were aloft on CAP, and one was returning from search patrol, leaving 43 on board at 1025. From *Kaga*'s 63, five had been killed in combat—leaving 58. Twelve were on CAP, and one was on search patrol, leaving 45 on board. From *Soryu*'s 56 (augmented to 57 when one of *Hiryu*'s Kates returned to *Soryu* after aborting soon after takeoff for the Midway attack), four had been killed in combat and three had been downed but rescued by destroyers—leaving 50. Nine were on CAP, and one was on search patrol, leaving 40 on board. Thus, out of a total of 161 pilots still with the three carriers at 1025, 33 were in the air—leaving 128 on board when their carriers were bombed. (The breakdown is 59 torpedo plane, 54 dive-bomber, and 15 Zero pilots.)[42]

As for how many of those pilots were killed by the bombing and fires, or were drowned on or off the carriers, that can only be a matter of conjecture. No detailed accounting in Japanese records—if one was ever made after the battle—survived the war. However, responsible officers from each carrier did give estimates in interrogations after the war, but most of those estimates have generally been discounted as exaggerations. Those estimates can be refined by taking into account the following factors: the number of ship's crewmen reported missing on each carrier in Nagumo's Official Report compared with the carrier's estimated battle complement (this will give a rough proportion of aircrew killed) and the severity of the bombing of each carrier coupled with the likely location of the pilots when each carrier was bombed. (Pilots in especially vulnerable locations such as the hangars or ready rooms next to them would be more likely to be killed than crew deeper down in the ship.) To arrive at an estimate of the pilots killed on board, let us again take each carrier in order.

AKAGI
The most definitive of all the estimates of pilot casualties was given by Captain Aoka, commanding officer of *Akagi*, who stated that six *Akagi* pilots were killed in the bombing.[43] This is a fairly low number considering that at the time *Akagi* was bombed, 20 of the 43 pilots on board were in the attack group preparing for launch—seventeen torpedo planes and three Zeros. Those pilots were mostly in the hangar, or in the ready room. (Most of the remainder had

returned from the strike on Midway and were probably in their living or din-
ing quarters deeper down in the carrier.) However, although 20 pilots were in
very vulnerable locations, only two bombs hit, and one of them was far to the
rear. Also, extensive evacuation measures had taken place before she was scuttled. Because of this, only 221 out of 2,000 crewmen perished; accordingly, one
would expect that a similarly low proportion of aviators would have been
killed. Thus, six seems a reasonable estimate.

KAGA

Kaga's pilots did not fare nearly so well. Captain Amagai, air officer of *Kaga*,
gave his opinion that about 50 percent of the pilots on board *Kaga* were lost.[44]
As there were 45 pilots on board at the time the carrier was bombed, this would
suggest that 20–25 were killed. This estimate is generally considered to be way
too high—a tally closer to *Akagi*'s six is deemed more likely. However, *Kaga*'s
pilots were exposed to far greater peril than those of *Akagi*. Four bombs hit
Kaga (one 1,000-pounder and three 500-pounders), and when they exploded
almost two-thirds of her pilots were preparing for launch (twenty-six torpedo
plane, three Zero). They were probably in the hangar or in the ready room
next to it. The carrier also went down suddenly when she blew up, before
evacuation could be completed, taking 800 out of a complement of 2,016
down with her. Thus, a higher proportion of *Kaga*'s aviators probably perished. Even if Amagai's estimate is on the high side, it seems reasonable to
reckon that around 20 were killed.

SORYU

The factors for *Soryu* were similar to those of *Kaga*, and the losses were propor-
tionately even worse. Captain Ohara, executive officer of *Soryu*, stated that of
the approximately 700 lost when *Soryu* was bombed and sank "about 30" were
pilots.[45] As there were 40 pilots on board, three-quarters of them being killed
may seem high. However, three 1,000-pound bombs hit this smaller carrier, and
when they exploded 21 pilots were preparing for launch (eighteen dive-bomber,
three Zero). They were on the flight deck, in the hangar, or in the ready room.
Moreover, like *Kaga*, *Soryu* blew up and sank before evacuation could be completed, and even a higher proportion of her complement perished—718 out of
1,100 crewmen were reported killed or missing. Thus, even if Ohara's estimate
is a bit high it is still likely that more than half of *Soryu*'s pilots were killed—at
least two dozen.

HIRYU

Now we come to the final carrier, bombed at around 1700 in the afternoon. It is
much more difficult to arrive at an estimate of the number of pilots killed on
board *Hiryu* when she was bombed than for the other carriers—and there is no

testimony giving such an estimate. Captain Kawaguchi, air officer of *Hiryu*, stated only that *Hiryu* lost a total of "about 60" pilots in the battle.[46] As *Hiryu* originally had only fifty-four operational aircraft of her own, this estimate, presumably, included pilots inherited from the other carriers. Also, as *Hiryu* had lost 32 of her own pilots before she had been bombed, this would appear to leave, under Kawaguchi's estimate, about 28 who were lost as a result of the bombing. This seems too high, but to refine the estimate let us begin by determining the number of pilots who were on board *Hiryu* when she was bombed.

Prior to the time *Hiryu* was bombed she had inherited twenty-seven Zeros from the other carriers that had been on CAP (there had been thirty aloft from those carriers, but three had been shot down after 1025). *Hiryu* also inherited the Kate search plane from *Akagi* and the Judy search plane from *Soryu* (*Kaga*'s Kate search plane had crash-landed alongside the carrier). Thus, in addition to what was left of her own original complement of 54 planes, she had 29 from the other carriers.

The deductions from these 83 planes to determine the number on board at the time of the bombing are somewhat complex as *Hiryu* sent off two attack groups against *Yorktown* in addition to the planes sent on the Midway attack. Nine pilots had been killed in the attack on Midway and on morning combat air patrol, one had been downed but rescued by a destroyer, and one had returned to *Soryu*; 23 had been killed in the two attacks on *Yorktown*, and two more had crashed on return but been rescued by destroyers; 14 were aloft on CAP when she was bombed—for a total of 50 pilots who were not on the carrier. This left 33 pilots on board at 1700 (though there were only fifteen operational planes remaining).

When *Hiryu* was bombed, perhaps as many as 15 pilots were in the hangar or ready room—those assigned to the third strike. Four bombs—most of them 1,000-pounders—struck this smaller carrier and detonated in the hangar, which would probably have killed most of the pilots there or in adjoining compartments. As for the remaining 18 pilots, it is not known where they were, but if they were deeper down in the vessel most would probably have survived. Unlike *Soryu*, *Hiryu* did not sink suddenly but was scuttled only after extensive evacuation measures had been taken; only 416 out of 1,100 crewmen were listed as killed or missing. Thus, it seems unlikely that 28 of the 33 pilots on board would have been killed. About half seems a more reasonable estimate.

In summary, it appears that a grand total of about 161 pilots were on board the four carriers when they were bombed. My estimate of the number of pilots killed on each carrier by the bombing and its aftermath is: *Akagi*, six of the 43; *Kaga*, 20 of 45; *Soryu*, 24 of 40; and *Hiryu*, 15 of 33—for a total of about 65. (Though higher than usually given, this estimate is actually conservative; if the testimony of the officers of the four carriers cited were taken at face value the number would be closer to 85.)

TABLE 8.2.
Summary of Japanese Carrier Plane and Pilot Losses, June 4

		Launched	Shot down	Crashed	Recovered	Operational	Pilots lost
Attack on	Zeros	36	2	0	34	29	2
Midway:	Vals	36	1	0	35	29	1
	Kates	36	5	3	28	19	5
		(108)	(8)	(3)	(97)	(77)	(8)
Search:	Kates & Judy	3	0	1	2	2	0
CAP—	Zeros	39	13	3	23	20?	12
morning:	Zeros-MW*	16	2	0	14	12?	1
		(55)	(15)	(3)	(37)		(13)
Hiryu's	Zeros	6	3	1	2	2	3
first attack:	Vals	18	13	0	5	4	13
		(24)	(16)	(1)	(7)	(6)	(16)
Hiryu's	Zeros	6	2	1	3	3	2
second	Kates	10	5	0	5	1	5
attack:		(16)	(7)	(1)	(7)	(4)	(7)
CAP—							
afternoon:	Zeros	14	0	14**	0	0	0
Total:			46	23			44

* First-wave Zeros relaunched for CAP
** Crashed from fuel exhaustion after *Hiryu* was bombed

Pilots lost when carriers bombed:

Akagi: 6
Kaga: 20
Hiryu: 15
Soryu: 24
    65+

Lost in combat: 44
Total pilots killed: 110

Permanently disabled: 15
Total lost: 125

Note: Total number of carrier planes lost: approximately 272 (including spares and Sixth Air Group). In addition, two cruiser float planes were shot down. Ten carrier planes and seven pilots were lost in the Aleutians.

We have already seen that the number of pilots from the four carriers killed in combat was about 44. This makes a grand total of about 110 pilots lost in the battle.[47] In addition to those killed, there were probably a substantial number who were permanently disabled because of battle wounds and, especially, burns when the carriers erupted in flames. Rear Admiral Takata, who was in charge of reorganizing the air fleet after the battle, stated that 40 percent of the pilots at Midway had been injured.[48] The number permanently disabled is unknown, but if it amounted to a sixth of those injured—5 to 10 percent of the total carrier pilots—then at least 15 seems a reasonable guess. (Fuchida was among those injured seriously enough to never see flight duty again.) This makes a total of about 125 carrier pilots—over half lost in the bombing—who would no longer be available to the Japanese navy in future carrier battles.

*   *   *

When it was all over, over half the 230 Japanese carrier pilots who entered the battle were lost. They were never replaced. As we will see in the next chapter—"Aftermath"—the loss of experienced carrier pilots at Midway turned out to be more costly to the Japanese navy than the loss of four carriers. There simply were not enough first-line pilots left to provide the two remaining attack carriers—*Shokaku* and *Zuikaku*—and the soon to be completed *Hiyo* with high-quality air groups, as became evident in the carrier battles that followed Midway. Although it was not fully realized at the time, Japan lost its war with the United States on June 4, 1942.

CHAPTER NINE

AFTERMATH

YAMAMOTO'S ALEUTIAN PLOY

Yamamoto had one more card to play: to entice the two remaining American carriers north to the Aleutian area, where a newly constituted carrier force would lie in wait. That new force would consist of *Junyo* and the light carrier *Ryujo* of the Second Mobile Force, already in the Aleutians—reinforced by the light carrier *Zuiho* from the Midway Invasion Force and, he hoped, the large attack carrier *Zuikaku*, still in home waters. (*Zuikaku* had been held back from the Midway operation because its air group had been decimated at Coral Sea a month earlier.) We saw in chapter 3 that Yamamoto had originally opposed the Aleutian operation as an unwise dilution of his carrier forces, but now that his Midway operation was a failure he looked at the Aleutians as his last hope for another crack at the American carriers. Perhaps an invasion of strategic Aleutian Islands would serve as the "bait" for Nimitz's carriers that had been envisioned for Midway.

On June 6 *Zuiho* was ordered north to join Rear Admiral Kakuji Kakuta's Second Mobile Force, along with the fast battleships *Kongo* and *Hiei* and the heavy cruisers *Tone* and *Chikuma* from Nagumo's now carrierless Mobile Force. *Zuikaku* was also ordered to join Kakuta's carrier force as soon as its air group was reconstituted (and possibly augmented by air crews from her sister *Shokaku*, which was still undergoing repairs from the damage at Coral Sea). Even without *Zuikaku*, the three smaller carriers still had about eighty-three operational aircraft among them: *Junyo* probably had fifteen Val dive-bombers and sixteen Zeros (contrary to some accounts, she carried no Kate torpedo planes in this campaign);[1] and *Ryujo* had about seventeen Kate attack planes and eleven Zeros.[2] *Zuiho* would add twelve Kate attack planes and twelve Zeros.

The Aleutian operation had begun on June 3—the day before the attack on Midway—by an air strike on Dutch Harbor on the eastern Aleutian island of Unalaska. Thirty-six planes had been launched from *Junyo* and *Ryujo* to bomb army and navy installations: nine Zeros and twelve Val dive-bombers from *Junyo*; six Zeros and nine bomb-laden Kate attack planes (which each carried one 250-kilogram bomb and up to four 60-kilogram bombs) from *Ryujo*. *Junyo*'s twenty-one planes had been forced to return because of foul weather, leaving only *Ryujo*'s nine Kates to do any bombing. The following day Dutch Harbor was hit again by thirty-two planes—all of which reached their target. The two attacks destroyed an army barracks, an aircraft hangar, a hospital, and a tank farm—and killed forty-three soldiers and sailors (more than died on the ground at Midway). Japanese losses had been light—only ten carrier planes shot down or crashed at sea, with only seven pilots lost.[3] (Most of the casualties were inflicted by Major John Chennault's army P-40s based at nearby Otter Point, an airstrip that had been unknown to the Japanese.)

After Dutch Harbor was bombed, Adak, Attu, and Kiska in the western Aleutians were scheduled to be invaded on June 7 and occupied by 2,500 army and navy troops and construction workers. However, on the afternoon of June 4—after Nagumo's carriers had been destroyed—Yamamoto, in a fit of despair, canceled those troop landings and ordered the invasion force to return to Japan. (Kakuta's carriers and the four battleships of the screening force had already been ordered south to join in a fleet action against the American task force.) But by evening Yamamoto changed his mind and ordered Vice Admiral Hosogaya, commander of the Northern Operation, to resume preparations to invade the western Aleutian Islands. He decided that at least some face could be salvaged from the Midway disaster by occupying American territory in the Aleutians. Moreover, it was the only prospect he had for luring the two American carriers north, where they could be engaged by his reconstituted carrier force. (Although without *Zuikaku*—which might arrive too late for the battle—his carrier force of just the three smaller carriers would not pack much of a punch, it was reckoned that the two American carriers would arrive with greatly diminished air groups.) The next day, June 5, Yamamoto ordered Kakuta's Second Mobile Force—which was then heading for Midway—to return north to a standby area some 600 miles south of Kiska to await the arrival of *Zuiho* (which was due on June 12).

That same day an event occurred that almost fulfilled Yamamoto's dreams of luring the American carrier force north—but for a completely different reason than he contemplated: Nimitz received a report from an American patrol plane sighting what appeared to be two large Japanese carriers, accompanied by two heavy cruisers and eight destroyers, steaming toward Dutch Harbor from the Bering Sea north of the Aleutians. As Kakuta's two carriers were known to be operating south of the Aleutians, it was feared that these new carriers were *Zuikaku* and a hastily repaired *Shokaku*—an altogether much more threatening prospect than Kakuta's weak force. Nimitz may not have thought that the small bases at Adak, Attu, and Kiska were worth risking carriers for, but Dutch Harbor was a different matter; it was a substantial base with even more military personnel (5,400) than Midway had. Frantic efforts were made by army and navy planes to locate and attack those carriers, but they could not be found.

On June 7, Captain Parker, whose dwindling PBY Catalinas at Dutch Harbor were being run ragged in fruitless efforts to find the supposed carriers, sent an urgent message to Nimitz warning that the Aleutian islands were in grave danger unless more planes—preferably carrier-based—were sent to the area. That was the very day landings were made on Attu and Kiska; Adak was scratched at the last minute by Hosogaya because it was too close to a newly discovered American airfield. Nimitz responded by ordering Spruance to head north with *Enterprise* and *Hornet* to engage the Japanese carrier force as soon as their depleted air groups could be replenished from *Saratoga*. (That carrier, which had just been repaired from the damage sustained by a torpedo from a Japanese submarine in January, had left Pearl Harbor that day with a fresh load of planes, under orders to rendezvous with Spruance's carriers.) On the morning of June 11, thirty-four replacement planes—nineteen Dauntless dive-bombers and fifteen torpedo planes—were taken on board *Enterprise* and *Hornet*. This gave Spruance at least 146 operational planes.[4] He then set course for due north.

About this time, however, Nimitz was having second thoughts. The occupation of Attu and Kiska had already been completed; Dutch Harbor had not been attacked since the 4th, and no new Japanese carriers had been located following the contact report on June 5. (It turned out that the sighting report was completely false. There were no Japanese carriers or any other warships in the Bering Sea. As Kakuta's Second Mobile Force was hundreds of miles to the south of Dutch Harbor, it is a mystery what the search plane saw and how the reported position could be so far off base. Both sides had been plagued by inaccurate sighting reports in the war so far, but this one probably takes the cake for inaccuracy.) Nimitz began to suspect that Yamamoto was setting a trap to ambush his carriers with a new carrier force if Spruance steamed into the Aleutians. (Indeed, if *Zuikaku* could have been brought into play it would have been a deadly trap.) He then changed his mind about getting involved up north and, late in the morning of June 11, ordered Spruance back to Pearl Harbor. Yamamoto's final ploy had failed, and the Battle of Midway was finally over.

In retrospect, had Yamamoto urged his Northern Force commanders to apply more pressure on Dutch Harbor—after Attu and Kiska were taken—with further carrier plane attacks, bombardment from battleships, and a threatened invasion, he might have succeeded in drawing Spruance's carriers up north. Nimitz would probably have felt compelled to come to the rescue of such a valuable asset as Dutch Harbor. But had this ploy succeeded, what sort of opportunity would Yamamoto really have gained? The two light carriers and *Junyo* by themselves would have stood no chance against *Enterprise* and *Hornet*—especially after their air groups had been replenished from *Saratoga* (a circumstance not known by Yamamoto). The Japanese would have had only about fifteen operational dive-bombers—all on *Junyo*—against at least seventy-five operational Dauntless SBDs on Spruance's carriers. *Ryujo* and *Zuiho* had some twenty-seven to thirty operational Kate attack planes, but they were not equipped with torpedoes; they carried a maximum of one 250- and four 60-kilogram bombs. Those Kates could have been used only as level bombers, which were virtually worthless against fast-moving ships.[5] (Spruance's eighteen torpedo bombers—with their defective torpedoes—would have been almost as worthless.)

Only if *Zuikaku* could have been brought into the fray would Yamamoto have had a realistic chance of winning a carrier battle against *Enterprise* and *Hornet*. (*Saratoga* would not have been available; during its long layover for repairs most of the pilots of its air group had been transferred to the other carriers, and it was being used mainly to ferry planes.) If *Zuikaku*'s air group was at full strength, it would have added twenty-seven torpedo planes and twenty-seven more dive-bombers—for a total of about seventy offensive planes against about seventy-five (effective) offensive planes for Spruance. But as twenty-seven Kates would carry the deadly Type 91 aerial torpedo, the Japanese would have to be favored. The problem, however, was that *Zuikaku* may not have been ready for deployment until much later in the month, which would have been too late to participate in any carrier battle with Spruance's carriers.[6] Without *Zuikaku* Yamamoto stood to lose even more carriers without the prospect of seriously damaging Spruance's carriers.

As it was, the Battle of Midway—and its Aleutian adjunct—was finally over for Yamamoto. All that had been gained from the fiasco were a couple of frozen islands, totally worthless in all but symbolic value. The disaster at Midway immediately became a top secret in Japan. The government publicly proclaimed the campaign a glorious victory—especially the conquests in the Aleutians. When the remnants of the shattered Mobile Force limped back into home waters all its personnel were sequestered and kept incommunicado —virtually made prisoners of war by their own government.[7] Nagumo's official battle report was prepared in secret, and after having been seen by only the highest officers in the navy and government it was impounded for the duration of the war.

IMPACT OF ALEUTIAN OPERATION ON MIDWAY OUTCOME

A question that has been raised many times is whether the carrier air power diverted to the Aleutian campaign prejudiced Nagumo's prospects at Midway and contributed to his defeat. *Junyo* and *Ryujo* would not actually have contributed very much to the fleet attack firepower of the Mobile Force. This is because neither carrier embarked torpedo-bearing Kate attack planes. (*Ryujo*'s flight deck was too short, and *Junyo* was too slow, for Kates to safely lift off with a 1,872-pound load.) The only Kates on board were with *Ryujo*, and they carried bombs (one 250-kilogram and up to four 60-kilogram bombs).

Does this mean then that those two carriers would not have been useful at Midway? Certainly not. We have seen that the one thing Nagumo was short of at Midway (apart from timely intelligence) was Zeros—he was about a dozen short. It limited his options at 0830 on the morning of the battle when he had to make a decision whether to launch an immediate strike against the American carrier, just reported by *Tone* 4, with Yamaguchi's dive-bombers or postpone until after the Midway strike force was landed. Lack of any Zeros for escort was a major factor in the decision to postpone. Even when he later organized a grand-scale strike force, he could spare only twelve Zeros for escort—twenty-four would have been the usual number for the seventy-two to eighty-one bombers being sent.

But most crucially, when the American dive-bombers arrived over the Mobile Force at 1020, there were no Zeros left on high-level patrol to counter them. They had all been drawn down to defend against the third wave of American torpedo bombers. Thus, Nagumo did not even have enough Zeros to protect his carriers in the event they were subjected to a tightly sequenced series of attacks. It is certainly possible that with another dozen Zeros available for combat air patrol Nagumo could have been spared at least some of the devastation wreaked on his carriers that morning.

It would not have been necessary for either of the Northern Force carriers to have been attached to the Mobile Force to provide for additional Zeros. (That would not have been desirable as *Junyo* was too slow to keep up, and *Ryujo*'s short range would have necessitated frequent refuelings.) Those carriers —or perhaps only one of them—could have been attached to the Midway invasion force, and carried all thirty-three of the land-based Zeros of the Sixth Air Group—relieving Nagumo's carriers of the twenty-one they had been saddled with. This would have freed up hangar space on the Mobile Force carriers so they could add at least a dozen more Zeros to their carrier air groups. Those Zeros could have come from just one of the Northern Force carriers, along with the dozen best pilots from those carriers.

Thus, the Aleutian operation probably did impact the Midway operation adversely. The price paid for it may have been much greater than Yamamoto had feared, or even could have contemplated, back when he opposed it as a risky dilution of his carrier strength.

BACK TO THE SOUTH SEAS

After Midway, the focus shifted from the northeast Pacific back to the south-west Pacific. With the loss of four of its six attack carriers at Midway, the Japanese navy had lost its capability to mount further offensive operations against the American carrier force, which came out of the battle still possessing four attack carriers. Gone was Japan's hope of extending its defensive perimeter eastward in the Pacific and of neutralizing Hawaii. From here on out the Japanese navy would be forced into a defensive posture closer to home. The best that could be hoped for was that its still formidable battleship and cruiser force, and the remaining carriers—especially the powerful *Shokaku* and *Zuikaku*—could keep the American naval and ground forces out of the vital resource-rich South Seas area so Japan could get its newly acquired resources, especially oil, back to the home islands. This, after all, had been the reason Japan went to war with America.

The Midway operation—by using almost every large warship in the Japanese navy—had substantially depleted Japan's oil stocks. About six months' of normal wartime oil consumption had been squandered in that operation. The Japanese navy was facing the prospect of running out of fuel oil and aviation gas by soon after the end of the year unless it could begin transporting oil from the Dutch East Indies back to Japan.[8] For this, it needed to control the sea lanes between the East Indies and Japan, a route that ran between the Indo-China peninsula and the Philippines, and on up along the coast of China. American air power had to be kept out of that area by Japan's preempting the islands on the eastern periphery of the vital sea lanes. While Japanese offensive naval capability had been decimated, American naval and ground forces had yet to prove that they had the capability of dislodging Japanese ground forces from their defensive bastions in the Pacific.

GUADALCANAL AND THE SOLOMON ISLANDS

The Japanese interest in the Solomon Islands, and Guadalcanal in particular, was mainly to build airfields to better defend the sea lanes of the South Seas. With most of the large carriers gone, those sea lanes would be have to be defended mostly by land-based naval air power, and for that Japan would need lots of island airfields. From this point in the war, the emphasis would shift from carrier-based to land-based naval air power, of which Japan still possessed formidable strength.

By the end of June Japanese construction workers had arrived at Guadalcanal to build an airfield—a project that was discovered by Allied reconnaissance on July 4. Plans for an American invasion of the Solomons had been in the works since before Midway—to shore up the defense of Australia and provide a starting point for the long march back to the Philippines—but the discovery at Guadalcanal put the heat on what would be known as "Operation Watchtower." This was not a welcome prospect. Guadalcanal, a fairly large island— about 80 miles long and 25 miles wide—was mountainous and covered with dense jungle. It was a sweltering, humid, and disease-ridden place. Neither side would have wanted to touch it unless compelled to by strategic necessity.

THE LANDINGS ON GUADALCANAL

In the early morning hours of August 7, around 19,000 marines aboard twenty-three transports—commanded by Major General Alexander A. Vandegrift, USMC—began landings on the northwest coast of Guadalcanal and two small islands, Tulagi and Gavutu, some 18 miles across the Savo Sound. This invasion force, under the command of Rear Admiral Richmond K. Turner, was the first large American amphibious operation since 1898 at Cuba in the Spanish-American War. The transports were escorted by six heavy cruisers (two of them Australian), two light cruisers (one Australian), and fifteen destroyers. Air support was provided by the three carriers of the "Expeditionary Force"—*Saratoga*, *Enterprise*, and *Wasp*—under the command of now Vice Admiral Frank Jack Fletcher (he had been promoted since Midway). These carriers embarked 240 aircraft, and were escorted by the new battleship *North Carolina*, five heavy cruisers, a light anti-aircraft cruiser, and sixteen destroyers.

The largest Marine force—11,000 troops—landed on Guadalcanal near the nearly completed airfield. The airfield, yet without planes, was defended by only 550 Japanese army troops (there were also 1,700 naval construction workers there). As the landings were a surprise to the Japanese and the Americans had total air superiority over the area, resistance was light, and by the next morning the airfield was taken with few casualties. The surviving Japanese troops and construction workers disappeared into the surrounding jungle.

On "Tulagi-side" about 5,000 marines had also been landed on August 7, with another 3,000 following the next day. As there was a functioning seaplane base (with twenty-one planes) there, the small islands were more heavily defended— by 900 troops and another 600 armed laborers—and resistance was much fiercer than on Guadalcanal. The marines received support from cruiser gun fire and also from dive-bombers from Fletcher's carriers, but the Japanese fought almost to the last man, with over 90 percent of the 1,500 troops being killed by the end of the next day when the islands were secured. The marines suffered about 250 casualties.

The transports and escorting ships of the amphibious force did not, however, escape attack from Japanese aircraft. Although there were no Japanese carriers in the area, there was a large naval air base at Rabaul in New Britain about 550 miles to the northwest. It contained about one hundred aircraft in the Twenty-fifth Air Flotilla—more than fifty Betty twin-engine light bombers, about eighteen dive-bombers and perhaps thirty-six Zeros. After Rear Admiral Yamada, commander of the Twenty-fifth Air Flotilla, learned of the American landings, he dispatched an attack force of twenty-seven bomb-laden Bettys, escorted by eighteen Zeros, at 0900 on the 7th, shortly followed by sixteen dive-bombers, to attack the landing force. The attacks did little damage because there were sixty Wildcats from *Enterprise* and *Saratoga* in the air over the landing zones. At least fourteen of the forty-three bombers from Rabaul, along with two Zeros, were shot down; the Americans lost eleven fighters along with an SBD dive-bomber from *Wasp* that was with a group of six bombing Tulagi. (The twenty-one seaplanes based there were destroyed.) Fletcher's carriers were operating about 60 miles away south of Guadalcanal and were not spotted by Japanese reconnaissance.

The next day Yamada sent about three dozen Bettys armed with torpedoes. Again, Wildcats from the American carriers were there to meet them, and they exacted an even heavier toll than the day before. By the end of August 8, Admiral Turner was pleased with results thus far: the beachhead on Guadalcanal had been secured and the airfield taken; the Tulagi-side islands were taken, and the Japanese forces there almost totally destroyed. American casualties had been relatively light—all because of surprise and air superiority.

Turner's optimism was short-lived. In the early hours of the following morning the Japanese counterattacked with a vengeance. A squadron containing five heavy cruisers had been sent down from Rabaul to wipe out the transports supplying the American force and destroy the Allied cruisers protecting the waters off Guadalcanal. This was to be in preparation for landings of Japanese troops to retake the island. (Six transports of troops had been dispatched from Rabaul on the 7th, along with the cruiser squadron. The next day they had been spotted by an American submarine, which torpedoed and sank one of them—with the loss of 342 men. The other five transports turned back to Rabaul. It was the first of several bungled attempts by the Japanese to get more troops to Guadalcanal before the American build-up became impregnable.) But the cruiser squadron, under the command of Vice Admiral Gunichi Mikawa, had slipped into the Savo Sound undetected. In a night action lasting just over one hour, four Allied heavy cruisers were sunk or sinking (the American *Astoria*, *Quincy*, and *Vincennes*, and the Australian *Canberra*; only the *Chicago* escaped with minor damage). More than one thousand sailors were killed—all but eighty-four of them American—in the worst American naval disaster at sea since the beginning of the war. Only slight damage had been inflicted on the Japanese cruisers—with but fifty-eight sailors killed.[9]

This—known as the Battle of Savo Island—had been a brilliant, lopsided victory for the Imperial Japanese Navy, and the most costly for the Americans in ships and manpower since Pearl Harbor. But the Japanese failed to achieve their main objective: the purpose of Mikawa's nighttime raid had been to destroy the

American transports and leave Vandegrift's marines stranded of supplies. The transports had not completed their unloading operations, and after the Allied cruisers had been eliminated they would have been sitting ducks. But, curiously, not a single transport was hit that night. After destroying the Allied cruiser force, Mikawa—like Nagumo at Pearl Harbor—declined to follow up his advantage and finish the job. Satisfied with the easy success already achieved, and not wanting to hang around and expose his ships to a possible counterattack from American carrier planes come daylight, Mikawa decided to retire and get an early start back to Rabaul.

Later in the day of the 9th, the reprieved transports finished their accelerated unloading schedule and then departed for New Caledonia. The marines on Guadalcanal and Tulagi were on their own and felt abandoned by the navy. They had been left with barely adequate supplies because Fletcher had withdrawn his carriers protecting the transports before they could get everything unloaded, causing them to depart prematurely. This resulted in a great deal of bitterness toward Fletcher, and badly damaged his reputation. Fortunately, however, some additional supplies—along with some reinforcements—soon did manage to get through to the island, even though the Japanese generally had naval and air superiority in the area. Also, the airstrip—renamed Henderson Field after a marine hero at Midway—was quickly completed and received its first planes on August 20.

The original Japanese garrison of 550 combat troops (and 1,700 construction workers) was still mostly intact and was holding the interior of the island. Some reinforcements had come in by destroyers at night several times since August 7—but only a few hundred at a time—and so at the end of August 21, there were only about 3,500 Japanese combat troops on Guadalcanal, opposed by 10,000 American combat troops.[10] The reason for piecemeal and totally inadequate forces being landed on Guadalcanal was that the Japanese high command grossly underestimated the size of the American force at Guadalcanal. They had estimated that there were only 2,000 combat troops there, and assumed that they could be eradicated at will.[11] By August 21, however, Tokyo began to take Guadalcanal more seriously. It was decided to land 1,500 more troops there on August 24.

But there was a problem: Fletcher's carriers were still within striking distance of Guadalcanal, and could scuttle any large amphibious operation. Yamamoto, therefore, decided to send his much-diminished Mobile Force—supported by other powerful elements of his Combined Fleet—south to attempt to neutralize the American carrier force. Vice Admiral Chuichi Nagumo, apparently rehabilitated from his disaster at Midway, commanded the carrier striking force, which consisted of the now repaired *Shokaku* and her sister *Zuikaku*. Although Nagumo would be outnumbered three attack carriers to two, Yamamoto believed that with guile, his superior aerial torpedoes, and possibly some help from land-based planes in the area, he at least had a chance of winning a carrier battle and redeeming the debacle at Midway. And, in any event—from the high command's perspective—even if Nagumo could not destroy the American carriers, at least he could tie them up—keeping their aircraft away from the Japanese troop transports. Thus, the main object of this rather huge operation appears to have been merely to safely land a measly 1,500 troops on Guadalcanal to reinforce the 3,500 already on the island—a number still woefully inadequate to dislodge the 17,000 Marines dug in there.

THE BATTLE OF THE EASTERN SOLOMONS

The upcoming battle was the first of two carrier battles that would be fought in the Solomon Islands area (the second being the Battle of the Santa Cruz Islands). These two carrier battles are being summarized in this chapter because they, like the Battle of the Coral Sea described in chapter 3, provide essential context for understanding the Japanese side of the Battle of Midway. It has become fashionable lately to attribute the Japanese defeat at Midway to defective carrier "doctrines"—such as using float planes for reconnaissance so as to reserve carrier bombers for strictly offensive operations,[12] and keeping flight decks clear for CAP operations rather than spotting a strike force that may or may not need to be launched immediately.[13] These "doctrines" appear to have been inferred from the very limited—and possibly anomalous—circumstances of Midway. I believe that only from all four carrier battles is it possible to deduce actual Japanese carrier warfare practice and place Midway in its proper context. (Although some changes in carrier fleet operations were made after Midway, in such matters as reconnaissance and strike force deployment the practices in the two post-Midway carrier battles closely parallel those of the pre-Midway Battle of the Coral Sea—with Midway being the anomaly.)

Back to the battle: On August 23, Yamamoto sent the Combined Fleet south from Truk and Rabaul. (Truk, in the Caroline Islands, had become the largest Japanese naval base outside the home islands; Yamamoto's flagship *Yamato* and a large portion of his Combined Fleet was now based there.) The Combined Fleet was broadly divided into two fleets. The first, under the command of Vice Admiral Gunichi Mikawa, was headed for Guadalcanal with five transports of the Reinforcement Group carrying 1,500 troops. Heavy support was provided by four heavy cruisers—the veterans of the Battle of Savo Island—and was under the direct command of Mikawa. Its role was to take on any Allied cuisers and transports that might be in the area of the Guadalcanal landings.

The second fleet contained the carrier striking force consisting of *Shokaku* and *Zuikaku*. They embarked 130 operational planes between them (26 Zeros, 14 Vals, and 18 Kates on *Shokaku*, and 27 Zeros, 27 Vals, and 18 Kates on *Zuikaku*).[14] While the carrier striking force was under the command of Nagumo, Nagumo himself was subordinate to Vice Admiral Nobutake Kondo for this operation. The carriers were protected by two fast battleships (*Hiei* and *Kirishima*), three heavy cruisers (*Chikuma, Kumano,* and *Suzuya*) and twelve destroyers led by a light cruiser. There was also a "Diversionary Group," which was centered around the light carrier *Ryujo* (with 30–35 planes) and accompanied by the heavy cruiser *Tone* and two destroyers. This redoubtable little carrier, a veteran of the Aleutian campaign and Japan's first purpose-built carrier, was given the ignominious mission of serving as "bait" to attract the attention of the American carriers away from *Shokaku* and *Zuikaku* (like the *Shoho* at Coral Sea). A third group was the "Advance Force" under the direct command of Kondo. It consisted mainly of five heavy cruisers, and its role was to proceed ahead of the Mobile Force into the waters of the eastern Solomons to flush out any American warships that might be in the path of the Mobile Force.

On the American side was Fletcher's carrier force. It contained three carriers— *Enterprise, Saratoga,* and *Wasp*. Their aircraft losses of August 7 and 8 had been replenished and on the 23rd they embarked a total of 253 planes (*Enterprise* had 36 Wildcat fighters, 36 Dauntless dive-bombers, and 15 Avenger torpedo bombers, *Saratoga* the same complement, and *Wasp* had 28 Wildcats, 36 Dauntlesses, and 15 Avengers). Not all were operational, however: it appears that only 65 of the 72 Dauntlesses and 27 of the 30 Avengers on *Enterprise* and *Saratoga* actually took part in the battle.[15] America's fourth, and last, fleet attack carrier— *Hornet*—had been patrolling the waters around Hawaii since June but on August 17 had been ordered by Nimitz to proceed to the Coral Sea. It would not arrive until after the battle. Fletcher's carrier force was supported by six heavy cruisers, one anti-aircraft light cruiser, and the new fast battleship *North Carolina* with nine 16-inch guns.

On the late afternoon of the 23rd, Fletcher made a decision that reduced his advantage for the upcoming carrier battle. Pacific Fleet intelligence out of Pearl Harbor had reported that the Mobile Force was still north of Truk, leading Fletcher to conclude that a carrier battle was several days away. As *Wasp's* destroyers were reported to be running low on fuel oil, he ordered the *Wasp* task force to proceed south for a refueling rendezvous—where they would be out of the area for the entire day of the battle. This would leave Fletcher with fewer than 164 operational carrier planes against about 160–165 for Kondo.

THE CARRIER BATTLE OF AUGUST 24

Unfortunately for Fletcher, Yamamoto ordered his Combined Fleet to make a high-speed run the night of the 23rd toward the eastern Solomons and Fletcher's carrier force. At 0400 on the 24th, the *Ryujo* Diversionary Group separated from Nagumo's striking force with orders to steam in the clear in the direction of the American carrier force. At 0905, the "bait" was, indeed, spotted by a Catalina—280 miles northwest of Fletcher's force. Fletcher was skeptical of the Catalina's report of a carrier, so he did not order an immediate strike. But at 1345 he launched from *Saratoga* twenty-nine Dauntless SBDs, eight Avenger TBFs, and perhaps a dozen fighter escorts, which found *Ryujo* at 1550. All twenty-nine of the dive-bombers dropped their bombs, and, although the first twenty-one were off-target, four of the last eight scored hits with 1,000-pounders. This was more than enough to destroy the light carrier. After she was a flaming wreck, five Avengers attacked with torpedoes. One hit was claimed, but cannot be confirmed. *Ryujo* burned for four hours and finally sunk at 2000.

Minutes after Fletcher had sent the *Saratoga* strike group off at 1345, Nagumo's two large carriers were spotted some 60 miles northeast of *Ryujo* by search planes. Because of communications foul-ups (radio reception had been terrible all day) Fletcher failed to receive the sighting reports directly. When he finally heard of them from other ships—apparently after 1500—he attempted to redirect *Saratoga*'s strike group to attack the *Shokaku* and *Zuikaku*, but could not get through to the group commander on the radio. He had very few planes left on board his two carriers with which to form another strike group—just fourteen SBDs and twelve TBFs. *Wasp*'s air group was now sorely missed.

Fletcher pondered whether to launch a small strike group against Nagumo's large carriers but decided against it. Apart from the lateness of the hour and distance to the Mobile Force—230 miles—which would have required a night landing upon return, he could not spare any Wildcats to escort the bombers as he was expecting an attack on his carriers from Nagumo's force at any moment. (Two of Fletcher's carriers had been discovered by a search plane from the cruiser *Chikuma* at 1405.)

Nagumo delayed his launch for over an hour waiting for the third American carrier (the absent *Wasp*) to be located, but at 1537 a first-wave attack group from *Shokaku* and *Zuikaku* was in the air. The composition of that attack group is a matter of conjecture because the Japanese records are fragmentary—*Shokaku*'s records for that day are missing. My reconstruction, based on American accounts of the air battles and prior Japanese practice, is that *Zuikaku* probably launched its entire dive-bomber squadron of twenty-seven Vals (though *Zuikaku*'s records account for only nine), along with six Zeros for escort.[16] It is known that *Shokaku* provided *some* Kate torpedo planes, and though only nine are recorded it is more likely that its full squadron of eighteen was launched, along with twelve Zeros. This would give a total of sixty-three planes in the strike group—a conservative estimate in view of the fact that these same two carriers are known to have launched a strike group of sixty-nine the next day.

When this strike group reached Fletcher's carrier force it was in for a nasty surprise. Fletcher had prepared for the attack by putting fifty-three Wildcats in the air for combat air patrol, and many of them had been stationed many miles from the carriers in the path of the incoming strike group. No Japanese carrier strike group had ever had to run such a gauntlet—not at Pearl Harbor, not at

Coral Sea, nor at Midway. They were shot to pieces. The Vals had come in at 12,000 feet—probably in three divisions of nine dive-bombers each, with about a dozen Zeros covering them from above and below. About 25 miles out the three divisions of Vals separated and climbed to 18,000 feet preparatory to making their dives. At about 15 miles from *Enterprise,* one division of nine Vals was met by Wildcats, and seven planes were shot down. Another division lost three dive-bombers before it could begin its dive.

Of the seventeen Vals that got through to make their dives, it appears that about fourteen dove on *Enterprise* and three targeted the battleship *North Carolina.* At least three more Vals were shot down while making their dives, mostly by antiaircraft gunfire. Three bombs hit *Enterprise*—the first two were delay-fuse (¹⁄₁₀ second) armor-piercing bombs, which penetrated about forty feet before exploding. They caused extensive damage, holing the hull and causing fires and flooding; seventy-four men were killed and another ninety-five wounded. The third bomb was an instant-detonation high-explosive bomb that blew a hole in the flight deck ten feet in diameter. Three more bombs were near misses close enough to rupture hull plating.

Enterprise—which had never been hit before—was quite badly damaged. Although the flight deck was easily repaired so flight operations could proceed, the carrier was put in peril by delayed effects of the bombs. Flooding had caused a steering motor to "ground," jamming the rudder, which left the carrier turning helplessly in a tight circle at about the time Nagumo's second-wave attack was due to come in. The other target of the dive-bombing attack—*North Carolina*—came out of it unscathed. While returning to their carrier, four more Vals were shot down, but in this case not by Wildcats but by Dauntlesses from *Saratoga* returning from their strike on *Ryujo.* All in all, the dive-bomber attack was not impressive. Although the bombing was a bit more accurate than that by the Americans, three hits from seventeen planes was below the usual standards for Japanese carrier dive-bombers achieved earlier in the war.

The greatest mystery of the battle is, what happened to the torpedo planes from *Shokaku?* With their deadly Type-91 aerial torpedoes, Kates had been the carrier-killers at Coral Sea and Midway—and a couple of torpedoes put into *Enterprise* might have finished her off. But none of *Shokaku's* Kates even made it to Fletcher's carrier force, let alone made any torpedo runs on the American carriers. As *Shokaku's* records for the battle are missing, they cannot shed any light on the mystery—it is not even known how many torpedo planes were launched, or when they were launched. The usual Japanese practice was to send off a coordinated attack with the dive-bombers and torpedo planes in the same formation until they separated near the target to make their run-ins. But the one thing that is known for certain is that no Kates were with the Vals, or flying below them, when contact was first made by the American combat air patrol 15–20 miles out from the carriers. Wildcats had been stationed at low altitude as well as high, and had been specifically instructed to keep a sharp eye out for torpedo planes. There were no Kates in the vicinity when the Vals came in; thus, there was no coordinated attack as was expected.

Why the Kates missed the battle has been a matter of conjecture. Some speculate that the torpedo plane squadron got lost en route and could not find the American carrier force. Others suggest that it was met by Wildcats and destroyed some distance from the target (it being assumed that there were only nine Kates in the group).[17] My conjecture is a combination of the two: that the torpedo plane squadron (with eighteen Kates, escorted by no more than six Zeros) did not fly with the dive-bombers, but proceeded separately—and later— toward the target, and was met by Wildcats some distance out from the American carrier force; that it was then shot up (American Wildcat pilots claimed to have shot down four), and the survivors were dispersed and unable to find the American force. There is, however, no explanation for why *Shokaku*'s Kates were not launched at the time as the Vals from *Zuikaku* and why they did not proceed with the Vals most of the way to the target, as was the usual Japanese practice. But, as there are no records from *Shokaku*, this mystery may never be solved.

In any case, this attack effort must stand as the worst executed by Japanese carrier planes in the first year of the war. What can account for such an uncharacteristically subpar effort? We know that *Shokaku* and *Zuikaku* had lost a large part of their air groups in the Battle of the Coral Sea. It has, however, been assumed that those air groups were replenished to a large extent with quality survivors of the air groups of *Akagi, Kaga, Hiryu,* and *Soryu* after the Battle of Midway. Almost half of the approximately 230 pilots from those four carriers survived, which would seem more than enough to fill out the air groups of *Shokaku* and *Zuikaku* (even after deducting those carrier pilots who were transferred to land-based air groups in the South Pacific after Midway).

But what may not be fully appreciated is that the dive-bomber and torpedo plane crews lost at Midway included a large proportion of the most experienced carrier pilots in the Japanese navy and, even more crucial, squadron and air group leaders—such as Mitsuo Fuchida, Michio Kobayashi and Joichi Tomonaga—who could not be replaced, and who made coordinated attacks work. (Tomonaga and Kobayashi had been killed in the attack on *Yorktown;* Fuchida had been severely injured when *Akagi* was bombed.)[18] Thus, it is possible that the leadership in *Shokaku*'s and *Zuikaku*'s air groups at the Battle of the Eastern Solomons was nowhere nearly as good as in the previous carrier battles, which just might account for the subpar performance in this battle.

Nagumo's problems for the day were not over. Less than an hour after his first-wave attack was launched, a second-wave had been sent off at around 1630. While the exact composition of that attack group is unknown—the records are missing—it appears to have consisted of *Shokaku*'s dive-bomber squadron of fourteen Vals and *Zuikaku*'s torpedo plane squadron of eighteen Kates, along with perhaps only six Zeros for escort.[19] The second wave should have reached Fletcher's carriers around 1800—before the fires set off by the first attack on *Enterprise* had been brought under control. However, mercifully for Fletcher, it never found the American carrier force and had to return home empty-handed.[20]

When added to the failure of the first wave's torpedo squadron to find the American force, this was a most miserable performance in target acquisition for the Japanese carrier plane crews. Almost two-thirds of the planes sent off by Nagumo that day failed to find the American carrier force—far exceeding in futility anything previously recorded. It was worse than the misadventures at Coral Sea, where both sides had difficulty in finding the other's carriers, and worse than at Midway, where *Hornet*'s dive-bomber squadrons got lost. Fletcher's airmen had almost as bad a time of it; although the little *Ryujo* was found and successfully attacked, no full strike group found Nagumo's big carriers. Only a few of the scattered search planes from *Enterprise* found those carriers, and no hits were scored. At the end of the day, after recovering planes from the second strike group, Fletcher decided that he had had enough and retreated south. A few hours later Kondo also decided that he had had enough and reversed course to return to Truk.

The Japanese troop transport group (five transports and a light cruiser) had not been molested during the carrier battles of the 24th and was still pressing on toward Guadalcanal. At 0935 on the 25th a squadron of Marine SBDs from Henderson Field found it and scored direct hits on the light cruiser *Jintsu* and the large troop transport *Kinryu Maru*. *Jintsu* was not sunk, but was put out of action and forced to retreat back to Truk. The damage to *Kinryu Maru*, loaded with 800 troops, was more serious. It was set ablaze and brought to a complete stop. This aborted the troop landings on Guadalcanal—frustrating at least temporarily a principal purpose of Yamamoto's naval operation in the Solomons.

This concluded the Battle of the Eastern Solomons. It had been a victory for the Americans, badly needed after the drubbing at Savo Island two and a half weeks earlier, but it was hardly a resounding one as Nagumo's large carriers escaped serious damage. Fletcher had sustained substantial damage to one carrier—*Enterprise*—which would put her out of action for a month, and had lost seventeen carrier aircraft. Yamamoto, on the other hand, had lost a light carrier and a destroyer, and had a light cruiser and large transport badly damaged. More grievously, he had lost about forty carrier planes with their virtually irreplaceable pilots.

In many ways, however, the battle was a sorry performance on both sides. Japanese carrier air power had clearly lost its punch after the debacle at Midway—not just in the greatly reduced numbers of planes, but in quality as well. Most notably, they appear to have lost their vaunted capability to mount a coordinated attack. And it was made clear that the Americans also still had much to learn, especially in the areas of reconnaissance and radio communications. But the Americans were growing stronger day by day and had time to learn from the mistakes made at the Eastern Solomons; the Japanese carrier fleet was grow- ing weaker day by day and running out of time.

Any American satisfaction over the outcome of the battle, however, was soon tempered: on the last day of August *Saratoga* was torpedoed. She was on patrol some 260 miles southeast of Guadalcanal when a Japanese submarine put one torpedo into her, wounding eleven men, including Admiral Fletcher. While structural damage to the carrier was minor, the damage to her finicky electric propulsion system was more serious. *Saratoga* was out of action for over two months and would be sorely missed. Two weeks later there was a more serious setback, and by far the costliest loss in the campaign to date: *Wasp* was torpe- doed and sunk by a Japanese submarine. She and *Hornet*—the only operational fleet carriers left in the Pacific with *Enterprise* and *Saratoga* undergoing repairs—were on patrol in the "torpedo alley" area between Guadalcanal and Espiritu Santo. They were there to protect against Yamamoto's carriers and battleships a group of six transports carrying a marine regiment from Espiritu Santo to reinforce the First Marine Division at Guadalcanal. But the waters of the eastern Solomons were also infested by at least twenty submarines—with their deadly long-range oxygen-fueled Long Lance torpedoes.[21]

At 1430 on September 15, two of those submarines—I-15 and I-19—happened to find *Wasp* just as she was in the vulnerable position of launching twenty-six planes for combat air and antisubmarine patrol. Just as the launch was nearing completion at 1445, I-19 fired a spread of four torpedoes. Because they were oxygen-fueled they left no telltale bubble trail, which made them very difficult to detect. Three of them struck *Wasp*, immediately setting off uncontrollable fires in the engine rooms and gasoline tanks, and destroying the forward water mains, which made effective firefighting impossible. As she was fairly light for a fleet carrier—at only 14,700 tons—she was less able than larger carriers to withstand such an assault (though three torpedo hits would imperil any car- rier), and it soon became apparent that she was doomed. The order to abandon ship was given a half-hour after the strike, though she stayed afloat until late at night, when she was sunk by torpedoes from one of her own destroyers. Of the 2,247 crew on board, 193 had been killed and 366 wounded.

Wasp was not the only casualty. The second Japanese submarine—I-15—also fired a spread of torpedoes at *Hornet*. Though they missed the carrier, one tor- pedo hit *North Carolina*. The battleship escaped fatal damage but was put out of action for two months for repairs at Pearl Harbor. Thus, if the casualties of the Japanese submarine attacks of August 31 and September 15 are included with the Battle of the Eastern Solomons, the Japanese would be the clear vic- tors: counting only capital ships, the Americans lost one fleet carrier and had two others, along with a battleship, put out of action, while the Japanese lost only a light carrier.

*   *   *

Things were not going very well on the ground at Guadalcanal either. Although a Japanese assault on Henderson Field (by 3,500 newly landed troops) had been beaten back by the marines on September 14, by mid-October the troop landings had intensified. The Japanese high command had formulated a new and much more threatening battle plan: there would be two massive operations in a joint army-navy offensive: first, Henderson Field would be taken by powerful units of the Seventeenth Army commanded by Lieutenant General Harukichi Hyakutake. "Y-Day," when the Rising Sun flag was to be planted on the airstrip, was set for October 22. Second, the Combined Fleet—including all its carriers— would sail from Truk and seek out and engage the American carrier force in a battle of annihilation. This climactic sea battle was set for October 25.

Japanese troop strength on Guadalcanal had been built up to over 20,000.[22] American strength, including support troops, was around 23,000 marines and GIs. The numbers of combat troops appear to have been roughly equal, at around 13,000 apiece. (American units, even marine, had a much larger proportion of noncombat "support" troops than did the Japanese units—or for that matter than did the militaries of all the other nations of the world.)

On October 21 the battle for Henderson Field began. It lasted five days and involved the fiercest fighting of the war to date—some of it hand-to-hand combat at night in the jungle. On the morning of October 26 the battle for Henderson Field was over. The American perimeter had held. In fact, the Japanese had been soundly trounced. In the final analysis, their attacks had been poorly coordinated, an insufficient number of troops had been committed, and the infantry had little artillery support—most of the guns and mortars having been abandoned in the jungle. The total number of Japanese casualties will probably never be known for certain, but a conservative estimate would be over 2,000 killed and a similar number wounded. American deaths exceeded 400.[23] This battle would turn out to be the decisive battle on Guadalcanal, and the high-water mark in the Japanese efforts to oust the marines from Henderson Field. There were other fierce battles yet to be fought, but Henderson Field would never again be seriously threatened.

The fact of the matter is that the Japanese high command waited too long to launch an all-out offensive on the island. Had the forces deployed for this battle in late October been sent to Guadalcanal in September—before marine and army regiments were brought in to reinforce the original garrison—the Japanese probably could have overrun Henderson Field and ousted the Americans ground forces from the Solomons. But by the end of October it was too late. The Japanese had lost the battle for Guadalcanal—though neither they nor the Americans yet realized it.

THE BATTLE OF THE SANTA CRUZ ISLANDS

While the land battle on Guadalcanal was raging, the second operation of the Japanese high command's combined offensive to chase the Americans out of the Solomons was in motion. Most of the Combined Fleet had been sent south from Truk in two task forces: the Advance Force and the carrier Striking Force. The Advance Force, under Admiral Kondo, was to clear a path for the Striking Force. It consisted of two fast battleships (*Kongo* and *Haruna*, which had just recently had radar installed), four heavy cruisers, and fourteen destroyers led by a light cruiser. It also contained the carrier *Junyo* in the Second Carrier Division, commanded by Admiral Kakuta of Aleutians fame.[24] (The newly commissioned *Hiyo*—sister of *Junyo*—was also originally included but developed engine trouble on October 22 and had to return to Truk.)

The Striking Force, still under Nagumo, was the main force to engage the American carriers, which were now under the command of Vice Admiral William Halsey. Nagumo's force contained the two fleet attack carriers, *Shokaku* and *Zuikaku*, and also the light, but fairly fast, *Zuiho*. The operational plane complements were: *Shokaku*—18 Zeros, 20 Val dive-bombers, and 23 Kate torpedo planes (61 total); *Zuikaku*—27 Zeros, 27 Vals, and 18 Kates (72 total); *Zuiho*—18 Zeros and 6 Kates (24 total). This came to a grand total of 157 aircraft.[25] The carriers were supported by two fast battleships (*Hiei* and *Kirishima*), four heavy cruisers (including *Tone* and *Chikuma*), and seven destroyers led by the light cruiser *Nagara*. It will be noted that most of these ships were in the Mobile Force at Midway. However, since that battle, part of those support ships were put in a separate "Vanguard Group," which was to steam about 60 miles in front of the carriers so as to position itself between Nagumo's carriers and the American carriers; in effect to act as a decoy for any American air strike force that might be heading toward the Striking Force.

On the American side was Halsey's South Pacific Force, containing Task Force 16, under Rear Admiral Thomas Kinkaid, built around *Enterprise* (which had just rejoined the fleet on October 24 after repairs for damage sustained at Eastern Solomons) and supported by the battleship *South Dakota*, the heavy cruiser *Portland*, the antiaircraft light cruiser (CLAA) *San Juan*, and eight destroyers in the screen; and Task Force 17, under Rear Admiral George Murray, built around *Hornet* and supported by two heavy cruisers (*Northampton* and *Pensacola*), two CLAAs (*San Diego* and *Juneau*), and six destroyers in its screen. Kinkaid was in overall command of both carrier groups.

On the 25th both sides began looking for each other's carriers. At noon, a PBY Catalina sighted two Japanese carriers but because of stormy weather was unable to maintain contact. Kinkaid then dispatched a twelve-plane search group from *Enterprise* at 1330, and an hour later an attack group of twenty-nine Dauntlesses. They were unable to find Nagumo's carriers (which had reversed course after spotting the Catalina) and, returning after dark, lost seven planes while attempting to land at night. That night Yamamoto ordered Nagumo to find and attack the American carrier force the next morning. Halsey, after receiving a PBY report in the early hours of the 26th sighting a Japanese carrier force 200 miles to the northwest of his own, sent the following message to his carrier commanders: "Attack—Repeat—Attack." The knives were now unsheathed.

THE CARRIER BATTLE OF OCTOBER 26

The ensuing battle would be the fourth and last carrier air battle of the year. There would be only one more in the war (and probably in all of history), and that would not take place until June of 1944. The action began at daybreak when both Kinkaid and Nagumo launched search patrols. A Catalina sighting report earlier that morning did not reach Kinkaid until after a two-hour delay and after he had launched his own search planes. Had he received it earlier he could have gotten off a strike group at daybreak and possibly caught Nagumo's carriers with most of their planes still on board—as at Midway. As it was, sixteen SBD scouts with 500-pound bombs were launched from *Enterprise* at 0500 to search, in pairs, a sector between southwest and due north.[26] Nagumo launched eight Kates from *Shokaku* at around the same time, along with sixteen cruiser float planes to search a sector covering the southeast quadrant. (Again, as at Coral Sea, when the Japanese expected enemy carriers to be in the area they were not loath to use carrier-based bombers for search duty.)

At 0617, a pair of SBDs sighted Abe's Vanguard Group; moments later, a Japanese float plane sighted *Hornet*, which, along with *Enterprise*, was about 80 miles north of the main Santa Cruz island. (Apparently, however, the Japanese sighting report was garbled, because Nagumo did not act on it.) At 0650, Nagumo's carrier force was spotted by another pair of SBDs at about 185 miles northwest of *Enterprise*. As the two SBDs were preparing to attack Nagumo's carriers eight Zeros jumped them, forcing them to abort the attack and seek the safety of clouds, but not before shooting down three of the Zeros. Another pair of SBDs, having received the sighting report by radio, rushed to the scene and dove on the light carrier *Zuiho*. One of the two 500-pound bombs hit the little carrier—blasting a fifty-foot hole in the flight deck aft—but as she had already just launched her strike group the damage was not serious, though she would not be able to land planes that day.

At 0658, Nagumo received a definitive sighting report from one of *Shokaku*'s Kates and beat Kinkaid to the punch by getting his strike group off first, at 0710. (It will be noted that these planes were already on the flight decks ready for launch.) A total of sixty-five planes were launched from the three carriers.

Eighteen Zeros and twenty Val dive-bombers took off from *Shokaku*; *Zuikaku* launched eighteen Kate torpedo planes, and *Zuiho* contributed nine Zeros. Twenty minutes later, Kinkaid launched his first strike group. *Hornet* sent off eight Wildcat fighters, fifteen Dauntless dive-bombers (with 1,000-pound bombs) and six Avenger torpedo bombers. Thirty minutes later, at 0800, *Enterprise* launched eight Wildcats, three Dauntlesses, and eight Avengers. Fifteen minutes later, *Hornet* launched a second deckload of nine Wildcats, nine Dauntlesses, and seven Avengers, bringing the total number of planes in the strike force to seventy-three. (*Enterprise*'s contribution was relatively modest, because she already had sixteen Dauntlesses in the air on search duty and had lost seven during the night landing the night before.)

Nagumo's strike group was the first to reach its target. It was picked up on radar at 0857 when it was 45 miles out. The American combat air patrol numbered thirty-eight Wildcats, substantially fewer than had been aloft at the Battle of the Eastern Solomons. Moreover, the Wildcats were poorly positioned—too near the carriers, and most were too low. (They were under the control of *Enterprise*'s fighter director officer, who was new to the job, Halsey having taken that carrier's veteran fighter director for service on his staff.) This poor positioning resulted in a much higher proportion of Vals and Kates getting through to make bombing dives and torpedo runs than at Eastern Solomons. Specifically, only one section of four Wildcats—from *Hornet*—intercepted *Shokaku*'s Vals before they began their dives. One was shot down, and another was hit and driven off the attack. As the remaining Vals were beginning their dives on *Hornet* at 0910, four *Enterprise* Wildcats that had overflown them further out finally caught up with them and shot down three Vals before they were able to release their bombs.

This left fifteen Vals to get through unmolested and drop their bombs. Four 550-pound bombs hit, the first striking the starboard side of *Hornet*'s flight deck aft and doing little damage. Another exploded on contact, blowing a large hole in the flight deck and destroying several planes in the hangar. Two more bombs, armor-piercing delayed-fuse types, penetrated forty feet before exploding in the bowels of the carrier, causing extensive damage. In addition, the squadron commander—Lieutenant Commander Mamoru Seki of *Shokaku*—having been disabled by an antiaircraft shell burst before he could release his bomb load, made a suicide crash on the carrier, and one of his 132-pound bombs exploded in the hangar (his main 550-pound bomb did not detonate).

Hornet almost certainly would have survived these bomb hits, but in this attack—unlike at Eastern Solomons—the torpedo planes came in simultaneously with the dive-bombers in a perfectly executed coordinated attack. The eighteen Kates from *Zuikaku*, having to come in low, fared less well against the American combat air patrol than did the dive-bombers. It appears that six were shot down or damaged enough to force them to retire, because only twelve were recorded as having attacked.[27] Of these, two scored torpedo hits on *Hornet* at the same time bombs from the Vals were dropping. The torpedoes ripped large holes in the carrier's thinly plated hull, flooding both fire rooms and the forward engine room. Propulsion failed immediately, and the ship was soon dead in the water and listing. The attack ended at 0917 when a Kate, blazing from an antiaircraft shell hit after releasing its torpedo, deliberately crashed into the carrier, setting off a dangerous fire. *Hornet*, though still floating, was seriously damaged, and her air group would have to land on *Enterprise* when it returned (and *Enterprise* would not have room for all of them). *Enterprise* escaped this first attack because as the Japanese planes were approaching she managed to find refuge under cloud cover. The highly successful Japanese attack was, however, not without its costs. Of the fifty-six planes that left *Shokaku* and *Zuikaku*, twenty-five were shot down—mostly Vals and Kates, and many by antiaircraft gunfire.

Meanwhile, the American strike force was approaching Nagumo's fleet. There were sixty-five planes in all the various groups (four TBFs and four Wildcats having been lost in a tangle with *Zuiho*'s Zeros on the way out). In contrast to the usual Japanese practice of launching separate attack waves, with each wave consisting of a single deckload from each of the participating carriers, the Americans launched all available planes from all the carriers—usually two deckloads for each carrier—for a single larger attack force. Unfortunately, however, the planes from the first deckload often did not wait for the second deckload (as was the case at Midway). Moreover, the planes from the different carriers—even if they were launched at the same time—often did not join up with each other (also as was the case at Midway). That was what happened on this day. *Hornet*'s two deckloads proceeded separately toward the target, and separately from *Enterprise*'s planes. Thus, the American strike force was split up into several distinct smaller groups, out of sight of each other. This total lack of coordination resulted in only the dive-bomber squadron from *Hornet*'s first launch finding Nagumo's carriers.

These were the fifteen SBDs led by Lieutenant Commander Gus Widhelm. He radioed his sighting of the Japanese carriers at 0930, but none of the leaders of the other groups picked up his broadcast—which was repeated twice—because the radios in the American planes were still lacking crystal-controlled receivers and tended to drift off frequency.[28] (This was the same communications problem that had plagued the American airmen at Eastern Solomons. The Japanese airmen, on the other hand, were equipped with crystal radios and had no such problem with inter-plane communications.) As Widhelm's squadron approached Nagumo's carrier force, it was jumped on by a swarm of Zeros. It was without fighter escort because a few minutes before the carriers were sighted the squadron had been intercepted by nine Zeros of the advance combat air patrol and the four Wildcat escorts got tangled up in a dogfight, leaving the dive-bombers to proceed alone. Two SBDs were shot down and two more were hit and put out of action—including Widhelm's. Widhelm had to ditch because a severed oil line caused his engine to seize up, but he and his gunner survived and were later rescued in their rubber raft.

The remaining eleven Dauntlesses, now led by Lieutenant James Vose, fought their way through to the push-over point. The target was *Shokaku*. *Zuikaku* had become separated and was out of sight to the east. (*Zuikaku* has to be the luckiest carrier in the war. This was the third carrier battle—beginning with Coral Sea—in which she escaped notice by American dive-bombers.) At about 0940 Vose's SBDs began their dives. In the most remarkable dive-bombing performance of the war so far by American dive-bomber pilots, three to six of the eleven 1,000-pound bombs dropped hit *Shokaku* (the best estimate is four). Her flight deck and hangars were almost completely destroyed, most of her guns were knocked out, and fires burned through a number of compartments. However, as the American navy still did not have armor-piercing delay-fuse bombs, none of the bombs reached the vitals deep in the carrier. Without the good fortune of catching a Japanese carrier with planes on board—loaded with fuel and ordnance as at Midway—it was very difficult for American dive-bombers to destroy a large carrier. *Shokaku* had launched her second wave at 0822, leaving no operational bombers on board. (No keeping her flight deck clear for CAP operations here.) This probably saved her, but even so, she was badly damaged and unable to conduct any further flight operations. Some of her planes were sent over to *Junyo*. *Shokaku* was out of action for repairs for four months.

If any of the other small groups of dive-bombers and torpedo planes in the fragmented American strike force had found *Shokaku* they might have been able to finish her off. But the best they could do was find Abe's Vanguard Group. The only ship hit was the cruiser *Chikuma*, which took three bombs but did not sink. (Given all the attention paid to the Vanguard Group, Kondo's ploy to use it as a decoy, rather than deploy it as part of the screen for the carrier force, appears to have paid off.)

All in all, except for Widhelm's dive-bomber squadron from *Hornet*, which performed brilliantly, the two American carrier air groups put in a disappointing performance on October 26. It should be noted in passing that *Hornet*'s air group generally outperformed *Enterprise*'s in the battle. This is noteworthy because it was a complete reversal of the relative performance of the two carriers at Midway. The prior June, *Hornet* was a new carrier with a green air group crew, while *Enterprise* had a veteran air group; by October, *Hornet*'s air group had profited from extensive training while *Enterprise* had lost some of its veteran air officers to the staff of its former skipper Halsey.

The day's action was not over yet. The second-wave strike force from *Shokaku* and *Zuikaku* approached the American carrier force at around 1000. It consisted of twenty Val dive-bombers and sixteen Zeros from *Zuikaku*, followed by twelve Kate torpedo planes from *Shokaku*. One of the Vals broke ranks and dove on the crippled *Hornet*. The bomb missed, but it disrupted efforts by the heavy cruiser *Northampton* to take her in tow.

The remaining nineteen Vals headed for *Enterprise*, 20 miles eastward. Again, the combat air patrol was positioned too low, and all the Vals got through to their push-over point above *Enterprise*. The main defense, however, was not the Wildcats but the newly installed 40-mm Bofors quad antiaircraft guns on both *Enterprise* and *South Dakota*. These were far superior to the 20-mm and 1.1-inch guns they replaced (and *Hornet* still had) and accounted for most of the Vals shot down in the attack. Two Vals were shot down, and two more were damaged and driven off before they could release their bombs. However, approximately sixteen of them dropped bombs, but only two hit *Enterprise*—along with a very close near-miss that opened a seam in the hull. This was a subpar dive-bombing performance by the usual Japanese standard, but may be accounted for by the effectiveness of the Bofors quads in getting shell bursts at a higher than expected altitude, thereby throwing off the aim of the Val pilots. The two direct hits caused considerable damage and jammed the forward elevator, but *Enterprise* was still operational. The Val squadron paid a heavy price. After dropping their bombs well over half were shot down and others damaged, mostly by antiaircraft gunfire. Of the twenty Vals that left *Zuikaku*, only four returned in a serviceable condition.

The dive-bombing attack was over at 1019. It was not, unlike the first-wave attack, accompanied by a coordinated torpedo plane attack (which accounts for some of the high mortality rate for the Vals). For some reason, the twelve Kates from *Shokaku* arrived twenty minutes after the dive-bombers. This made them more vulnerable to the American combat air patrol, and it appears that six were shot down—including that of the squadron leader Shigeharu Murata—before they got close enough to release their torpedoes. Of the six that got through, three more were fatally hit by antiaircraft shellfire before dropping their torpedoes. It appears that only three dropped their torpedoes—at least in an aimed fashion—none of which hit *Enterprise*, and one of those planes was shot down by ship gunfire. This attack, which began about 1035, was over ten minutes later. The lack of a coordinated attack by the second wave cost Nagumo dearly. Eleven of the twelve Kates were lost, along with at least a dozen Vals out of the twenty. Five Zeros from *Zuikaku* were also shot down.

Enterprise had not sustained any further damage from the torpedo plane attack—and had the damage from the dive-bombing attack well under control—but after a forty-minute respite she had to face a third attack. This was from *Junyo*, her very first engagement against carriers. (As has been noted, *Junyo* had been intended as a "support" carrier—to bomb land targets. But after the loss of four fleet attack carriers at Midway she got pressed into fleet attack duty.) Shortly after 0900, *Junyo* had launched a strike group of twelve Zeros and seventeen to eighteen dive-bombers. When the *Junyo* Vals attacked the *Enterprise* task force at 1121, there were few Wildcats covering her as most had landed for refueling and gun reloading. However, the antiaircraft gun batteries on *Enterprise* and *South Dakota* were as deadly as before and shot down eight Vals—some before they could release their bombs. About half the Vals dove on *Enterprise*; no bombs hit, but a near-miss exploded close enough to do some damage to her hull. The rest of the Vals dove on *South Dakota* and *San Juan*, and had better success. One bomb hit *South Dakota*'s No. 1 turret, jamming it, and another hit the light cruiser, causing minor damage.

The excitement was over for *Enterprise*. After the attack ended at around 1130, she landed the strike group planes that had returned from attacks on the Japanese fleet, both hers and *Hornet*'s. But the inoperative forward elevator slowed recovery operations considerably, and several planes ran out of gas and had to make water landings. To make room for the extra planes from *Hornet*, thirteen SBDs were flown off for Espiritu Santo. At 1400, *Enterprise* retired from the battle zone.

The grief was not over for *Hornet*. At 1315 *Junyo* sent off another strike group—apparently launched in two deckloads. Its composition is in dispute (and the record of it practically nonexistent) but it appears to have been a mixed group of planes including some refugees from *Shokaku* along with *Junyo*'s own air group.

Around six torpedo-laden Kates—probably originally from *Shokaku*—arrived in the vicinity of Task Force 17 a little after 1500. At that time *Hornet* was being towed by the heavy cruiser *Northampton*, and, as *Enterprise* had already departed from the battle zone, there was no combat air patrol. At 1515 the Kates made torpedo attacks on both *Hornet* and *Northampton*. A couple were shot down by antiaircraft shellfire, but most got their torpedoes off. *Northampton* quickly cut loose her tow and was able to evade the torpedoes directed at her. However, at 1523, one of the torpedoes aimed at *Hornet* struck home.

This was the third torpedo to hit *Hornet* on the day, and it administered the coup de grace. A violent explosion tore open the hull, flooding the engine room and causing her to list dangerously. Her captain gave the order for the crew to stand by to abandon ship. Seventeen minutes later, at 1540, five Vals showed up and made dive-bombing attacks on *Hornet*, but, although she was dead in the water, all the bombs missed. Ten minutes later, six Kates—probably launched from *Junyo* in a second deckload along with the dive-bombers—arrived and made a horizontal bombing run on the immobile *Hornet* as she was putting her crew over the side.[29] One bomb hit the aft starboard corner of the flight deck but caused no casualties.

There was one final attack on the thoroughly besieged *Hornet*. At 1702 four dive-bombers from *Zuikaku*—all the serviceable Vals she had left—attacked and delivered one more bomb on the abandoned derelict.[30] It was redundant, as all of *Hornet*'s crew had been safely evacuated. When it was decided to put the gutted carrier out of her misery, one of the destroyers in the screen fired eight torpedoes into her. Only three hit, and they did not sink her. A second destroyer fired another eight, six of which hit but also failed to sink her. (It appears that American ship-launched torpedoes were not a whole lot more effective than the American aerial torpedoes at this stage in the war.) The two destroyers then resorted to shellfire, pumping 430 rounds into *Hornet*. Although this set her ablaze from stem to stern, she still did not sink. Later, Japanese destroyers in Abe's Vanguard Group arrived on the scene and put four Long Lance torpedoes into her. She sank—at 0135 on October 27. One hundred eleven of her crew had been killed, and 108 wounded.

THE ACCOUNTING

The Battle of the Santa Cruz Islands was over. It had been a clear victory for the Japanese. The first attack on *Hornet* had been a masterpiece in coordinated attack execution, the best they had achieved in the war. The American performance, on the other hand—except for that of Widhelm's dive-bomber squadron—had been generally poor. With the sinking of *Hornet* the Japanese navy had evened the score in fleet carriers lost to four apiece. But it was too late in the year for the Japanese carrier force to regain the initiative lost at Midway. Also, on the very day of its greatest victory at sea the Japanese had lost the battle for Henderson Field on Guadalcanal. Moreover, even their naval victory came at an intolerable price: sixty-nine carrier planes had been shot down and another twenty-three lost in crash landings in the water. The Americans lost twenty-three planes shot down and another fifty-one in water landings or onboard *Hornet* when she went down—a total of seventy-four American planes against ninety-two for the Japanese.[31]

More critically for Japan, about seventy irreplaceable carrier pilots had been lost. Perhaps more costly than the gross number of carrier pilots lost in the battle was the loss of the air group and squadron leaders. The torpedo plane squadron leaders of both *Shokaku* and *Zuikaku* had been lost, as were the dive-bomber squadron leaders of *Shokaku* and *Junyo*. Yamamoto's carrier force would never win another battle, nor would its airmen ever again even sink another American capital ship. Thus, the Japanese victory at Santa Cruz was in many ways a Pyrrhic one. After the battle, *Shokaku* and *Zuiho* had been sent back to Japan for repairs, and *Zuikaku* (for the second time in her short career) returned home to replenish her air group. Only *Junyo* and her recently arrived sister *Hiyo* remained in the area. (And all Halsey had was a damaged *Enterprise*.)

LAST BIG NAVAL BATTLE

There was one major naval battle yet to come—the Battle of Guadalcanal in mid-November. (It was part of the last attempt by the Japanese to land a substantial number of reinforcements on the island. It did not succeed, and most of the troop transports were sunk.) The naval battle was notable for a couple of things: the first Japanese battleship to be sunk in the war—*Hiei*—was sunk there. It was dive-bombed by SBDs from Henderson and torpedoed by Avengers from *Enterprise* on November 13 after having been disabled by over fifty hits from American cruiser guns in an engagement the night before; its steering gear had been wrecked, making it a sitting duck. (Two American light cruisers had been lost in the battle.)

The second event was the first and only battlewagon duel in the Pacific. *Kirishima* (and two heavy cruisers) slugged it out with *Washington* and *South Dakota* on the night of the 14th. It was an unequal battle; the two American battleships each sported nine 16-inch guns, *Kirishima* but eight 14-inch guns. *Kirishima* took nine hits and later sank (but managed to put *South Dakota* out of action).

It is curious that Yamamoto did not send his more powerful battleships—the *Yamato*-class with its 18.1-inch guns or even the *Nagato*-class with 16-inch guns—to take on the American battlewagons. Yamamoto was surely aware that the Americans had two of its new 16-inch-gunned battleships in the area; it seems inexcusable that he did not take advantage of his overwhelming superiority in large-gunned battleships. But as mentioned earlier, one possible explanation is that Yamamoto did not think he could afford the fuel oil to send the heavier battleships to the Solomons unless absolutely necessary. He apparently gambled that the *Kongo*-class ships could—with their superior speed—avoid contact with the American battleships.[32] Thus, while the Guadalcanal campaign opened with a sea battle that was disastrous for the Americans—the Battle of Savo Island—the final major sea battle in that campaign was even more disastrous for the Japanese.

FINAL ACCOUNTING IN THE SOLOMONS

Overall, the American navy had been roughly handled in the Solomons. In capital ships, the loss of two fleet carriers (*Wasp* and *Hornet*) was not compensated for by the loss of two battleships and a light carrier by the Japanese. In cruisers, the Americans lost five heavy cruisers (along with an Australian) and two light cruisers—compared with three heavy cruisers and one light cruiser for Yamamoto. Even in destroyers the disparity was fourteen to eleven. Only in transport losses did the Americans have the advantage. In losses of the real capital ships of the Pacific War—fleet carriers—the Japanese had evened the tally at four apiece (all Japanese losses being at Midway). Each side was down to two fleet carriers—*Shokaku* and *Zuikaku* for Yamamoto, and *Enterprise* and *Saratoga* for Nimitz—and only one for each side was operational at the end of 1942.

However, the decimated American carrier fleet was about to be replaced by superior carriers: the 27,100-ton *Essex* was commissioned on the last day of the year, and would be joined by others of that class at about two-month intervals. Although it would take several months after commissioning for *Essex* and her sisters to become operational, by the end of 1943 there would be four—with another six added in 1944.[33] These superb fleet carriers would be supplemented by nine light carriers of the *Independence* class (converted from cruiser hulls). Five of those would become operational in 1943, the remaining four in early 1944.

The Japanese fleet carrier losses of 1942 would never be made good. They had not planned for a long war and, thus, had made no provisions for replacing the six fleet carriers they had on hand at the beginning of the war. Only one new fleet carrier hull had been laid down before the war began—*Taiho*—and only it would become operational before the war's end. (This was an armored-deck version of the *Shokaku* class laid down in July 1941, in response to the British armored-deck *Illustrious*-class carriers.) It became operational in June 1944, just in time to be sunk in the Battle of the Philippine Sea. After Midway, six improved *Hiryu*-class fleet carriers were laid down.[34] However, only three would be completed before the end of the war (*Unryu*, *Amagi*, and *Katsuragi*), and none would become operational in the sense of embarking an air group. The only new Japanese carriers after the Solomon Islands battles to enter service before 1944 were three light carriers: *Ryuho* in November 1942, and two carriers converted from seaplane carriers in 1943—*Chitose* and *Chiyoda*.

Even more debilitating and irreplaceable than the fleet carrier losses was the destruction of Japan's carrier pilot cadre. We saw that 40 pilots had been lost in the Battle of the Eastern Solomons, and around 70 more in the Battle of the Santa Cruz Islands. After Santa Cruz another 25 carrier pilots were lost from *Junyo* and *Hiyo*, bringing the total number lost in the Solomon Islands battles to around 135—exceeding the toll of Midway. (Another 200-plus land-based naval pilots, some of them carrier-qualified, had also been lost in the Solomons.) When added to the approximately 240 carrier pilots lost in prior battles, the tally reached about 375 since the war began. Of that number, roughly 325 could be regarded as "first-line" pilots. Thus, over 80 percent of the elite group of 400 who were on hand at the beginning of the war (and who participated in the attack on Pearl Harbor) were gone. As we saw in an earlier chapter, Yamamoto had known at the outset that if he was going to achieve the objective of eliminating the American navy in the Pacific in the first year of the war, those 400 elite carrier pilots would have to do it; he had come up short. And, as earlier mentioned, even more costly than the raw number of carrier pilots lost was the almost total destruction of the top echelon who were the squadron and air group leaders. They were the ones who made precision, coordinated attacks possible.

These elite pilots could not be replaced because after 1942 Japan lacked the aviation fuel to provide pilot trainees with the hundreds of hours of flight time required to become highly skilled pilots. Not enough oil from the Dutch East Indies was getting back to Japan because of the accelerating interdiction of tankers by American aircraft and, especially, submarines. Although increasing numbers of pilots were coming out of Japan's naval pilot training program at Kasumigaura, their combat performance would prove to be mediocre. After 1942 the Japanese navy went for quantity over quality in carrier pilots. But in a numbers game against the United States, Japan did not stand a chance. Moreover, while the number of highly trained Japanese carrier pilots was dwindling to almost nothing, the number of experienced American carrier pilots was rapidly expanding. The skill advantage possessed by Japanese carrier pilots in the first year of the war would be more than reversed when the next—and last—carrier battle took place at the Philippine Sea in June 1944. In that battle, known as the "Marianas Turkey Shoot," about 292 Japanese carrier planes were lost in combat compared with 37 for the Americans.

While the American navy had been roughly handled at sea around Guadalcanal, on land it was the Japanese who were roughly handled. They lost every major battle, and the casualty tally was far more lopsided in America's favor than was the Japanese advantage at sea. The Americans had suffered only 1,592 killed in action out of the 60,000 army and Marine Corps troops committed to Guadalcanal. Of the 36,000 Japanese troops who fought there, over two-thirds were killed or died from disease: 14,800 were killed in action, 9,000 died of disease, and another 1,000 were taken prisoner.[35] (This does not include several thousand more who went down in sunken transports while attempting to land on the island.)

On January 4, 1943, six weeks after the abortive naval Battle of Guadalcanal, the Japanese high command finally threw in the towel and ordered Guadalcanal to be evacuated. The Americans were unaware of this, and there was another month of fighting—including an especially bloody battle to finally take the totemic Mount Austen. But on February 7—six months to the day after the marines landed on the island—the last of the 11,000 surviving Japanese soldiers was pulled out that night. The battle for Guadalcanal was finally over.

FINAL PERSPECTIVE

While the Battle of Midway was pivotal in that it destroyed Japanese offensive naval power and shifted Japan to the defensive, American armed forces still had to prove that they could take and hold Japanese territory. Thus, Guadalcanal was also pivotal in that it established that American naval, marine, and army forces could do just that. The Japanese evacuation of Guadalcanal coincided with the German surrender at Stalingrad and the final Anglo-American push in North Africa. Roosevelt proclaimed this encouraging period "the turning point"; Churchill, "the end of the beginning." Even the Japanese high command admitted that the outcome of the struggle for Guadalcanal was "the fork in the road which leads to victory for them or for us."[36] Actually, the Japanese were finished. Although it would take another two and a half years of bloody fighting before they surrendered, they would never win another major naval or land battle in the Pacific War.

Yamamoto had foretold that his carrier force could "run wild for twelve months" but thereafter would have a rough time surviving against an American carrier force that was bound to double and redouble in strength. Accordingly, his strategy had been simple: eliminate American naval power from the Pacific in the first year of the war. If that could be done, then the strategic resources of the South Seas, especially oil, that would be quickly captured by the army could be transported back to Japan, and stockpiled, before a rebuilt American navy could take control of the vital sea lanes. But it was not to be. At the end of Yamamoto's twelve-month deadline, American military, naval, and air power was firmly entrenched on the flanks of the vital sea lanes of the southwest Pacific and poised to roll back the Japanese conquests.

CHAPTER TEN

POSTMORTEM

WE HAVE SEEN THAT the disaster that befell Nagumo's Mobile Force at Midway was one from which the Japanese navy never recovered. It was not only one of the most lopsided naval victories in history, but the turning point of the Pacific War. However, it is generally accepted that had Nagumo gotten his grand-scale attack launched against the American carrier force before his Mobile Force was bombed at 1025 he probably would have won the Battle of Midway. This would have radically changed the course of the war in the Pacific, but in exactly what ways can only be imagined. I will later attempt to construct a scenario for such a hypothetical Japanese victory at Midway had Nagumo's strike force gotten launched, and its likely consequences in the Pacific War. But, of course, he did not get his strike force off his carriers in time, and solving the mystery of why he could not has been the central focus of this "inquest."

We saw that the key to unraveling this mystery has been around for over fifty years, but has generally been disregarded by American commentators on the battle—as well as the official Japanese history: acceptance of Nagumo's claim in his official report that he did not receive the *Tone* 4 sighting report discovering the presence of the American fleet until about 0800. This is around twenty minutes later than generally assumed, and meant that the rearming operation he had ordered at 0715—to change the torpedoes on his attack planes to land bombs for a second strike on Midway—proceeded that much longer before being suspended or reversed. We saw that this resulted in twenty minutes' more work having to be done to restore the torpedoes in twenty minutes' less time— a swing of forty minutes—making it impossible for Nagumo to get a strike force launched before the fatal American attack on his carriers.

BLUNDERS THAT COST NAGUMO
THE BATTLE OF MIDWAY

How did Nagumo get into this fix; were there avoidable blunders to blame? By "avoidable blunders" I do not mean the ordinary mistakes and inefficiencies that attend all battles and can be said to be part of the fog of war. For example, while it might appear that the real cause for Nagumo's inability to get a strike launched in time was the thirty-minute delay in getting the *Tone* 4 sighting report to him, we saw that such communications inefficiency was endemic to both navies at that time in the war. (It had taken thirty-three minutes to get the American search plane sighting report to the American carrier force commander.) It now appears that thirty minutes was pretty much a normal time for decrypting and relaying an *initial* sighting report at that time—especially if unexpected. The need to streamline this procedure simply had not been foreseen in either navy until after Midway. Thus, although Nagumo's flexibility to respond to an American carrier threat was clearly constrained by this delay, it cannot be fairly considered an avoidable blunder under the circumstances of those days.

As for other blunders often alleged, such as deficiencies in the search effort that are assumed to have prevented an earlier discovery of the American carrier force, we saw (in chapter 4) that a more thorough, higher-density search plan probably would not have produced an earlier sighting of the American fleet by Japanese search planes: a Japanese search plane in fact flew almost right over *Yorktown* at 0630, but clouds obscured the carrier. Nor would an earlier launch of the *Tone* 4 search plane have produced an earlier discovery. We saw that, paradoxically, its late launch probably resulted in an *earlier* discovery than would have occurred had *Tone* 4 been launched on time—at 0430 instead of 0500. We now know that *Tone* 4 shortened its course—apparently to make up for lost time—and ran into the American ships on its new return route about an hour earlier than it otherwise would have.

Several other purported blunders have been cited by commentators on the battle, but they too do not hold up under close scrutiny. (Lately, as previously mentioned, it has become fashionable to attribute the Japanese defeat to defective carrier "doctrines"—such as using float planes for reconnaissance instead of carrier bombers; but we have seen that no such "doctrine" existed.)

There has also been a lingering tendency over the years since the war to blame the Japanese defeat at Midway on a generalized ineptitude on the part of the Japanese commanders—brought on, it has been said, by "victory disease" (resulting from too many easy victories prior to Midway). This idea came from the first published postmortems of the battle after the war—largely from Japanese veterans, and most notably Mitsuo Fuchida in his book *Midway*. Coming from Japanese veterans, this gave the notion of pervasive incompetence a ring of credibility to many American historians. But one should be leery of postmortems of a war, by losers as well as winners, so soon after the event. There is a natural tendency on the part of the vanquished toward self-flagellation and scapegoating, which can produce explanations as biased as those tinged by jingoism on the part of the victors.

As is apparent by now, I have labored under the possibly naive notion that the Japanese commanders at Midway were actually quite intelligent and well trained —easily on a par with their American counterparts. Therefore, I have sought explanations for what went wrong on the Japanese side that do not require one to assume that the Japanese commanders, especially Nagumo, were stupid. However, though generally competent, they did commit some serious blunders—all military commanders do.

What, then, were the real avoidable blunders that cost the Japanese the battle? There were two that were especially serious: Yamamoto's communications failure, and Nagumo's decision to rearm the torpedo planes. We saw that Yamamoto failed to ensure that Nagumo had the benefit of radio intelligence that Yamamoto received during the sortie from Japan, indicating that the Americans had discovered Yamamoto's Midway operation and, even more critically, indicating that American carriers might actually be at Midway when Nagumo got there. Yamamoto had declined advice from his staff to forward crucial intelligence to Nagumo, preferring to maintain radio silence under the assumption that Nagumo's flagship *Akagi* had also received the radio transmissions. This turned out to be a fatal assumption; *Akagi*'s radio equipment was inadequate to receive long-distance radio signals, and no alternative arrangements had been made.

However, unlike the delay in forwarding initial sighting reports from search planes, this problem of poor radio equipment on *Akagi* had been foreseen. We saw that before the departure from Japan, Nagumo's chief of staff, Kusaka, had warned Yamamoto's staff that *Akagi* might not receive long-wave radio signals, and had urged Yamamoto to relay to *Akagi* from his flagship *Yamato* any important radio intelligence he received. Yamamoto ignored this plea in the interests of radio silence. This was a clear blunder and the one most responsible for the disaster that befell Nagumo's Mobile Force at Midway. It left Nagumo assuming, on the morning of June 4, that there would be no American carriers at Midway—and that he was therefore free to give his full attention to neutralizing Midway in preparation for the amphibious invasion scheduled for June 6. Had he known what Yamamoto—and almost everyone else in the Japanese high command—knew, he most certainly would not have ordered the torpedoes to be stripped from his standby torpedo planes for a second strike on Midway.

But Nagumo must share some of the blame for the debacle. While a second strike on Midway was called for after Nagumo received the report from the leader of the first strike urging one, we saw that it was not necessary that the standby torpedo planes be used for it. This is because the most important target at Midway was American aircraft; they had not been caught on the ground by the first attack, and would have to be hit after they returned from their attacks on the Mobile Force. The most effective planes, however, for attacking those aircraft after they had returned to their airstrips were not torpedo planes in the role of high-level horizontal bombers, but dive-bombers and Zeros—as, indeed, they had been at Hawaii on December 7 when the airfields of Oahu were attacked. We saw that although the doctrine of coordinated attack with all three types of aircraft was deeply imbedded in the consciousness of Japanese carrier commanders, Nagumo should have deviated from it on this occasion.

Moreover, we saw that before he left Japan Nagumo had been expressly directed by Yamamoto to keep one-half of his torpedo planes on standby at all times equipped with torpedoes in the event that American carriers suddenly appeared at Midway. We saw in chapter 4 that there was a good reason for this: the rearming of torpedo planes from torpedoes to 800-kilogram land bombs was a much lengthier procedure than is commonly assumed—taking at least one and a half hours *after* the planes and bombs were already in the hangar. During this extended period, the torpedo planes—by far the most effective anti-carrier weapon the Japanese navy possessed when equipped with the deadly Type 91 torpedoes—would be out of commission if an American carrier threat were to suddenly emerge. On the other hand, dive-bombers could be easily and quickly rearmed with land bombs, and could also be quickly reversed back to armor-piercing bombs should American carriers be discovered. (For this reason, Yamamoto's "standing order" did not apply to them.) Thus, Nagumo still could have made his second strike on Midway—while at the same time complying with Yamamoto's standing order regarding the torpedo planes. His decision to rearm the torpedo planes must, therefore, also be judged an avoidable blunder that cost him the battle.

WHAT IFS

The biggest "what if" is what is likely to have happened in the battle had Nagumo *not* rearmed his torpedo planes. While it might be assumed that Nagumo would easily have been able to launch his strike force before being bombed by American carrier dive-bombers at 1025, actually there would have been difficulties. In the first place, an immediate attack after Nagumo received the *Tone* 4 sighting report at 0800 must be ruled out. This is because at that time it is almost certain that all his torpedo planes were in the hangars of *Akagi* and *Kaga*—even if they were not being rearmed. (The flight decks had to be cleared for combat air patrol operations before the torpedo bombers from Midway arrived at 0700.) Most, if not all, the dive-bombers were also in the hangars of *Hiryu* and *Soryu*, and they would have been rearmed with land bombs by 0800. Thus, Nagumo would have been in no position to launch an immediate attack at that time even had he suspected American carriers in the area.

The next question, then, is whether it would have been possible for Nagumo to have launched an attack in the next half-hour or so—before the Midway strike force, which was beginning to return, had to be landed. Had there been no attacks by American bombers from Midway during that period this might have been possible. We know that Yamaguchi's dive-bombers on *Hiryu* and *Soryu* could have been launched soon after 0830;[1] and if both the aft and midship elevators were used, the torpedo planes could have been raised to the flight decks and launched by about the same time.[2] Thus, if the order to prepare for launch of a strike group had been given at 0805, it appears that it would have been possible to have gotten all the planes off all four carriers by around 0840 —leaving the flight decks clear to land the Midway strike force—*if* there were no American attacks from Midway.

But there were attacks from Midway. Sixteen Marine Dauntless dive-bombers began their attack almost immediately after Nagumo received the *Tone* 4 sighting report—and before he had received clarification on the composition of the American ships. While this attack—and the two to follow—would not have prevented the raising to the flight deck, spotting, and launching of the strike force (fifteen Zeros were spotted and launched during the attacks), the radical evasive maneuvering of the carriers would certainly have slowed such operations. The launch would surely have been delayed beyond 0840—by how much could not have been foreseen at 0805.

Would Nagumo have still ordered preparations for a launch? There is, of course, no way of knowing, but given his cautious demeanor it seems unlikely. More likely is that he would have postponed the decision at least until he got word back from *Tone* 4 on whether there were any carriers among the American ships sighted. When he was told (at 0811) that the American ships consisted only of five destroyers and five cruisers there may have been a sigh of relief among some of Nagumo's staff that there was no longer any urgency to launch an attack. But we saw that the wiser heads (such as Kusaka) did not believe that those cruisers and destroyers would be there unless they were escorting carriers. By that time, however, American heavy bombers were spotted at high altitude beginning their bombing run; several Zeros were launched to intercept them—including the last available for escorting any strike force that might be launched to attack the American ships. At this point, it would seem that the mood in headquarters would have favored waiting until the attacks were over—

and even waiting until the first-wave planes back from Midway were landed before assembling the strike force on the flight decks.

Many of the same arguments in favor of postponement that actually prevailed at 0830 that morning would still have applied in this hypothetical situation: First, there were no longer any Zeros available for escort—every single one had been committed to the combat air patrol to defend against the attacks from Midway. And without an adequate escort the strike force would sustain far greater losses, and inflict less damage on the American carrier fleet, than could be achieved by a later, adequately escorted strike. Second, it would have appeared that there was time to organize an adequately escorted strike—with even more torpedo planes—after the Midway strike force had been landed. This is because the American ships were calculated to be too far away, based on the coordinates given in *Tone* 4's sighting report, for any carriers among them to launch an escorted attack of their own until around 0830.

When Nagumo received *Tone* 4's report identifying a carrier at 0830, there may have been considerable angst in headquarters, but it would have been too late to reverse the decision to postpone the launch of the strike force. This all leads us to perhaps an astonishing conclusion: even if the torpedo planes had *not* been ordered to be rearmed at 0715 for a second strike on Midway, Nagumo probably still would have postponed any attack against the American carrier force until after the Midway strike force had been landed.

Now, the larger question is posed: could Nagumo have got his grand-scale attack off his carriers before they were bombed at 1025 even had his torpedo planes never been stripped of their torpedoes? The answer to that question might seem obvious—of course they could have been launched in time. But it would not have been as easy as it might first appear. Operations to raise the strike force planes back to the flight decks could not have begun until the Midway strike force planes—and Zeros on combat air patrol—had been landed. Although the last dive-bomber was landed on *Akagi* at 0859 (and about the same time on *Kaga*), Zeros were still being taken aboard *Akagi* and *Kaga* as late as 0910.[3] On *Hiryu* and *Soryu* landing operations took longer; apparently they were delayed by Yamaguchi's reluctance to abandon his hopes for a strike with his dive-bombers. In any case, landing operations were not completed on those carriers until after 0918.

Thus, operations to spot torpedo planes on *Akagi* and *Kaga* could not have begun until at least 0910, and operations for the dive-bombers on *Hiryu* and *Soryu* could not have begun until around 0920. A worse problem would have been that, unlike at 0835, only one elevator on each carrier could be used to raise the strike force planes because the hangars were full of planes, blocking access to the second elevator. We saw that it would take forty minutes to raise, spot, and prepare for launch a squadron of torpedo planes on *Akagi*, using only the rear elevator. The elevators on *Hiryu* and *Soryu* were a little faster, but it still would have taken about thirty-five minutes, using only the midship eleva-tors.[4]

But these spotting times are based on the assumption that the carriers are free from attacks. We have seen that, contrary to Nagumo's estimate—based on the erroneous *Tone* 4 sighting report—that American carrier planes would not ar-rive until after 1000, a torpedo bomber attack actually came in at 0930, followed by another at 0940. This would not have prevented the elevator and spotting operations, but would have slowed them down—adding at least five minutes to time it took to complete them. This would mean that the torpedo planes on *Akagi* and *Kaga*—and the dive-bombers on *Hiryu* and *Soryu*—would not have been ready for launch until around 1000. But they would have made, just barely, the fifteen-minute window between 1000 and 1015—between the end of the second American torpedo bomber attack and the beginning of the third—during which they absolutely had to be launched to avoid destruction by American dive-bombers.[5]

This situation would almost exactly parallel the one posed in chapter 6, where it was shown what could have been done had the torpedo planes been ordered rearmed with land bombs at 0715, but reversed at 0745—as claimed by Senshi Sosho. The seventeen torpedo planes on *Akagi*, and perhaps nineteen of the twenty-six on *Kaga*, along with the thirty-six dive-bombers on *Hiryu* and *Soryu*, could have been spotted on the flight decks by 1000, with engines warm-ing up ready for takeoff. By that time, there would also have been three Zeros from each carrier for escort spotted at the front of the flight decks. However, Nagumo would have faced the same quandary regarding *Kaga*: it would have taken another fifteen to twenty minutes to raise and spot the remaining seven or eight torpedo planes on the flight deck. Would Nagumo have commenced the launch at 1000—when the second torpedo bomber attack was over—with what was ready to go, or would he have delayed until all twenty-six of the tor-pedo planes on *Kaga* could be launched? We saw that with American dive-bombers expected momentarily, Nagumo would probably have opted for an immediate launch.

But it can be seen that any assumption that had the torpedo planes *not* been rearmed, a launch could have been easily made before the fatal bombing is not well founded. Still, it would have been achievable, and thus Nagumo's blunder of rearming his torpedo planes cost him the ability to get a strike force launched before the fatal bombing at 1025.

WHAT IF THE STRIKE FORCE
HAD BEEN LAUNCHED?

In the foregoing hypothetical case, the strike force would have gotten off the flight decks a little before 1015—just before the arrival of *Yorktown*'s torpedo

bombers forced Nagumo's carriers to make evasive maneuvers. Thirty-six torpedo planes (assuming that nineteen from *Kaga* got spotted along with *Akagi*'s
seventeen), thirty-six dive-bombers from *Hiryu* and *Soryu*, and twelve Zeros
(three from each carrier) would have been launched. The escort would still be
a bit thin, but it would have been a formidable strike force nevertheless; the
American carriers would have been in for a rough time. Let us now consider
what might have happened to the American carriers, and then to Nagumo's carriers when they were bombed at around 1025.

One would intuitively suspect—based on what actually happened to *Yorktown* in the attacks by planes from just one Japanese carrier—that the American
carriers would have been hit by enough of the deadly Type 91 aerial torpedoes—
supplemented by numerous armor-piercing bombs—in this initial attack to destroy perhaps two of the three carriers—either sinking them during the battle or
rendering them so helpless that they would be easy prey for Japanese submarines. (Recall that *Yorktown* was destroyed by just eighteen dive-bombers and
ten torpedo planes from *Hiryu*. And at Coral Sea, *Lexington* was destroyed by
the planes from two carriers whose pilots were generally regarded by the Japanese as second-rate.)

However, it might be interesting to attempt to quantify the outcome of this
hypothetical carrier battle by using a simplified war-gaming model of the kind
employed by the Japanese in their war-gaming exercises. The rules for such a
war-gaming model are set out in Appendix D. (The values built into this
model—relating to hit ratios for bombs and torpedoes dropped, and damage to
the American carriers—were derived largely from the statistics of the actual carrier battles of 1942: from Coral Sea to Midway to the Santa Cruz Islands.) In this
chapter, I will just give a summary of the results indicated by application of the
rules to the various attacks by both sides that would ensue under this hypothetical. (A more detailed scenario is set out in the appendix for anyone who might
be interested.)

The Japanese strike force—consisting of thirty-six Val dive-bombers and
thirty-six Kate torpedo planes, escorted by twelve Zeros—would have arrived
in the vicinity of the American carriers around 1120. It would have been picked
up on radar while it was about 30 miles out and, thus, would have been confronted by a combined American combat air patrol of about thirty-six Wildcats. The application of the war game rules indicates that enough bombers
would get through to deliver roughly eight bombs and three torpedoes on target. This attack would likely result in one American carrier being destroyed
(burning dead in the water and sinking), another being damaged severely
enough to be put out of action for the duration of the battle, and the third sustaining only light damage that could be patched up after an hour or so.

The rules indicate that Japanese losses in the attack would be in the neighbor-
hood of thirteen Vals, twenty-one Kates, and six Zeros. About one-third of the

twenty-three Vals, fifteen Kates, and six Zeros that returned to their carriers would probably have been damaged too badly to make further attacks. American plane losses would be about sixteen Wildcats; half lost in combat and half destroyed on the bombed carriers (a few Dauntless dive-bombers would also be destroyed on the carriers).

THE AMERICAN ATTACK ON THE MOBILE FORCE

Within minutes after the hypothetical Japanese attack force was launched (by around 1010) American dive-bombers from *Enterprise* and *Yorktown* bombed three carriers of Nagumo's Mobile Force. What would have been the results of that attack had the strike force been off those carriers? There is no reason to assume that the number of bomb hits would have been any different than actually occurred—four on *Kaga*, two on *Akagi*, and three on *Soryu*. But what we most definitely can assume is that there would have been a substantial difference in the damage those bomb hits would have caused to the carriers with the strike force off the carriers. There would have been eighteen fewer torpedo planes loaded with fuel and torpedoes on each of the carriers *Akagi* and *Kaga*, and eighteen fewer dive-bombers on *Soryu*. We saw in chapter 8 that it was all this fuel and ordnance on board the carriers that made them extraordinarily vulnerable to American bombs that, with $\frac{1}{100}$-second fuses, exploded about four feet into the upper hangars.

With this lessened vulnerability, the rules indicate that the four bomb hits (one 1,000-pounder and three 500-pounders) *Kaga* took would have been sufficient to knock her out of action for the duration of battle, but not destroy her. She would not have been able to launch or recover any of her planes (and most of the aircraft remaining on board would have been destroyed). The two bomb hits (both 1,000-pounders) *Akagi* took would have badly damaged her, but not put her out of action. The damage to her flight deck could have been patched up in a couple of hours, and she then could have launched and recovered planes—though at a reduced pace. (In the actual attack, *Akagi*'s midship elevator was knocked out, so even if *Akagi* had not been destroyed by fire, that elevator would have been inoperable.) Most of the Val dive-bombers in the hangar would have been destroyed or rendered inoperable. As for *Soryu*, however, the rules indicate that the lessened vulnerability would not have saved her. The three 1,000-pound bomb hits she took would still have been sufficient to destroy this smaller carrier.

Thus, this model indicates that in the American attack after the hypothetical Japanese strike force had been launched, Nagumo would have lost but one carrier (compared to the three he actually lost in the first attack), and would have had a second put out of action. He would have had two carriers remaining to continue operations against the American carrier force. The Americans, as we saw, would have lost one carrier and had a second put out of action in the attack (compared with only one destroyed after the actual two attacks from *Hiryu*). Spruance would have had only one carrier remaining to carry on with the battle. But there would have been more attacks to come.

SUBSEQUENT JAPANESE ATTACKS

While our hypothetical Japanese attack on the American carriers was taking place, *Hiryu*—which had not been attacked by the American dive-bombers— would have been preparing for a second attack. *Hiryu* had nine operational tor- pedo planes remaining after the Midway strike, and had inherited one from *Akagi* (the one that had been on search duty, but could not land on that carrier on its return because of the American bombing). These planes would have been rearmed with torpedoes and spotted on the flight deck after the first strike force had departed. They would have been ready to go soon after 1200, along with some Zeros for escort.

In this second strike force, however—unlike the actual one—there would have been some dive-bombers from *Akagi* to accompany the torpedo planes; how many is difficult to estimate. There had been about sixteen operational Val dive-bombers on *Akagi* in the process of being rearmed with 250-kilogram anti- ship bombs when the bombs hit at 1025. We have seen in our hypothetical that the damage from two bombs would not have been fatal as the torpedo planes were off the carrier, but the bomb that hit the midship elevator destroyed a num- ber of dive-bombers in the upper hangar. Let us assume, however, that six Vals were undamaged and could have been ready to launch at around the same time as *Hiryu*'s torpedo planes—shortly after 1200. As for Zeros for escort, there were plenty available; *Hiryu* and *Akagi* would have inherited those from *Kaga* and *Soryu* on combat air patrol when those carriers were bombed. The problem would have been getting them landed and serviced immediately. Because of the damage to *Akagi*, Zeros could be landed, and turned around in a reasonable time, only on *Hiryu*. It will be assumed that nine Zeros could have been made ready on *Hiryu* soon enough for a launch to accompany the bombers.

As the surviving planes from the hypothetical first strike on the American car- riers would return around 1230 and need to be landed immediately—many would have been shot up—it would have been necessary to complete the launch of the second strike by that time.[6] Let us therefore assume that the sec- ond strike force would have been launched by around 1230. It would have con- sisted of ten torpedo planes from *Hiryu* and six dive-bombers from *Akagi*, and been escorted by nine Zeros, all launched from *Hiryu*.

When that strike force got to the American carrier fleet at around 1330, it would have seen one smoldering, badly listing carrier dead in the water, and apparently finished (which we will suppose was *Yorktown*); a second carrier— also smoldering, but apparently still steaming at normal speed (which we will suppose was *Hornet*); and a third carrier with no obvious damage, which appeared to be conducting normal flight operations. (Let us suppose that the third carrier was the lucky *Enterprise*, which would have been damaged by bomb hits from the previous attack at around 1130, but by an hour later her flight deck would have been patched.) There would have been about a dozen Wildcats in the air—all from *Enterprise*.

Application of the rules indicate that enough bombers would get through to deliver one to two bombs and one to two torpedoes on target. This would have been sufficient to knock *Enterprise* out of action and inflict more damage on the already out-of-action *Hornet* but not destroy her. Two Vals, three Kates, and two Zeros would probably have been lost; the Americans would probably have lost five Wildcats.

But now, all three of the American carriers would be out of the battle, unable to conduct further flight operations. Nagumo's carriers would be free from further attack from those carriers for, at least, the remainder of the day. However, Midway itself would still be alive; the six operational marine Dauntlesses and five Vindicator dive-bombers would have been supplemented by eleven Dauntlesses from *Hornet* (which would not have returned to their carrier because of the attack on it). There also would have been about sixteen Wildcats: four survivors of the morning attack on Midway, along with about twelve that would have been unable to land on an overcrowded *Enterprise* after the first attack had disabled the other two carriers—they would have been directed to fly to Midway. Although refueling on Midway would be very slow, as the gasoline pumping system had been knocked out in the morning attacks, it seems that it still would have been possible for an ad hoc strike force to be prepared for an attack on Nagumo's carriers later in the afternoon.

In the meantime, the first Japanese strike force, which had completed its hypothetical attack on the American carriers around 1145, would have returned to *Akagi* and *Hiryu* around 1230, just after the smaller second strike force had been launched. We saw that about twenty-three dive-bombers, fifteen torpedo planes, and six Zeros could be expected to have returned. But, as many would have sustained damage, it is likely that only about two-thirds of them would have been available for further duty. Let us suppose that sixteen Vals and ten Kates—along with nine Zeros—could be sent on a third attack. As the turn-around time for the planes having returned from a prior strike was a little over three hours—a good part of it required to give the crews some rest and nourishment—we will assume that the third strike force could have been launched at around 1545.

When this third strike force would have arrived over the crippled American carriers, there would have been no combat air patrol to meet it. Thus, all of the dive-bombers and torpedo planes could be expected to release their ordnance. About five bombs and two torpedoes are likely to have hit the two out-of-action carriers. This would have been more than enough finish off those carriers. Now, all three of Nimitz's carriers would have been sinking, or so helpless as to be easy prey for Japanese submarines. But Nagumo's remaining carriers were not home free just yet. Less than an hour after the third strike force had been launched, an American attack from Midway would have been spotted coming in.

MIDWAY STRIKES BACK

By around 1530, an ad hoc strike force would have been assembled and ready to take off to attack the Mobile Force. The eleven Marine dive-bombers (armed with 500-pound bombs) would have been joined by the eleven *Hornet* Dauntlesses (equipped with 1,000-pound bombs). They would be escorted by ten of the refugee Wildcats from the carrier force.

When this strike force would have reached the Mobile Force at around 1630, it would probably have run into a Japanese combat air patrol launched from *Akagi* and *Hiryu*—let us suppose sixteen Zeros. The rules indicate that of the *Hornet* dive-bombers that got through, only one would deliver a bomb on target (due to the relative inexperience of the *Hornet* pilots). If we assume that the larger and slower *Kaga* would have been the recipient of that 1,000-pounder, it would have been enough to finish her off—as she had already sustained enough damage in the 1025 attack to put her out of action. The even less experienced marine dive-bomber pilots would probably have had less success, scoring zero to one hit with a 500-pounder. Even assuming that *Akagi* took this possible hit, it would not have done enough additional damage to put her out of action.

Yamamoto would now have lost two carriers—*Kaga* and *Soryu*—and *Akagi* would have been badly beaten up, though still operational after temporary repairs to her flight deck. Only *Hiryu* would have remained unscathed. But this would be enough to finish the job at Midway. Of the twenty-two American dive-bombers that left Midway for this hypothetical attack, the rules indicate that at least eight would have been downed. Of the dozen or so that would have made it back to Midway, about half would have been damaged too severely to be operational. There would not be enough left to seriously threaten the Mobile Force again. Nagumo's second strike on Midway—postponed at 0805 that morning—could now take place the next morning, though at greatly reduced strength, and would probably have resulted in the destruction of the remaining operational planes on Midway. The attack would also soften up the gun emplacements and other defense installations, leaving the islands vulnerable to an amphibious invasion.

MOP-UP

With the American carriers out of the way, the invasion would have proceeded on schedule the early morning of the 6th of June. The Japanese landing forces, however, would have been in for a rough time, as Nimitz had beefed up the garrison to about 3,000 troops. The approximately 5,000 Japanese troops would most likely have suffered very heavy casualties as they hit the beaches. Only with tactical air support (supplemented by planes from the light carrier *Zuiho*) and bombardments from the battleships and cruisers of the supporting fleets would the Japanese troops have eventually been able to prevail, and only after a ferocious battle that might have taken several days. We do not want to speculate on the fate of the captured marines.

Before the fleets of the Midway and Aleutian operations would have returned to Japan, the surviving carriers would have shed their Zeros of the Sixth Air Group to take up residence on the airstrip at Midway: six from *Akagi*, three from *Hiryu*, and twelve from *Junyo*, down from the Aleutians. These would be needed to defend the base from anticipated bombing raids by B-17s from Hawaii. Long-range Emily flying boats would also be flown in from Kwajalein to take up residence in the lagoon. These could each carry 4,000 pounds of bombs, and could be used to harass Pearl Harbor with nighttime bombing raids.

*   *   *

The foregoing scenario may seem fanciful, but it has been constructed from capabilities on the two sides that are known to have existed. Most analysts of Midway have concluded that had Nagumo been able to get his grand-scale attack launched, he would have won the battle. I have merely added some details to show just how that battle might have played out—and what the toll in carriers and planes for both sides might have been. My scenario also shows, however, that unlike the actual lopsided American victory, a Japanese victory would probably have been a fairly close-run thing: three American carriers lost versus two for the Japanese, with a third badly damaged but able to make it back to Japan.

FINAL ACCOUNTING

The cost to the Japanese for their victory, especially in terms of irreplaceable carrier pilots, would have been enormous—almost as many killed or disabled in this hypothetical as in the actual battle that they lost. In our various hypothetical attacks, a total of fifty-three Japanese carrier planes and pilots would have been shot down (as compared with twenty-three in the actual two attacks by *Hiryu*). As the same number of pilots (eight) would have been lost in the morning attack on Midway, and presumably the same number of Zero pilots on combat air patrol would have been lost in the various morning attacks on the Mobile Force (thirteen), this would bring to seventy-four the total number of pilots killed, compared to the forty-four actually lost in combat. On the other hand, with the Japanese strike force off the carriers when three of them were bombed at 1025, there would have been far fewer pilots onboard, and substantially less damage—especially from fire—done to the carriers. Therefore, instead of the approximately sixty-five pilots who were killed in the actual bombings, it could be expected that only about twenty would have been killed on the three carriers hit—and none on *Hiryu*.

This would bring the total number of pilots killed to approximately 95, as compared to the actual 110.[7] If we assume that another 10 would have been permanently disabled (fewer than was actually the case), then the total lost for future carrier battles would have been around 105—compared to the approximately 125 actually lost. And those killed in combat would still have been the most experienced carrier pilots in the Japanese Navy. The approximately 125 who would have survived to fight another day would not have been enough to fill out the air groups of the four fleet carriers that remained. (It will be recalled that *Shokaku* and *Zuikaku*'s air groups had been largely depleted in the Battle of the Coral Sea and were later augmented by Midway survivors; with *Akagi* and *Hiryu* surviving the battle, there would have been very few Midway veterans available for *Shokaku* and *Zuikaku*.) American carrier pilot losses, in this scenario, though somewhat greater than they actually were (roughly 76 instead of 61), would still leave over 150 pilots to form a seasoned nucleus for a new carrier fleet.

Although the hypothetical Japanese victory I have posed would have been close—two Japanese carriers lost in exchange for three for the Americans—the one-carrier margin would have been one that Nimitz could ill afford, having already lost a fleet carrier at Coral Sea. This would have left Yamamoto with four fleet attack carriers as against two for Nimitz (the recently repaired *Saratoga*, and *Wasp*, en route from the Atlantic). The balance of carrier superiority, however, would not shift over to Yamamoto until *Shokaku*, and now *Akagi*, were repaired—which would take at least another two months.

WHAT NEXT?

Had the Japanese won the Battle of Midway, what would have happened in the Pacific War? Although the long-term consequences can scarcely be imagined, the immediate aftermath is fairly easy to reconstruct from Japanese records. The general outlines of the Japanese "Basic Plan" for the first year of the war are known. It had been promulgated to the fleets by the Naval General Staff in December 1941 (though modifications were later made as circumstances evolved). The Basic Plan divided projected naval operations for the first year into three phases.[8] The objectives of the first phase were to cripple the American Pacific Fleet—especially its aircraft carriers—at Pearl Harbor, and then to seize the resource-rich islands and peninsulas of the South Seas—especially the oil-rich Dutch East Indies. (To secure this area, British military power in Singapore and

Hong Kong and American power in the Philippines were also to be eliminated.) This phase was to be completed by April 1942. While the objectives in the South Seas had been achieved on schedule, the failure to catch and destroy American aircraft carriers at Pearl Harbor meant that the objective of eliminating American naval air power would have to be carried over into the next phase.

The second phase of the Basic Plan, which began May 1, was originally intended to consolidate and extend the defensive perimeter in the western Pacific and South Seas to protect the sea lanes back to Japan.[9] The Combined Fleet's draft plan for this phase envisioned three periods or stages: the objectives of the first stage were to capture Tulagi in the Solomon Islands to establish a seaplane base and, more important, to capture Port Moresby on the south coast of Papua New Guinea. This would eliminate a strategic Allied base and establish in its place a Japanese base from which Australia could be threatened. Although Tulagi had been taken on schedule, the American navy had frustrated — in the Battle of the Coral Sea—the main objective of taking Port Moresby. This operation would have to be postponed to a later stage.

The objectives of the second stage (in the second phase) were to capture Midway and the western Aleutians. While the original purpose of these operations had been to extend the defensive perimeter eastward, we saw that it had later been amended to also serve as bait to lure the American carrier fleet into a decisive battle in order to finish what had eluded the Mobile Force at Pearl Harbor: destruction of the bulk of American carrier air power in the Pacific. With a victory in the Battle of Midway, this objective would have been achieved. Completion of the second phase objectives (taking Port Moresby) and fulfillment of the remaining objectives of the Basic Plan could then proceed. What were they?

The final objective of the second phase was to cut off Australia from American supply lines. This would greatly diminish the capability of Allied land-based air power in Australia to threaten the sea lanes of the South Seas, and even make northern Australia vulnerable to invasion. It would be accomplished by extending control over New Guinea and the Solomon Islands (including Guadalcanal) in the northern approaches to Australia, and then by seizing Fiji, Samoa, the New Hebrides, and New Caledonia to the east to preempt the Allies from establishing bases on the eastern flank of Australia.

The third phase in the Basic Plan—envisioned for the latter half of the first year—was more nebulous: to conduct offensive operations to destroy the Americans' will to fight. Among those operations contemplated: invasion of Hawaii—or at least the neutralization of Pearl Harbor—and the enticement of the Americans into a "decisive fleet battle" to destroy any carriers remaining after Midway. (This was actually war-gamed in early May.) Also contemplated (though never expressly articulated or war-gamed) was knocking out the Panama Canal. These operations, it was hoped, would force an early settlement of the war with the United States. No specific details of these tentative third-phase operations were ever promulgated—as the defeat at Midway consigned that phase to the ash heap.

But had the Japanese won at Midway, one can easily imagine operations to neutralize Pearl Harbor, to invade northeast Australia, and, more ominously, to destroy the Panama Canal. The destruction of just one key lock would have made the canal unusable for at least a year—and possibly two. This, obviously, would have seriously impaired the American navy's ability to get its new *Essex*-class carriers from the shipyards of the east coast into the Pacific. It would also have been highly demoralizing and, along with the elimination of Pearl Harbor as a forward base, would have made it very difficult for the United States to continue the war in the Pacific.

Now, let us turn to what America would *probably* have been in for in the summer of 1942 had Nagumo won the Battle of Midway. Although possible operations in the third phase can only be speculated, the implementation of the remaining stages of the second phase is a virtual certainty. As soon as possible after its return to Japan for refitting, the Combined Fleet would have moved south and taken up anchorage at its new main base at Truk in the Caroline Islands. The unfinished business of the first stage of the second phase—the capture of Port Moresby on the south coast of Papua New Guinea—would have received the first attention of the Japanese high command.

COULD AMERICA HAVE INTERVENED IN THE SOUTHWESTERN PACIFIC?
We saw in the previous chapter that, in actual fact, the invasion of Port Moresby had been derailed by the American landings on Guadalcanal and Tulagi in early August. This had forced the Japanese army to dilute its troop strength in Papua New Guinea to respond to this new threat. The next "what if," then, is: would the Americans have been able to invade the Solomon Islands in 1942 had they lost the Battle of Midway? We saw that Nimitz sent three carriers—*Enterprise*, *Saratoga*, and *Wasp*—to provide air superiority over the landing areas of Guadalcanal and Tulagi (*Hornet* was kept in Hawaiian waters). Although it turned out that they were not needed in the early stages of the invasion, as the Japanese were taken by surprise and did not have any carriers within striking distance, it is almost certain that an invasion would not have been attempted without those carriers being available. If three American carriers had been lost at Midway—instead of just one—just where would the necessary air superiority over Guadalcanal have come from?

Under our scenario, Nimitz would still have had two fleet carriers—*Saratoga* and *Wasp*; could they have been used in the southwest Pacific to support a landing in the Solomons? Probably not. With Hawaii now being threatened with invasion from Midway, Nimitz would need to hold back those carriers to defend Hawaii. (If they were going to be used to support any invasion of Japanese-held islands any time soon, it would be Midway, not the Solomons.) Thus, the first strategic casualty of an American defeat at Midway would have been the Guadalcanal campaign in 1942. Any invasion of that island, or anywhere else in the southwestern Pacific, would have to wait until late 1943 at the earliest—until a sufficient number of the new *Essex*-class carriers came on line. Until then, the Japanese would have been free to proceed with implementation of the remaining stages of the Basic Plan.

PROJECTED JAPANESE OPERATIONS

Even before *Shokaku* and *Akagi* would have been repaired, landings near Port Moresby in Papua New Guinea could have taken place—perhaps by mid-July—supported by *Zuikaku, Hiryu, Junyo,* and *Ryujo*. Even in the face of Australian resistance, with no American carriers in the area, this operation could have been completed by early August. At the same time, the Japanese presence in the Solomon Islands would have been strengthened with the occupation of Guadalcanal and construction of an airbase there. With that accomplished, the Combined Fleet could then have proceeded with the invasion of the Allied-held ring of islands to the east of Australia—Fiji, Samoa, the New Hebrides, and New Caledonia. As those islands were not heavily defended at the time, they probably would have been in Japanese hands by mid-August. In the meantime, the Japanese airfield on Guadalcanal would have been completed and stocked with aircraft.

The new Japanese bases in the islands off the east coast of Australia would have been added to those already established in the Marshalls, Marianas, Carolines, and Gilberts—as well as those in New Guinea, New Britain, and the Bismarcks to the north of the continent. Australia would have been largely cut off from the supplies and reinforcements that had been coming in from the United States. MacArthur's army would have been virtually marooned. Allied airbases in north Queensland and the Northern Territories of Australia would have been subject to bombing raids from Port Moresby and other Japanese airfields in the newly acquired islands. Even MacArthur's headquarters and the vital submarine base at Brisbane in southern Queensland would now have been within bombing range.

Although the Japanese would not have been ready to invade Australia, with American supply lines to it largely severed, the sea lanes from the East Indies and other strategic points in the South Seas area to Japan would have been much more secure. By the fall of 1942, oil from the oil fields of the East Indies would be flowing again (though full production would not be restored until 1943). Attacks on Japanese tankers and transports by air would have been greatly diminished, and even attacks from American submarines would have been substantially curtailed by the loss of refueling stations in the area. However, submarines could still be deployed from Pearl Harbor, and, although the length of time they could spend on patrol in the southwestern Pacific area would have been reduced, they still could have harassed Japanese convoys—especially in the sea lanes closer to the Japanese home islands. American submarines would, thus, remain a serious problem for the oil tankers and transports as long as Pearl Harbor remained operational. Something would have to be done about that, and soon.

By September, plans to neutralize Pearl Harbor probably would have been well advanced. Although an invasion of Hawaii had been war-gamed in Combined Fleet headquarters—and tentatively set for October—it is unlikely that a frontal assault on Oahu would have actually been attempted. American troop strength on the island had been massively built up since the December 7 attack, and would have been formidable by the fall of 1942. Moreover, the Japanese navy lacked the capability to transport the large number of troops that would be required for a major amphibious landing. But what was within Japanese capabilities would have been bad enough for the Americans: carrier bomber attacks on the oil tank farms, repair docks, and submarine pens at Pearl Harbor. This could make good the failure to hit those vital facilities in a third attack on December 7. Such a carrier-borne assault also had the potential of drawing the remaining American carriers into this arena for a final carrier battle of 1942 that would have eliminated all of Nimitz's carriers in the Pacific for about a year.

For such an operation against Hawaii, Yamamoto would have had available his four remaining attack carriers—*Akagi, Hiryu, Shokaku,* and *Zuikaku.* He would also have had the light carriers *Ryujo, Zuiho,* and *Junyo.* But, as we have seen, he would not have had enough carrier pilots to provide full-strength air groups for all his carriers. Of the 400 first-line pilots who participated in the attack on Pearl Harbor, no more than 220 would still be in service. There would have been another 80–90 second-line carrier pilots available—most of them recent graduates from the carrier pilot training program—but most of these would be adequately trained only for support operations with the light carriers. Thus, it seems unlikely that the air groups of the four attack carriers would be at full strength (which would be 72 planes each for *Shokaku* and *Zuikaku,* 63 for *Akagi,* and 57 for *Hiryu*—for a total of 264). Let us assume that those carriers would have nominal complements of only 234 operational planes (63, 63, 54, and 54, respectively) for this operation. Even at that lesser strength, over a dozen of these planes would have to be flown by second-line pilots taken from the light carriers.

This would leave only about 70 second-line pilots—barely enough for two light carriers. Let us assume that only *Junyo* and *Ryujo*—veterans of the Aleutian campaign—would be sent to Hawaii. Although these carriers would not be expected to engage in attacks on American carriers, they would be useful in making attacks against land targets—which, requiring less skill, was their main role anyway. The four attack carriers of Nagumo's Mobile Force would probably be supported by two or three *Kongo*-class fast battleships and three to four heavy cruisers (along with the usual destroyer screen).

As Nimitz would have had, by September, three modern fast battleships at his disposal (*North Carolina, Washington,* and *South Dakota*), one might expect that Yamamoto would also send a separate battleship fleet—as he had done in the Midway Operation. He had available in heavy battleships—disregarding the four obsolete *Fuso*-class battlewagons—two 16-inch-gunned *Nagato*-class battleships, and two *Yamato*-class behemoths with 18.1-inch guns (*Musashi* would have just joined the fleet). However, we saw that after the profligate expenditure of fuel oil for the Midway and Aleutians operations, the Japanese navy was faced with a serious fuel-oil shortage problem. Because of this, Yamamoto may have preferred to leave his heavy battleships at home (as he did in the actual naval battles of Guadalcanal) until oil stockpiles improved. In any case, they would not be needed; the main objectives of the hypothetical upcoming Hawaiian operation would be to eliminate, by carrier air power, Pearl Harbor as a functioning base for submarine deployment and, if the opportunity arose, to destroy the remaining American carriers.

THE SECOND ATTACK ON HAWAII

An attack on Pearl Harbor would have to begin by eliminating the land-based aircraft on Oahu. This would be a daunting undertaking as the Americans would have built up substantial air power on the island; Hickam and Wheeler airfields would be crawling with army bombers and fighters, and Ford Island and Ewa would be well stocked with navy and marine dive-bombers, torpedo planes, and fighters. Although American aircraft production had not yet reached top gear, the losses suffered in the December 7 attack and at Midway would have been more than made up by September. There would have been at least three hundred first-line combat aircraft on Oahu for the Japanese to contend with. The airfields and other facilities around Pearl Harbor may have received some softening up from bombing raids by flying boats from Midway, but Yamamoto's six carriers would still have faced an enormous task that could not be accomplished by just a couple of air strikes, as was the case at Midway. A prolonged series of attacks—extending over several days—would have been required. In the meantime, the Japanese carriers would have been subjected to counterattacks from the target—as they had been at Midway, but on a much larger scale.

Even with substantial air power on Oahu, unless Nimitz committed his two carriers to the battle, Yamamoto's carriers would probably have succeeded in wearing down, and eventually destroying, most of that air power. Fixed airbases cannot hold out for long against mobile ones—land targets can be hit even at night, while carriers are difficult to locate even during the day. Though the

Japanese would suffer heavy aircraft losses, and perhaps even some carriers, the bulk of the carrier air power would probably survive, and in the end the air power on Oahu would almost certainly have been destroyed. (The oil tank farms, submarine pens, and other vital facilities would also have taken a beating.) In view of such a dire prospect, would Nimitz have committed his remaining two carriers to the fray? Given the aggressive disposition he showed in earlier carrier battles it seems likely that he would have, even at the risk losing them. While he would have been even more heavily outnumbered in carriers than he was at Midway, he would have had much more support from land-based aircraft than he had in that battle. Moreover, he would have had an opportunity to exploit the same sort of problem that had bedeviled Nagumo at Midway: using carrier bombers and torpedo planes to attack land targets on Oahu while, at the same time, maintaining readiness to attack any American carriers that might show up.

Without war-gaming such a hypothetical carrier battle, let us assume that Nimitz would have found a way to exploit Nagumo's tactical dilemma and—with help from land-based bombers—would have managed to sink two or three Japanese carriers (let us say *Akagi, Hiryu,* and *Ryujo*), but would have ended up losing *Saratoga* and *Wasp.* In such a case, Nimitz would then have been completely bereft of any fleet carriers for the time being, while Yamamoto would still have two attack carriers and two light carriers. And when the battle was over Nagumo probably would have succeeded in destroying the oil tank farms, submarine pens, and repair docks of Pearl Harbor—along with most of the air power on Oahu. Japanese submarines could then be used to cordon off the islands to make resupplies of oil and dockyard equipment from the mainland very difficult and costly. Nimitz would probably have been forced to abandon Pearl Harbor and withdraw the Pacific Fleet to San Diego.[10]

The American army, however, almost certainly would have stayed to defend Oahu from invasion. It is possible that the Japanese could have made small-scale troop landings on the outer islands—perhaps even on the main island of Hawaii—but any attempt to get a foothold on Oahu would probably have been repelled. That strategic island, though stripped of most of its naval support facilities, would most likely have remained in American hands.

This hypothetical second Hawaii operation could have been completed by the end of September. Yamamoto's goal of eliminating the American carrier force from the Pacific in the first year of the war would finally have been achieved. Also, with American submarines having been forced to deploy all the way from the west coast of America—along with the elimination of most of the Allied land-based air power from the southwest Pacific—the vital sea lanes from the South Seas to Japan would have been made relatively secure. This would have achieved the major aim of the Japanese warlords in going to war with the United States in the first place: to acquire resources in the south—especially oil—to make Japan self-sufficient in natural resources. But a problem would have remained: what to do about the new carriers and other warships that America could deploy after the first year of war?

THE PANAMA CANAL

There would have been one major target left, one that gave America the ability to get new carriers from the shipyards of the east coast into the Pacific Ocean in a short time—the Panama Canal. As mentioned, the destruction of just one of its key locks would put it out of commission for at least a year, and require new ships from America's east coast (where all the *Essex*-class carriers were built) to make a long, treacherous voyage around the horn of South America. Although an attack on the Panama Canal would be an extremely hazardous operation, the two fast, long-ranged *Shokaku*-class carriers that Yamamoto still had—under our scenario—could probably have done the job.[11] Let us assume—in a worst-case scenario—that the canal was, indeed, knocked out before the end of 1942.

Had all this happened, by the end of 1942 Japan would have appeared invincible to the whole world, and America would have reached its lowest point since the Civil War. But the final "what if" is: would this have been enough to achieve the final goal of the Japanese warlords—to force America to abandon the war with Japan? Almost certainly not. At the end of 1942 the war in Europe was approaching a turning point: Anglo-American landings had been made in North Africa and were pushing Rommel's army back toward Tunis; a large German army was trapped at Stalingrad by the Red Army. As bad as things in the Pacific would have looked in Washington, D.C., Winston Churchill would no doubt have reminded the American people that Britain had gone through much worse and survived. At the end of that dark year, the Allies were beginning to get the upper hand against Germany, and Japan's turn would come in due course. This would not have been the time for America to throw in the towel in the Pacific.

THE GERMAN FACTOR

When the Japanese warlords decided in the autumn of 1941 to attack the United States, their hope that a quick destruction of the Pacific Fleet would force America to make a settlement was founded not just on that fact alone, but also on their assessment that Germany would win the war in Europe.[12] At that time, the German armies appeared to be routing the Soviet armies, and it was assumed that after a German victory on the Eastern Front, the British would surely succumb soon. This would leave America with no strong allies—and leave Japan with one very powerful one. In the face of such odds, it was expected, America would be compelled to gird itself for an assault from across the Atlantic and would lose the will to fight on in the Pacific. That was the not too-wishful thinking in Tokyo when the finishing touches were being made on the plan to attack Pearl Harbor.

Without venturing to speculate on what would have happened to America's war strategy had Germany won in Europe, it suffices to say that by the end of 1942 Germany was losing. Thus, Japan's warlords had made two fundamental miscalculations when they decided to go to war against the United States. The first is well known: underestimating the will of an enraged American public to fight to the end to avenge a "sneak attack" on Pearl Harbor—no matter how devastating an initial defeat. But the second miscalculation is less appreciated: the assumption that Germany would win the war in Europe.

On that point, curiously, the relationship between Germany's war in Europe —especially on the Eastern Front—and Japan's war in the Pacific does not appear to have been well thought out in Tokyo. We saw in chapter 2 that although Japan had entered into an alliance with Germany and Italy with the signing of the Tripartite Pact in September of 1940, Japan had effectively betrayed that alliance in April of 1941 by signing a nonaggression treaty with Germany's chief adversary in Europe, the Soviet Union. (This was just two months before Hitler's Operation Barbarossa was launched.) While the purpose of the pact with the Soviet Union was to free up Soviet pressure on the Manchurian border so that Japanese troops could be redeployed in the South Seas—Japan did not have enough army strength to fight in both areas simultaneously—this pact also freed Stalin to redeploy those crack divisions in the east to the Moscow front in the late autumn of 1941. This probably saved Moscow. It also probably cost Germany victory on the Eastern Front. And as a result, one of the premises for a Japanese victory over America in the Pacific—a German victory in Europe—was fatally undermined by the Japanese themselves just months before they went to war with the United States. This has to rank as one of the great ironies of World War II.

In any case, although the United States would have been in terrible shape in the Pacific at the end of 1942—her carriers gone and the rest of the fleet backed up to the west coast—things were finally looking much brighter in Europe. Even more hopeful, the first of the new *Essex*-class carriers was coming on line (*Essex* was commissioned the last day of the year), along with a new generation of battleships and carrier aircraft—and thousands of new carrier pilots. The conversion of America's industrial might into a colossal armaments foundry—that would soon outproduce the rest of the world combined—was now gaining a momentum that would have awed even the most doleful elements in the American government. There was now absolutely no chance that America would bail out of the Pacific.

THE NEW LONG ROAD TO
VICTORY OVER JAPAN

Though the war against Japan would surely have continued, in 1943 America would have faced a formidable challenge in the Pacific. A defeat at Midway would have set back the schedule for the advance across the Pacific by at least a year. Instead of Nimitz being able to attack Japanese strongholds in the Gilberts and Marshalls with his new carrier force in the fall of 1943, and instead of MacArthur's army pressing forward in New Guinea and the Solomons, America would have had to begin its thrust against the Japanese almost from its west coast. It would first have to secure Hawaii and restore Pearl Harbor as the principal naval base, and then evict the Japanese from Midway and the Aleutians. After that it would face the tougher task of opening up the supply lines to Australia, and to MacArthur's army, by retaking the island groups east of Australia—Fiji, Samoa, the New Hebrides, and New Caledonia. All of this, along with reopening the Panama Canal, would have to be done just to get America back to the position it was in the summer of 1942.

America would, however, have had powerful new naval forces with which to accomplish these tasks in the Pacific. By the summer of 1943, four *Essex*-class carriers were operational (*Essex, Yorktown* II, *Lexington* II, and *Bunker Hill*), along with three of the new *Independence*-class light carriers.[13] For battleship support, six modern fast battleships (two *North Carolina*-class and four *South Dakota*-class) would also be available. These new assets would probably have enabled America to achieve these preliminary goals by late fall of 1943, and by the end of the year, an invasion of New Guinea and the Solomon islands (including Guadalcanal) could have been underway. By the summer of 1944, the operational strength of the new carrier force would have been increased to ten *Essex*-class fleet carriers and nine *Independence*-class light carriers, and two *Iowa*-class super-battleships would join the six existing new battleships in support. By fall of 1944, America could have begun its assault on the main Japanese perimeter islands of the western Pacific, beginning with the Gilberts and Marshalls—about one year later than the actual schedule.

But all this would have been much more costly in blood and ship hulls than it was in the actual event. This is because in the meantime, under this scenario, the Japanese would have been able to build up substantially greater strength than they were actually able to do. Much more oil and other raw materials would have reached Japan. By spring of 1944, the Japanese would have managed to largely rebuild their own carrier fleet. Under our post-Midway scenario, Yamamoto would have lost about the same number of carriers in 1942 as he actually did (but with much more to show for it). The fleet attack carriers *Shokaku* and *Zuikaku* would probably have survived—along with the light carriers *Junyo* and *Zuiho*. In the fall of 1942 a sister of *Junyo* (*Hiyo*) and another light carrier (*Ryuho*) had come on line, and in 1943 the *Chitose* and *Chiyoda* were converted from seaplane carriers into light carriers.

More significantly, in the spring of 1944 *Taiho*—a 29,000-ton improved *Shokaku*-class carrier, but with an armored deck—would have joined the fleet (as it actually did) and would soon be followed by three improved *Hiryu*-class fleet carriers of the *Unryu* class, and the super-heavy *Shinano*—converted from a *Yamato*-class battleship hull. Three more carriers of the *Unryu* class had actually been launched, but work had been suspended in early 1945 because of shortages and disruptions caused by American bombing.[14] Without those impediments these carriers probably would have been completed by the end of 1944. In addition, two more *Taiho*-class carriers had been authorized, but not built because of shortages in resources. They most likely would have been built and come on line in 1945. But by summer of 1945 the Americans, on the other hand, would have deployed seventeen *Essex*-class carriers—each capable of carrying one hundred operational aircraft—along with nine *Independence*-class light carriers. Between the fall of 1942 and mid-1945, the Americans would have outbuilt the Japanese in carriers by twenty-six to fourteen—a ratio of almost two to one (but less than the three to one ratio they actually did).

However, the increased production of Japanese carriers and aircraft is not the only difference that the Americans would have faced under this scenario. Plentiful oil from the East Indies would have avoided the crippling shortage of aviation gasoline that actually occurred beginning in 1943. This would have enabled the Japanese to produce more and far better trained carrier pilots after 1942 to replace the losses of 1942 than they were actually able to do. Thus, any carrier battle in the summer of 1944 (probably in the Marshalls rather than in the Marianas closer to Japan) is unlikely to have been the "turkey shoot" that the American carrier pilots actually enjoyed in the Mariana campaign of June 1944.

In the thrust across the Pacific, the cost of America's losing the Battle of Midway gets even worse. Marine and army casualties would almost certainly have been much higher in taking the Japanese-held islands than in the actual event. In the actual Pacific campaigns, the Americans were able to win battles with relatively low casualties compared with those sustained in the European theater. Six months of fighting on Guadalcanal in 1942 cost only 1,600 dead. Even at Tarawa in November 1943—considered to have been the bloodiest battle in the Pacific in terms of casualties per day and per acre—only 1,000 marines lost their lives.[15] And in the costliest campaign of the Pacific—the battle for Okinawa in the spring of 1945—only 12,500 Americans were killed. While these numbers are horrific to those involved, they pale in comparison to the American casualties in the battles of the European theater. In total, less than 75,000 Americans died in combat in the Pacific, as against about 220,000 in Europe and the Mediterranean area.

Against a better equipped and better supplied Japanese army and navy, however, and in a much longer war in the Pacific, American casualties probably would have been several times heavier than they actually were—and this does not include the cost of invading the Japanese home islands, had that proved necessary. But, as we will see, the cost to the Japanese in this hypothetical prolonged war would also have been much greater than it actually was.

THE LAST CARRIER BATTLE

By the end of 1944, let us assume that the Gilbert and Marshall islands were finally taken—after much bloodier battles—along with the main islands of the Solomons—including Guadalcanal. Port Moresby would have been retaken, and MacArthur's army would have been advancing northwest through New Guinea—toward the Philippines. In the spring of 1945, the first assaults by air on the Mariana Islands probably would have been made—a year later than the actual schedule. Another big carrier battle is likely to have taken place. This is because the key islands in this group—Saipan, Tinian, and Guam—would be the first to be within bombing range of Japan by B-29 heavy bombers; they would have been defended with everything the Japanese could muster—as they actually were in 1944. However, the Americans would have had a two-to-one advantage in carriers and a three-to-one advantage in carrier aircraft (around 2,000 to 700). Although the Japanese carrier force would have been stronger than any the Americans actually faced, it still would have been overwhelmed. Let us suppose a decisive victory for the Americans (though at a cost of some *Essex*-class carriers): most of the Japanese carriers sent to the bottom of the ocean, and their carrier air power decimated—all this about one year behind the actual schedule.

After this last carrier battle, let us suppose that an amphibious landing would have taken place on Saipan—the most heavily defended island in the Marianas—in early summer of 1945. In the actual battle the summer of 1944, the Americans lost 3,000 killed in combat. In this bloodier and longer hypothetical battle a year later it is likely that the cost would have been closer to 10,000 dead. But Saipan would have been taken—let us assume by early August 1945.

GÖTTERDAMMERUNG

By midsummer of 1945 one can imagine that the American leadership would probably have faced a quandary in deciding what to do next. The war in Europe would be over. (Although after a defeat at Midway there might have been a reassessment of the "Germany first" policy, let us assume that it was decided to continue with it, and that Germany was defeated on schedule in May.) As of August 1945, it would have appeared that at least another year of savage fighting in the Pacific would be required to defeat Japan, and at a projected cost of hundreds of thousands of American casualties. On the other hand, America would have just acquired the atomic bomb—successfully tested on July 16—and it was clear that the awesome new weapon would revolutionize warfare. What to do with this new weapon? The answer might seem obvious: drop it on Japan and force her to surrender—as actually happened in August 1945.

It would not, however, have been that simple under the changed circumstances of our scenario. As of August 1945, America possessed only two bombs (one uranium and one plutonium) and would not yet have been within range of Japan to deliver them by air. Though Saipan would have been in American hands, it would still take several more months before the Japanese were evicted from the remaining islands in the Marianas. This would be necessary before the large airstrips required for B-29s could be safely constructed in these islands. And even if some way could have been devised to drop two atomic bombs on Japan right away, she would not yet have been prostrate as was the case in August 1945.

In fact, under this scenario, Japan's defensive war-fighting capability would have barely been dented, so it might have taken more than two atomic bombs to convince her government to throw in the towel. If the bombs were used prematurely, the American leadership could have been faced with a dire prospect: that Japan, after recovering from the initial shock of two—or even three—bombings by the fearsome new weapon, and after realizing that the Americans did not have sufficient stockpiles of them for further frequent bombings, would dig its heels in. (As it actually did in the spring of 1945, after conventional fire-bombing raids had done even more damage to Tokyo than the atomic bomb did to Hiroshima.)

So, would the American president (presumably Harry Truman) have waited until more atomic bombs were available? The test at Alamogordo, New Mexico, in July had proved that plutonium bombs would work. That type of atomic bomb could be produced at a much faster rate than Uranium-235 bombs.[16] Although the production details are still classified, let us suppose that plutonium bombs could have been made at a rate of at least one a month. It would have been projected that by spring of 1946, the Mariana Islands would be secure, along with Iwo Jima as a way station. With those islands then turned into airbases, large-scale B-29 bombing raids on Japanese cities could be staged by the next spring. So, Truman might well have postponed a decision on the use of atomic bombs until then.

But when the spring of 1946 arrived, it can be imagined that President Truman would have been presented with a dilemma far more gut-wrenching than he actually faced in August 1945: the destructiveness of large numbers of atomic bombs would be so horrible that there would be a risk of revulsion, not just by world opinion—such as it was in 1946—but perhaps even by the American public as well. (Efforts to keep the bombings secret for very long can be expected to fail.) On the other hand, if they were not used and American servicemen thereafter suffered heavy casualties invading the Japanese home islands, there would be outrage in America that a weapon that might have shortened the war was not used. In these circumstances it is not inconceivable that the president would have played for time.

A complicating factor in all of this would have been the Soviet Union. At the Yalta Conference in February 1945, Stalin had promised to enter the war against Japan three months after Germany surrendered. That pledge was reaffirmed at the Potsdam Conference in mid-July—at the time of the successful A-bomb test, of which Stalin was informed. In actual fact, the Soviet Union honored that pledge on August 8 by attacking Japanese forces in Manchuria. At that time—when Japan was actually on its knees, and it appeared that Japan would soon surrender without Soviet help—American policy makers were ambivalent about Soviet intervention in the Pacific. (And it had already been decided that American troops alone would occupy Japan.) Under our hypothetical scenario of a defensively stronger Japan, however, America is more likely to have welcomed Soviet participation in the invasion of Japan to lessen the burden on American troops.

In any case, by the spring of 1946 the Americans would have reclaimed the Philippines; the Soviets would probably have conquered Manchuria and Korea, and possibly even made landings on the northern Japanese islands. The Japanese navy would mostly be on the bottom of the ocean, and by the summer— even had the atomic bombs not yet been used—firebombing raids by thousands of B-29s would have reduced the centers of most large Japanese cities to ashes—as was the actual case a year earlier. America would have built up a stockpile of at least a dozen atomic bombs. Assuming that an ultimatum was then issued to Tokyo: surrender unconditionally or America would begin using atomic bombs on Japan (and the Soviets would invade her home islands)—what is the likely response?

There is, of course, no way of knowing. But what is likely is that in the summer of 1946 Japan would still have had more oil and other war-making materiel stockpiled than it actually had in August 1945 when Emperor Hirohito decided that enough was enough. Its victory at Midway would have given it over a year more time to get those resources up from the South Seas, and thus it would have been better able to fight on to defend its home islands. In these circumstances— without already having experienced the horror of nuclear weapons—it is not inconceivable that the Japanese government would have rejected the ultimatum. In such a case it seems likely that the American president would finally have felt compelled to use those new super-bombs. Instead of just two, possibly as many as twenty could have been dropped on Japan over the next month or so. All her major cities would have been reduced to rubble; millions of Japanese civilians would have perished.

By early autumn—with the Japanese government not knowing how many more atomic bombs America had, and with the Soviet army closing in on the main home island of Honshu from the northern island of Hokkaido—one would hope that the Japanese emperor would have decided that his people had suffered enough. (And decided that it was preferable to have the bulk of the home islands occupied by Americans than by Russians.) Thus, a bloody invasion of Japan by American troops might still have been averted.

The scenario for what might have happened had America lost the Battle of Midway need not be belabored further. In the end, Japan would still have been defeated, and justice served—though it probably would have taken over a year longer. However, it is almost certain that American casualties would have been several times higher than they actually were—making the Pacific War more costly for the Americans than the European theater had been. But the Japanese would also have been much worse off than they actually were: in addition to greater devastation of their cities, the home islands would have been occupied —and not just by the relatively benevolent Americans, but by the Soviets as well. Japan, almost certainly, would have been divided into zones as Germany had been, and likewise would have become a pawn in the Cold War still likely to follow. Its economy would have taken much longer to recover (for one thing, there probably would not have been a Korean War to give it a big boost, as the communists would have already controlled the entire Korean peninsula).

In a chronicle replete with ironies and paradoxes, the final irony is that Japan's defeat would almost certainly have been much more horrible had it won the Battle of Midway than it was having lost it. All in all, it is difficult to escape the conclusion that Japan was lucky to lose at Midway. Such are the vagaries of war.

APPENDIX A

NAGUMO'S OFFICIAL REPORT (EXCERPTS)

EXCERPTS FROM THE Office of Naval Intelligence translation of Vice Admiral Nagumo's official report on the Battle of Midway—"Mobile Force's Detailed Battle Report #6." The translation was published in June 1947 under the title "The Japanese Story of the Battle of Midway." (OPNAV P32–1002.)

The first 21 pages of the translation are reproduced here in their entirety, and verbatim (though some translator's notes are omitted.) Even the translator's typographical errors and inconsistencies in punctuation are preserved. There is, however, a change in format—made in the interests of readability due to the smaller pages of this book: the original double-columned text has been converted to conventional single-columned text so that a larger typeface can be used. This changes the pagination of the document, and also requires that footnotes be put in brackets where the original footnote numbers were, rather than at the bottom of the page. But, so that citations made in this book to the original document can be precisely located, the original pagination is inserted in brackets—and in bold face—where the original pages began.

The Japanese Story of the Battle of Midway

MILITARY SECRET
> *First Air Fleet* Secret #38 of 6.
> > 15 June 1942

(sent on 1 Feb)
(Seal of CinC First Air Fleet)
Copy #7 of 20

> *Mobile Force's* Detailed Battle Report #6.
> *First Air Fleet's* Detailed Battle Report #6.
> > Midway operation From 27 May to 9 June 1942.

Headquarters, First Air Fleet.

CINC FIRST AIR FLEET DETAILED BATTLE REPORT NO. 6

TABLE OF CONTENTS

PART I. EXISTING CONDITIONS AND TRENDS:
  1. General Situation of the Enemy.
  2. Situation in the Midway area.
  3. *Mobile Force* Commander's Estimate of the Situation.
PART II. PLANS:
  1. Fleet Organization and Composition immediately prior to Motivation of this Operation:
      (a) Organization.
      (b) Organization of Attack Units:
          (1) Attack on Midway.
          (2) First Attack on Enemy Carriers.
          (3) Second Attack on Enemy Carriers.
      (c) Organization of Reconnaissance Units.
  2. High Command's Operation Orders.
  3. Preparation for Operation.
  4. Outline of Movement of Commander and Men during the Period of Preparation for the Operation.
PART III. DESCRIPTION OF THE OPERATION:
  1. Direction of Operation by the Commander and his Movements.
  2. Outline of Developments (Excerpts).
  3. Actual Condition of the Enemy:
      (a) Actual Conditions in the Midway area.
      (b) Enemy Carriers.
      (c) Attacking planes of the Enemy.
  4. Conditions and Circumstances which Affected the Operation.
  5. Outstanding Events during the Operations:
      (a) Attack on Midway.
      (b) First Attack on Enemy Carriers.
      (c) Second Attack on Enemy Carriers.
      (d) Action of Cover Units.

      (e) Action of AA Units.

      (f) Enemy Action and Damages suffered by us.

  6. General Situation at Conclusion of Operations and the Commander's Estimate concerning it.

  7. Movement and Action Charts:

      Supplementary Table #1: Track Chart.

      Supplementary Table #2: Action Chart.

PART IV: ORDERS, REPORTS, ETC.:

  War Diary (Abbreviated). [*This part is missing from the document.—Ed.*]

[P. 2]

PART V: RESULTS:

  1. Attack on Midway:

      (a) Military Installations.

      (b) Aircraft.

  2. Attacks on Carriers.

  3. Action of Air Cover Units (Supplementary Tables 3 and 4).

  4. Action of AA Units (Supplementary Tables 3 and 4).

  5. Recapitulation of Results Obtained during Midway Operation.

  6. Damage Sustained:

      (a) Surface Vessels (Outline).

      (b) Aircraft (destroyed).

      (c) Personnel (killed).

PART VI: RECOGNITION OF MERITORIOUS ACTIONS.

PART VII: REFERENCE MATERIAL:

  1. Battle Lessons (Separate Volume).

  2. Weather Charts.

  3. *Mobile Force's* Operation Order #34.

SUPPLEMENT TO FIRST AIR FLEET SECRET FILE #37 OF 6.
MOBILE FORCE DETAILED BATTLE REPORT #6.
FIRST AIR FLEET DETAILED BATTLE REPORT #6.
OCCUPATION OF MIDWAY OPERATIONS, 27 MAY 1942–6 JUNE 1942.

PART I. EXISTING CONDITIONS AND TRENDS

1. *General Situation of the Enemy*

Because of developments during the First Phase Operations, the enemy's outposts which he had relied on to be his first line of defense, collapsed one after another until he began to feel direct threats even to such areas as India, Australia, and Hawaii. The enemy was exerting every pressure to stem this tide by stepping up his submarine strength in the waters controlled by us and by increasing his air strength in the Australian area. He employed these to carry on guerilla type tactics. Task force thrusts were also made in the Western and Southwestern Pacific.

These seemed to indicate that the enemy was planning on more positive actions than heretofore.

Subsequent to the beating he received in the Coral Sea on 7–8 May, the enemy was temporarily subdued, but by the end of May—by the time the Fleet was about to sortie from Hashera Jima—the enemy again began to show considerable life in all areas, particularly in the Australian area.

2. *Situation in the Midway Area*

Midway acts as a sentry for Hawaii. Its importance was further enhanced after the loss of Wake and it was apparent that the enemy was expediting the reinforcing of its defensive installations, its air base facilities, and other military installations as well as the personnel.

Estimate of existing conditions there were as follows:

(a) Air strength:

    Recco. Flying Boats --------------2 squadrons.
    Army Bombers -------------------1 squadron.
    Fighters------------------------1 squadron.

The above estimated strength could be doubled in an emergency.

(b) Strict Air Patrols were maintained both day and night to the West to a distance of about 600 miles. About three fighters covered the Island at all times.

(c) Some surface vessels patrolled the area and some submarines were active to the West.

(d) Of the enemy's carriers, the *Ranger* was apparently in the Atlantic. According to some prisoners' statements, the *Lexington* had been sunk. There were others, however, who claimed that she was under repair on the West Coast.

(e) The *Enterprise* and the *Hornet* were definitely placed in the Pacific, but we could get no reliable information as the whereabouts of the *Wasp*.

(f) About six auxiliary carriers had been completed and there were indications that about half of this number were in the Pacific. However, they were known to be inferior in speed and could not be effectively employed for positive action.

[P. 3]

(g) Air strength in the Hawaii area was estimated to be as follows:

    Flying Boats --------------------About 60.
    Bombers ------------------------About 100.
    Fighters -----------------------About 200.

These could be used for the speedy reinforcement of Midway.

(h) Enemy surface units in the Hawaii area were estimated to be in about the strength noted below. It was likely that these units could sortie in the event of an attack on Midway.

    Aircraft Carriers-------------------2 to 3.
    Special Carriers-------------------2 to 3.
    Battleships-----------------------2.
    Type A Cruisers ------------------4 to 5.
    Type B Cruisers ------------------3 to 4.
    Light Cruisers--------------------4.
    Destroyers----------------------About 30.
    Submarines---------------------25.

(i) Shore Defense Installations on Midway

Large numbers of various types of level and high angle large caliber guns as well as high angle machine guns had been installed. Marines had also been landed and all in all, the island was very strongly defended.

3. *Mobile Force Commander's Estimate of the Situation*

(a) Although the enemy lacks the will to fight, it is likely that he will counter attack if our occupation operations progress satisfactorily.

(b) The enemy conducts air reconnaissance mainly to the West and to the South but does not maintain a strict vigil to the Northwest or to the North.

(c) The enemy's patrol radius is about 500 miles.

(d) The enemy is not aware of our plans. (We were not discovered until early in the morning of the 5th at the earliest.)

(e) It is not believed that the enemy has any powerful unit, with carriers as its nucleus, in the vicinity.

(f) After attacking Midway by air and destroying the enemy's shore based air strength to facilitate our landing operations, we would still be able to destroy any enemy task force which may choose to counter attack.

(g) The enemy's attempt to counter attack with use of shore based aircraft could be neutralized by our cover fighters and AA fire.

PART II. PLANS

1. *Fleet Organization and Composition Immediately Prior to Motivation of the Operation.*

(a) **Organization:**

Tactical organization		Commander	Composition	Duties
Air Attack Force		CinC *1st Air Fleet*	1st Air Fleet (less 4Sf, 5Sf, 10S)[1]	To attack and destroy enemy fleet, support Occupation force
Supporting Force		Comdr. CruDiv. 8	CruDiv 8, 2nd section of BatDiv 3	To destroy enemy fleet; Cover Air Attack Force
Screening Unit		Comdr. DesRon 10	DesRon 10 (less Desdiv 7), DesDiv. 4	Screen; to destroy enemy fleet
Supply Force	1st Supply Unit Group	Comdr. Sp. Service Ship *Kyokuto Maru*	*Kyokuto M*[2] *(1)*, *Shin Koku M (2)*, *Toho M (3)*, *Nippon M (4)*, *Kokuyo M (5)*	Supply
	2nd Supply Unit Group	Under Direct Command	Nichiro M (9), #2 Kyoei M(10), Hoko M (11)	Duty
Reserve Unit		Comdr. CaDiv 5	CarDiv 5	Maintenance; Training. *Zuikaku* to prepare for Third-Phase Operations

[1] 4Sf is CarDiv 4. 5Sf is Cardiv 5. 10S is DesRon 10.
[2] M is *Maru*.

[P. 4]
(b) Organization of Attack Units:

(1) Attack on Midway

Composition [Organization No. 5]			Command			Number of Aircraft[1]	Notes
First Wave	Second Group	Third Attack Unit	Direct Command	Air Officer *Hiryu*	Div. Comdr. *Soryu*	F^o × 18 plane	1 torpedo from *Hiryu* returned due to engine trouble.
		Fourth Attack Unit				F^o × 18	
Second Wave	Fifth Group	11th Attack Unit	Div. Comdr. *Kaga*	Div. Comdr. *Kaga*	Div. Comdr. *Akagi*	F^b × 18	
		12th Attack Unit				F^b × 18	
Third Wave	Eighth Group	1st Air Control Unit	Div. Comdr. *Soryu*	Div. Comdr. *Akagi*		F^e × 9	[Strike Group led by Air Officer *Hiryu*]
		2nd Air Control Unit		Div. Comdr. *Kaga*		F^e × 9	
	Ninth Group	3rd Air Control Unit		Div. Comdr. *Soryu*		F^e × 9	
		4th Air Control Unit		Div. Comdr. *Hiryu*		F^e × 9	

[1] F^o is attack plane; F^b is bomber; F^e is fighter.

(2) First Attack on Enemy Carriers

Organization	Commander	Number of Aircraft	Notes
14th Attack Unit	*Hiryu* Division Comdr.	F^b × 18	2 planes of the Air Control Unit encountered and destroyed enemy torpedo planes en route, and did not join in the attack.
4th Air Control Unit	*Hiryu* Division Comdr.	F^e × 6	

(3) *Second Attack on Enemy Carriers*

Organization	Commander	Number of Planes	Notes
4th Attack Unit	Air Officer *Hiryu*	F° × 9	*Akagi*'s attack planes failed to use their torpedoes and brought them back.
Akagi Attack Planes	Warrant Officer *Nishimori*	F° × 1	
4th Air Control Unit	Division Comdr. *Hiryu*	Fᵉ × 4	
Kaga Air Control Unit	A Yamamoto	Fᵉ × 2	

[P. 5]

(c) Organization of Reconnaissance Units (see Supplementary Table):

Organization	Search Line No.	Ship	Plane Type	Number	Commander	Notes
Recco Unit[1]	1	*Akagi*	Type 97, ship based attack.	1	Commander of respective planes.	1. Take offs from *Tone* were greatly delayed. 2. Due to bad weather, *Chikuma*'s #6 *Search* line returned at 0335.
	2	*Kaga*	Type 97, ship based attack.	1		
	3	*Tone*	Type-0 Float	1		
	4		Recco	1		
	5	*Chikuma*	Type-0 Float	1		
	6		Recco	1		
	7	*Haruna*	Type-95 Float Recco	1		

[1] Other reccos were carried out by type 13 experimental ship based bombers from CruDiv 8 and 2d Div. Of BatDiv 3.

2. *High Command's Operation Orders*

(a) Secret *Combined Fleet* OpOrd #12. *Combined Fleet's* Second Phase Operation Order.

(b) Secret *Combined Fleet* OpOrd #13. Communication plans of *Combined Fleet* for Second Phase Operation.

(c) Secret *Combined Fleet* OpOrd #14. Coordination of Movements of Various Forces involved in the MI (Midway) and AL (Aleutians) Operations.

3. *Preparations for the Operation*

Upon their return to home ports on 22 and 23 April, the ships immediately underwent repair and maintenance operations.

From the latter part of April, the carrier planes engaged in training at Kagoshima (*Akagi*), Kanoya (*Kaga*), Tomitaka (*Hiryu*), Kasanohara (*Soryu*), and Iwakuni (bomber leaders).

Float plane training was conducted at Kagoshima from 6 May.

Although the flight training program was conducted without any major incident, since there had been a considerable turn-over in personnel, practically no one got beyond the point of basic training. Inexperienced fliers barely got to the point where they could make daytime landings on carriers. It was found that even some of the more seasoned fliers had lost some of their skill. No opportunity was available to carry out joint training, which, of course made impossible any coordinated action between contact units, illumination units, and attack units. The likelihood of obtaining any satisfactory results from night attacks, therefore, was practically nil.

(a) Torpedo Attacks:

During the middle part of May, mock torpedo attacks were carried out, with judges from the Yokosuka Air Group acting as referees. The records during these tests were so disappointing that some were moved to comment that is was almost a mystery how men with such poor ability could have obtained such brilliant results as they had in the Coral Sea.

On 18 May, actual tests were made against CruDiv 8 traveling at high speed. In spite of the fact that the speed was 30 knots with only 45-degree turns, the records made by the fliers were again exceedingly poor. With water depth at 40 to 50 meters, about a third of the torpedoes were lost.

(b) Level bombing:

Bomber leaders were concentrated at Iwakuni and practiced level bombing using the *Settsu* as a target ship. The men attained a fair degree of skill, but they had no opportunity participate in any formation bombing drills.

(c) Dive Bombing:

Since the *Settsu* was limited to the waters in the vicinity of Naikai Seibu (Western Inland Sea) valuable time was wasted by the fliers in coming and going. The men could not participate in more than one dive bombing drill a day without seriously interfering with their basic training. Even this minimum practice could not be conducted satisfactorily because the men were kept busy with maintenance work.

[P. 6]

(d) Air Combat:

Men engaged in this phase were able to get no further than to actual firing and basic training for lone air combat operations. The more experienced were employed in formation air combat tactics, but even they were limited to about a three-plane formation.

(e) Landing:

Since the carriers were undergoing repair and maintenance operations, the only available ship for take-off and landing drills was the *Kaga*. She was kept busy from early morning to nightfall but even at that the young fliers barely were able to learn the rudiments of carrier landings. The more seasoned fliers were given about one chance each to make dusk landings.

(f) Night flying:

Insofar as the weather permitted, men were trained in this phase every day. Due to maintenance needs and because of the limited time, only the very fundamentals were learned by the inexperienced flyers.

Because of the need for replacements and transfers of personnel, the combat efficiency of each ship had been greatly lowered. Moreover, since most of the ships were undergoing maintenance and repair work until only a few days before departure, the men's efficiency suffered greatly.

Training in group formations would not be satisfactorily conducted because of the limitation in time. This was particularly true of the newly formed DesRon 10. Some of the units in it underwent training as anti-air-screening ships, while others were assigned antisub duties. The squadron as a whole never had the opportunity to carry out joint drills.

That was the situation as far as fleet training was concerned. Added to this, we had practically no intelligence concerning the enemy. We never knew to the end where or how many enemy carriers there were. In other words, we participated in this operation with meager training and without knowing the enemy.

4. *Outline of Movements of Commander and Men During the Period of Preparation for the Operation*

Since the *Akagi* was undergoing repairs, the Flag was transferred to the *Kaga* during the early part of May after instructions session with the *Combined Fleet* had been completed. The Flag was moved back to the *Akagi* during the middle of the month upon her return to Hashira Anchorage.

Because the *Soryu* was undergoing repairs, the Flag CarDiv 2 was transferred to the *Hiryu* at Sasebo during early May. Later the latter ship was permanently assigned as Flagship.

During the early part of May, CruDiv 8 assembled at Hashira Jima, and then in order DesRon 10, CarDiv 1, CarDiv 2, and the second section of Batdiv 3 arrived at the same anchorage. It was not until only a few days before the force was scheduled to sortie during the latter part of May, that all units were assembled.

On 24 May aircraft were taken aboard and on the 26th operation plans were agreed upon. At 0600 27 May the force departed for its operations area.

During this entire time, I [Admiral Nagumo] was at Naikai Seibu (Western Inland Sea), directing training operations and attempting to coordinate intelligence.

PART III. DESCRIPTION OF THE OPERATION

1. *Direction of Operation by the Commander and his Movements*

The *Mobile Force* departed Hashira Jima at 0600 17 May. Maintaining strict anti-sub screen and a rigid radio silence, the force headed for the area to the northwest of Midway following course 1 as given in *Mobile Force* Secret OpOrd 35.

On 1 and 2 June, all ships were refueled. [These Japanese dates of course would be reckoned as 31 May and 1 June in U. S. reports. It should be noted that all dates in this report and all times are in Tokyo time, plus 9.]

Visibility steadily decreased from about 1000 2 June so that by 2300 on the 3d, all ships were being navigated blindly. No visual signals could be employed during this period. Since there seemed little likelihood of the fog's lifting, the radio was used as a last resort at 1030 on the 3d (long wave) to give change of course.

Shortly after this, the fog lifted somewhat, making visual signals barely possible. By the morning of the 4th visibility on the surface improved greatly, but there were scattered clouds overhead.

At 1640 the *Tone* reported sighting about 10 enemy planes bearing 260 degrees. Three fighters immediately took off from the *Akagi* in pursuit of these but they were unable to sight the enemy. There is some element of doubt in the reported sighting.

At about 2330 on the same day, the *Akagi* twice sighted what was thought to be enemy planes
[P. 7]
weaving in and out of the clouds. All hands were immediately ordered to battle stations. There is considerable doubt as the reliability of this sighting.

At 0130 on the 5th [0430 June 4th by U. S. reckoning], under command of flight officer of the *Hiryu*, Lieut. Tomonaga, Organization #5 composed of 36 ship-based fighters, 36 ship-based bombers, and 36 ship-based torpedo planes, took off to attack Midway.

Between 0130 and 0200, 1 ship-based torpedo plane each from *Akagi* and *Kaga*, 2 Type 0 Float Recco each from *Tone* and *Chikuma* (distance 300 miles, to the left 60 miles) and 1 Type-95 Float Recco from the *Haruna* (distance 150 miles, to the left 40 miles), took off in search of enemy task forces to the South and to the East.

From about 0230, two to three enemy flying boats maintained continuous contact with us.

Shortly after taking off, the attack unit was contacted by enemy flying boats. When about 30 miles short of the target on Midway, the above mentioned flying boats suddenly dropped illumination bombs over our attack plane units to attract overhead cover fighters.

Thereafter, while engaging in bitter air combats, bombs were dropped on military installations on Midway between about 0345 and 0410. Fires resulted. All but 2 ship-based fighters, 1 ship-based bomber and 3 ship-based torpedo planes returned to their carriers by about 0600.

After our attack unit had taken off, enemy flying boats maintained contact with us. At about 0400 the first enemy wave attacked. From then until about 0730, the enemy attacked almost continuously. We counter attacked with fighters and AA fire and were able to bring most of the attackers down by 0645. About 30 carrier-based bombers then attacked us resulting in fires aboard the *Akagi*, *Kaga* and *Soryu*, forcing them to fall behind and leaving only the *Hiryu* untouched.

Prior to this and subsequent to the take off of the initial attack unit, the fleet had Organization Number 4 (ship-based torpedo planes) stand by in readiness to act against any enemy surface vessels. however, at 0415, the command plane of the *Hiryu* radioed that:

"There is a necessity for carrying out a second attack (0400)."

It was decided, therefore, that a second attack would be directed against Midway. Orders were issued for the ship-based attack planes to remove their torpedoes and replace them with #80 land bombs.

At about 0500, *Tone's* #4 plane reported:

"Sighted what appears to be the enemy composed of 10 (ships), bearing 10 degrees, distance 240 miles from Midway, on course 150 degrees, speed 20 knots (0428)."

Two subsequent reports concerning the weather (0440) and the enemy's course and speed (0455) were received but since we had not been advised of details, the plane was ordered to:

"Advise ship types."

At 0530, *Tone's* plane reported:

"The enemy is accompanied by what appears to be a carrier in a position to the rear of the others (0520)."

and again at about 0540:

"Sight what appears to be 2 cruisers in position bearing 8 degrees, distance 250 miles from Midway; course, 150 degrees; speed 20 knots (0530)."

Thus, it was definitely established that enemy carriers were operating in the vicinity. The following dispatch was, therefore, sent to CinC *Combined Fleet*:

"(Info: CinC 2nd Fleet) At 0500, the enemy composed of 1 carrier, 5 cruisers and 5 destroyers, was sighted in position bearing 10 degrees, distance 240 miles from Midway. We are heading for it."

Under orders issued at 0415, the ship-based attack planes were already being re-equipped with #80 land bombs which made immediate take-offs of the ship-based attack planes in Organization Number 4, impossible. It was therefore decided that we would await the return of the Midway attack unit and then carry out a grand scale air attack. The Fleet was advised as follows:

"After taking on the returning planes, we shall proceed north to contact and destroy the enemy task force."

This was sent at 0605.

In reply to this CarDiv 1 advised that its ship-based attack planes (torpedo equipped) would be ready for the take-off at 0730 and CarDiv 2 that its ship-based attack planes (to be equipped with torpedoes upon their return from the first attack), would be ready for the take-off by from 0730 to 0800. Subsequent to this, every effort was made to expedite completing preparations for the take-off of Organization Number 4. (*Akagi:* 3 ship-based fighters; 18 ship-based attack planes. *Kaga:* 3 ship-based fighters; 27 ship-based attack planes. *Hiryu:* 3 ship-based fighters; 18 ship-based bombers. *Soryu:* 3 ship-based fighters; 18 ship-based bombers).
[P. 8]

While we were engaged in this, the enemy struck. Communication facilities were knocked out of all damaged ships. There was little likelihood of the fires being extinguished in the immediate future. For these reasons, I decided to direct the operations from *Nagara*, and transferred to her at 0830.

After our ships had been damaged, the commander of CarDiv 2 decided to carry out the attack against the enemy carrier sighted by *Tone's* float recco plane. At 0758, *Hiryu's* attack unit (6 fighters and 18 bombers) took off and carried out the attack. Direct hits by 5 #25 ordinary and 1 land bombs were scored on an *Enterprise* class carrier, inflicting serious damage to her (possibly sinking her).

Prior to this, at 0530, a type 13 experimental ship-based bomber from the *Soryu* was ordered to maintain contact with the enemy carrier but due to breakdown in radio facilities, it was not known until the return of this plane that, in addition to the aforementioned, there was a task force which had as its nucleus a carrier of the *Enterprise* class and another of the *Hornet* class. This task force was operating in waters to the north of the other one.

With this information at hand, the *Hiryu* attack unit (4 fighters and 9 torpedo planes, supplemented by 2 fighters from the *Kaga* and 1 torpedo plane from the *Akagi*) was ordered to the attack. Three torpedo hits were scored on a carrier of the *Enterprise* class, seriously damaging her. Heavy damages were also inflicted on a heavy cruiser of the *San Francisco* class.

NOTES

Report of Chikuma's recco plane at 1413, 5[th:]

(a) Sighted an enemy carrier of the *Enterprise* class listing and stopped in position 30–15N, 176–50W. (No evidence of fire. No damage to flight deck.) Three cruisers and 5 destroyers were in the vicinity. At about 1420, leaving the carrier on the scene, the others proceeded eastward on course 80 degrees, speed 20 knots.

(b) Sighted 2 enemy carriers (*Yorktown* or *Hornet* class) at 1510, in position 30–23N, 176–05W. Each was being directly escorted by 2 cruisers and 4 destroyers. Distance between the two groups, 3 miles; course 270 degrees; speed 12 knots.

(c) Two other carriers (class undetermined) escorted by 5 cruisers and 6 destroyers sighted at 1516 in a position about 4 miles to the south of the others. Course 260 degrees, speed 12 knots.

(d) Since the above sightings were made by the #2 plane while it was proceeding southward on a course of about 180 degrees from about 1500, and were seen one after another along this line, there is no chance of duplication. [There was duplication, nevertheless. The carriers sighted, of course, were *Enterprise* and *Hornet*.] Moreover, sightings described in (b) and (c) above, were from below cloud level, or at about 300 meters altitude.

Judging from these reports, it seemed probable that the carrier damaged by torpedoes remained adrift until the following morning.

Subsequent searches failed to locate the carrier damaged by 5 ordinary bombs and 1 land bomb.

From these evidences, it was possible to estimate that one carrier was sunk by bombing while another was seriously damaged by torpedoes. The damaged carrier was sunk the following day by submarine torpedoes.

The three attacks resulted in the loss of most of *Hiryu's* attack unit. At 1240, she only had 6 fighters, 5 bombers, and 4 torpedo planes left. Contact was maintained, however, with *Soryu's* Type 13 experimental ship-based bomber (the plane which was ordered to the *Hiryu* because of fire on board the *Soryu* after returning from reconnaissance). Preparations were pressed for a fourth attack, aimed at the destruction of the *Hornet* class carrier.

During this time, the *Hiryu* had the planes of her air cover maintain constant cover. At 1403, at the very moment when a type 13 experimental ship-based bomber was about to take off, the *Hiryu* was subjected to dive bombing attacks from 13 enemy ship-based bombers. The *Hiryu*, also, broke out in flames.

Damages to our carriers up to this time were as follows:

(a) AKAGI

The enemy attack unit which carried out a sustained attack from about 0400 was almost totally destroyed by friendly cover fighters. Up to 0650, our surface units had suffered practically no damage and the skies were clear of enemy planes.

At 0700, the second wave struck. Fourteen enemy torpedo planes, splitting into two groups approached from the northwest. One group carried out a torpedo attack against the *Kaga* and was followed up with several planes dive-bombing her.

At 0706, enemy torpedo planes were sighted bearing 118 degrees. To minimize the target area, the *Akagi* turned to course 300 degrees and stayed on this course. At a time when all of our surface

[P. 9]

units had maneuvered themselves into maximum defense against the torpedo planes, enemy dive bombers were suddenly noted among the clouds overhead at 0726. Resorting to evasive tactics, every effort was made to avoid the bombs, but one direct hit was sustained on the aft rim of the lift amidship and another on the rear guard of the port flight deck. (Neither were fatal hits.)

Since the *Akagi* was at the time preparing to carry out the second attack, the fire spread over the entire hangar area and with induced explosions, the fire gradually moved from the aft quarters, forward with great intensity, spreading even to the immediate vicinity of the bridge.

Ammunition rooms were immediately ordered flooded, and all hands were ordered to fire-fighting stations. The pump system aboard, however, failed to function and it became apparent that the fire would not be extinguishable in the immediate future. The headquarters, therefore, was moved to the *Nagara* at 0746. Subsequent to this, every effort was made to bring the fire under control but it became increasingly evident that there would be little hope of success.

At 1038, the Emperor's portrait was transferred to the destroyer *Nowake*. By 1620, the situation was deemed hopeless, and the captain of the *Akagi* decided to order all hands to abandon ship. A report to that effect was made to the commander of the *Mobile Force* and the order was issued at 1625. Personnel began transferring to the destroyers *Arashi* and *Nowake* at 1700. At 1925 CinC *Combined Fleet* ordered: "Delay disposition." While standing by awaiting further orders, CinC *Combined Fleet* ordered: "Dispose," at 0150 on the 6th. In accordance with this order, the ship was scuttled at 0200, in position 30–30N, 178–40W.

(b) KAGA

Against enemy torpedo plane attacks which were carried out after 0400, AA fire and evasive action proved completely successful. While still engaged in evasive action at about 0715 against the persistent enemy torpedo planes, 9 enemy dive bombers were suddenly sighted among the clouds at 0722. Every effort was made to counter these through evasive action and AA fire cover. These efforts were successful against the first, second, and third bombs, but #4 hit starboard, aft, while #7 was a direct hit in the vicinity of the forward elevator. Glass on the bridge was shattered and because of the smoke from the bombs, visibility from that point was reduced to zero. The captain ordered emergency steering apparatus put in operation. Bomb #8 hit in the vicinity of the forward elevator. Practically nothing of the bridge remained after this hit. All persons who were on the bridge at the time, including the captain, were killed in action. Bomb #9 also hit amidship. Fire-fighting was conducted under the direction of the air officer, but since there seemed to be little hope of getting the fire under control, the Emperor's portrait was transferred to the *Hagikaze* at 1025. The situation became hopeless by 1340 and all hands were ordered to abandon ship. They were transferred to the destroyers *Hagikaze* and *Maikaze*. The fire on board spread to both the forward and aft fuel tanks by 1625, causing two great explosions and the ship's sinking. Position of *Kaga's* sinking: 30–20.3N, 179–17.2W.

(c) HIRYU

Fire broke out as a result of dive-bombing attacks by 13 enemy dive bombers at 1403. From then until 1803 she resorted to evasive action under battle speed #1, while efforts were made to escape from the battle area and to fight fires. The flames could not be brought under control, however, and the fires killed one man after another in the engine rooms until further operation of the ship became impossible. Telephone communications with the engine rooms were maintained until the last. The manner in which the engine room personnel from Engineer Commander Kunizo Aimune down to the last man, carried on in the face of death which finally overtook them, can only be described as heroic.

The ship's list, due to shipping water, constantly increased to about 15 degrees.

At 2058, it seemed as if the fires might be brought under control, but at that time there was another induced explosion and the fierce fires were rekindled. It became evident that further fire-fighting operations were useless and all hands were ordered to prepare to abandon ship at 2330. At 2350 Captain Tomeo Kaki and Squadron Commander Rear-Admiral Tamon Yamaguchi delivered messages to the crew. This was followed by expressions of reverence and respect to the Emperor, the shouting of Banzai's, the lowering of the battle flag and command flag. At 0015, all hands were ordered to abandon ship, His Imperial Highness' portrait removed, and the transfer of personnel to the destroyers *Kazagumo* and *Makigumo* put under way. The transfer of portrait and men was completed at 0130.
[P. 10]

After completion of the transfer operations, the Division Commander and Captain remained aboard ship. They waved their caps to their men and with complete composure joined their fate with that of their ship.

At 0210 the *Hiryu* was scuttled by torpedo (1) from the *Makigumo*. Position of *Hiryu's* scuttling: 31–27.5N, 179–23.5W.

(d) SORYU

The *Soryu* was attacked by 13 dive bombers from 0725. Three hits were scored on her at 0725, 0726 and 0728. By 0730, the fires quickly spread and caused induced explosions from the bomb-storage room, torpedo-storage room, AA and machine-gun-ammunition rooms as well as from gasoline tanks. Fires enveloped the entire ship in no time. By 0740 both engines had stopped. At 0743, attempts were made to steer her, but with the entire ship in flames, she was helpless. "Abandon ship" was ordered at 0745.

While most of the officers and men, including the Executive officer, had congregated on deck, having been forced to leave their posts due to the flames, a terrific explosion occurred. The explosion sent them flying into the water.

Every effort was made to pick these men up and put them on the forward deck. Medical aid was given to those needing it there. Transfers to the destroyers *Hamakaze* and *Isonami* were completed at about 1600.

As soon as the fires broke out aboard ship, the captain, Ryusaku Yanagimoto, appeared on the signal tower to the starboard of the bridge. He took command from this post and pleaded that his men seek shelter and safety. He would allow no man to approach him. Flames surrounded him but he refused to give up his post. He was shouting "Banzai" over and over again when heroic death overtook him.

Fires died down somewhat by about 1600, and the air officer who was the acting commander, organized fire fighters with the intention of reboarding the ship. However, the ship sank at 1613 and there was a great underwater explosion at 1620. Position: 30–42.5N, 178–37.5W.

At 0828, after the headquarters had been transferred to the *Nagara*, a plane from the *Chikuma* reported: "The enemy is in a position bearing 70 degrees, distance 90 miles from us (0810)." It was decided that the enemy would be destroyed in a daytime attack. Therefore, the following order was issued at 0853: "We are now going to attack. Assemble." At 0900, our course was set at 60 degrees, speed 16 knots; at 0945, course 0 degrees, speed 20 knots; 1000, speed 24 knots.

At 1045, the enemy changed its course to 90 degrees and the opportunity for battle seemed to be close at hand. Somewhat later, *Tone's* #4 plane reported: "The enemy is in a position bearing 114 degrees, distance 110 miles from my position of 1230." From this it became evident that the enemy was trying to put distance between himself and us.

It was deemed that if under these conditions, the enemy chose to strike, we would be at a distinct disadvantage in that we would be unable to carry out a decisive battle.

We, therefore, turned about and proceeded westward, with the expectation of destroying the enemy in a night encounter.

Prior to this, at 1120, the following order was issued to the *Second Mobile Force*:

"The *First Mobile Force* is in (grid) position TO E WO 33 at 1100, 5th. After destroying enemy striking force to the east, we plan to proceed northward. The *Second Mobile Force* will rendezvous with us as soon as possible. Our (grid) position at 1130 will be: YU YU KE 44, on course 285, speed 24 knots. Plan to rendezvous with *Landing Force* at 1600."

While thus laying plans for a night attack, the *Hiryu* also broke out in flames at 1405. That meant that while all four of our carriers had been lost, the enemy had at least one. Moreover, as long as we were in the operational radius of their shore-based air, we would be at a very distinct disadvantage.

By 1433, the enemy began to retreat to the east on course 70, speed 20 knots, which further reduced our hopes for a night engagement. However, we still were determined to carry it out. *Nagara's* plane was ordered to prepare for a take-off and all the ships were ordered to assemble in the vicinity of the *Nagara*. At 1450, CinC *Second Fleet*, issued the orders for the night battle.

At 1530, the commander of DesDiv 4 ordered the destroyers under his command to stand by the various carriers assigned to them and to protect them from enemy submarines and task forces.

At about this time the commander of the *Chikuma* made the following report: "This ship's #2 plane reports that at about 1530 he sighted 4 enemy carriers, 6 cruisers and 15 destroyers proceeding westward in a position about 30 miles east of the listing and burning enemy carrier."

[P. 11]

This was the first inkling we had of the overwhelming superiority of the enemy's carrier strength. Since we were not able to maintain contact with this task force after sundown, our hopes of a successful night engagement were further reduced.

At 1615, the following order was received from CinC *Combined Fleet*:

"*Combined Fleet* Secret Despatch #298.

"*Combined Fleet* DesOpOrd #158:

"1. The enemy task force has retired to the east. Its carrier strength has practically been destroyed.

"2. The *Combined Fleet* units in that area, plan to overtake and destroy this enemy, and, at the same time, occupy AF (Midway).

"3. The Main Body was in position (grid) FU ME RI 32 at 0000, 6th. Course 90 degrees, speed 20 knots.

"4. The *Mobile Force, Occupation Force* (less CruDiv 7) and *Advance Force* [Submarine] will contact and destroy the enemy as soon as possible."

It was evident that the above message was sent as a result of an erroneous estimate of the enemy, for he still had 4 carriers in operational condition and his shore-based air on Midway was active. Therefore, the following message was sent:

"*Mobile Force* Secret despatch #560.

"Enemy has a total of 5 carriers, 6 cruisers, and 15 destroyers which are proceeding west from the vicinity of (grid) position TO SU WA 15 (at 1530). While offering protection to the *Hiryu* we are retiring northwestward. Speed 18 knots. 1830 (grid) position: FU N RE 55."

Although we had already reported the existing situation, we again sent the following despatch at 1950:

"Re *Combined Fleet* DesOpOrd #158.

"The enemy still has 4 carriers (may include special type carriers), 6 cruisers, and 15 destroyers which are at present proceeding westward. All the carriers of our force have become inoperational. We plan to contact the enemy with float reconnaissance planes tomorrow morning."

A follow-up message reading: "*Mobile Force* Secret despatch #562. Re *Mobile Force* Secret Despatch #561: 2 of the carriers involved are of the *Hornet* class, speed 24 knots. Type of the other two are unknown," was sent.

We were not in contact with the enemy at that time and our destroyers had been assigned to the damaged carriers. Moreover, the enemy was approximately 100 miles away which made a night engagement by us almost out of the question. Every effort, instead, was made to save the *Hiryu*.

At 2040, the following order was received from Com*Occupation Force*:

"*Second Fleet* Secret Despatch #761.

"1. The support for the *Occupation Force* reached position (grid) TO E WA 12 at 0000, 6th. We plan to carry out searches to the east and to participate in the night attack described in *Mobile Force's* Secret Despatch #560.

"2. The *Mobile Force* (excepting the *Hiryu*, *Akagi*, and their respective escorts), will immediately turn about and participate in the *Occupation Force's* night engagement."

While complying with the orders issued by the *Combined Fleet* and the *Second Fleet*, orders were received from the *Combined Fleet* to rendezvous, which were complied with.

The following was received from the *Combined Fleet* at 0430, 6th:

"*Combined Fleet's* Secret Despatch #310.

"Has the *Hiryu* sunk? Advise situation and position."

So, it became evident that the *Hiryu's* sinking was not as yet certain to CinC *Combined Fleet*. Moreover, a friendly plane reported that the *Hiryu* was still afloat. Therefore, a plane from the *Nagara* was sent out in search for her and at the same time the destroyer *Tanikaze* was despatched to dispose of her. Neither could sight the target, so it was assumed that she had sunk.

From about 1500, 6th, the *Tanikaze* was subjected to attacks from about 50 enemy planes. She fought well without any support from any other units, and managed to down 4 of the enemy planes.

The carrier of the *Yorktown* type which had been hurt by our efforts (apparently no damage had been inflicted on her flight deck) was definitely sunk by subsequent submarine action.

2. *Outline of Events* (Excerpts).

3 June

0000	Course, 70; speed, 9.
1030	Despatch from Comdr. *Mobile Force* to *Mobile Force* (radio): "Course, 125."
1200	Refuelling of DesRon 10 begun.
1250	Fog gradually lifts.
1330	Course, 130. Position: 37–1.5N, 171–7.0E.
1350	Fog bank.
1530	Message by signal from Comdr. *Mobile Force* to *Mobile Force*: "*Mobile Force* SigOrd #97. Method one will be employed in

[P. 12]

the attack on the 5th. There will seven search lines: #1, 181 degrees, *Akagi*; #2, 158 degrees, *Kaga*; #3, 123 degrees; #4, 100 degrees; #5, 77 degrees; #6, 54 degrees; all four to be carried out by planes of CruDiv 8. Search distance, 300 miles and 60 miles to the left. #7, to bear 31 degrees, distance 150 miles and 40 miles to left. Besides the above, the *Akagi* will have ready a weather observation plane. Times of take-offs will be ordered later."

1640	Message by signal from Comdr. CruDiv 8 to CruDiv 8, info *Mobile Force*: "CruDiv 8 SigOrd #28. With regards to *Mobile Force* SigOrd #97. *Tone* will supply planes for searches on lines 3 and 4 and *Chikuma* for lines 5 and 6."
2350	Fog clears.

4 June

0307	Supply Unit and *Akigumo* detached. Course, 130; speed, 12.
0525	Signal message from Comdr. CruDiv 8 to CruDiv 8, BatDiv 3. Info, *Mobile Force*:

"CruDiv 8 Sig Ord #29. The following revisions made for antisub air patrol for tomorrow, the 5th:

"1. Take-off times: Watch 1, 0130; Watch 2, 0430; Watch 3, 0730.

"2. 1 plane each from the *Kirishima* and *Chikuma* (3-seat float recco's, if needed) will undertake the flights for Watch 2. *Kirishima's* will be the #1 duty plane, *Chikuma's* #2 duty plane."

0615	Screen cruising disposition #5.
1025	Signal message from Comdr. *Mobile Force* to *Mobile Force*:
	"*Mobile Force* SigOrd #100. Movements of the fleet subsequent to the take-off

[Army Air Force photo of *Akagi* being attacked omitted]

[P. 13]

of the attack units tomorrow, will be as follows:

"1. For three hours and 30 minutes following the first wave's take-off, the fleet will proceed on course 135 degrees, speed, 24 knots. Thereafter, if the prevailing winds are from the east, course will be 45 degrees, speed 20; if west winds prevail, course will be 270 degrees, speed, 20 knots.

"2. Change in plans may be necessitated by enemy actions. Bear this in mind in making preparations for assembling and taking aboard the air control units.

"3. Unless otherwise specified, the search units will take off at the same time as the attack units.

1117	Signal message from Comdr. *Mobile Force* to *Mobile Force*: "#25. Maintain 26 knot momentary stand-by and maximum battle speed 20 minute stand-by from 0100, 5th."
1200	Speed, 24 knots.
1230	Signal message from Comdr. *Mobile Force* to *Mobile Force*:
	"*Mobile Force* Sig Ord #101: Disposition #1 will be employed in carrying out float plane antisub patrols tomorrow, the 5th."
1350	Signal message from Comdr. CruDiv 8 to CruDiv 8 and BatDiv 3. Info, *Mobile Force*:
	"Following changes will be made in the antisub air patrols for tomorrow, the 5th:
	"1. Allocation: For Watches 1 and 3, one plane each from all ships of CruDiv 8. For Watches 2 and 4, one plane each from all ships of BatDiv 3. For Watch 5, one plane each from *Chikuma* and *Kirishima*.
	"2. Take off times (from Watch 1 through Watch 5 in order): 0130, 0430, 0730, 1030, 1330."
1630	Enemy plane sighted. *Tone* opens fire.
1631	3 fighters take off from the *Akagi*.
1640	Signal message from Comdr. CruDiv 8 to Comdr. *Mobile Force*: "Lost enemy planes in direction bearing 260 degrees. About 10 planes."
1654	Fighters return to *Akagi*.
2350	Twice sighted, but almost immediately lost, what appeared to be enemy planes.

5 June

0030	Screen cruising disposition #1. Course, 130 degrees.
0032	Signal message from Comdr. *Mobile Force* to *Mobile Force*: "#1. Plan movements for west winds."
0054	Speed, 20 knots.
0100	All hands ordered to stations.
0130	Midway attack units take off.

0135   *Chikuma* plane takes off on #5 search line.

0138   Signal message from Comdr. *Mobile Force* to *Mobile Force*: "*Chikuma's* plane takes off on #6 search line."

0138   *Tone's* antisub direct escort plane takes off.

0142   *Tone's* plane takes off on #3 search line.

0142   Course, 135.

0150   *Chikuma's* antisub direct escort plane takes off.

0150   Speed, 24 knots.

0200   *Tone's* plane takes off on #4 search line.

0220   Signal message from Comdr. *Mobile Force* to *Mobile Force*: "Unless unforeseen changes in the situation occur, the second attack wave, in Organization #4 (under command of Air Officer of *Kaga*), will be carried out today."

0232   *Nagara* lays down smoke screen.

0232   Speed, 26 knots.

0234   *Kirishima* lays down smoke screen.

0242   Sight one enemy flying boat in position bearing 166 degrees, distance, 40 kilometers.

0243   Fighters take off from all ships.

0245   Radio message from *Tone's* #4 plane to *Mobile Force*: "#1. Sight two surfaced enemy submarines in position bearing 120 degrees, distance 80 miles from my take-off point. Subs' course, 120 degrees. (0220)."

0251   *Tone* sights one enemy flying boat bearing 45 degrees to port, distance 32 kilometers, at high elevation.

0253   Above flying boat lost when he entered a squall zone.

0255   Radio message from *Tone's* plane on #4 search line to *Mobile Force*: "15 enemy planes are heading towards you."

0300   Message from Condr. CarDiv 2 to *Mobile Force*: "Sight enemy planes bearing 90 degrees." Fighters take off from all ships. Sight enemy planes bearing 50 degrees to port (90 degree direction), distance 42.5 kilometers.

0309   Speed, 28 knots.

0331   Course, 140 degrees.

[P. 14]

0336   Radio message from Com. *Attack Unit* to *Attack Unit*: "Assume penetration formation."

0343   *Tone* sights three enemy planes. Lays down smoke screen.

0344   Above planes enter clouds.

0345   Radio message from *Hiryu's* attack unit Comdr. *Mobile Force*: "We have completed our attack and are homeward bound."

0349   Message from *Chikuma's* plane of #4 search line to Comdr. *Mobile Force*: "#1. Because of bad weather, I am returning. Position 350 miles from point of origin (Bearing 11 degrees from Midway) (0335)."

0349   Several enemy planes sighted overhead by *Tone*.

0350   Signal message from Comdr. *Mobile Force* to *Mobile Force*: "Assume Air Alert Disposition #1, Method B."

0355   Three fighters take off from the *Akagi*.

0358	Radio message from plane of *Hiryu* to *Mobile Force*: "I have been hit and have ordered each squadron to act separately."
0359	Three fighters return to the *Akagi*.
0400	Radio message from Air Officer, *Hiryu* to *Mobile Force*: "#2. There is need for a second attack wave."
0405	Message from Comdr. *Mobile Force* to CruDiv 8. "Have all planes assume standby disposition #1."
0405	*Akagi* sights 9 enemy planes bearing 150 degrees, distance 25,000 meters, elevation 0.5 degrees. Assumed battle speed #5, heading into the above mentioned planes.
0405	*Tone* sights 10 enemy heavy bombers bearing 35 degrees to port, elevation 15 degrees, distance, 1800.
0406	*Chikuma* sights about 10 PBY's 36 kilometers dead ahead.
0407	Radio message from Air Officer, *Kaga* to Comdr. of *Mobile Force*: "Sand Island bombed, and great results obtained. (340)."
0407	*Akagi* commences firing with her starboard AA gun.
0407	*Tone* commences firing her main guns.
0408	About 10 friendly fighters head for the enemy.
0410	Three fighters take off from the *Akagi*. Enemy torpedo planes divide into two groups.
0410	Enemy flying boat brought down by friendly fighters.
0411	*Akagi* heads into the planes to the starboard.
0411	Friendly fighters in air combat with enemy aircraft.
0412	*Akagi* notes that enemy planes loosed torpedoes. Counters with AA machine gun fire. Enemy machine gun strafing seriously injures two men manning the #3 AA gun. Revolving mechanism of said gun damaged (repaired about half an hour later). Both transmitting antennas cut. Unable to use port . . . (?)."
0412	*Akagi* makes full turn to evade, successfully, the torpedo to starboard, and another full turn evades another to port. Noted one torpedo to starboard, two to port (of which one exploded automatically) on parallel courses, and other which crossed astern.
0417	Three planes brought down by AA fire.
0412	*Tone* sights a group of enemy planes heading for our carriers. Three planes heading for this ship, bearing 160 degrees to starboard, elevation 10 degrees.
0412.5	Hold main gun fire. Commence AA gun fire.
0413	Air battle over the carriers.
0414	Enemy planes carry out level bombing attack on carriers. No hits sustained.
0414	*Chikuma* changes course to starboard of enemy plane formation.
0415	Message from CinC *First Air Fleet*: "Planes in second attack wave stand by to carry out attack today. Re-equip yourselves with bombs."
0415	Torpedo dropped ahead of the *Akagi*. No hit sustained.
0416	*Chikuma* turns her main guns on enemy planes which were escaping from friendly fighters. Enemy planes cut to three.
0418	*Tone* ordered to hold fire.
0420	*Akagi* takes one fighter aboard.

0420   *Chikuma* sights an enemy flying boat near the horizon. Elevation 0.5 degrees.

0421   *Chikuma* holds fire.

0422   *Tone* sights one enemy twin-engined plane making a getaway bearing 45 degrees to starboard. Friendly fighter takes after it. Main gun ammunition expended: 54. No casualties to men or machines.

0424   One enemy flying boat brought down by friendly fighters.

[P. 15]

0426   *Akagi* assumes battle speed #4. Ammunition box attached to her #2 machine gun damaged by machine gun fire. (Emergency repairs completed in about 10 minutes).

0428   Radio message from *Tone's* plane on #4 Search Line to Comdr. *Mobile Force:* "#3. Sight what appears to be 10 enemy surface ships, in position bearing 10 degrees distance 240 miles from Midway. Course 150 degrees, speed over 20 knots."

0431   *Chikuma* sights enemy flying boat bearing 50 degrees to port, distance 25 kilometers. Recedes, gradually. (Total of six enemy flying boats sighted of which five were shot down.)

0436   Four fighters return to *Akagi.*

0438   Note the return of friendly attack units.

0439   *Tone* assumes patrol disposition #1.

0439   *Chikuma* on course 100 degrees. *Soryu* completes taking her planes aboard.

0439   Course 100 degrees.

0445   Message from Comdr. *Mobile Force* to *Mobile Force:* "Prepare to carry out attacks on enemy fleet units. Leave torpedoes on those attack planes which have not as yet been changed to bombs."

0447   Radio message from Comdr. *Mobile Force* to *Tone's* plane on #4 Search Line: "1. Ascertain ship types, and maintain contact."

0448   *Chikuma* changes course to port and carries out AA combat to port. Message from Comdr. aboard the *Soryu* to *Mobile Force:* "Sight 6 to 9 enemy planes bearing 320 degrees."

0449   Course, 120 degrees.

0450   *Chikuma* commences firing on the 6 to 9 enemy planes bearing 320 degrees.

0453   *Chikuma* ceases firing.

0453   *Tone* sights one enemy flying boat bearing 90 degrees, elevation 1 degree, distance, 24,000 meters.

0453.5 *Tone* advises that enemy flying boat disappears into clouds. Bombs dropped bearing 0 degrees.

0453.5 *Kirishima* lays down smoke screen.

0454   Message from *Haruna* to *Mobile Force:* "Sight enemy plane bearing 100 degrees."

0454   Course, 150 degrees.

0455   Enemy bombs *Soryu* (9 or 10 bombs). No hits.

0455   Message from Comdr. aboard the *Soryu* to *Mobile force:* "14 enemy twin-engined planes flew over us at 270 degrees, altitude 30,000 meters." (sic).

0456   Noted that the *Akagi* and *Hiryu* were being subjected to bombings.

0458   Radio message from *Tone's* plane on #4 Search Line to Comdr. *Mobile Force:* "#5. At 0455, the enemy is on course 80 degrees, speed 20 knots. (0458)."

0458   *Hiryu's* fighter comes aboard.

0500   *Akagi* sights 16 enemy planes bearing 85 degrees, elevation 7 degrees, distance 17,000 meters. She assumes #5 battle speed.

0500   Radio message from Comdr. *Mobile Force* to *Tone's* plane on #4 Search Line: "Advise ship types (0500)."

0500   *Soryu* lays down smoke screen. Stopped.

0504   *Chikuma* sights a group of enemy planes bearing 30 degrees to port.

0506   *Tone* sights a group of enemy planes bearing 280 degrees, elevation 2 degrees, distance 25,000 meters.

0506   *Chikuma* reports that enemy planes bearing 25 degrees to port heading for the fleet concentration. (Carrier-based planes. These were the first carrier-based planes noted by this ship.) Main guns, AA guns and machine guns commence firing.

0507   Three heavy bombers appear over the *Soryu.*

0508   *Soryu* reports sighting 10 enemy planes.

0508   Three fighters take off from the *Akagi.* She goes into evasive tactics.

0509   Radio message from *Tone's* plane on #4 search line to Comdr. *Mobile Force:* "Enemy is composed of 5 cruisers and 5 destroyers."

0509   *Chikuma* reports shooting down one enemy carrier-based attack plane (torpedo) bearing 100 degrees to starboard, 200 meters distance.

0510   Maximum battle speed at momentary standby ordered.
        Bomb hits on *Akagi* and *Hiryu* were noted.

0510   Enemy plane dives on *Soryu. Tone's* plane hoisted up.

0510   Course 140 degrees.
        Chikuma holds fire.

0511   *Chikuma* reports dozens of friendly and enemy planes carrying out a great air combat.

[P. 16]

0511   Radio message from *Tone's* plane on #4 search line to Comdr.
        Mobile Force: "The enemy is composed of 5 cruisers and 5 destroyers. (0509)."

0512   *Akagi* opens fire on enemy plane bearing 90 degrees to port.

0512   Bomb falls astern of the *Kaga.* Miss.

0513   Sight bombs fall in position bearing 120 degrees to port, distance 500 meters from the *Akagi.*

0513   Bomb falls in position bearing 50 degrees to port distance 1,500 from the *Tone. Tone* counters with port guns.

0513   Battle speed #1.

0514   *Tone* opens AA fire.

0515   *Tone* sights 3 enemy planes overhead. These immediately disappear in the clouds.

0519   Bomb dropped in position bearing 100 degrees to port, distance 4,000 meters from the *Tone*. *Soryu* and *Hiryu* countering with fierce gun fire. Many bombs being dropped in the vicinity of *Soryu*.

0520   Radio message from *Tone's* plane on #4 search line to Comdr. *Mobile Force*: "The enemy is accompanied by what appears to be a carrier."

0520   Course, 270 degrees. Bomb dropped astern of the *Akagi*. Miss.

0520   *Soryu* bombed. No hits.

0521   *Akagi* completes maximum battle speed, momentary standby.

0521   *Hiryu* bombed. No hits.

0522   *Akagi* heads into the enemy torpedo planes to port at maximum battle speed.

0523   *Nagara* lays down smoke screen.

0524   Noted that the *Soryu* was subjected to bombing attack. *Tone* turns to 270 degrees.

0527   *Akagi* goes into evasive tactics. Enemy planes dive on the *Haruna*. No bomb hits.

0529   *Chikuma* sights 3 enemy planes bearing 15 degrees to port proceeding to starboard. Evasive action. Speed, 30 knots.

0530   Message from Comdr. *Mobile Force* to *Mobile Force*: "Carrier-based bombers will prepare for second attack. Equip yourselves with 250 kilogram bombs."

0530   Radio message from *Tone's* plane on #4 search line to Comdr. *Mobile Force*: "#8. Sight two additional enemy cruisers in position bearing 8 degrees, distance 250 miles from Midway. Course, 150 degrees, speed, 20 knots. (0530)."

0530   10 enemy planes dive on the *Haruna*. No hits. Friendly fighters engaged in air combat with the enemy.

0531   *Tone* ordered to hold fire.

0532   4 fighters take off from the *Akagi*.

0533   *Chikuma's* main guns commence directional firing.

0534   Radio message from *Tone's* plane on #4 search line to Comdr. of *Mobile Force*: "#9. I am now homeward bound."

0536   *Chikuma* holds fire.

0537   *Akagi* on battle speed #3. Commences taking planes on board.

0539   *Akagi* sights enemy torpedo plane bearing 10 degrees to port, elevation 2 degrees. Landing operations halted, and evasive action at top battle speed started.

0539   *Chikuma* sights two enemy planes bearing 90 degrees to port.

0540   *Akagi* resumes #3 battle speed and landing operations.

0545   Message from Comdr. CruDiv 8 to Comdr. of *Chikuma*, info Comdr. *Mobile Force*: "#2. Have type-o float recco plane take off and contact enemy sighted by *Tone's* plane on #4 search line."

0545   Radio message from *Tone's* plane on #4 search line to the *Akagi*:
        "Sight what appears to be two additional enemy cruisers in position bearing 8 degrees, distance 250 miles from Midway. Course 150 degrees, speed 20 knots."

0545   Assumed patrol disposition #1. Course, 160 degrees.

0548   Course, 120 degrees.

0548   Radio message from *Tone's* plane on #4 search line to *Akagi*:
        "I am now homeward bound."

0550   Radio message from *Tone's* plane on #4 search line to Comdr. *Mobile Force:* "Sight what appears to be two additional enemy cruisers in position bearing 8 degrees, distance 250 miles from Midway. Course 150 degrees, speed 20 knots."

0550   Radio message from *Tone's* plane on #4 search line to Comdr. *Mobile Force:* "I am now homeward bound. (0540)."

0554   Radio message from Comdr. (*Mobile Force*) to *Tone's* plane on #4 search line: "Go on the air with transmitter for DF purposes."

[P. 17]

0555   Radio message from ComCruDiv 8 to *Tone's* plane on #4 search line: "Postpone your homing."

0555   Radio message from *Tone's* plane on #4 search line to Com*Mobile Force* (received at 0601): "Orders received. 10 enemy torpedo planes are heading toward you. (0555)."

0555   Course 90 degrees.

0555   Stopped.

0555   Radio message from ComCruDiv 8 to *Tone's* plane on #4 search line: "2. Maintain contact with enemy until arrival of four *Chikuma* planes. Go on the air with your long wave transmitter."

0555   Blinker from Com*Mobile Force* to *Mobile Force* (received at 0613): "#10. After completing homing operations, proceed northward. We plan to contact and destroy the enemy task force."

0555   Blinker from *Chikuma* to ComCruDiv 8 (received at 0620): "Take-offs planned for 0630."

0555   Blinker from *Chikuma* to ComCruDiv 8 (received 0653): "#5. Plane #5 launched (0635)."

0555   Radio message from Com*Mobile Force* to CinC *Combined Fleet*, Info *Second Fleet* (received at 0630): "#336. Enemy composed of 1 carrier, 5 cruisers, and 5 destroyers sighted at 5 A. M. in position bearing 10 degrees, distance 240 miles from AF (Midway). We are heading for it."

0559   Homing of all bombers completed.

0600   Blinker from ComCruDiv 8 to *Chikuma:* "Have your type-0 float recco plane take off and establish contact with the enemy sighted by *Tone's* plane on #4 search line."

0602   *Chikuma* takes aboard two planes.

0602   Speed, 9 knots.

0605   #4 battle speed (*Akagi*).

0605   Radio from ComCruDiv 8 to *Tone's* plane on #4 search line: "Maintain contact until arrival of *Chikuma's* planes. Go on the air with your long wave transmitter."

0605   Message from *Tone's* plane on #4 search line to Com*Mobile Force:* "Sight 10 enemy attack (torpedo) planes heading toward you. (0555)."

0605	Blinker from ComMobile Force to all ships: "Proceed northward after taking on your planes. We plan to contact and destroy the enemy task force."
0607	Message from Tone to Tone's plane on #4 search line: "Maintain contact until Chikuma's four planes arrive. Use your long wave transmitter. (0555)."
0610	12 fighters taken aboard.
0617	Course 70 degrees. #3 battle speed.
0618	Maximum battle speed. (Noted enemy plane sighting signals from all ships.)
0618	Completed taking aboard the attack units.
0618	Chikuma sights 16 enemy planes bearing 52 degrees to starboard, elevation 2 degrees, distance 35 kilometers.
0618	Speed 30 knots.
0618	Destroyer lays down smoke screen 30 degrees to port of the Tone. AA action readied. Several enemy planes sighted in position bearing 66 degrees to starboard, elevation 2 degrees, distance 20,000 meters. Smoke screen laid down. (Tone). #4 battle speed.
0619	Akagi resorts to evasive action.
0620	Main gun directional firing commenced (Chikuma)
0622	Firing ceased.
0622	Speed 30 knots.
0623	Akagi sights 18 enemy planes in position bearing 122 degrees to starboard, elevation 0.5 degrees, distance 40,000 meters.
0624	Message from CinC First Air Fleet to CinC Combined Fleet: "At 0500 sighted enemy composed of one carrier, 5 cruisers and 5 destroyers in position bearing 10 degrees, distance 240 miles from Midway. We are heading for it. (0600)."
0625	So as to bring the enemy torpedo planes astern, the Akagi was swung around.
0625	18 enemy flying boats sighted bearing 20 degrees, elevation 1 degree, distance 35 kilometers. (Chikuma).
0625	Chikuma lays down two curtains of smoke.
0625	Main guns' directional firing commenced (Chikuma).
0625	Enemy planes bearing 75 degrees to starboard, elevation 1 degree, coming closer. (Chikuma).
0627	Firing of main guns on planes to starboard commenced.

[P. 18]

0627	The 6 enemy planes mentioned above proceeding to starboard (Chikuma).
0627	Tone sights 15 enemy planes bearing 115 degrees to starboard, elevation 0.2 degrees.
0628	Course, 115 degrees.
0629	Chikuma commences firing her AA guns.
0629	Tone commences firing her main guns on enemy planes. Kaga's fighters take off.

0629.5   Radio from *Tone's* plane on #4 search line to *Tone:* "My fuel is getting low. I am breaking off the contact and am returning home."

0630   AA guns go into action (*Akagi*).

0630   Firing ceased (*Chikuma*).

0630   Radio from Com*Mobile Force* to CinC *Combined Fleet:* "Sighted enemy composed of 1 carrier, 5 cruisers and 5 destroyers in position bearing 10 degrees, distance 240 miles from AF (Midway) at 0500. We are heading for it."

0630   Radio from *Tone's* plane on #4 search line to ComCruDiv 8 (received at 0640): "#10. My fuel supply is running low. I am breaking off the contact and returning home."

0630   Radio from destroyer *Arashi* to *Mobile Force* (received at 0610): "Received an enemy submarine's torpedo attack in position (grid) HE E A 37 at 0610. Countered immediately with depth charges, but results unknown."

0630   Blinker from Com*Mobile Force* to *Mobile Force* (received 0910): "Battleships in 10–8–3 order. Course 70, speed 12."

0630   Blinker from Com*Mobile Force* to *Mobile Force* (received 0915): "Plan to destroy the enemy in a daylight engagement."

0632   Five fighters take off (*Akagi*).

0632   Flying boats to port form a line (*Chikuma*).

0632   The planes to starboard go into bombing formation (*Chikuma*).

0634   Main and AA guns open fire (*Chikuma*).

0634   Two of the enemy flying boats bearing 90 degrees to port, shot down by friendly fighters.

0635   Planes to port gradually retire (*Chikuma*).

0635   Radio from ComCruDiv 8 to *Tone's* plane on #4 search line: "Wait until 0700."

0636   Firing halted on seeing that friendly fighters were shooting them down. (*Akagi*).

0636   Firing of main and AA guns held up (*Chikuma*).

0637   *Tone's* plane on #4 search line to ComCruDiv 8: "My fuel is running low. I am breaking off the contact and returning (0637)."

0638   *Chikuma's* plane #5 catapulted off to establish contact with enemy fleet. (To relieve *Tone's* #4 plane.)

0638   Blinker from *Chikuma* to ComCruDiv 8: "Plane off at 0638."

0638   *Tone's* plane #4 to *Tone:* "I can't do it."

0638   Sight 14 enemy planes in position bearing 142 degrees to port, elevation 4 degrees, distance 25,000 meters.

0638   Course, 300 degrees.

0639   From ComCruDiv 8 to *Tone's* #4 plane: "Wait until 0700. (0630)."

0640   Sight 14 enemy torpedo planes in position bearing 140 degrees to port, elevation 1 degree, distance 40,000 meters. (*Akagi*).

0640   *Tone* opens fire with her main guns on the above planes. Two directional salvos.

0641   Radio from *Tone's* #4 plane to ComCrudiv 8: "I can't."

0641   Course, 320 degrees.

0642   Noted that all of the above-mentioned torpedo planes were brought down by friendly fighters. (*Akagi*).

0642   Friendly fighters bring down 1 flying boat. (*Chikuma*).

0644   Same as above.

0645   Friendly fighters engaging enemy flying boats bearing 40 degrees to starboard. (About 32 enemy flying boats already brought down). (*Chikuma*).

0646   Noted that the torpedo plane group to port was attacking CarDiv 2 (*Akagi*).

0649   Sight 14 enemy planes in position bearing 24 degrees to port, elevation 1 degree, distance 50 kilometers. (*Chikuma*).

0651 to 0700   Took aboard two fighters. Noted that 10 of the torpedo plane group were brought down by friendly fighters (*Akagi*).

0652   *Chikuma* lays down two smoke curtains.

0652   Sight enemy planes bearing 135 degrees to port. We are their target (*Tone*).

0653   Port AA and main guns of *Chikuma* commence directional firing against enemy planes bearing 75 degrees to port, elevation 2 degrees, distance 45 kilometers.

0653   Main guns open fire on enemy planes bearing 140 degrees (*Tone*).

[P. 19]

0655   *Tone* ceases main gun firing.

0658   Radio from ComCruDiv 8 to planes of CruDiv 8: "At 0630, we are in position bearing 137 degrees distance 96 miles from take-off point. We are on a northerly course, speed 24 knots."

0658   14 enemy planes divided in two groups are heading for us, particularly for CarDiv 1. One section carry out torpedo attacks against the *Kaga*. *Kaga* successfully evades. This attack is followed up with dive bombing attacks. Friendly surface units are heading into the enemy planes and engaging them with starboard main gun fire.

0659   Course, 340 degrees.

0700   From *Soryu's* recco plane to Com*Mobile Force* (received 0715): "#1. Fail to sight enemy. I am in position bearing 20 degrees, distance 290 miles from Midway (0700)."

0700   Radio from CinC *First Air Fleet* to CinC *Combined Fleet*, CinC *Second Fleet*, CinC *Sixth Fleet*, ComDesRon 2; info (others): "#337. Carried out air attack of AF (Midway) at 0330. Many enemy shore-based planes attacked us subsequent to 0415. We have suffered no damages. At 0428, enemy composed of 1 carrier, 7 cruisers and 5 destroyers sighted in (grid) position TO SHI RI 34, on course southwest, speed 20 knots. After destroying this, we plan to resume our AF (Midway) attack. Our position at 0700 is (grid) HE E A oo, course 30 degrees, speed 24 knots."

0702   Sight a dozen or more enemy planes bearing 150 degrees to starboard, elevation 2 degrees, distance 35 kilometers.

0704   Holding fire (*Tone*).

0705	Starboard AA guns commence directional firing (*Chikuma*).
0705	*Tone* sights enemy planes bearing 60 degrees on the horizon.
0706	*Akagi* sights 15 enemy planes bearing 48 degrees starboard (118 degrees), distance 45,000 meters.
0706	*Tone* sees enemy planes dropping bombs in position bearing 140 degrees to port, distance 20,000 meters. 7 friendly fighters take off to engage the enemy planes.
0607	(T. N. in error for 0707?) *Tone* reports sighting 15 enemy planes bearing 20 degrees to starboard, elevation 9 degrees, distance 29,000, heading for her. Goes into evasive action to starboard then opens directional firing with her main guns.
0609	(T. N. in error for 0709?) Wigwag from ComDesRon 10 to all units: "Sight a dozen or more planes bearing 60 degrees." (*Chikuma*).
0710	*Akagi* takes three fighters aboard.
0710	*Chikuma* opens directional fire with her main guns.
0710	Course, 90 degrees.
0711	*Akagi* swings around to place the starboard group of torpedo planes to her stern.
0714	*Akagi* settles on course 300 degrees.
0714	*Chikuma* opens fire on enemy planes bearing 100 degrees to starboard, elevation 2 degrees.
0714	*Tone* sights enemy planes bearing 25 degrees to starboard, elevation 2 degrees. Bombs drop on both sides of *Akagi*. No hits.
0715	*Akagi* sights enemy torpedo plane group of 12 planes in position bearing 170 degrees to port, distance 45,000 meters.
0716	*Chikuma* opens AA fire.
0717	*Chikuma* reports that her AA guns shot down 4 enemy torpedo planes.
0718	*Chikuma* reports that two enemy planes shot down by friendly fighters.
0718	*Tone* sights enemy planes bearing 41 degrees to port, elevation 5 degrees.
0718.5	*Tone* opens fire.
0719	*Chikuma* reports shooting down one enemy plane by her AA fire.
0719	*Tone* ceases firing. Friendly fighters carry on the engagement (2 planes).
0720	*Akagi* reports sighting bomber bearing 30 degrees directly over the *Kaga* and goes into a maximum turn.
0720	*Chikuma* reports seeing enemy torpedo planes drop torpedoes. No hits.
0721	*Chikuma* reports seeing two enemy planes downed by friendly fighters.
0722	*Akagi* sees *Kaga* being dive bombed. Fighters ordered to take off as soon as readied.
0723	*Tone* opens machine gun and AA gun fire on enemy approaching from 40 degrees to port. Several enemy planes suddenly emerge from clouds and dive on *Akagi*.
0723	*Chikuma* ceases firing.
0723	Course, 350 degrees.

[P. 20]

| 0724 | Noting that the two torpedo plane groups to starboard of the *Akagi* were preparing to launch their torpedoes, she goes into evasive action. Then, |

seeing that she was about to be dive bombed, she makes maximum reverse turn.

0724   Fires break out aboard *Kaga*.

0725   *Akagi* notes fire aboard *Kaga* and also that fighters were commencing to take off.

0725   *Chikuma* reports dive bombing attacks on *Akagi*.

0726   Three bombers dive on *Akagi* from position bearing 80 degrees to port, altitude about 2,000 meters (angle of dive, about 50 degrees). At about 500 meters altitude, the bombs were loosed. First was a near miss about 10 meters abeam of the bridge; second hit near the elevator amidship (fatal hit); third hit the flight deck on the portside, aft (damage: several holes to after deck, 1 emergency personnel killed.)

0726   *Chikuma* reports fires aboard the *Akagi*.

0726   *Tone* opens fire with forward machine guns on enemy planes approaching from dead ahead.

0728   *Chikuma* sights one enemy plane bearing 16 degrees to starboard on the horizon, and proceeding to port. *Soryu* sustains bomb hits.

0729   Induced explosions from torpedoes stored in *Akagi's* hangars begins (ammunition and bomb storage rooms ordered flooded). The forward groups were successfully flooded immediately, but because of valve damages to those in the aft sections, none could be automatically flooded except the ammunition room for #2 main turret. (They were finally flooded two and half hours later.)

0730   *Chikuma* sights 2 enemy flying boats bearing 63 degrees to starboard and proceeding along her starboard.

0732   *Akagi* ordered to battle speed #3 and activation of carbon dioxide gas fire fighting apparatus.

0733   *Akagi* sights 4 enemy torpedo planes bearing 80 degrees to port, elevation 4 degrees. She goes into a maximum turn and settled on course 0.

0734   *Chikuma* opens directional fire with her main guns on the above planes.

0734   *Tone* on course 0 degrees.

0736   *Akagi's* starboard aft engine damaged. Able to proceed at cruising speed.

0737   *Chikuma* fires her starboard AA guns on 10 enemy planes bearing 70 degrees to her starboard and proceeding along her starboard.

0737   *Tone* assumes battle speed #5.

0740   *Akagi* sights 1 torpedo plane bearing 20 degrees to starboard, and heads into it.

0742   *Akagi's* steering apparatus damaged. Engines stopped (all hands ordered to fire fighting station). By this time, the only guns which could keep up defensive fire were the first and second machine gun groups and 1 AA gun.

0742   Enemy planes retreat. *Chikuma* ceases firing.

0743   Fighter aboard the *Akagi* to starboard of the bridge catches fire and spreads to bridge. Pumps ordered into action. Engine room ordered to put ship under full speed.

0745   Destroyer *Nowalke* approaches the *Akagi* to transfer the headquarters.

0745   Radio from #5 plane of the *Chikuma* to ComMobile Force (received at 0818): "#1. Sight 5 additional cruisers and 5 destroyers in position bearing 10 degrees, distance 130 miles from point of origin. They are on course 275 degrees, speed 24 knots. (0745)."

0746   CinC and other headquarters officers abandon bridge of the *Akagi* and commence transfer operations.

0747   Radio from Com*Mobile Force* to CinC *Combined Fleet*: "Sighted enemy composed of 1 carrier, 5 cruisers and 5 destroyers in position bearing 10 degrees, distance 240 miles from Midway. We are heading for it."

0749   *Tone* sights a periscope bearing 45 degrees to starboard, distance 1,000. Turns about and commences evasive maneuvers.

0750   *Chikuma* sights 5 enemy carrier-based attack planes (torpedo) bearing 130 degrees to port, elevation 2 degrees, distance 40 kilometers.

0750   Radio from ComCruDiv 8 to CinC *Combined Fleet* and CinC *Second Fleet*: "#40. Fires are raging aboard the *Kaga*, *Soryu* and *Akagi* resulting from attacks carried out by enemy land-based and carrier-based attack planes. We plan to have the *Hiryu* engage the enemy carriers. In the meantime,

[P. 21]

we are temporarily retiring to the north, and assembling our forces. My position (grid) is TO WA N 55 (0750)."

0750   Radio from ComCruDiv 8 to ComCarDiv 2: "Attack the enemy carriers."

0750   Blinkers from ComCarDiv 2 to ComCruDiv 8 (received at 0758): "All our planes are taking off now for the purpose of destroying the enemy carriers."

0754   *Chikuma* reports that first wave took off from the *Hiryu*.

0755   From *Chikuma's* #5 plane to Com*Mobile Force*: "Sighted an additional 5 cruisers and 5 destroyers in position bearing 10 degrees, 130 miles from point of origin. They are on course 275 degrees, speed 24 knots. (0745)."

0757   *Tone* sights several enemy planes bearing 80 degrees to starboard, elevation 2 degrees, distance 34,000 meters. These were immediately lost in the clouds.

0757   Course, 80 degrees; basic speed.

0758   *Chikuma* reports that take-offs of *Hiryu's* planes were completed.

0758   From *Hiryu* to *Tone*: "All my planes are taking off now for the purpose of destroying the enemy carriers."

0800   Radio from ComCruDiv 8 to *Chikuma's* #5 plane: "Advise position of enemy carriers. Lead the attack unit to it."

[The remainder of the composite message log is omitted.]

[P. 40]

3. *Actual Condition of the Enemy*

(a) Actual conditions in the Midway area:

The enemy apparently anticipated our attack and had their attack planes and flying boats take off. They also concentrated about 50 fighters (all Grummans), and intercepted our first attack wave at a point approximately 30 miles short of our target. When we subjected these to fierce counterattacks, however, they were put on the defensive and engaged, for the most part, in evasive maneuvers. Our ship-based attack planes and bombers suffered no casualties from enemy interceptors while the greater part of their fighters were brought down by us. Results we obtained were 41 enemy ship-based fighters, 1 ship-based bomber and 1 float recco shot down. We lost 4 planes from the exceedingly hot enemy AA fire, so our total losses including 2 which were scuttled during air engagements, were 6 planes.

Twelve bomb hits were scored by us on two enemy runways with #80 land bombs, but these were insufficient to render them inoperational, since the large shore-based attack planes were very active subsequently. We are of the opinion that it is impractical to attempt to render such air fields as these inoperational through bombings.

Intelligence obtained from enemy POW's with regards to Midway is as follows (POW taken aboard the *Makigumo*):

(1) POW's names and ranks:

Ensign. [Ed. Note.—Names given, but are purposely omitted from this translation.]

Aviation Machinist Mate.

(2) Defenses of Midway:

(i) About 5,000 Marines. No Army troops.

(ii) About 150 planes.

Fighters (Grummans and Buffalos) - - - - - - - - - 55
Bombers (B-18's) -50
Flying Boats (Consolidated PBY's) - - - - - - - - - -30

(iii) There are gun emplacements along the entire perimeter of the island. Guns are 20 mm., 30 mm., 50 mm., and 5-inch, of which the 20 mm.'s are the most numerous.

(iv) There are 5 torpedo boats in the harbor.

(v) The air field on Eastern Island is situated at the northern tip and is built in a triangular shape. Runways are 200 feet wide and 3,000 feet long.

(vi) Flying boats carry out air patrols to a distance of 700 miles each morning and evening. They are out for 14 hours each.

(3) Midway has never been used as a carrier base.

(4) The *Alabama* has apparently recently been commissioned.

(5) The United States apparently does not announce losses of her carriers.

(6) Douglas SBD's are used for patrol planes as well as dive bombers.

(b) Enemy carriers:

Our search planes were scheduled to take off at 0130 or 30 minutes before dawn, but the take offs of the float recco planes were delayed as shown below:

Search line	Time of take-off	Notes
#3	0142	*Tone's* #1 plane; sighted no enemy.
#4	0200	*Tone's* #4 plane; sighted enemy.
#5	0135	*Chikuma's* #1 plane; sighted no enemy.
#6	0138	*Chikuma's* #4 plane; sighted no enemy.

[P. 41]

Moreover, as can clearly be seen by the search chart, the search plane on #5 search line which should have sighted the enemy failed to do so while the plane on the #4 search line sighted him at 0428 while on his return run and reported it as follows: "Sight what appears to be the enemy composed of 10 ships in position bearing 10 degrees, distance 240 miles from Midway. He is on course 150 degrees, speed 20 knots. (0428.)" Subsequently he advised us of the weather conditions in the vicinity of the enemy, and again that "The enemy has changed to course 80 degrees, speed 20 knots." Since, however, he failed to report on the type of ships that he had sighted, he was ordered to do so. At 0509 he reported that the enemy was composed of 5 cruisers and 5 destroyers and again at 0520 that the above formation was accompanied by what appeared to be a carrier to its rear. This was the first reference to an enemy carrier. Subsequent to this and until the ship based recco plane returned, we received conflicting reports, numbering the carriers at three, making it impossible for us to estimate the enemy strength.

Later, at 0910, 4 fighters and 18 bombers from CarDiv 2 (less *Soryu*) bombed and sunk (seriously damaged) an enemy carrier. At 1000, it was learned from an enemy POW who was an air crew member from the *Yorktown*, that 3 carriers; namely, *Yorktown*, *Enterprise*, and *Hornet* were in the vicinity. This information together with our air recco made it possible for us to estimate that the enemy carrier strength was 3.

At 1145, 6 fighters and 10 torpedo planes from the *Hiryu* carried out the second attack on enemy carriers and succeeded in seriously damaging (sinking) another carrier.

This should have left only 1 enemy carrier in a healthy condition. But at 1530, the captain of the *Chikima* reported that according to his #2 plane, there were 4 enemy carriers, 6 cruisers, and 15 destroyers in position about 30 miles to the east of the listing and burning enemy carrier. This sighting was made at 1413. The ships were reportedly proceeding westward.

Then we were at a complete loss as to estimating the number of remaining enemy carriers.

The enemy carrier which was bombed by us at 0910 was hit with 5 #25 ordinary and 1 #25 land bomb. Judging from the hour of the enemy's first attack on us, it is estimated that he was preparing for his second attack wave. Therefore, we probably inflicted considerable damage on him.

Subsequent searches failed to locate the damaged carrier so the probability of its sinking is very good. The damaged carrier which was located by *Chikuma's* #4 plane at 0352 on the 6th and later sunk by our submarine was most likely the carrier torpedoed by our planes at 1145, judging from the fact that her flight decks were undamaged.

Pertinent fact concerning the POW picked up by the *Arashi*, and his testimony were as follows:

His plane which was from the U. S. carrier *Yorktown*, was shot down in position 30–30N, 178–40W on 5 June. He died on 6 June and was buried at sea. The following information was obtained from him:

(1) POW's name and rank: [Names given, but are purposely omitted from this translation.]

(2) Place of birth: Chicago.

(3) Age: 23.

(4) Point of debarkation: Pearl Harbor.

(5) Destination: Vicinity of Midway.

(6) Other items:

(i) Enemy task force strength:

    3 carriers (*Yorktown*, *Enterprise*, *Hornet*).

    6 cruisers; about 10 destroyers.

(ii) The *Yorktown*, 2 cruisers, and 3 destroyers formed one group, and was separated from the other forces.

(iii) Sortied from Pearl Harbor during the morning of 31 May, arriving in the vicinity of Midway on 2 June. Since then, this group had been carrying out a mobile patrol along a north-south line.

(iv) There were no battleships in Pearl Harbor on 31 May. (The POW engaged in base training until 31 May, and therefore had no detailed knowledge of battleship movements in the Hawaii area.)

(v) Air strength on the island of Oahu:

Navy had about 200 to 300 planes (including 20 flying boats); the principal base was on Ford Island; POW had no detailed knowledge of the army, but believed that it had several hundred planes there.

(vi) Base for carrier plane drills: Kaneohe, on Oahu.

(vii) Types (numbers) of aircraft on the *Yorktown*: Bombers (18); Recco (18); Torpedo planes (12); Fighters (27).

[P. 42]

(Reference material):

Matters pertaining to battleships (in Hawaii area):

BB's in port before the war	Damages sustained during Battle of Hawaii	Subsequent movements	Destination
Pennsylvania	Medium damage	Departed about February	Seattle
Nevada	Sunk	Refloated and departed about May	Do.
West Virginia	do	do	Do.
California	do	do	Do.
Arizona	do		
Utah	do		
Name unknown	do		

(i) Apparently no battleships have arrived since the outbreak of hostilities.

(ii) As for the subsequent movements noted in the above table, they are all this POW's guesses.

(c) Enemy air attacks are described in Supplementary Table #3; the number shot down are shown in Supplementary Table #4.

4. *Conditions and Circumstances Which Affected the Operation.*

(a) Weather:

(1) Visibility gradually became worse from 2 June until we were completely closed in. All the heavier ships, not to mention the destroyers, were forced to participate in the operation without a full load of fuel.

(2) We were still fog-bound on the morning of 3 June. Were we to proceed on our course and speed, we would be unable to meet the operation schedule for N-day. We finally broke radio silence, therefore, at 1030 to order a change of course. We presume that this gave the enemy an opportunity to detect us. The fog lifted somewhat by 1250, but this was after we had gone on the air.

(3) during the search carried out on 5 June, *Chikuma's* #1 plane failed to sight the large enemy force which should have been sighted. Although, of course, it is deemed

essential that strict lookouts should be maintained along lines at right angles to the course of the plane, it is quite possible in view of the prevailing weather conditions, that the enemy was obscured from vision by clouds. Even if *Tone's* #4 plane had sighted this enemy on his outward flight (*Tone's* #4 plane's take-off had already been delayed by twenty to thirty minutes), we could have carried out an operation with the advantage with us. The weather of the day certainly was not a friend of our search planes.

Under such weather conditions, it is believed that the number of recco planes should be increased.

(4) After 0400, the enemy took advantage of existing clouds in contacting us. This delayed our sighting them. Enemy dive bombers, in particular, seem to very frequently come to the attack from behind clouds, placing us in a very disadvantageous position.

(b) Communication:

Tone's #4 plane's message, reporting the sighting of the enemy, was filed at 0428 but was not delivered until about 0500. *Hiryu's* Air Officer's message stating that there was a need for a second attack was filed at 0400 and delivered 4 or 5 minutes later. The messages ordering the carrying out of the second attack wave today, and to have the stand-by planes change from torpedoes to bombs, were all delivered by 0415. The delay in the delivery of message from *Tone's* #4 plane greatly affected our subsequent attack preparations.

5. *Outstanding Events During the Operation*
(a) Attack on Midway:

[The remainder of this report—which ends on page 68—is omitted.]

SRMN-012, TRAFFIC
INTELLIGENCE SUMMARIES,
PP. 499–505

THE SRMN-012 TRAFFIC INTELLIGENCE Summaries of radio intercepts at Hawaii for June 4, 1942 (pp. 499–505) are reproduced in this appendix. As discussed in chapter 5, one of the log entry summaries (the one for 0447) has been cited as proof that Admiral Nagumo received the crucial *Tone* 4 sighting report before 0745—contradicting Nagumo's (and my) claim of an 0800 receipt time. My view is that these summaries were sloppily rendered, and some are patently inaccurate—making them extremely unreliable. Therefore, the summary in question should be given little or no weight to impeach Nagumo's claim of an 0800 receipt time. But because of the central importance of this issue, these summaries are made available in this appendix so readers can make their own judgment as to the reliability of the summary in question. (Note that there is no page 503. It was a duplicate of page 502, and has been omitted.)

June 4, 1942

RUNNING LOG OF MIDWAY
OPERATIONS

TOKYO(-9)
TIME

0255   MEKU4 believed to be a plane sent to MARI the control
station:

RIHIHI.HIHITE.15 KIKI. Ø255

This was intercepted by   coming out of Tokyo (UTSU).
This is first record of action. It is believed to be
reporting 15 American planes (dive bombers?).

0335   Fleet unit HAMI4 sends to MARI the controlling or senior
station a four kana despatch - his NR 1 on 711Ø kcs.

The frequency 711Ø kcs rapidly became the primary or at
least most active frequency. The following units are on
this channel:

MARI   - (in command - ComBatDiv 3?)
SESO   - Carrier -
HAMI 4 - Fleet Unit.
MU N 3 - Maru tanker ?
KIMU 1 - Base Force line in garble table.
EN I 1 - Fleet Unit.
WIMI 1 - ?
MEKU 4 - Plane
MAHI   - Sub ?
KAHA 1 - Fleet Unit.
MASO   - ?

Oahu bearings on eight of above units were 297-315 degrees.
HAMI 4 bore 315, others 297-305. This indicated a
separation into at least two groups.

D/F stations reported WISA2 a Maru and KOO also on this
circuit but unheard.

0330   Ominato broadcasts to 5th Fleet the first despatch about
15 KIKI drafted at 0255.

0335   MAHI 4 a fleet unit sends a four kana nigori to MARI.
HAMI4's NR 1 on 711Ø.

0346   WISA 1 sends his NR 1 as follows:

SUTI SUTI SUIT. BIHISIHIHIHI 0346

Tokyo broadcasts at 0400.

(=9)
TIME

0400   KIMU 1 on 7110 kcs sends his NR 2:

KAWAKAWAKAWA 0400

0340   ENI 1 sends despatch on 7110 ending with:

KOTASINNOTAME.KOTE.KERI. 0340

0350   MUN 3 sends to MUN 1 his NR 1 on 7110:

SIFU" SISA" SESU 0350

0420   Reports from Midway say first attack on Midway at 1920 GCT -
        0420 Tokyo time; second attack at 2020 GCT - 0520 Tokyo
        time.

0430   Midway reports HOKI 1 bearing 325 degrees on frequency
        7035. Shortly after Midway reported HOTI bearing 320 or
        142 on 7035. It is believed his 7035 and our (correct)
        7110 are the same frequency.

0415   WIMI 1 originates NR 3 (according to Tokyo UTSU) KASEKI.
        YUUOTO" USERI. 0415(WIMI 1)

0422   WIMI 1 on 7110 sends to KIMU 1 his NR 3
        SAN SAN SAN ? 0 0422

0440   MEKU 4 sends on 7110 to MARI a 4 kana nigori despatch -
        his Nr 3 at 0440.

0447   MARI comes back to MEKU 4 with plain text "Retain contact".

0458   MEKU 4 report to MARI in his Nr 4
        0455.N. 080. SO. 20. 0458
        Meaning course 080 speed 20 (N a garble?)

0459   Carrier SASO on 6826 kcs (cardiv 2 frequency?) opens up
        with his NR 1 to his plane SAMIMU
        HATUKO" SI 135 SO 24 SA SA SA
        Meaning after Launching my course 135 speed 24.

        The following units on 6825 kcs.
                SASO carrier (SORYU or HIRYU?)
                WITI Carrier or heavy unit. Homes planes.
                MUN 3 plane?
                MUN 1 Plane?

        MARI goes to MAMI 4 on 7110 kcs his #2 a 4 kana nigori.

(-9)
TIME

0500   ////// 19th Air (MEMO 8) goes to 7 KHA   ½ a plane
        at Ponape on9080 with a code.

0540   Garbled call goes to MARI and MEKU 4 on 7110 MIRA MIRA
        MIRA 0540.

0600   Carrier SESO goes to MEKU 4 on 7110 with his Nr 1.
                KITO. MATE 0600

0555   MEKU 4 to MARI on 7110
                HI JII HI HI. KOKI.1Ø. PKI 0555
        10 enemy planes sighted by MEKU 4.

0605   On 6826 WITI goes to MUN 3 _____ followed by HOTE 1 HOTE 1
        the latter means "Make MO's for homing".

0630   MEKU 4 sends to SESO (a carrier) his #9,
        "Our planes which are short of fuel will stop the contact
        (SHOKUSETSU). Am now returning."
        This makes MEKU 4 a squadron leader on board SESO?

0630   Carrier goes back to MEKU 4 with #3
        0700 MATE 0630   meaning "Wait till 0700 to land"?

0700   WITI goes to MUN 3 on 6825 with his NR 2.

                YOSOSI. 125. MA 84. 0700

        Something bearing 125 distant 84 miles at 0700.

0712   On 6825 plane MUN 3 goes to WITI

                ???? YOYO NOSISIROSIRA

        What is your course?

0713   Carrier or heavy ship WITI answeres with 135 degrees.

0711   MARI on 7110 to MISE 1.

                234.10A

        Meaning your (unidentified Mise 1) bears 234 degrees
        from me 10 minutes after 0700. Excellent bearing.

        This makes MARI look like a carrier. At least he homes
        planes or possibly MISE 1 is a surface vessel making a
        junction with flagship MARI.

0745   SESO (believed should be MASO)sent NR 1 to MEKU 4

                "Inform us of position of enemy carrier."

TOKYO(-9)
TIME

0905   Jaliut Radio first observed on 7110 kcs. with SeSo carriers.
            Jaliut sends his NR 3

                        TOYA TOYA TOYA 0905

1000   MUTE 3 on 7110 kcs. to WANE Ø (Plane?)

            HONOSI Ø1Ø . 8 . SI ØØ . SO 24 . 1000

            ? ? bearing 10° distant 8 miles course North speed 24
            at 1000 (Report of US ships??)

1059   Carrier SESO sends his NR 21 to Jaliut

            (HI 3) FU KU SI YA SE YO
            "Do something with frequency HI 3"

1135   MEKU 4 NR 1 to Carrier SESO on 7110

            MOMOMO. 090. 40 MA . N . 180 . HE Ø 1135

            Enemy bears 90 distant 40 miles on course 180   (HE Ø ??)

1215   MEKU 4 NR 3 to SESO

                TATATA. WI. 102. 120 MA.N.280.SO 24.1215

                Enemy (WI?) bearing 102 distant 120 miles on course
                280 speed 24 at 1215.

1215   SESO a carrier placed by good DF position in 31-40 N
            179-20 W.

1500   HAMI 2 sent NR 6 to TAYO

                HOHOHO 1. 103 MA 85 TENA.TETETE.SI"3 KU 6 N 70
                TESO 20 TAIRUI

                1 carrier 103 miles (bearing 85?) 3 cruisers
                6 destroyers on course 70 speed 20 in formation.

1510   HAMI 2 sent NR 8 to TAYO

                TETETE KOHO" 1 SI" 2 KU 4 YONO SI 95 MA 105 1510

                1 Enemy carrier 2 cruisers 4 destroyers (YONO?)
                course 95 105 miles at 1510.

TOKYO (-9)
TIME

1516   HAMI 2 sent NR 9 to TAYO

       SARA KOHO" 1. N 170 1516

       Also 1 carrier course 170 degrees.

1520   HAMI 2 sent NR 10

       HOHO 3 YONO SI 95 MA 105 1520

       3 carriers (YONO ?) course 95 miles 105 1520.

1540   MAHI sent to HAMI 2 NR 26 a 4 kana nigori ending up with
       1415 (SESO). It is believed the real originator was
       carrier SESO at 1415 and may mean this carrier now sunk
       or damaged.

1630   SESO believed a possibility as casualty now more active
       than ever still placed by D/F in very much same position
       as before 31 N 179 W.

1630   HAMI 2 asks carrier SESO for bearings - SESO (MAHI) directs
       him to use 397 Kcs then tells him to use HI24 (8030 Kcs)
       and gives him bearings of 330 and 160 at 1630-5. This
       indicates HAMI 2 returns to his carrier but carrier not
       knowing which direction gives reciprocal bearings.

1630   (average time). Oahu D/F reports FUN 3 flagship of DesRon
       2 and several 2 kana units on 6440 kcs., bearing ten degrees
       lower than carrier SESO. The bearings:

SESO	(Carrier)	7110 & 6580	301°	
FUN 3	(JINTSU f/s Des- ron 2)	6440	292	
NKA	Unidentified	6440	289	
KONO	Possible sub	6440	292	
NOHA	Unidentified	6440	291	
SESA	Garble for SESO?	5964	301	26/N/175/E
MAU	Unidentified (sub)	5964		26 N 175 E
KONO	Sub ?	5964	302	
SIYO	Sub ?	5964		30 N 178 W
SEHE	Sub	5964	325 fm Palmyra	
WOFU	Sub	5964	300	
NESO2	Maru f/s of MUMI5	5964	284	

TOKYO (-9)
TIME

1700   Tokyo Radio sends the following to SubForce

        "KA" 1. 1700" Received at 1733.

1745   Comdr. of the submarines Unit=TEKA 9 (believed a Squadron)
        originated a long urgent tactical despatch to ComSubFor
        CinC Combined Fleet, Sub unit KOSI 66 information to Comdr
        1st Air Fleet, RITI 11, CinC Second Fleet, ComSbBRon 3
        ComSubRon 5 and Sub unit TAE 22.

        Calls appearing on 6440 Kcs are as follows:

            FUN 3 (JINTSU(Flag DesRon 2 ?)
            HOWI
            IWA
            KINA
            KIHI
            KONO
            KOU
            MERA
            MINI (Includes HOWO-Garble for HOWI ?)
            MOKA
            MERA
            NKA
            NEHE
            NOHA
            RUKI
            SEKE
            SIYO
            UKE
            WOFU

1900   Direction Finder positions obtained on METO a submarine
        unit on 6100 Kcs.

        24 N 164 W (Excellent fix at 1900 (/-9-)

2000   Activity on 6440 continuing with tactical traffic being
        favored. Most of this from HOWI.

2115   CinC Combined Fleet originated tactical code to RISU 4
        (associated with 4th Air Attack Corps), TAYU 1 less
        SEME 9 which appears to be "All Major Commanders less the
        Comdr Dutch Indies Force" information to General Staff.

RECONSTRUCTION OF JAPANESE CAP ACTIVITY[1]

Time	Akagi TO	Akagi Land	Kaga TO	Kaga Land	Soryu TO	Soryu Land	Hiryu TO	Hiryu Land	Total launched first time	Left on board	In air	Shot down	Total shot down
0430	3a[2]		2a		3a		3a		11	27[3]	11		
0515							3b		14	24	14		
0543	3b								17	21	17		
0600					3b				20	18	20		
0612							3c		23	15	23		
0655	3c								26	12	26		
0659		3a									23		
0700			3b					2a				1Ha	1
			2c					1c[4]	31	7	24		
0705–	3a2[5]				3c								
0710	2m								36	2	32		
0720		1c									31		
0730				3b	3a[6]			2b*					
					3b						20		
0736		3a2											
		1b									16		

Time	Akagi TO	Akagi Land	Kaga TO	Kaga Land	Soryu TO	Soryu Land	Hiryu TO	Hiryu Land	Total launched first time	Left on board	In air	Shot down	Total shot down
0750		2b									14		
0759			2a					1b*					
			2c								9		
0800					3a2*		2a2						
					3b2*		3b2*				20		
0808	3b2										23		
0810												1Ac	
												1Hc	
											20	1Sc	4
0815			3b2										
			2d						38	0	25		
0830			2a2										
			1c2								28		
0832	3a3												
	1c2										32		
0840								1c	38	0	31		4
0859		1c											
		2m									28		
0910		1b2	3b2				2a2*						
			2d				3b2*				17		
0920			3b3										
			2d2										
			1c2								23		
0930					3a2*							1Kc	5
					2c						17		
0932	1b3											1Aa	6
	1c2												
	2m2												
	1m[7]								39		21		
0937							3b3						
							1c2			29[8]	25		
0945	4r				2c2								
					1r				44	24	32		
0951		2c2									29	1Aa	7
1000			6r		3a3				50	18	38		
1010		1a3											
		2b2									35		
1013							2a3						
							1r		51	17	38		
1015					3r				54	14	41		
1015–												2Kd	
1030											36	3S	12

Time	Akagi TO	Land	Kaga TO	Land	Soryu TO	Land	Hiryu TO	Land	Total launched first time	Left on board	In air	Shot down	Total shot down
1024	1r[9]								55	13	37		
1030–1045										6(H) (7 lost on A,K&S)	31	1Ar 3H 2Kr	18
1100								5A 3S			23		
1130								10K 4H			9		
1330								6S 3A (31)			0		18[10]

NOTES

1. This data is compiled from the carrier Action Reports (WDC 160985-B), Nagumo's Official Report (Mobile Force's Detailed Battle Report #6, translated as "The Japanese Story of the Battle of Midway," OPNAV P32-1002), and Senshi Sosho. Where records are missing or incomplete I have made a guess as to missing patrols that most likely were launched and landed. Specifically, there is no mention of the second and fourth patrols in *Hiryu*'s report, and as the records of *Soryu*'s Twelfth *Shotai* were transferred to *Junyo* (and missing) there is no record of its CAP activity after its first patrol. The Official Report and Senshi Sosho have filled some of the gaps, but not all. For example, Senshi Sosho notes that *Hiryu* launched Zeros for CAP in the 0800–0808 period (when the American dive-bombers from Midway attacked) and that all available Zeros were launched from other carriers as well during that period, but does not say how many or from which carriers. I have assumed that *Hiryu* and *Soryu* launched patrols at that time—even though this is not mentioned in their fragmentary Action Reports. An * marks the patrols I have inserted.

2. Lower-case letters identify groups of Zeros called *shotais* (sections) so the planes can be tracked when they land and are relaunched on subsequent patrols. Each carrier had nine Zeros left from its operational air group after the Midway strike force departed, and most were divided into three *shotais* of three planes each, with the *shotais* designated as "a," "b," and "c." However, *Kaga* divided its CAP into four *shotais* and, thus, "d" indicates the fourth. In addition, *Akagi* used some Zeros from the Sixth Air Group (which were intended for the defense of Midway after its capture); they are indicated by "m." Later on, Zeros that returned from the strike on Midway were used for CAP; they are indicated by "r." The number after the *shotai* designation indicates recycling of those Zeros for CAP. Capital letters A, H, K and S (in the "shot down" column, for example) indicate Zeros from the carriers *Akagi*, *Hiryu*, *Kaga*, and *Soryu*, respectively.

3. After the Midway strike force departed it was reckoned that thirty-eight operational Zeros remained on board (thirty-six in the Second Wave plus two from the Sixth Air Group deemed to be carrier qualified.) After the Midway strike force returned, its Zeros became available—along with (apparently) a third Zero from the Sixth Air Group.

4. It appears that this plane from *Hiryu* developed engine trouble and returned early. Senshi Sosho, p. 315. It apparently remained out of action.

5. The short "turn around" time indicates that they landed for refueling only, which could be done on the flight deck. (The reloading of guns had to be done in the hangar deck, which required over 30 minutes.)

6. *Soryu*'s Action Report has return times of both 0430 (0730), WDC 160985-B, p. 14, and 0630 (0930), p. 15. As this *shotai* was launched at 0130 (0430), the latter return time cannot be correct because the planes did not carry enough fuel to stay aloft for five hours. I am assuming they were landed at 0730, relaunched around 0800 to attack the American planes from Midway, and landed again at 0930. (As they would have been available for relaunch soon after 0800, I think it reasonable to assume that they would have been launched then when 16 dive-bombers from Midway arrived over the Mobile Force.)

7. The Official Report and *Akagi*'s Action Report state that five fighters took off at 0932. As only four planes were landed recently landed on *Akagi*, it is not clear where this fifth plane came from. Although Senshi Sosho makes note only of two Sixth Air Group Zeros being used for CAP, Hata and Izawa claim that three participated. I am guessing that this accounts for the fifth Zero.

8. By this time, all the Zeros in the Midway strike force had been taken aboard and were being serviced. They would then become available for CAP and escort duty for the attack planned for 1030. Of the original thirty-six, two had failed to return and five had returned damaged, and apparently were out of action. Of the twenty-nine serviceable Zeros, *Akagi* had five, *Kaga* eight, *Soryu* nine, and *Hiryu* seven.

9. This is not mentioned in *Akagi*'s Action Report. According to Senshi Sosho it was launched seconds before *Akagi* was bombed. Apparently, two others were ready to launch — but destroyed by the bombing.

10. This total includes three that made "emergency landings" in the ocean as a result of battle damage. Though the planes were lost, the pilots were rescued. Of the fifteen Zeros actually shot down, the pilots of two of them bailed out and were rescued. Thus, only thirteen pilots were killed. Of the eleven Zeros that went down during the climactic battle of 1010–1045, nine were shot down; six by the Wildcats of Fighting Three, one by Torpedo Three, one by the dive-bombers from *Enterprise*, and one by friendly AA gunfire.

A WAR GAME EXERCISE

THE FOLLOWING WAR GAME RULES, though simpler than those used in such institutions as the Naval War College, simulate the carrier battles of 1942 with quite uncanny accuracy. This is because the values built into them—relating to hit ratios for bombs and torpedoes dropped from the various types of aircraft used in 1942, and damage to the carriers of both sides—were derived largely from the statistics of the actual carrier battles of 1942. Those battles were at Coral Sea, Midway, Eastern Solomons, and Santa Cruz Islands. (The most relevant statistics are, of course, from the battles that took place at Midway; but as they are sparse for the Japanese attacks, those from the other carrier battles are necessary to flesh out the values.)

But before we get to "hit ratios" and damage caused by bombs and torpedoes, we have to get the attacking planes through the air defenses. We must first attempt to simulate the effectiveness of fighter escorts in protecting the dive-bombers and torpedo planes from opposing fighters on combat air patrol over the enemy carriers. We know that escorted bombers suffered far fewer casualties and inflicted much more damage than unescorted ones. How do we quantify this? Also, we know that in dogfights between Zeros and Wildcats, except for a few tactical geniuses such as John Thach, most American Wildcat pilots at this time in the war were at a disadvantage against the more agile Zeros handled by more experienced pilots. Then we have to account for the affect of carrier antiaircraft (AA) gunfire on bombers that get through the combat air patrol. (Not that many planes were actually shot down by AA gunfire in early carrier battles, but there were some.)

RULES

1. It will be assumed that each of the escorting Zeros would keep one Wildcat away from the Japanese bombers—shooting down half the Wildcats engaged and chasing away the other half; one Zero would be lost for every one and one-half Wildcats shot down.[1]

2. Each of the remaining Wildcats would destroy or divert from their target one Val dive-bomber or one and one-half Kate torpedo planes—with three-quarters of them shot down. For every eight Vals, or every twelve Kates, shot down or diverted, one Wildcat would be lost to the gunfire of the bombers.

3. Of the Vals and Kates that got through the Wildcats, one plane would be shot down by the antiaircraft gunfire of each carrier attacked.[2] (If three carriers were attacked by dive-bombers and torpedo planes simultaneously, a total of three planes would be shot down—apportioned between the Vals and Kates one and two, reflecting the greater vulnerability of torpedo planes.)

4. Of the planes that got through both the CAP and AA gunfire to drop their bombs or torpedoes, one-third of the dive-bombers and one-fifth of the torpedo planes would score hits on the carriers. (These "hit ratios" are a little higher than the averages for all the carrier battles of 1942 and reflect the fact that the Japanese carrier pilots at Midway were the "A-Team.")

5. Each 250-kilogram bomb hit would do one point of damage to a carrier, and each torpedo hit would do 3 points of damage. If three carriers are attacked, the damage points are presumed to be distributed among them in proportions of 3-2-1. (This unequal distribution is based on the observation that in the carrier battles of 1942 when more than one carrier was attacked, there was a tendency to concentrate on the closest carrier.) If two carriers are attacked, the damage points are distributed 2-1.

6. Nine points of damage, in either a single or successive attacks, would destroy an American *Yorktown*-class carrier (all three at Midway were of this class), and 5 points would put the carrier out of action for the duration of the battle. ("Destroy" means that the carrier would either sink before the end of the day—possibly from internal explosions—or, more likely, be left badly listing and without power, which would make it easy prey for enemy submarines—or require it to be scuttled. "Out of action" means that the carrier cannot conduct flight operations or defend itself.) It is assumed that damage from less than 5 points can be temporarily patched up to allow flight operations after an hour or two—depending on the amount of damage.

7. After releasing bombs or torpedoes, one more plane would be shot down by the AA gunfire of each carrier, apportioned as in Rule 3. In addition, every four Wildcats remaining in excess of the surviving Zeros would, in the pursuit of fleeing bombers, shoot down one plane—apportioned equally between dive-bombers and torpedo planes. (This rule, though not affecting the attack on the carriers, is necessary for calculating the total plane losses for the battle—and the number available for subsequent battles.)

APPLICATION TO HYPOTHETICAL ATTAC

The Japanese strike force—thirty-six dive-bombers, thirty-six torpedo planes, and twelve Zeros—would have arrived in the vicinity of the American carriers around 1120 (forty minutes earlier than the actual first wave from *Hiryu*). It would have been picked up on radar at least ten minutes earlier while it was about 30 miles from the carriers. Although the two American task forces were about 30 miles apart at this time, it will be assumed that both task forces would have been spotted by the strike force and that all three carriers would have been attacked almost simultaneously. Also, it is assumed that the combat air patrol of the three carriers could have been shared among the two task forces.[3]

We must now ascertain the status of the American combat air patrol fighters at that time. On the morning of the battle, the three carriers had 79 operational Wildcats—27 each on *Enterprise* and *Hornet*, and 25 on *Yorktown*. Twenty-six Wildcats were away on escort duty (10 each from *Enterprise* and *Hornet*, and 6 from *Yorktown*), leaving 53 on board. Of these, approximately 50 fighters would have been available for combat air patrol (16 each for *Enterprise* and *Hornet*, 18 for *Yorktown*). However, not all could have been deployed at the same time on short notice. At the time the Japanese strike force would have been detected, some of the fighters would have been on deck being refueled after earlier patrols, and some in the air might have been low enough on fuel to have required landing for refueling before they could engage in aerial combat. (In the actual battle with *Hiryu*'s first wave at 1200, only 12 of *Yorktown*'s 18 Wildcats could be launched, and only 10 of them were launched in time to engage the Japanese planes.)

Thus, for purposes of our war-gaming model, it will be assumed that less than three-fourths of the 50 operational Wildcats on the three carriers would actually be able to engage the Japanese strike force—let us say 36 (12 over *Yorktown*'s Task Force, and 24 over the Task Force containing *Enterprise* and *Hornet*.) With that last critical parameter in place, we can now apply the gaming rules to make an estimate of the outcome of the hypothetical Japanese attack on the three American carriers.

We will assume that half the American combat air patrol (18 Wildcats) would be deployed at high level to defend against the 36 Val dive-bombers, and the other half would be at low level to take on the 36 torpedo planes. Correspondingly, we will assume that the 12 Zero escorts are also divided—6 each protecting the dive-bombers and torpedo planes. Taking the dive-bombers and their escorts first, 6 Zeros could be expected to deflect 6 Wildcats from the Vals, shooting down 3—at a cost of 2 Zeros. The remaining 12 Wildcats would deflect 12 Vals from their targets—with 9 shot down—while losing one more Wildcat. This would leave 24 Vals to get through the CAP, with one then being shot down by AA gunfire. The remaining 23 would drop bombs—with roughly eight (one in three) hitting the carriers. Eight points of damage, rounded-off, would be inflicted among the three carriers.

The real punch from the Japanese attack would come from the 36 torpedo planes—attacking simultaneously with the dive-bombers. The 6 Zeros escorting them would deflect 6 of the 18 Wildcats on low-level patrol from the Kates, shooting down 3 at a cost of 2 Zeros. The remaining 12 Wildcats would deflect 18 Kates from their targets, shooting down 14 while losing another Wildcat. This would leave 18 Kates getting through the CAP, but 2 would be shot down by AA gunfire. The remaining 16 would launch torpedoes and, on average, a little over three (one in five) would hit, inflicting roughly 10 points of damage.

When added to the bomb damage, a total of about 18 points worth of damage would have been sustained by the three carriers. Under Rule 3, the damage would be apportioned among the carriers 3-2-1, equating to 9, 6, and 3 points, respectively. As 9 points will destroy a carrier, and 5 will put it out of action, this would result in one carrier being destroyed (let us suppose it was *Yorktown*), one being put out of action (assume *Hornet*), and the third being damaged, but not put out of action (which we will assume was the "lucky" *Enterprise*.) After an hour or so of damage control and deck-hole patching this third carrier could resume carrier operations. This allocation of the total damage inflicted would represent two torpedo and three bomb hits on *Yorktown*, one torpedo and three bomb hits on *Hornet*, and two bomb hits (plus the equivalent of a third of a torpedo) on *Enterprise*. Thus, after this first attack only one American carrier has been destroyed under these rules—but, alas, there are more attacks to come.

As for the aircraft casualties of the battle: about 10 Vals, 16 Kates, and 6 Zeros would have been shot down before the bombs and torpedoes were released. After that one more Val and 2 more Kates would be shot down by AA gunfire. Eight Wildcats and 6 Zeros would also have been shot down, leaving 28 and 6, respectively, for an excess of 22 Wildcats over Zeros. During the postattack pursuit, every four of those Wildcats would then shoot down one bomber, for a total of 2 Vals and 3 Kates. This would bring the total bomber losses to 13 Vals and 21 Kates (along with the 6 Zeros), for a total of 40 Japanese planes lost. Of the 23 Vals, 15 Kates, and 6 Zeros that will be presumed to have made it back to their carriers, at least a third would be damaged too severely to make further attacks in the battle. American aircraft losses would have been about 8 Wildcats lost in combat, with about the same number, along with a few Dauntless dive-bombers, lost on the destroyed and damaged carriers (for a total of 16 Wildcats.)

THE AMERICAN ATTACK ON
THE MOBILE FORCE

Within minutes after the hypothetical Japanese attack force was launched (by around 1015) American dive-bombers from *Enterprise* and *Yorktown* bombed three carriers of Nagumo's Mobile Force. What would have been the results of that attack had the strike force been off those carriers? There is no reason to assume that the number of bomb hits would have been any different than actually occurred—four on *Kaga*, two on *Akagi*, and three on *Soryu*. But what we most definitely can assume is that there would have been a substantial difference in the damage those bomb hits would have caused to the carriers. There would have been eighteen fewer torpedo planes loaded with fuel and torpedoes on each of the carriers *Akagi* and *Kaga*, and eighteen fewer dive-bombers on *Soryu*. Moreover, without any rearming operation on the torpedo planes, there also would not have been eighteen 800-kilogram land bombs lying on the hangar deck of *Akagi* (and probably also of *Kaga*). We saw in chapter 8 that it was all this fuel and this ordnance on board the carriers that made them extraordinarily vulnerable to American bombs, which, with 1/100-second fuses, exploded about four feet into the upper hangars.

In our gaming model, this extraordinary vulnerability is reflected by the assumption that a "vulnerable" carrier can be destroyed with less than half the damage points required to destroy a non-vulnerable one. (Two 1,000-pound bombs destroyed *Akagi* at Midway, but at Coral Sea, three 1,000-pound bombs did not destroy the non-vulnerable *Shokaku*, nor did even four or more destroy her at Santa Cruz Islands, though the carrier was put out of action.) For purposes of our model, a carrier can be deemed "vulnerable" if over half its torpedo planes or dive-bombers are on board laden with fuel and ordnance.

However, even with the strike force off the carriers under our hypothetical case, the Japanese carriers would not have been freed of all hazards from ordnance and fuel in case they were bombed. *Kaga* would still have had about seven torpedo planes in her hangar armed with torpedoes, and probably fueled. Also, most of her dive-bombers from the first wave back from Midway were being armed with 250-kilogram bombs at 1025 (though the bombers probably would not yet have been refueled.) Thus, *Kaga* must be deemed at least partially vulnerable—making it subject to being destroyed by fewer bomb hits than would be required if it was completely free of these hazards.

Soryu would also have been "partially vulnerable" at 1025. About half of her first-wave torpedo planes back from Midway were being armed with torpedoes (the other half had been shot down or rendered inoperable by combat.) In addition there were about twelve 250-kilogram land bombs still stacked in the hangar, because under this hypothetical we are assuming that the dive-bombers had still been rearmed for a second strike on Midway—and reversed back to antiship bombs—but that the land bombs had not been returned to the magazine.

Only *Akagi* can be deemed to have been relatively non-vulnerable; it had no fueled bombers on board at 1025, and no torpedoes in the hangar. Though, like *Kaga*, most of its first-wave dive-bombers were being armed with 250-kilogram antiship bombs, that by itself would not have been especially hazardous. Armor-piercing bombs had smaller explosive charges than did the 242-kilogram high-explosive land bombs on *Soryu*, and much smaller than the torpedoes on both *Soryu* and *Kaga*. Thus, the presence of perhaps a dozen 250-kilogram antiship bombs in the hangar of *Akagi* would not have been enough of a hazard to render that carrier even "partially vulnerable" for purposes of the gaming model.

(It may be noted that degrees of "vulnerability" did not figure in the rules for modeling a Japanese attack on the American carriers. This is because neither *Enterprise* nor *Hornet* had any operational dive-bombers or torpedo planes left on board at the time of the hypothetical attack on them. Though *Yorktown* did have a squadron of seventeen armed and fueled dive-bombers left on board after its strike force departed for Nagumo's carriers, it is presumed that they—or most of them—would have been launched when our hypothetical Japanese attack was detected on radar soon after 1100; they had been ready for launch since before 1000.)[4]

The rules, then, for modeling American attacks against Japanese carriers are different than for Japanese attacks against American carriers. In addition to the "vulnerability factor" there are other differences: As there were no escorts for American dive-bombers and no Japanese combat air patrol to meet them, no rules are necessary for aerial combat. Also, as the actual number of bomb hits on each of the Japanese carriers is known (and it is known that no torpedoes hit), it is not necessary to calculate hit ratios. (Of the forty-three bombs that may have been dropped, only nine actually hit.) Thus, all that is necessary is to estimate the damage those bomb hits would have inflicted, and the likely consequences to the carriers, under the changed circumstances. The only variables are the size of the American bombs (1,000 or 500 pounds) and the size of the Japanese carriers (they ranged from the 15,900-ton *Soryu* to the 38,200-ton *Kaga*). The rules:

1. Each 1,000-pound bomb hit would do 1.5 points of damage to a carrier, and each 500-pound bomb would do 0.75 point. (American torpedoes—if they ever hit—would do 3 points of damage.)
2. Eight points of damage, in either a single or successive attacks, would be re-

quired to destroy *Akagi* or *Kaga* if they were non-vulnerable, and 4 points would put them out of action for the duration of the battle. (As the damage-control systems on the older *Akagi* and *Kaga* were not as effective as those on the American *Yorktown*-class carriers, slightly fewer damage points are sufficient to destroy them.) If those carriers were "partially vulnerable," 5 points would destroy them and 3 points would put them out of action. If they were fully vulnerable—such as in the actual attack—only 3 points (two 1,000-pound bomb hits) would be required to destroy them, and 2 points would put them out of action.

3. For the smaller *Soryu* and *Hiryu*, 6 points would be required to destroy them if they were non-vulnerable, and 3 points would put them out of action. If they were "partially vulnerable," 4 points would destroy them, and 2 points would put them out of action. (If they were fully vulnerable, only 3 points would be required to destroy them, and 1.5 points would put them out of action.)

APPLICATION

The *Kaga* would have been "partially vulnerable" and took four bomb hits—one 1,000-pounder and three 500-pounders. This would total 3.75 points and be sufficient to knock her out of action for the duration of battle, but not destroy her. She would not have been able to launch or recover any of her planes (and most of the aircraft remaining on board would have been destroyed.) *Akagi* took two 1,000-pound bomb hits (3 points), but would not have been vulnerable. Accordingly, though she would have been badly damaged, she would not have been put out of action. The damage to her flight deck could have been patched up in a couple of hours, and she then could have launched and recovered planes—though at a reduced pace. (In the actual attack, *Akagi*'s midship elevator was knocked out, so even if *Akagi* had not been destroyed by fire, that elevator would have been inoperable.) Most of the Val dive-bombers in the hangar would have been destroyed or rendered inoperable.

Soryu took three 1,000-pound bomb hits (4.5 points), and, as she would have been "partially vulnerable," she would still have been destroyed. Thus, this model indicates that in the American attack after the hypothetical Japanese strike force had been launched, Nagumo would have lost but one carrier (compared to the three he actually lost in the first attack), and would have had a second put out of action. He would have had two carriers remaining to continue operations against the American carrier force. The Americans, as we saw, would have lost one carrier and had a second put out of action in the attack (compared with only the one hit and destroyed after the actual two attacks from *Hiryu*.) Spruance would have had only one carrier remaining to carry on with the battle. But there would have been more attacks to come. (Note that much of the running commentary here on the various attacks largely duplicates the text of chapter 10, but it is included in this appendix to provide context in applying the war game rules.)

SUBSEQUENT JAPANESE ATTACKS

While our hypothetical Japanese attack on the American carriers was taking place, *Hiryu*—which had not been attacked by the American dive-bombers—would have been preparing for a second attack. *Hiryu* had nine operational torpedo planes remaining after the Midway strike, and had inherited one from *Akagi* (the one that had been on search duty, but could not land on that carrier on its return because of the American bombing.) These planes would have been rearmed with torpedoes and spotted on the flight deck after the first strike force had departed. They would have been ready to go soon after 1200, along with some Zeros for escort. (In the actual event, they were not ready until 1245, but as *Hiryu*'s dive-bombers had been launched forty minutes earlier under our hypothetical than they actually were, it is assumed that the torpedo planes could have been ready about that much earlier.)

In this second strike force, however—unlike the actual one—there would have been some dive-bombers from *Akagi* to accompany the torpedo planes; how many is difficult to estimate. There had been about sixteen operational Val dive-bombers on *Akagi* in the process of being rearmed with 250-kilogram antiship bombs when the bombs hit at 1025. We have seen in our hypothetical that the damage from two bombs would not have been fatal as the torpedo planes were off the carrier and there were no 800-kilo-gram land bombs lying on the hangar deck. Indeed, the bomb hit recorded as "fatal" in *Akagi*'s damage report was the one that exploded in the rear port corner of the hangar. It apparently had ignited armed and fueled torpedo planes—causing raging fires to sweep through the hangar. Without those planes there, the damage to the flight deck aft would have been quite easily repaired—permitting landing operations. The damage from the other bomb would prove to be more serious. Not only had it destroyed the midship elevator, but most of the dive-bombers—which were in the vicinity of that elevator—would have been destroyed even if the carrier survived.

As for how many Vals would have survived, we can only speculate. *Akagi*, like all Japanese fleet carriers (but unlike the American ones at Midway), had two levels of hangar decks. The dive-bombers were probably split between the upper and lower hangars. It is almost certain that all the Vals in the middle section of the upper hangar— where the bomb exploded—would have been destroyed. Most of the Vals in the lower hangar, however, might have survived—as the hangar floors were made of steel and the bomb exploded about eight feet above the floor of the upper hangar. Let us assume that about six dive-bombers in *Akagi*'s lower hangar remained operational.

There would have been problems getting those Vals up to the flight deck and launching them, as *Akagi*'s midship elevator—normally used to raise dive-bombers— could not be used and a large hole had been blown in the center of the flight deck, which would have taken time to patch. However, the aft elevator could be used, as the torpedo planes were no longer in the hangar, and almost two hours would have been available for a makeshift repair to the flight deck.

In such a case, let us assume that the six Vals could have been ready to launch at around the same time as *Hiryu*'s torpedo planes—shortly after 1200. As for Zeros for escort, there were plenty available; *Hiryu* and *Akagi* would have inherited those from *Kaga* and *Soryu* on combat air patrol when those carriers were bombed. The problem would have been getting them landed and serviced immediately. Because of the damage to *Akagi*, Zeros could be landed, and turned around in a reasonable time, only on *Hiryu*. It will be assumed that nine Zeros could have been made ready on *Hiryu* soon enough for a launch to accompany the bombers.

As the surviving planes from the hypothetical first strike on the American carriers would have returned around 1230 and need to be landed immediately—most would have been shot up—it would have been necessary to complete the launch of the second strike by that time.[5] Let us therefore assume that the second strike force would have been launched by around 1230. It would have consisted of ten torpedo planes from *Hiryu* and six dive-bombers from *Akagi*; it would have been escorted by nine Zeros, all launched from *Hiryu*.

When that strike force got to the American carrier fleet at around 1330, it would have seen one smoldering, badly listing carrier dead in the water, and apparently finished; a second carrier—also smoldering, but apparently still steaming at normal speed; and a third carrier with no obvious damage, which appeared to be conducting normal flight operations. (That third carrier, which we are supposing was the lucky *Enterprise*, would have, in hypothetical fact, been damaged by bomb hits from the previous attack at around 1130, but by an hour later her flight deck would have been patched.)

Enterprise would have been crammed with aircraft. As the only carrier able to land planes after our hypothetical Japanese first attack, she would have had to accommodate the planes from all three carriers—not only those that had returned from the morning attack on the Mobile Force, but the fighters that had been on combat air patrol. Not all could have been taken on board: of the seventy-four planes that had returned, perhaps only the first sixty could have been recovered—with the fourteen later returnees, most of them *Enterprise* Dauntlesses out of fuel, which could not wait in the "queue," having to ditch. (The eleven Dauntlesses from *Hornet* that landed on Midway after failing to find the Mobile Force would remain there.) Of the twenty-eight Wildcats that had been on combat air patrol, and survived the Japanese attack (eight had been shot down in our hypothetical), there would be room on board for only about half of them. Let us assume that around a dozen would have been ordered to fly to Midway—where they would join the eleven *Hornet* dive-bombers already there—and sixteen would have landed on *Enterprise* for reservicing just before our second hypothetical Japanese attack arrived at 1330.

RESULTS OF SECOND ATTACK

When the small second strike force (of ten Kates, six Vals, and nine Zeros) would have been detected on radar at around 1320, there would have been a mad scramble—because of the cluttered flight deck—to get some Wildcats launched for air defense. But let us assume that some had already been relaunched after refueling, and that perhaps a half-dozen more could have been launched in time to engage the incoming planes, for a total of twelve.

APPLICATION OF RULES

Nine Zeros could be expected to divert nine of the Wildcats from the bombers (shooting down four to five, while losing two Zeros), leaving one Wildcat to take on the six Vals and two to attack the ten Kates. One Val and three Kates would be deflected from their target—with three-quarters shot down—leaving five Vals and eight Kates to get through. One (let us assume a Kate) would be shot down by the AA gunfire of *Enterprise*, leaving five Vals and seven Kates to drop ordnance on *Enterprise* and *Hornet*. One to two bombs and one to two torpedoes would hit, inflicting around 6 points of damage. If we apportion the points 2-1 between *Enterprise* and *Hornet*, respectively, 4 points of damage would be added to the 2 points already sustained by *Enterprise* from the first attack—knocking her out of action. The remaining 2 points of damage added to the 6 already sustained by *Hornet* would not be enough to destroy it—just leave it out of action. The cost in aircraft for the Japanese—adding a Val lost to AA gunfire after the attack—would have been about seven (two Vals, three Kates, and two Zeros.) The Americans would have lost five Wildcats.

But now, all three of the American carriers would be out of the battle, unable to conduct further flight operations. Nagumo's carriers would be free from further attack from those carriers for, at least, the remainder of the day. However, Midway itself would still be alive; the six operational Marine Dauntlesses and five Vindicator dive-bombers would have been supplemented by eleven Dauntlesses from *Hornet*, along with about sixteen Wildcats (twelve of which would also have become refugees from the carrier force.) Although refueling would be very slow, as the gasoline pumping system had been knocked out in the morning attacks, it seems that it still would have been possible for an ad hoc strike force to be prepared for an attack on Nagumo's carriers later in the afternoon.

THIRD ATTACK

In the meantime, the first Japanese strike force, which had completed its hypothetical attack on the American carriers around 1145, would have returned to *Akagi* and *Hiryu* a little after 1230, just after the smaller second strike force had been launched. We saw that about twenty-three dive-bombers, fifteen torpedo planes, and six Zeros could be expected to have returned. But, as many would have sustained damage, it is likely that only about two-thirds of them would have been available for further duty. Let us suppose that sixteen Vals and ten Kates—along with nine Zeros—could be sent on a third attack. As the turn-around time for the planes having returned from a prior strike was a little over three hours—a good part of it required to give the crews some rest and nourishment—we will assume that the third strike force could have been launched at around 1545.

When this third strike force would have arrived over the crippled American carriers, there would have been no combat air patrol to meet it. Thus, all of the dive-bombers and torpedo planes could be expected to release their ordnance. Five bombs and two torpedoes are likely to have hit the two out-of-action carriers—inflicting around 11 points of damage. This would have been more than enough finish off those carriers. Now, all three of Nimitz's carriers would have been sinking, or so helpless as to be easy prey for Japanese submarines. But Nagumo's remaining carriers were not home free just yet. Less than an hour after the third strike force had been launched, an American attack from Midway would have been spotted coming in.

MIDWAY STRIKES BACK

Earlier at Midway, eleven Dauntlesses from *Hornet*'s "Bombing-Eight" had landed on the airstrip at 1135. We also saw that around a dozen Wildcats from the CAP of the American carrier force would have been diverted to the atoll after the first Japanese attack had, in our hypothetical, disabled two carriers. Let us assume that they would have landed on Midway around 1400. Although refueling with hand pumps would have taken awhile, it would seem that some of them could have been made ready to escort the dive-bombers on an attack on the Mobile Force by around 1530.

In the meantime, the eleven *Hornet* Dauntlesses could have been refueled and armed with bombs—and their crews given some rest and sustenance—so they could also have been ready to go by then. They could have been joined by the eleven Marine dive-bombers. As for the size of the bombs that would be carried, the planes of "Bomb-ing-Eight" had jettisoned their 1,000-pound bombs before landing, and it is not clear whether Midway had any 1,000-pound bombs available. Let us assume that it had some and that *Hornet*'s eleven dive-bombers would be so equipped. (All the Marine dive-bombers would have been armed with the usual 500-pounders.) Let us also assume that ten Wildcats would be assigned for escort (with the remainder standing by for combat air patrol over the islands.)

When this strike force — twenty-two dive-bombers and ten Wildcats — would have reached the Mobile Force at around 1630, it would probably have run into a Japanese combat air patrol launched from *Akagi* and *Hiryu* — let us suppose sixteen Zeros. In order to model this hypothetical air combat and bombing attack, we have to devise some rules that were not necessary for evaluating the first (and actual) American attack on the Mobile Force:

1. Let us assume that each escorting Wildcat would keep one Zero away from the bombers — shooting down half and chasing away the other half, and that one and a half Wildcats would be lost for every Zero shot down.
2. Each of the remaining Zeros would destroy, or divert from their target, one dive-bomber, with half of them being shot down. For every six dive-bombers shot down or diverted, one Zero would be shot down by the bombers.
3. Of the dive-bombers that got through the Zeros, one would be shot down by the AA gunfire of each carrier attacked.
4. Of the bombers that got through both the CAP and AA gunfire to drop their bombs, one in seven dropped by the *Hornet* dive-bombers would hit, and one in twelve of those dropped by the Marine dive-bombers would hit. (These low hit rates reflect the inexperience of the Marine pilots — most of whom had to resort to glide-bombing because of lack of practice in making near-vertical dives. Also, the hit rate of *Hornet* dive-bomber pilots must be assumed to be lower than that of the *Enterprise* and *Yorktown* pilots — which would have been around one in five — because of the relative inexperience of the newly formed *Hornet* air group.) As with the earlier rules, each 1,000-pound bomb hit would do 1.5 points of damage and each 500-pounder would do 0.75 point.

APPLICATION

In the tussle with the Japanese combat air patrol, the ten Wildcats would engage ten Zeros, keeping them from the bombers. Five Zeros and seven Wildcats would be shot down. The remaining six Zeros would deflect six dive-bombers from their targets, shooting down three of them (while losing one more Zero.) Of the remaining sixteen dive-bombers, two would be shot down by the AA gunfire of *Akagi* and *Hiryu*. Let us assume that seven *Hornet* Dauntlesses and seven of the Marine dive-bombers would get through to drop bombs. It can be expected that one of the bombs dropped by the *Hornet* dive-bombers would hit — a 1,000-pounder (inflicting 1.5 points of damage) — along with one-half of a Marine 500-pounder. Let us suppose that the larger and slower out-of-action *Kaga* would have been the recipient of the 1,000-pound bomb. As she had already taken 3.75 points of damage while "partially vulnerable," another 1.5 points would have been enough to finish her off. It does not much matter who would take the smaller (and par-tial) bomb hit, as less than 0.5 point of damage would accrue; let us give it to *Akagi*.

Nagumo would now have lost two carriers — *Kaga* and *Soryu* — and *Akagi* would have been badly beaten up, though still operational after temporary repairs to her flight deck. Only *Hiryu* would have remained unscathed. But the carriers would be enough to finish the job at Midway. Of the twenty-two American dive-bombers that began this hypothetical attack, five would have been shot down before releasing their bombs, and roughly three more would have been shot down afterward by AA gunfire and pursuing Zeros. Of the dozen or so that would have made it back to Midway, about half would have been damaged too severely to be operational. There would not be enough left to seriously threaten the Mobile Force again. Nagumo's second strike on Midway—postponed at 0805 that morning—could now take place the next morning, though at greatly reduced strength, and would probably have resulted in the destruction of the remaining operational planes on Midway.

NOTES

1. This 1.5:1 ratio favoring Zeros over Wildcats would not have applied against *Yorktown*'s fighters—whose pilots had far more combat experience (from Coral Sea) than those of *Enterprise* and *Hornet*. Moreover, it would not obtain where the Zeros were greatly outnumbered—such as in the actual combat that took place over *Yorktown* in the first attack from *Hiryu* at 1200, when only four Zeros showed up. But, with an adequate number of Zeros—such as the twelve in this hypothetical—engaging inexperienced Wildcat pilots, this is a realistic ratio.

2. Although cruisers (and in the case of the Japanese carrier force, battleships) accounted for some casualties on attacking bombers, they were so few that we can disregard them in the interests of simplicity.

3. In the two actual air battles over *Yorktown*, Wildcats from *Enterprise* and *Hornet* were sent to augment *Yorktown*'s CAP.

4. Ten of *Yorktown*'s dive-bombers actually were launched at 1150, just before the real Japanese dive-bomber attack from *Hiryu* arrived. As for any that remained in the hangar with 1,000-pound bombs attached (as seven actually were), this probably would not have made *Yorktown* even partially "vulnerable." This is because, unlike the American bombs—which exploded about four feet into the hangar—most of the bombs carried by Japanese dive-bombers were armor-piercing and fused to detonate about forty feet deep into the ship, which did not have much impact in the hangar. As for the few high-explosive bombs carried by dive-bombers, they exploded on contact. Though this could blow holes in the flight deck and destroy planes on it, these bombs did not do much damage to aircraft in the high-ceilinged American hangars. (In the actual attack by *Hiryu*'s dive-bombers, one high-explosive bomb blew an eleven-foot hole in *Yorktown*'s flight deck—but, apparently, did not ignite the bombs or fuel of any of the Dauntless SBDs in the hangar.)

5. In the actual second attack by *Hiryu*'s torpedo planes, Yamaguchi had delayed the launch until around 1320—just before the Vals and Zeros from the actual first strike had to be landed—because he had been waiting for a search plane report identifying the carrier hit by the first attack and assessing the damage. In our hypothetical, however, it will be assumed that the second-strike planes would have been launched earlier, without waiting for the damage report.

NOTES

1. WHY THIS INQUEST

1. Nagumo's carrier force has been variously called Mobile Force, Striking Force, First Air Fleet or, in Japanese, *Kido Butai*.

2. John B. Lundstrom, *The First Team: Pacific Naval Air Combat from Pearl Harbor to Midway* (Annapolis: Naval Institute Press, 1984), p. 330.

3. Commander in Chief U.S. Pacific Fleet, "Battle Report," 28 June 1942, Serial 01849, part 1, p. 27.

4. The Japanese called their torpedo bombers "attack planes" (reflecting their dual role as torpedo carriers and level bombers) or "torpedo planes." Those terms will be used in this book when referring to Japanese aircraft rather than "torpedo bomber," which will be reserved for the American counterpart. In Japanese sources "carrier bomber" always refers to dive-bombers.

5. In chronological order: Samuel Eliot Morison, *Coral Sea, Midway and Submarine Actions, May 1942–August 1942*, vol. 4 of *History of United States Naval Operations in World War II* (Boston: Little, Brown, 1949); Mitsuo Fuchida and Masatake Okumiya, *Midway: The Battle That Doomed Japan*, ed. Clarke K. Kawakami and Roger Pineau (Annapolis: Naval Institute Press, 1955); Walter Lord, *Incredible Victory* (New York: Harper and Row, 1967); Gordon W. Prange, *Miracle at Midway*, ed. Donald M. Goldstein and Katherine V. Dillon (New York: McGraw-Hill, 1982); and Lundstrom (note 2, above).

6. Hitoshi Tsunoda, *Middowe Kaisen* [Midway Sea Battle], vol. 43 of Senshi Sosho [War History Series] (Tokyo: Asagumo Shimbunsha, 1971) (hereafter Senshi Sosho). (Under the American Library Classification system, the Midway volume is number 34.)

7. This order was not included in the Mobile Force's Midway operation order but was given to Nagumo orally before the fleets sortied from Japan. Yamamoto's staff officers Kameto Kuroshima and Yasuji Watanabe regretted after the battle that the order had not been put in writing. Prange, *Miracle at Midway*, p. 214.

8. In Japanese, *Kiroku Middowe Kaisen* (Tokyo: Bungei Shinju, 1986).

9. Sawachi, p. 22.

10. Senshi Sosho, pp. 281, 313.

11. Sawachi, p. 23.

12. Fuchida and Okumiya, *Midway* (American ed.), p. 161; Prange, *Miracle at Midway*, p. 214.

13. Mobile Force's Detailed Battle Report #6, translated and published by the Office of Naval Intelligence under the title "The Japanese Story of Midway," OPNAV P32-1002 (hereafter Official Report), p. 7.

14. Prange, *Miracle at Midway*, p. 214, says one hour or less; Fuchida and Okumiya, *Midway* (American ed.), p. 167, and Lord, p. 119, say that the rearming was half done thirty minutes after it began.

15. Senshi Sosho, p. 314.

16. Official Report, p. 42.

17. Morison, *Coral Sea*, p. 107.

18. Senshi Sosho, p. 308.

19. Fuchida and Okumiya, *Midway* (American ed.), p. 165; Prange, *Miracle at Midway*, p. 218; John Toland, *But Not in Shame* (New York: Random House, 1961), p. 382.

20. Official Report, p. 15.

21. Fuchida and Okumiya, *Midway* (American ed.), p. 167; Lord, p. 119; Lundstrom, p. 337.

22. Senshi Sosho, p. 313.

23. Sawachi, p. 23.

24. Senshi Sosho, p. 314.

25. Senshi Sosho, pp. 329, 372, and 377.

26. Ryunosuke Kusaka, *Rengo Kantai* [Combined Fleet] (Tokyo: Mainichi, 1952), p. 84; Minoru Genda, *Kaigun Kokutai Shimatsuki (Sento-hen)* [Short History of Naval Air Force: Battle volume] (Tokyo: Bungei Shunju, 1962), p. 141.

27. Fuchida and Okumiya, *Midway* (American ed.), p. 168; Lord, p. 124.

28. Prange, *Miracle at Midway*, p. 225.

29. Lord, p. 131; Lundstrom, p. 338.

30. Official Report, p. 7, "from about 0230 [0530 Midway time] two to three enemy flying boats maintained continuous contact with us."

31. Lord, p. 132.

32. Fuchida and Okumiya, *Midway* (American ed.), p. 154.

33. Senshi Sosho, pp. 296–97.

34. Senshi Sosho does not specify the number of Zeros in the Sixth Air Group; this number is from Ikuhiko Hata and Yasuho Izawa, *Japanese Naval Aces and Fighter Units in World War II* (Annapolis: Naval Institute Press, 1989), p. 148.

35. Senshi Sosho, p. 289.

36. Prange, Miracle at Midway, p. 218.

37. Senshi Sosho, p. 289.

38. Ibid., p. 290.

39. Ibid. (recollection of Minoru Genda).

40. Ibid., p. 291.

41. Ibid., p. 309. (See chart #29 therein.)

42. Lord, p. 128.

43. Senshi Sosho, pp. 308, 312.

44. Washington, D.C.: Potomac Books, 2005.

45. Ibid., p. 205.

46. Ibid., p. 230.

47. Mitsuo Fuchida and Masatake Okumiya, *Midway* (Kyoto: Nippon Shuppan, 1951).

48. Ibid., p. 172 (p. 271 in the 1982 edition).

49. Fuchida and Okumiya, *Midway* (American ed.), p. xix (Editors' Preface).

50. OPNAV P32-1002. Two versions of this report were published. One is in the May 1947 issue of the ONI Review, and the other was published as a separate booklet by ONI in June 1947. The latter is easiest to obtain, and for that reason I cite to it. Unfortunately, the pagination is different—which causes confusion, as some authorities cite to the ONI Review version. The Japanese language source for both versions (along with the unpublished carrier Action Reports cited in the next note) is JD-1, which is on microfilm at the U.S. Naval Historical Center.

51. WDC 160985-B. These translations were produced by the Washington Document Center and can be found in the U.S. Naval Historical Center, Operational Archives Branch, Washington, D.C.

52. Senshi Sosho, p. 284.

53. Doc. No. 34488. The Midway Operations Monograph was translated by General MacArthur's Allied Translator and Interpreter Section (ATIS).

54. The relevant text from pages 38 and 39 of the monograph is as follows: "Our reconnaissance plane discovers naval surface crafts of the enemy: At about 0500 hours [0800 Midway time] hours, the first message in respect to the discovery of the enemy, dispatched by the *Tone* plane of the fourth search line, which was reported to be greatly delayed, was received. . . . Therefore, at 0500 [0800] hours, we requested information on the type of naval ship. . . . At 0530 [0830] hours, it was reported that the enemy was accompanied by something resembling an aircraft carrier. . . . It was decided to launch an all-out attack on the enemy aircraft carriers after uniting with the Midway assault unit."

55. Japanese Monograph No. 93, "Midway Operations" is referred to by Japanese commentators as the "Detailed Report of Mobile Force Battles: The Second Demobilization / Deactivation Department." See Sawachi, p. 18.

56. The following Mobile Force air group veterans were interviewed in Japan in October 1992 and July 1993: Katutaro Akimoto, torpedo mechanic, *Akagi*; Takeshi Arakawa, dive-bomber mechanic, *Hiryu*; Mr. Dairoku, dive-bomber mechanic, *Soryu*; Fukuji Inoue, torpedo plane pilot, *Akagi*; Mr. Itazu, dive-bomber gunner, *Hiryu*; Yaroku Jinnouchi, Zero mechanic, *Hiryu*; Yuichi Kobayashi, chief of fighter squadron maintenance, *Hiryu*; Takeshi Maeda, torpedo plane pilot, *Kaga*; Tokayoshi Morinaga, torpedo plane pilot, *Kaga*; Mr. Motake, torpedo mechanic, *Soryu*; Yasaharu Mouri, dive-bomber mechanic, *Hiryu*; Tatsuya Ohtawa, torpedo plane pilot, *Soryu*; Moushichi Santou, dive-bomber mechanic, *Akagi*; Kanzo Sawada, dive-bomber mechanic, *Akagi*; Makato Tutumi, torpedo plane mechanic, *Hiryu*. Other Midway veterans with helpful information on events during the rearming operation were Hiseo Mandai, engineer, *Hiryu*; and Chuichi Yoshioka, staff officer, *Akagi* (who compiled Nagumo's Official Report.) Other veterans, not at Midway, who contributed to my investigation were Jiro Yoshida, Zero pilot, and, most importantly, Hitoshi Tsunoda, who served on the headquarters staff of the Naval Air Force in Tokyo at the time of the battle and was the principal author of the Senshi Sosho volume on Midway.

2. PRELUDE

1. Herbert Feis, *The Road to Pearl Harbor* (Princeton, N.J.: Princeton University Press, 1950), p. 268.

2. Data on Japan's oil imports, consumption, domestic production and reserves are taken from: Feis, pp. 268–69; David C. Evans and Mark R. Peattie, *Kaigun: Strategy, Tactics, and Technology in the Imperial Japanese Navy 1887–1941* (Annapolis: Naval Institute Press, 1997), pp. 410–13. (Note: Evans and Peattie use the Japanese measurement

for quantity of oil—kiloliters instead of barrels. Their figures have been converted to 42-gallon barrels in this book. For example, the Cabinet Planning Board's estimate of total petroleum reserves in late 1941 is listed as 8.4 million kiloliters. As there are roughly 160 liters in a 42-gallon barrel of oil, 8.4 billion liters divided by 160 = 52.5 million barrels—close to the quantity cited by Feis.)

3. Crude oil production in the Dutch East Indies was 65.1 million barrels in 1940. Daniel Yergin, *The Prize: The Epic Quest For Oil, Money and Power* (New York: Touchstone: Simon and Schuster, 1993), p. 356. British Borneo (Sarawak and Brunei) added another 7–8 million barrels. *The World Almanac and Book of Facts for 1941*, New York World-Telegram, p. 601. This was more than double Japan's estimated petroleum needs of 30–35 million barrels.

4. Samuel Eliot Morison, *The Rising Sun in the Pacific*, vol. 3 of *History of United States Naval Operations in World War II* (Boston: Little, Brown, 1988), p. 70.

5. Gordon W. Prange, *At Dawn We Slept* (New York: Penguin Books, 1982), p. 321.

6. B. H. Liddell Hart, *History of the Second World War* (New York: Putnam, 1970), p. 209.

7. David Bergamini, *Japan's Imperial Conspiracy* (New York: William Morrow, 1971), p. 300.

8. Morison, *Rising Sun*, p. 10.

9. Hansgeorg Jentschura, Dieter Jung, and Peter Mickel, *Warships of the Imperial Japanese Navy 1869–1945* (Annapolis: Naval Institute Press, 1992), p. 37.

10. Stefan Terzibaschitsch, *Battleships of the U.S. Navy in World War II* (New York: Bonanza Books, 1977), pp. 110–13.

11. Ibid., p. 93.

12. For a good summary of the treaty limitations, see Roger Chesneau, ed., *Conway's All the World's Fighting Ships, 1922–1946* (Annapolis: Naval Institute Press, 1980), p. 2.

13. Morison, *Rising Sun*, p. 16.

14. Bergamini, p. 17.

15. Bergamini estimates 150,000 (p. 44). Iris Chang, *The Rape of Nanking* (New York: Basic Books, 1997), p. 102, gives 260,000 as the total number killed.

16. It was later learned that the reign of terror in Nanking was in fact planned at a very high level in Tokyo for the purpose of intimidating the Chinese army and public into forsaking Chiang Kai-shek for a leader more amenable to Japanese will. Bergamini, p. 35.

17. *Ranger's* operational deficiencies are rarely mentioned, but James H. Belote and William M. Belote, *Titans of the Seas* (New York: Harper and Row, 1975), p. 113, is in accord with this assessment.

18. There were different carrier design philosophies between the two countries. American carriers (except for *Ranger*) vented their smoke vertically through funnels in the "island." Japanese carriers (up to *Junyo*) vented their smoke out of the side of the hull (which is why the island superstructure was so small.) The purpose of this was to keep the flight deck clear of smoke to make takeoff and landing operations less hazardous. The disadvantage was that smoke got into the hangars—and even crew's quarters—causing considerable discomfort, especially during battle-speed conditions. Japanese carrier flight decks were also relatively smaller than American ones. This is because aircraft were not parked on the flight deck as was the practice on American carriers; the Japanese usually kept their planes in the hangars between flight operations. (And their hangar decks were generally double-level compared with the large, but single-level, hangars of the American carriers.)

19. *Jane's Fighting Ships of World War II* (New York: Military Press, 1989; reprint of 1946–47 ed.), p. 187.

20. This was a class of carriers not yet built by the United States. However, in addition to *Hosho* and *Ryujo*, Japan had deployed *Zuiho*, and its sister *Shoho* (later sunk at Coral Sea) was nearing completion. (Both had been converted from submarine tenders.) Two more conversions—from ocean liners—would soon be completed: *Junyo* and *Hiyo*. It is difficult to classify these two carriers. In size they were CVs of 24,100 tons, but because of their slow speed (originally rated at 25.5 knots, but actually achieved only 22–23, see Jentschura, p. 52) they could not launch a full squadron of carrier torpedo planes. Thus, like *Ranger*, they functioned more like large light carriers—that is, to support amphibious troop landing operations. They also carried fewer planes than *Soryu* and *Hiryu*— only 53, with 48 operational.

When comparing carrier strength between the two countries it is not particularly useful to use the conventional designations of CV and CVL. *Soryu* was light, but as it could launch a full attack air group it was a full-fledged CV (though sometimes designated a CVL.) *Junyo* was much heavier than *Soryu*, but functioned as a light carrier. *Ranger* was designated a CV but also functioned more as a large CVL. More useful classifications to distinguish the various carriers would be between "attack" and "support" fleet carriers—the former fully capable of attacking large ships, the latter performing the role of giving fighter support to amphibious landings and providing combat air patrol. (This was the role of "CV" *Ranger*, and also *Junyo* until it was necessary to press it into fleet attack duty after the carrier losses at Midway.)

21. Bergamini, p. 921 n. 20.

22. The naval limitation treaties also imposed limitations on the number of heavy cruisers (with 8-inch guns) each nation could have, but allowed large 6-inch-gunned cruisers to be built, which though technically "light cruisers" were as heavy as "heavy cruisers," and thus referred to as "treaty" cruisers. The American treaty cruisers were the *Brooklyn* class; the Japanese the *Mogami* class.

23. For a much more detailed treatment of the technological developments that made carrier-based naval air power feasible, see Evans and Peattie, chap. 9 ("To Strike from the Sky")

24. See U.S. Naval Technical Mission to Japan, *Ordnance Targets, Japanese Torpedoes and Tubes*, Index No. O-01-2.

25. Morison, *Rising Sun*, p. 23.

26. Lundstrom, p. 140.

27. Before the war, all basic pilot training for the navy was done at Kasumigaura ("Misty Lagoon") on a lake 50 miles northeast of Tokyo. It was Japan's Pensacola, Florida.

28. Compiled from Hata and Izawa, Appendix C.

29. Although Japan had a total of about 3,500 naval pilots, the vast majority were land-based aircraft or seaplane pilots. The estimate of just under 500 that I use for carrier pilots is based on the total number of aircraft in the complements indicated in the "Japanese Navy Wartime Organization Table" for the six CVs and three CVLs as of December, 1941. Masatake Okumiya and Jiro Horikoshi, *Zero!* (New York: Ballantine Books, 1957), pp. 30–35. (In that table, the six CVs in the First Air Fleet had a total of 378, the three CVLs a total of 87, for a grand total of 465. Other sources add nine dive-bombers to *Kaga*'s complement.) To this a few more pilots can be added who were presumably awaiting assignment to the soon to be commissioned *Shoho*. The 400 carrier pilots who were in the First Air Fleet in the Pearl Harbor operation (355 assigned to the attack—plus about 45 for CAP) included around 20 of the most experienced pilots from the light carriers. Morison, *Rising Sun*, p. 85. These 400 can be considered "first-line" in the sense that they were available for fleet attack operations; however, only

about 250 (in the First and Second Carrier Divisions) were regarded as "first-line" by the Japanese carrier airmen.

30. Belote and Belote, p. 3; Lundstrom, p. 452.

31. In the British navy, carriers had even a lesser role. Although the British had built the first carrier, and had more of them at the beginning of the war than either America or Japan, they had not developed modern carrier aircraft (their torpedo bomber—the Swordfish—was a biplane). This was largely due to the fact that the Royal Navy was not permitted to have its own air arm and had to rely on the Royal Air Force (and development of carrier aircraft had a low priority with the RAF.) Thus, the British carrier fleet had no capability to attack other carrier fleets.

32. Compiled largely from Stefan Terzibaschitsch, *Aircraft Carriers of the U.S. Navy* (Annapolis: Naval Institute Press, 1989, pp. 323–325; Okumiya and Horikoshi, p. 32. Aircraft complement numbers vary among the sources, especially for the Japanese carriers. The numbers given, therefore, are a synthesis. Also, in actual carrier operations, the numbers of the various types of planes differed from the nominal complements. For example, the number of operational dive-bombers carried by *Kaga* is often given as 18, but for all its actual combat operations—beginning with Pearl Harbor—it carried 27. For the American carriers, the total number of aircraft usually given for *Lexington* and *Saratoga* exceeds 80 (which because of their huge flight decks they could easily ferry.) However, because of their cramped hangars, in actual combat operations they carried closer to 70. Also, the standard fighter squadron was increased from 18 to 27 when the folding-wing model of the Wildcat F4F came on line in late spring of 1942 (increasing the operational complements from 72 to 81 planes for most of the American carriers.)

33. Joseph C. Grew, *Ten Years in Japan* (New York: Simon and Schuster, 1944), p. 327.

34. Indeed, it was so inviting that many Japanese Pacific War veterans—and some historians as well—believe that the move was made by President Roosevelt to lure Japan into attacking Pearl Harbor so America could enter the war. Chuichi Yoshioka (one of Vice Admiral Nagumo's staff officers) expressed this view with passion in an interview in Kobe, Japan, 1993. Munehiro Miwa says that the notion that President Roosevelt enticed Japan into starting the war is very popular among the Japanese military history community. This notion is not confined to Japan. See Robert B. Stinnett, *Day of Deceit: The Truth about FDR and Pearl Harbor* (London: Constable, 2000; also American ed., New York: Free Press, 2000.) I have concluded that there is no hard evidence for this theory.

35. Prange, *At Dawn We Slept*, p. 159. (When Japanese aerial torpedoes were launched at the preferred altitude and speed—250 feet at over 200 mph—they dove between 100 and 300 feet deep before rising to the surface.)

36. Commander Mitsuo Fuchida, who would later lead the air strike on Pearl Harbor, was in charge of training the torpedo plane crews (however, Genda became personally involved in the later stages). The training was done at Kagoshima Bay at the southern tip of Kyushu—a bay that was similar to Pearl Harbor. The special launch technique for shallow water required a very slow speed for the plane—100 knots compared with the usual 200—and a drop from about 50 feet—compared with the usual 250. See Prange, *At Dawn We Slept*, pp. 321, 324, and 332.

37. Prange, *At Dawn We Slept*, p. 161.

38. According to Feis, p. 269, by the beginning of December, the oil reserve had been drawn down from around 50 million barrels in September to just 43 million. But estimates differ: Evans and Peattie have the total reserves at the beginning of the war as 52.5 million barrels (8.4 million kiloliters.) It is interesting to note, however, that after the war began the shortage of fuel oil, in fact, became so severe by the fall of 1942 that the Japanese navy was reluctant to deploy its largest battleships in battle. (The deployment of all

eleven battleships in the Midway operation had consumed far more oil than planned prewar.) Only two of the light *Kongo*-class battleships were used at the sea Battle of Guadalcanal on November 14–15, where, with their 14-inch guns, they were no match against the American *Washington* and *South Dakota* battleships with 16-inch guns. The super-battleships *Yamato* and *Musashi*—each with 18-inch guns—would probably have easily sunk the American battleships, but were kept in port.

39. Feis, p. 270.

40. Prange, *At Dawn We Slept*, p. 282.

41. Ibid., p. 296.

42. Translations of the various cautionary statements made by Yamamoto differ. What I have given is a composite of the various versions. See Morison, *Rising Sun*, p. 46.

43. Although Yamamoto has acquired a reputation in America as being an almost pro-American anti–Pacific war pacifist, he has—according to Munehiro Miwa—a reputation among many of the veterans who knew him as having been one of the more pro-war members of the naval high command, at least in the months leading up to December 7. However, direct evidence of Yamamoto's opinions in favor of war with the United States, and optimism concerning his Pearl Harbor plan, during 1941 is very difficult to come by. There is widespread belief among younger Japanese historians that many of Yamamoto's letters were destroyed—and that some of those which survived were "doctored"—after the surrender, to place the war hero in a better light with the Allies. Miwa presented an argument for this unpopular theory in a symposium edition of the Yomiuri newspaper, "The 20th Century—What Kind of Century Is It?" (Tokyo, 1999), pp. 72–73. However, Miwa concedes that there is, as yet, no conclusive proof of this. But it is known that Yamamoto was a prolific letter writer, and thus it is curious that so few of his letters written in 1941 have been found. (An even more extensive "sanitizing" of the Emperor Hirohito took place to minimize his role in leading the war effort, but modern historians have begun to pierce this veil of deception. See Bergamini and, more recently, Herbert P. Bix, *Hirohito and the Making of Modern Japan* (New York: Harper Collins, 2000.)

44. This optimism is rarely mentioned by Western historians, but two who do are Robert Cowley in *What If? Military Historians Imagine What Might Have Been* (London: Macmillan, 2000), pp. 332, 337, and Philip D. Grove, *Midway 1942* (London: Brassey's, 2004).

45. Morison, *Rising Sun*, p. 130. Not only were there no radio transmissions from the First Air Fleet, there were none from Yamamoto that specifically identified it. Edwin T. Layton, *"And I Was There": Pearl Harbor and Midway: Breaking the Secrets* (New York: Quill, William Morrow, 1985), pp. 230, 505–6.

46. Stinnett has contended in *Day of Deceit*, pp. 45–47 (in British ed.), that a radio message from Yamamoto ordering a carrier task force to advance into Hawaiian waters and attack the United States fleet was received and decoded by the American naval intelligence station at Pearl Harbor. However, no such message—decoded before the Pearl Harbor attack—can be found in official American records (Stinnett claims deliberate withholding by the American government.) And Edwin T. Layton, who was Admiral Kimmel's intelligence chief at the time, has testified that no such message was intercepted (which Stinnett dismisses as a cover-up.)

More credible is a contention that on November 25 a British naval intelligence unit—the Far East Combined Bureau (FECB)—in Singapore picked up and decoded a message from Yamamoto instructing a task force (unidentified) to move out of Tankan Bay in the Kuriles the next morning and advance to a standby location for refueling eight days later. (The coordinates for that refueling location—which happened to be in the north Pacific about three-quarters of the way to Pearl Harbor—were included, but they were in a special code that apparently had not been broken by the FECB.) The British government refuses to confirm this intercept or release any relevant documents. See James Rusbridger and Eric Nave, *Betrayal At Pearl Harbor* (New York: Touchstone, Simon and Schuster, 1992.) This message from Yamamoto would, if actually intercepted and decoded, indicate that an attack had been planned on a distant target—though not necessarily Pearl Harbor; there were other equally distant possible targets, such as Singapore. Edwin Layton denies that the message was decoded by American naval intelligence at the time but believes that it was received by Roosevelt from Churchill. Layton, p. 207. Rusbridger, on the other hand, speculates that Churchill—treacherously—did not pass this message on to Roosevelt; he wanted Pearl Harbor to be a shocking surprise to better ensure America's entry into the war. Rusbridger and Nave, p. 144.

47. Morison, *Rising Sun*, p. 77.

48. Ibid., p. 78. (This belies the idea that the Japanese intended a totally "sneak" attack. They counted on surprise—and 30 minutes notice would not have given the Americans time to organize a defense—but they wanted to conform at least nominally to diplomatic conventions.)

49. Donald M. Goldstein and Katherine V. Dillon, eds., *The Pearl Harbor Papers* (New York: Brassey's, 1993), pp. 42–43.

50. *Akagi* was designed to have the same aircraft capacity as *Kaga*, but for the Pearl Harbor and Midway operations carried fewer planes. This was because its fuel oil tanks were smaller than *Kaga's*; to give it the same range, *Akagi* carried extra oil in drums, which were stored in the lower hangar—reducing space for airplanes. Interview with Tokayoshi Morinaga (torpedo plane pilot on *Kaga*), July 1993.

51. United States Strategic Bombing Survey (Pacific), Naval Analysis Division, *The Campaigns of the Pacific War* (Washington, D.C.: Government Printing Office, 1946), pp. 13–14. (The text states *Ryujo* and *Ryuho*; however *Ryuho* was not completed until November 1942, and the only operational carrier of that class—as of December 1941—was *Zuiho*.)

52. Morison, *Rising Sun*, pp.120, 211; Prange, *At Dawn We Slept*, p. 460.

53. Torpedo and bomb damage data is compiled from Prange, *At Dawn We Slept*, p. 512 (Fuchida's damage chart); and Morison, *Rising Sun*, pp. 103–114.

54. Varying figures have been given, and because of the difficulty of distinguishing planes destroyed from those badly damaged, and distinguishing those destroyed in the first wave attack from those in the second, the exact number may never be known. These figures are compiled from Morison, *Rising Sun*, pp. 120–24.

55. At the time the first wave of the strike force was launched, eight seaplanes were launched from the cruisers *Tone* and *Chikuma*, and the battleships *Hiei* and *Kirishima*, to search the area around the Mobile Force to a radius of 180 miles. Genda, *Pearl Harbor Papers*, p. 42.

56. Layton, p. 498. Admiral Nimitz expressed the opinion that if the oil tank farms had been destroyed, it could have prolonged the war by as much as two years. Yergin, p. 327.

57. Prange, *At Dawn We Slept*, p. 550.

58. Lundstrom, pp. 16–18.

59. Those ships were *Maryland, Pennsylvania,* and *Tennessee*, and had been joined by *Colorado* (which was being overhauled on the west coast at the time of the attack.) Three equally obsolete ships of the *New Mexico* class had also been brought in from the Atlantic.

60. Admiral Ernest J. King, commander in chief of the United States Fleet, noted in his endorsement on the Report of the Naval Court of Inquiry in 1944 that "It is evident, in retrospect, that the capabilities of Japanese aircraft torpedoes were seriously underestimated." Morison, *Rising Sun*, p. 139.

61. Captain W. D. Puleston (former director of the Office of Naval Intelligence), writing shortly before Pearl Harbor, noted that no capital ship had been sunk by an air bomb. Puleston, *The Armed Forces of the Pacific* (New Haven: Yale University Press, 1941), pp. 228–30.

62. This racial slur is not included here gratuitously. It was taken from a recent television documentary on the Pacific War and is typical of the attitude admitted to by veterans interviewed in many other such documentaries.

63. See Puleston, pp. 183–85, for the most detailed assessment of Japanese carrier strength from the American navy's perspective in 1941. Captain Puleston had gathered his data from *The Japan Year Book, Brassey's Naval Annual, Jane's Fighting Ships,* and the *United States Naval Institute Proceedings.* As a retired naval officer who had been director of the Office of Naval Intelligence, he was in a unique position to know what was known in the West about the Japanese naval capabilities and how they were assessed by the American naval high command prior to the Pearl Harbor attack. (See Layton, p. 59.) The gist of his assessment of the Japanese carrier force is that America did not have much to worry about. Among comments that probably reflect the thinking of the American naval high command at the time are: "As a group the American carriers are larger, speedier and carry more planes than the Japanese" (p. 184); "Japan has been energetic in her efforts to create naval aviation, but she is usually a phase behind" (p. 226); "capital ships have not been sunk by air bombs" (p. 230); "In design, contemporary American planes are faster, more maneuverable. . . . American personnel have more natural aptitude for flying and . . . are more thoroughly trained" (p. 232).

64. Yergin, p. 316.

65. Rusbridger, p. 131.

66. The translation—made after the war—of the exact text of this message from Yamamoto was: "The Task Force, keeping its movement strictly secret, shall leave Hitokappu Bay on the morning of 26 November and advance to 42° N. 170° E. on the afternoon of 3 December and speedily complete refueling." United States Strategic Bombing Survey, *Campaigns,* p. 50. It should be noted that the compass coordinates could not be decoded by any of the Allies before the war. Also, although this version purports to be addressed to the First Air Fleet, in fact, the actual message prefixes did not identify the First Air Fleet (Nagumo's carrier striking force) but, rather, were to other fleets not involved in the Pearl Harbor operation, namely: Second Fleet, Third Fleet, Fourth Fleet, Combined Fleet, and Eleventh Air Fleet (containing only land-based aircraft). See Rusbridger, p. 138–39. No copy of this message exists in American or British wartime communications records—or at least none has been disclosed. This text was retrieved from the wreck of the Japanese cruiser *Nachi.* Rusbridger, p. 273 n. 28. Although there is compelling evidence that it was received and decoded (except for the refueling location coordinates) by British naval intelligence, as discussed in a previous note it is not known whether it was received and decoded by American naval intelligence prior to the Pearl Harbor attack.

3. THE RUN-UP TO MIDWAY

1. Only 22 planes (13 dive-bombers and 9 Zeros) were launched. Morison, *Rising Sun,* p. 169. As previously mentioned, some of *Ryujo*'s normal aircraft complement (37–40 aircraft) had been stripped off to strengthen the Mobile Force.

2. *Timewatch,* "Death of the Battleship," BBC/History Channel co-production (January 2001).

3. Belote and Belote, p. 35.

4. Yergin, p. 356.

5. Although 15 hits on the cruiser *Cornwall* were claimed by the Japanese airmen, the British recorded only eight. Belote and Belote, p. 61.

6. The F4F-4 model of the Wildcat was not, however, received with great enthusiasm by the pilots. The 400-pounds of extra weight substantially degraded its performance (and the increase in guns from four to six resulted in a shorter duration of shell fire.) The Japanese Zero pilots zealously—and successfully for a time—opposed measures to increase their protection at the expense of added weight. They believed that their chances for survival in dogfights depended more on greater maneuverability. This trade-off worked until they ran out of highly trained pilots after the first year of the war.

7. The North American B-25 had a loaded weight of 35,000-pounds and was powered by two 1,700-h.p. engines. Of the two medium bombers in service at the time—the other being the Martin B-26—the B-25 was chosen because it had a longer range: 1,500 miles compared with 1,150 for the B-26. Elke C. Weal, John A. Weal, and Richard F. Barker, *Combat Aircraft of World War Two* (New York: Macmillan, 1977), p. 205.

8. See Thomas Wildenberg, "Midway: Sheer Luck or Better Doctrine?" *Naval War College Review* 58, no. 1 (Winter 2005), p. 130. (This idea originated with Mitsuo Fuchida.) While it was true that the Japanese preferred to use cruiser-launched float planes instead of carrier-based attack planes in situations where they did not expect to find American carriers—such as at Midway—the ensuing account of the battle at Coral Sea shows that when enemy carriers were known to be in the area the Japanese commanders were not at all reluctant to use carrier-based attack planes to locate them.

9. This count is derived from Lundstrom's table (in *First Team*) for aircraft strength on May 7 (given on p. 190), by adding the aircraft losses incurred on May 4 in the attack on Tulagi.

10. Ibid., p. 188.

11. Ibid., p. 209.

12. Ibid., p. 217, has them landing safely, but most commentators have most of them ditching in the sea. Morison, *Coral Sea*, p. 44; Belote and Belote, p. 77. (Lundstrom notes that the claim of exaggerated losses by ditching comes from a postwar interview with VADM Hara, who lacked the relevant documents. Lundstrom, p. 511 n. 11.)

13. Different accounts give different numbers of planes available for May 8. The numbers I give come from Lundstrom, p. 221. (He counts 117 operational planes at the end of May 7. However, one *Yorktown* fighter counted as inoperable was repaired the next morning and saw duty, so I count it as operational.)

14. Ibid., p. 246.

15. Belote and Belote, p. 81.

16. Some accounts—beginning with Morison—state that this was an 800-pound bomb (*Coral Sea*, p. 55.) However, the largest bomb carried by Vals weighed 250 kilograms (550 pounds).

17. The aircraft losses for both sides that I have enumerated were compiled from Lundstrom, chap. 12.

18. See ibid., p. 280.

19. The various phases of the Japanese "Basic Plan" promulgated by the Naval General Staff in December 1941 are discussed in detail in the final chapter of this book, and are taken from Senshi Sosho, pp. 63–69.

20. Lord, p. 5.

21. Actually less than 40 percent of the text could be read, depending on how often the code books were changed. See Layton, p. 420. However, many Japanese veterans assume

we could read 100 percent—even before Pearl Harbor (among them is Hitoshi Tsunoda, who wrote the Senshi Sosho volume on Midway.)

22. Indeed, Admiral King, Cominch U.S. Fleet, disagreed with Nimitz's deduction that Midway was the target. He had Nimitz's HYPO intelligence, but interpreted it differently. He initially thought that indication of a Midway operation was a ruse to cloak a strike to the south or on west coast naval installations. Layton, p. 414.

23. It is not known how many were reassigned, but one of the veterans interviewed by me, Katuturo Akimoto, a torpedo plane weapons mechanic, had been transferred from *Shokaku* to *Akagi*.

24. I define "attack carriers" as only those that carried a complete air group of at least one full squadron each of torpedo planes, dive-bombers, and fighters and could launch a full squadron of at least 18 fully loaded torpedo planes in one deckload in calm weather. The fairly light *Hiryu* and *Soryu* (17,300 and 15,900 tons respectively) are sometimes designated CVLs. However, because of their tremendous speed they met the foregoing criteria and, thus, qualified as full-fledged attack carriers. On the other hand, *Junyo* and *Hiyo*, though usually designated CVs because of their displacement (over 24,000 tons) could not carry a complete air group and, because of their slow speed (rated at 25.5 knots, but actually no more than 23) and relatively short flight deck (less than 700 feet), they could not launch 18 loaded torpedo planes in one deckload in calm weather. (They never carried more than 10 Kates.) Thus, I classify them as "support" carriers, along with *Ryujo* and *Zuiho*. Their role was mainly to support amphibious invasions, rather than attack ships.

25. Most of the pilots of these Zeros were not carrier-qualified. However, it appears that three of them (all from *Akagi*) participated in the combat air patrol after all the regular Zeros had been deployed and things became desperate after successive attacks on the Mobile Force. See Hata and Izawa, p. 149. Also, *Soryu* carried two special experimental dive-bombers (later known as "Judy") to be used for high-speed reconnaissance. Thus, there may actually have been about 230 operational planes available to Nagumo. (For the aircraft complements on each carrier, see "Orders of Battle" later in this chapter.)

26. *Ryujo* carried 16 fighters and 21 torpedo planes. The exact plane complement of *Junyo* is unknown, and varying numbers are given. The best estimate is from Okumiya in his statement given in the United States Strategic Bombing Survey, Naval Analysis Division, *Interrogations of Japanese Officials*, OPNAV P-03-100, p. 93: 51 planes—30 fighters and 21 dive-bombers (no torpedo planes.)

27. It will be noted that all the capital ships—battleships and fleet attack carriers—were in Hiroshima Bay. Hashirajima anchorage was the Japanese counterpart to Pearl Harbor. Also on Hiroshima Bay were the major port and shipbuilding city of Kure; Eta Jima, home of the Japanese Naval Academy; and Hiroshima, counterpart to Honolulu.

28. Fuchida and Okumiya, *Midway* (this and all citations hereafter are to the American ed.), pp. 119–20, 129; and Admiral Matome Ugaki, *Fading Victory: The Diary of Admiral Matome Ugaki* (Pittsburgh: University of Pittsburgh Press, 1991), p. 135 (hereafter Ugaki Diary).

29. Fuchida and Okumiya, *Midway*, p. 124. (It should be noted that *Akagi*'s antenna—which was rigged on the side of the flight deck—appears to have been even shorter than those of the other three carriers, possibly heightening Kusaka's worries.)

30. Jonathan Parshall and Anthony Tully (in *Shattered Sword: The Untold Story of the Battle of Midway* [Washington, D.C.: Potomac Books, 2005], at pp. 99–102) argue that Nagumo had, in fact, received all the important radio intelligence indicating the possible presence of American carriers in the Midway area. To the claim by Fuchida (in his

book *Midway*) that Nagumo had not received it, Parshall and Tully say, essentially, that he lied. (Fuchida did stretch the truth about some things—such as the "fateful five minutes"—but this does not mean that he lied about everything.) They offer no proof whatever that Nagumo had received this vital intelligence; they merely assume that because the battleships and some other ships in the Mobile Force had the capability of receiving long-distance radio transmissions they must have received all important radio intelligence and relayed it to Nagumo.

Fuchida, however, is not the only one to claim that Nagumo did not receive this intelligence: Chuichi Yoshioka (one of Nagumo's staff officers and the principal author of the Official Report), in an interview with me in July 1993, stated that *Akagi* did not receive any "long wave" radio transmissions prior to the battle. (He related how he and Kusaka had been interrogated by some members of Yamamoto's staff as to these communications at an informal inquiry in 1953—following the publication of Fuchida's book in Japan. Those staff officers had been shocked to learn that Nagumo had not received those crucial long-wave transmissions.)

It is, of course, impossible to know what Nagumo knew before the battle. But in his Official Report he complained that before the battle he "had practically no intelligence concerning the enemy" (p. 6), and had been led to believe that there were no American carriers in the vicinity (p. 3). This, I suppose, can be dismissed as lies also.

But Nagumo's known behavior on the morning of the battle certainly is not that of someone who had reason to believe that American carriers might be in the vicinity: the minimal precautionary search effort (compared to the extensive searches at the Coral Sea, where American carriers were expected); the rearming of the torpedo planes at 0715—rendering them impotent against any American carriers that might be discovered. As to why Nagumo did not act on this intelligence he supposedly received by altering his search plan to make it more thorough and refrain from rearming his torpedo planes, Parshall and Tully offer no explanation other than suggesting Nagumo's inability to adapt and general incompetence. (One of the purposes of my book is to present a scenario that explains why the Japanese lost the battle that is not premised on blatant stupidity on the part of the Japanese commanders.)

31. Layton, p. 415.

32. Ibid., p. 433.

33. Nagumo's Official Report, p. 3.

34. Prange, *Miracle at Midway*, p. 146 (citing interview with Kuroshima.) See also Lord, p. 44.

35. Senshi Sosho, p. 286.

36. The only explanation I can find for this failure to provide Nagumo with adequate radio equipment is that in none of the prior campaigns—Pearl Harbor, Indian Ocean, Coral Sea—had it been necessary for the carrier force commander to receive last-minute information from *long-distance* radio signals. Thus, the problem simply may have not been anticipated by Yamamoto. Still, however, it seems that Yamamoto should have found some way to brief Nagumo on the eve of the battle to make certain that he was aware of the possibility that American carriers might be at Midway.

37. Official Report, p. 3.

38. See Lundstrom, pp. 309–20, for detailed account.

39. These Action Reports are contained in WDC 160985–B, on file at the Naval Archives in Washington, D.C. They are unpublished and the translation is poor, but a wealth of detail concerning the deployment of the Japanese carrier aircraft can be gleaned from them. Senshi Sosho is also very helpful in filling in gaps and resolving ambiguities in the Action Reports regarding the aircraft complements.

40. Hata and Izawa, p. 148. (Although *Japanese Naval Aces and Fighter Units in World War II* was first published in Japanese in 1970, it was not available in English until 1989, when published by the Naval Institute Press.)

41. The very concept of "spares" was peculiar to the Japanese navy at the time of Midway; American carrier squadrons in the first year of the war generally did not have them. Because of the limited number of Japanese carrier pilots, it was essential that there be a plane available for each able-bodied pilot. And as carrier planes were easily damaged during carrier operations, the solution was to carry extra planes. (Japan produced more planes than carrier pilots.) In the American navy, on the other hand, especially in the early months of the war, the problem was reversed: the most serious shortage was with carrier aircraft; there were not enough to go around for the pilots on hand. Because of this, American carrier plane squadrons often carried not extra planes, but extra pilots—called "supernumeraries." See Lundstrom, p. 320.

42. Ohtawa interview. (He also noted that some disassembled spares were hung from the hangar ceiling.)

43. Lt. Tomonaga of *Hiryu* replaced Cdr. Mitsuo Fuchida as commander of the Midway strike force after Fuchida became disabled from an appendicitis operation.

44. This includes three Zeros from the Sixth Air Group that participated in the combat air patrol and, thus, could be regarded as operational.

45. The data is ambiguous on how many operational Zeros *Kaga* had. Senshi Sosho states that after 36 Zeros had departed for the Midway strike there were 9 remaining on each carrier. But it later states that after 3 had been launched from each carrier for combat air patrol at 0430, there were 7 remaining on board *Kaga*. (See p. 315.) However, it also notes that one Zero launched from either *Hiryu* or *Soryu* around 0600 had returned with engine trouble. It does not state from which carrier the Zero originated, or to which carrier it returned, but it appears that it landed on *Kaga* and was included in the count of 7 Zeros. The CAP schedule in *Kaga*'s Action Report (WDC 160985B) is also confusing. It states that *Kaga* had 16 Zeros for CAP, but the numbers given for the various "watches" (patrols) for Zeros deployed for the first time add up to much less than that.

46. These were experimental models of the Yokosuka D4Y "Suisei" (Comet) dive-bomber (later known to the Americans as "Judy"). At 343 mph it was the fastest plane at Midway.

47. On June 3, *Akigumo* was detached to escort the Supply Unit.

48. The following data is from Lundstrom, p. 330.

49. The destroyer *Gwin* was delayed and joined on June 5.

50. Different numbers have been given for many of the plane types at Midway. My data is a synthesis from Bates's Naval War College analysis; Morison, *Coral Sea*; and Lord.

51. These were Consolidated Catalina flying boats. About half were model PBY-5a, which were amphibians and could also be land-based. The number operational is an estimate (two were damaged on May 31).

4. THE FATAL DECISION

1. Senshi Sosho (p. 314) says 12 Zeros, 3 from each carrier, were launched. However, *Kaga*'s Action Report states that *Kaga* launched only 2 Zeros for combat air patrol at 0430, which would make a total of 11. WDC 160985-B.

2. The actual launch times for the *Tone* and *Chikuma* search planes were: *Chikuma* #5—0435; *Chikuma* #6—0438; *Tone* #3—0442; *Tone* #4—0500. Senshi Sosho, p. 304.

3. Most accounts—including Nagumo's Official Report—have 45 torpedo planes

left. I accept Senshi Sosho's version that the 2 used for search duty came from the regular operational complements, p. 287. It does seem odd, however, that the planes were not taken from the 6 spares. Apparently, there were only 45 torpedo plane pilots on *Akagi* and *Kaga*—reflecting the broader pilot shortage problem bedeviling the Japanese navy at that time.

4. See Action Reports of the carriers (especially *Hiryu's*). WDC 160985–B.

5. Fuchida and Okumiya, *Midway* (American ed.), p. 152.

6. Richard W. Bates, *The Battle of Midway Including the Aleutian Phase, June 3 to June 14, 1942: Strategical and Tactical Analysis* (Naval War College, 1948), p. 122. (This is unpublished but available at selected libraries.) The Catalina PBY that discovered the Mobile Force was 4V58. It is not known why it, or other PBYs drawn to the area soon after, failed to monitor the Mobile Force and send updates after 0552. American carrier commanders did not know that four carriers were in a single group until after 1000, when dive-bombers from *Enterprise* arrived over the Mobile Force.

7. This search plane was erroneously identified in Nagumo's Official Report as the one on the "#4 search line." Senshi Sosho (p. 307) points out that *Tone* 4's course of 100° made it impossible for it to have seen planes coming from Midway. Only *Tone* 1, on the #3 search line (course of 123°), could have seen these planes. Moreover, the recorded time was in error. The planes were probably 16 dive-bombers—which did not take off from Midway until after 0600 and form up until around 0610. The only group of American planes anywhere near this numerous that were in the air at 0555 were 14 B-17s, but they were too far west to be seen by any Japanese search planes.

8. Most of the details of Japanese losses come from Action Reports of the Mobile Force's carrier air groups, translated into WDC 160985–B, and from Senshi Sosho.

9. See Action Reports, WDC 160985–B.

10. Although Nagumo's Official Report (at p. 7) indicates that Tomonaga's report was received in headquarters at 0715, most commentators—apparently believing that this was a misprint or translation error—put the time of receipt earlier. Fuchida and Okumiya, *Midway*, pp. 159–60; Lundstrom, p. 337. As *Akagi's* radio was monitoring the strike group's radio frequencies, the report should not have taken 15 minutes to reach Nagumo, and as he made his decision to rearm the second-wave planes for another strike on Midway at 0715 based on Tomonaga's recommendation, it seems reasonable to assume that it took several minutes to make that decision. Thus, 0705 seems the best guess for time of receipt.

11. Plane and pilot losses, including planes that returned inoperable, are from Senshi Sosho, p. 302.

12. Bates, p. 114; Lord, p. 126.

13. Senshi Sosho, p. 315. (Most of the pilots in the Sixth Air Group with carrier experience were on *Junyo* in the Aleutian campaign.)

14. Ibid., p. 315; Action Reports of *Akagi* and *Hiryu*, WDC 160985B.

15. Senshi Sosho, p. 287. (This order is logged in the Official Report, p. 13, but is much more cryptic and does not mention Midway.)

16. Sawachi, *Record of the Midway Sea Battle*, p. 23. Sawachi also notes that there is no other record in the surviving radio logs of Mobile Force ships of Tomonaga's message.

17. Senshi Sosho interprets the 0520 directive as merely being a precautionary order to alert the second-wave commanders of the possibility of a second strike on Midway. It suggests that Nagumo entered the morning suspecting that surprise for the first attack might have been lost when the Transport Group was discovered the day before. Senshi Sosho, pp. 286–87.

18. Bates, p. 110.

19. For contact with Mobile Force to be made at 0534, even assuming it had advanced toward Midway 20 nautical miles since the launch of the Midway strike force, and even assuming that the PBY was 40 miles away when the sighting was made, the PBY would be about 150 nautical miles from Midway. As the PBY flew at 100 knots, it would take one and a half hours to get that far.

20. The heavy reliance by the Japanese on cruiser-based float planes, rather than carrier-based bombers, for reconnaissance at sea has also been criticized. This criticism is ill founded because it is based on a misconception of the nature of the float planes used. The assumption appears to be that the Japanese float planes were something comparable to the American cruiser-based Vought "Kingfisher" float plane. (This plane clearly was unsuitable for long-range surface ships searches and was used only for anti-submarine patrol.) On the other hand, the Aichi E13 "Jake" float plane deployed from *Tone* and *Chikuma* at Midway was a new-type reconnaissance plane. It was much larger, much faster, more powerful, and of longer range than the American Kingfisher.

In fact, the Jake was in almost every respect relevant to reconnaissance comparable to the Kate torpedo plane (which was the Japanese carrier plane most suitable for reconnaissance.) The Jake's range was slightly longer than the Kate's, its cruising speed was almost as fast, its weight and armament about the same, and its crew of three the same as the Kate's. It was eminently suitable as a search plane. At Midway, the Japanese did use older float planes of a lower performance comparable to the Kingfisher for anti-submarine patrol, and one of them from battleship *Haruna* was used for the seventh, shorter, line of the surface ship search.

21. Senshi Sosho, p. 305. See also Bates, p. 126.

22. Bates, p. 126.

23. Official Report, p. 42.

24. Senshi Sosho, pp. 309, 311. Senshi Sosho was not the first authority to conclude that *Tone* 4 had shortened its course. Bates, 25 years earlier in his Naval War College analysis, had noticed the same thing (see his Diagram D-2).

25. Yoshiji Doi, *The Pacific War Which I Saw* (Japan, 1975), pp. 134–38. (Translation of excerpt obtained from Munehiro Miwa; full Japanese citation unavailable.)

26. Official Report, p. 14.

27. Fuchida and Okumiya, *Midway*, p. 161; Prange, *Miracle at Midway*, p. 214.

28. Interview with Akimoto at Sakura, Chiba, Japan, on August 4, 1993.

29. Prange, *Miracle at Midway*, p. 214 (based on interviews with Yamamoto's staff officers Kuroshima and Watanabe.)

30. If landing operations began at 0835 on *Akagi* and *Kaga*, it would take 15 minutes to land the dive-bombers and another 15–20 minutes to land the Zeros (including those on combat air patrol needing rearming.) It would then take about 40 minutes to raise the torpedo planes from the hangar decks and spot them on the flight decks for launch.

31. Although the Japanese did not know the schedule for the American bombers from Midway, their fear that a 1000 launch for the second strike would fail to catch the American bombers on the ground was well-founded: the American dive-bombers took off from Midway at about 0605. The first group of dive-bombers finished their attack around 0815, and the second (slower) group around 0840. They got back around 0915 and 0950, respectively. Therefore, if a second-wave attack had arrived at 1000, it probably would have caught most of them on the runway. By 1100, however, they could have been refueled and rearmed and, given sufficient warning time, been off the ground.

32. Senshi Sosho, pp. 313–14. (It reports the results of an experiment done on *Hiryu* in the Indian Ocean campaign in April to determine how long it would take to change between different types of ordnance on a squadron of torpedo planes.)

33. Ibid., p. 290.

34. Ugaki Diary, p. 140.

35. It appears that from the earliest hours of the day of the battle Yamaguchi took the threat of American carriers more seriously than did Nagumo: there is evidence that on the morning of June 4 he kept his torpedo planes armed with torpedoes until the last minute before rearming them with bombs for the first strike on Midway. Also, he may have learned of the presence of American ships—by monitoring radio messages from the search planes—before Nagumo did, and ordered that the rearming of his dive-bombers be reversed back to antiship bombs before Nagumo reversed the rearming of his torpedo planes. Interview with Tsunoda (author of Senshi Sosho volume on the Battle of Midway) in Chiba, Japan, on August 3, 1993.

36. Official Report, p. 3.

37. Official Report, p. 6.

38. The testimony from the Kaga veterans was divided on the number of torpedo planes that had been equipped with torpedoes that morning and, thus, had to be re-armed; some said the entire squadron of 27 (actually 26 because of the Kate used for reconnaissance), while others were adamant that only 18 had torpedoes on. I found the evidence for 18 more credible.

39. Morison, Fuchida, Lord, and Prange are the most prominent authorities having the torpedo planes on the flight decks at 0715—with a "breaking of the spot" by striking the planes below in order to rearm them. As the testimony of the veterans on this issue was inconsistent, I, too, assumed this in my article "The Battle of Midway: Why the Japanese Lost," published in the Summer 2000 issue of the Naval War College Review. After discussions with John Lundstrom I have since changed my mind.

40. The various procedures involved in the rearming operation and the approximate times they took were obtained from the following Mobile Force air group veterans during interviews conducted in Japan in October 1992 and July 1993: Katutaro Akimoto, torpedo mechanic, Akagi; Takeshi Arakawa, dive-bomber mechanic, Hiryu; Mr. Dairoku, dive-bomber mechanic, Soryu; Fukuji Inoue, torpedo plane pilot, Akagi; Mr. Itazu, dive-bomber gunner, Hiryu; Yaroku Jinnouchi, Zero mechanic, Hiryu; Yuichi Kobayashi, chief of Zero squadron maintenance, Hiryu; Takeshi Maeda, torpedo plane pilot, Kaga; Tokayoshi Morinaga, torpedo plane pilot, Kaga; Mr. Motake, torpedo mechanic, Soryu; Yasaharu Mouri, dive-bomber mechanic, Hiryu; Tatsuya Ohtawa, torpedo plane pilot, Soryu; Moushichi Santou, dive-bomber mechanic, Akagi; Kanzo Sawada, dive-bomber mechanic, Akagi; Makato Tutumi, torpedo plane mechanic, Hiryu. Other Midway veterans with helpful information on events during the rearming operation were Hiseo Mandai, engineer, Hiryu; and Chuichi Yoshioka, staff officer in Nagumo's headquarters.

41. Interviews with Akimoto, Inoue, Kobayashi, Morinaga, and Motake. The testimony from these veterans was divided on whether Akagi's 18 torpedo planes were re-armed in groups of 6 or 9. Akagi's torpedo plane squadron was divided into three chutais of 6 planes each, so it would be natural for the planes to be processed by chutais. As Kaga's larger squadron of 27 planes (divided into three chutai of 9 each) had more carrier cars and weapons mechanics, it appears more likely that Kaga's torpedo planes were processed 9 at a time.

42. This time-consuming procedure of changing the launcher when changing from torpedoes to land bombs has not been mentioned by any American commentators, but was described by several torpedo plane pilots and torpedo mechanics: Akimoto, Inoue, Maeda, Morinaga, and Ohtawa. The 800-kilogram armor-piercing bombs, having been modified from 16-inch battleship shells, were more slender than land bombs and required even a different launcher.

43. The testimony from the veterans was that launcher-changing procedure took 20 minutes, but it became apparent that the veterans tended to underestimate the time a particular procedure took. For the various procedures they described in the rearming operation to add up to one and a half hours, I found it necessary to increase the times they recalled for each procedure by about 50 percent.

44. This rearming schedule has been premised on the torpedo planes already being in the hangars when the rearming order was given by Nagumo at 0715. Had they been on the flight decks of *Akagi* and *Kaga* at 0715—as is widely assumed—the first step in the procedure would have been to lower the planes to the hangars. According to the testimony of the veterans, it would have taken about 7 minutes for the first plane to be rolled to the elevator, positioned, lowered, and manhandled to its arming station in the hangar. Thereafter, as two elevators would probably have been used, the planes would have arrived at their stations at about one-minute intervals. Thus, it took about 25 minutes to lower and position at their arming stations a squadron of 18 torpedo planes. However, the weapons mechanics would not have waited until all the planes were in the hangar; as each plane arrived at its station, the work would have begun. Accordingly, as the last plane of *Akagi*'s first *chutai* (the sixth plane) would be ready for rearming 12 minutes into the operation—and the remaining planes would be at their arming stations before the carrier cars became available to remove their torpedoes—the net delay would only have been 12 minutes, not 25. But this would have delayed each of the times given in my rearming schedule by 12 minutes, meaning, for example, that the torpedoes from the last planes in the squadron would not have been removed and deposited on the heavy weapons rack until 0810—instead of 0758.

45. See Jonathan B. Parshall, David D. Dickson, and Anthony P. Tully, "Doctrine Matters: Why the Japanese Lost at Midway," *Naval War College Review* (Summer 2001): 142, citing a letter from Nisohachi Hyodo.

46. Four of the veterans interviewed assisted with the rearming of the dive-bombers: Kobayashi, Jinnouchi, and Mouri from *Hiryu*, and Dairoku from *Soryu*. Kobayashi and Jinnouchi stated that half the bombers were rearmed on the flight deck and half in the hangar. Mouri and Dairoku thought that all were rearmed on the flight deck.

47. Yuichi Kobayashi, chief of fighter squadron maintenance on *Hiryu*, stated that a small number of Zeros could be landed even though there were some dive-bombers on the flight deck, if the dive-bombers were moved in front of the crash barrier. (But no more than 9 dive-bombers would fit in front of *Hiryu*'s crash barrier, which was only about one-fourth of the flight deck back from the front.)

48. Tatsuya Ohtawa, torpedo plane pilot from *Soryu*, stated that when he returned to the Mobile Force after the attack on Midway at around 0800, the flight decks of *Hiryu* and *Soryu* were clear. Also, photographs from B-17s taken sometime between 0810 and 0825 show the flight decks of *Hiryu* and *Soryu* clear of dive-bombers.

5. GAMBLE LOST

1. Morison and Lord say 0728 (Bates 0730); Fuchida (American edition), Prange and Toland say around 0740 (Senshi Sosho appears to agree); Nagumo's Official Report, Genda, and Kusaka (Nagumo's staff officers) say 0800.

2. Morison, *Coral Sea*, p. 107.

3. Official Report, p. 42.

4. This report was produced in Japan in 1947 under the direction of General MacArthur's Allied Translator and Interpreter Section (ATIS), and was most likely written by Nagumo's staff officers—most prominently Kusaka. However, it was never published

and is rarely cited. It is on file at the Naval Historical Center (Operational Archives Branch), Washington Navy Yard, Washington, D.C.

5. Fuchida and Okumiya, *Midway* (1951 Japanese ed.), p. 172 (p. 271 in the 1982 edition).

6. Fuchida and Okumiya, *Midway* (American ed.), p. 165.

7. Sawachi's *Record of the Midway Sea Battle* is discussed in chapter 1.

8. This is the opinion of Munehiro Miwa, a Japanese history professor who assisted me with research in Japan.

9. Kusaka, p. 84; Genda, *Kaigun Kokutai Shimatsuki*, p. 141.

10. Interview of Tsunoda in August 1993, Tokyo, Japan. Tsunoda, nevertheless, chose to accept a pre-0745 receipt time for the *Tone* 4 sighting report. This was based largely on Yoshioka's recollection, which Tsunoda found more credible than Kusaka's and Genda's. (Yoshioka had compiled the composite log of the Official Report.)

11. Senshi Sosho, p. 284. (Although *Akagi*'s headquarters log was lost, the logs of some of *Akagi*'s air group squadrons apparently survived, from which the carrier Action Reports—translated in WDC 160985B—were derived.)

12. This translation and interpretation of the title was provided by Captain Noritaka Kitazawa, who is the head librarian for the Military History Department, National Institute for Defense Studies, Tokyo, Japan. Letter dated 7 December 2000.

13. This is Munehiro Miwa's view, and he believes it typical among young Japanese scholars.

14. It is not known who wrote the narrative portion of the Official Report. My suppositions come from Miwa.

15. Fuchida and Okumiya, *Midway* (American edition), p. 168; Lord, p. 124; and Prange, *Miracle at Midway*, p. 223.

16. Official Report, p. 7.

17. Parshall and Tully, pp. 160–61.

18. These summaries were released as RG (Record Group) 457, and are kept at the National Archives Annex in College Park, Maryland. The document in question is "SRMN-012, 14th Naval District Combat Intelligence Unit, Traffic Intelligence Summaries with Comments by CINCPAC, Part III, 1 Apr–30 June 1942," pp. 499–505. It is reproduced in Appendix B.

These summaries are *not* primary records and are notoriously unreliable. See caveat in Layton, pp. 577–78. (Layton was an intelligence officer at HYPO and was able to compare some of the original messages with the later summaries.) The message in question is a case in point. The original message from Nagumo to *Tone* 4 was: "Ascertain ship types, and maintain contact." This has been rendered in the summary as merely "Retain contact." But as it is the reliability of the time noted in the summary that is at issue here, another summary on the same page sheds some light on that issue: "0420 'Reports from Midway say first attack on Midway at 1920 GCT—0420 Tokyo time; second attack at 2020 GCT—0520 Tokyo time.'" (These times would be 0720 and 0820 Midway time.) Apart from the fact that the attacks on Midway came much earlier, how could a message supposedly sent at 0420 contain information occurring at 0520?

The summaries in question (pp. 499–505) also do not give the time the radio transmissions were received by the American radio intelligence unit in Hawaii (Hawaii time was two hours later than Midway time.) On the left margin of each page there is a time noted, but it is *Tokyo* time (used by the Japanese at Midway, but three hours earlier than Midway time, and the next day) and was usually taken from the text of the Japanese radio message itself. (A typical example, also on p. 500, is: "0400 'KIMU 1 on 7110 kcs sends his NR 2: *KAWAKAWAKAWA* 0400.'") When the Japanese messages lacked a time sent, it is not known where the compiler of the summary got the time.

19. It should be noted that the message from Nagumo to *Tone* 4 logged at 0447 (0747 Midway time) in the "composite log" of Nagumo's report does not contain the time sent in the message itself, but a similar message logged at 0500 (0800) does. (This latter entry is, therefore, "self-authenticating" as to time sent.) It is curious that the American summaries in the document in question do not include the 0500 (0800) message from *Akagi*. As it appears that American radio intelligence was closely monitoring messages from *Akagi* at this time, this would seem to be further evidence that there was only one reply from Nagumo to *Tone* 4's initial sighting report, and the question is, what time was it sent?

20. Official Report, p. 13. The message is reported in the log as having come from *Tone* 4—which flew nowhere near Midway. However, Senshi Sosho points out that it was actually the *Tone* plane on the #3 search line (also designated *Tone* 1) that did fly near Midway. Senshi Sosho, p. 307. It should be noted that Parshall and Tully (note 52 for p. 133) say "Senshi Sosho is wrong on this point, because American radio intelligence picked up *Tone* No. 4's signal, as well as Amari's particular call sign (MEKU 4), at exactly 0555." For this they cite "HYPO Log, p. 499." Not only are these radio intelligence summaries quite unreliable, as previously explained, but Parshall and Tully have read way too much into this one. The text of the summary is: "0255 'MEKU 4 believed to be a plane sent to MARI the control station: *HIHIHI.HIHIHI.15 KIKI. 0255.* This was intercepted by [word deleted] coming out of Tokyo (UTSU). This is first record of action. It is believed to be reporting 15 American planes (dive-bombers?).'" Note that this summary does not say that the radio transmission was received directly from MEKU 4 (*Tone* 4); rather it was from Tokyo UTSU. (A summary of a later radio message says, "WIMI 1 originates NR 3 (according to Tokyo UTSU . . .).") Apparently, Tokyo UTSU was a Japanese navy radio facility in Tokyo that picked up weak radio transmissions (such as from Japanese search planes) and rebroadcast them with a stronger signal to the fleet. It is not known whether the original radio message was merely amplified and instantly relayed back to the fleet, or whether it was received, transcribed, and broadcast as a new signal. (The latter process could, of course, introduce transcription errors.) In any case, there is clearly something wrong with both the identity of the search plane and the time the message was supposedly sent. (Parshall and Tully concede that *Tone* 4 could not possibly have seen a group of planes coming out of Midway, but speculate that what was seen was a PBY search plane.) Senshi Sosho is undoubtedly correct in concluding that the search plane was misidentified in this case. And I believe I am correct in inferring that the 0255 (0555) time given was in error—either it was mislogged or the sender's clock was inaccurate—and that the message was actually sent 15–20 minutes later.

21. Lord, p. 98; Prange, *Miracle at Midway*, p. 219; and Robert D. Heinl, Jr., *Marines at Midway* (N.p.: Marine Corps Monographs, 1948), p. 27.

22. Official Report, p. 15.

23. Ugaki Diary p. 149.

24. Tsunoda interview; see also William Ward Smith, *Midway, Turning Point of the Pacific* (New York: Thomas Y. Crowell, 1966), p. 90.

25. Senshi Sosho, p. 308.

26. Official Report, p. 7. Parshall and Tully assume that this 0740 message was *Tone* 4's *initial* sighting report (p. 159). For this they again rely on the "HYPO Log." Actually the SRMN summary says only "MEKU 4 sends on 7110 to MARI a 4 kana nigori despatch—his Nr 3 at 0440," which gives no clue as to the contents of the message. (Kana is the Japanese syllabary more suitable for Morse code messages than the Chinese-derived kanji.) Senshi Sosho translates this dispatch as commenting on the weather conditions, which supplemented the previous sighting report sent at 0428 (0728.) It is curious that there is

no entry in the SRMN summary for that crucial 0428 (0728) report. It is even more strange that Parshall and Tully treat the SRMN summaries as preempting more authoritative sources.

27. Bates' Naval War College analysis, p. 122.

28. The first elements of the Midway strike force returned at 0750. Senshi Sosho, p. 301.

29. Senshi Sosho, p. 288.

30. Lord, p. 119; Lundstrom, p. 337; Thaddeus V. Tuleja, *Climax at Midway*, (New York: Jove Books, 1960), p. 109.

31. Senshi Sosho, pp. 313–14.

32. Official Report, p. 15.

33. Prange, *Miracle at Midway*, pp. 224–25 (citing to Kusaka, p. 84.) One staff officer, Ono, is said by Prange (p. 224) to have doubted the presence of carriers, and expressed relief that *Tone* 4's response confirmed this, but the prevailing opinion in Nagumo's headquarters appears to have been that carriers were likely. See Senshi Sosho, p. 288.

34. Senshi Sosho, p. 313. (Practice runs during training had showed that the hit ratio for torpedoes was six times better than that for bombs dropped by torpedo planes in level bombing—60 percent to 10 percent.)

35. After Nagumo received that sighting report at about 0800 he certainly would not have wanted any more torpedoes removed—even if he was not ready to reverse the operation. But, as we have seen, all the torpedoes had probably already been removed by then—though just barely. (It appears—according to the veterans involved in that rearming operation on *Akagi*—that Nagumo and his staff would not have known the exact armament status of the torpedo planes at 0800, but it would not have been unreasonable to assume that some torpedo planes still had torpedoes attached.)

36. Sawachi contends—based on Fuchida and Okumiya's original *Midway*—that the order reversing the rearming operation was probably issued at around 0840. See Sawachi, p. 25. It should be noted that there is more than one version of Nagumo's Official Report, and more than one version of the countermand order. There were twenty copies rendered of the original report, with the American translation having been made from "No. 7 of 20." The countermand order in one of the copies in the War History Library of the Japanese Defense Agency in Tokyo contains only the sentence "Prepare to carry out attacks on enemy fleet units," with no mention of anything like "Leave torpedoes on those attack planes which have not as yet been changed to bombs." It should also be noted that the "copies" are not exact copies—such as photocopies—of the original report, but rather are hand-transcribed renditions of it, which vary somewhat from copy to copy. Thus, apart from the question of when the order was given, it is by no means clear what the countermand order (or orders) actually said. As already explained, *Akagi*'s headquarters log—which would have contained all of Nagumo's orders—did not survive, and the only record of the countermand order came from a log of another ship in the Mobile Force.

37. This assumes that *Kaga*'s torpedo planes were rearmed 9 at a time because of its larger squadron—with more torpedo mechanics and carrier cars. It also assumes that only 18 of its 27 torpedo planes had been armed with torpedoes in the first place.

38. There is some confusion over the time of this B-17 attack. Some Japanese sources have it beginning before 0800, but authoritative American sources have it beginning after 0810. Bates says that the order to attack was given just after 0810, p. 114. Lord says that the bombing commenced at 0814 and ended at 0820, pp. 126–27. There is also confusion as to the number of bombers, most accounts giving 14. It appears that 16 B-17s took off, but 2 returned because of some sort of malfunction. Bates, p. 114.

39. Senshi Sosho, p. 316. Nagumo's Official Report (p. 16) notes a plane described as a "torpedo plane" attacking *Akagi* at 0839, requiring high-speed evasive action. It could only have been one of the Vindicators coming in at a low-angle bombing run.

40. Different figures have been given for the number of Vindicators shot down, ranging from 2 to 4. Lundstrom and Heinl state 3. There is also confusion as to the number involved in the attack, with some saying 12 but most agreeing on 11. It appears that 12 took off but one returned because the cowling blew off. It is clear that 5 returned operational, as they took off for another attack later in the day.

41. This is the version of the 0820 sighting report given in the narrative of the Official Report (p. 7.) The entry in the composite log (p. 16) omits the phrase "in a position to the rear of the others."

42. Lord, p. 128.

43. Senshi Sosho, pp. 308, 312.

44. Bates, p. 126. (Overcast sky at 0700; sky clouding rapidly at 0730.)

45. At 30 miles, for instance, with the search plane flying at 5,000 feet, the angle of view would be extremely narrow—about 2°. This angle would be too acute for the exact course to be seen.

46. The heavy cruisers were *Minneapolis, New Orleans, Northampton, Pensacola,* and *Vincennes.* The light cruiser was *Atlanta.*

47. Action Report, Commander Cruiser Division Six, A16–3, Serial 058, June 11, 1942 (Enclosure A, p. 1).

48. This was known as "Formation 11V." See ibid., p. 1.

49. Ibid., pp. 1–2.

50. Ibid., p. 1.

51. Ibid. (Enclosure A), p. 2.

52. *Minneapolis*'s track chart does not show such a course change. However, this does not mean that none of the other escorts made a course change (and it possible that *Minneapolis* was not one of the five cruisers seen by *Tone* 4).

53. From Enclosure A of Cruiser Division Six's Action Report (times converted to Midway time): 0615: "Sky heavily overcast"; 0648: "overcast sky"; 0732: "Sky clouding rapidly. Heavy detached clouds predominate blue sky." But by 0857: "Sky overhead clear."

54. Senshi Sosho, p. 324.

55. Doi, pp. 134–38. (Doi was an officer on cruiser *Tone* in charge of the search plane operations.)

56. Herman Wouk, *War and Remembrance* (Boston: Little, Brown, 1978), p. 406.

57. Bates, pp. 120–21.

58. The light carriers were *Ryujo* and *Zuiho* (the obsolete *Hosho* would not be deployed again); the heavy "support" carriers were *Junyo* and its soon to be completed sister *Hiyo.*

59. As explained in chapter 2, *Ranger*—though designated a CV—was not capable at that time of deploying a full offensive air group, and was really just a large "support" carrier. Thus, it would not have been an adequate replacement for a *Yorktown*-class carrier.

6. TO LAUNCH OR NOT TO LAUNCH

1. Nagumo's Official Report, p. 7. This report was received at 0820 by cruiser *Tone* and relayed to Nagumo, rather than being received by *Akagi* directly. (*Akagi*'s limited radio equipment was probably still tuned to receive communications from the commander of the Midway strike force.)

2. Other reasons for postponing given by commentators: need to immediately land the Midway strike force to avoid losses from ditching (the main concern of Minoru Genda, Nagumo's air officer); contempt for the ability of American aviators to inflict serious damage on his carriers.

3. Fuchida and Okumiya, *Midway*, p. 169; Prange, *Miracle at Midway*, p. 232.

4. Prange, *Miracle at Midway*, p. 218.

5. Lundstrom, p. 338.

6. Lord, pp. 131–32.

7. Fuchida, pp. 168–69; Prange, *Miracle at Midway*, p. 232; Lord, p. 131; and Senshi Sosho, p. 289.

8. Senshi Sosho, p. 289.

9. Ibid., p. 313.

10. Though some accounts say that there were torpedo planes—as many as a half squadron—on the flight deck of *Akagi* at 0830, I conclude that this is very implausible. The decision to land the Midway strike force was not made until after Nagumo received, at 0830, the *Tone* 4 report identifying an American carrier. It is very unlikely that this decision was made before 0835. Landing operations commenced on *Akagi* at 0837. As it would have taken at least ten minutes to lower nine torpedo planes from the flight deck; there was not time to have done it.

11. Senshi Sosho, p. 289.

12. Lundstrom (p. 338) suggests that there were six Zeros available for escort duty at 0830. These would have been the planes from the first two CAP patrols from *Soryu*, which are recorded in *Soryu*'s action report (WDC 160985–B) as having landed at 0730—but there is no record of them being relaunched before 1000. It is apparent that *Soryu*'s CAP log is incomplete (and some of the records were transferred to *Junyo*—and then lost.) Thus, not all of *Soryu*'s CAP launches are necessarily in its action report. It seems very likely that the six Zeros recorded as landing at 0730 were actually relaunched soon after 0800 when dive-bombers from Midway attacked (especially as there were only nine Zeros on CAP at the time). Senshi Sosho states that all "available Zeros"—from all four carriers—were launched immediately after 0800 (but does not specify the carriers). This seems reasonable, and I accept it.

13. Bates, p. 82; Fuchida and Okumiya, p. 154. Had Nagumo actually had anywhere near 90 operational Zeros available to him, he would have had enough to provide an escort for any bombers available for launch at 0830.

14. Senshi Sosho, p. 297. The main problem with determining the total number of Zeros in the four air groups of the Mobile Force is the state of *Kaga*'s records. *Kaga*'s Action Report (WDC 160985–B) states that its "Combat Air Patrol was made up of sixteen type zero fighters." However, this seems in error. Its CAP schedule accounts for only 7 Zeros being launched before 0815. This can lead to an inference that the total number of operational Zeros in its fighter squadron—at least early on—was 16, with 9 in the Midway attack unit. (It appears that 2 of *Kaga*'s Zeros were not operational until after 0900.)

15. Senshi Sosho, p. 315. (These Sixth Air Group Zeros were launched at 0710.) See also Hata and Izawa, p. 148–49. They have 3 available, all on *Akagi*; there is no evidence that any of the others, including the 9 on *Kaga*, were used for CAP.

16. See Appendix C for reconstruction of Mobile Force's CAP activity.

17. These 3 Zeros from *Akagi* on CAP had landed but ten minutes earlier and, apparently, needed only refueling (which in an emergency could be done on the flight deck). Had the guns needed reloading, it would have been necessary to lower them to the hangar deck for that operation, which would have added another 30 minutes to the turnaround time.

18. The record is fragmentary as to the number of Zeros launched for CAP at this time. *Akagi*'s action report states that 3 were launched from *Akagi* at 0808 (confirmed by the Official Report). *Senshi Soshi* (p. 316) states that *Hiryu* launched some at around 0800, but *Hiryu*'s Action Report does not mention any. (There is no record whatever of *Hiryu*'s fourth patrol—which should have been launched at about this time. Its Zeros would have been those of the first patrol after they had landed and been reserviced.) There would have been 5 Zeros available on *Hiryu*—having landed from the previous two patrols—which I assume were launched around 0800. *Soryu*'s action report, as mentioned in an earlier note, is silent on what was done with 6 Zeros from prior patrols which were on board at 0800. But as that report is obviously incomplete—and *Senshi Sosho* states that *all available* Zeros from *all* the carriers were launched to attack the dive-bombers that arrived from Midway (which seems reasonable)—I assume that *Soryu*'s 6 Zeros were launched around that time.

19. Some might wonder whether these 7 Zeros could have been used instead to escort the dive-bombers. Actually, they were not available for escort duty. Apart from the fact that they were being launched at the time Nagumo received *Tone* 4's report sighting a carrier, they had been committed to the combat air patrol and were under the control of the air defense officer. They were taking off at 0830 was to defend against the last wave of dive-bombers from Midway—which had just arrived over the Mobile Force. Moreover, it appears that those 7 Zeros may have been the only Zeros on combat air patrol with any 20-mm cannon ammunition left at that time—all the other Zeros having exhausted their cannon ammunition in the air battles that had been going on since 0800. Even if Nagumo could have stopped their launch, or called them back immediately, he would not have done so. His Mobile Force was facing a new attack, and he had to give priority to the preservation of his carriers.

20. Fuchida and Okumiya, p. 173.

21. The Kate torpedo plane had a nominal range of 1,237 miles compared with 915 miles for the Val dive-bomber. (The actual combat radius is roughly one-forth the nominal range.) Thus, the torpedo planes could stay in the air for at least an hour longer than could the dive-bombers—and, in fact, according to *Soryu*'s Action Report, the last torpedo planes back from Midway did not land until 0950.

22. Statements of Mogi, Zero mechanic, *Akagi*; and of Jinnouchi, Zero mechanic, *Hiryu*.

23. Senshi Sosho, p. 313. Practice runs had shown the Japanese that 800-kilogram bombs dropped from torpedo planes by "glide bombing" had only one-sixth as much chance of hitting a ship as a torpedo.

24. Ugaki Diary p. 140.

25. For a summary of the "phases" of the Japanese "Basic Plan" for the first year of the war, see chapter 10.

26. There are several versions, and interpretations, of this famous pronouncement. This version comes from Bergamini, p. 739.

27. Shigeru Nohara, A6M *Zero in Action* (Carrollton, Tex.: Squadron/Signal Publications, No. 59, 1983), p. 31.

28. For example, production of ingot steel in Japan for 1940 was 7.5 million metric tons; for the United States it was 61 million metric tons. Evans and Peattie, p. 364.

29. Various estimates have been given for how long Japan's oil and gasoline reserves would last during wartime consumption. The Japanese navy had estimated that its 6.5 million tons (40,625,000 barrels) of petroleum on hand on December 1941 would last for two years (Evans and Peattie, p. 410.) For "full-scale" naval and air warfare, however, based on the actual consumption in the first year (4.85 million tons, or 30,312,500 bar-

rels) the Japanese navy actually began the war with only enough petroleum for one year and four months.

30. No fleet carriers were even laid down between May 1938 (when *Zuikaku* was laid down), and July 1941 (when *Taiho* was laid down). And except for *Taiho*, none were laid down until after the Battle of Midway, when construction of several of the *Unryu* class (improved *Hiryu*) was begun in August 1942. *Junyo* and *Hiyo*, which were completed in 1942, are often classified as CVs because of their large displacement (24,000 tons). However, they were too slow and too short to launch a full squadron of torpedo planes in calm weather and, thus, were not really "attack carriers." Rather, they were intended for use—like light carriers—primarily to support amphibious invasion operations, such as the Aleutian campaign. After Midway, however, their role was—of necessity—expanded, but even then they never really functioned as full-fledged attack carriers.

31. Lundstrom, p. 339; Prange, *Miracle at Midway*, p. 234.

32. Official Report, p. 7; Senshi Sosho, p. 291.

33. Nagumo states in his Official Report that because the torpedo planes could not be launched at 0830, "it was therefore decided that we would await the return of the Midway attack unit and then carry out a grand scale air attack," p. 7.

34. See Senshi Sosho, pp. 290, 309.

35. Genda's statement. Senshi Sosho, p. 290. But there is an irony here: when the American attack came, the Dauntless dive-bombers were without escorts, but there were no Zeros at high level to oppose them.

36. Senshi Sosho, p. 291.

37. Hiroshi Yoshii, *The Pacific War*, vol. 7: *History of Showa Told by the Eyewitnesses* (Tokyo: Shin Jinbutsu Oraisha, 1989), p. 39. (Kusaka's recollections, cited from *Rengo Kantai*.)

38. Though one might expect that Nagumo would be aware of the problems the re-arming crews in the hangar decks were having, the evidence from the veterans who did the rearming was that he was not. The torpedo mechanics were quite scornful about how little the "brass" in headquarters knew about what went on down below. Interview with Akimoto, torpedo mechanic on *Akagi*.

39. Sawachi, p. 25. (Based on Fuchida's original Japanese version of "Midway.")

40. Senshi Sosho, p. 289: "Provided that the torpedo planes had been fully equipped, it would take at least 40 minutes to bring all of them up from the hangar, position them on the flight deck and then finish preparations for launch." Note: This assumes that only one elevator—the aft—could be used to raise the torpedo planes, which would be the case after 0920 as dive-bombers would block access to the midship elevator. It took almost 2 minutes of elevator time per plane, for a total of about 30 minutes to raise 17 torpedo planes. Once they were spotted on the flight deck, engine warm-up took 10–15 minutes, but could begin while the last few planes were being raised. Thus, the extra 10 minutes required (in addition to the 30 to raise them) was for engine warm-up for the last planes to be spotted.

41. Senshi Sosho, pp. 372–78.

42. Ibid., pp. 329–30.

43. Sawachi, pp. 23–25.

44. *Akagi*'s Action Report, WDC Doc No 160985–B, pp. 5–6.

45. Ibid., pp. 11, 13.

46. *Hiryu*'s action report does not state when its torpedo planes and Zeros were "recovered"—only that they "returned to the carrier" at 0905. Ibid., p. 21.

47. Ibid., p. 18. (See also Senshi Sosho, p. 292.)

48. Statement of Ohtawa, torpedo plane pilot, *Soryu*. (He stated that when he re-

turned to the vicinity of the carriers at about 0750, his landing was delayed for one and a half hours; he landed at 0918.)

49. *Soryu*'s Action Report, WDC 160985-B, p. 17.

50. At Pearl Harbor, the carriers of the Mobile Force launched aircraft at a rate of one every 28 seconds. Prange, *At Dawn We Slept*, p. 490. Therefore, the approximately 21 planes each from *Akagi, Kaga*, and *Hiryu* could have been launched in around 10 minutes.

7. IRONIES

1. Combat radii of warplanes can only be roughly calculated and, in actual practice, vary widely depending on the circumstances of each mission. It is generally accepted that the F4F-4 Wildcat had a combat radius of less than 200 miles—with some estimates as low as 175 miles. The starting point is with its nominal range, which is specified in published sources as 770 miles (670 nautical miles). Allowing for fifteen minutes of combat at the target, and several minutes of full-throttle speed to escape pursuing enemy fighters, the combat radius would usually be a little over one-fourth the range—about 175 to 190 miles. The TBD Devastator, on the other hand, had a loaded range of 435 miles (378 nautical miles). However, because it did not need to spend as much time at the target, and because its range was increased considerably after it dropped its torpedo, its radius was almost one-half its loaded range. But this still gave it a combat radius of only about 175 miles.

2. Bates, p. 121.

3. Ibid., p. 123.

4. Although in the launch commencing at 0705, the torpedo bombers were launched last—about 45 minutes into the launch operation—the distance from the Mobile Force would not have closed any by then because the carriers had to turn into the wind during the launch—135°. This would have kept them roughly parallel to the course of the Mobile Force during the entire launch.

5. The Mobile Force's course change at 0920 would have put it on a course roughly parallel to that of the *Enterprise* dive-bombers, though in the opposite direction, and approximately 12 miles apart. See Search & Course Chart.

6. The first wave of torpedo bombers—*Hornet*'s "Torpedo Eight"—actually attacked at 0930, having been launched at about the same time as the *Enterprise* dive-bombers departed. But had they been launched 30 minutes later, there is no reason to believe that they would have reached the Mobile Force before the dive-bombers, as they were considerably slower. However, they too would probably have spotted the Japanese carriers before reaching the "interception point"—perhaps at around 0950.

7. Bates, p. 124.

8. While this is the generally accepted launch sequence—see Bates, p. 123; Morison, *Coral Sea*, p. 114—John Lundstrom, in his *The First Team*, p. 333, gives a radically different scenario for the launch of the *Hornet* air group based on research by Bowen P. Weisheit. According to this scenario, the first deckload consisted of 20 fighters (8 for combat air patrol—plus 2 spares—and 10 for escort), 34 dive-bombers, and 6 torpedo bombers—for a total of 60 planes (with 58 being launched.) The second deckload supposedly consisted of but 9 torpedo bombers.

Although there is some evidence from *Hornet*'s air group veterans for this scenario, it is inconsistent with the official record and, therefore, not conclusive. In any case, such a launch sequence seems dubious. Even had it been possible to launch 58 planes in one deckload from *Hornet* it would seem very foolish to have done it. According to the scenario, 6 torpedo bombers were launched in the first deckload, and then had to orbit over the carrier until the remaining 9 torpedo bombers in the squadron were raised from the hangar deck and launched to join them. It would take about 20 minutes to raise and spot 9 torpedo bombers, and another 5 to launch them. The orbiting torpedo bombers would consume enough fuel in 25 minutes to cut around 40 miles off their range. Given the concern over the short range of the Devastator TBD, it would not make sense to split the torpedo bombers into two launches, and launch some of them in the first deckload—making them wait for 25 minutes.

It would have made even less sense to have launched the 10 Wildcat fighters designated for escort duty in the first deckload. After launch, they would have had to wait for the 34 dive-bombers and 6 torpedo bombers to be launched, which would take about 15 minutes, and then wait another 25 minutes for the second deckload of 9 TBDs to be raised, spotted, and launched. This 40-minute waiting time would be about 30 minutes longer than if they were launched in the second deckload along with 15 TBDs, as would normally be expected. Given the already limited range of the Wildcat, adding 30 minutes of extra orbiting time—which would cut about 60 miles off that range—seems completely irrational.

Thus, because of the limited range of the TBD and Wildcat, it seems only sensible to launch them last—in the second deckload—as was done on *Enterprise*. In correspondence with this author, Lundstrom admits that *Hornet*'s launch sequence was irrational and points to some other fairly strange things that are known to have happened during the maiden sortie of *Hornet*'s air group—many of which engendered rancor among its surviving members that persists to this day. While it is possible that the Wildcat escorts were launched in the first deckload—however irrational it might seem—it should be noted that the primary records, though not explicit on the point, indicate a launch sequence for *Hornet* similar to that of *Enterprise*. (Spruance, in his battle report, dated 16 June 1942, serial 0144–A, p. 1, states that for both carriers in TF 16 the fighters for escort were launched *after* the bombers.)

9. According to the Lundstrom-Weisheit scenario, the launch of the *Hornet* air group was completed at 0742, and it departed for the target at 0746, instead of the more generally accepted time of around 0800. But this earlier departure time is premised on 58 planes being launched in the first deckload and only 9 in the second, which—as discussed in the previous note—is dubious. If the launch sequence was similar to that of *Enterprise* (with the 10 fighter escorts and all the torpedo bombers launched in the second deckload), as most commentators assume, then the departure time for *Hornet*'s air group would have been closer to 0800. (There is evidence from the records of cruiser *Vincennes*—which was in the screen for TF 16—for a departure time of 0755 for *Hornet*'s air group, which I adopt.)

10. Bates, p. 126.

11. Ibid., p. 127.

12. Ibid., p. 128.

13. Prange, *Miracle at Midway*, p. 257.

14. Statement of Captain Amagai, air officer on *Kaga*, United States Strategic Bombing Survey [Pacific], Naval Analysis Division, *Interrogations of Japanese Officials*, vol. 1 (OPNAV P-03-100), p. 2; statement of Captain Aoki, commanding officer of *Akagi*, ibid., p. 14.

15. *Kaga* action report, WDC 160985–B, p. 12. (Deployed at three levels: 1,000, 3,000, and 6,000 meters; 6,000 meters is 19,800 feet.)

16. The commander of Fighting Six reported that he did not see any Zeros during his time over the Mobile Force (between 0930 and 1000.) Bates, p. 128. From this, it has

been inferred that the Japanese stationed no Zeros at high level to defend against dive-bombers. It is more likely, however, that there had been some Zeros at high altitude but they had dropped down to help out with the attacking torpedo bombers immediately prior to the arrival of Fighting Six.

17. Of the 17 Zeros on combat air patrol at 0918 when Torpedo Eight was spotted, 2 had been in the air since 0710, and another 8 since between 0800 and 0808; only 7 had been launched since 0830. See Appendix C.

18. For a detailed description of the "Thach weave," see Lundstrom, pp. 352–55.

19. See Lundstrom for a detailed account of the reorganization and composition of *Yorktown*'s air group.

20. Bates, p. 133.

21. Nimitz's battle report of 28 June 1942, serial 01849, p. 12. Bates (p. 134) is in accord, and states that the dive-bombers were directed to circle over *Yorktown* for 12 minutes to give the torpedo planes a head start. It should be noted, however, that Lundstrom has the torpedo planes being launched first — ahead of the dive-bombers (p. 340). But as the Devastator was carrying a 2,200-pound torpedo (versus a 1,000-pound bomb) and was underpowered compared to the Dauntless dive-bomber, it needed more flight deck to safely launch than the Dauntless. In view of this, the launch sequence in Nimitz's report seems more likely.

22. While Bombing Three could not see the torpedo bombers below the clouds, it seems odd that it did not see the fighters flying at 6,000 feet change course and follow them. There is a possible explanation: Wildcat fighters could not fly as slow as the Devastators that they were escorting — about 100 knots — and maintain altitude without seriously compromising fuel efficiency. Thus, to keep pace they made broad S-turns, which allowed them to fly at a higher speed without getting ahead of the torpedo bombers. (See Lundstrom, p. 349.) Because of this irregular pattern, perhaps along with some intervening clouds, the course change by those fighters to follow the torpedo bombers may not have been obvious to the commander of Bombing Three.

23. It should be noted that some accounts of the battle state that the commander of Bombing Three saw Torpedo Three and its escorts make the course change and followed them to the target. See Lord, p. 157; Lundstrom, p. 351. However, the most authoritative chronology of the attack (that of Bates's Midway Analysis, supported by Japanese records) has Torpedo Three reaching the Mobile Force and beginning its torpedo attack run-up at 1016, while Leslie's dive-bombers did not attack until 1024. See Bates, pp. 134, 135. The 8-minute difference in arrival time can only be explained by assuming that the dive-bombers made their turn north several minutes later than Torpedo Three.

24. Lundstrom, p. 364. The pilots of Fighting Three claimed a total of 6 Zeros shot down. However, the Japanese records show a total of 5 Zeros being lost during the period of these skirmishes, which may be more accurate. As one was shot down by a Devastator, that would leave 4 to have been shot down by Wildcats. See Action Reports, WDC 160985–B.

25. Lundstrom, p. 358. (Though some American authorities say that no Devastators were shot down in the approach.)

26. Bates, p. 131. See Search & Course Chart.

27. The rate of climb for the A6M2 Zero was 2,750 feet per minute (at sea level), and it took 7 minutes and 27 seconds to climb to 19,685 feet (6,000 meters). Rene J. Francillon, *Japanese Aircraft of the Pacific War* (Annapolis: Naval Institute Press, 1990), p. 377.

28. Spruance, who was normally reluctant to criticize his subordinates, went out of his way in his battle report to comment that *Hiryu* probably could have been destroyed in the morning attack had *Hornet*'s dive-bombers not got lost — thus forestalling the

fatal attacks on *Yorktown*. Serial 0144–A (Enclosure B of Enclosure D of Nimitz's battle report), pp. 2–3.

29. Lord, p. 151.

30. Lundstrom, pp. 335, 346.

31. Under the Lundstrom-Weisheit scenario, Torpedo Eight approached the Mobile Force from the northeast, rather than from the southeast as generally assumed. It should be noted, however, that according to the log of Nagumo's Official Report (at p. 17), at 0918 cruiser *Chikuma* sighted "16 enemy planes bearing 52 degrees to starboard." Unless bearings are indicated to be true compass direction (T), they are considered to be relative to the observer's course. (And "bearing 52 degrees *to starboard*" plainly seems to be meant this way.) In such a case, as *Chikuma* was on a course of 70° at the time (logged at 0917), the true compass direction (T) of the approaching planes would be 122° — which is from the southeast.

32. "Lost Letter of Midway," *United States Naval Institute: Proceedings* 125, no. 8 (August 1, 1999): 29.

33. There, apparently, is a record of Waldron (commander of Torpedo Eight), soon after departure, radioing Ring, "you are going the wrong way!" Letter from John Lundstrom.

34. It is well known that the Japanese were devoted to the doctrine of coordinated attack, but the American navy espoused it as well (though less experienced in implementing it). Bates, p. 125. Moreover, American tactical doctrine (as well as Japanese) held that in a coordinated attack the dive-bombers should precede the torpedo planes because the more vulnerable torpedo planes needed to have enemy fighters drawn away from them to survive long enough to launch their torpedoes. Bates, p. 130.

35. A 20-mm bullet is 0.787-inch in diameter, compared with 0.5-inch for a 50-caliber bullet. This gives it almost four times the mass of a 50-caliber bullet (0.787 cubed v. 0.5 cubed.) Even with a lower muzzle velocity, a 20-mm round had two to three times the destructive power of a 50-caliber round.

36. Francillon, p. 367.

37. Parshall and Tully (in *Shattered Sword*) downplay the role of the first two waves of American torpedo bombers in wearing down the Japanese combat air patrol. Rather, they argue that the principal role those torpedo bomber attacks played in the Japanese defeat was to deter Nagumo from spotting his strike force on his flight decks between 0920 and 1000 — which they contend, without any evidence, was fully rearmed with torpedoes and ready to go at 0920! (They claim that keeping the flight decks clear in case some Zeros on CAP needed to be landed had higher priority than launching a strike force against the American carriers.) I explained in chapter 1 why I find this theory to be specious.

8. DENOUEMENT

1. Many more planes on both sides had been shot up and were out of action for at least the rest of the day. Twenty Japanese planes returned from Midway with severe enough damage to make them inoperable (almost half the torpedo planes.) See Senshi Sosho, p. 302. For the Americans, 6 Marine fighters had been rendered useless (leaving only 3 operational), and the single TBF and 2 B-26s that returned were out of action, as were 5 of the 16 dive-bombers.

2. Lundstrom, p. 388.

3. United States Strategic Bombing Survey, *Interrogations of Japanese Officials*, p. 14. Captain Amagai, air officer of *Kaga*, also testified that dive-bomber attacks were most feared because their bombs could not be dodged. Ibid., p. 2.

4. *Kaga*'s Action Report states that having planes stationed at 6,000, 3,000 and 1,000 meters was an effective arrangement. WDC 160985–B, p. 12. (This would put the highest level patrol at almost 20,000 feet.)

5. Lord, p. 178; Prange, *Miracle at Midway*, p. 260.

6. There has been confusion over the relative position of *Kaga* and *Akagi*. I accept Lord's findings (p. 292) based on conversations with Nagumo's chief of staff, Kusaka.

7. Different times for the first bomb hit on *Kaga* have been recorded in the various reports. Senshi Sosho's reconciliation is convincing, p. 328.

8. Official Report, p. 52.

9. Official Report, pp. 9, 53.

10. Lord, p. 175.

11. Observers on *Kaga* counted only 9 planes diving at *Kaga*. Official Report, p. 9. It has been suggested that the Japanese "gave up counting" after the fourth hit, as the ship was by then being engulfed by flames. But although they may have stopped counting the bomb misses after that, it seems likely that any direct hits would have been recorded.

12. Robert J. Cressman, et al., *A Glorious Page in Our History: The Battle of Midway 4–6 June 1942* (Missoula, Mont.: Pictorial Histories Publishing Company, 1990), p. 102.

13. Ensign Frank O'Flaherty and his gunner, Bruno Gaido, of Scouting Six went down near the Mobile Force and were picked up by a Japanese destroyer. (After being interrogated, they were weighted down and thrown overboard to drown.) Two more SBDs, those of Delbert Halsey and Norman Vandivier of Bombing Six, went down from battle damage soon after leaving the Mobile Force and perished at sea. (I count them as having been "shot down.") Six more SBDs ran out of gas—some from holed gas tanks—while trying to find the *Enterprise* and ditched, and their crews were never heard of again: John Lough, Carl Peiffer, James Shelton, and Charles Ware, of Scouting Six, and John Van Buren and Bertram Varian of Bombing Six. See Cressman, pp. 108–15.

14. Bates, p. 133.

15. Lord, p. 167.

16. Cressman, p. 102.

17. Lord resolved this controversy, p. 290. *Soryu* was much larger than assumed by American carrier pilots at Midway. The assumption that *Soryu* was a "light" carrier was based on deceptive prewar Japanese reports that it had a displacement of only 10,000 tons (instead of 15,900.) Actually, at 746 feet it was almost as long as *Kaga* (though not nearly as wide), and as the islands of both carriers were on the starboard side it was easy to mistake one for the other.

18. Of the 13 SBDs that ditched after having run out of gas, it appears that 6 had sustained punctured fuel tanks from shellfire. (The other seven appear to have just run out of gas without fuel tank damage because they got lost attempting to find their carrier.) Those that lost fuel rapidly because of battle damage, and went down close to the Mobile Force, can be regarded as battle casualties, and it seems only a matter of semantics whether or not they are said to have been "shot down."

19. Several Zeros were claimed to have been shot down by *Enterprise*'s dive-bombers, including McClusky's gunner and wingmen. But reconciliation with Japanese records indicate that probably only one Zero was shot down by SBDs, though others may have received enough damage from them to force later emergency landings. See Appendix C regarding Zero CAP activity.

20. Four of the 6 SBDs that ditched and whose crews were lost were with a group of Scouting Six planes led by Charles Ware. Along with Ware and his gunner, Lough, Peiffer, and Shelton and their gunners, were never found. The other two lost were from Bombing Six—Van Buren and Varian, and their gunners. The 4 SBDs that ditched but

whose crews were rescued were piloted by Clarence Dickinson, Joe Penland, Thomas Ramsey, and John McCarthy.

21. The records from *Enterprise* relating to the number and identity of the SBDs that landed are incomplete and confusing. However, a reconstruction by Cressman is as follows: From the Air Group Commander's Section: McClusky, Pittman, and Jaccard; from Scouting Six: Gallaher, Stone, Kleiss, Dexter, West, and Micheel; from Bombing Six: Best, Kroger, Weber, Hopkins; and Anderson; Cressman, p. 115. Eleven of these were operational, and later launched for the attack on *Hiryu*; Lundstrom, p. 411.

22. Senshi Sosho, p. 302; *Hiryu* Action Report, WDC 160985–B.

23. I rely heavily on Lundstrom's meticulous account of the CAP battle over *Yorktown*, pp. 374–90.

24. Lord, p. 198. Although *Shokaku* and *Zuikaku*—whose aircraft *Yorktown*'s AA gunners had seen at the Battle of the Coral Sea—were the newest and best carriers the Japanese had, as we saw in an earlier chapter, their air groups were inexperienced at the beginning of the war, and their pilots were derided as second rate by many aviators in the older First and Second Carrier Divisions.

25. There is confusion regarding how many returned operable. My numbers are from *Hiryu*'s Action Report in WDC 160985–B.

26. See Appendix C for CAP details.

27. The Judy dive-bomber is referred to in Japanese Midway records as a Type 13 reconnaissance plane. It later became the Yokosuka D4Y dive-bomber known as the Suisei (Comet). Francillon, p. 454.

28. A report from Destroyer Division 4, at 1300, based on an interrogation of a bailed-out Torpedo Three pilot, also confirmed composition of American carrier force. Official Report, p. 24.

29. The Type 91 torpedo, though the fastest and most deadly aerial torpedo in the world, was not long-ranged or oxygen-powered like the "Long Lance" torpedoes fired by Japanese destroyers and submarines. (The Type 91—like its American counterpart—had its pressure vessel charged with ordinary air, under very high pressure—to mix with kerosene.) Longer range had been traded off to achieve very high speed—42 knots. This required the torpedo plane to drop it relatively close to the target (optimally 800 yards.) The American Mark 13, in contrast, had a longer range but much slower speed—33.5 knots. For complete specifications of Japanese aerial torpedoes see "Ordnance Targets: Japanese Torpedoes and Tubes," U.S. Naval Technical Mission to Japan, Index No. 0–01–2.

30. *Enterprise*'s VF-6 still had 26 operational fighters, and *Hornet*'s VF-8 15. *Yorktown*'s VF-3 still had around 10, now on the other two carriers. Lundstrom, p. 418.

31. After Midway's gasoline pumping system was damaged refueling was done from 55-gallon drums using hand pumps. Heinl, p. 39.

32. There are varying estimates of the number of *Hiryu*'s planes still operational. *Hiryu*'s Action Report says that of the 5 dive-bombers that returned "one plane made useless by shell damage, two planes made serviceable by repairs after shell damage." This implies that the other 2 returned undamaged. Of the 5 torpedo planes that returned, "four planes made useless by shell damage. One plane made serviceable by repairs after shell damage." WDC 160985B.

33. Lundstrom, p. 414.

34. Official Report, p. 9.

35. Different numbers for plane losses have been given by the various authorities. These figures are my own synthesis, taken largely from Bates, Cressman, Lundstrom, and Senshi Sosho.

36. Nagumo's last message to Yamamoto that day stated that he was still being pursued by four carriers! Official Report, p. 36.

37. This brave pilot was Captain Richard Fleming, USMC. Morison, *Coral Sea*, p. 145.

38. It had been reported that the USS *Nautilus* torpedoed *Soryu*, actually sinking her. This turned out to be mistaken; the carrier targeted by the submarine was *Kaga*, but the torpedo failed to explode. Lord, p. 295.

39. Nagumo's Official Report, p. 67, itemizes the losses for all four carriers.

40. Lord, p. 109.

41. Cressman, p. 220.

42. The breakdown of plane types on board each carrier at 1025 is: *Akagi*: 17 torpedo planes, 18 dive-bombers, and 8 fighters; *Kaga*: 26 torpedo planes, 17 dive-bombers, and 2 fighters; *Soryu*: 16 torpedo planes, 19 dive-bombers, and 5 fighters. On *Hiryu* at 1700: 8 torpedo planes, 6 dive-bombers, and 19 fighters.

43. United States Strategic Bombing Survey, *Interrogations of Japanese Officials*, p. 14.

44. Ibid., p. 3.

45. Ibid., p. 168.

46. Ibid., p. 6. In another report, Captain Kawaguchi states that of the 150 flying personnel on board *Hiryu* only 20 survived. ATIS Report No. 1.

47. United States Strategic Bombing Survey, *Campaigns of the Pacific*, p. 60, concludes that around 100 pilots were lost. Also, Hata and Izawa, in *Japanese Naval Aces*, list 23 Zero pilots killed at Midway, but concede that their accounting is not complete.

48. *Interrogations of Japanese Officials*, p. 262. It should also be noted that in addition to injuries from obvious causes, even repeated dives from high altitude by dive-bombers caused debilitating inner ear damage to some dive-bomber pilots.

9. AFTERMATH

1. The plane complements given for *Junyo* by Morison, *Coral Sea*, p. 172, showing ten torpedo planes, are for July 1942.

2. The original plane complements for *Junyo* and *Ryujo* in the Aleutian campaign were: *Junyo*—21 Val dive-bombers (18 operational) and about 30 Zeros, of which only 18 were operational. (Twelve Zeros from the Sixth Air Group—a land-based contingent intended for Midway after its capture—were being carried, but very few of its pilots were carrier-qualified. See Hata and Izawa, p. 149.) *Ryujo*—21 Kate attack planes and 16 Zeros—18 and 12 of which, respectively, were operational. (A total of 66 operational planes on the two carriers.) These complements are from USSBS, *Interrogations of Japanese Officials*, p. 93 (Okumiya statement.) Of the 10 carrier planes that were shot down or crashed at sea in the Dutch Harbor operation: *Junyo* lost 4 dive-bombers and 2 Zeros; *Ryujo* lost 3 Kate attack planes and one Zero. However, the aircrews of at least two Kates and probably one Val were rescued. As the carriers had "spares," I am assuming that these pilots would be able to use them—boosting the number of operational planes from 56 to 59.

3. A Zero from Ryuju was forced to make a crash landing on Akutan Island. Its pilot was killed when the Zero flipped over on the marshy ground, but the plane was only slightly damaged. It became famous as the "Koga Zero." It was recovered by the Americans and shipped to California, revealing the secrets of its remarkable performance (and also its weaknesses.) This knowledge proved invaluable as it helped American fighter pilots adopt tactics to better engage the Zero in dogfights—and may even have improved American fighter aircraft design. It was by far Japan's most costly loss in the Aleutian

campaign. See Jim Rearden, *Cracking the Zero Mystery* (Harrisburg, Penn.: Stackpole Books, 1990.)

4. This is my computation after subtracting the number of planes known to be shot down, crashed at sea, or returned damaged, in the various operations at Midway—plus those sunk with *Yorktown*—from the operational complements at the outset. (See "Summary of American plane and pilot losses June 4–6.") This would leave 112 planes (from the original complements of 221) to which the 34 planes received from *Saratoga* are then added. It is possible, however, that some of the planes reported as returning damaged were soon repaired. Lundstrom (p. 431) gives a slightly higher estimate of the number of "apparently operational" planes as of June 11.

5. Even if *Ryujo* and *Zuiho*'s Kates could have been supplied with torpedoes, those carriers lacked the capability of launching more than a handful of torpedo-bearing Kates because of their short flight decks. Also, even if the larger *Junyo* carried Kates—which it did not in this campaign—it was too slow to develop sufficient wind speed over the flight deck for Kates to safely lift off with a 1,872-pound torpedo load. (Though *Junyo* was designed to have a top speed of 25.5 knots, its engines did not work properly and it was never able to achieve more than 22–23 knots. See Jentschura, Jung, and Mickel, p. 52.) Accordingly, in subsequent campaigns where *Junyo* carried up to ten Kates it appears that they were equipped with 250-kilogram bombs rather than torpedoes.

6. Morison (*Coral Sea*, p. 184) has *Zuikaku* joining Kakuta's Second Mobile Force on June 12, but it almost certainly has been confused with *Zuiho*. Okumiya's statement in *Interrogations of Japanese Officials*, p. 95, makes it fairly clear that *Zuikaku* did not join up with Kakuta's force until June 30. However, it is possible that had Yamamoto remained serious about luring American carriers up north he could have advanced that date somewhat, but by how much is problematic.

7. Fuchida, *Midway* (American version), p. xvi (author's preface.)

8. United States Strategic Bombing Survey, *Interrogations of Japanese Officials* (Toyoda statement), p. 316: "We used very much fuel at that time, more than we had expected would be necessary; and the effect of that was felt right through afterwards."

9. For a tabulation of Allied casualties see Samuel Eliot Morison, *History of United States Naval Operations in World War II*, vol. 5: *The Struggle for Guadalcanal, August 1942–February 1943* (Boston: Little, Brown, 1989), p. 63; for Japanese casualties, p. 60.

10. Paul S. Dull, *A Battle History of the Imperial Japanese Navy* (Annapolis: Naval Institute Press, 1978), p. 238. (There were another 7,000 American support troops, for a total of 17,000.)

11. Morison, *Struggle for Guadalcanal*, p. 70.

12. Wildenberg.

13. Parshall and Tully.

14. Plane numbers from WDC 161,709. (*Shokaku*'s dive-bomber squadron apparently was still grossly under strength on August 24.)

15. See Morison, *Struggle for Guadalcanal*, p. 88.

16. See WDC 161,709. Japanese practice was to launch an entire squadron of carrier bombers or attack planes in one deckload if they were available, and *Zuikaku* certainly had the deck length and speed to launch 27 Vals along with 6 Zeros. It would be totally irrational for *Zuikaku* to launch only 9 bombers in the first wave. Also, the main accounts of the battle have at least 27 Vals in the first wave. Belote and Belote, though stating that only 18 dive-bombers were launched, appear (on p. 126) to have 27 attacking in three nine-plane divisions, which I believe is the likely number. I believe that *Zuikaku*'s records showing 9 Vals launched in the first wave and 18 in the second wave are in error.

The 18 bombers launched in her second wave were most likely torpedo planes, not dive-bombers, despite what the WDC 161,709 translation says.

17. Belote and Belote, p. 128, say that the torpedo squadron got lost; Morison, *Struggle for Guadalcanal*, p. 99, says that it was shot down.

18. Fuchida, *Midway*, p. xvi. (After Fuchida got out of the hospital his leg never healed properly, so he was reassigned from the fleet to instructor duty at the Japanese Naval War College.)

19. Morison (*Struggle for Guadalcanal*, p. 100) has this second wave composed of 18 dive-bombers, 9 torpedo planes and 3 Zeros; Belote and Belote say 18 dive-bombers, "some Kates," and 6 Zeros. It would have been irrational for less than the entire squadron of Kates to have been launched (as aerial torpedoes were the principal ship-sinking weapon for the Japanese), and *Zuikaku* had 18 Kates. Also, as already mentioned, the entry in WDC 161,709 stating that 18 dive-bombers were launched in the second wave from *Zuikaku* appears to be in error—they were more likely torpedo planes.

20. That attack group's course of 140° had originally headed straight for *Enterprise* but, for some unexplained reason, a course change from 140 to 180° was made a little after 1725, which took the group westward of the American force by 50 miles. Morison, *Struggle for Guadalcanal*, p. 100.

21. The Long Lance torpedo had an incredible 24,000-yard range at 49 knots and had a powder charge of 225-pounds. This compares with a range of 4,360 yards at 48 knots, with a powder charge of 135-pounds, for the American torpedo. Dull, pp. 60, 76–78.

22. Ibid., p. 238.

23. Morison (*Struggle for Guadalcanal*, at p. 198) has the Seventh Regiment suffering 182 deaths and the 164th Regiment 166, but gives no figures for the First Regiment.

24. The precise aircraft complement of *Junyo* is uncertain. It appears to have carried 24 Zeros and 21 Val dive-bombers (with 21 and 18, respectively, being operational), but whether it carried any Kate attack planes equipped with torpedoes, as generally assumed, is problematic. It apparently took on 10 Kates in July after returning home from the Aleutian campaign and is assumed to have retained that number for the Battle of the Santa Cruz Islands. However, it appears that *Junyo's* Kates were equipped with 250-kilogram bombs, rather than torpedoes.

25. These complements are from Morison, *Struggle for Guadalcanal*, p. 206.

26. This time is zone minus 11. Some commentators use the time for the next zone to the east, which would give a launch time of 0600.

27. Belote and Belote, p. 139.

28. Ibid., p. 142.

29. There is confusion over the type of aircraft making this horizontal bombing attack: Belote and Belote (p. 149) say they were twin-engine Bettys. Morison (*Struggle for Guadalcanal*, p. 221) says they were Kates.

30. There is yet more confusion regarding the source of the dive-bombers. Morison (*Struggle for Guadalcanal*, p. 221) and Dull (p. 230) say they were from *Junyo*. Belote and Belote (p. 150) say they were from *Zuikaku*. I believe it more likely that they were from *Zuikaku*—the survivors of *Zuikaku's* second strike—as that carrier's air crews were much more experienced at attacking ships than *Junyo's*.

31. Belote and Belote, p. 150.

32. Some have commented that Yamamoto should also have been more aggressive with his two carriers—*Junyo* and *Hiyo*—as Halsey had only one still-damaged carrier in the area. But American commentators have tended to overestimate the capabilities of those slow converted carriers in fleet actions. As mentioned earlier, the 9 torpedo planes on each carrier were primarily used for horizontal bombing of land targets; their crews

were inexperienced in torpedo attacks (and may not even have had torpedoes available.) Also, though those two carriers had a full squadron of dive-bombers, their crews were likewise trained primarily for the less-exacting task of bombing of land targets.

33. See Terzibaschitsch, *Aircraft Carriers of the U.S. Navy*, 2nd ed., pp. 59–79, 319–321.

34. Jentschura, Jung and Mickel, pp. 56–57.

35. Morison, *Struggle for Guadalcanal*, p. 372.

36. From a captured Japanese document quoted in the Cincpac Action Report on the Solomons.

10. POSTMORTEM

1. Senshi Sosho, p. 289, 290. (See discussion in chapter 6, "To Launch or Not to Launch.")

2. While, normally, it would take around 40 minutes to raise and spot a squadron of torpedo planes to *Akagi*'s flight deck—when the hangars contained a full air group, and only the aft elevator could be used—on this occasion, however, things were different. As the dive-bombers were off the carrier, both the aft and midship elevators could have been used, reducing the time to 20–25 minutes. (This was the opinion of Ohtawa, torpedo plane pilot, *Soryu*, who stated that when both the aft and midship elevators were used, the total time to raise and spot 18 torpedo planes on the flight deck was about 25 minutes. Maeda, torpedo plane pilot, *Kaga*, believed that it took only about 20 minutes to raise 18 torpedo planes with both elevators. Interviews in Tokyo, October 1992.) Engines could have been warmed up and the entire squadron launched in about another 15 minutes. (On *Kaga*, though there were 26 torpedo planes in her squadron, it appears that only 18 had been armed with torpedoes earlier that morning; those could have been launched at the same time as *Akagi*'s squadron.)

3. Official Report, p. 17; Action Reports of *Akagi* and *Kaga*, WDC 160985–B, pp. 5, 6, and 11.

4. *Soryu*'s records show that some Zeros were landed at around 0930. *Soryu* Action Report, WDC 160985–B, p. 15. But it is assumed that they could have been brought down earlier if a decision to raise the dive-bombers to the flight deck at 0920 had been made.

5. Although bombs from the American dive-bombers did not actually hit the carriers until shortly after 1020, when the third-wave torpedo bombers from *Yorktown* began their attack at 1015, the carriers had to turn sharply away from the wind to present their sterns to the torpedoes, which would have disrupted the launch of the heavily laden torpedo planes. (Wind was from the southeast at around 1020; the carriers turned to the northwest (300°) to evade the torpedo bombers. Official Report, p. 19.)

6. In the actual second attack by *Hiryu*'s torpedo planes, Yamaguchi had delayed the launch until around 1320—just before the Vals and Zeros from the actual first strike had to be landed—because he had been waiting for a search plane report identifying the carrier hit by the first attack and assessing the damage. In our hypothetical, however, it will be assumed that the second-strike planes would have been launched earlier, without waiting for the damage report.

7. See the computation at the end of chapter 8 ("Denouement.")

8. United States Strategic Bombing Survey, *Campaigns of the Pacific War*, p. 3.

9. The second phase operations and its three periods are discussed in detail in Senshi Sosho, pp. 63–89.

10. Admiral Kimmel stated that had the Japanese destroyed the oil tank farms in a third attack on December 7, it would have been necessary to withdraw to the west coast. Prange, *At Dawn We Slept*, p. 549.

11. Hector Bywater, in a book published fifteen years earlier entitled *The Great Pacific War*, had set out such a scenario for knocking out the Panama Canal in graphic detail. First published in 1925, it was republished by Houghton Mifflin Company in 1942.

12. United States Strategic Bombing Survey, *Interrogations of Japanese Officials*, p. 385 (Nomura statement).

13. For dates of deployments of the new American carriers, see Terzibaschitsch, pp. 304–308.

14. Jentschura, Jung, and Mickel, p. 57.

15. These casualty numbers are from Morison, *Struggle for Guadalcanal*, and *History of United States Naval Operations in World War II*, Vol. 7: *Aleutians, Gilberts and Marshalls* (Boston: Little, Brown, 1990).

16. Apparently, it took many months back in 1945 to separate enough of the fissionable U-235 isotope from ordinary uranium (which is over 99 percent non-fissionable U-238) to make just one bomb. Plutonium, on the other hand, could be produced in large quantities from plentiful Uranium-238 in heavy water reactors. But the problem was learning how to make it explode. Unlike U-235, which will naturally sustain a chain reaction when sufficient quantities are brought together to form a "critical mass," plutonium must be violently imploded in a very precise manner in order to sustain a chain reaction. (See Peter Goodchild, *Edward Teller: The Real Dr. Strangelove* [London: Weidenfeld and Nicolson, 2004], pp. 85–87.) This presented a daunting engineering challenge, but once the tricky design puzzle was solved—and proved to work in the Alamogordo test—plutonium bombs could be produced in quantity. (While there were as few as three fission bombs in the U.S. atomic arsenal at the end of 1945, by October 1949, this had grown to 169—mostly plutonium. See Goodchild, pp. 146, 210.)

SELECTED BIBLIOGRAPHY

BOOKS

Barker, A. J. *Midway*. New York: Galahad Books, 1981.

Bates, Richard W. *The Battle of Midway Including the Aleutian Phase, June 3 to June 14, 1942: Strategical and Tactical Analysis*. Naval War College, 1948 (unpublished).

Belote, James H., and William M. Belote. *Titans of the Seas*. New York: Harper and Row, 1975.

Bergamini, David. *Japan's Imperial Conspiracy*. New York: William Morrow, 1971.

Bicheno, Hugh. *Midway*. London: Cassell, 2000.

Bix, Herbert P. *Hirohito and the Making of Modern Japan*. Harper Collins, 2000.

Boyne, Walter J. *Clash of Titans: World War II at Sea*. New York: Simon and Schuster, 1995.

Bywater, Hector. *The Great Pacific War*. Boston: Houghton Mifflin, 1942.

Chang, Iris. *The Rape of Nanking*. New York: Basic Books, 1997.

Chesneau, Roger, ed. *Conway's All the World's Fighting Ships 1922–1946*. Annapolis: Naval Institute Press, 1980.

Coale, Griffith Baily. *Victory at Midway*. New York: Farrar and Rinehart, 1944.

Cowley, Robert. *What If? Military Historians Imagine What Might Have Been*. London: Macmillan, 2000.

Cressman, Robert, et al. *A Glorious Page in Our History: The Battle of Midway 4–6 June 1942*. Missoula, Mont.: Pictorial Histories Publishing Co., 1990.

Doi, Yoshiji. *The Pacific War Which I Saw*. Japan, 1975. (Translation of excerpt obtained from Munehiro Miwa; full Japanese citation unavailable.)

Dull, Paul S. *A Battle History of the Imperial Japanese Navy*. Annapolis: Naval Institute Press, 1978.

Evans, David C, and Mark R. Peattie. *Kaigun: Strategy, Tactics, and Technology in the Imperial Japanese Navy 1887–1941*. Annapolis: Naval Institute Press, 1997.

Feis, Herbert. *The Road to Pearl Harbor*. Princeton University Press, 1950.

Francillon, Rene J. *Japanese Aircraft of the Pacific War*. Annapolis: Naval Institute Press, 1990.

Fuchida, Mitsuo, and Masatake Okumiya. *Midway: The Battle That Doomed Japan*, ed. Clarke K. Kawakami and Roger Pineau. Annapolis: Naval Institute Press, 1955.

———. *Midway*. Kyoto: Nippon Shuppan, 1951.

Genda, Minoru. *Kaigun Kokutai Shimatsuki (Sento-hen)* [Short History of Naval Air Force: Battle volume]. Tokyo: Bungei Shunju, 1962.

Goldstein, Donald, and Katherine Dillon, eds. *The Pearl Harbor Papers*. New York: Brassey's, 1993.

Goodchild, Peter. *Edward Teller: The Real Dr Strangelove*. London: Weidenfeld and Nicolson, 2004.

Greene, Jack. *The Midway Campaign*. Conshohocken, Penn.: Combined Books, 1995.

Grew, Joseph C. *Ten Years in Japan*. New York: Simon and Schuster, 1944.

Harrington, Pat Frank, and Joseph D. Harrington. *Rendezvous at Midway*. New York: Paperback Library, 1968.

Hart, B. H. Liddell. *History of the Second World War*. New York: Putnam, 1970.

Hata, Ikuhiko, and Yasuho Izawa. *Japanese Naval Aces and Fighter Units in WWII*. Annapolis: Naval Institute Press, 1989.

Heinl, Robert D. *Marines at Midway*. N.p.: Marine Corps Monographs, 1948.

Hoyt, Edwin P. *Yamamoto*. New York: Warner Books, 1990.

Ito, Masanori. *The End of the Imperial Japanese Navy*. Westport, Conn.: Greenwood Press, 1984.

Jane's Fighting Ships of World War II. New York: Military Press, 1989.

Jentschura, Hansgeorg, Dieter Jung, and Peter Mickel. *Warships of the Imperial Japanese Navy, 1869–1945*. Annapolis: Naval Institute Press, 1992.

Karig, Walter, and Welbourn Kelley. *Battle Report: Pearl Harbor to Coral Sea*. New York: Farrar and Rinehart, 1944.

Keegan, John. *The Price of Admiralty: The Evolution of Naval Warfare*. New York: Viking, 1989.

Kernan, Alvin. *The Unknown Battle of Midway: The Destruction of the American Torpedo Squadrons*. New Haven: Yale University Press, 2005.

Kusaka, Ryunosuke. *Rengo Kantai* [Combined Fleet]. Tokyo: Mainichi, 1952.

Layton, Edwin T. *"And I Was There": Pearl Harbor and Midway: Breaking the Secrets*. New York: Quill, William Morrow, 1985.

Lewin, Ronald. *The American Magic: Codes, Ciphers and the Defeat of Japan*. New York: Farrar Straus Giroux, 1982.

Lord, Walter. *Incredible Victory*. New York: Harper and Row, 1967.

Lundstrom, John B. *The First Team: Pacific Naval Air Combat from Pearl Harbor to Midway*. Annapolis: Naval Institute Press, 1984.

Morison, Samuel Eliot. *History of United States Naval Operations in World War II*. Vol. 3: *The Rising Sun in the Pacific, 1931–April 1942*. Boston: Little, Brown, 1988.

———. *History of United States Naval Operations in World War II*. Vol. 4: *Coral Sea, Midway and Submarine Actions, May 1942–August 1942*. Boston: Little, Brown, 1988.

———. *History of United States Naval Operations in World War II*. Vol. 5: *The Struggle for Guadalcanal, August 1942–February 1943*. Boston: Little, Brown, 1989.

———. *History of United States Naval Operations in World War II*. Vol. 7: *Aleutians, Gilberts and Marshalls*. Boston: Little, Brown, 1990.

Nohara, Shigeru. *A6M Zero in Action*. Carrollton, Tex.: Squadron/Signal Publications, No. 59, 1983.

Okumiya, Masatake, and Jiro Horikoshi. *Zero! The Story of Japan's Air War in the Pacific: 1941–45*. New York: Ballantine Books, 1957.

Parshall, Jonathan, and Anthony Tully. *Shattered Sword: The Untold Story of the Battle of Midway*. Washington, D.C.: Potomac Books, 2005.

Prange, Gordon W. *Miracle at Midway*, ed. Donald M. Goldstein and Katherine V. Dillon. New York: McGraw-Hill, 1982.

——. *At Dawn We Slept*. New York: Penguin Books, 1982.

Puleston, W. D. *The Armed Forces of the Pacific*. New Haven: Yale University Press, 1941.

Rearden, Jim. *Cracking the Zero Mystery*. Harrisburg, Penn.: Stackpole Books, 1990.

Rusbridger, James, and Eric Nave. *Betrayal At Pearl Harbor*. New York: Touchstone, Simon and Schuster, 1992.

Sakai, Saburo. *Samurai!* New York: Pocket Books, Simon and Schuster, 1996.

Sawachi, Hisae. *Kiroku Middowe Kaisen* [Record of the Midway Sea Battle]. Tokyo: Bungei Shunju, 1986.

Senshi Sosho. *See under* Tsunoda, Hitoshi.

Smith, Peter C. *The Battle of Midway*. Staplehurst, U.K.: Spellmount, 1996.

Smith, William Ward. *Midway, Turning Point of the Pacific*. New York: Thomas Y. Crowell, 1966.

Spector, Ronald H. *Eagle against the Sun: The American War with Japan*. London: Cassell, 2000.

Stephan, John J. *Hawaii under the Rising Sun*. Honolulu: University of Hawai'i Press, 1984.

Stinnett, Robert B. *Day of Deceit: The Truth about FDR and Pearl Harbor*. London: Constable, 2000.

Taylor, Theodore. *The Battle Off Midway Island*. New York: Avon Books, 1981.

Terzibaschitsch, Stefan. *Aircraft Carriers of the U. S. Navy*. 2nd ed. Annapolis: Naval Institute Press, 1989.

——. *Battleships of the U. S. Navy in World War II*. New York: Bonanza Books, 1977.

Tillman, Barrett. *The Dauntless Dive Bomber of World War II*. Annapolis: Naval Institute Press, 1976.

Toland, John. *But Not in Shame*. New York: Random House, 1961.

Tsunoda, Hitoshi. *Middowe Kaisen* [Midway Sea Battle]. Senshi Sosho [War History Series], Boeikenshujo Senshishitsu, eds., vol. 43. Tokyo: Asagumo Shimbunsha, 1971.

Tuleja, Thaddeus V. *Climax at Midway*. New York: Jove Books, 1983.

Ugaki, Matome. *Fading Victory: The Diary of Admiral Matome Ugaki*. Pittsburgh: University of Pittsburgh Press, 1991.

United States Strategic Bombing Survey. *The Campaigns of the Pacific War*. Washington, D.C.: Government Printing Office, 1946.

Weal, Elke C., John A. Weal, and Richard F. Barker. *Combat Aircraft of World War Two*. New York: Macmillan, 1977.

Werstein, Irving. *The Battle of Midway*. New York: Thomas Y. Crowell, 1961.

Wouk, Herman. *War and Remembrance*. Boston: Little, Brown, 1978.

Yergin, Daniel. *The Prize: The Epic Quest for Oil, Money and Power*. New York: Touchstone: Simon and Schuster, 1993.

Yoshii, Hiroshi. *The Pacific War*. Vol. 7: *History of Showa Told by the Eyewitnesses*. Tokyo: Shin Jinbutsu Oraisha, 1989.

ARTICLES

Isom, Dallas Woodbury. "The Battle of Midway: Why the Japanese Lost." *Naval War College Review* (Summer 2000): 60–100.

——. "They Would Have Found a Way." *Naval War College Review* (Summer 2001): 158–63.

Parshall, Jonathan B., David D. Dickson, and Anthony P. Tully. "Doctrine Matters: Why the Japanese Lost at Midway." *Naval War College Review* (Summer 2001): 139–51.
Ring, Stanhope. "Lost Letter of Midway." *United States Naval Institute: Proceedings* 125, no. 8 (August 1, 1999): 29.
Wildenberg, Thomas. "Midway: Sheer Luck or Better Doctrine?" *Naval War College Review* 58, no. 1 (Winter 2005): 121–35.

OFFICIAL DOCUMENTS

Action Report, Commander, Cruiser Division Six. A16–3. 11 June 1942, Serial 058.
Allied Translator and Interpreter Section (Kusaka's statement). ATIS Doc. No. 16647–B
Battle Report, Commander in Chief U.S. Pacific Fleet (Admiral Nimitz). 28 June 1942, Serial 01849.
Japanese Monograph No. 93. "Midway Operations May–June 1942." ATIS Doc. No. 34488.
"Meritorious Citation for CV *Ryujo*," WDC 161709.
"Merit Rating Standards, CV *Ryujo*," WDC 161733.
"The Midway Operation" (Action Reports of Mobile Force carriers), WDC 160985–B.
Office of Naval Intelligence. "The Japanese Story of the Battle of Midway" (Translation of Mobile Force's Detailed Battle Report #6), ONI, OPNAV P32-1002. (Admiral Nagumo's official report on the Battle of Midway).
Record Group 457, SRMN-012, Part III, Combat Intelligence Unit, 14th Naval District. Traffic Intelligence Summaries, 1 Apr–30 June, pp. 499–505. National Archives, Washington, D.C.
United States Strategic Bombing Survey. *Interrogations of Japanese Officials*. OPNAV P-03-100.
U.S. Naval Technical Mission to Japan. *Ordnance Targets, Japanese Torpedoes and Tubes*. Index No. O-01-2.

INTERVIEWS CONDUCTED BY AUTHOR IN JAPAN

Akimoto, Katutaro, torpedo mechanic, *Akagi*.
Arakawa, Takeshi, dive-bomber mechanic, *Hiryu*.
[Mr.] Dairoku, dive-bomber mechanic, *Soryu*.
Inoue, Fukuji, torpedo plane pilot, *Akagi*.
[Mr.] Itazu, dive-bomber gunner, *Hiryu*.
Jinnouchi, Yaroku, Zero mechanic, *Hiryu*.
Kobayashi, Yuichi, chief of fighter squadron maintenance, *Hiryu*.
Maeda, Takeshi, torpedo plane pilot, *Kaga*.
Mandai, Hiseo, engineer, *Hiryu*.
[Mr.] Mogi, Zero mechanic, *Akagi*.
Morinaga, Tokayoshi, torpedo plane pilot, *Kaga*.
[Mr.] Motake, torpedo mechanic, *Soryu*.
Mouri, Yasaharu, dive-bomber mechanic, *Hiryu*.
Ohtawa, Tatsuya, torpedo plane pilot, *Soryu*.
Santou, Moushichi, dive-bomber mechanic, *Akagi*.
Sawada, Kanzo, dive-bomber mechanic, *Akagi*.
Tutumi, Makato, torpedo plane mechanic, *Hiryu*.
Tsunoda, Hitoshi, author of Midway volume of Senshi Sosho.
Yoshida, Jiro, Zero pilot (not at Midway.)
Yoshioka, Chuichi, compiler of Admiral Nagumo's official report.

INDEX

Abe, Hiraoki, 255, 261
action reports: *Akagi,* 178, 210, 340nn7,9,
    370n11, 372n36; description and transla-
    tion, 24, 100, 355n50, 364n39; *Hiryu,*
    375n18, 376n46, 382nn25,32; *Kaga,* 159,
    178, 365nn1,45, 374n14, 378n15, 381n4; *So-
    ryu,* 178, 340n6, 374n12, 375nn18,21,
    386n4. *See also* Nagumo's Official Re-
    port; Senshi Sosho
Adak Island, 92, 238–40
Advance (Submarine) Force, 94–95
aerial combat. *See under* Midway, Battle of,
    June 4 phase
aerial torpedoes. *See* torpedoes
Aichi D3A1. *See* Val dive-bomber
air power, emergence of, 50–53, 79–80, 151, 242
aircraft carriers: aircraft launch rate (Japan),
    377n50; attack carrier designation (Ja-
    pan), 35, 236, 363n24, 376n30; building
    programs, 48–50, 357n20; comparable
    strengths, 357n20, 361n63; comparative
    aircraft complements, 53t, 358n32,
    363n24; design philosophies, 356n18,
    357n20; role in British navy, 358n31;
    vulnerability of, 4, 344. *See also specific
    carriers*
Akagi: action report, 178, 210, 340nn7,9,
    370n11, 372n36; aircraft complement, 2,
    53t, 62, 93, 101, 360n50, 377n50, 383n42;
    aircraft launch rate, 377n50; American
    attack on, 142–43, 210, 373n39; armament
    status, 20, 22, 141–42, 156–57, 168–69, 172–
    80, 372n35; building program, 42–43, 46–
    48; combat air patrol, 127–28, 159, 169,

337–39t, 339n2, 374nn15,17, 375n18; dam-
    age report, 307; decision to rearm, 116–18,
    365n3, 366n10; destroyed, 5, 22, 185, 209–
    12, 228–29, 307, 340n9, 344; headquarters
    log, 133; Midway battle losses, 231–34,
    235t; Operation Hawaii/Pearl Harbor, 62,
    64–65, 377n50; ordnance, 106; pilot
    cadre, 231–33, 235t, 365n3; radio limita-
    tions, 96–98, 130, 137, 268, 363nn29–30,
    364n36, 373n1; rearming procedure, 124–
    27, 157, 177–80, 272, 368n41, 369n44,
    386n2; receipt of sighting report, 137–38,
    147, 160, 366n10; relanding/recovery of
    Midway Strike Force, 155, 169, 178, 271,
    367n30, 374n10; survivors, 250. *See also*
    rearming operation; war game exercise
Akigumo, 365n47
Akimoto, Katutaro, 117, 363n23
Akutan Island, 383n3
Alamogordo, N. M., 291, 387n16
Aleutian Operation, 237–41; Adak-Attu Inva-
    sion Force, 94; concept and strategy, 92,
    93, 280, 384n6; deployment of combined
    fleet, 93–103; fleet components, 94,
    376n30, 382n2; impact on Midway opera-
    tion, 161, 241, 366n13; Kiska Invasion
    Force, 94; "Koga Zero," 383n3; losses,
    235t, 383nn2–3; Northern Aleutian
    Force, 94
Amagai, Takehisa, 233, 380n3
Amagi, 42, 263
American Pacific Fleet, 182–203; aircraft com-
    plements, 3, 53t, 102–103, 384n4; carrier
    striking force, 102–103t; coordinated at-

Dallas Woodbury Isom is a retired professor of law.